BASEBALL AMERICA'S 1991 ALMANAC

A Comprehensive Review
Of The 1990 Season,
Featuring Statistics
And Commentary

Copyright © 1991 by American Sports Publishing, Inc.

Distributed by Simon & Schuster

No portion of this book may be reprinted or reproduced without the written consent of the publishers. For additional copies, send $9.95 to American Sports Publishing, P.O. Box 2089, Durham, NC 27702.

BASEBALL AMERICA'S 1991 ALMANAC

PUBLISHED BY
Baseball America

PUBLISHER
Miles Wolff

EDITOR
Allan Simpson

ASSISTANT EDITOR
Jennifer McCarthy

PRODUCTION MANAGER
Shannon Cain

PRODUCTION ASSISTANT
Susan Merrell

ASSOCIATE EDITORS
Jon Scher, Jim Callis, Dean Gyorgy

CONTRIBUTING EDITORS
*Tracy Ringolsby, Nick Cafardo, Paul Hagen,
George Rorrer, Patti Singer, Mike Klis, Phil Bowman,
Rubin Grant, Ted Bakamjian, Maureen Delany,
David Jones, Curt Rallo, Gene Sapakoff,
Peter Conradi, Howie Stalwick, Wayne Graczyk*

PHOTOGRAPHERS
*Ken Babbitt, Mel Bailey, Tom DiPace, Wayne Eastburn,
Simon Griffiths, Gary Halpern, Reed Hoffman,
Paul Jasienski, Larry Kinker, Richard C. Lewis,
David McIntyre, Mike Ponzini, Lee R.Schmid,
Ron Schreier, Bruce Schwartzman, John Spear,
Bernard Troncale, Ron Vesely.*

**STATISTICAL PRODUCTION
CONSULTANT**
*Howe Sportsdata International, Inc.
Boston, Mass.*

CONTENTS

THE MAJOR LEAGUES

THE MINOR LEAGUES

AND THERE'S MORE

THE MAJOR LEAGUES

1990 IN REVIEW

Nolan Ryan, 43, won his 300th game in 1990 and also spun his sixth career no-hitter.

Off-field recriminations tarnish game's image

By DEAN GYORGY

Sports pages these days are too often invaded by the real world. No longer simply an innocent escape, baseball has had its nose bloodied the last couple of years. And still attendance records are set. Detroit Tigers manager Sparky Anderson said during the Pete Rose scandal something to the effect of, "We've tried and tried to ruin this game, and we just can't do it."

History looks for labels. And in this age of sex and drugs and million-dollar shoe contracts, 1990 could easily go down as the Year of the Lockout, or of the George Steinbrenner banishment, or Pete Rose goes to prison. It's unfair to ask baseball to live up to utopian dreams, but for true lovers of the game, the glass is always half full.

So, if we may, let's label 1990 as the Year of the No-hitter.

Enough for everybody

Nine no-hitters were thrown in 1990, setting a new major league record. Nolan Ryan, the legendary Texan, extended his career record to six with a 5-0 blanking of the A's on June 5. He was 43, the oldest pitcher ever to throw a no-hitter.

Toronto's Dave Stieb, after coming oh-so-close in the past by losing three no-hit bids in the ninth inning, finally etched his name in the books when he beat Cleveland on Sept. 2. It was the first no-hitter for a Blue Jays pitcher in the 14-year history of the franchise.

Oakland's Dave Stewart, who won 20 games for the fourth straight year, never winning a Cy Young Award, took a step toward immortality with a no-hit win over Toronto on June 29. On the same day, Fernando Valenzuela of the Dodgers shut down the Cardinals. It was the first time this century two pitchers threw no-hitters in different games the same day.

The no-hit madness all began in the first week of the season, when California's Mark Langston and Mike Witt combined to blank the Mariners on April 11. Seattle's Randy Johnson got his on June 2 against Detroit.

On July 1, the Yankees' Andy Hawkins became only the second pitcher in major league history to pitch a no-hitter and lose. Three errors by his teammates led to a 4-0 loss, but Hawkins still held the White Sox hitless.

The White Sox' Melido Perez no-hit the Yankees on July 12. Terry Mulholland of the Phillies no-hit his former teammates, the San Francisco Giants, on Aug. 15.

Labor troubles

After dealing in 1989 with the death of his predecessor, Bart Giamatti, and the earthquake that shook that year's World Series, commissioner Fay Vincent didn't have things any easier in 1990.

He was forced to preside, in varying degrees, over an owner's lockout that essentially wiped out spring training, and the investigation and eventual banishment of Steinbrenner, the long-time Yankees owner, for involvement with admitted gambler Howard Spira.

"If it is right that nobody has had a year like this, the comfort should be that there shouldn't be another one," Vincent said.

A lockout, George Steinbrenner's banishment and Pete Rose's imprisonment made it a tough year for commissioner Fay Vincent.

With a new stadium as a backdrop, 81-year-old Comiskey Park was phased out as the home of the White Sox.

"I just don't know what's ahead. I only know what I've experienced in baseball, and it's been difficult."

The Basic Agreement between players and owners expired on Dec. 31, 1989, seemingly giving plenty of time for a new one to be hammered out before the 1990 season was to start.

But since the pact was signed in 1985, the owners were found guilty of collusion, conspiring against the players to hold free-agent salaries down. An air of mistrust abounded.

Months of grandstanding and verbal potshots ensued, and as spring training grew nearer, the players and owners grew farther apart on the issues. The owners brought to the table proposed widespread changes. They talked about salary caps and pay-for-performance, limiting arbitration awards and revenue sharing. The Players Association talked about minor adjustments to the system, to be written in stone.

The last three labor disputes resulted in mid-season strikes by the players. So this time, the owners took the lead and instituted a lockout of spring training sites.

Baseball fans waited and wondered.

A new Basic Agreement was finally signed on March 19, canceling the first 32 days of spring training. It forced a one-week delay on Opening Day, although the 162-game schedule was spared.

The players got a higher minimum salary (from $68,000 to $100,000) and increased benefit-plan contributions from the owners. And the two sides compromised on the biggest obstacle, eligibility for salary arbitration.

The season was finally on. But perhaps the biggest losers in the whole affair were the spring-training communities. It was estimated that spring training annually pumps $300 million into the economy of Florida, and $150 million into Arizona. Those states certainly felt the brunt of the lockout.

Gates still spinning

For the most part, fans didn't have any trouble deciding on which side of the labor dispute their loyalties fell. They were for the game itself. They didn't see it as players vs. owners, but as hallowed institution vs. greed. They developed a throw-up-their-hands attitude that surfaced in several fan-organized movements to boycott major league games.

But of course, the lure of the game was too strong, and fans

Yankees general partner George Steinbrenner was slapped with a lifetime ban for making payments to gambler Howard Spira.

once again swallowed their disdain. Major League Baseball enjoyed another banner season at the gate in 1990.

With a total of 54,871,718 fans, baseball just missed setting a single-season attendance record for the sixth straight year. The ends of the spectrum were Toronto, which drew 3,885,284 to the first full season at SkyDome, and Atlanta, which for the second straight year was the only team to draw less than 1 million, at 980,129.

Steinbrenner falls

When the position of baseball commissioner was created in the wake of the 1919 Black Sox scandal, a rule was written into the mission that gave the man power to act in matters not in the best interest of baseball.

Steinbrenner, in his 17½ years as general partner of the New York Yankees, made 18 managerial changes. In the previous 71 years of the franchise, there were only 19 changes.

But his merry-go-round search for the perfect manager wasn't the cause of his final downfall. It was his association with admitted gambler Howard Spira.

On July 30, after a four-month investigation by the commissioner's office, Steinbrenner accepted a lifetime ban from running the club.

In an 11-page decision from the commissioner, baseball found that Steinbrenner had paid Spira $40,000 for damaging information on then-Yankees outfielder Dave Winfield.

Vincent's original penalty was to be a two-year suspension followed by a three-year probation for Steinbrenner, forcing him to sell a percentage of the team and dropping him from general partner to limited partner.

But Steinbrenner, 60, mysteriously, wanted a lifetime ban. He didn't fully explain his decision, but sources close to him reportedly offered a few possibilities: He wanted to avoid the stigma of a suspension for a second time. Steinbrenner was suspended for two years in the 1970's by commissioner Bowie Kuhn for illegal campaign contributions to Richard Nixon. Another possibility was that the clean break might help

AL wins sluggish affair for fourth win in 5 games

Baseball's 61st all-star spectacle was hardly that. In fact, it was something of a bust in 1990.

The game at Chicago's Wrigley Field was interrupted by 85 minutes of rain delays, but the American League finally came out on top for the fourth time in five years, winning the pitchers duel, 2-0.

Pitchers, indeed. The National League used a record nine hurlers. Only the starter, Cincinnati's Jack Armstrong, went more than one inning.

In the seventh inning, the rains came, this time for 68 minutes. CBS television cut to a rerun of *Rescue 911*. Many fans called it a night.

When play resumed, the Rangers'

Julio Franco ...MVP

Julio Franco immediately greeted Reds reliever Rob Dibble with a two-run double that earned Franco MVP honors.

Kansas City's Bret Saberhagen, the third of six AL pitchers, got the win. The loser's two hits was the lowest total in all-star game history.

American 2, National 0

AMERICAN	ab	r	h	bi	bb	so	NATIONAL	ab	r	h	bi	bb	so
Henderson lf	3	0	0	0	0	1	Dykstra cf	4	0	1	0	0	0
Guillen ss	2	0	0	0	0	0	Sandberg 2b	3	0	0	0	0	0
Boggs 3b	2	0	2	0	1	0	R.Alomar 2b	1	0	0	0	0	0
Gruber pr-3b	1	0	0	0	1	0	Clark 1b	3	0	1	0	0	0
Canseco rf	4	0	0	0	1	1	Myers p	0	0	0	0	0	0
C.Ripken ss	2	0	0	0	0	0	Jo.Franco p	0	0	0	0	0	0
Bell ph-lf	2	0	0	0	0	1	Williams ph	1	0	0	0	0	1
Griffey, cf	2	0	0	0	1	0	Mitchell lf	2	0	0	0	0	1
Puckett ph-cf	1	0	1	0	0	0	Viola p	0	0	0	0	0	0
McGwire 1b	2	0	0	0	0	2	Wallach 3b	2	0	0	0	0	0
Fielder ph-1b	1	0	0	0	1	0	Dawson rf	2	0	0	0	0	1
S.Alomar c	3	1	2	0	0	0	Strawberry rf	1	0	0	0	0	1
Thigpen p	0	0	0	0	0	0	Sabo 3b	2	0	0	0	0	0
Trammell ph	1	0	0	0	0	0	D.Smith p	0	0	0	0	0	0
Finley p	0	0	0	0	0	0	Brantley p	0	0	0	0	0	0
Eckersley p	0	0	0	0	0	0	Dibble p	0	0	0	0	0	0
Sax 2b	1	0	0	0	1	0	Bonilla 1b	1	0	0	0	0	0
Saberhagen p	0	0	0	0	0	0	Scioscia c	2	0	0	0	0	1
Parrish ph-c	1	1	1	0	1	0	GregOlson ph-c	1	0	0	0	0	1
Welch p	0	0	0	0	0	0	O.Smith ss	1	0	0	0	0	0
Jacoby ph	1	0	0	0	0	0	De.Martinez p	0	0	0	0	0	0
Stieb p	0	0	0	0	0	0	Bonds lf	1	0	0	0	1	0
Ju.Franco ph-2b	3	0	1	2	0	0	Armstrong p	0	0	0	0	0	0
							R.Martinez p	0	0	0	0	0	0
							Gwynn ph	0	0	0	0	1	0
							Larkin pr-ss	0	0	0	0	0	0
							Dunston ss	2	0	0	0	0	0
TOTALS	32	2	7	2	7	5	**TOTALS**	29	0	2	0	2	6

American	. . . .	000 000 200—2
National	. . . .	000 000 000—0

E—Strawberry. DP—National 2. LOB—American 10, National 4. 2B— Julio Franco. SB—Sax, Larkin, Gruber 2, Canseco.

American	IP	H	R	ER	BB	SO	National	IP	H	R	ER	BB	SO
Welch	2	1	0	0	0	2	Armstrong	2	1	0	0	0	2
Stieb	2	0	0	0	1	1	R.Martinez	1	0	0	0	2	1
Saberhagen W	2	0	0	0	0	1	De.Martinez	1	0	0	0	0	1
Thigpen	1	0	0	0	0	0	Viola	1	1	0	0	0	0
Finley	1	0	0	0	1	1	D.Smith	⅔	1	0	0	2	1
Eckersley S	1	1	0	0	0	1	Brantley L	⅓	2	2	2	0	0
							Dibble	1	1	0	0	1	0
							Myers	1	1	0	0	2	0
							Jo.Franco	1	0	0	0	0	0

Brantley pitched to 2 batters in 7th.
T—2:53. A—39,071.

Baseball's all-time hits leader, Pete Rose, was sent to prison in 1990 for income tax evasion.

Steinbrenner retain his position as vice-president of the U.S. Olympic Committee.

Whatever the case, the Boss was out. There was a standing ovation when word hit Yankee Stadium.

Rose wilts

Baseball banished its all-time hits leader in August 1989. And in 1990, society slapped Pete Rose as well.

Rose pleaded guilty to income tax evasion in a Cincinnati court on July 19. U.S. District Judge S. Arthur Spiegel sentenced him to five months in prison, three months in a half-way house, 1,000 hours of community service and a $50,000 fine.

Rose was sent to a minimum-security facility in Marion, Ill. In a pre-sentencing statement, the addicted gambler and admitted felon apologized for the tarnishing of his legend.

"I think I'm perceived as a very aggressive, arrogant type of individual," Rose said. "But I want people to know that I do have emotion, I do have feelings, and I can be hurt like everybody else.

"And I hope no one has to go through what I went through the last year and a half. I lost my dignity, I lost my self-respect, I lost a lot of dear fans and almost lost some very dear friends."

The question that remains is will Rose be elected to the Hall of Fame when he becomes eligible in December, 1991.

Two join Hall

There certainly were moments of warm reflection in 1990, as two of the most popular and dominant players of the 1970's were inducted into the Hall of Fame in Cooperstown, N.Y.

Joe Morgan, the second-base catalyst of the Big Red Machine, and Jim Palmer, longtime ace of the Baltimore Orioles, joined the ranks of the immortals in an Aug. 6 ceremony.

Morgan was named National League MVP in 1975 and '76, both years in which his Cincinnati club captured the World Series. He established records for most home runs by a second baseman (266) and most seasons played at the position (22).

Newest members of baseball's Hall of Fame: Joe Morgan and Jim Palmer.

He is third on the all-time walks list with 1,865, behind only Babe Ruth (2,056) and Ted Williams (2,019).

Palmer won 20 games eight times. He won three Cy Young Awards, threw a no-hitter against the A's in 1969, and beat Sandy Koufax in Game Two of the 1966 World Series at the age of 20. He had a career winning percentage of .658 (268-152), ranking fourth-best all-time. And in 558 games, Palmer never surrendered a grand slam home run.

Comiskey passes on

Baseball bid farewell to one of the game's grand old ball parks in 1990. Comiskey Park in Chicago, home of the White Sox for 81 years, faced the winter-time wrecking ball as a new Comiskey was going up across the street. Only the infield dirt will make the trip across 35th Street.

The White Sox flirted with giving Comiskey one last postseason dance, as they valiantly chased the American League West champion A's. The White Sox fell short in the end, but 2,002,359 fans usually enjoyed an exciting game as they paid their final respects to Comiskey Park.

With Comiskey gone, Fenway Park and Tiger Stadium now rank as the oldest of all major league parks. Both were dedicated on April 20, 1912.

Milestones

Opening Day, though delayed by the lockout, provided some historic firsts. U.S. president George Bush and Canadian prime minister Brian Mulroney both threw out the first pitches in Toronto's home opener against Texas. It marked the first time two national leaders were simultaneously given the honor. Seattle opened the Kingdome with the first home sellout in franchise history. And Sam Horn of the Orioles tied a major league record with six RBIs against the Royals . . . Eddie Murray of the Dodgers homered from both sides of the plate on April 18. It was the ninth time in his career he'd accomplished the feat, one short of Mickey Mantle's record . . . On May 9, Baltimore's Cal Ripken Jr. became only the third shortstop in history to hit 200 home runs, joining Ernie Banks and Vern Stephens. Ripken also moved into second place on the all-time games played list in 1990, as he again appeared in all 162 . . . Ryne Sandberg of the Cubs ended his records for consecutive errorless games (123) and consecutive errorless chances (582) . . . The Philadelphia Phillies retired Mike Schmidt's No. 20 . . . On May 29, Oakland's Rickey Henderson broke Ty Cobb's AL stolen base record with his 893rd. Henderson stole 50 bases for the 10th straight season, extending his AL record. He finished the season just two stolen bases shy of Lou Brock's all-time mark . . . On June 4, the Dodgers' Ramon Martinez struck out 18 Braves batters, tying a club record . . . On July 17, the Minnesota Twins became

Obituaries

Billy Martin, 61, always a Yankee no matter where he played or managed, died in an automobile accident on Christmas Day, 1989. Martin's truck was driven by a friend, William Reedy, who was later convicted of driving while intoxicated. Martin was the Yankees' starting second baseman for much of the 1950's, when he was a part of three championships. He went on to manage five different American League clubs, and in 1977 guided the Yankees to their first World Series victory in 15 years. Martin was hired and fired as Yankees manager five different times by owner George Steinbrenner, as the feuds between the two men became legendary.

Billy Martin
. . . fighter to the end

Tony Conigliaro, 45, was a rising-star outfielder for the Boston Red Sox in the mid-1960's when his career was hampered by a tragic beaning in 1967. Although he came back to the Sox and hit 36 homers in 1970, his vision was permanently impaired. A heart attack in 1982 left him brain damaged, and he was confined to his bed for the last eight years of his life. He died of pneumonia and kidney failure in a Boston hospital on Feb. 24.

Johnny Neun, 89, spent more than 60 years in baseball as player, coach, manager and scout. He is one of only eight players to be credited with an unassisted triple play, turning the trick while with the Tigers in 1927. He ran the Kansas City Royals Baseball Academy for two years, and retired from baseball in 1989, working last as a scout for the Brewers. He died March 28 in Baltimore.

Glen Gorbous, 59, is credited in the Guiness Book of World Records for the longest baseball throw in history. Gorbous played briefly in the major leagues in the mid-1950's. But at Omaha Stadium on Aug. 1, 1957, he threw a ball 445 feet, 10 inches on the fly with a six-step running start. he won $200 for his feat.

R.R.M "Bob" Carpenter, 74, owned the Philadelphia Phillies for 29 years, from 1943-1972. Carpenter was one of the first proponents of signing bonuses for minor league prospects. He died at his home in Delaware on July 8.

Wilbert (Junior) Miner, 64, minor league manager and coach since 1970 with the Mets, Yankees, Orioles and Expos, died Aug. 21. Miner managed Gastonia to the 1983 South Atlantic League championship, and built a reputation in player development.

Roger (Doc) Cramer, 85, played in big league outfields from 1929-1948 with the Athletics, White Sox, Red Sox, Senators and Tigers. Cramer is the only AL player to have gone 6-for-6 in a game twice. He was selected to five all-star teams and finished his career with a .296 average and 2,705 hits.

Wally Moses, 80, was an outfielder for 17 years with the Athletics, White Sox and Red Sox from 1934-1951. He went on to become a successful batting coach, presiding over Richie Ashburn's batting titles with the Phillies in 1955 and '58, and the home run derby of Mantle and Maris with the Yankees in 1961. He retired from baseball in 1975. He died Oct. 10 in his home state of Georgia.

Cleveland catcher Sandy Alomar Jr., who hit .290 with 66 RBIs, was named Baseball America's 1990 Rookie of the Year.

the first team ever to turn two triple plays in one game, against Boston at Fenway Park . . . The Rangers' Nolan Ryan won his 300th game on July 31 against the Brewers, making him only the 20th pitcher to reach the plateau . . . With his 328th career homer, the White Sox' Carlton Fisk passed Johnny Bench for No.1 on the all-time list for catchers . . . On Aug. 25, Cecil Fielder became the first Tigers player and the third ever to hit a ball over the left-field roof at Tiger Stadium. Fielder, who spent 1989 in Japan, hit his 50th and 51st homers on the last day of the season, becoming the first American Leaguer since 1961 to reach the half-century mark . . . On Aug. 31, the Mariners' Ken Griffey and Ken Griffey Jr. became the first father-son combo to get a hit for the same team in the same game. No fathers and sons had ever played together before . . . Bobby Thigpen of the White Sox set a major league saves record with his 47th of the season on Sept. 3. Thigpen finished the year with 57.

Rob Dibble, member of Cincinnati's Nasty Boys, helps hold Oakland to a .207 average.

Reds pull huge upset; beat Oakland 4 straight

By TRACY RINGOLSBY

For the doubters, the Cincinnati Reds found the answer—a 1990 World Series championship.

A wire-to-wire, first-place finish—something no National League team had done since the advent of the 162-game schedule in 1962 and which only one (the 1923 New York Giants) had done before that—didn't earn the Reds the respect they wanted.

A six-game disposal of the favored Pittsburgh Pirates in the NL playoffs didn't convince anyone that a new version of the Big Red Machine had been unveiled in Cincinnati, either.

But once the World Series was complete, and the Reds had swept the mighty Oakland Athletics, 4-0, the Reds finally earned the respect due a team that didn't just beat the highly-favored A's, but swept away the talk of an Oakland dynasty.

"We didn't fold, did we?" said Reds manager Lou Piniella. "I never expected us to. When we were in first everyone expected this team to be caught. I argued that we wouldn't. They were fooled by the fact we played .500 baseball for the last 100 games or so. But whenever we had to win a big game, we did, and that's a good sign. Our club can play. I've always known that."

"They said all year we had no heart, no soul, no team leaders," reliever Rob Dibble said. "The people in this clubhouse knew differently."

Rijo, bullpen too tough for A's

The Reds left little doubt about what they knew in stunning a team which came into the World Series thinking sweep—and a chance to become the first repeat champion since the

1977-78 New York Yankees—only to be beaten in every phase of the game.

Cincinnati left the A's in a state of confusion and consternation, underscored when Jose Canseco, bothered by a sore back and bruised middle finger on his right hand, was benched for the final game.

Anchored by Series MVP Jose Rijo, who allowed one earned run in 15⅔ innings in winning Games One and Four, and a nasty bullpen, which allowed only one earned run in 31 post-season innings and none in 13 World Series innings, the Reds compiled a 1.70 ERA, holding the A's to just eight runs and a .207 average. The A's never scored a run after the third inning.

Meanwhile, A's pitchers, who compiled a major-league low 3.18 ERA during the regular season, gave up 22 runs, including 14 in the 14 innings the starters worked in the first three games. The Reds hit .317, including a .750 average for outfielder Billy Hatcher, who set a World Series record with hits in his first seven official at-bats.

Jose Rijo
...MVP

And what the Reds didn't take, the A's gave away.

For the A's, the Series was epitomized in the eighth inning of Game Four. Dave Stewart, atoning for a four-inning, four-run effort in the A's 7-0 opening game loss, had the Reds shut out for seven innings, and was nursing a 1-0 lead.

But a lead-off single by Barry Larkin and two bunts (Herm Winningham's two-strike attempt going for a base hit, and Paul O'Neill's sacrifice that Stewart threw away) loaded the bases. A double-play ball that couldn't be turned and Hal Morris' scoring fly ball gave the Reds the two runs they needed for a 2-1 win, enabling them to become the 15th team in history to sweep a series.

Reds wash away bad taste

With the sweep of the A's, the Reds swept away growing frustrations of their recent existence.

Shut out of post-season play during the '80s—a decade in which every NL team except the Reds and their NL playoff opponent, Pittsburgh, made it at least once—Cincinnati lived through unmet expectations in finishing second in the NL West four years running before the debacle of 1989.

Not only did they finish fifth in the division that year, but manager Pete Rose, baseball's all-time hit leader, was given a lifetime ban from the game for his involvement with gamblers.

With 1990, however, came a new decade, and a new approach administered by Piniella, hired after a two-year apprenticeship covering two terms as manager of the Yankees.

Piniella came to Cincinnati with something to prove, and found a team with the talent he was confident could prove itself.

"If I didn't feel I could manage, I wouldn't have taken this job," said Piniella.

Piniella realized as soon as the lockout-delayed spring training began that he had a special team.

"I saw a very athletic club," Piniella said. "We could run. We could throw. We could hit. We had good speed. We just had to get it all together. My message to the players, simply stated, was: 'You've played together four or five years now. It's time this club goes out and wins. It's your turn. Let's gear ourselves up for that.' That's exactly what we did."

A team effort

The Reds did it in style—both during the regular season and the post-season. This was a team that was built on the team concept—no Reds player was a legitimate candidate for any post-season award—and maintained that image in the post-season.

While Rijo, with seven shutout innings in Game One and a Game Four performance in which he retired the final 20 batters he faced, and the bullpen were the big guns, the Reds provided a different set of heroes for each victory.

Eric Davis and Chris Sabo had five RBIs apiece, but eight other Reds drove in at least one run. Hatcher went 9-for-12 before a bruised left hand, suffered when he was hit by a Stewart pitch in the first inning of Game Four, knocked him out. Four other Reds regulars hit .286 or better.

Rijo set the pace in the opener, a 7-0 victory. But it was Davis, slowed by a bruised left shoulder and hip injury suffered in a late-season collision with the outfield fence at Riverfront Stadium, who got the Reds going. He delivered a two-run home run in the first, and added an RBI-single in the Reds' three-run fifth against reliever Todd Burns.

It was Davis' first home run since Sept. 26 and came after a 4-for-23 struggle in the NL playoffs, a slump that had Piniella contemplating hitting Davis leadoff instead of cleanup for Game One.

"It's hard for Eric right now," Hatcher said. "He's injured and not producing. People want to blame the injury, but Eric says, 'I'm just not doing the job.' I think Lou made him a little upset by saying he wanted to bat Eric leadoff. When Eric hit the home run, he was telling Lou, 'Hey, I want to bat fourth.' "

Davis became the 22nd player in history to homer in his first World Series at-bat.

It was his way of telling the A's that they may have been

WORLD SERIES CHAMPS

1990—Cincinnati (NL)	1946—St. Louis (NL)
1989—Oakland (AL)	1945—Detroit (AL)
1988—Los Angeles (NL)	1944—St. Louis (NL)
1987—Minnesota (AL)	1943—New York (AL)
1986—New York (NL)	1942—St. Louis (NL)
1985—Kansas City (AL)	1941—New York (AL)
1984—Detroit (AL)	1940—Cincinnati (NL)
1983—Baltimore (AL)	1939—New York (AL)
1982—St. Louis (NL)	1938—New York (AL)
1981—Los Angeles (NL)	1937—New York (AL)
1980—Philadelphia (NL)	1936—New York (AL)
1979—Pittsburgh (NL)	1935—Detroit (AL)
1978—New York (AL)	1934—St. Louis (NL)
1977—New York (AL)	1933—New York (NL)
1976—Cincinnati (NL)	1932—New York (AL)
1975—Cincinnati (NL)	1931—St. Louis (NL)
1974—Oakland (AL)	1930—Philadelphia (AL)
1973—Oakland (AL)	1929—Philadelphia (AL)
1972—Oakland (AL)	1928—New York (AL)
1971—Pittsburgh (NL)	1927—New York (AL)
1970—Baltimore (AL)	1926—St. Louis (NL)
1969—New York (NL)	1925—Pittsburgh (NL)
1968—Detroit (AL)	1924—Washington (AL)
1967—St. Louis (NL)	1923—New York (AL)
1966—Baltimore (AL)	1922—New York (NL)
1965—Los Angeles (NL)	1921—New York (NL)
1964—St. Louis (NL)	1920—Cleveland (AL)
1963—Los Angeles (NL)	1919—Cincinnati (NL)
1962—New York (AL)	1918—Boston (AL)
1961—New York (AL)	1917—Chicago (AL)
1960—Pittsburgh (NL)	1916—Boston (AL)
1959—Los Angeles (NL)	1915—Boston (AL)
1958—New York (AL)	1914—Boston (NL)
1957—Milwaukee (NL)	1913—Philadelphia (AL)
1956—New York (AL)	1912—Boston (AL)
1955—Brooklyn (NL)	1911—Philadelphia (AL)
1954—New York (NL)	1910—Philadelphia (AL)
1953—New York (AL)	1909—Pittsburgh (NL)
1952—New York (AL)	1908—Chicago (NL)
1951—New York (AL)	1907—Chicago (NL)
1950—New York (AL)	1906—Chicago (AL)
1949—New York (AL)	1905—New York (NL)
1948—Cleveland (AL)	1903—Boston (AL)
1947—New York (AL)	

Reds outfielder Billy Hatcher set a Series record by hitting safely in his first seven at-bats.

heavy favorites, having come into the Series with 10 consecutive post-season wins and starting a pitcher (Stewart) who had won six post-season starts in a row, but the Reds weren't impressed.

Plenty of motivation for Rijo

Rijo had a special motive of his own.

Traded by the A's to Cincinnati after the 1987 season, he had livened up the pre-Series days by saying he felt misused in Oakland, where he bounced between the minors and big leagues, and the bullpen and rotation. He also said he was insulted by pitching coach Dave Duncan.

He made his point particularly well, pitching out of jams and setting the tone for an anemic Oakland team that went 3-for-40 with men in scoring position during the four games. Rijo gave up seven hits and two walks in seven innings, but no runs.

The A's left eight men on base against him. Rijo induced Mark McGwire to ground out to end the third with runners on first and third and to pop up to end the fifth with the bases loaded.

Relievers to the rescue

Reds starter Danny Jackson was a third-inning knockout victim in Game Two. He allowed all four A's runs in what became a 5-4, 10-inning victory for the Reds.

Four relievers combined to shut out the A's on four hits the remaining 7⅓ innings—including three innings of one-hit relief by Jack Armstrong in his lone post-season appearance.

Meanwhile, Joe Oliver, who doubled and scored the Reds third run in the fourth, singled home the game-winner in the 10th. And the bench came through. Pinch-hitter Ron Oester singled to drive in Oliver in the fourth. Pinch-hitter Glenn Braggs tied the game, 4-4, with a fielder's choice grounder in the eighth. And pinch-hitter Billy Bates, in his first post-season at-bat after a September of pinch-running, beat out the infield chopper for the first of three consecutive 10th-inning hits off A's relief ace Dennis Eckersley that produced the game-winning rally.

Closed it out in Oakland

Having won the first two games on their own Riverfront Stadium turf, the Reds headed to Oakland for Game Three with renewed confidence.

"I felt all along once we won our division, that club would

stick its chest out a little and really feel confident about itself," said Piniella. "The experience of being in first place from day one until the end of the year, like we were, where you're under scrutiny every day, where people are trying their hardest to beat you, makes you a better ballclub."

Sabo, who had driven in two runs in Game One, keyed the Reds victory in Game Three. He became the first NL player to homer in back-to-back World Series innings. He gave the Reds a 1-0 lead with home run No. 1 in the second, and put them on top 5-2 with a two-run shot that highlighted a seven-run third inning against starter Mike Moore and reliever Scott Sanderson. Sabo also set a World Series record for a third baseman with 10 errorless chances.

Game Four had a painful beginning for Cincinnati.

Jose Canseco
. . . 1-for-12

Hatcher was hit on the hand in the top of the first, and Davis suffered a bruised right hip and kidney attempting to make a diving catch in the bottom of the first. Both came out of the game in the second. But the replacements came to the rescue again in the 2-1 victory.

It was Winningham, who replaced Hatcher, who beat out the bunt single after Larkin's lead-off single in the eighth. And with the bases loaded, it was Braggs, who replaced Davis, delivering the game-tying fielder's choice grounder ahead of the game-winning sacrifice fly by Morris.

"We wanted to make a statement that we're a good team, too," said O'Neill.

And the Reds made it emphatically.

WORLD SERIES BOX SCORES

Game One: Reds 7, Athletics 0

OAKLAND	ab	r	h	bi	bb	so	CINCINNATI	ab	r	h	bi	bb	so
R.Henderson lf	5	0	3	0	0	1	Larkin ss	4	1	0	0	1	0
McGee cf	5	0	1	0	0	0	Hatcher cf	3	3	3	1	1	0
Canseco rf	2	0	0	0	2	1	O'Neill rf	2	1	0	1	2	1
McGwire 1b	3	0	0	0	1	0	Davis lf	4	2	2	3	0	0
Lansford 3b	4	0	2	0	0	0	Morris 1b	4	0	1	0	0	1
Steinbach c	4	0	1	0	0	1	Sabo 3b	3	0	1	2	1	1
Randolph 2b	4	0	1	0	0	0	Oliver c	4	0	1	0	0	0
Gallego ss	4	0	0	0	0	2	Duncan 2b	3	0	1	0	1	1
Stewart p	1	0	0	0	0	1	Rijo p	3	0	1	0	0	0
Jennings ph	1	0	1	0	0	0	Dibble p	0	0	0	0	0	0
Burns p	0	0	0	0	0	0	Benzinger ph	1	0	0	0	0	0
Nelson p	0	0	0	0	0	0	Myers p	0	0	0	0	0	0
Hassey ph	1	0	0	0	0	0							
Sanderson p	0	0	0	0	0	0							
Eckersley p	0	0	0	0	0	0							
D.Henderson ph	1	0	0	0	0	0							
TOTALS	**35**	**0**	**9**	**0**	**3**	**7**	**TOTALS**	**31**	**7**	**10**	**7**	**6**	**4**

Oakland 000   000   000—0
Cincinnati 202   030   00x—7

E—Gallego. DP—Oakland 2, Cincinnati 1. LOB—Oakland 11, Cincinnati 6. 2B—R.Henderson 2, Hatcher 2. HR—Davis. SB—McGee, Lansford.

Oakland	IP	H	R	ER	BB	SO	Cincinnati	IP	H	R	ER	BB	SO
Stewart L	4	3	4	4	4	3	Rijo W	7	7	0	0	2	5
Burns	⅔	4	3	3	1	0	Dibble	1	1	0	0	1	0
Nelson	1⅓	2	0	0	1	0	Myers	1	1	0	0	0	2
Sanderson	1	1	0	0	0	0							
Eckersley	1	0	0	0	0	1							

WP—Dibble. T—2:38. A—55,830.

Game Two: Reds 5, Athletics 4

OAKLAND	ab	r	h	bi	bb	so
R.Henderson lf	4	1	1	0	1	0
Lansford 3b	4	0	1	0	0	0
Canseco rf	5	1	1	2	0	2
McGwire 1b	4	1	2	0	1	2
D.Henderson cf	4	1	2	0	1	0
Steinbach c	0	0	0	0	0	0
Randolph 2b	4	0	0	0	1	0
Hassey c	4	0	2	1	0	0
Bordick pr-ss	0	0	0	0	0	0
Gallego ss	4	0	1	1	0	0
Baines ph	1	0	0	0	0	1
Eckersley p	0	0	0	0	0	0
Welch p	3	0	0	0	0	2
Honeycutt p	0	0	0	0	0	0
McGee cf	0	0	0	0	0	0
TOTALS	37	4	10	4	4	7

CINCINNATI	ab	r	h	bi	bb	so
Larkin ss	5	1	3	0	0	0
Hatcher cf	4	2	4	1	1	0
O'Neill rf	4	0	0	0	1	0
Davis lf	5	0	1	0	0	0
Morris 1b	3	0	0	0	0	0
Braggs ph	1	0	0	1	0	0
Dibble p	0	0	0	0	0	0
Bates ph	1	1	1	0	0	0
Sabo 3b	5	0	3	0	0	1
Oliver c	5	1	2	1	0	0
Duncan 2b	3	0	0	0	1	0
Jackson p	1	0	0	0	0	1
Scudder p	0	0	0	0	0	0
Oester ph	1	0	1	0	0	0
Armstrong p	0	0	0	0	0	0
Winningham ph	1	0	0	0	0	0
Charlton p	0	0	0	0	0	0
Benzinger 1b	1	0	0	0	0	0
TOTALS	40	5	14	5	3	2

Oakland	103	000	000	0—4
Cincinnati	200	100	010	1—5

E—McGwire, Hassey, Oliver, Jackson. DP—Cincinnati 1. LOB—Oakland 10, Cincinnati 10. 2B—Larkin, Hatcher 2, Oliver. 3B—Hatcher. HR—Canseco. SB—R.Henderson, Lansford. S—Welch, Lansford. SF—Hassey.

Oakland	IP	H	R	ER	BB	SO
Welch	7⅓	9	4	4	2	2
Honeycutt	1⅔	2	0	0	1	0
Eckersley L	⅓	3	1	1	0	0

Cincinnati	IP	H	R	ER	BB	SO
Jackson	2⅔	6	4	3	2	0
Scudder	1⅓	0	0	0	2	2
Armstrong	3	1	0	0	0	3
Charlton	1	1	0	0	0	0
Dibble W	2	2	0	0	0	2

One out when winning run scored.
T—3:31. A—55,832.

Game Three: Reds 8, Athletics 3

CINCINNATI	ab	r	h	bi	bb	so
Larkin ss	5	0	2	1	0	0
Hatcher cf	5	1	1	0	0	0
O'Neill rf	3	1	1	0	2	0
Davis lf	5	1	2	1	0	0
Morris dh	4	0	1	1	1	0
Sabo 3b	4	2	2	3	1	0
Benzinger 1b	5	1	2	0	0	0
Oliver c	5	1	2	1	0	1
Duncan 2b	4	1	1	1	0	0
TOTALS	40	8	14	8	4	1

OAKLAND	ab	r	h	bi	bb	so
R.Henderson lf	3	1	1	1	1	1
Lansford 3b	3	0	0	0	1	0
Canseco rf	4	0	0	0	0	0
D.Henderson cf	4	1	0	0	0	0
Baines dh	4	1	1	2	0	1
McGwire 1b	4	0	1	0	0	1
Steinbach c	4	0	0	0	0	0
Randolph 2b	4	0	3	0	0	0
Gallego ss	2	0	0	0	0	0
McGee ph	1	0	0	0	0	1
Bordick ss	0	0	0	0	0	0
Blankenship ph	1	0	0	0	0	1
TOTALS	34	3	7	3	2	5

Cincinnati	017	000	000—8	
Oakland	021	000	000—3	

E—Oliver, McGwire. DP—Oakland 2. LOB—Cincinnati 9, Oakland 6. 2B—Oliver, D.Henderson. 3B—Larkin. HR—Sabo 2, R.Henderson, Baines. SB—O'Neill, Duncan, R.Henderson, Randolph.

Cincinnati	IP	H	R	ER	BB	SO
Browning W	6	6	3	3	2	2
Dibble	1⅔	0	0	0	0	2
Myers	1⅓	1	0	0	0	0

Oakland	IP	H	R	ER	BB	SO
Moore L	2⅔	8	6	2	0	1
Sanderson	⅔	3	2	2	1	0
Klink	0	0	0	0	1	0
Nelson	3⅔	1	0	0	1	0
Burns	1	1	0	0	1	0
Young	1	1	0	0	0	0

Klink pitched to 1 batter in 4th. Browning pitched to 1 batter in 7th.
WP—Burns, Sanderson. T—3:01. A—48,269.

Game Four: Reds 2, Athletics 1

CINCINNATI	ab	r	h	bi	bb	so
Larkin ss	3	1	1	0	1	0
Hatcher cf	0	0	0	0	0	0
Winningham cf	3	1	2	0	0	0
O'Neill rf	3	0	0	0	0	1
Davis lf	0	0	0	0	0	0
Braggs ph-lf	3	0	1	1	0	0
Morris dh	3	0	1	0	0	0
Sabo 3b	4	0	3	0	0	0
Benzinger 1b	4	0	0	0	0	0
Oliver c	4	0	1	0	0	0
Duncan 2b	4	0	0	0	0	1
TOTALS	31	2	7	2	2	2

OAKLAND	ab	r	h	bi	bb	so
R.Henderson lf	3	0	0	0	1	2
McGee rf	4	1	1	0	0	1
D.Henderson cf	4	0	0	0	0	2
Baines dh	2	0	0	0	1	0
Canseco ph	1	0	0	0	0	1
Lansford 3b	4	0	1	1	0	0
Quirk c	3	0	0	0	0	2
McGwire 1b	3	0	0	0	0	1
Randolph 2b	3	0	0	0	0	0
Gallego ss	1	0	0	0	1	1
Hassey ph	1	0	0	0	0	0
Bordick ss	0	0	0	0	0	0
TOTALS	29	1	2	1	3	9

Cincinnati	000	000	020—2	
Oakland	100	000	000—1	

E—Oliver, Stewart. DP—Oakland 1. LOB—Cincinnati 7, Oakland 4. 2B—Sabo, Oliver, McGee. SB—R.Henderson, Gallego. S—O'Neill. SF—Morris.

Cincinnati	IP	H	R	ER	BB	SO	Oakland	IP	H	R	ER	BB	SO
Rijo W	8⅓	2	1	1	3	9	Stewart L	9	7	2	1	2	2
Myers S	⅔	0	0	0	0	0							

HBP—Hatcher (by Stewart). T—2:48. A—48,613.

WORLD SERIES COMPOSITE BOX

OAKLAND

Player, Pos.	AVG	G	AB	R	H	2B	3B	HR	RBI	BB	SO	SB
Doug Jennings, ph	1.000	1	1	0	1	0	0	0	0	0	0	0
Rickey Henderson, lf	.333	4	15	2	5	2	0	1	1	3	4	3
Ron Hassey, c	.333	3	6	0	2	0	0	0	1	0	0	0
Carney Lansford, 3b	.267	4	15	0	4	0	0	0	1	1	0	1
Willie Randolph, 2b	.267	4	15	0	4	0	0	0	0	1	0	1
Dave Henderson, cf	.231	4	13	2	3	1	0	0	1	1	3	0
Mark McGwire, 1b	.214	4	14	1	3	0	0	0	0	2	4	0
Willie McGee, cf	.200	4	10	1	2	1	0	0	0	0	2	1
Harold Baines, dh	.143	3	7	1	1	0	0	1	2	1	2	0
Terry Steinbach, c	.125	3	8	0	1	0	0	0	0	0	1	0
Mike Gallego, ss	.091	4	11	0	1	0	0	0	1	1	3	1
Jose Canseco, rf	.083	4	12	1	1	0	0	1	2	2	3	0
Jamie Quirk, c	.000	1	3	0	0	0	0	0	0	0	2	0
Bob Welch, p	.000	1	3	0	0	0	0	0	0	0	2	0
Dave Stewart, p	.000	2	1	0	0	0	0	0	0	0	1	0
Lance Blankenship, ph	.000	1	1	0	0	0	0	0	0	0	1	0
Mike Bordick, ss	.000	3	0	0	0	0	0	0	0	0	0	0
TOTALS	.207	4	135	8	28	4	0	3	8	12	28	7

Pitcher	W	L	ERA	G	GS	CG	SV	IP	H	R	ER	BB	SO
Gene Nelson	0	0	0.00	2	0	0	0	5	3	0	0	2	0
Rick Honeycutt	0	0	0.00	1	0	0	0	1⅔	2	0	0	1	0
Curt Young	0	0	0.00	1	0	0	0	1	1	0	0	0	0
Joe Klink	0	0	0.00	1	0	0	0	0	0	0	0	1	0
Dave Stewart	0	2	3.46	2	2	1	0	13	10	6	5	6	0
Bob Welch	0	0	4.91	1	1	0	0	7⅓	4	4	2	2	2
Mike Moore	0	1	6.75	1	1	0	0	2⅔	8	6	2	0	1
Dennis Eckersley	0	1	6.75	2	0	0	0	1⅓	3	1	1	0	1
Scott Sanderson	0	0	10.80	2	0	0	0	1⅔	4	2	2	1	0
Todd Burns	0	0	16.20	2	0	0	0	1⅔	5	3	3	2	0
TOTALS	0	4	4.33	4	4	1	0	35⅓	45	22	17	15	9

CINCINNATI

Player, Pos.	AVG	G	AB	R	H	2B	3B	HR	RBI	BB	SO	SB
Billy Bates, ph	1.000	1	1	1	1	0	0	0	0	0	0	0
Ron Oester, ph	1.000	1	1	0	1	0	0	0	1	0	0	0
Billy Hatcher, cf	.750	4	12	6	9	4	1	0	2	2	0	0
Chris Sabo, 3b	.563	4	16	2	9	1	0	2	5	2	2	0
Herm Winningham, cf	.500	2	4	1	2	0	0	0	0	0	0	0
Barry Larkin, ss	.353	4	17	3	6	1	1	0	1	2	0	0
Joe Oliver, c	.333	4	18	2	6	3	0	0	2	0	1	0
Jose Rijo, p	.333	2	3	0	1	0	0	0	0	0	0	0
Eric Davis, of	.286	4	14	3	4	0	0	1	5	0	0	0
Todd Benzinger, 1b	.182	4	11	1	2	0	0	0	0	0	0	0
Mariano Duncan, 2b	.143	4	14	1	2	0	0	0	1	2	2	1
Paul O'Neill, rf	.083	4	12	2	1	0	0	0	1	5	2	1
Hal Morris, 1b	.071	4	14	0	1	0	0	0	2	1	1	0
Glenn Braggs, lf	.000	2	4	0	0	0	0	0	0	2	1	0
Danny Jackson, p	.000	1	1	0	0	0	0	0	0	0	1	0
TOTALS	.317	4	142	22	45	9	2	3	22	15	9	2

Pitcher	W	L	ERA	G	GS	CG	SV	IP	H	R	ER	BB	SO
Rob Dibble	1	0	0.00	3	0	0	0	4⅔	3	0	0	1	4
Randy Myers	0	0	0.00	3	0	0	1	3	2	0	0	0	3
Jack Armstrong	0	0	0.00	1	0	0	0	3	1	0	0	0	3
Scott Scudder	0	0	0.00	1	0	0	0	1⅓	0	0	0	2	2
Norm Charlton	0	0	0.00	1	0	0	0	1	1	0	0	0	0
Jose Rijo	2	0	0.59	2	2	0	0	15⅓	9	1	1	5	14
Tom Browning	1	0	4.50	1	1	0	0	6	6	3	3	2	2
Danny Jackson	0	0	10.13	1	1	0	0	2⅔	6	4	3	2	0
TOTALS	4	0	1.70	4	4	0	1	37	28	8	7	12	28

Oakland	2	2	4	0	0	0	0	0	0	0 — 8
Cincinnati	4	1	9	1	3	0	0	3	0	1 — 22

E—Hassey, McGwire 2, Gallego, Stewart, Oliver 3, Jackson. DP—Oakland 5, Cincinnati 2. LOB—Oakland 31, Cincinnati 32. S—Lansford, Welch, O'Neill. SF—Hassey, Morris. HBP—Hatcher (by Stewart). WP—Burns, Sanderson, Dibble. Umpires—Frank Pulli (NL), Rocky Roe (AL), Jim Quick (NL), Ted Hendry (AL), Randy Marsh (NL), Larry Barnett (AL), Bruce Froemming (NL). Official Scorers—Glenn Sample (University of Cincinnati); Gordon Verrell (BBWAA President); John Hickey (Hayward Daily Review); Dave Nightingale (The Sporting News).

New-look White Sox year's biggest surprise

By NICK CAFARDO

It was a year of silver linings and lights at the end of the tunnel. It was a year when first impressions were often wrong.

For instance, Comiskey Park was about to be demolished and general manager Larry Himes was axed. But the Chicago White Sox were the rags-to-riches story of the 1990 season, going from 69-92 and 29½ games behind the Oakland A's in 1989 to a record (94-68) that showed almost a 180-degree turnaround. They finished nine games behind the predictably powerful A's, who won 103 games and won the West and the American League pennant for the third straight year.

You thought that when Oakland and the Boston Red Sox met in the American League Championship Series for the second time in three years, the Red Sox would put up more of a fight. Rewind your VCR. The A's swept the Red Sox again.

But the Red Sox were more than met the eye, too.

The Red Sox' starting rotation to start the 1990 season consisted of John Dopson, Mike Rochford and Wes Gardner to go along with mainstays Roger Clemens and Mike Boddicker. Eek! Look again. Before it was over, the Red Sox had the best starting rotation in the league with a league-low 3.32 ERA thanks to improbables such as Tom Bolton, Dana Kiecker and Greg Harris—household names in Sleepy Eye, Minn., Brentwood, Tenn. and Laguna Niguel, Calif.

LEAGUE CHAMPIONS

Playoff Champions, Where Applicable

1990—Oakland	1960—New York	1930—Philadelphia
1989—Oakland	1959—Chicago	1929—Philadelphia
1988—Oakland	1958—New York	1928—New York
1987—Minnesota	1957—New York	1927—New York
1986—Boston	1956—New York	1926—New York
1985—Kansas City	1955—New York	1925—Washington
1984—Detroit	1954—Cleveland	1924—Washington
1983—Baltimore	1953—New York	1923—New York
1982—Milwaukee	1952—New York	1922—New York
1981—New York	1951—New York	1921—New York
1980—Kansas City	1950—New York	1920—Cleveland
1979—Baltimore	1949—New York	1919—Chicago
1978—New York	1948—Cleveland	1918—Boston
1977—New York	1947—New York	1917—Chicago
1976—New York	1946—Boston	1916—Boston
1975—Boston	1945—Detroit	1915—Boston
1974—Oakland	1944—St. Louis	1914—Philadelphia
1973—Oakland	1943—New York	1913—Philadelphia
1972—Oakland	1942—New York	1912—Boston
1971—Baltimore	1941—New York	1911—Philadelphia
1970—Baltimore	1940—Detroit	1910—Philadelphia
1969—Baltimore	1939—New York	1909—Detroit
1968—Detroit	1938—New York	1908—Detroit
1967—Boston	1937—New York	1907—Detroit
1966—Baltimore	1936—New York	1906—Chicago
1965—Minnesota	1935—Detroit	1905—Philadelphia
1964—New York	1934—Detroit	1904—Boston
1963—New York	1933—Washington	1903—Boston
1962—New York	1932—New York	1902—Philadelphia
1961—New York	1931—Philadelphia	1901—Chicago

AL CHAMPS

Members of the American League champion Oakland Athletics included, **bottom row**, left to right, Merv Rettenmund (coach), Art Kusnyer (coach), Tommie Reynolds (coach), Rene Lachemann (coach), Tony LaRussa (manager), Dave Duncan (coach), Dave McKay (coach), Rickey Henderson, Stan Javier. **Second row**, Frank Ciensczyk (equipment manager), Mickey Morabito (traveling secretary), Mike Gallego, Walt Weiss, Jim Corsi, Carney Lansford, Rick Honeycutt, Lance Blankenship, Mike Bordick, Joe Klink, Steve Vucinich (equipment manager), Barry Weinberg (trainer). **Third row**, Terry Steinbach, Ron Hassey, Felix Jose, Dennis Eckersley, Gene Nelson, Curt Young, Todd Burns, Ken Phelps, Larry Davis (trainer). **Top row**, Mark McGwire, Scott Sanderson, Bob Welch, Dave Stewart, Dave Otto, Jose Canseco, Dave Henderson, Mike Norris. Not pictured—Harold Baines, Reggie Harris, Doug Jennings, Willie McGee, Mike Moore, Willie Randolph.

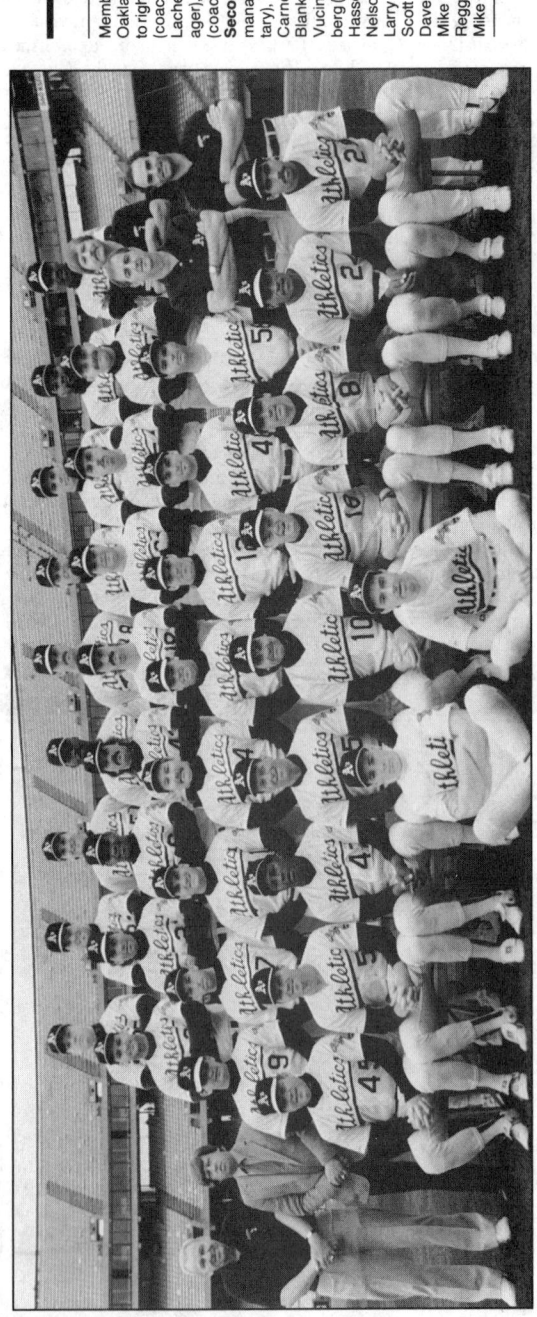

Dave Stewart, a 20-game winner four years in a row, beat Boston twice in the AL playoffs.

White Sox chase A's

Manager of the year Jeff Torborg led a White Sox team whose average age was less than 27 years old. The White Sox pressed the A's most of the year and owned the distinction of being the only team which beat the A's in their seasons series, 8-5.

Bobby Thigpen amassed a record you can close the books on—58 saves. Carlton Fisk set a record for most home runs by a catcher, with 328. The White Sox pulled as close as 4½ games in late August, but the A's then acquired Willie McGee and former White Sox outfielder Harold Baines in seperate deals, both on Aug. 29, and began to pull away again.

Curious, to say the least, was the move by owner Jerry Reinsdorf to fire Himes on Sept. 15. Himes had built up the White Sox farm system to a point where farmhands Greg Hibbard, Jack McDowell, Thigpen, Frank Thomas, Robin Ventura, etc. were all making significant contributions. Reinsdorf said while Himes had "taken us from Point A to Point B", he needed someone else to take them from "Point B to Point C."

But Reinsdorf had no idea who that was. He ran the team himself the remainder of the year.

It didn't matter. Oakland, coming off a World Series championship in 1989, was healthy for most of 1990 until the final month.

Jose Canseco still managed to hit 37 homers and drive in 101 runs, but back problems hindered his productivity, especially in the post-season against Boston and then Cincinnati in the World Series. But the A's were a well-oiled machine otherwise.

Rickey Henderson had an MVP type season (.325, 28 homers and 65 stolen bases) and broke Ty Cobb's American League record for steals. With 936 steals, he was two short of tying Lou Brock's all-time record.

Welch won 27 games, more than any pitcher in the majors and more than anyone since Steve Carlton won 27 for the 1972 Philadelphia Phillies. Dave Stewart won 20 or more games for the fourth straight year, the most since Jim Palmer strung four straight 20-game seasons (1975-78).

Dennis Eckersley had an almost perfect season for a reliever. He saved 48 games in 50 opportunities. His ERA was 0.61.

White Sox reliever Bobby Thigpen saved 58 games, shattering the major league record.

Red Sox, Blue Jays go the wire

The AL East, a division which has bordered on pathos since 1986, proved to be the most exciting race of all in 1990. Only the Red Sox and Blue Jays would sport winning records in 1990.

The two teams were tied for first on July 31. Boston built a quick 6½ game lead, only to slump badly and by Sept. 18 had fallen a game behind Tortonto. The Sox swoon coincided with Clemens leaving the lineup Sept. 4 because of a bout with severe tendinitis. Clemens won 21 games and had a league-leading ERA of 1.93, but did not pitch again until Sept. 29.

The Red Sox and Blue Jays met the final weekend of the 1990 season at Fenway Park and the Sox took two out of three with Clemens returning to put the Sox two games up. The Red Sox then beat the White Sox two out of three to end their season with an 88-74 record, two games ahead of Toronto.

Red Sox exit on sour note

The A's-Red Sox ALCS ended in controversy when home plate umpire Terry Cooney ejected Clemens in the second inning of Game Four. The Red Sox were trailing, 1-0, down three games to none, with Mike Gallego up and runners at first and second with one out when Clemens, in the stretch position, started mouthing expletives at Cooney. Without hesitation, Cooney ejected Clemens.

The righthander, not knowing he had been ejected, remained on the mound while catcher Tony Pena and manager Joe Morgan protested vigorously. When Clemens finally realized he had been ejected, he rushed Cooney, shoving aside umpire Jim Evans who was trying to be a mediator.

Meanwhile, Red Sox second baseman Marty Barrett threw a Gatorade container and bucket of gum and sunflower seeds onto the field. He also shoved coach Dick Berardino down the dugout steps after Berardino tried to calm Barrett down so the veteran second baseman would not be ejected. But umpire Vic Voltaggio had already ejected Barrett.

Boston argued how dare Cooney eject their star from a game of such magnitude without a verbal warning? The A's argued that Clemens' words warranted ejection and Oakland third baseman Carney Lansford said, "The Red Sox are an embarrassment to my profession."

Gallego doubled to score two runs off Bolton, who relieved

Clemens, and it was enough to beat and eliminate the Red Sox, 3-1.

Couldn't beat Stewart

The Red Sox had put all their hopes on beating Stewart, the eventual ALCS MVP (2-0, 1.13 ERA), in Game One. The feeling was, if the Sox got to Stewart, it would set the tone.

Stewart had beaten the Red Sox in nine straight starts. He was 6-0 against Clemens, the Game One starter. But nothing would change. Clemens, who had pitched just once since Sept. 4 when he lost to the A's, lasted six innings. He left with a 1-0 lead. The A's tied it in the seventh on Rickey Henderson's sacrifice fly off Larry Andersen. Lansford singled in the go-ahead run in the eighth, making it 2-1. And then the A's pummelled the Red Sox bullpen for seven runs in the ninth, for a 9-1 win.

The bullpen exploded on the Red Sox again in Game Two, in a 4-1 loss. Dana Kiecker and Bob Welch engaged in a 1-1 pitcher's duel through six, but a Baines ground ball got the second A's run in the seventh. The A's struck again in the ninth, getting two more.

The series shifted to Oakland for Game Three. Just like 1988. Mike Boddicker again was the pitcher for Boston, and pitched well enough to win, but the silent Red Sox bats produced just one run off Mike Moore and the A's bullpen. Oakland won 4-1.

The A's outscored the Red Sox 20-4. The Red Sox hit .183. And that pretty much told the story.

Life in the slow lane

Detroit's Trumbull Avenue in 1990 was like Main Street on the Moon—a ghost town. There were more folks feasting on Domino's Pizza on any given night than watching the Tigers finish below .500 again.

But the Tigers boasted a serious, yet unexpected player of the year candidate. He was the find of the year—the player that each and every GM in baseball, except the Tigers' Bill Lajoie, can look back and kick himself for.

Cecil Fielder, the big, loveable Blue Jays castaway, who found his stroke in the Far East in 1989, brought it to Detroit in 1990,

Detriot's Cecil Fielder became the Japanese import of the year, slugging 51 homers.

Kansas City's George Brett recovered from a slow start to win his third American League batting title.

producing a memorable season reminiscent of something out of 1961, when Mickey Mantle and Roger Maris went on a home run rampage. Fielder hit 51 homers and knocked in 132 runs.

But the folks in Detroit longed for a winner and the streets of downtown Detroit became more solemn as the summer turned to fall. The Tigers finished ahead of only Cleveland in attendance.

The Kansas City Royals spent a fortune in the off-season on 1989 National League Cy Young winner Mark Davis, who was a bust, going 2-7 with a 5.11 ERA and saving only six games.

The Royals also got old. Veterans Frank White and Bob Boone were released following the season. Willie Wilson lost a step or two. Only George Brett rebounded. He hit .386 after the all-star break to win his third American League batting title, finishing at .329.

Yankees hit bottom

Once again, it was a news-filled season for the New York Yankees.

Manager Bucky Dent was unceremoniously fired by Yankees owner George Steinbrenner. He was the only manager let go during the 1990 season. It was June 6, in Boston of all places, which coincidentally was the first time the Red Sox went into first place.

Dent is Boston's eternal villain. Little children, who are now adults, still remember the three-run homer Dent hit off Mike Torrez in October, 1978 in the playoff game for the AL East title. When Dent was fired in Boston The Wall seemed to exude a sinister grin.

There was no 'Stump Magic' under new skipper Stump Merrill, as the Yanks lost 95 games, their worst season since 1912, and finished in last place 21 games behind the Red Sox.

The team underwent a major change when commissioner Fay Vincent forced Steinbrenner out of baseball because of his involvement with reputed gambler Howard Spira, whom he hired and allegedly paid $40,000 to discredit Dave Winfield.

1990 FINAL STANDINGS

East	W	L	Pct.	GB
Boston	88	74	.543	—
Toronto	86	76	.531	2
Detroit	79	83	.488	9
Cleveland	77	85	.475	11
Baltimore	76	85	.472	11½
Milwaukee	74	88	.457	14
New York	67	95	.414	21
West				
Oakland	103	59	.636	—
Chicago	94	68	.580	9
Texas	83	79	.512	20
California	80	82	.494	23
Seattle	77	85	.475	26
Kansas City	75	86	.466	27½
Minnesota	74	88	.457	29

1990 GENERAL INFORMATION

League Championship Series: Oakland defeated Boston 4-0 in best-of-7 series for the league pennant.

Regular-Season Attendance: Toronto, 3,885,284; Oakland, 2,900,217; California, 2,555,688; Boston, 2,528,986; Baltimore, 2,415,189; Kansas City, 2,244,956; Texas, 2,057,887; New York, 2,006,436, Chicago, 2,002,359; Milwaukee, 1,752,900; Minnesota, 1,750,964; Seattle, 1,509,705; Detroit, 1,495,785, Cleveland, 1,225,241.

Managers: Baltimore—Frank Robinson; **Boston**—Joe Morgan; **California**—Doug Rader; **Chicago**—Jeff Torborg; **Cleveland**—John McNamara; **Detroit**—Sparky Anderson; **Kansas City**—John Wathan; **Milwaukee**—Tom Trebelhorn; **Minnesota**—Tom Kelly; **New York**—Bucky Dent, Stump Merrill; **Oakland**—Tony LaRussa; **Seattle**—Jim Lefebvre; **Texas**—Bobby Valentine; **Toronto**—Cito Gaston.

1990 All-Star Team (by Baseball America): C—Carlton Fisk, Chicago. **1B**—George Brett, Kansas City. **2B**—Jody Reed, Boston. **3B**—Kelly Gruber, Toronto. **SS**—Alan Trammell, Detroit. **OF**—Rickey Henderson, Oakland; Ellis Burks, Boston; Ken Griffey Jr., Seattle. **DH**—Cecil Fielder, Detroit. **P**—Roger Clemens, Boston; Bob Welch, Oakland; Dave Stewart, Oakland; Bobby Thigpen, Chicago; Dennis Eckersley, Oakland. **Player of Year**—Rickey Henderson, Oakland. **Pitcher of Year**—Roger Clemens, Boston. **Manager of Year**—Jeff Torborg, Chicago. **Rookie of Year**—Sandy Alomar Jr., Cleveland. **Executive of Year**—Sandy Alderson, Oakland.

1990 BATTING, PITCHING STATS

CLUB BATTING

	AVG	G	AB	R	H	2B	3B	HR	BB	SO	SB
Boston	.272	162	5516	699	1502	298	31	106	598	795	53
Cleveland	.267	162	5485	732	1465	266	41	110	458	836	107
Kansas City	.267	161	5488	707	1465	316	44	100	498	879	107
Minnesota	.265	162	5499	666	1458	281	39	100	445	749	96
Toronto	.265	162	5589	767	1479	263	50	167	526	970	111
California	.260	162	5570	690	1448	237	27	147	566	1000	69
Seattle	.259	162	5474	640	1419	251	26	107	596	749	105
Texas	.259	162	5469	676	1416	257	27	110	575	1054	115
Detroit	.259	162	5479	750	1418	241	32	172	634	952	82
Chicago	.258	162	5402	682	1393	251	44	106	478	903	140
Milwaukee	.256	162	5503	732	1408	247	36	128	519	821	164
Oakland	.254	162	5433	733	1379	209	22	164	651	992	141
Baltimore	.245	161	5410	669	1328	234	22	132	660	962	94
New York	.241	162	5483	603	1322	208	19	147	427	1027	119

CLUB PITCHING

	ERA	G	CG	SHO	SV	IP	H	R	ER	BB	SO
Oakland	3.18	162	18	16	64	1456	1287	570	514	494	831
Chicago	3.61	162	17	10	68	1449	1313	633	582	548	914
Boston	3.72	162	15	13	44	1442	1417	664	596	519	997
Seattle	3.72	162	21	7	41	1443	1319	680	597	606	1064
California	3.81	162	21	13	42	1454	1482	706	616	544	944
Toronto	3.84	162	6	9	48	1454	1434	661	620	445	892
Texas	3.83	162	25	9	36	1445	1343	696	615	623	997
Kansas City	3.93	161	18	8	33	1421	1449	709	621	560	1006

White Sox catcher Carlton Fisk enjoyed an all-star season in 1990 at age 42, hitting .285 with 18 homers.

	ERA	G	CG	SHO	SV	IP	H	R	ER	BB	SO
Baltimore	4.07	161	10	5	43	1435	1445	698	649	537	776
Milwaukee	4.11	162	23	13	42	1445	1558	760	660	469	771
Minnesota	4.14	162	13	13	43	1436	1509	729	660	489	872
New York	4.23	162	15	6	41	1445	1430	749	679	618	909
Cleveland	4.27	162	12	10	47	1427	1491	737	677	518	860
Detroit	4.39	162	15	12	45	1430	1401	754	697	661	856

INDIVIDUAL BATTING LEADERS
(Minimum 502 Plate Appearances)

BATTING	AVG	G	AB	R	H	2B	3B	HR	RBI	BB	SO	SB
*Brett, George, KC	.329	142	544	82	179	45	7	14	87	56	63	9
Henderson, Rickey, Oak	.325	136	489	119	159	33	3	28	61	97	60	65
*Palmeiro, Rafael, Texas	.319	154	598	72	191	35	6	14	89	40	59	3
Trammell, Alan, Detroit	.304	146	559	71	170	37	1	14	89	68	55	12
*Boggs, Wade, Boston	.302	155	619	89	187	44	5	6	63	87	68	0
Martinez, Edgar, Seattle	.302	144	487	71	147	27	2	11	49	74	62	1
*Griffey, Ken Jr., Seattle	.300	155	597	91	179	28	7	22	80	63	81	16
*McGriff, Fred, Toronto	.300	153	557	91	167	21	1	35	88	94	108	5
James, Chris, Cleveland	.299	140	528	62	158	32	4	12	70	31	71	4
Puckett, Kirby, Minnesota	.298	146	551	82	164	40	3	12	80	57	73	5

INDIVIDUAL PITCHING LEADERS
(Minimum 162 Innings)

	W	L	ERA	G	GS	CG	SV	IP	H	R	ER	BB	SO
Clemens, Roger, Boston	21	6	1.93	31	31	7	0	228	193	59	49	54	209
*Finley, Chuck, Calif	18	9	2.40	32	32	7	0	236	210	77	63	81	177
Stewart, Dave, Oakland	22	11	2.56	36	36	11	0	267	226	84	76	83	166
Appier, Kevin, KC	12	8	2.76	32	24	3	0	186	179	67	57	54	127
Stieb, Dave, Toronto	18	6	2.93	33	33	2	0	209	179	73	68	64	125
Welch, Bob, Oakland	27	6	3.06	35	35	2	0	238	214	90	78	77	127
*Wells, David, Toronto	11	6	3.14	43	25	0	3	189	165	72	66	45	115
*Hibbard, Greg, Chicago	14	9	3.16	33	33	3	0	211	202	80	74	55	92
Hanson, Erik, Seattle	18	9	3.24	33	33	5	0	236	205	88	85	68	211
McCaskill, Kirk, Calif	12	11	3.25	29	29	2	0	174	161	77	63	72	78

Cumulative Statistics, Multi-team Players

BATTING	AVG	G	AB	R	H	2B	3B	HR	RBI	BB	SO	SB
*Baines, Harold, Texas-Oak	.284	135	415	52	118	15	1	16	65	67	80	0
Bradley, Phil, Balt-Chi	.256	117	422	59	108	14	2	4	31	50	61	17
Coles, Darnell, Sea-Det	.209	89	215	22	45	7	1	3	20	16	38	0
Gallagher, Dave, Chi-Balt	.254	68	126	12	32	4	1	0	7	7	12	1
#Jefferson, Stan, Balt-Clev	.231	59	117	22	27	8	0	2	10	10	26	9
Jones, Tracy, Det-Sea	.260	75	204	23	53	8	1	6	24	9	25	1
Kittle, Ron, Chi-Balt	.231	105	338	33	78	16	0	18	46	26	91	0
#Liriano, Nelson, Tor-Minn	.234	103	355	46	83	12	9	1	28	38	44	8
#McLemore, Mark, Calif-Clev	.150	28	60	6	9	2	0	0	2	4	15	1
*Nokes, Matt, Det-NY	.248	136	351	33	87	9	1	11	40	24	47	2
*Phelps, Ken, Oak-Clev	.150	56	120	10	18	2	0	1	6	22	21	1
*Polonia, Luis, Calif-NY	.337	120	403	52	136	7	9	2	35	25	43	21
*Walker, Greg, Chi-Balt	.154	16	39	2	6	0	0	0	2	3	11	1
*Washington, Claudell, Calif-NY	.167	45	114	7	19	2	1	1	9	4	25	4
Winfield, Dave, NY-Calif	.267	132	475	70	127	21	2	21	78	52	81	0

PITCHING	W	L	ERA	G	GS	CG	SV	IP	H	R	ER	BB	SO
Bitker, Joe, Oak-Texas	0	0	2.25	9	0	0	0	12	8	3	3	4	8
*Black, Bud, Clev-Tor	13	11	3.57	32	31	5	0	207	181	86	82	61	106
*Candelaria, John, Minn-Tor	7	6	3.95	47	3	0	5	80	87	36	35	20	63
McCullers, Lance, NY-Det	2	0	3.02	20	1	0	0	45	32	19	15	19	31
Parker, Clay, NY-Det	3	3	3.58	29	3	0	0	73	64	29	29	32	40
*Powell, Dennis, Sea-Mil	0	4	7.02	11	7	0	0	42	64	40	33	21	23
Reed, Jerry, Sea-Bos	2	2	4.82	33	0	0	2	52	63	31	28	19	19
Witt, Mike, Calif-NY	5	9	4.00	26	16	2	1	117	106	62	52	47	74

BALTIMORE

BATTING

BATTING	AVG	G	AB	R	H	2B	3B	HR	RBI	BB	SO	SB
*Anderson, Brady	.231	89	234	24	54	5	2	3	24	31	46	15
#Bell, Juan	.000	5	2	1	0	0	0	0	0	0	1	0
Bradley, Phil	.270	72	289	39	78	9	1	4	26	30	35	10
Brown, Marty	.200	9	15	1	3	0	0	0	0	1	7	0
Devereaux, Mike	.240	108	367	48	88	18	1	12	49	28	48	13
*Finley, Steve	.256	142	464	46	119	16	4	3	37	32	53	22
Gallagher, Dave	.216	23	51	7	11	1	0	0	2	4	3	1
Gomez, Leo	.231	12	39	3	9	0	0	0	1	8	7	0
Gonzales, Rene	.214	67	103	13	22	3	1	1	12	12	14	1
Hoiles, Chris	.190	23	63	7	12	3	0	1	6	5	12	0
*Horn, Sam	.248	79	246	30	61	13	0	14	45	32	62	0
Hulett, Tim	.255	53	153	16	39	7	1	3	16	15	41	1
#Jefferson, Stan	.000	10	19	1	0	0	0	0	0	2	8	1
Kittle, Ron	.164	22	61	4	10	2	0	2	3	2	14	0
Komminsk, Brad	.238	46	101	18	24	4	0	3	8	14	29	1
McKnight, Jeff	.200	29	75	11	15	2	0	1	4	5	17	0
Melvin, Bob	.243	93	301	30	73	14	1	5	37	11	53	0
Milligan, Randy	.265	109	362	64	96	20	1	20	60	88	68	6
Nixon, Donell	.250	8	20	1	5	2	0	0	2	1	7	5
*Orsulak, Joe	.269	124	413	49	111	14	3	11	57	46	48	6
Ripken, Bill	.291	129	406	48	118	28	1	3	38	28	43	5
Ripken, Cal	.250	161	600	78	150	28	4	21	84	82	66	3
#Segui, David	.244	40	123	14	30	7	0	2	15	11	15	0
#Tettleton, Mickey	.223	135	444	68	99	21	2	15	51	106	160	2
*Walker, Greg	.147	14	34	2	5	0	0	0	2	3	9	1
Worthington, Craig	.226	133	425	46	96	17	0	8	44	63	96	1

PITCHING

PITCHING	W	L	ERA	G	GS	CG	SV	IP	H	R	ER	BB	SO
Aldrich, Jay	1	2	8.25	7	0	0	1	12	17	13	11	7	5
*Ballard, Jeff	2	11	4.93	44	17	0	0	133	152	79	73	42	50
Bautista, Jose	1	0	4.05	22	0	0	0	27	28	15	12	7	15
*Boone, Dan	0	0	2.79	4	1	0	0	10	12	3	3	3	2
Harnisch, Pete	11	11	4.34	31	31	3	0	189	189	96	91	86	122
*Hickey, Kevin	1	3	5.13	37	0	0	1	26	26	16	15	13	17
Holton, Brian	2	3	4.50	33	0	0	0	58	68	31	29	21	27
Johnson, Dave	13	9	4.10	30	29	3	0	180	196	83	82	43	68
McDonald, Ben	8	5	2.43	21	15	3	0	119	88	36	32	35	65
Mesa, Jose	3	2	3.86	7	7	0	0	47	37	20	20	27	24
Milacki, Bob	5	8	4.46	27	24	1	0	135	143	73	67	61	60
Mitchell, John	6	6	4.64	24	17	0	0	114	133	63	59	48	43
Olson, Gregg	6	5	2.42	64	0	0	37	74	57	20	20	31	74
*Price, Joe	3	4	3.58	50	0	0	0	65	62	29	26	24	54
Schilling, Curt	1	2	2.54	35	0	0	3	46	38	13	13	19	32
Smith, Mike	0	0	12.00	2	0	0	0	3	4	4	4	1	2
Taylor, Dorn	0	1	2.45	4	0	0	0	4	4	3	1	2	4
Telford, Anthony	3	3	4.95	8	8	0	0	36	43	22	20	19	20
Tibbs, Jay	2	7	5.68	10	10	0	0	51	55	34	32	14	23
Weston, Mickey	0	1	7.71	9	2	0	0	21	28	20	18	6	9
Williamson, Mark	8	2	2.21	49	0	0	1	85	65	25	21	28	60

FIELDING

Catcher
Catcher	PCT	G	PO	A	E
Hoiles	1.000	7	21	4	0
Melvin	.997	76	364	25	1
Tettleton	.991	90	425	37	4

First Base
First Base	PCT	G	PO	A	E
Hoiles	1.000	6	41	2	0
Horn	.970	10	58	6	2
Kittle	1.000	5	26	1	0
McKnight	1.000	15	89	11	0
Melvin	1.000	1	1	1	0
Milligan	.990	98	846	87	9
Segui	.990	36	283	26	3
Tettleton	.971	5	32	2	1
Walker	1.000	1	14	1	0

Second Base
Second Base	PCT	G	PO	A	E
Brown	1.000	3	1	1	0
Gonzales	.994	43	61	94	1
Hulett	.986	16	27	45	1
McKnight	1.000	5	8	8	0
B. Ripken	.987	127	250	366	8

Third Base
Third Base	PCT	G	PO	A	E
Brown	1.000	2	0	2	0

	PCT	G	PO	A	E
Gomez	.886	12	11	20	4
Gonzales	.929	16	3	10	1
Hulett	.961	24	17	56	3
Worthington	.945	131	90	218	18

Shortstop
Shortstop	PCT	G	PO	A	E
Bell	1.000	1	1	1	0
Gonzales	1.000	9	4	10	0
McKnight	1.000	1	1	1	0
C. Ripken	.996	161	242	435	3

Outfield
Outfield	PCT	G	PO	A	E
Anderson	.987	63	149	3	2
Bradley	.987	70	149	3	2
Devereaux	.983	104	281	4	5
Finley	.977	133	290	4	7
Gallagher	.980	20	46	2	1
Gonzales	.000	1	0	0	0
Jefferson	1.000	5	9	0	0
Komminsk	1.000	40	67	2	0
McKnight	1.000	8	8	0	0
Nixon	1.000	4	5	0	0
Orsulak	.989	109	267	5	3
Tettleton	1.000	1	1	0	0

BOSTON

BATTING

	AVG	G	AB	R	H	2B	3B	HR	RBI	BB	SO	SB
Barrett, Marty	.226	62	159	15	36	4	0	0	13	15	13	4
*Boggs, Wade	.302	155	619	89	187	44	5	6	63	87	68	0
Brunansky, Tom	.267	129	461	61	123	24	5	15	71	54	105	5
*Buckner, Bill	.186	22	43	4	8	0	0	1	3	3	2	0
Burks, Ellis	.296	152	588	89	174	33	8	21	89	48	82	9
*Cooper, Scott	.000	2	1	0	0	0	0	0	0	0	1	0
Evans, Dwight	.249	123	445	66	111	18	3	13	63	67	73	3
*Gedman, Rich	.200	10	15	3	3	0	0	0	0	5	6	0
Greenwell, Mike	.297	159	610	71	181	30	6	14	73	65	43	0
*Heep, Danny	.174	41	69	3	12	1	1	0	8	7	14	0
Kutcher, Randy	.230	63	74	18	17	4	1	1	5	13	18	3
*Lancellotti, Rick	.000	4	8	0	0	0	0	0	0	1	3	0
Marshall, Mike	.286	30	112	10	32	6	1	4	12	4	26	0
Marzano, John	.241	32	83	8	20	4	0	0	6	5	10	0
Naehring, Tim	.271	24	85	10	23	6	0	2	12	8	15	0
Pena, Tony	.263	143	491	62	129	19	1	7	56	43	71	8
*Plantier, Phil	.133	14	15	1	2	1	0	0	3	4	6	0
Quintana, Carlos	.287	149	512	56	147	28	0	7	67	52	74	1
Reed, Jody	.289	155	598	70	173	45	0	5	51	75	65	4
Rivera, Luis	.225	118	346	38	78	20	0	7	45	25	58	4
*Robidoux, Billy Jo	.182	27	44	3	8	4	0	1	4	6	14	0
Romine, Kevin	.272	70	136	21	37	7	0	2	14	12	27	4
*Stone, Jeff	.500	10	2	1	1	0	0	0	0	0	1	0

PITCHING

	W	L	ERA	G	GS	CG	SV	IP	H	R	ER	BB	SO
Andersen, Larry	0	0	1.23	15	0	0	1	22	18	3	3	3	25
Boddicker, Mike	17	8	3.36	34	34	4	0	228	225	92	85	69	143
*Bolton, Tom	10	5	3.38	21	16	3	0	120	111	46	45	47	65
Clemens, Roger	21	6	1.93	31	31	7	0	228	193	59	49	54	209
Dopson, John	0	0	2.04	4	4	0	0	18	13	7	4	9	9
Gardner, Wes	3	7	4.89	34	9	0	0	77	77	43	42	35	58
Gray, Jeff	2	4	4.44	41	0	0	9	51	53	27	25	15	50
Harris, Greg	13	9	4.00	34	30	1	0	184	186	90	82	77	117
*Hesketh, Joe	0	4	3.51	12	2	0	0	26	37	12	10	11	26
Hetzel, Eric	1	4	5.91	9	8	0	0	35	39	28	23	21	20
Irvine, Daryl	1	1	4.67	11	0	0	0	17	15	10	9	10	9
Kiecker, Dana	8	9	3.97	32	25	0	0	152	145	74	67	54	93
Lamp, Dennis	3	5	4.68	47	1	0	0	106	114	61	55	30	49
Leister, John	0	0	4.76	2	1	0	0	6	7	5	3	4	3
*Murphy, Rob	0	6	6.32	68	0	0	7	57	85	46	40	32	54
Reardon, Jeff	5	3	3.16	47	0	0	21	51	39	19	18	19	33
Reed, Jerry	2	1	4.80	29	0	0	2	45	55	27	24	16	17
*Rochford, Mike	0	1	18.00	2	1	0	0	4	10	10	8	4	0
Smith, Lee	2	1	1.88	11	0	0	4	14	13	4	3	9	17

FIELDING

Catcher	PCT	G	PO	A	E
Gedman	.970	9	27	5	1
Marzano	1.000	32	153	14	0
Pena	.995	142	864	74	5

First Base	PCT	G	PO	A	E
Buckner	1.000	15	75	6	0
Heep	.963	5	23	3	1
Lancellotti	1.000	2	20	2	0
Marshall	1.000	8	42	7	0
Pena	1.000	1	2	0	0
Quintana	.987	148	1188	137	17
Robidoux	.981	11	49	4	1

Second Base	PCT	G	PO	A	E
Barrett	.992	60	90	147	2
Kutcher	1.000	5	8	11	0
Naehring	.000	1	0	0	0
Pankovits	.000	2	0	0	0
Jo. Reed	.990	119	215	374	6
Rivera	1.000	3	1	0	0

Third Base	PCT	G	PO	A	E
Barrett	1.000	1	0	1	0
Boggs	.946	152	108	241	20
Kutcher	1.000	11	6	15	0
Naehring	.923	5	3	9	1
Rivera	.000	1	0	0	0

Shortstop	PCT	G	PO	A	E
Naehring	.918	19	33	57	8
Jo. Reed	.944	50	63	104	10
Rivera	.965	112	186	310	18

Outfield	PCT	G	PO	A	E
Brunansky	.982	121	267	7	5
Burks	.994	143	324	7	2
Greenwell	.977	159	287	13	7
Heep	1.000	14	19	1	0
Kutcher	1.000	34	41	0	0
Marshall	.929	8	13	0	1
Plantier	.000	1	0	0	0
Quintana	1.000	3	2	0	0
Romine	.976	64	81	0	2

CALIFORNIA

BATTING

	AVG	G	AB	R	H	2B	3B	HR	RBI	BB	SO	SB
Anderson, Kent	.308	49	143	16	44	6	1	1	5	13	19	0
Bichette, Dante	.255	109	349	40	89	15	1	15	53	16	79	5
Coachman, Pete	.311	16	45	3	14	3	0	0	5	1	7	0
#Davis, Chili	.265	113	412	58	109	17	1	12	58	61	89	1
DiSarcina, Gary	.140	18	57	8	8	1	1	0	0	3	10	1
Downing, Brian	.273	96	330	47	90	18	2	14	51	50	45	0
#Hill, Donnie	.264	103	352	36	93	18	2	3	32	29	27	1
*Howell, Jack	.228	105	316	35	72	19	1	8	33	46	61	3
*Joyner, Wally	.268	83	310	35	83	15	0	8	41	41	34	2
#McLemore, Mark	.146	20	48	4	7	2	0	0	2	4	9	1
Orton, John	.190	31	84	8	16	5	0	1	6	5	31	0
Parrish, Lance	.268	133	470	54	126	14	0	24	70	46	107	2
*Polonia, Luis	.336	109	381	50	128	7	9	2	32	25	42	20

Angels pitcher Chuck Finley became one of the AL's top lefthanders by going 18-9 with a 2.40 ERA.

	AVG	G	AB	R	H	2B	3B	HR	RBI	BB	SO	SB
#Ray, Johnny	.277	105	404	47	112	23	0	5	43	19	44	2
Rose, Bobby	.385	7	13	5	5	0	0	1	2	2	1	0
Schofield, Dick	.255	99	310	41	79	8	1	1	18	52	61	3
Schroeder, Bill	.224	18	58	7	13	3	0	4	9	1	10	0
Schu, Rick	.268	61	157	19	42	8	0	6	14	11	25	0
*Stevens, Lee	.214	67	248	28	53	10	0	7	32	22	75	1
Tingley, Ron	.000	5	3	0	0	0	0	0	0	1	1	0
*Venable, Max	.259	93	189	26	49	9	3	4	21	24	31	5
*Washington, Claudell	.176	12	34	3	6	1	0	1	3	2	8	1
#White, Devon	.217	125	443	57	96	17	3	11	44	44	116	21
Winfield, Dave	.275	112	414	63	114	18	2	19	72	48	68	0

PITCHING	W	L	ERA	G	GS	CG	SV	IP	H	R	ER	BB	SO
*Abbott, Jim	10	14	4.51	33	33	4	0	212	246	116	106	72	105
*Bailes, Scott	2	0	6.37	27	0	0	0	35	46	30	25	20	16
Blyleven, Bert	8	7	5.24	23	23	2	0	134	163	85	78	25	69
Clear, Mark	0	0	5.87	4	0	0	0	8	5	7	5	9	6
*Corbett, Sherm	0	0	9.00	4	0	0	0	5	8	5	5	3	2
Eichhorn, Mark	2	5	3.08	60	0	0	13	85	98	36	29	23	69
Fetters, Mike	1	1	4.12	26	2	0	1	68	77	33	31	20	35
*Finley, Chuck	18	9	2.40	32	32	7	0	236	210	77	63	81	177
Fraser, Willie	5	4	3.08	45	0	0	2	76	69	29	26	24	32
Grahe, Joe	3	4	4.98	8	8	0	0	43	51	30	24	23	25
Harvey, Bryan	4	4	3.22	54	0	0	25	64	45	24	23	35	82
*Langston, Mark	10	17	4.40	33	33	5	0	223	215	120	109	104	195
Lewis, Scott	1	1	2.20	2	2	1	0	16	10	4	4	2	9
McCaskill, Kirk	12	11	3.25	29	29	2	0	174	161	77	63	72	78
*McClure, Bob	2	0	6.43	11	0	0	0	7	7	6	5	3	6
Minton, Greg	1	1	2.35	11	0	0	0	15	11	4	4	7	4
Richardson, Jeff	0	0	0.00	1	0	0	0	1	0	0	0	0	0
Witt, Mike	0	3	1.77	10	0	0	1	20	19	9	4	13	14
*Young, Cliff	1	1	3.52	17	0	0	0	31	40	14	12	7	19

FIELDING

Catcher	PCT	G	PO	A	E
Orton	.987	31	139	15	2
Parrish	.993	131	760	88	6
Schroeder	1.000	15	74	7	0
Tingley	1.000	5	12	0	0

First Base	PCT	G	PO	A	E
Hill	1.000	3	23	2	0
Howell	1.000	1	2	0	0
Joyner	.995	83	727	62	4
Parrish	1.000	4	34	2	0
Schroeder	1.000	3	26	3	0
Schu	.989	15	85	4	1
Stevens	.994	67	597	36	4

Second Base	PCT	G	PO	A	E
Anderson	.955	5	10	11	1
Coachman	.857	2	1	5	1
DiSarcina	1.000	3	3	8	0
Hill	.990	60	128	173	3
McLemore	1.000	8	14	15	0
Ray	.987	100	241	295	7
Rose	1.000	4	1	2	0
Schu	.750	1	3	3	2

Third Base	PCT	G	PO	A	E
Anderson	.944	16	12	39	3
Coachman	.958	9	5	18	1
Hill	.891	21	8	33	5
Howell	.939	102	70	193	17
Rose	1.000	3	2	5	0
Schu	.918	38	16	74	8

Shortstop	PCT	G	PO	A	E
Anderson	.964	29	53	79	5
DiSarcina	.940	14	14	49	4
Hill	.965	24	35	47	3
Howell	.875	1	4	3	1
Schofield	.966	99	170	318	17

Outfield	PCT	G	PO	A	E
Bichette	.965	105	183	12	7
Davis	.965	52	77	5	3
Polonia	.980	85	144	3	3
Schu	.000	4	0	0	0
Venable	.975	77	112	3	3
Washington	1.000	9	19	1	0
White	.972	122	302	11	9
Winfield	.989	108	165	7	2

CHICAGO

BATTING	AVG	G	AB	R	H	2B	3B	HR	RBI	BB	SO	SB
*Boston, Daryl	.000	5	1	0	0	0	0	0	0	0	0	1
Bradley, Phil	.226	45	133	20	30	5	1	0	5	20	26	7
Calderon, Ivan	.273	158	607	85	166	44	2	14	74	51	79	32
Fisk, Carlton	.285	137	452	65	129	21	0	18	65	61	73	7
Fletcher, Scott	.242	151	509	54	123	18	3	4	56	45	63	1
Gallagher, Dave	.280	45	75	5	21	3	1	0	5	3	9	0
Grebeck, Craig	.168	59	119	7	20	3	1	1	9	8	24	0
*Guillen, Ozzie	.279	160	516	61	144	21	4	1	58	26	37	13
Johnson, Lance	.285	151	541	76	154	18	9	1	51	33	45	36
Karkovice, Ron	.246	68	183	30	45	10	0	6	20	16	52	2
Kittle, Ron	.245	83	277	29	68	14	0	16	43	24	77	0
*Lyons, Steve	.192	94	146	22	28	6	1	1	11	10	41	1
Martinez, Carlos	.224	92	272	18	61	6	5	4	24	10	40	0
McCray, Rodney	.000	32	6	8	0	0	0	0	0	1	4	6
*Pasqua, Dan	.274	112	325	43	89	27	3	13	58	37	66	1
Sosa, Sammy	.233	153	532	72	124	26	10	15	70	33	150	32
Stark, Matt	.250	8	16	0	4	1	0	0	3	1	6	0
Thomas, Frank	.330	60	191	39	63	11	3	7	31	44	54	0
*Ventura, Robin	.249	150	493	48	123	17	1	5	54	55	53	1
*Walker, Greg	.200	2	5	0	1	0	0	0	0	0	2	0
*Willard, Jerry	.000	3	3	0	0	0	0	0	0	0	2	0

PITCHING	W	L	ERA	G	GS	CG	SV	IP	H	R	ER	BB	SO
*Edwards, Wayne	5	3	3.22	42	5	0	2	95	81	39	34	41	63
Fernandez, Alex	5	5	3.80	13	13	3	0	88	89	40	37	34	61
Hibbard, Greg	14	9	3.16	33	33	3	0	211	202	80	74	55	92
Hillegas, Shawn	0	0	0.79	7	0	0	0	11	4	1	1	5	5
Jones, Barry	11	4	2.31	65	0	0	1	74	62	20	19	33	45
King, Eric	12	4	3.28	25	25	2	0	151	135	59	55	40	70
Kutzler, Jerry	2	1	6.03	7	7	0	0	31	38	23	21	14	21
Long, Bill	0	1	6.35	4	0	0	0	6	6	5	4	2	2
McDowell, Jack	14	9	3.82	33	33	4	0	205	189	93	87	77	165
Pall, Donn	3	5	3.32	56	0	0	2	76	63	33	28	24	39
*Patterson, Ken	2	1	3.39	43	0	0	2	66	58	27	25	34	40
Perez, Melido	13	14	4.61	35	35	3	0	197	177	111	101	86	161
Peterson, Adam	2	5	4.55	20	11	2	0	85	90	46	43	26	29
*Radinsky, Scott	6	1	4.82	62	0	0	4	52	47	29	28	36	46
*Rosenberg, Steve	1	0	5.40	6	0	0	0	10	10	6	6	5	4
Thigpen, Bobby	4	6	1.83	77	0	0	57	89	60	20	18	32	70

FIELDING

Catcher	PCT	G	PO	A	E
Fisk	.994	116	660	63	4
Karkovice	.994	64	296	31	2
Willard	.000	1	0	0	0

First Base	PCT	G	PO	A	E
Calderon	1.000	2	1	0	0
Kittle	.987	25	150	5	2
Lyons	.991	61	206	19	2
Martinez	.988	82	632	38	8
Thomas	.989	51	428	26	5
Ventura	.000	1	0	0	0

Second Base	PCT	G	PO	A	E
Fletcher	.988	151	305	436	9
Grebeck	1.000	6	6	12	0
Lyons	.951	15	29	29	3

Third Base	PCT	G	PO	A	E
Grebeck	.987	35	17	58	1

	PCT	G	PO	A	E
Lyons	1.000	5	0	4	0
Ventura	.939	147	116	268	25

Shortstop	PCT	G	PO	A	E
Grebeck	.953	16	13	28	2
Guillen	.977	159	252	474	17
Lyons	1.000	1	0	1	0

Outfield	PCT	G	PO	A	E
Boston	.000	1	0	0	0
Bradley	.973	38	70	1	2
Calderon	.975	130	268	7	7
Gallagher	.981	37	50	1	1
Johnson	.973	148	353	5	10
Lyons	1.000	7	9	0	0
Martinez	.000	1	0	0	0
McCray	1.000	13	8	0	0
Pasqua	.962	43	71	5	3
Sosa	.962	152	315	14	13

CLEVELAND

BATTING	AVG	G	AB	R	H	2B	3B	HR	RBI	BB	SO	SB
Allred, Beau	.188	4	16	2	3	1	0	1	2	2	3	0
Alomar, Sandy	.290	132	445	60	129	26	2	9	66	25	46	4
#Baerga, Carlos	.260	108	312	46	81	17	2	7	47	16	57	0
Belle, Albert	.174	9	23	1	4	0	0	1	3	1	6	0
Brookens, Tom	.266	64	154	18	41	7	2	1	20	14	25	0
#Browne, Jerry	.267	140	513	92	137	26	5	6	50	72	46	12
*Cole, Alex	.300	63	227	43	68	5	4	0	13	28	38	40
Fermin, Felix	.256	148	414	47	106	13	2	1	40	26	22	3
*Hernandez, Keith	.200	43	130	7	26	2	0	1	8	14	17	0
Jacoby, Brook	.293	155	553	77	162	24	4	14	75	63	58	1
James, Chris	.299	140	528	62	158	32	4	12	70	31	71	4
*James, Dion	.274	87	248	28	68	15	2	1	22	27	23	5
#Jefferson, Stan	.276	49	98	21	27	8	0	2	10	8	18	8
Maldonado, Candy	.273	155	590	76	161	32	2	22	95	49	134	3
Manto, Jeff	.224	30	76	12	17	5	1	2	14	21	18	0
#McLemore, Mark	.167	8	12	2	2	0	0	0	0	0	6	0
*Phelps, Ken	.115	24	61	4	7	0	0	0	0	10	11	1
Santana, Rafael	.231	7	13	3	3	0	0	1	3	0	0	0
Skinner, Joel	.252	49	139	16	35	4	1	2	16	7	44	0
Snyder, Cory	.233	123	438	46	102	27	3	14	55	21	118	1

Knuckleballer Tom Candiotti paced the Cleveland Indians with 15 victories.

	AVG	G	AB	R	H	2B	3B	HR	RBI	BB	SO	SB
Springer, Steve	.167	4	12	1	2	0	0	0	1	0	6	0
#Ward, Turner	.348	14	46	10	16	2	1	1	10	3	8	3
#Webster, Mitch	.252	128	437	58	110	20	6	12	55	20	61	22

PITCHING	W	L	ERA	G	GS	CG	SV	IP	H	R	ER	BB	SO
*Bearse, Kevin	0	2	12.91	3	3	0	0	8	16	11	11	5	2
*Black, Bud	11	10	3.53	29	29	5	0	191	171	79	75	58	103
Candiotti, Tom	15	11	3.65	31	29	3	0	202	207	92	82	55	128
Farrell, John	4	5	4.28	17	17	1	0	97	108	49	46	33	44
Gozzo, Goose	0	0	0.00	2	0	0	0	3	2	0	0	2	2
Guante, Cecilio	2	3	5.01	26	1	0	0	47	38	26	26	18	30
Jones, Doug	5	5	2.56	66	0	0	43	84	66	26	24	22	55
*Kaiser, Jeff	0	0	3.55	5	0	0	0	13	16	5	5	7	9
Nagy, Charles	2	4	5.91	9	8	0	0	46	58	31	30	21	26
Nichols, Rod	0	3	7.88	4	2	0	0	16	24	14	14	6	3
Nipper, Al	2	3	6.75	9	5	0	0	24	35	19	18	19	12
Olin, Steve	4	4	3.41	50	1	0	1	92	96	41	35	26	64
*Orosco, Jesse	5	4	3.90	55	0	0	2	65	58	35	28	38	55
Seanez, Rudy	2	1	5.60	24	0	0	0	27	22	17	17	25	24
Shaw, Jeff	3	4	6.66	12	9	0	0	49	73	38	36	20	25
*Swindell, Greg	12	9	4.40	34	34	3	0	215	245	110	105	47	135
*Valdez, Efrain	1	1	3.04	13	0	0	0	24	20	10	8	14	13
Valdez, Sergio	6	6	4.75	24	13	0	0	102	109	62	54	35	63
Walker, Mike	2	6	4.88	18	11	0	0	76	82	49	41	42	34
Ward, Colby	1	3	4.25	22	0	0	1	36	31	17	17	21	23
*Wickander, Kevin	0	1	3.65	10	0	0	0	12	14	6	5	4	10

FIELDING

Catcher	PCT	G	PO	A	E
Alomar	.981	129	686	46	14
Skinner	.996	49	222	16	1

	PCT	G	PO	A	E
Manto	1.000	5	6	6	0
McLemore	1.000	4	1	2	0
Springer	1.000	3	2	3	0

First Base	PCT	G	PO	A	E
Brookens	1.000	2	3	1	0
Hernandez	.994	42	340	20	2
Jacoby	.997	78	584	28	2
D. James	.996	35	228	17	1
Manto	.990	25	179	18	2
Phelps	1.000	14	87	7	0
Webster	.895	3	15	2	2

Shortstop	PCT	G	PO	A	E
Baerga	.942	48	24	41	4
Brookens	1.000	3	5	4	0
Fermin	.975	147	213	422	16
McLemore	.882	8	15	15	4
Santana	1.000	7	2	9	0
Snyder	.923	5	5	7	1

Second Base	PCT	G	PO	A	E
Baerga	.898	8	22	22	5
Brookens	.989	21	40	48	1
Browne	.985	139	286	382	10
Fermin	1.000	1	1	2	0
McLemore	1.000	3	7	7	0

Outfield	PCT	G	PO	A	E
Allred	.833	4	5	0	1
Belle	.000	1	0	0	0
Cole	.961	59	145	3	6
C. James	1.000	14	25	1	0
D. James	.947	33	54	0	3
Jefferson	.985	34	61	4	1
Maldonado	.993	134	293	9	2
Snyder	.975	120	224	11	6
Ward	.957	13	20	2	1
Webster	.991	118	330	1	3

Third Base	PCT	G	PO	A	E
Baerga	.944	50	33	101	8
Brookens	.923	35	9	51	5
Jacoby	.981	99	44	158	4

Alan Trammell 304-14-89

Jack Morris ... 15 wins

Lou Whitaker ... 18 homers

BATTING	AVG	G	AB	R	H	2B	3B	HR	RBI	BB	SO	SB
*Bergman, Dave	.278	100	205	21	57	10	1	2	26	33	17	3
Coles, Darnell	.204	52	108	13	22	2	0	1	4	12	21	0
#Cuyler, Milt	.255	19	51	8	13	3	1	0	8	5	10	1
Fielder, Cecil	.277	159	573	104	159	25	1	51	132	90	182	0
Fryman, Travis	.297	66	232	32	69	11	1	9	27	17	51	3
Heath, Mike	.270	122	370	46	100	18	2	7	38	19	71	7
Jones, Tracy	.229	50	118	15	27	4	1	4	9	6	13	1
Lemon, Chet	.258	104	322	39	83	16	4	5	32	48	61	3
Lindeman, Jim	.219	12	32	5	7	1	0	2	8	2	13	0
*Lusader, Scott	.241	45	87	13	21	2	0	2	16	12	8	0
*Moseby, Lloyd	.248	122	431	64	107	16	5	14	51	48	77	17
*Nokes, Matt	.270	44	111	12	30	5	1	3	8	4	14	0
Paredes, Johnny	.125	6	8	2	1	0	0	0	0	1	0	0
#Phillips, Tony	.251	152	573	97	144	23	5	8	55	99	85	19
Romero, Ed	.229	32	70	8	16	3	0	0	4	6	4	0
Rowland, Rich	.158	7	19	3	3	1	0	0	0	2	4	0
*Salas, Mark	.232	74	164	18	38	3	0	9	24	21	28	0
*Sheets, Larry	.261	131	360	40	94	17	2	10	52	24	42	1
#Shelby, John	.248	78	222	22	55	9	3	4	20	10	51	3
Trammell, Alan	.304	146	559	71	170	37	1	14	89	68	55	12
Ward, Gary	.256	106	309	32	79	11	2	9	46	30	50	2
*Whitaker, Lou	.237	132	472	75	112	22	2	18	60	74	71	8
Williams, Kenny	.133	57	83	10	11	2	0	0	5	3	24	2

PITCHING	W	L	ERA	G	GS	CG	SV	IP	H	R	ER	BB	SO
*Aldred, Scott	1	2	3.77	4	3	0	0	14	13	6	6	10	7
*DuBois, Brian	3	5	5.09	12	11	0	0	58	70	37	33	22	34
*Gibson, Paul	5	4	3.05	61	0	0	3	97	99	36	33	44	56
*Gleaton, Jerry Don	1	3	2.94	57	0	0	13	83	62	27	27	25	56
Henneman, Mike	8	6	3.05	69	0	0	22	94	90	36	32	33	50
Kinzer, Matt	0	0	16.20	1	0	0	0	2	3	3	3	3	1
Lugo, Urbano	2	0	7.03	13	1	0	0	24	30	19	19	13	12
McCullers, Lance	1	0	2.73	9	1	0	0	30	18	11	9	13	20
Morris, Jack	15	18	4.51	36	36	11	0	250	231	144	125	97	162
Nosek, Randy	1	1	7.71	3	2	0	0	7	7	7	6	9	3
Nunez, Edwin	3	1	2.24	42	0	0	6	80	65	26	20	37	66
Parker, Clay	2	2	3.18	24	1	0	0	51	45	18	18	25	20
Petry, Dan	10	9	4.45	32	23	1	0	150	148	78	74	77	73
Ritz, Kevin	4	11	4.05	4	4	0	0	7	14	12	9	14	3
Robinson, Jeff	10	9	5.96	27	27	1	0	145	141	101	96	88	76
Schwabe, Mike	0	0	2.45	1	0	0	0	4	5	1	1	0	1
*Searcy, Steve	2	7	4.66	16	12	1	0	75	76	44	39	51	66
*Tanana, Frank	9	8	5.31	34	29	1	1	176	190	104	104	66	114
Terrell, Walt	6	4	4.54	13	12	0	0	75	86	39	38	24	30
Wapnick, Steve	0	0	6.43	4	0	0	0	7	8	5	5	10	6

FIELDING

Catcher	PCT	G	PO	A	E
Heath	.980	117	585	54	13
Nokes	.984	19	55	7	1
Rowland	.967	5	29	0	1
Salas	.988	57	227	22	3

First Base	PCT	G	PO	A	E
Bergman	.995	27	203	13	1
Coles	.955	4	18	3	1
Fielder	.989	143	1190	111	14
Lindeman	1.000	1	5	0	0
Ward	1.000	2	7	0	0

Second Base	PCT	G	PO	A	E
Paredes	.917	4	4	7	1
Phillips	.996	47	91	135	1
Whitaker	.991	130	286	372	6

Third Base	PCT	G	PO	A	E
Coles	.926	8	6	19	2
Fryman	.915	48	23	95	11
Phillips	.931	104	69	200	20
Romero	.982	27	15	41	1

	PCT	G	PO	A	E
Salas	1.000	1	0	1	0
Shortstop	**PCT**	**G**	**PO**	**A**	**E**
Fryman	.961	17	24	50	3
Heath	1.000	1	1	0	0
Phillips	.978	11	12	33	1
Trammell	.979	142	232	409	14
Outfield	**PCT**	**G**	**PO**	**A**	**E**
Bergman	.000	5	0	0	0
Coles	1.000	11	11	0	0
Cuyler	.976	17	38	2	1
Heath	1.000	3	2	0	0
Jones	.952	27	37	3	2
Lemon	.973	96	209	7	6
Lindeman	.000	1	0	0	0
Lusader	.982	42	53	1	1
Moseby	.983	116	288	9	5
Phillips	.889	8	8	0	1
Sheets	.981	79	98	7	2
Shelby	.973	68	138	5	4
Ward	.988	85	157	2	2
Williams	1.000	47	67	5	0

Rafael Palmeiro
... hits leader

Tony Fernandez
... 17 triples

BATTING

RUNS
Rickey Henderson, Oakland ... 119
Cecil Fielder, Detroit 104
Harold Reynolds, Seattle 100
Robin Yount, Milwaukee 98
Tony Phillips, Detroit 97

HITS
Rafael Palmeiro, Texas 191
Wade Boggs, Boston 187
Roberto Kelly, New York 183
Mike Greenwell, Boston........ 181
George Brett, Kansas City 179
Ken Griffey Jr., Seattle 179

TOTAL BASES
Cecil Fielder, Detroit 339
Kelly Gruber, Toronto 303
Fred McGriff, Toronto 295
Ken Griffey Jr., Seattle 287
Ellis Burks, Boston............ 286

DOUBLES
George Brett, Kansas City....... 45
Jody Reed, Boston 45
Wade Boggs, Boston 44
Ivan Calderon, Chicago 44
Brian Harper, Minnesota 42

TRIPLES
Tony Fernandez, Toronto 17
Sammy Sosa, Chicago.......... 10
Lance Johnson, Chicago 9
Nelson Liriano, Tor./Minn. 9
Luis Polonia, NY/California 9

HOME RUNS
Cecil Fielder, Detroit 51
Mark McGwire, Oakland 39
Jose Canseco, Oakland........ 37
Fred McGriff, Toronto 35
Kelly Gruber, Toronto 31

RUNS BATTED IN
Cecil Fielder, Detroit 132
Kelly Gruber, Toronto 118
Mark McGwire, Oakland 108
Jose Canseco, Oakland 101
Ruben Sierra, Texas 96

SACRIFICE BUNTS
Mike Gallego, Oakland 17
Billy Ripken, Baltimore 17
Ozzie Guillen, Chicago......... 15
Three tied at 13

SACRIFICE FLIES
Dave Parker, Milwaukee 14
Kelly Gruber, Toronto 13
George Bell, Toronto........... 11
Jerry Browne, Cleveland 11
Three tied at 9

WALKS
Mark McGwire, Oakland 110
Mickey Tettleton, Baltimore ... 106
Tony Phillips, Detroit 99
Rickey Henderson, Oakland..... 97
Fred McGriff, Toronto 94

INTENTIONAL WALKS
Wade Boggs, Boston 19
Cal Ripken Jr., Baltimore 17

George Brett, Kansas City....... 14
Don Mattingly, New York........ 13
Ruben Sierra, Texas 13

HIT BY PITCH
Phil Bradley, Baltimore/Chicago. 11
Pete Incaviglia, Texas 9
Kelly Gruber, Toronto 8
Eight tied at 7

STRIKEOUTS
Cecil Fielder, Detroit 182
Mickey Tettleton, Baltimore ... 160
Jose Canseco, Oakland 158
Jesse Barfield, New York 150
Sammy Sosa, Chicago 150

STOLEN BASES
Rickey Henderson, Oakland..... 65
Steve Sax, New York 43
Roberto Kelly, New York 42
Alex Cole, Cleveland........... 40
Gary Pettis, Texas 38

CAUGHT STEALING
Lance Johnson, Chicago........ 22
Ozzie Guillen, Chicago......... 17
Roberto Kelly, New York 17
Ivan Calderon, Chicago 16
Harold Reynolds, Seattle 16
Sammy Sosa, Chicago......... 16

GIDP
Ivan Calderon, Chicago 26
Rafael Palmeiro, Texas 24
Tony Pena, Boston 23
Gary Gaetti, Minnesota 22
Three tied at 20

PINCH HITS
Kevin Reimer, Texas 12
Carlos Baerga, Cleveland 11
Scott Bradley, Seattle 10
Jack Daugherty, Texas.......... 10
Five tied at 8

HITTING STREAKS
Brian Harper, Minnesota 25
Paul Molitor, Milwaukee 19
Kent Hrbek, Minnesota......... 17
Kevin Seitzer, Kansas City 17
Three tied at 16

MULTI-HIT GAMES
George Brett, Kansas City....... 59
Wade Boggs, Boston 54
Ellis Burks, Boston............ 54
Mike Greenwell, Boston......... 53
Four tied at 52

SLUGGING PERCENTAGE
Cecil Fielder, Detroit .... .592
Rickey Henderson, Oakland... .577
Jose Canseco, Oakland .... .543
Fred McGriff, Toronto .... .530
George Brett, Kansas City ..... .515

ON-BASE PERCENTAGE
Rickey Henderson, Oakland... .439
Fred McGriff, Toronto .... .400
Edgar Martinez, Seattle........ .397
George Brett, Kansas City..... .387
Alvin Davis, Seattle............ .387

KANSAS CITY

BATTING	AVG	G	AB	R	H	2B	3B	HR	RBI	BB	SO	SB
Berry, Sean	.217	8	23	2	5	1	1	0	4	2	5	0
Boone, Bob	.239	40	117	11	28	3	0	0	9	17	12	1
*Brett, George	.329	142	544	82	179	45	7	14	87	56	63	9
Conine, Jeff	.250	9	20	3	5	2	0	0	2	2	5	0
*Eisenreich, Jim	.280	142	496	61	139	29	7	5	51	42	51	12
Jackson, Bo	.272	111	405	74	110	16	1	28	78	44	128	15
#Jeltz, Steve	.155	74	103	11	16	4	0	0	10	6	21	1
Macfarlane, Mike	.255	124	400	37	102	24	4	6	58	25	69	1
*Mayne, Brent	.231	5	13	2	3	0	0	0	1	3	3	0
#McRae, Brian	.286	46	168	21	48	8	3	2	23	9	29	4
Morman, Russ	.270	12	37	5	10	4	2	1	3	3	3	0
Palacios, Rey	.232	41	56	8	13	3	0	2	9	5	24	2
Pecota, Bill	.242	87	240	43	58	15	2	5	20	33	39	8
*Perry, Gerald	.254	133	465	57	118	22	2	8	57	39	56	17
*Schulz, Jeff	.258	30	66	5	17	5	1	0	6	6	13	0
Seitzer, Kevin	.275	158	622	91	171	31	5	6	38	67	66	7
Shumpert, Terry	.275	32	91	7	25	6	1	0	8	2	17	3
Stillwell, Kurt	.249	144	506	60	126	35	4	3	51	39	60	0
Tabler, Pat	.272	75	195	12	53	14	0	1	19	20	21	1
Tartabull, Danny	.268	88	313	41	84	19	0	15	60	36	93	1
Thurman, Gary	.233	23	60	5	14	3	0	0	3	2	12	1
White, Frank	.216	82	241	20	52	14	1	2	21	10	32	1
#Wilson, Willie	.290	115	307	49	89	13	3	2	42	30	57	24

PITCHING	W	L	ERA	G	GS	CG	SV	IP	H	R	ER	BB	SO
Appier, Kevin	12	8	2.76	32	24	3	0	186	179	67	57	54	127
Aquino, Luis	4	1	3.16	20	3	1	0	68	59	25	24	27	28
Baller, Jay	0	1	15.43	3	0	0	0	2	4	4	4	2	1
*Campbell, Jim	1	0	8.38	2	2	0	0	10	15	9	9	1	2
Codiroli, Chris	0	1	9.58	6	2	0	0	10	13	11	11	17	8
Crawford, Steve	5	4	4.16	46	0	0	1	80	79	38	37	23	54
*Davis, Mark	2	7	5.11	53	3	0	6	69	71	43	39	52	73
Davis, Storm	7	10	4.74	21	20	0	0	112	129	66	59	35	62
Dotson, Rich	0	4	8.48	8	7	0	0	29	43	29	27	14	9
Encarnacion, Luis	0	0	7.84	4	0	0	0	10	14	10	9	4	8
Farr, Steve	13	7	1.98	57	6	1	1	127	99	32	28	48	94
Filson, Pete	0	4	5.91	8	7	0	0	35	42	31	23	13	9
Gordon, Tom	12	11	3.73	32	32	6	0	195	192	99	81	99	175
Gubicza, Mark	4	7	4.50	16	16	2	0	94	101	48	47	38	71
Maldonado, Carlos	0	0	9.00	4	0	0	0	6	9	6	6	4	9
McGaffigan, Andy	4	3	3.09	24	11	0	1	79	75	40	27	28	49
McWilliams, Larry	0	0	9.72	13	0	0	0	8	10	9	9	9	7
Montgomery, Jeff	6	5	2.39	73	0	0	24	94	81	36	25	34	94
Saberhagen, Bret	5	9	3.27	20	20	5	0	135	146	52	49	28	87
*Sanchez, Israel	0	0	8.38	11	0	0	0	10	16	9	9	3	5
Smith, Darryl	0	1	4.05	2	1	0	0	7	5	3	3	4	6
Stottlemyre, Mel	0	1	4.88	13	2	0	0	31	35	18	17	12	14
Wagner, Hector	0	2	8.10	5	5	0	0	23	32	24	21	11	14

FIELDING

Catcher	PCT	G	PO	A	E
Boone	.985	40	243	19	4
Macfarlane	.991	112	660	23	6
Mayne	.970	5	29	3	1
Palacios	.992	27	113	6	1

First Base	PCT	G	PO	A	E
Brett	.993	102	865	66	7
Conine	.977	9	39	4	1
Morman	1.000	3	19	3	0
Palacios	1.000	7	8	0	0
Pecota	1.000	4	19	1	0
Perry	.986	51	394	40	6
Tabler	1.000	5	31	1	0

Second Base	PCT	G	PO	A	E
Jeltz	.977	34	28	57	2
Pecota	.986	50	82	122	3
Seitzer	.974	10	18	19	1
Shumpert	.977	27	56	74	3
White	.978	79	142	218	8

Third Base	PCT	G	PO	A	E
Berry	.944	8	7	10	1
Brett	1.000	1	1	0	0
Jeltz	1.000	3	1	1	0

	PCT	G	PO	A	E
Palacios	1.000	3	1	1	0
Pecota	1.000	11	5	15	0
Seitzer	.953	152	100	262	18
Tabler	.875	6	2	5	1

Shortstop	PCT	G	PO	A	E
Jeltz	.969	23	23	39	2
Pecota	.981	21	44	57	2
Stillwell	.957	141	181	350	24

Outfield	PCT	G	PO	A	E
Brett	1.000	9	14	1	0
Eisenreich	.996	138	261	6	1
Jackson	.952	97	230	8	12
Jeltz	1.000	13	6	1	0
McRae	1.000	45	120	1	0
Morman	1.000	8	8	1	0
Palacios	.000	1	0	0	0
Pecota	1.000	6	10	0	0
Schulz	.943	22	33	0	2
Tabler	.986	42	68	4	1
Tartabull	.965	52	81	1	3
Thurman	1.000	21	32	0	0
White	.000	1	0	0	0
Wilson	1.000	106	187	2	0

MILWAUKEE

BATTING	AVG	G	AB	R	H	2B	3B	HR	RBI	BB	SO	SB
*Bates, Billy	.103	14	29	6	3	1	0	0	2	4	7	4
Braggs, Glenn	.248	37	113	17	28	5	0	3	13	12	21	5
*Brock, Greg	.248	123	367	42	91	23	0	7	50	43	45	4
*Canale, George	.077	10	13	4	1	1	0	0	0	2	5	0
Deer, Rob	.209	134	440	57	92	15	1	27	69	64	147	2

Bo Jackson
...28 homers

Ted Higuera
...11-10, 3.76

BATTING	AVG	G	AB	R	H	2B	3B	HR	RBI	BB	SO	SB
Diaz, Edgar	.271	86	218	27	59	2	2	0	14	21	32	3
#Felder, Mike	.274	121	237	38	65	7	2	3	27	22	17	20
*Francona, Terry	.000	3	4	1	0	0	0	0	0	0	0	0
*Gantner, Jim	.263	88	323	36	85	8	5	0	25	29	19	18
*Hamilton, Darryl	.295	89	156	27	46	5	0	1	18	9	12	10
McIntosh, Tim	.200	5	5	1	1	0	0	1	1	0	2	0
Molitor, Paul	.285	103	418	64	119	27	6	12	45	37	51	18
O'Brien, Charlie	.186	46	145	11	27	7	2	0	11	11	26	0
*Parker, Dave	.289	157	610	71	176	30	3	21	92	41	102	4
Polidor, Gus	.067	18	15	0	1	0	0	0	1	0	1	0
Sheffield, Gary	.294	125	487	67	143	30	1	10	67	44	41	25
*Spiers, Billy	.242	112	363	44	88	15	3	2	36	16	46	11
*Surhoff, B.J.	.276	135	474	55	131	21	4	6	59	41	37	18
#Sveum, Dale	.197	48	117	15	23	7	0	1	12	12	30	0
Vaughn, Greg	.220	120	382	51	84	26	2	17	61	33	91	7
Yount, Robin	.247	158	587	98	145	17	5	17	77	78	89	15

PITCHING	W	L	ERA	G	GS	CG	SV	IP	H	R	ER	BB	SO
August, Don	0	3	6.55	5	0	0	0	11	13	10	8	5	2
Bosio, Chris	4	9	4.00	20	20	4	0	133	131	67	59	38	76
*Brown, Kevin	1	1	2.57	5	3	0	0	21	14	7	6	7	12
Capel, Mike	0	0	135.00	2	0	0	0	0	6	6	5	1	1
Crim, Chuck	3	5	3.47	67	0	0	11	86	88	39	33	23	39
Edens, Tom	4	5	4.45	35	6	0	2	89	89	52	44	33	40
*Elvira, Narciso	0	0	5.40	4	0	0	0	5	6	3	3	5	6
Filer, Tom	2	3	6.14	7	4	0	0	22	26	17	15	9	8
*Fossas, Tony	2	3	6.44	32	0	0	0	29	44	23	21	10	24
*Higuera, Ted	11	10	3.76	27	27	4	0	170	167	80	71	50	129
Knudson, Mark	10	9	4.12	30	27	4	0	168	187	84	77	40	56
*Krueger, Bill	6	8	3.98	30	17	0	0	129	137	70	57	54	64
*Lee, Mark	1	0	2.11	11	0	0	0	21	20	5	5	4	14
Machado, Julio	0	0	0.69	10	0	0	3	13	9	1	1	8	12
*Mirabella, Paul	4	2	3.97	44	2	0	0	59	66	32	26	27	28
Navarro, Jamie	8	7	4.46	32	22	3	1	149	176	83	74	41	75
*Plesac, Dan	3	7	4.43	66	0	0	24	69	67	36	34	31	65
*Powell, Dennis	0	4	6.86	9	7	0	0	39	59	37	30	19	23
Robinson, Ron	12	5	2.91	22	22	7	0	148	158	60	48	37	57
Sebra, Bob	1	2	8.18	10	0	0	0	11	20	10	10	5	4
Veres, Randy	0	3	3.67	26	0	0	1	42	38	17	17	16	16
Wegman, Bill	2	2	4.85	8	5	1	0	30	37	21	16	6	20

FIELDING

Catcher	PCT	G	PO	A	E
McIntosh	.875	4	6	1	1
O'Brien	.992	46	217	24	2
Surhoff	.985	125	615	53	10

First Base	PCT	G	PO	A	E
Brock	.995	115	885	63	5
Canale	1.000	6	32	4	0
Deer	.986	21	130	11	2
Francona	1.000	2	6	0	0
Molitor	.986	37	325	25	5
Parker	.960	3	24	0	1
Sveum	1.000	5	17	0	0

Second Base	PCT	G	PO	A	E
Bates	.962	14	18	33	2
Diaz	.945	15	23	29	3
Felder	1.000	1	2	0	0
Gantner	.982	80	164	220	7
Molitor	.988	60	136	190	4
Polidor	1.000	2	1	2	0
Sveum	.981	16	22	30	1

Third Base	PCT	G	PO	A	E
Diaz	1.000	7	1	5	0
Felder	1.000	1	0	1	0
Gantner	.920	9	3	20	2
Molitor	.900	2	2	7	1
Polidor	1.000	14	1	10	0
Sheffield	.934	125	98	254	25
Surhoff	.867	11	4	9	2
Sveum	.918	22	17	28	4

Shortstop	PCT	G	PO	A	E
Diaz	.950	65	101	163	14
Polidor	1.000	2	0	1	0
Spiers	.976	111	159	326	12
Sveum	.889	5	3	5	1

Outfield	PCT	G	PO	A	E
Braggs	.965	32	81	1	3
Deer	.970	117	243	14	8
Felder	.972	109	165	8	5
Hamilton	.992	72	120	1	1
Vaughn	.967	106	195	8	7
Yount	.991	157	422	3	4

Kirby Puckett
... .298-12-80

Kent Hrbek
... .287-22-79

Kevin Tapani
... 12 wins

BATTING	AVG	G	AB	R	H	2B	3B	HR	RBI	BB	SO	SB
#Baker, Doug	.000	3	1	0	0	0	0	0	0	0	0	0
*Bush, Randy	.243	73	181	17	44	8	0	6	18	21	27	0
Castillo, Carmen	.219	64	137	11	30	4	0	0	12	3	23	0
*Dwyer, Jim	.190	37	63	7	12	0	0	1	5	12	7	0
Gaetti, Gary	.229	154	577	61	132	27	5	16	85	36	101	6
Gagne, Greg	.235	138	388	38	91	22	3	7	38	24	76	8
Gladden, Dan	.275	136	534	64	147	27	6	5	40	26	67	25
*Hale, Chip	.000	1	2	0	0	0	0	0	0	2	0	1	0
Harper, Brian	.294	134	479	61	141	42	3	6	54	19	27	3
*Hrbek, Kent	.287	143	492	61	141	26	0	22	79	69	45	5
#Larkin, Gene	.269	119	401	46	108	26	4	5	42	42	55	5
Leius, Scott	.240	14	25	4	6	1	0	1	4	2	2	0
#Liriano, Nelson	.254	53	185	30	47	5	7	0	13	22	24	5
Mack, Shane	.326	125	313	50	102	10	4	8	44	29	69	13
Manrique, Fred	.237	69	228	22	54	10	0	5	29	4	35	2
#Moses, John	.221	115	172	26	38	3	1	1	14	19	19	2
Munoz, Pedro	.271	22	85	13	23	4	1	0	5	2	16	3
#Newman, Al	.242	144	388	43	94	14	0	0	30	33	34	13
Ortiz, Junior	.335	71	170	18	57	7	1	0	18	12	16	0
Puckett, Kirby	.298	146	551	82	164	40	3	12	80	57	73	5
*Sorrento, Paul	.207	41	121	11	25	4	1	5	13	12	31	1
Webster, Lenny	.333	2	6	1	2	1	0	0	0	1	1	0

PITCHING	W	L	ERA	G	GS	CG	SV	IP	H	R	ER	BB	SO
Abbott, Paul	0	5	5.97	7	7	0	0	35	37	24	23	28	25
Aguilera, Rick	5	3	2.76	56	0	0	32	65	55	27	20	19	61
*Anderson, Allan	7	18	4.53	31	31	5	0	189	214	106	95	39	82
Berenguer, Juan	8	5	3.41	51	0	0	0	100	85	43	38	58	77
*Candelaria, John	7	3	3.39	34	1	0	4	58	55	23	22	9	44
*Casian, Larry	2	1	3.22	5	3	0	0	22	26	9	8	4	11
Drummond, Tim	3	5	4.35	35	4	0	1	91	104	46	44	36	49
Erickson, Scott	8	4	2.87	19	17	1	0	113	108	49	36	51	53
Garces, Rich	0	0	1.59	5	0	0	2	6	4	2	1	4	1
*Guthrie, Mark	7	9	3.79	24	21	3	0	145	154	65	61	39	101
Leach, Terry	2	5	3.20	55	0	0	2	82	84	31	29	21	46
Savage, Jack	0	2	8.31	17	0	0	1	26	37	26	24	11	12
Smith, Roy	5	10	4.81	32	23	1	0	153	191	91	82	47	87
Tapani, Kevin	12	8	4.07	28	28	1	0	159	164	75	72	29	101
*Wayne, Gary	1	1	4.19	38	0	0	1	39	38	19	18	13	28
*West, David	7	9	5.10	29	27	2	0	146	142	88	83	78	92
Yett, Rich	0	0	2.08	4	0	0	0	4	6	2	1	1	2

FIELDING

Catchers	PCT	G	PO	A	E
Harper	.985	120	672	53	11
Ortiz	1.000	68	247	25	0
Webster	1.000	2	9	0	0

	PCT	G	PO	A	E
Leius	.000	1	0	0	0
Newman	.945	28	13	39	3
Puckett	.000	1	0	0	0

First Base	PCT	G	PO	A	E
Bush	1.000	6	12	2	0
Gaetti	1.000	2	23	0	0
Harper	1.000	2	13	3	0
Hrbek	.997	120	1057	81	3
Larkin	.992	28	222	13	2
Moses	1.000	6	5	0	0
Sorrento	.992	15	118	7	1

Shortstop	PCT	G	PO	A	E
Gaetti	1.000	2	1	0	0
Gagne	.976	135	184	377	14
Leius	1.000	12	20	25	0
Liriano	.000	1	0	0	0
Newman	.949	48	57	92	8
Puckett	.000	1	0	0	0

Second Base	PCT	G	PO	A	E
Baker	1.000	3	1	2	0
Hale	1.000	1	2	6	0
Liriano	.968	50	83	128	7
Manrique	.974	67	104	155	7
Newman	.993	89	118	173	2
Puckett	.000	1	0	0	0

Outfield	PCT	G	PO	A	E
Bush	1.000	32	52	1	0
Castillo	.923	21	24	0	2
Dwyer	1.000	2	2	0	0
Gagne	.000	1	0	0	0
Gladden	.980	133	286	12	6
Larkin	1.000	47	77	5	0
Mack	.988	109	230	8	3
Moses	1.000	85	103	2	0
Munoz	.972	21	34	1	1
Newman	1.000	3	2	0	0
Puckett	.989	141	354	9	4

Third Base	PCT	G	PO	A	E
Gaetti	.959	151	102	318	18
Harper	1.000	3	1	2	0
Hrbek	1.000	1	0	2	0

Boston's Roger Clemens led **AL** in **ERA** (1.93) while posting a 21-6 record.

PITCHING

GAMES
Bobby Thigpen, Chicago 77
Jeff Montgomery, Kansas City ... 73
Duane Ward, Toronto 73
Mike Henneman, Detroit 69
Kenny Rogers, Texas 69

GAMES STARTED
Jack Morris, Detroit 36
Dave Stewart, Oakland.......... 36
Melido Perez, Chicago 35
Bob Welch, Oakland 35
Three tied at 34

COMPLETE GAMES
Jack Morris, Detroit 11
Dave Stewart, Oakland.......... 11
Five tied at 7

SHUTOUTS
Roger Clemens, Boston 4
Dave Stewart, Oakland 4
Kevin Appier, Kansas City 3
Jack Morris, Detroit 3
Melido Perez, Chicago 3

SAVES
Bobby Thigpen, Chicago 57
Dennis Eckersley, Oakland..... 48
Doug Jones, Cleveland 43
Gregg Olson, Baltimore 37
Dave Righetti, New York 36

WINS
Bob Welch, Oakland 27
Dave Stewart, Oakland 22
Roger Clemens, Boston 21
Chuck Finley, California 18
Erik Hanson, Mariners 18
Dave Stieb, Toronto 18

LOSSES
Tim Leary, New York............ 19
Allan Anderson, Minnesota..... 18
Jack Morris, Detroit 18
Matt Young, Seattle 18
Mark Langston, California 17
Todd Stottlemyre, Toronto....... 17

INNINGS PITCHED
Dave Stewart, Oakland 267
Jack Morris, Detroit 250
Bob Welch, Oakland........... 238
Chuck Finley, California 236
Erik Hanson, Seattle 236

HITS ALLOWED
Jim Abbott, California 246
Greg Swindell, Cleveland 245
Jack Morris, Detroit 231
Dave Stewart, Oakland 226
Mike Boddicker, Boston....... 225

RUNS ALLOWED
Jack Morris, Detroit 144
Mark Langston, California 120
Jim Abbott, California 116
Mike Moore, Oakland 113
Melido Perez, Chicago........ 111

HOME RUNS ALLOWED
Dave Johnson, Baltimore 30
Scott Sanderson, Oakland 27
Greg Swindell, Cleveland 27
Randy Johnson, Seattle 26
Jack Morris, Detroit 26
Bob Welch, Oakland 26

WALKS
Randy Johnson, Seattle....... 120
Charlie Hough, Texas.......... 119
Bobby Witt, Texas 110
Matt Young, Seattle 107
Mark Langston, California 104

HIT BATSMEN
Charlie Hough, Texas 11
Mike Boddicker, Boston 10
Dave Stieb, Toronto............ 10
Dana Kiecker, Boston 9
Frank Tanana, Detroit 9

STRIKEOUTS
Nolan Ryan, Texas 232
Bobby Witt, Texas 221
Erik Hanson, Seattle 211
Roger Clemens, Boston 209
Mark Langston, California 195

WILD PITCHES
Tim Leary, New York............ 23
Jack Morris, Detroit 16
Jeff Robinson, Detroit 16
Matt Young, Seattle 16
Greg Cadaret, New York 14

BALKS
Jaime Navarro, Milwaukee 5
Melido Perez, Chicago 4
Five tied at 3

OPPONENTS BATTING AVERAGE
Nolan Ryan, Texas............ .188
Randy Johnson, Seattle ...... .216
Roger Clemens, Boston ...... .228
Dave Stieb, Toronto .... .230
Dave Stewart, Oakland .... .231

NEW YORK

BATTING

	AVG	G	AB	R	H	2B	3B	HR	RBI	BB	SO	SB
*Azocar, Oscar	.248	65	214	18	53	8	0	5	19	2	15	7
Balboni, Steve	.192	116	266	24	51	6	0	17	34	35	91	0
Barfield, Jesse	.246	153	476	69	117	21	2	25	78	82	150	4
Blowers, Mike	.188	48	144	16	27	4	0	5	21	12	50	1
Cerone, Rick	.302	49	139	12	42	6	0	2	11	5	13	0
Dorsett, Brian	.143	14	35	2	5	2	0	0	2	4	0	
Espinoza, Alvaro	.224	150	438	31	98	12	2	2	20	16	54	1
Geren, Bob	.213	110	277	21	59	7	0	8	31	13	73	0
*Hall, Mel	.258	113	360	41	93	23	2	12	46	6	46	0
Kelly, Roberto	.285	162	641	85	183	32	4	15	61	33	148	42
Leyritz, Jim	.257	92	303	28	78	13	1	5	25	27	51	2
*Maas, Kevin	.252	79	254	42	64	9	0	21	41	43	76	1
*Mattingly, Don	.256	102	394	40	101	16	0	5	42	28	20	1
Meulens, Hensley	.241	23	83	12	20	3	0	3	10	9	25	1
*Nokes, Matt	.238	92	240	21	57	4	0	8	32	20	33	2
*Polonia, Luis	.318	11	22	2	7	0	0	0	3	0	1	1
*Sanders, Deion	.158	57	133	24	21	2	2	3	9	13	27	8
Sax, Steve	.260	155	615	70	160	24	2	4	42	49	46	43
#Tolleson, Wayne	.149	73	74	12	11	1	1	0	4	6	21	1
Velarde, Randy	.210	95	229	21	48	6	2	5	19	20	53	0
#Walewander, Jim	.200	9	5	1	1	1	0	0	1	0	0	1
*Washington, Claudell	.163	33	80	4	13	1	1	0	6	2	17	3
Winfield, Dave	.213	20	61	7	13	3	0	2	6	4	13	0

PITCHING

	W	L	ERA	G	GS	CG	SV	IP	H	R	ER	BB	SO
*Adkins, Steve	1	2	6.38	5	5	0	0	24	19	18	17	29	14
*Cadaret, Greg	5	4	4.15	54	6	0	3	121	120	62	56	64	80
*Cary, Chuck	6	12	4.19	28	27	2	0	157	155	77	73	55	134
Eiland, Dave	2	1	3.56	5	5	0	0	30	31	14	12	5	16
*Guetterman, Lee	11	7	3.39	64	0	0	2	93	80	37	35	26	48
Habyan, John	0	0	2.08	6	0	0	0	9	10	2	2	2	4
Hawkins, Andy	5	12	5.37	28	26	2	0	158	156	101	94	82	74
Jones, Jimmy	1	2	6.30	17	7	0	0	50	72	42	35	23	25
*LaPoint, Dave	7	10	4.11	28	27	2	0	158	180	84	72	57	67
Leary, Tim	9	19	4.11	31	31	6	0	208	202	105	95	78	138
Leiter, Mark	1	1	6.84	8	3	0	0	26	33	20	20	9	21
McCullers, Lance	1	0	3.60	11	0	0	0	15	14	8	6	6	11
Mills, Alan	1	5	4.10	36	0	0	0	42	48	21	19	33	24
Monteleone, Rich	0	1	6.14	5	0	0	0	7	8	5	5	2	8
Parker, Clay	1	1	4.50	5	2	0	0	22	19	11	11	7	20
Perez, Pascual	1	2	1.29	3	3	0	0	14	8	3	2	3	12
Plunk, Eric	6	3	2.72	47	0	0	0	73	58	27	22	43	67
*Righetti, Dave	1	1	3.57	53	0	0	36	53	48	24	21	26	43
Robinson, Jeff	3	6	3.45	54	4	1	0	89	82	35	34	34	43
Witt, Mike	5	6	4.47	16	16	2	0	97	87	53	48	34	60

FIELDING

Catcher	PCT	G	PO	A	E
Cerone	.995	35	177	14	1
Dorsett	1.000	9	31	0	0
Geren	.993	107	487	55	4
Leyritz	.983	11	55	4	1
Nokes	.995	46	181	27	1

	PCT	G	PO	A	E
Velarde	.945	74	43	128	10
Walewander	1.000	2	1	1	0

First Base	PCT	G	PO	A	E
Balboni	.984	28	183	7	3
Maas	.983	57	486	35	9
Mattingly	.997	89	800	78	3

Shortstop	PCT	G	PO	A	E
Espinoza	.977	150	268	447	17
Tolleson	.983	45	43	72	2
Velarde	.979	15	21	26	1
Walewander	1.000	1	0	2	0

Second Base	PCT	G	PO	A	E
Cerone	1.000	1	2	0	0
Sax	.987	154	292	457	10
Tolleson	1.000	13	14	14	0
Velarde	.833	3	0	5	1
Walewander	1.000	2	3	2	0

Outfield	PCT	G	PO	A	E
Azocar	.991	57	105	4	1
Barfield	.973	151	305	16	9
Hall	.973	50	70	2	2
Kelly	.988	160	420	5	5
Leyritz	.955	14	19	2	1
Mattingly	.000	1	0	0	0
Meulens	.963	23	49	3	2
Nokes	1.000	2	1	0	0
Sanders	.973	42	69	2	2
Velarde	1.000	5	6	0	0
Washington	1.000	21	42	2	0
Winfield	1.000	12	12	0	0

Third Base	PCT	G	PO	A	E
Blowers	.899	45	26	63	10
Leyritz	.929	69	43	101	11
Tolleson	.000	3	0	0	0

OAKLAND

BATTING

	AVG	G	AB	R	H	2B	3B	HR	RBI	BB	SO	SB
Afenir, Troy	.143	14	14	0	2	0	0	0	2	0	6	0
*Baines, Harold	.266	32	94	11	25	5	0	3	21	20	17	0
Blankenship, Lance	.191	86	136	18	26	3	0	0	10	20	23	3
Bordick, Mike	.071	25	14	0	1	0	0	0	0	1	4	0
Canseco, Jose	.274	131	481	83	132	14	2	37	101	72	158	19
Canseco, Ozzie	.105	9	19	1	2	1	0	0	1	1	10	0
Gallego, Mike	.206	140	389	36	80	13	2	3	34	35	50	5
*Hassey, Ron	.213	94	254	18	54	7	0	5	22	27	29	0
Hemond, Scott	.154	7	13	0	2	0	0	0	1	0	5	0
Henderson, Dave	.271	127	450	65	122	28	0	20	63	40	105	3
Henderson, Rickey	.325	136	489	119	159	33	3	28	61	97	60	65

Rickey Henderson paced Oakland to the AL pennant by hitting .325 with 28 homers and stealing 65 bases.

	AVG	G	AB	R	H	2B	3B	HR	RBI	BB	SO	SB
Howard, Steve	.231	21	52	5	12	4	0	0	1	4	17	0
*Howitt, Dann	.136	14	22	3	3	0	1	0	1	3	12	0
#Javier, Stan	.242	19	33	4	8	0	2	0	3	3	6	0
*Jennings, Doug	.192	64	156	19	30	7	2	2	14	17	48	0
#Jose, Felix	.264	101	341	42	90	12	0	8	39	16	65	8
Lansford, Carney	.268	134	507	58	136	15	1	3	50	45	50	16
Lewis, Darren	.229	25	35	4	8	0	0	0	1	7	4	2
#McGee, Willie	.274	29	113	23	31	3	2	0	15	10	18	3
McGwire, Mark	.235	156	523	87	123	16	0	39	108	110	116	2
*Phelps, Ken	.186	32	59	6	11	2	0	1	6	12	10	0
*Quirk, Jamie	.281	56	121	12	34	5	1	3	26	14	34	0
Randolph, Willie	.257	93	292	37	75	9	3	1	21	32	25	6
Steinbach, Terry	.251	114	379	32	95	15	2	9	57	19	66	0
#Weiss, Walt	.265	138	445	50	118	17	1	2	35	46	53	9

PITCHING	W	L	ERA	G	GS	CG	SV	IP	H	R	ER	BB	SO
Bitker, Joe	0	0	0.00	1	0	0	0	3	1	0	0	1	2
Burns, Todd	3	3	2.97	43	2	0	3	79	78	28	26	32	43
Chitren, Steve	1	0	1.02	8	0	0	0	18	7	2	2	4	19
Eckersley, Dennis	4	2	0.61	63	0	0	48	73	41	9	5	4	73
Harris, Reggie	1	0	3.48	16	1	0	0	41	25	16	16	21	31
*Honeycutt, Rick	2	2	2.70	63	0	0	7	63	46	23	19	22	38
*Klink, Joe	0	0	2.04	40	0	0	1	40	34	9	9	18	19
Moore, Mike	13	15	4.65	33	33	3	0	199	204	113	103	84	73
Nelson, Gene	3	3	1.57	51	0	0	5	75	55	14	13	17	38
Norris, Mike	1	0	3.00	14	0	0	0	27	24	10	9	9	16
*Otto, Dave	0	0	7.71	2	0	0	0	2	3	3	2	3	2
Sanderson, Scott	17	11	3.88	34	34	2	0	206	205	99	89	66	128
Stewart, Dave	22	11	2.56	36	36	11	0	267	226	84	76	83	166
Welch, Bob	27	6	3.06	35	35	2	0	238	214	90	78	77	127
*Young, Curt	9	6	4.85	26	21	0	0	124	124	70	67	53	56

FIELDING

Catcher	PCT	G	PO	A	E
Afenir	1.000	12	13	0	0
Hassey	.997	59	307	18	1
Quirk	.977	37	151	17	4
Steinbach	.988	83	396	31	5

First Base	PCT	G	PO	A	E
Blankenship	.000	1	0	0	0
Hassey	1.000	3	5	0	0
Howitt	1.000	5	18	1	0
Jennings	1.000	4	28	0	0
Lansford	1.000	5	28	1	0
McGwire	.997	154	1329	95	5
Phelps	.964	5	24	3	1
Quirk	1.000	8	13	0	0
Steinbach	1.000	3	5	0	0

Second Base	PCT	G	PO	A	E
Blankenship	1.000	20	20	32	0
Bordick	1.000	7	2	4	0
Gallego	.990	83	153	258	4
Hemond	.000	1	0	0	0
Randolph	.982	84	148	240	7

Third Base	PCT	G	PO	A	E
Blankenship	.947	28	17	37	3
Bordick	1.000	1	2	3	0
Gallego	.882	27	10	35	6

	PCT	G	PO	A	E
Hemond	1.000	7	2	5	0
Howitt	.000	1	0	0	0
Lansford	.970	126	100	194	9
Quirk	.833	8	4	1	1

Shortstop	PCT	G	PO	A	E
Bordick	1.000	9	5	1	0
Gallego	.977	38	43	86	3
Weiss	.979	137	194	373	12

Outfield	PCT	G	PO	A	E
Baines	.833	2	5	0	1
Blankenship	.935	28	29	0	2
J. Canseco	.995	88	182	7	1
O. Canseco	1.000	2	3	0	0
Gallego	1.000	1	1	0	0
D. Henderson	.988	116	319	5	4
R. Henderson	.983	118	289	5	5
Howard	.933	14	14	0	1
Howitt	1.000	11	16	0	0
Javier	1.000	13	19	0	0
Jennings	.984	45	62	1	1
Jose	.977	92	212	5	5
Lewis	1.000	23	33	0	0
McGee	.986	28	72	1	1
Quirk	.000	1	0	0	0

BATTING

BATTING	AVG	G	AB	R	H	2B	3B	HR	RBI	BB	SO	SB
*Bradley, Scott	.223	101	233	11	52	9	0	1	28	15	20	0
*Briley, Greg	.246	125	337	40	83	18	2	5	29	37	48	16
#Brumley, Mike	.224	62	147	19	33	5	4	0	7	10	22	2
Buhner, Jay	.276	51	163	16	45	12	0	7	33	17	50	2
#Cochrane, Dave	.150	15	20	0	3	0	0	0	0	0	8	0
Coles, Darnell	.215	37	107	9	23	5	1	2	16	4	17	0
Cotto, Henry	.259	127	355	40	92	14	3	4	33	22	52	21
*Davis, Alvin	.283	140	494	63	140	21	0	17	68	85	68	0
Giles, Brian	.232	45	95	15	22	6	0	4	11	15	24	2
*Griffey, Ken Jr.	.300	155	597	91	179	28	7	22	80	63	81	16
*Griffey, Ken Sr.	.377	21	77	13	29	2	0	3	18	10	3	0
Jones, Tracy	.302	25	86	8	26	4	0	2	15	3	12	0
Leonard, Jeffrey	.251	134	478	39	120	20	0	10	75	37	97	4
Martinez, Edgar	.302	144	487	71	147	27	2	11	49	74	62	1
*Martinez, Tino	.221	24	68	4	15	4	0	0	5	9	9	0
*O'Brien, Pete	.224	108	366	32	82	18	0	5	27	44	33	0
#Reynolds, Harold	.252	160	642	100	162	36	5	5	55	81	52	31
Schaefer, Jeff	.206	55	107	11	22	3	0	0	6	3	11	4
Sinatro, Matt	.300	30	50	2	15	1	0	0	4	4	10	1
Valle, Dave	.214	107	308	37	66	15	0	7	33	45	48	1
#Vizquel, Omar	.247	81	255	19	63	3	2	2	18	18	22	4

PITCHING

PITCHING	W	L	ERA	G	GS	CG	SV	IP	H	R	ER	BB	SO
Bankhead, Scott	0	2	11.08	4	4	0	0	13	18	16	16	7	10
Burba, Dave	0	0	4.50	6	0	0	0	8	8	6	4	2	4
*Clark, Bryan	2	0	3.27	12	0	0	0	11	9	4	4	10	3
*Comstock, Keith	7	4	2.89	60	0	0	2	56	40	22	18	26	50
DeLucia, Rich	1	2	2.00	5	5	1	0	36	30	9	8	9	20
*Eave, Gary	0	3	4.20	8	5	0	0	30	27	16	14	20	16
Gardiner, Mike	0	2	10.66	5	3	0	0	13	22	17	15	5	6
Hanson, Erik	18	9	3.24	33	33	5	0	236	205	88	85	68	211
Harris, Gene	1	2	4.74	25	0	0	0	38	31	25	20	30	43
Holman, Brian	11	11	4.03	28	28	3	0	190	188	92	85	66	121
Jackson, Mike	5	7	4.54	63	0	0	3	77	64	42	39	44	69
Johnson, Randy	14	11	3.65	33	33	5	0	220	174	103	89	120	194
Knackert, Brent	1	1	6.51	24	2	0	0	37	50	28	27	21	28
*Lovelace, Vance	0	0	3.86	5	0	0	0	2	3	1	1	6	1
Medvin, Scott	0	1	6.23	5	0	0	0	4	7	4	3	2	1
Melendez, Jose	0	0	11.81	3	0	0	0	5	8	8	7	3	7
*Powell, Dennis	0	0	9.00	2	0	0	0	3	5	3	3	2	0
Reed, Jerry	0	1	4.91	4	0	0	0	7	8	4	4	3	2
Schooler, Mike	1	4	2.25	49	0	0	30	56	47	18	14	16	45
*Swan, Russ	2	3	3.64	11	8	0	0	47	42	22	19	18	15
Swift, Bill	6	4	2.39	55	8	0	6	128	135	46	34	21	42
*Young, Matt	8	18	3.51	34	33	7	0	225	198	106	88	107	176

FIELDING

Catcher	PCT	G	PO	A	E		PCT	G	PO	A	E
Bradley	.995	63	349	24	2	Coles	.815	6	2	20	5
Cochrane	.000	1	0	0	0	Giles	1.000	1	0	3	0
Sinatro	.992	28	112	16	1	Martinez	.928	143	89	259	27
Valle	.997	104	631	44	2	Schaefer	.933	26	17	39	4

First Base	PCT	G	PO	A	E		Shortstop	PCT	G	PO	A	E
Bradley	1.000	1	2	0	0	Brumley	.983	47	58	111	3
Cochrane	1.000	3	7	1	0	Cochrane	1.000	5	0	1	0
Davis	.994	52	435	31	3	Giles	.978	37	51	80	3
Martinez	1.000	23	155	12	0	Schaefer	.988	24	34	47	1
O'Brien	.995	97	850	76	5	Vizquel	.980	81	102	239	7
Valle	1.000	1	2	0	0						

Second Base	PCT	G	PO	A	E		Outfield	PCT	G	PO	A	E
Brumley	1.000	6	3	7	0	Briley	.989	107	177	4	2
Giles	1.000	2	6	5	0	Brumley	1.000	2	1	0	0
Reynolds	.978	160	331	499	19	Buhner	.966	40	55	1	2
Schaefer	1.000	3	1	1	0	Coles	.970	20	32	0	1
						Cotto	.990	118	194	4	2
Third Base	PCT	G	PO	A	E	Griffey Jr.	.980	151	330	8	7
Bradley	1.000	5	3	6	0	Griffey Sr.	.963	20	25	1	1
Brumley	.750	3	1	5	2	Jones	1.000	18	31	0	0
Cochrane	1.000	3	1	8	0	Leonard	.983	79	118	0	2
						O'Brien	1.000	6	2	0	0

BATTING

BATTING	AVG	G	AB	R	H	2B	3B	HR	RBI	BB	SO	SB
*Baines, Harold	.290	103	321	41	93	10	1	13	44	47	63	0
Belcher, Kevin	.133	16	15	4	2	1	0	0	0	2	6	0
*Bosley, Thad	.138	30	29	3	4	0	0	1	3	4	7	1
Buechele, Steve	.215	91	251	30	54	10	0	7	30	27	63	1
Coolbaugh, Scott	.200	67	180	21	36	6	0	2	13	15	47	1
#Daugherty, Jack	.300	125	310	36	93	20	2	6	47	22	49	0
#Espy, Cecil	.127	52	71	10	9	0	0	0	1	10	20	11
Franco, Julio	.296	157	582	96	172	27	1	11	69	82	83	31
Gonzalez, Juan	.289	25	90	11	26	7	1	4	12	2	18	0
Green, Gary	.216	62	88	10	19	3	0	0	8	6	18	1

At age 20, Ken Griffey Jr. became one of the AL's top players in 1990, hitting .300 with 22 homers.

BATTING	AVG	G	AB	R	H	2B	3B	HR	RBI	BB	SO	SB
Haselman, Billy	.154	7	13	0	2	0	0	0	3	1	5	0
*Huson, Jeff	.240	145	396	57	95	12	2	0	28	46	54	12
Incaviglia, Pete	.233	153	529	59	123	27	0	24	85	45	146	3
Kreuter, Chad	.045	22	22	2	1	1	0	0	2	8	9	0
Kunkel, Jeff	.170	99	200	17	34	11	1	3	17	11	66	2
*Palmeiro, Rafael	.319	154	598	72	191	35	6	14	89	40	59	3
*Petralli, Geno	.255	133	325	28	83	13	1	0	21	50	49	0
#Pettis, Gary	.239	136	423	66	101	16	8	3	31	57	118	38
*Reimer, Kevin	.260	64	100	5	26	9	1	2	15	10	22	0
Russell, John	.273	68	128	16	35	4	0	2	8	11	41	1
#Sierra, Ruben	.280	159	608	70	170	37	2	16	96	49	86	9
Stanley, Mike	.249	103	189	21	47	8	1	2	19	30	25	1

PITCHING	W	L	ERA	G	GS	CG	SV	IP	H	R	ER	BB	SO
Alexander, Gerald	0	0	7.71	3	2	0	0	7	14	6	6	5	8
Arnsberg, Brad	6	1	2.15	53	0	0	5	63	56	20	15	33	44
*Barfield, John	4	3	4.67	33	0	0	1	44	42	25	23	13	17
Bitker, Joe	0	0	3.00	5	0	0	0	9	7	3	3	3	6
*Bohanon, Brian	0	3	6.62	11	6	0	0	34	40	30	25	18	15
Brown, Kevin	12	10	3.60	26	26	6	0	180	175	84	72	60	88
Chiamparino, Scott	1	2	2.63	6	6	0	0	38	36	14	11	12	19
Hoover, John	0	0	11.57	2	0	0	0	5	8	6	6	3	0
Hough, Charlie	12	12	4.07	32	32	5	0	219	190	108	99	119	114
*Jeffcoat, Mike	5	6	4.47	44	12	1	5	111	122	57	55	28	58
Manon, Ramon	0	0	13.50	1	0	0	0	2	3	3	3	3	0
McMurtry, Craig	0	3	4.32	23	3	0	0	42	43	25	20	30	14
Mielke, Gary	0	3	3.73	33	0	0	0	41	42	17	17	15	13
Moyer, Jamie	2	6	4.66	33	10	1	0	102	115	59	53	39	58
*Rogers, Kenny	10	6	3.13	69	3	0	15	98	93	40	34	42	74
Russell, Jeff	1	5	4.26	27	0	0	10	25	23	15	12	16	16
Ryan, Nolan	13	9	3.44	30	30	5	0	204	137	86	78	74	232
Witt, Bobby	17	10	3.36	33	32	7	0	222	197	98	83	110	221

FIELDING

Catcher	PCT	G	PO	A	E
Haselman	1.000	1	8	0	0
Kreuter	.977	20	39	4	1
Petralli	.991	118	599	43	6
Russell	.980	31	135	11	3
Stanley	.985	63	244	20	4

First Base	PCT	G	PO	A	E
Daugherty	.990	30	175	18	2
Palmeiro	.995	146	1215	91	7
Russell	1.000	3	8	0	0
Stanley	1.000	6	14	1	0

Second Base	PCT	G	PO	A	E
Buechele	1.000	4	2	3	0
Espy	.000	1	0	0	0
Franco	.975	152	310	444	19
Huson	1.000	12	14	20	0
Kunkel	1.000	13	12	18	0
Petralli	1.000	3	2	2	0

Third Base	PCT	G	PO	A	E
Buechele	.966	88	70	157	8
Coolbaugh	.941	66	42	117	10

	PCT	G	PO	A	E
Huson	.955	36	12	30	2
Kunkel	.950	15	10	28	2
Petralli	1.000	7	1	1	0
Russell	.000	1	0	0	0
Stanley	1.000	8	3	4	0

Shortstop	PCT	G	PO	A	E
Green	.972	58	61	112	5
Huson	.960	119	157	254	17
Kunkel	.958	67	77	126	9

Outfield	PCT	G	PO	A	E
Belcher	1.000	9	12	0	0
Bosley	1.000	9	4	0	0
Daugherty	.982	42	50	4	1
Espy	1.000	39	56	1	0
Gonzalez	1.000	16	33	0	0
Incaviglia	.974	145	290	12	8
Kunkel	1.000	5	2	0	0
Pettis	.993	128	285	10	2
Reimer	.857	9	12	0	2
Russell	1.000	6	5	0	0
Sierra	.967	151	283	7	10

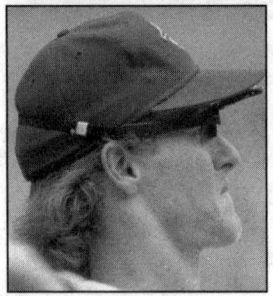

Kelly Gruber
... .274-31-118

Fred McGriff
... .300-35-88

BATTING	AVG	G	AB	R	H	2B	3B	HR	RBI	BB	SO	SB
Bell, George	.265	142	562	67	149	25	0	21	86	32	80	3
Borders, Pat	.286	125	346	36	99	24	2	15	49	18	57	0
Diaz, Carlos	.333	9	3	1	1	0	0	0	0	0	2	0
*Ducey, Rob	.302	19	53	7	16	5	0	0	7	7	15	1
*Eppard, Jim	.200	6	5	0	1	0	0	0	0	0	2	0
#Felix, Junior	.263	127	463	73	122	23	7	15	65	45	99	13
#Fernandez, Tony	.276	161	635	84	175	27	17	4	66	71	70	26
Gruber, Kelly	.274	150	592	92	162	36	6	31	118	48	94	14
Hill, Glenallen	.231	84	260	47	60	11	3	12	32	18	62	8
Lawless, Tom	.083	15	12	1	1	0	0	0	1	0	1	0
#Lee, Manny	.243	117	391	45	95	12	4	6	41	26	90	3
#Liriano, Nelson	.212	50	170	16	36	7	2	1	15	16	20	3
*McGriff, Fred	.300	153	557	91	167	21	1	35	88	94	108	5
*Mulliniks, Rance	.289	57	97	11	28	4	0	2	16	22	19	2
*Myers, Greg	.236	87	250	33	59	7	1	5	22	22	33	0
*Olerud, John	.265	111	358	43	95	15	1	14	48	57	75	0
Quinlan, Tom	.500	1	2	0	1	0	0	0	0	0	1	0
Sojo, Luis	.225	33	80	14	18	3	0	1	9	5	5	1
Virgil, Ozzie	.000	3	5	0	0	0	0	0	0	0	3	0
*Whiten, Mark	.273	33	88	12	24	1	1	2	7	7	14	2
Williams, Kenny	.194	49	72	13	14	6	1	0	8	7	18	7
#Wilson, Mookie	.265	147	588	81	156	36	4	3	51	31	102	23

PITCHING	W	L	ERA	G	GS	CG	SV	IP	H	R	ER	BB	SO
Acker, Jim	4	4	3.83	59	0	0	1	92	103	49	39	30	54
*Black, Bud	2	1	4.02	15	3	2	0	16	10	7	7	3	3
Blair, Willie	3	5	4.06	27	6	0	0	69	66	33	31	28	43
*Candelaria, John	0	3	5.48	13	2	0	1	21	32	13	13	11	19
*Cerutti, John	9	9	4.76	30	23	0	0	140	162	77	74	49	49
Cummings, Steve	0	0	5.11	6	2	0	0	12	22	7	7	5	4
*Flanagan, Mike	2	2	5.31	5	5	0	0	20	28	14	12	8	5
Gilles, Tom	1	0	6.75	2	0	0	0	1	2	1	1	0	1
Henke, Tom	2	4	2.17	61	0	0	32	75	58	18	18	19	75
Key, Jimmy	13	7	4.25	27	27	0	0	155	169	79	73	22	88
*Kilgus, Paul	0	0	6.06	11	0	0	0	16	19	11	11	7	7
*Leiter, Al	0	0	0.00	4	0	0	0	6	1	0	0	2	5
Luecken, Rick	0	0	9.00	1	0	0	0	1	2	1	1	1	0
*MacDonald, Rob	0	0	0.00	4	0	0	0	2	0	0	0	2	0
Stieb, Dave	18	6	2.93	33	33	2	0	209	179	73	68	64	125
Stottlemyre, Todd	13	17	4.34	33	33	4	0	203	214	101	98	69	115
Ward, Duane	2	8	3.45	73	0	0	11	128	101	51	49	42	112
*Wells, David	11	6	3.14	43	25	0	3	189	165	72	66	45	115
Wills, Frank	6	4	4.73	44	4	0	0	99	101	54	52	38	72

FIELDING

Catcher	PCT	G	PO	A	E
Borders	.993	115	515	46	4
Diaz	1.000	9	13	3	0
Myers	.993	87	411	30	3
Virgil	1.000	2	1	0	0

First Base	PCT	G	PO	A	E
McGriff	.996	147	1246	126	6
Mulliniks	1.000	3	11	0	0
Olerud	.986	18	132	10	2

Second Base	PCT	G	PO	A	E
Lawless	1.000	1	4	1	0
Lee	.993	112	260	286	4
Liriano	.983	49	93	132	4
Sojo	.969	15	16	15	1

Third Base	PCT	G	PO	A	E
Gruber	.955	145	123	280	19
Lawless	.800	4	1	3	1
Mulliniks	.949	22	12	25	2

	PCT	G	PO	A	E
Quinlan	1.000	1	0	1	0
Sojo	.875	4	2	5	1

Shortstop	PCT	G	PO	A	E
Fernandez	.989	161	297	480	9
Lee	1.000	9	6	15	0
Sojo	.842	5	6	10	3

Outfield	PCT	G	PO	A	E
Bell	.979	106	226	4	5
Ducey	1.000	19	37	0	0
Felix	.966	125	242	11	9
Gruber	1.000	6	6	0	0
Hill	.983	60	115	4	2
Lawless	1.000	2	6	0	0
Sojo	1.000	5	10	1	0
Whiten	1.000	30	60	3	0
Williams	1.000	30	36	0	0
Wilson	.992	141	372	5	3

Oakland's Bob Welch (27-6) became the first big league pitcher to win 27 games since Steve Carlton in 1972.

ALCS BOX SCORES

Game One: Athletics 9, Red Sox 1

OAKLAND	ab	r	h	bi	bb	so	BOSTON	ab	r	h	bi	bb	so
R.Henderson lf	5	1	2	3	0	0	Reed 2b-ss	3	0	0	0	0	0
McGee cf	4	1	0	0	1	2	Quintana 1b	4	0	0	0	0	0
Canseco rf	2	1	1	1	2	0	Boggs 3b	4	1	1	1	0	2
Baines dh	3	1	1	0	1	0	Burks cf	4	0	1	0	0	1
Lansford 3b	5	1	3	2	0	0	Greenwell lf	4	0	0	0	0	0
Steinbach c	5	1	3	1	0	1	Evans dh	2	0	0	0	1	0
McGwire 1b	3	1	0	0	2	0	Brunansky rf	3	0	1	0	0	0
Weiss ss	3	2	0	0	2	1	Pena c	3	0	0	0	0	0
Gallego 2b	1	0	1	0	1	0	Rivera ss	2	0	1	0	0	0
Quirk ph	1	0	1	0	0	0	Marshall ph	1	0	1	0	0	0
Randolph pr-2b	2	0	1	1	0	0	Kutcher pr	0	0	0	0	0	0
							Barrett 2b	0	0	0	0	0	0
TOTALS	34	9	13	8	9	4	TOTALS	30	1	5	1	1	3

```
Oakland . . . . . . . . . . . . . . . . . . . . . . . . . . . . . . . . . . . . . 000  000  117—9
Boston  . . . . . . . . . . . . . . . . . . . . . . . . . . . . . . . . . . . . . 000  100  000—1
```

E—Gray. DP—Oakland 1, Boston 1. LOB—Oakland 11, Boston 4. 2B—Lansford, Burks. HR—Boggs. SB—R.Henderson, McGee, Canseco. S—McGee, Baines, Reed. SF—Canseco, R.Henderson.

Oakland	IP	H	R	ER	BB	SO	Boston	IP	H	R	ER	BB	SO
Stewart W	8	4	1	1	1	3	Clemens	6	4	0	0	4	4
Eckersley	1	1	0	0	0	0	Andersen L	1	2	2	2	1	0
							Bolton	1/3	0	0	0	0	0
							Gray	2/3	3	2	1	1	0
							Lamp	1/3	2	4	4	2	0
							Murphy	2/3	2	1	1	1	0

Andersen pitched to 1 batter in 8th. Gray pitched to 2 batters in 9th.
WP—Clemens. PB—Pena. T—3:25. A—35,192.

Game Two: Athletics 4, Red Sox 1

OAKLAND	ab	r	h	bi	bb	so	BOSTON	ab	r	h	bi	bb	so
R.Henderson lf	4	0	1	0	0	0	Reed 2b-ss	4	0	1	0	0	0
McGee cf	5	2	2	0	0	0	Quintana 1b	3	0	1	0	0	0
Canseco rf	3	1	1	0	2	1	Boggs 3b	4	0	2	0	0	1
Baines dh	5	0	2	3	0	0	Burks cf	3	0	1	0	1	0
Blnknship pr-dh	0	0	0	0	0	0	Greenwell lf	3	0	0	0	1	1
McGwire 1b	5	0	2	1	0	1	Evans dh	4	0	1	0	0	1
Lansford 3b	5	0	3	0	0	0	Brunansky rf	3	0	0	0	1	1
Hassey c	3	0	1	0	1	0	Pena c	4	0	0	0	0	0
Weiss ss	3	0	0	0	0	1	Rivera ss	2	1	1	0	0	1
Randolph 2b	0	0	0	0	0	0	Marshall ph	1	0	0	0	0	0
Gallego 2b-ss	3	1	1	0	0	0	Barrett 2b	0	0	0	0	0	0
							Heep ph	1	0	0	0	0	0
TOTALS	36	4	13	4	3	3	TOTALS	32	1	6	1	3	6

```
Oakland . . . . . . . . . . . . . . . . . . . . . . . . . .  000  100  102—4
Boston . . . . . . . . . . . . . . . . . . . . . . . . . . . 001  000  000—1
```

E—Weiss. DP—Oakland 1, Boston 2. LOB—Oakland 12, Boston 8. 2B—McGee, Baines, Evans, Rivera. SB—McGee, Burks. SF—Weiss, R.Henderson, Quintana.

Oakland	IP	H	R	ER	BB	SO	Boston	IP	H	R	ER	BB	SO
Welch W	7⅓	6	1	1	3	4	Kiecker	5⅔	6	1	1	1	2
Honeycutt	⅓	0	0	0	0	0	Harris L	⅓	3	1	1	0	0
Eckersley S	1⅓	0	0	0	0	2	Andersen	1	1	0	0	1	0
							Reardon	2	3	2	2	1	0

Harris pitched to 2 batters in 7th. Andersen pitched to 1 batter in 8th.
HBP—Hassey (by Reardon), Gallego (by Kiecker). T—3:42. A—35,070.

Game Three: Athletics 4, Red Sox 1

BOSTON	ab	r	h	bi	bb	so	OAKLAND	ab	r	h	bi	bb	so
Reed 2b-ss	4	0	0	0	0	1	R.Henderson lf	4	0	1	0	0	0
Quintana 1b	4	0	0	0	0	0	Lansford 3b	3	0	0	0	0	0
Boggs 3b	4	0	2	0	0	0	Canseco rf	3	1	0	0	1	2
Burks cf	4	0	1	0	0	0	Baines dh	3	2	1	0	1	0
Greenwell lf	3	1	0	0	1	1	McGwire 1b	3	0	0	0	0	2
Evans dh	4	0	2	0	0	2	D.Henderson cf	2	0	1	1	0	1
Brunansky rf	3	0	0	1	0	1	Steinbach c	3	1	0	0	1	1
Pena c	4	0	3	0	0	0	Randolph 2b	4	0	2	2	0	0
Kutcher pr	0	0	0	0	0	0	Gallego ss	3	0	1	0	0	1
Rivera ss	2	0	0	0	0	1							
Marshall ph	1	0	0	0	0	0							
Barrett 2b	0	0	0	0	0	0							
Heep ph	1	0	0	0	0	0							
TOTALS	34	1	8	1	1	6	TOTALS	28	4	6	3	3	7

```
Boston . . . . . . . . . . . . . . . . . . . . . . . . . . . 010  000  000—1
Oakland . . . . . . . . . . . . . . . . . . . . . . . . . .  000  202  00x—4
```

E—Pena, Rivera, Boddicker. DP—Boston 1. LOB—Boston 8, Oakland 7. 2B—Boggs. SB—Canseco, Baines, D.Henderson. S—Lansford. SF—Brunansky, D.Henderson.

Boston	IP	H	R	ER	BB	SO	Oakland	IP	H	R	ER	BB	SO
Boddicker L	8	6	4	2	3	7	Moore W	6	4	1	1	1	5
							Nelson	1⅔	3	0	0	0	0
							Honeycutt	⅓	0	0	0	0	0
							Eckersley S	1	1	0	0	0	1

HBP—McGwire (by Boddicker), D.Henderson (by Boddicker). T—2:47. A—49,026.

Game Four: Athletics 3, Red Sox 1

BOSTON	ab	r	h	bi	bb	so	OAKLAND	ab	r	h	bi	bb	so
Burks cf	4	1	1	0	0	0	R.Henderson lf	3	0	1	0	1	2
Reed 2b	4	0	1	1	0	0	D.Henderson cf	4	0	0	0	0	1
Boggs 3b	4	0	2	0	0	0	Canseco rf	3	0	0	0	0	2
Greenwell lf	4	0	0	0	0	0	Jennings rf	1	0	0	0	0	0
Pena c	3	0	0	0	0	0	Baines dh	3	0	1	0	0	1
Evans dh	3	0	0	0	0	0	McGee pr-dh	0	0	0	0	0	0
Brunansky rf	3	0	0	0	0	1	Hassey ph	0	0	0	0	1	0
Quintana 1b	2	0	0	0	1	0	Blankenship pr	0	0	0	0	0	0
Rivera ss	3	0	0	0	0	0	Lansford 3b	3	1	1	0	0	1
							Steinbach c	3	0	2	0	0	0
							McGwire 1b	2	1	0	1	1	0
							Randolph 2b	2	1	0	0	1	0
							Gallego ss	3	0	1	2	0	0
TOTALS	30	1	4	1	1	1	TOTALS	27	3	6	3	4	7

```
Boston . . . . . . . . . . . . . . . . . . . . . . . . . . . 000  000  001—1
Oakland . . . . . . . . . . . . . . . . . . . . . . . . . .  030  000  00x—3
```

E—Greenwell. DP—Boston 2, Oakland 1. LOB—Boston 3, Oakland 5. 2B—Burks, Gallego. SB—R.Henderson, Blankenship. S—Lansford.

Boston	IP	H	R	ER	BB	SO	Oakland	IP	H	R	ER	BB	SO
Clemens L	1⅔	3	3	3	1	0	Stewart W	8	4	1	1	1	1
Bolton	2⅔	2	0	0	2	3	Honeycutt S	1	0	0	0	0	0
Gray	2⅔	1	0	0	0	2							
Andersen	1	0	0	0	0	2							

Stewart pitched to 2 batters in 9th.
T—3:02. A—49,052.

ALCS COMPOSITE BOX

BOSTON

Player, Pos.	AVG	G	AB	R	H	2B	3B	HR	RBI	BB	SO	SB
Wade Boggs, 3b	.438	4	16	1	7	1	0	1	1	0	3	0
Mike Marshall, ph	.333	3	3	0	1	0	0	0	0	0	0	0
Ellis Burks, cf	.267	4	15	1	4	2	0	0	0	1	1	1
Dwight Evans, dh	.231	4	13	0	3	1	0	0	1	1	3	0
Luis Rivera, ss	.222	4	9	1	2	1	0	0	0	0	2	0
Tony Pena, c	.214	4	14	0	3	0	0	0	0	0	0	0
Jody Reed, 2b	.133	4	15	0	2	0	0	0	1	0	2	0
Tom Brunansky, rf	.063	4	12	0	1	0	0	0	1	1	3	0
Mike Greenwell, lf	.000	4	14	1	0	0	0	0	0	2	2	0
Carlos Quintana, 1b	.000	4	13	0	0	0	0	0	1	1	0	0
Danny Heep, ph	.000	2	2	0	0	0	0	0	0	0	0	0
TOTALS.............	.183	4	126	4	23	5	0	1	4	6	16	1

Pitcher	W	L	ERA	G	GS	CG	SV	IP	H	R	ER	BB	SO
Tom Bolton............	0	0	0.00	2	0	0	0	3	2	0	0	2	3
Dana Kiecker	0	0	1.59	1	1	0	0	5⅔	6	1	1	1	2
Mike Boddicker	0	1	2.25	1	1	0	0	8	6	4	2	3	7
Jeff Gray	0	0	2.70	2	0	0	0	3⅓	4	2	1	1	2
Roger Clemens	0	1	3.52	2	2	0	0	7⅔	7	3	3	5	4
Larry Andersen	0	1	6.00	3	0	0	0	3	3	2	2	3	3
Jeff Reardon	0	0	9.00	1	0	0	0	2	3	2	2	1	0
Rob Murphy	0	0	13.49	1	0	0	0	⅔	2	1	1	1	0
Greg Harris	0	1	27.00	1	0	0	0	⅓	3	1	1	0	0
Dennis Lamp	0	0	108.00	1	0	0	0	⅓	2	4	4	2	0
TOTALS	0	4	4.50	4	4	0	0	34	38	20	17	19	21

OAKLAND

Player, Pos.	AVG	G	AB	R	H	2B	3B	HR	RBI	BB	SO	SB
Jamie Quirk, ph	1.000	1	1	0	1	0	0	0	0	0	0	0
Terry Steinbach, c	.455	3	11	2	5	0	0	0	1	1	2	0
Carney Lansford 3b	.438	4	16	2	7	1	0	0	2	0	1	0
Mike Gallego, ss	.400	4	10	1	4	1	0	0	2	1	1	0
Willie Randolph, 2b	.375	4	8	1	3	0	0	0	3	1	0	0
Harold Baines, dh	.357	4	14	2	5	1	0	0	3	2	1	1
Ron Hassey, c	.333	2	3	0	1	0	0	0	0	0	0	0
Rickey Henderson, lf	.294	4	17	1	5	0	0	0	3	1	2	2
Willie McGee, cf	.222	3	9	3	2	1	0	0	0	1	2	2
Jose Canseco, rf	.182	4	11	3	2	0	0	0	1	5	5	2
Dave Henderson, cf	.167	2	6	0	1	0	0	0	1	0	2	1
Mark McGwire, 1b	.154	4	13	2	2	0	0	0	2	3	3	0
Walt Weiss, ss	.000	2	7	2	0	0	0	0	0	2	2	0
Doug Jennings, rf	.000	1	1	0	0	0	0	0	0	0	0	0
Lance Blankenship, pr	.000	3	0	1	0	0	0	0	0	0	0	1
TOTALS...............	.299	4	127	20	38	4	0	0	18	19	21	9

Pitcher	W	L	ERA	G	GS	CG	SV	IP	H	R	ER	BB	SO
Dennis Eckersley	0	0	0.00	3	0	0	2	3⅓	2	0	0	0	3
Rick Honeycutt	0	0	0.00	3	0	0	1	1⅔	0	0	0	0	0
Gene Nelson	0	0	0.00	1	0	0	0	1⅔	3	0	0	0	0
Dave Stewart	2	0	1.13	2	2	0	0	16	8	2	2	2	4
Bob Welch	1	0	1.23	1	1	0	0	7⅓	6	1	1	3	4
Mike Moore	1	0	1.50	1	1	0	0	6	4	1	1	1	5
TOTALS	4	0	1.00	4	4	0	3	36	23	4	4	6	16

Boston	0	1	1		1	0	0		0	0	1 — 4
Oakland	0	3	0		3	0	2		2	1	9 — 20

E—Weiss, Rivera, Pena, Greenwell, Boddicker, Gray. **DP**—Boston 6, Oakland 3. **LOB**—Boston 23, Oakland 35. **S**—Reed, Baines, McGee, Lansford 2. **SF**—R.Henderson, Canseco, Quintana, Brunansky, D.Henderson. **PB**—Pena. **HBP**—Gallego (by Kiecker), Hassey (by Reardon), McGwire (by Boddicker), D.Henderson (by Boddicker). **WP**—Clemens. **Umpires**—Garcia, Hirschbeck, Evans, Cooney, Voltaggio, McCoy. **Official Scorers**—Charles Scoggins (Lowell, Mass.); Glenn Schwarz (San Francisco).

NATIONAL LEAGUE

Bizarre turns routine in wacky '90 season

By PAUL HAGEN

The National League batting champion, Willie McGee of the Cardinals, spent the last six weeks of the season playing in the safe haven of the American League.

Before the postseason, Reds manager Lou Piniella got almost as much attention for how far he could throw first base than for keeping Cincinnati in first place every day of the season.

The Dodgers took an eight-run lead into the top of the ninth ... and lost to the Phillies.

The Pirates became the first team to sweep five straight doubleheaders since the 1906 Yankees.

The Cubs scored 10 runs in an inning before they made an out.

Mets righthander David Cone held the ball while arguing a call at first base, allowing two runs to score.

In one game against the Reds, Cubs slugger Andre Dawson was intentionally walked five times, twice with a runner on first.

Pirates switchhitter Bobby Bonilla became so frustrated trying to hit off Cardinals lefthander John Tudor that he turned around and tried batting lefthanded ... and homered.

Pitchers Fernando Valenzuela of the Dodgers and Kevin Gross of the Expos homered. In the same inning. Off each other.

Don Robinson of the Giants became the first pitcher to pinch-

LEAGUE CHAMPIONS

Playoff Champions, Where Applicable
(Since 1900)

1990—Cincinnati	1959—Los Angeles	1928—St. Louis
1989—San Francisco	1958—Milwaukee	1927—Pittsburgh
1988—Los Angeles	1957—Milwaukee	1926—St. Louis
1987—St. Louis	1956—Brooklyn	1925—Pittsburgh
1986—New York	1955—Brooklyn	1924—New York
1985—St. Louis	1954—New York	1923—New York
1984—San Diego	1953—Brooklyn	1922—New York
1983—Philadelphia	1952—Brooklyn	1921—New York
1982—St. Louis	1951—New York	1920—Brooklyn
1981—Los Angeles	1950—Philadelphia	1919—Cincinnati
1980—Philadelphia	1949—Brooklyn	1918—Chicago
1979—Pittsburgh	1948—Boston	1917—New York
1978—Los Angeles	1947—Brooklyn	1916—Brooklyn
1977—Los Angeles	1946—St. Louis	1915—Philadelphia
1976—Cincinnati	1945—Chicago	1914—Boston
1975—Cincinnati	1944—St. Louis	1913—New York
1974—Los Angeles	1943—St. Louis	1912—New York
1973—New York	1942—St. Louis	1911—New York
1972—Cincinnati	1941—Brooklyn	1910—Chicago
1971—Pittsburgh	1940—Cincinnati	1909—Pittsburgh
1970—Cincinnati	1939—Cincinnati	1908—Chicago
1969—New York	1938—Chicago	1907—Chicago
1968—St. Louis	1937—New York	1906—Chicago
1967—St. Louis	1936—New York	1905—New York
1966—Los Angeles	1935—Chicago	1904—New York
1965—Los Angeles	1934—St. Louis	1903—Pittsburgh
1964—St. Louis	1933—New York	1902—Pittsburgh
1963—Los Angeles	1932—Chicago	1901—Pittsburgh
1962—San Francisco	1931—St. Louis	1900—Brooklyn
1961—Cincinnati	1930—St. Louis	
1960—Pittsburgh	1929—Chicago	

hit a home run since 1971. This is the same Robinson off whom Cincinnati's Paul O'Neill hit five of his 16 home runs.

The Phillies and Braves each played five games in which the losing team scored 10 or more runs.

One of the most controversial moves made by Tom Werner, new owner of the Padres, was inviting Roseanne Barr to sing the National Anthem.

Yeah, it was just another routine year in the National League in 1990.

The hunt for Red October

By June 3, Cincinnati had a 33-12 record and led the rest of the Western Division by 10 games. The Reds held on to become wire-to-wire leaders despite injuries that forced Jose Rijo, Tom Browning and Danny Jackson to miss starts.

Pittsburgh's Barry Bonds enjoyed a banner '90 season, hitting .301 with 33 homers and 52 stolen bases.

All three were healthy for the playoffs. Still, the Reds were considered underdogs to the Cinderella Pirates when the National League Championship Series opened at Riverfront Stadium.

Just over a week later, the Reds were headed to their first World Series since 1976 after beating the Pirates, four games to two.

The Pirates departure from postseason play was a farewell to arms—the arms of the Nasty Boys in the Reds bullpen, that is, and the arms in the Reds outfield.

The teams split the first two games, with the pivotal play in each being misjudged fly balls by two of the game's best leftfielders.

In the opener, it was Eric Davis of the Reds who misplayed Andy Van Slyke's fly ball into a ground-rule double, allowing the winning run to score in a 4-3 Pittsburgh victory.

In Game Two, it was Barry Bonds losing Paul O'Neill's fly

NL CHAMPS

Members of the National League champion Cincinnati Reds included, **bottom row**, left to right, Chris Sabo, Billy Hatcher, Luis Quinones, Jackie Moore (coach), Tony Perez (coach), Lou Piniella (manager), Sam Perlozzo (coach), Stan Williams (Coach), Larry Rothschild (coach), Bill Doran, Todd Benzinger. **Middle row**, Bernie Stowe (equipment manager), Dave Reynolds (batboy), Danny Jackson, Hal Morris, Jose Rijo, Terry Lee, Rob Dibble, Glenn Braggs, Paul O'Neill, Joe Oliver, Norm Charlton, Jeff Reed, Eric Davis, Joel Pieper (traveling secretary), Larry Starr (trainer), **Top row**, Randy Myers, Tim Layana, Scott Scudder, Jack Armstrong, Ron Oester, Rick Mahler, Tom Browning, Herm Winningham, Mariano Duncan, Barry Larkin, Dan Wright (assistant trainer).

Chicago's Ryne Sandberg had an all-star season at second base, hitting .306 with 40 homers.

ball in the sun. Herm Winningham scored and the Reds won, 2-1.

But just as big was another play by O'Neill, gunning down Van Slyke trying to advance from second to third on a fly to right in the sixth. O'Neill threw Van Slyke out, snuffing Pittsburgh's last, best chance to come back.

The Reds cruised to a 6-3 win in Game Three as the heart of the Pirates order—Bonds, Van Slyke, Bobby Bonilla—continued to struggle.

The play that defined the NLCS, however, came in the eighth inning of Game Four.

The Reds led, 4-2, going into the bottom of the inning when Jay Bell led off with a homer to pull Pittsburgh within one. Randy Myers relieved starter Rijo and the first batter he faced, Van Slyke, flied out after hitting a long shot into the seats that barely faded into foul territory.

Bonilla smashed a line drive off the wall, just beyond the reach of centerfielder Billy Hatcher, who crumpled to the ground. Bonilla rounded second and kept on running.

But Davis, hustling all the way, retrieved the ball, whirled and threw a strike to third. Bonilla was out and so, as it turned out, were the Pirates. Bonds followed with a single that would have tied the score. Instead, Myers survived his uncharacteristically shaky inning and the Reds ended up winning, 5-3.

"I was thinking three bases all the way," Bonilla would say later. "But I guess you have to tip your hat to Eric Davis for making the defensive play of the year."

Said Davis: "I knew I had to get into the gap as quickly as possible. When I made the throw, I knew it was on line. It was just a matter of whether or not it would get there on time."

That was the second key outfield throw made by the Reds.

In the fourth, Hatcher threw out Sid Bream trying to score from second on a single.

"You usually don't see this many putouts all year long," said Pirates manager Jim Leyland. "But they've put some throws on the money when they had to."

The Pirates stayed alive with a 3-2 win in Game Five when the series shifted back to Cincinnati, but a strong six innings from Jackson and another bullpen assist lifted the Reds to a 2-1 win and the pennant in Game Six.

Myers and Rob Dibble, who made up the Nasty Boys bullpen along with Norm Charlton, were named co-MVP of the playoffs.

Walking the plank

After a disappointing and injury-plagued fifth-place finish in 1989, hopes were not high for the Pirates. But Bonds blossomed and Bonilla made a successful transition from third base to right field to give the Pirates, along with Van Slyke in center, one of baseball's best outfields.

Lefthander Neal Heaton carried the rotation in the first half. And when he faded after the all-star break, Doug Drabek came on strong. Finally, down the stretch, the Pirates traded for lefthander Zane Smith, who won six games.

The Pirates still lost money and there was some concern that short-term moves had cost the team a long-range future. But at least a franchise that had been moribund only a few years

Bobby Bonilla hit 32 homers and drove in 120 runs to lead Pittsburgh to an NL East title.

Whitey Herzog, left, and Jack McKeon stepped down at midseason from managerial jobs in St. Louis and San Diego.

earlier had come back to life.

The Mets, once again, disappointed their followers. They led the league in runs scored, home runs and pitching and still finished second. Manager Davey Johnson was replaced by Bud Harrelson at midseason and the Mets improved, but they couldn't win the big games in crunch time.

Cardinals owner August Busch Jr. told manager Whitey Herzog after St. Louis won the pennant in 1985: "I'm giving you a lifetime contract." Quipped Herzog: "My lifetime or yours?" The answer became evident in 1990. Busch died in September, 1989. Herzog resigned at midseason, his club in last place.

The defending NL East champion Cubs were never a factor, and pitching was the main reason. Rick Sutcliffe was hurt most of the year. Greg Maddux got off to a slow start. Mike Bielecki didn't come close to matching his 1989 numbers. Mike Harkey was hurt. And Mitch Williams struggled after saving 36 games.

Nobody expected the Expos to do anything after losing Mark Langston, Bryn Smith, Pascual Perez and Hubie Brooks to free agency. But manager Buck Rodgers, with the help of rookies like Delino DeShields, Larry Walker, Bill Sampen and Chris Nabholz came home a strong third.

The Phillies got a terrific year out of Lenny Dykstra. Kenny Howell, projected as the No. 1 starter missed most of the year with a sore shoulder. The improvement of Jose DeJesus gives hope for the future.

How the West wasn't won

The Dodgers stayed in contention all year despite injuries to Orel Hershiser (early) and Tim Belcher (late). Ramon Martinez emerged as a star and future Cy Young candidate.

The underachieving Padres changed owners, Joan Kroc to Tom Werner; general managers, Jack McKeon to Joe McIlvaine; and managers, McKeon to Greg Riddoch. It didn't stop there. By the end of the World Series more than 20 employees including the trainer, public relations director and group sales director, had been fired.

The Braves hired John Schuerholz away from the Kansas City Royals to be the general manager and gave him a free hand to make sweeping changes.

The Giants failed to defend their NL championship, despite being able to bat Will Clark, Kevin Mitchell and Matt Williams, who accounted for 87 homers and 310 RBIs, in the middle of their order. The main reason: undependable starting pitching.

The Astros were reportedly up for sale. But there were no buyers and, for a team that has played a pat hand for years, no help when the pitching got old and first baseman Glenn Davis went on the disabled list.

East	W	L	Pct.	GB
Pittsburgh	95	67	.586	—
New York	91	71	.562	4
Montreal	85	77	.525	10
Philadelphia	77	85	.475	18
Chicago	77	85	.475	18
St. Louis	70	92	.432	25
West				
Cincinnati	91	71	.562	—
Los Angeles	86	76	.531	5
San Francisco	85	77	.525	6
San Diego	75	87	.463	16
Houston	75	87	.463	16
Atlanta	65	97	.401	26

1990 GENERAL INFORMATION

League Championship Series: Cincinnati defeated Pittsburgh 4-2 in best-of-7 series for the league pennant.

Regular-Season Attendance: Los Angeles, 3,002,396; New York, 2,732,745; St. Louis, 2,573,495; Cincinnati, 2,400,892; Chicago, 2,243,291; Pittsburgh, 2,049,908; Philadelphia, 1,992,484; San Francisco, 1,975,571; San Diego, 1,856,395; Montreal, 1,421,388; Houston, 1,310,927; Atlanta, 980,129.

Managers: Atlanta—Russ Nixon, Bobby Cox; **Chicago**—Don Zimmer; **Cincinnati**—Lou Piniella; **Houston**—Art Howe; **Los Angeles**—Tommy Lasorda; **Montreal**—Buck Rodgers; **New York**—Davey Johnson, Bud Harrelson; **Philadelphia**—Nick Leyva; **Pittsburgh**—Jim Leyland; **St. Louis**—Whitey Herzog, Red Schoendienst, Joe Torre; **San Diego**—Jack McKeon, Greg Riddoch; **San Francisco**—Roger Craig.

1990 All-Star Team (by Baseball America): C—Mike Scioscia, Los Angeles. **1B**—Eddie Murray, Los Angeles. **2B**—Ryne Sandberg, Chicago. **3B**—Matt Williams, San Francisco. **SS**—Barry Larkin, Cincinnati. **OF**—Barry Bonds, Pittsburgh; Bobby Bonilla, Pittsburgh; Lenny Dykstra, Philadelphia. **P**—Doug Drabek, Pittsburgh; Ramon Martinez, Los Angeles; Frank Viola, New York; Rob Dibble, Cincinnati; Jose Rijo, Cincinnati. **Player of Year**—Barry Bonds, Pittsburgh. **Pitcher of Year**—Doug Drabek, Pittsburgh. **Manager of Year**—Jim Leyland, Pittsburgh. **Rookie of Year**—Dave Justice, Atlanta. **Executive of Year**—Dave Dombrowski, Montreal.

1990 BATTING, PITCHING STATS

CLUB BATTING

	AVG	G	AB	R	H	2B	3B	HR	BB	SO	SB
Cincinnati	.265	162	5525	693	1466	284	40	125	466	913	166
Chicago	.263	162	5600	690	1474	240	36	136	406	869	151
San Francisco	.262	162	5573	719	1459	221	35	152	488	973	109
Los Angeles	.262	162	5491	728	1436	222	27	129	538	951	141
Pittsburgh	.259	162	5388	733	1395	288	42	138	582	915	137
San Diego	.257	162	5554	673	1429	243	35	123	509	902	138
New York	.256	162	5504	775	1410	278	21	172	536	851	110
St. Louis	.256	162	5462	599	1398	255	41	73	517	844	221
Philadelphia	.255	162	5535	646	1410	237	27	103	582	915	108
Atlanta	.250	162	5504	682	1376	263	26	162	473	1010	92
Montreal	.250	162	5452	662	1363	227	43	114	576	1024	235
Houston	.242	162	5379	573	1301	209	32	94	548	997	179

CLUB PITCHING

	ERA	G	CG	SHO	SV	IP	H	R	ER	BB	SO
Montreal	3.37	162	18	11	50	1473	1349	598	551	510	991
Cincinnati	3.39	162	14	12	50	1456	1338	597	549	543	1029
Pittsburgh	3.40	162	18	8	43	1447	1367	619	546	413	848
New York	3.43	162	18	14	41	1440	1339	613	548	444	1217
Houston	3.62	162	12	6	37	1450	1396	656	583	496	854
San Diego	3.68	162	21	12	35	1462	1437	673	598	507	928
Los Angeles	3.74	162	29	12	29	1442	1364	685	599	478	1021
St. Louis	3.88	162	8	13	39	1443	1432	698	622	475	833
San Francisco	4.08	162	14	6	45	1446	1477	710	655	553	788
Philadelphia	4.09	162	18	7	35	1449	1381	729	659	651	840
Chicago	4.34	162	13	7	42	1443	1510	774	695	572	877
Atlanta	4.58	162	17	8	30	1430	1527	821	728	579	938

Ramon Martinez
. . . 20-8, 223 K's

Lenny Dykstra
. . . .325 average

INDIVIDUAL BATTING LEADERS
(Minimum 502 Plate Appearances)

	AVG	G	AB	R	H	2B	3B	HR	RBI	BB	SO	SB
#McGee, Willie, St. Louis ...	.335	125	501	76	168	32	5	3	62	38	86	28
#Murray, Eddie, LA	.330	155	558	96	184	22	3	26	95	82	64	8
*Magadan, Dave, New York	.328	144	451	74	148	28	6	6	72	74	55	2
*Dykstra, Lenny, Phil	.325	149	590	106	192	35	3	9	60	89	48	33
Dawson, Andre, Chicago ..	.310	147	529	72	164	28	5	27	100	42	65	16
#Roberts, Bip, San Diego ..	.309	149	556	104	172	36	3	9	44	55	65	46
*Grace, Mark, Chicago	.309	157	589	72	182	32	1	9	82	59	54	15
*Gwynn, Tony, San Diego ..	.309	141	573	79	177	29	10	4	72	44	23	17
*Butler, Brett, SF	.309	160	622	108	192	20	9	3	44	90	62	51
Sandberg, Ryne, Chicago ..	.306	155	615	116	188	30	3	40	100	50	84	25

INDIVIDUAL PITCHING LEADERS
(Minimum 162 Innings)

	W	L	ERA	G	GS	CG	SV	IP	H	R	ER	BB	SO
Darwin, Danny, Hou	11	4	2.21	48	17	3	2	163	136	42	40	31	109
*Smith, Zane, Mtl.-Pitt	12	9	2.55	33	31	4	0	215	196	77	61	50	130
Whitson, Ed, San Diego ..	14	9	2.60	32	32	6	0	229	215	73	66	47	127
*Viola, Frank, New York ...	20	12	2.67	35	35	7	0	250	227	83	74	60	182
Rijo, Jose, Cincinnati	14	8	2.70	29	29	7	0	197	151	65	59	78	152
Drabek, Doug, Pittsburgh ..	22	6	2.76	33	33	9	0	231	190	78	71	56	131
Martinez, Ramon, LA	20	6	2.92	33	33	12	0	234	191	89	76	67	223
Boyd, Oil Can, Montreal ..	10	6	2.93	31	31	3	0	191	164	64	62	52	113
Martinez, Dennis, Mon	10	11	2.95	32	32	7	0	226	191	80	74	49	156
*Hurst, Bruce, San Diego ..	11	9	3.14	33	33	9	0	224	188	85	78	63	162

Cumulative Statistics, Multi-team Players

BATTING	AVG	G	AB	R	H	2B	3B	HR	RBI	BB	SO	SB
Alou, Moises, Pitt-Mtl	.200	16	20	4	4	0	1	0	0	0	3	0
#Doran, Bill, Hous-Cinc ...	.300	126	403	59	121	29	2	7	37	79	58	23
*Fletcher, Darrin, LA-Phil ..	.130	11	23	3	3	1	0	0	1	1	6	0
#Herr, Tommy, Phil-NY	.261	146	547	48	143	26	3	5	60	50	58	7
Hudler, Rex, Mon-StL	.282	93	220	31	62	11	2	7	22	12	32	18
Lyons, Barry, NY-LA	.235	27	85	9	20	0	0	3	9	2	10	0
Martinez, Carmelo, Phil-Pitt	.240	83	217	26	52	9	0	10	35	30	42	2
McClendon, Lloyd, Chi-Pitt	.164	53	110	6	18	3	0	2	12	14	22	1
McGriff, Terry, Cinc-Hous .	.000	6	9	0	0	0	0	0	0	0	1	0
*Meadows, Louie, Hous-Phil	.107	30	28	4	3	0	0	0	0	3	6	0
Mercado, Orlando, NY-Mtl .	.214	50	98	10	21	1	0	3	7	8	12	0
Murphy, Dale, Atl-Phil	.245	154	563	60	138	23	1	24	83	61	130	9
Roomes, Rolando, Cinc-Mtl	.227	46	75	6	17	0	1	2	8	1	26	0
Trevino, Alex, Hous-NY-Cinc	.221	58	86	3	19	5	0	1	13	7	11	0
Vatcher, Jim, Phil-Atl	.260	57	73	7	19	2	1	1	7	5	15	0

PITCHING	W	L	ERA	G	GS	CG	SV	IP	H	R	ER	BB	SO
Boever, Joe, Atl-Phil	3	6	3.36	67	0	0	14	88	77	35	33	51	75
Camacho, Ernie, SF-StL ..	0	0	5.17	14	0	0	0	16	17	10	9	9	5
*Cook, Dennis, Phil-LA	9	4	3.92	47	16	2	1	156	155	74	68	56	64
Costello, John, StL-Mtl	0	0	5.91	8	0	0	0	11	12	8	7	2	2
Freeman, Marvin, Phil-Atl ..	1	2	4.31	25	3	0	1	48	41	24	23	17	38
Grant, Mark, SD-Atl	2	3	4.73	59	1	0	3	91	108	53	48	37	69
Greene, Tommy, Atl-Phil ..	3	3	5.08	15	9	0	0	51	50	31	29	26	21
*Hammaker, Atlee, SF-SD ..	4	9	4.36	34	7	0	0	87	85	44	42	27	44
*Hesketh, Joe, Mtl-Atl	1	2	5.29	33	0	0	5	34	32	23	20	14	24
Kerfeld, Charley, Hous-Atl .	3	3	6.62	30	0	0	2	34	40	28	25	29	31
Kramer, Randy, Pitt-Chi ...	0	3	4.50	22	4	0	0	46	47	25	23	21	27
*Lilliquist, Derek, Atl-SD ...	5	11	5.31	28	18	1	0	122	136	74	72	42	63
Parrett, Jeff, Phil-Atl	5	10	4.64	67	5	0	2	109	119	62	56	55	86
*Ruskin, Scott, Pitt-Mtl	3	2	2.75	67	0	0	2	75	75	28	23	38	57
*Schatzeder, Dan, Hous-NY .	1	3	2.20	51	2	0	0	70	66	23	17	23	39
*Smith, Zane, Mtl-Pitt	12	9	2.55	33	31	4	0	215	196	77	61	50	130

BATTING	AVG	G	AB	R	H	2B	3B	HR	RBI	BB	SO	SB
*Bell, Mike	.244	36	45	8	11	5	1	1	5	2	9	0
Berroa, Geronimo	.000	7	4	0	0	0	0	0	0	1	1	0
Blauser, Jeff	.269	115	386	46	104	24	3	8	39	35	70	3
Cabrera, Francisco	.277	63	137	14	38	5	1	7	25	5	21	1
Davis, Jody	.071	12	28	0	2	0	0	0	1	3	3	0
Esasky, Nick	.171	9	35	2	6	0	0	0	0	4	14	0
Gant, Ron	.303	152	575	107	174	34	3	32	84	50	86	33
*Gregg, Tommy	.264	124	239	18	63	13	1	5	32	20	39	4
Infante, Alexis	.036	20	28	3	1	1	0	0	0	7	7	0
*Justice, Dave	.282	127	439	76	124	23	2	28	78	64	92	11
*Kremers, Jimmy	.110	29	73	7	8	1	1	1	2	6	27	0
Lemke, Mark	.226	102	239	22	54	13	0	0	21	21	22	0
Mann, Kelly	.143	11	28	2	4	1	0	1	2	0	6	0
*McDowell, Oddibe	.243	113	355	47	74	14	0	7	25	21	53	13
Murphy, Dale	.232	97	349	38	81	14	0	17	55	41	84	9
Olson, Greg	.262	100	298	36	78	12	1	7	36	30	51	1
Presley, Jim	.242	140	541	59	131	34	1	19	72	29	130	1
Rosario, Victor	.143	9	7	3	1	0	0	0	0	1	1	0
Smith, Lonnie	.305	135	466	72	142	27	9	9	42	58	69	10
Thomas, Andres	.219	84	278	26	61	8	0	5	30	11	43	2
*Treadway, Jeff	.283	128	474	56	134	20	2	11	59	25	42	3
Vatcher, Jim	.259	21	27	2	7	1	1	0	3	1	9	0
*Whitt, Ernie	.172	67	180	14	31	8	0	2	10	23	27	0

PITCHING	W	L	ERA	G	GS	CG	SV	IP	H	R	ER	BB	SO
*Avery, Steve	3	11	5.64	21	20	1	0	99	121	79	62	45	75
Boever, Joe	1	3	4.68	33	0	0	8	42	40	23	22	35	35
*Castillo, Tony	5	1	4.23	52	3	0	1	77	93	41	36	20	64
Clary, Marty	1	10	5.67	33	14	0	0	102	128	72	64	39	44
Freeman, Marvin	1	0	1.72	9	0	0	0	16	7	3	3	3	12
*Glavine, Tom	10	12	4.28	33	33	1	0	214	232	111	102	78	129
Grant, Mark	1	2	4.64	33	1	0	3	52	61	30	27	18	40
Greene, Tommy	1	0	8.03	5	2	0	0	12	14	11	11	9	4
Henry, Dwayne	2	2	5.63	34	0	0	0	38	41	26	24	25	34
*Hesketh, Joe	0	2	5.81	31	0	0	5	31	30	23	20	12	21
Kerfeld, Charley	3	1	5.58	25	0	0	2	31	31	22	19	23	27
*Leibrandt, Charlie	9	11	3.16	24	24	5	0	162	164	72	57	35	76
*Lilliquist, Derek	2	8	6.28	12	11	0	0	62	75	45	43	19	34
Luecken, Rich	1	4	5.77	36	0	0	1	53	73	36	34	30	35
Marak, Paul	1	2	3.69	7	7	1	0	39	39	16	16	19	15
*Mercker, Kent	4	7	3.17	36	0	0	7	48	43	22	17	24	39
Parrett, Jeff	1	1	3.00	20	0	0	1	27	27	11	9	19	17
Richards, Rusty	0	0	27.00	1	0	0	0	1	3	3	3	1	0
Sisk, Doug	0	0	3.86	3	0	0	0	2	1	1	1	4	1
Smith, Pete	5	6	4.79	13	13	3	0	77	77	45	41	24	56
Smoltz, John	14	11	3.85	34	34	6	0	231	206	109	99	90	170
*Stanton, Mike	0	3	18.00	7	0	0	2	7	16	16	14	4	7
Valdez, Sergio	0	0	6.75	3	0	0	0	5	6	4	4	3	3

FIELDING

Catcher	PCT	G	PO	A	E
Cabrera	1.000	3	5	0	0
Davis	1.000	4	17	1	0
Kremers	.992	27	107	10	1
Mann	1.000	10	40	3	0
Olson	.987	97	501	43	7
Whitt	.991	59	296	42	3

First Base	PCT	G	PO	A	E
Bell	.981	24	97	9	2
Cabrera	.990	48	264	19	3
Davis	1.000	6	45	5	0
Esasky	.944	9	79	5	5
Gregg	.987	50	334	34	5
Justice	.981	69	488	38	10
Presley	.989	17	77	11	1

Second Base	PCT	G	PO	A	E
Blauser	1.000	14	23	25	0
Infante	.964	10	14	13	1
Lemke	.984	44	70	120	3
Rosario	.000	1	0	0	0
Treadway	.976	122	241	360	15

Third Base	PCT	G	PO	A	E
Blauser	1.000	9	5	6	0
Infante	1.000	4	0	3	0
Lemke	.989	45	21	72	1
Olson	.000	1	0	0	0
Presley	.930	133	101	231	25
Thomas	1.000	5	1	7	0

Shortstop	PCT	G	PO	A	E
Blauser	.961	93	140	257	16
Infante	.941	3	8	8	1
Lemke	1.000	1	0	1	0
Rosario	1.000	3	3	4	0
Thomas	.967	72	103	193	10

Outfield	PCT	G	PO	A	E
Berroa	1.000	3	1	0	0
Blauser	.000	1	0	0	0
Gant	.978	146	357	7	8
Gregg	.957	20	22	0	1
Justice	.968	61	116	4	4
McDowell	.971	72	134	2	4
Murphy	.981	97	208	3	4
Smith	.956	122	254	6	12
Vatcher	1.000	6	7	0	0

BATTING	AVG	G	AB	R	H	2B	3B	HR	RBI	BB	SO	SB
#Berryhill, Damon	.189	17	53	6	10	4	0	1	9	5	14	0
*Clark, Dave	.275	84	171	22	47	4	2	5	20	8	40	7
#Dascenzo, Doug	.253	113	241	27	61	9	5	1	26	21	18	15
Dawson, Andre	.310	147	529	72	164	28	5	27	100	42	65	16
Dunston, Shawon	.262	146	545	73	143	22	8	17	66	15	87	25
Girardi, Joe	.270	133	419	36	113	24	2	1	38	17	50	8

Atlanta outfielder Ronnie Gant became a 30-30 player in 1990, hitting 32 homers and stealing 33 bases.

	AVG	G	AB	R	H	2B	3B	HR	RBI	BB	SO	SB
*Grace, Mark	.309	157	589	72	182	32	1	9	82	59	54	15
*May, Derrick	.246	17	61	8	15	3	0	1	11	2	7	1
McClendon, Lloyd	.159	49	107	5	17	3	0	1	10	14	21	1
Ramos, Domingo	.265	98	226	22	60	5	0	2	17	27	29	0
Salazar, Luis	.254	115	410	44	104	13	3	12	47	19	59	3
Sandberg, Ryne	.306	155	615	116	188	30	3	40	100	50	84	25
*Smith, Dwight	.262	117	290	34	76	15	0	6	27	28	46	11
#Smith, Greg	.205	18	44	4	9	2	1	0	5	2	5	1
*Varsho, Gary	.250	46	48	10	12	4	0	0	1	1	6	2
Villanueva, Hector	.272	52	114	14	31	4	1	7	18	4	27	1
Walton, Jerome	.263	101	392	63	103	16	2	2	21	50	70	14
#Wilkerson, Curtis	.220	77	186	21	41	5	1	0	16	7	36	2
Wrona, Rick	.172	16	29	3	5	0	0	0	0	2	11	1
*Wynne, Marvell	.204	92	186	21	38	8	2	4	19	14	25	3

PITCHING	W	L	ERA	G	GS	CG	SV	IP	H	R	ER	BB	SO
*Assenmacher, Paul	7	2	2.80	74	1	0	10	103	90	33	32	36	95
Bielecki, Mike	8	11	4.93	36	29	0	1	168	188	101	92	70	103
Blankenship, Kevin	0	2	5.84	3	2	0	0	12	13	10	8	6	5
Boskie, Shawn	5	6	3.69	15	15	1	0	98	99	42	40	31	49
Coffman, Kevin	0	2	11.29	8	2	0	0	18	26	24	23	19	9
*Dickson, Lance	0	3	7.24	3	3	0	0	14	20	12	11	4	4
Harkey, Mike	12	6	3.26	27	27	2	0	174	153	71	63	59	94
*Kraemer, Joe	0	0	7.20	18	0	0	0	25	31	25	20	14	16
Kramer, Randy	0	2	3.98	10	2	0	0	20	20	10	9	12	12
Lancaster, Les	9	5	4.62	55	6	1	6	109	121	57	56	40	65
Long, Bill	6	1	4.37	42	0	0	5	56	66	29	27	21	32
Maddux, Greg	15	15	3.46	35	35	8	0	237	242	116	91	71	144
Nunez, Jose	4	7	6.53	21	10	0	0	61	61	47	44	34	40
Pavlas, Dave	2	0	2.11	13	0	0	0	21	23	7	5	6	12
Pico, Jeff	4	4	4.79	31	8	0	2	92	120	53	49	37	37
Sutcliffe, Rick	0	2	5.91	5	5	0	0	21	25	14	14	12	7
Wilkins, Dean	0	0	9.82	7	0	0	1	7	11	8	8	7	3
*Williams, Mitch	1	8	3.93	59	2	0	16	66	60	38	29	50	55
*Wilson, Steve	4	9	4.79	45	15	1	1	139	140	77	74	43	95

FIELDING

Catcher	PCT	G	PO	A	E
Berryhill	.978	15	87	3	2
Girardi	.985	133	653	61	11
Villanueva	.991	23	108	6	1
Wrona	.970	16	55	9	2

First Base	PCT	G	PO	A	E
Grace	.992	153	1324	180	12
Villanueva	.985	14	62	4	1

Second Base	PCT	G	PO	A	E
Ramos	.000	1	0	0	0
Sandberg	.989	154	278	469	8
G. Smith	1.000	7	10	17	0
Wilkerson	.946	14	24	29	3

Third Base	PCT	G	PO	A	E
Ramos	.932	66	23	46	5
Salazar	.950	91	55	136	10
Wilkerson	.888	52	25	62	11

Shortstop	PCT	G	PO	A	E
Dunston	.970	144	255	392	20
Ramos	.949	21	39	54	5
G. Smith	.912	7	10	21	3
Wilkerson	1.000	1	0	2	0

Outfield	PCT	G	PO	A	E
Clark	1.000	39	60	2	0
Dascenzo	1.000	107	174	2	0
Dawson	.981	140	250	10	5
Lancaster	.000	1	0	0	0
May	.972	17	34	1	1
McClendon	.980	23	49	0	1
Salazar	.955	28	41	1	2
D. Smith	.986	81	139	4	2
Varsho	1.000	3	2	0	0
Walton	.977	98	247	3	6
Wilkerson	.000	1	0	0	0
Wynne	.991	66	108	3	1

CINCINNATI

BATTING	AVG	G	AB	R	H	2B	3B	HR	RBI	BB	SO	SB
#Bates, Billy	.000	8	5	2	0	0	0	0	0	0	2	2
#Benzinger, Todd	.253	118	376	35	95	14	2	5	46	19	69	3
Braggs, Glenn	.299	72	201	22	60	9	1	6	28	26	43	3
Davis, Eric	.260	127	453	84	118	26	2	24	86	60	100	21
#Doran, Bill	.373	17	59	10	22	8	0	1	5	8	5	5
Duncan, Mariano	.306	125	435	67	133	22	11	10	55	24	67	13
*Griffey, Ken	.206	46	63	6	13	2	0	1	8	2	5	2
Hatcher, Billy	.276	139	504	68	139	28	5	5	25	33	42	30
Larkin, Barry	.301	158	614	85	185	25	6	7	67	49	49	30
Lee, Terry	.211	12	19	1	4	1	0	0	3	2	2	0
McGriff, Terry	.000	2	4	0	0	0	0	0	0	0	1	0
*Morris, Hal	.340	107	309	50	105	22	3	7	36	21	32	9
*O'Neill, Paul	.270	145	503	59	136	28	0	16	78	53	103	13
#Oester, Ron	.299	64	154	10	46	10	1	0	13	10	29	1
Oliver, Joe	.231	121	364	34	84	23	0	8	52	37	75	1
#Quinones, Luis	.241	83	145	10	35	7	0	2	17	13	29	1
*Reed, Jeff	.251	72	175	12	44	8	1	3	16	24	26	0
Roomes, Rolando	.213	30	61	5	13	0	0	2	7	0	20	0
Sabo, Chris	.270	148	567	95	153	38	2	25	71	61	58	25
Sutko, Glenn	.000	1	1	0	0	0	0	0	0	0	1	0
Trevino, Alex	.429	7	7	0	3	1	0	0	1	0	0	0
*Winningham, Herm	.256	84	160	20	41	8	5	3	17	14	31	6

PITCHING	W	L	ERA	G	GS	CG	SV	IP	H	R	ER	BB	SO
Armstrong, Jack	12	9	3.42	29	27	2	0	166	151	72	63	59	110
*Birtsas, Tim	1	3	3.86	29	0	0	0	51	69	24	22	24	41
Brown, Keith	0	0	4.76	8	0	0	0	11	12	6	6	3	8
Browning, Tom	15	9	3.80	35	35	2	0	228	235	98	96	52	99
*Charlton, Norm	12	9	2.74	56	16	1	2	154	131	53	47	70	117
Dibble, Rob	8	3	1.74	68	0	0	11	98	62	22	19	34	136
Gross, Kip	0	0	4.26	5	0	0	0	6	6	3	3	2	3
*Hammond, Chris	0	2	6.35	3	3	0	0	11	13	9	8	12	4
*Jackson, Danny	6	6	3.61	22	21	0	0	117	119	54	47	40	76
Layana, Tim	5	3	3.49	55	0	0	2	80	71	33	31	44	53
Mahler, Rick	7	6	4.28	35	16	2	4	135	134	67	64	39	68
*Minutelli, Gino	0	0	9.00	2	0	0	0	1	0	1	1	2	0
*Myers, Randy	4	6	2.08	66	0	0	31	87	59	24	20	38	98
Rijo, Jose	14	8	2.70	29	29	7	0	197	151	65	59	78	152
Robinson, Ron	2	2	4.88	6	5	0	0	31	36	18	17	14	14
*Rodriguez, Rosario	0	0	6.10	9	0	0	0	10	15	7	7	2	8
Scudder, Scott	5	5	4.90	21	10	0	0	72	74	41	39	30	42

FIELDING

Catcher	PCT	G	PO	A	E
McGriff	1.000	1	4	2	0
Oliver	.992	118	686	59	6
Reed	.987	70	358	26	5
Sutko	1.000	1	3	0	0
Trevino	1.000	2	9	0	0

First Base	PCT	G	PO	A	E
Benzinger	.992	95	707	52	6
Griffey	.979	9	42	4	1
Lee	1.000	6	28	3	0
Morris	.995	80	589	53	3
Quinones	1.000	1	2	0	0
Trevino	.938	1	14	1	1

Second Base	PCT	G	PO	A	E
Bates	1.000	1	0	1	0
Doran	.985	12	28	37	1
Duncan	.973	115	245	287	15
Oester	.982	50	80	88	3
Quinones	.964	13	22	31	2

Third Base	PCT	G	PO	A	E
Doran	.667	4	0	4	2
Oester	.667	3	0	2	1
Quinones	.981	22	12	41	1
Sabo	.966	146	70	273	12

Shortstop	PCT	G	PO	A	E
Duncan	.914	12	16	16	3
Larkin	.977	156	254	469	17
Quinones	.875	9	8	13	3

Outfield	PCT	G	PO	A	E
Benzinger	1.000	10	26	0	0
Braggs	.968	60	110	10	4
Davis	.993	122	257	11	2
Duncan	1.000	1	4	0	0
Griffey	1.000	6	12	0	0
Hatcher	.997	131	308	10	1
Morris	.857	6	6	0	1
O'Neill	.993	141	271	12	2
Roomes	1.000	19	33	1	0
Winningham	1.000	64	89	3	0

HOUSTON

BATTING	AVG	G	AB	R	H	2B	3B	HR	RBI	BB	SO	SB
*Anthony, Eric	.192	84	239	26	46	8	0	10	29	29	78	5
*Baldwin, Jeff	.000	7	8	1	0	0	0	0	0	1	2	0
Biggio, Craig	.276	150	555	53	153	24	2	4	42	53	79	25
*Caminiti, Ken	.242	143	541	52	131	20	2	4	51	48	97	9
#Candaele, Casey	.286	130	262	30	75	8	6	3	22	31	42	7
Cedeno, Andujar	.000	7	8	0	0	0	0	0	0	0	5	0
Davidson, Mark	.292	57	130	12	38	5	1	1	11	10	18	0
Davis, Glenn	.251	93	327	44	82	15	4	22	64	46	54	8
#Doran, Bill	.288	109	344	49	99	21	2	6	32	71	53	18
*Gedman, Rich	.202	40	104	4	21	7	0	1	10	15	24	0
*Gonzalez, Luis	.190	12	21	1	4	2	0	0	0	2	5	0
Lombardozzi, Steve	.000	2	1	0	0	0	0	0	0	1	1	0
McGriff, Terry	.000	4	5	0	0	0	0	0	0	0	0	0
*Meadows, Louie	.143	15	14	3	2	0	0	0	0	2	4	0
Nichols, Carl	.204	32	49	7	10	3	0	0	11	8	11	0
*Oberkfell, Ken	.207	77	150	10	31	6	1	1	12	15	17	1

Eric Davis hit .260 with 24 homers and led World Series champion Cincinnati with 88 RBIs.

	AVG	G	AB	R	H	2B	3B	HR	RBI	BB	SO	SB
Ortiz, Jose	.273	30	77	7	21	5	1	1	10	12	11	1
*Puhl, Terry	.293	37	41	5	12	1	0	0	8	5	7	1
Ramirez, Rafael	.261	132	445	44	116	19	3	2	37	24	46	10
*Rhodes, Karl	.244	39	86	12	21	6	1	1	3	13	12	4
#Rohde, Dave	.184	59	98	8	18	4	0	0	5	9	20	0
Simms, Mike	.308	12	13	3	4	1	0	1	2	0	4	0
*Stubbs, Franklin	.261	146	448	59	117	23	2	23	71	48	114	19
Trevino, Alex	.188	42	69	3	13	3	0	1	10	6	11	0
Wilson, Glenn	.245	118	368	42	90	14	0	10	55	26	64	0
Yelding, Eric	.254	142	511	69	130	9	5	1	28	39	87	64
#Young, Gerald	.175	57	154	15	27	4	1	1	4	20	23	6

PITCHING	W	L	ERA	G	GS	CG	SV	IP	H	R	ER	BB	SO
*Agosto, Juan	9	8	4.29	82	0	0	4	92	91	46	44	39	50
Andersen, Larry	5	2	1.95	50	0	0	6	74	61	19	16	24	68
Clancy, Jim	2	8	6.51	33	10	0	1	76	100	58	55	33	44
Clark, Terry	0	0	13.50	1	1	0	0	4	9	7	6	3	2
Darwin, Danny	11	4	2.21	48	17	3	2	163	136	42	40	31	109
*Deshaies, Jim	7	12	3.78	34	34	2	0	209	186	93	88	84	119
Fisher, Brian	0	0	7.20	4	0	0	0	5	9	5	4	0	1
Gullickson, Bill	10	14	3.82	32	32	2	0	193	221	100	82	61	73
Hennis, Randy	0	0	0.00	3	1	0	0	10	1	0	0	3	4
Hernandez, Xavier	2	1	4.62	34	1	0	0	62	60	34	32	24	24
Kerfeld, Charley	0	2	16.20	5	0	0	0	3	9	6	6	6	4
Meyer, Brian	0	4	2.21	14	0	0	1	20	16	7	5	6	6
*Osuna, Al	2	0	4.76	12	0	0	0	11	10	6	6	6	6
Portugal, Mark	11	10	3.62	32	32	1	0	197	187	90	79	67	136
*Schatzeder, Dan	1	3	2.39	45	2	0	0	64	61	23	17	23	37
Scott, Mike	9	13	3.81	32	32	4	0	206	194	102	87	66	121
Smith, Dave	6	6	2.39	49	0	0	23	60	45	18	16	20	50

FIELDING

Catcher	PCT	G	PO	A	E
Biggio	.985	113	547	54	9
Gedman	1.000	39	180	25	0
McGriff	.900	4	9	0	1
Nichols	.986	15	64	9	1
Trevino	.992	30	124	7	1

First Base	PCT	G	PO	A	E
Davis	.995	91	796	55	4
Gonzalez	1.000	2	17	0	0
Nichols	.920	3	22	1	2
Oberkfell	.987	11	69	7	1
Puhl	1.000	1	1	0	0
Simms	1.000	6	20	1	0
Stubbs	.991	72	496	42	5
Wilson	1.000	1	2	0	0

Second Base	PCT	G	PO	A	E
Candaele	.989	49	75	107	2
Doran	.989	99	170	265	5
Oberkfell	1.000	11	12	14	0
Rhodes	.000	1	0	0	0
Rohde	1.000	31	27	63	0
Yelding	.953	10	21	20	2

Third Base	PCT	G	PO	A	E
Caminiti	.945	149	118	243	21
Candaele	1.000	1	0	1	0

	PCT	G	PO	A	E
Gonzalez	1.000	4	5	10	0
Oberkfell	.935	24	12	31	3
Rohde	1.000	4	0	5	0
Yelding	.667	3	0	2	1

Shortstop	PCT	G	PO	A	E
Candaele	.944	13	6	11	1
Cedeno	.833	3	3	2	1
Ramirez	.953	129	190	321	25
Rohde	1.000	2	1	2	0
Yelding	.958	40	64	97	7

Outfield	PCT	G	PO	A	E
Anthony	.970	71	124	5	4
Baldwin	1.000	3	1	0	0
Biggio	.967	50	111	6	4
Candaele	1.000	58	66	1	0
Davidson	.981	51	103	1	2
Meadows	1.000	9	7	0	0
Nichols	.000	1	0	0	0
Ortiz	.978	25	44	1	1
Puhl	1.000	8	8	0	0
Rhodes	.955	30	61	2	3
Stubbs	.991	71	112	1	1
Wilson	.973	108	225	12	6
Yelding	.971	94	230	5	7
Young	.990	50	99	4	1

BATTING	AVG	G	AB	R	H	2B	3B	HR	RBI	BB	SO	SB
Brooks, Hubie	.266	153	568	74	151	28	1	20	91	33	108	2
*Daniels, Kal	.296	130	450	81	133	23	1	27	94	68	104	4
Dempsey, Rick	.195	62	128	13	25	5	0	2	15	23	29	1
*Fletcher, Darrin	.000	2	1	0	0	0	0	0	0	0	1	0
*Gibson, Kirk	.260	89	315	59	82	20	0	8	38	39	65	26
Gonzalez, Jose	.232	106	99	15	23	5	3	2	8	6	27	3
#Griffin, Alfredo	.210	141	461	38	97	11	3	1	35	29	65	6
*Gwynn, Chris	.284	101	141	19	40	2	1	5	22	7	28	0
Hamilton, Jeff	.125	7	24	1	3	0	0	0	1	0	3	0
*Hansen, Dave	.143	5	7	0	1	0	0	0	1	0	3	0
*Harris, Lenny	.304	137	431	61	131	16	4	2	29	29	31	15
Hatcher, Mickey	.212	85	132	12	28	3	1	0	13	6	22	0
Hernandez, Carlos	.200	10	20	2	4	1	0	0	1	0	2	0
#Javier, Stan	.304	104	276	56	84	9	4	3	24	37	44	15
Lopez, Luis	.000	6	6	0	0	0	0	0	0	0	2	0
Lyons, Barry	.200	3	5	1	1	0	0	1	2	0	1	0
*Murray, Eddie	.330	155	558	96	184	22	3	26	95	82	64	8
#Offerman, Jose	.155	29	58	7	9	0	0	1	7	4	14	1
Randolph, Willie	.271	26	96	15	26	4	0	1	9	13	9	1
#Samuel, Juan	.242	143	492	62	119	24	3	13	52	51	126	38
*Scioscia, Mike	.264	135	435	46	115	25	0	12	66	55	31	4
Sharperson, Mike	.297	129	357	42	106	14	2	3	36	46	39	15
Shelby, John	.250	25	24	2	6	1	0	0	2	0	7	1
*Traxler, Brian	.091	9	11	0	1	1	0	0	0	0	4	0
#Vizcaino, Jose	.275	37	51	3	14	1	1	0	2	4	8	1

PITCHING	W	L	ERA	G	GS	CG	SV	IP	H	R	ER	BB	SO
Aase, Don	3	1	4.97	32	0	0	3	38	33	24	21	19	24
Belcher, Tim	9	9	4.00	24	24	5	0	153	136	76	68	48	102
*Cook, Dennis	1	1	7.53	5	3	0	0	14	23	13	12	2	6
Crews, Tim	4	5	2.77	66	2	0	5	107	98	40	33	24	76
Gott, Jim	3	5	2.90	50	0	0	3	62	59	27	20	34	44
Hartley, Mike	6	3	2.95	32	6	1	1	79	58	32	26	30	76
Hershiser, Orel	1	1	4.26	4	4	0	0	25	26	12	12	4	16
Holmes, Darren	0	1	5.19	14	0	0	0	17	15	10	10	11	19
Howell, Jay	5	5	2.18	45	0	0	16	66	59	17	16	20	59
Maddux, Mike	0	1	6.53	11	2	0	0	21	24	15	15	4	11
Martinez, Ramon	20	6	2.92	33	33	12	0	234	191	89	76	67	223
Morgan, Mike	11	15	3.75	33	33	6	0	211	216	100	88	60	106
*Munoz, Mike	0	1	3.18	8	0	0	0	6	2	2	2	3	2
*Neidlinger, Jim	5	3	3.28	12	12	0	0	74	67	30	27	15	46
*Perry, Pat	0	0	8.10	7	0	0	0	7	9	7	6	5	2
*Poole, Jim	0	0	4.22	16	0	0	0	11	7	5	5	8	6
*Searage, Ray	1	0	2.78	29	0	0	0	32	30	11	10	10	19
*Valenzuela, Fernando	13	13	4.59	33	33	5	0	204	223	112	104	77	115
*Walsh, Dave	1	0	3.86	20	0	0	1	16	15	12	7	6	15
*Wells, Terry	1	2	7.84	5	5	0	0	21	25	23	18	14	18
Wetteland, John	2	4	4.81	22	5	0	0	43	44	28	23	17	36

FIELDING

Catcher	PCT	G	PO	A	E
Dempsey	.992	53	213	27	2
Fletcher	.000	1	0	0	0
Hernandez	1.000	10	37	2	0
Lyons	1.000	2	3	0	0
Scioscia	.989	132	842	58	10

First Base	PCT	G	PO	A	E
Hatcher	1.000	25	73	7	0
Lopez	1.000	1	4	0	0
Murray	.992	150	1180	113	10
Sharperson	.983	6	55	2	1
Traxler	1.000	3	6	2	0

Second Base	PCT	G	PO	A	E
Harris	.985	44	62	70	2
Randolph	.969	26	50	73	4
Samuel	.972	108	195	258	13
Sharperson	.957	9	10	12	1
Vizcaino	1.000	6	4	3	0

Third Base	PCT	G	PO	A	E
Hamilton	1.000	7	3	12	0
Hansen	.500	2	0	1	1

	PCT	G	PO	A	E
Harris	.959	94	77	133	9
Hatcher	.813	10	3	10	3
Sharperson	.949	106	70	153	12

Shortstop	PCT	G	PO	A	E
Griffin	.959	139	221	382	26
Harris	1.000	1	0	2	0
Offerman	.946	27	30	40	4
Sharperson	.977	15	17	26	1
Vizcaino	.956	11	19	24	2

Outfield	PCT	G	PO	A	E
Brooks	.964	150	255	9	10
Daniels	.986	127	206	13	3
Gibson	.995	81	191	4	1
Gonzalez	1.000	81	62	1	0
Gwynn	1.000	44	39	1	0
Harris	1.000	2	1	0	0
Hatcher	1.000	10	10	0	0
Javier	1.000	87	204	2	0
Samuel	.965	31	79	4	3
Shelby	1.000	12	8	0	0

Gregg Jefferies ...40 doubles

Brett Butler ... 192 hits

Andres Galarraga ... 169 K's

BATTING

RUNS
Ryne Sandberg, Chicago 116
Bobby Bonilla, Pittsburgh 112
Brett Butler, San Francisco 108
Ron Gant, Atlanta 107
Lenny Dykstra, Philadelphia 106

HITS
Brett Butler, San Francisco 192
Lenny Dykstra, Philadelphia 192
Ryne Sandberg, Chicago 188
Barry Larkin, Cincinnati 185
Tim Wallach, Montreal 185

TOTAL BASES
Ryne Sandberg, Chicago 344
Bobby Bonilla, Pittsburgh 324
Ron Gant, Atlanta 310
Matt Williams, San Francisco ... 301
Tim Wallach, Montreal 295

DOUBLES
Gregg Jefferies, New York 40
Bobby Bonilla, Pittsburgh........ 39
Chris Sabo, Cincinnati 38
Howard Johnson, New York 37
Tim Wallach, Montreal 37

TRIPLES
Mariano Duncan, Cincinnati 11
Tony Gwynn, San Diego 10
Brett Butler, San Franicsco 9
Vince Coleman, St. Louis 9
Lonnie Smith, Atlanta............ 9

HOME RUNS
Ryne Sandberg, Chicago 40
Darryl Strawberry, New York 37
Kevin Mitchell, San Franicsco ... 35
Barry Bonds, Pittsburgh 33
Matt Williams, San Franicsco ... 33

RUNS BATTED IN
Matt Williams, San Francisco ... 122
Bobby Bonilla, Pittsburgh 120
Joe Carter, San Diego 115
Barry Bonds, Pittsburgh........ 114
Darryl Strawberry, New York ... 108

SACRIFICE BUNTS
Jay Bell, Pittsburgh 39
Dwight Gooden, New York 14
Jack Armstrong, Cincinnati 13
Eddie Whitson, San Diego 13
Oil Can Boyd, Montreal 12
Dennis Martinez, Montreal 12

SACRIFICE FLIES
Bobby Bonilla, Pittsburgh....... 15
Will Clark, San Franicsco 13
Hubie Brooks, Los Angeles 11
Pedro Guerrero, St. Louis 11
Three tied at 10

WALKS
Jack Clark, San Diego 104
Barry Bonds, Pittsburgh 93
Brett Butler, San Francisco...... 90
Lenny Dykstra, Philadelphia 89
Von Hayes, Philadelphia 87

INTENTIONAL WALKS
Andre Dawson, Chicago 21
Eddie Murray, Los Angeles 21
Tony Gwynn, San Diego 20

Jose Lind, Pittsburgh............ 19
Joe Carter, San Diego 18

HIT BY PITCH
Glenn Davis, Houston 8
Joe Carter, San Diego 7
Lenny Dykstra, Philadelphia 7
Barry Larkin, Cincinnati.......... 7
Matt Williams, San Francisco 7

STRIKEOUTS
Andres Galarraga, Montreal.... 169
Matt Williams, San Francisco .. 138
Dale Murphy, Atlanta/Phil 130
Jim Presley, Atlanta............ 130
Juan Samuel, Los Angeles 126

STOLEN BASES
Vince Coleman, St. Louis 77
Eric Yelding, Houston 64
Barry Bonds, Pittsburgh 52
Brett Butler, San Francisco..... 51
Otis Nixon, Montreal 50

CAUGHT STEALING
Eric Yelding, Houston 25
Delino DeShields, Montreal 22
Juan Samuel, Los Angeles 20
Brett Butler, San Francisco 19
Vince Coleman, St. Louis 17

GIDP
Dale Murphy, Atlanta/Phil 22
Jose Lind, Pittsburgh............ 20
Eddie Murray, Los Angeles 19
Garry Templeton, San Diego.....17
Roberto Alomar, San Diego 16
Glenn Wilson, Houston.......... 16

PINCH HITS
Tommy Gregg, Atlanta 18
Mickey Hatcher, Los Angeles ... 14
Chris Gwynn, Los Angeles 13
Luis Quinones, Cincinnati 13
Randy Ready, Philadelphia...... 12
Ernie Riles, San Francisco 12

HITTING STREAKS
Lenny Dykstra, Philadelphia 23
Willie McGee, St. Louis 22
Mark Grace, Chicago 18
Barry Larkin, Cincinnati 18
Darryl Strawberry, New York ... 18

MULTI-HIT GAMES
Eddie Murray, Los Angeles...... 58
Tim Wallach, Montreal 58
Ryne Sandberg, Chicago 57
Brett Butler, San Francisco 55
Ron Gant, Atlanta 55

SLUGGING PERCENTAGE
Barry Bonds, Pittsburgh .... .565
Ryne Sandberg, Chicago....... .559
Kevin Mitchell, San Francisco .. .544
Ron Gant, Atlanta .... .539
Andre Dawson, Chicago .... .535
Dave Justice, Atlanta.......... .535

ON-BASE PERCENTAGE
Lenny Dykstra, Philadelphia .... .418
Dave Magadan, New York..... .417
Eddie Murray, Los Angeles .... .414
Barry Bonds, Pittsburgh .... .406
Brett Butler, San Francisco .... .397

MONTREAL

BATTING

BATTING	AVG	G	AB	R	H	2B	3B	HR	RBI	BB	SO	SB
*Aldrete, Mike	.242	96	161	22	39	7	1	1	18	37	31	1
Alou, Moises	.200	14	15	4	3	0	1	0	0	0	3	0
*Bullock, Eric	.500	4	2	0	1	0	0	0	0	0	0	0
*DeShields, Delino	.289	129	499	69	144	28	6	4	45	66	96	42
Fitzgerald, Mike	.243	111	313	36	76	18	1	9	41	60	60	8
*Foley, Tom	.213	73	164	11	35	2	1	0	12	12	22	0
Galarraga, Andres	.256	155	579	65	148	29	0	20	87	40	169	10
*Goff, Jerry	.227	52	119	14	27	1	0	3	7	21	36	0
Grissom, Marquis	.257	98	288	42	74	14	2	3	29	27	40	22
Hudler, Rex	.333	4	3	1	1	0	0	0	0	0	1	0
#Johnson, Wallace	.163	47	49	6	8	1	0	1	5	7	6	1
*Martinez, Dave	.279	118	391	60	109	13	5	11	39	24	48	13
Mercado, Orlando	.250	8	8	0	2	0	0	0	0	0	1	0
#Nixon, Otis	.251	119	231	46	58	6	2	1	20	28	33	50
Noboa, Junior	.266	81	158	15	42	7	2	0	14	7	14	4
*Owen, Spike	.234	149	453	55	106	24	5	5	35	70	60	8
Paredes, Johnny	.333	3	6	0	2	1	0	0	1	1	1	0
#Raines, Tim	.287	130	457	65	131	11	5	9	62	70	43	49
Roomes, Rolando	.286	16	14	1	4	0	1	0	1	1	6	0
Santovenia, Nelson	.190	59	163	13	31	3	1	6	28	8	31	0
*Walker, Larry	.241	133	419	59	101	18	3	19	51	49	112	21
Wallach, Tim	.296	161	626	69	185	37	5	21	98	42	80	6

PITCHING

PITCHING	W	L	ERA	G	GS	CG	SV	IP	H	R	ER	BB	SO
Anderson, Scott	0	1	3.00	4	0	0	0	18	12	6	6	5	16
*Barnes, Brian	1	1	2.89	4	4	1	0	28	25	10	9	7	23
Boyd, Oil Can	10	6	2.93	31	31	3	0	191	164	64	62	52	113
Burke, Tim	3	3	2.52	58	0	0	20	75	71	29	21	21	47
Costello, John	0	0	5.68	4	0	0	0	6	5	5	4	1	1
Farmer, Howard	0	3	7.04	6	4	0	0	23	26	18	18	10	14
*Frey, Steve	8	2	2.10	51	0	0	9	56	44	15	13	29	29
Gardner, Mark	7	9	3.42	27	26	3	0	153	129	62	58	61	135
Gideon, Brett	0	0	9.00	1	0	0	0	1	2	1	1	4	0
Gross, Kevin	9	12	4.57	31	26	2	0	163	171	86	83	65	111
*Hall, Drew	4	7	5.09	42	0	0	3	58	52	35	33	29	40
Hesketh, Joe	1	0	0.00	2	0	0	0	3	2	0	0	2	3
Malloy, Bob	0	0	0.00	1	0	0	0	2	1	0	0	1	1
Martinez, Dennis	10	11	2.95	32	32	7	0	226	191	80	74	49	156
Mohorcic, Dale	1	2	3.23	34	0	0	2	53	56	21	19	18	29
*Nabholz, Chris	6	2	2.83	11	11	1	0	70	43	23	22	32	53
Rojas, Mel	3	1	3.60	23	0	0	1	40	34	17	16	24	26
*Ruskin, Scott	1	0	2.28	23	0	0	0	28	25	7	7	10	23
Sampen, Bill	12	7	2.99	59	4	0	2	90	94	34	30	33	69
Schmidt, Dave	3	3	4.31	34	0	0	13	48	58	26	23	13	22
*Smith, Zane	6	7	3.23	22	21	1	0	139	141	57	50	41	80
Thompson, Rich	0	0	0.00	1	0	0	0	1	1	0	0	0	0

FIELDING

Catcher	PCT	G	PO	A	E
Fitzgerald	.990	98	560	41	6
Goff	.963	38	196	13	8
Mercado	1.000	8	26	1	0
Santovenia	.980	51	264	24	6

First Base	PCT	G	PO	A	E
Aldrete	1.000	18	109	8	0
Foley	.000	1	0	0	0
Galarraga	.993	154	1300	94	10
Goff	1.000	3	19	0	0
Johnson	1.000	7	39	0	0

Second Base	PCT	G	PO	A	E
DeShields	.981	128	237	372	12
Foley	.940	20	18	29	3
Noboa	1.000	31	31	45	0
Paredes	.889	2	1	7	1

Third Base	PCT	G	PO	A	E
Foley	1.000	7	0	5	0
Goff	.833	3	1	4	1

	PCT	G	PO	A	E
Noboa	.714	8	3	2	2
Wallach	.954	161	128	308	21

Shortstop	PCT	G	PO	A	E
Foley	.987	45	61	89	2
Nixon	1.000	1	0	1	0
Noboa	1.000	7	4	4	0
Owen	.989	148	216	340	6

Outfield	PCT	G	PO	A	E
Aldrete	.982	38	51	4	1
Alou	1.000	5	6	1	0
Fitzgerald	1.000	6	5	1	0
Grissom	.988	87	165	5	2
Martinez	.989	108	257	6	3
Nixon	.994	88	149	5	1
Noboa	1.000	9	9	1	0
Raines	.976	123	239	3	6
Roomes	1.000	6	6	0	0
Walker	.985	124	249	12	4

NEW YORK

BATTING

BATTING	AVG	G	AB	R	H	2B	3B	HR	RBI	BB	SO	SB
Baez, Kevin	.167	5	12	0	2	1	0	0	0	0	4	0
*Boston, Daryl	.273	115	366	65	100	21	2	12	45	28	50	18
#Carr, Chuck	.000	4	2	0	0	0	0	0	0	0	2	1
Carreon, Mark	.250	82	188	30	47	12	0	10	26	15	29	1
Diaz, Mario	.136	16	22	0	3	1	0	0	1	0	3	0
Elster, Kevin	.207	92	314	36	65	20	1	9	45	30	54	2
#Herr, Tommy	.250	27	100	9	25	5	0	1	10	14	11	0
*Hughes, Keith	.000	8	9	0	0	0	0	0	0	0	4	0
#Hundley, Todd	.209	36	67	8	14	6	0	0	2	6	18	0
#Jefferies, Gregg	.283	153	604	96	171	40	3	15	68	46	40	11
Jelic, Chris	.091	4	11	2	1	0	0	1	3	0	3	0

Tim Wallach
... .296-21-98

Darryl Strawberry
... 37 homers

BATTING	AVG	G	AB	R	H	2B	3B	HR	RBI	BB	SO	SB
#Johnson, Howard	.244	154	590	89	144	37	3	23	90	69	100	34
Liddell, Dave	1.000	1	1	1	1	0	0	0	0	0	0	0
Lyons, Barry	.238	24	80	8	19	0	0	2	7	2	9	0
*Magadan, Dave	.328	144	451	74	148	28	6	6	72	74	55	2
Marshall, Mike	.239	53	163	24	39	8	1	6	27	7	40	0
McReynolds, Kevin	.269	147	521	75	140	23	1	24	82	71	61	9
Mercado, Orlando	.211	42	90	10	19	1	0	3	7	8	11	0
Miller, Keith	.258	88	233	42	60	8	0	1	12	23	46	16
O'Brien, Charlie	.162	28	68	6	11	3	0	0	9	10	8	0
*O'Malley, Tom	.223	82	121	14	27	7	0	3	14	11	20	0
Reed, Darren	.205	26	39	5	8	4	1	1	2	3	11	1
*Sasser, Mackey	.307	100	270	31	83	14	0	6	41	15	19	0
*Strawberry, Darryl	.277	152	542	92	150	18	1	37	108	70	110	15
Tabler, Pat	.279	17	43	6	12	1	1	1	10	3	8	0
Teufel, Tim	.246	80	175	28	43	11	0	10	24	15	33	0
*Torve, Kelvin	.289	20	38	0	11	4	0	0	2	4	9	0
Trevino, Alex	.300	9	10	0	3	1	0	0	2	1	0	0

PITCHING	W	L	ERA	G	GS	CG	SV	IP	H	R	ER	BB	SO
Brown, Kevin	0	0	0.00	2	0	0	0	2	2	0	0	1	0
Cone, David	14	10	3.23	31	30	6	0	212	177	84	.76	65	233
Darling, Ron	7	9	4.50	33	18	1	0	126	135	73	63	44	99
*Fernandez, Sid	9	14	3.46	30	30	2	0	179	130	79	69	67	181
*Franco, John	5	3	2.53	55	0	0	33	68	66	22	19	21	56
Gooden, Dwight	19	7	3.83	34	34	2	0	233	229	106	99	70	223
Innis, Jeff	1	3	2.39	18	0	0	1	26	19	9	7	10	12
Machado, Julio	4	1	3.15	27	0	0	0	34	32	13	12	17	27
*Musselman, Jeff	0	2	5.63	28	0	0	0	32	40	22	20	11	14
*Ojeda, Bob	7	6	3.66	38	12	0	0	118	123	53	48	40	62
Pena, Alejandro	3	3	3.20	52	0	0	5	76	71	31	27	22	76
*Schatzeder, Dan	0	0	0.00	6	0	0	0	6	5	0	0	0	2
Valera, Julio	1	1	6.92	3	3	0	0	13	20	11	10	7	4
*Viola, Frank	20	12	2.67	35	35	7	0	250	227	83	74	60	182
Whitehurst, Wally	1	0	3.29	38	0	0	2	66	63	27	24	9	46

FIELDING

Catcher	PCT	G	PO	A	E
Hundley	.988	36	162	8	2
Liddell	1.000	1	1	0	0
Lyons	.980	23	180	12	4
Mercado	.991	40	213	8	2
O'Brien	.986	28	191	21	3
Sasser	.975	87	498	43	14
Trevino	.929	7	25	1	2

First Base	PCT	G	PO	A	E
Magadan	.998	113	830	71	2
Marshall	.993	42	277	24	2
O'Malley	.938	3	15	0	1
Sasser	1.000	1	3	0	0
Teufel	.991	24	106	9	1
Torve	1.000	9	65	0	0

Second Base	PCT	G	PO	A	E
Diaz	.000	1	0	0	0
Herr	.979	26	35	59	2
Jefferies	.976	118	219	278	12
Miller	.972	11	19	16	1
Teufel	.970	24	29	35	2

Third Base	PCT	G	PO	A	E
Jefferies	.956	34	23	63	4
Johnson	.913	92	52	159	20

	PCT	G	PO	A	E
Magadan	.972	19	7	28	1
O'Malley	.983	38	26	33	1
Teufel	.952	10	6	14	1

Shortstop	PCT	G	PO	A	E
Baez	1.000	4	5	7	0
Diaz	.958	10	5	18	1
Elster	.960	92	159	251	17
Johnson	.972	73	98	176	8
Miller	1.000	4	3	4	0

Outfield	PCT	G	PO	A	E
Boston	.986	109	203	3	3
Carr	.000	1	0	0	0
Carreon	1.000	60	87	1	0
Hughes	1.000	5	5	0	0
Jelic	1.000	4	1	0	0
Marshall	.000	1	0	0	0
McReynolds	.988	144	237	14	3
Miller	.980	61	146	1	3
Reed	.955	14	20	1	1
Strawberry	.989	149	268	10	3
Tabler	1.000	10	20	1	0
Thornton	1.000	2	1	0	0
Torve	.000	1	0	0	0

Darren Daulton	Von Hayes	Terry Mulholland
....268-12-57	...281-17-73	...9-10, 3.34

BATTING	AVG	G	AB	R	H	2B	3B	HR	RBI	BB	SO	SB
*Booker, Rod	.221	73	131	19	29	5	2	0	10	15	26	3
Campusano, Sil	.212	66	85	10	18	1	1	2	9	6	16	1
Chamberlain, Wes	.283	18	46	9	13	3	0	2	4	1	9	4
*Daulton, Darren	.268	143	459	62	123	30	1	12	57	72	72	7
*Dykstra, Lenny	.325	149	590	106	192	35	3	9	60	89	48	33
*Fletcher, Darrin	.136	9	22	3	3	1	0	0	1	1	5	0
*Ford, Curt	.111	22	18	0	2	0	0	0	0	1	5	0
Hayes, Charlie	.258	152	561	56	145	20	0	10	57	28	91	4
*Hayes, Von	.261	129	467	70	122	14	3	17	73	87	81	16
#Herr, Tommy	.264	119	447	39	118	21	3	4	50	36	47	7
#Hollins, David	.184	72	114	14	21	0	0	5	15	10	28	0
*Jones, Ron	.276	24	58	5	16	2	0	3	7	9	9	0
Jordan, Ricky	.241	92	324	32	78	21	0	5	44	13	39	2
*Kruk, John	.291	142	443	52	129	25	8	7	67	69	70	10
Lake, Steve	.250	29	80	4	20	2	0	0	6	3	12	0
Martinez, Carmelo	.242	71	198	23	48	8	0	8	31	29	37	2
*Meadows, Louie	.071	15	14	1	1	0	0	0	0	0	1	2	0
*Morandini, Mickey	.241	25	79	9	19	4	0	1	3	6	19	3
Murphy, Dale	.266	57	214	22	57	9	1	7	28	20	46	0
Nieto, Tom	.167	17	30	1	5	0	0	0	4	3	11	0
Ready, Randy	.244	101	217	26	53	9	1	1	26	29	35	3
Thon, Dickie	.255	149	552	54	141	20	4	8	48	37	77	12
Vatcher, Jim	.261	36	46	5	12	1	0	1	4	4	6	0

PITCHING	W	L	ERA	G	GS	CG	SV	IP	H	R	ER	BB	SO
Akerfelds, Darrel	5	2	3.77	71	0	0	3	93	65	45	39	54	42
Boever, Joe	2	3	2.15	34	0	0	6	46	37	12	11	16	40
*Carman, Don	6	2	4.15	59	1	0	1	87	69	43	40	38	58
*Combs, Pat	10	10	4.07	32	31	3	0	183	179	90	83	86	108
*Cook, Dennis	8	3	3.56	42	13	2	1	142	132	61	56	54	58
DeJesus, Jose	7	8	3.74	22	22	3	0	130	97	63	54	73	87
Freeman, Marvin	0	2	5.57	16	3	0	1	32	34	21	20	14	26
Frohwirth, Todd	0	1	18.00	5	0	0	0	1	3	2	2	6	1
Greene, Tommy	2	3	4.15	10	7	0	0	39	36	20	18	17	17
Grimsley, Jason	3	2	3.30	11	11	0	0	57	47	21	21	43	41
Howell, Ken	8	7	4.64	18	18	2	0	107	106	60	55	49	70
Malone, Chuck	1	0	3.68	7	0	0	0	7	3	4	3	11	7
McDowell, Roger	6	8	3.86	72	0	0	22	86	92	41	37	35	39
*McElroy, Chuck	0	1	7.71	16	0	0	0	14	24	13	12	10	16
Moore, Brad	0	0	3.38	3	0	0	0	3	4	1	1	2	1
*Mulholland, Terry	9	10	3.34	34	33	26	6	0	181	172	78	67	42	75
Noles, Dickie	0	1	27.00	1	0	0	0	1	3	2	1	1	0
Ontiveros, Steve	0	0	2.70	5	0	0	0	10	9	3	3	3	6
Parrett, Jeff	4	9	5.18	47	5	0	1	82	92	51	47	36	69
*Ruffin, Bruce	6	13	5.38	32	25	2	0	149	178	99	89	62	79

FIELDING

Catcher	PCT	G	PO	A	E
Daulton	.989	139	683	70	8
Fletcher	1.000	6	30	3	0
Lake	.993	28	115	19	1
Nieto	.984	17	57	5	1

First Base	PCT	G	PO	A	E
C. Hayes	1.000	1	28	2	0
Hollins	1.000	1	8	1	0
Jordan	.995	84	744	36	4
Kruk	.996	61	402	43	2
Martinez	.994	43	318	24	2

Second Base	PCT	G	PO	A	E
Booker	.975	23	17	22	1
C. Hayes	1.000	1	2	3	0
Herr	.991	114	240	290	5
Morandini	.990	25	37	61	1
Ready	.985	28	46	84	2

Third Base	PCT	G	PO	A	E
Booker	.909	10	5	5	1

	PCT	G	PO	A	E
C. Hayes	.957	146	121	324	20
Hollins	.932	30	19	36	4

Shortstop	PCT	G	PO	A	E
Booker	.976	27	35	47	2
Thon	.964	148	222	439	25

Outfield	PCT	G	PO	A	E
Campusano	.976	47	40	1	1
Chamberlain	.958	10	23	0	1
Dykstra	.987	149	439	7	6
Ford	1.000	3	2	0	0
V. Hayes	.979	127	272	8	6
Jones	1.000	16	25	1	0
Kruk	.986	87	141	2	2
Martinez	1.000	20	32	1	0
Meadows	1.000	4	1	0	0
Murphy	.992	55	113	4	1
Ready	1.000	30	32	2	0
Vatcher	1.000	24	20	0	0

Pittsburgh righthander Doug Drabek led National League pitchers with 22 wins.

PITCHING

GAMES
Juan Agosto, Houston............ 82
Paul Assenmacher, Chicago 74
Greg Harris, San Diego 73
Roger McDowell, Philadelphia... 72
Darrel Akerfelds, Philadelphia ... 71

GAMES STARTED
Tom Browning, Cincinnati 35
Greg Maddux, Chicago 35
Frank Viola, New York 35
Three tied at 34

COMPLETE GAMES
Ramon Martinez, Los Angeles... 12
Doug Drabek, Pittsburgh 9
Bruce Hurst, San Diego 9
Greg Maddux, Chicago............ 8
Three tied at 7

SHUTOUTS
Bruce Hurst, San Diego 4
Mike Morgan, Los Angeles 4
Six tied at 3

SAVES
John Franco, New York 33
Randy Myers, Cincinnati 31
Lee Smith, St. Louis............. 27
Craig Lefferts, San Diego 23
Dave Smith, Houston 23

WINS
Doug Drabek, Pittsburgh 22
Ramon Martinez, Dodgers 20
Frank Viola, New York 20
Dwight Gooden, New York 19
Tom Browning, Cincinnati 15
Greg Maddux, Chicago 15

LOSSES
Jose DeLeon, St. Louis 19
Joe Magrane, St. Louis 17
Greg Maddux, Chicago 15
Mike Morgan, Los Angeles 15
Dennis Rasmussen, San Diego . 15

INNINGS PITCHED
Frank Viola, New York 250
Greg Maddux, Chicago 237
Ramon Martinez, Los Angeles . 234
Dwight Gooden, New York 233
Doug Drabek, Pittsburgh 231
John Smoltz, Atlanta........... 231

HITS ALLOWED
Greg Maddux, Chicago 242
Tom Browning, Cincinnati..... 235
Tom Glavine, Atlanta 232

Dwight Gooden, New York 229
Frank Viola, New York 227

RUNS ALLOWED
Greg Maddux, Chicago 116
Fernando Valenzuela, LA 112
Tom Glavine, Atlanta 111
Dennis Rasmussen, San Diego 110
John Smoltz, Atlanta........... 109

HOME RUNS ALLOWED
Dennis Rasmussen, San Diego . 28
Mike Scott, Houston............ 27
Tom Browning, Cincinnati 24
Ramon Martinez, Los Angeles .. 22
Five tied at 21

WALKS
John Smoltz, Atlanta 90
Pat Combs, Philadelphia 86
Jose DeLeon, St. Louis 86
Jim Deshaies, Houston 84
Tom Glavine, Atlanta 78
Jose Rijo, Cincinnati 78

HIT BATSMEN
Mark Gardner, Montreal 9
Jim Deshaies, Houston.......... 8
Joe Magrane, St. Louis.......... 8
Three tied at 7

STRIKEOUTS
Dave Cone, New York 233
Dwight Gooden, New York 223
Ramon Martinez, Los Angeles . 223
Frank Viola, New York 182
Sid Fernandez, New York...... 181

WILD PITCHES
John Smoltz, Atlanta 14
Fernando Valenzuela, LA 13
Mike Bielecki, Chicago 11
Joe Magrane, St. Louis......... 11
Frank Viola, New York 11

BALKS
Jack Armstrong, Cincinnati 5
Andy Benes, San Diego 5
Bob Kipper, Pittsburgh 5
Jose Rijo, Cincinnati 5
Dave Smith, Houston............ 5

OPPONENTS BATTING AVERAGE
Sid Fernandez, New York ..... .200
Jose Rijo, Cincinnati .... .212
Ramon Martinez, Los Angeles . .221
Danny Darwin, Houston .... .225
Doug Drabek, Pittsburgh ...... .225

PITTSBURGH

BATTING

BATTING	AVG	G	AB	R	H	2B	3B	HR	RBI	BB	SO	SB
Alou, Moises	.200	2	5	0	1	0	0	0	0	0	0	0
#Backman, Wally	.292	104	315	62	92	21	3	2	28	42	53	6
Bell, Jay	.254	159	583	93	148	28	7	7	52	65	109	10
Belliard, Rafael	.204	47	54	10	11	3	0	0	6	5	13	1
Bilardello, Dann	.054	19	37	1	2	0	0	0	3	4	10	0
Bonds, Barry	.301	151	519	104	156	32	3	33	114	93	83	52
#Bonilla, Bobby	.280	160	625	112	175	39	7	32	120	45	103	4
*Bream, Sid	.270	147	389	39	105	23	2	15	67	48	65	8
#Cangelosi, John	.197	58	76	13	15	2	0	0	1	11	12	7
*Carter, Steve	.200	5	5	0	1	0	0	0	0	0	1	0
Garcia, Carlos	.500	4	4	1	2	0	0	0	0	0	2	0
King, Jeff	.245	127	371	46	91	17	1	14	53	21	50	3
*LaValliere, Mike	.258	96	279	27	72	15	0	3	31	44	20	0
Lind, Jose	.261	152	514	46	134	28	5	1	48	35	52	5
Martinez, Carmelo	.211	12	19	3	4	1	0	2	4	1	5	0
McClendon, Lloyd	.333	4	3	1	1	0	1	0	1	2	0	1
#Merced, Orlando	.208	25	24	3	5	1	0	0	0	1	9	0
Prince, Tom	.100	4	10	1	1	0	0	0	0	0	1	0
Redus, Gary	.247	96	227	32	56	15	3	6	23	33	38	11
#Reynolds, R.J.	.288	95	215	25	62	10	1	0	19	23	35	12
*Ryal, Mark	.083	9	12	0	1	0	0	0	0	0	3	0
Slaught, Don	.300	84	230	27	69	18	3	4	29	27	27	0
*Van Slyke, Andy	.284	136	493	67	140	26	6	17	77	66	89	14

PITCHING

PITCHING	W	L	ERA	G	GS	CG	SV	IP	H	R	ER	BB	SO
Bair, Doug	0	0	4.81	22	0	0	0	24	30	15	13	11	19
Belinda, Stan	3	4	3.55	55	0	0	8	58	48	23	23	29	55
Drabek, Doug	22	6	2.76	33	33	9	0	231	190	78	71	56	131
*Heaton, Neal	12	9	3.45	30	24	0	0	146	143	66	56	38	68
Huismann, Mark	1	0	9.00	2	0	0	0	3	6	5	3	1	2
*Kipper, Bob	5	2	3.02	41	1	0	3	63	44	24	21	26	35
Kramer, Randy	0	1	4.91	12	2	0	0	26	27	15	14	9	15
Landrum, Bill	7	3	2.13	54	0	0	13	72	69	22	17	21	39
Palacios, Vicente	0	0	0.00	7	0	0	3	15	4	0	0	2	8
*Patterson, Bob	8	5	2.95	55	5	0	5	95	88	33	31	21	70
Power, Ted	1	3	3.66	40	0	0	7	52	50	23	21	17	42
Reed, Rick	2	3	4.36	13	8	1	1	54	62	32	26	12	27
*Reuss, Jerry	0	0	3.52	4	1	0	0	8	8	3	3	3	1
Roesler, Mike	1	0	3.00	5	0	0	0	6	5	2	2	2	4
Ross, Mark	1	0	3.55	9	0	0	0	13	11	5	5	4	5
*Ruskin, Scott	2	2	3.02	44	0	0	2	48	50	21	16	28	34
*Smiley, John	9	10	4.64	26	25	2	0	149	161	83	77	36	86
*Smith, Zane	6	2	1.30	11	10	3	0	76	55	20	11	9	50
Terrell, Walt	2	7	5.88	16	16	0	0	83	98	59	54	33	34
Tibbs, Jay	1	0	2.57	5	0	0	0	7	7	2	2	2	4
*Tomlin, Randy	4	4	2.55	12	12	2	0	78	62	24	22	12	42
Walk, Bob	7	5	3.75	26	24	1	1	130	136	59	54	36	73
York, Mike	1	1	4.84	4	1	0	0	13	13	5	4	5	4

FIELDING

Catcher	PCT	G	PO	A	E
Bilardello	1.000	19	69	9	0
LaValliere	.990	95	478	36	5
McClendon	1.000	8	13	2	0
Merced	.000	1	0	0	0
Prince	1.000	3	16	1	0
Slaught	.979	78	345	36	8

First Base	PCT	G	PO	A	E
Bonilla	1.000	3	16	1	0
Bream	.993	142	971	104	8
King	1.000	1	3	0	0
Martinez	1.000	5	22	4	0
McClendon	1.000	8	58	7	0
Redus	.988	72	447	35	6

Second Base	PCT	G	PO	A	E
Backman	1.000	15	22	32	0
Belliard	1.000	21	23	16	0
Lind	.991	152	330	449	7

Third Base	PCT	G	PO	A	E
Backman	.920	71	34	104	12

	PCT	G	PO	A	E
Belliard	1.000	5	3	3	0
Bonilla	.923	14	10	26	3
King	.938	115	58	215	18

Shortstop	PCT	G	PO	A	E
Bell	.970	159	260	459	22
Belliard	.933	10	11	17	2
Garcia	1.000	3	0	4	0

Outfield	PCT	G	PO	A	E
Alou	1.000	2	3	0	0
Bonds	.983	150	338	14	6
Bonilla	.961	149	289	8	12
Cangelosi	1.000	12	24	0	0
Carter	1.000	3	4	0	0
Martinez	1.000	2	2	0	0
McClendon	.000	1	0	0	0
Merced	.000	1	0	0	0
Redus	.882	7	14	1	2
Reynolds	.972	59	102	3	3
Ryal	1.000	4	4	0	0
Van Slyke	.976	133	326	6	8

ST. LOUIS

BATTING

BATTING	AVG	G	AB	R	H	2B	3B	HR	RBI	BB	SO	SB
*Brewer, Rodney	.240	14	25	4	6	1	0	0	2	0	4	0
Brunansky, Tom	.158	19	57	5	9	3	0	1	2	12	10	0
#Coleman, Vince	.292	124	497	73	145	18	9	6	39	35	88	77
#Collins, Dave	.224	99	58	12	13	1	0	0	3	13	10	7
Gilkey, Bernard	.297	18	64	11	19	5	2	1	3	8	5	6
Guerrero, Pedro	.281	136	498	42	140	31	1	13	80	44	70	1
Hudler, Rex	.281	89	217	30	61	11	2	7	22	12	31	18

66 • 1991 ALMANAC

St. Louis finished last, but Willie McGee, left, led the league in hitting while Vince Coleman was tops in steals.

	AVG	G	AB	R	H	2B	3B	HR	RBI	BB	SO	SB
*Jones, Tim	.219	67	128	9	28	7	1	1	12	12	20	3
#Jose, Felix	.271	25	85	12	23	4	1	3	13	8	16	4
*Lankford, Ray	.286	39	126	12	36	10	1	3	12	13	27	8
#McGee, Willie	.335	125	501	76	168	32	5	3	62	38	86	28
*Morris, John	.111	18	18	0	2	0	0	0	0	3	6	0
#Oquendo, Jose	.252	156	469	38	118	17	5	1	37	74	46	1
Pagnozzi, Tom	.277	69	220	20	61	15	0	2	23	14	37	1
#Pena, Geronimo	.244	18	45	5	11	2	0	0	2	4	14	1
#Pendleton, Terry	.230	121	447	46	103	20	2	6	58	30	58	7
#Smith, Ozzie	.254	143	512	61	130	21	1	1	50	61	33	32
Stephens, Carl	.133	5	15	2	2	1	0	1	1	0	3	0
*Thompson, Milt	.218	135	418	42	91	14	7	6	30	39	60	25
*Walling, Denny	.220	78	127	7	28	5	0	1	19	8	15	0
Wilson, Craig	.248	55	121	13	30	2	0	0	7	8	14	0
Zeile, Todd	.244	144	495	62	121	25	3	15	57	67	77	2

PITCHING	W	L	ERA	G	GS	CG	SV	IP	H	R	ER	BB	SO
Camacho, Ernie	0	0	7.94	6	0	0	0	6	7	6	5	6	7
Carpenter, Cris	0	0	4.50	4	0	0	0	8	5	4	4	2	6
*Clarke, Stan	0	0	2.70	2	0	0	0	3	2	1	1	0	3
Costello, John	0	0	6.23	4	0	0	0	4	7	3	3	1	1
*Dayley, Ken	4	4	3.56	58	0	0	2	73	63	32	29	30	51
DeLeon, Jose	7	19	4.43	32	32	0	0	183	168	96	90	86	164
*DiPino, Frank	5	2	4.56	62	0	0	3	81	92	45	41	31	49
Hill, Ken	5	6	5.49	17	14	1	0	79	79	49	48	33	58
Hilton, Howard	0	0	0.00	2	0	0	0	3	2	0	0	3	2
*Horton, Ricky	1	1	4.93	32	0	0	1	42	52	25	23	22	18
*Magrane, Joe	10	17	3.59	31	31	3	0	203	204	86	81	59	100
*Mathews, Greg	0	5	5.33	11	10	0	0	51	53	34	30	30	18
Niedenfuer, Tom	0	6	3.46	52	0	0	2	65	66	26	25	25	32
Olivares, Omar	1	1	2.92	9	6	0	0	49	45	17	16	17	20
Perez, Mike	1	0	3.95	13	0	0	1	14	12	6	6	3	5
*Sherrill, Tim	0	0	6.23	8	0	0	0	4	10	5	3	3	3
Smith, Bryn	9	8	4.27	26	25	0	0	141	160	81	67	30	78
Smith, Lee	3	4	2.10	53	0	0	27	69	58	20	16	20	70
Terry, Scott	2	6	4.75	50	2	0	2	72	75	45	38	27	35
Tewksbury, Bob	10	9	3.47	28	20	3	1	145	151	67	56	15	50
*Tudor, John	12	4	2.40	25	22	1	0	146	120	48	39	30	63

FIELDING

Catcher	PCT	G	PO	A	E
Pagnozzi	.989	63	334	38	4
Stephens	1.000	5	31	2	0
Zeile	.988	105	533	56	7

First Base	PCT	G	PO	A	E
Brewer	.981	9	46	6	1
Collins	1.000	49	80	0	0
Guerrero	.989	132	1083	73	13
Hudler	1.000	6	54	4	0
Pagnozzi	1.000	2	11	0	0
Walling	1.000	15	86	6	0
Wilson	1.000	1	1	0	0
Zeile	.991	11	104	8	1

Second Base	PCT	G	PO	A	E
Hudler	.946	10	9	26	2
Jones	.977	19	15	28	1
Oquendo	.996	150	285	393	3
Pena	.982	11	24	31	1
Wilson	1.000	9	5	8	0

Third Base	PCT	G	PO	A	E
Hudler	.929	6	5	8	1
Jones	1.000	6	0	3	0
Pendleton	.947	117	91	248	19

	PCT	G	PO	A	E
Walling	1.000	11	6	19	0
Wilson	.971	13	13	20	1
Zeile	.883	24	11	42	7

Shortstop	PCT	G	PO	A	E
Hudler	1.000	1	1	1	0
Jones	.944	29	28	74	6
Oquendo	.950	4	9	10	1
O. Smith	.980	140	212	378	12

Outfield	PCT	G	PO	A	E
Brunansky	.950	17	37	1	2
Coleman	.981	120	244	12	5
Collins	.900	12	9	0	1
Gilkey	.961	18	47	2	2
Hudler	.979	45	89	3	2
Jose	1.000	23	42	0	0
Lankford	.989	35	92	1	1
McGee	.957	124	341	13	16
Morris	1.000	6	4	0	0
Thompson	.971	116	232	4	7
Walling	1.000	8	11	1	0
Wilson	1.000	13	26	2	0
Zeile	.000	1	0	0	0

SAN DIEGO

BATTING	AVG	G	AB	R	H	2B	3B	HR	RBI	BB	SO	SB
Abner, Shawn	.245	91	184	17	45	9	0	1	15	9	28	2
#Alomar, Roberto	.287	147	586	80	168	27	5	6	60	48	72	24
Carter, Joe	.232	162	634	79	147	27	1	24	115	48	93	22
Clark, Jack	.266	115	334	59	89	12	1	25	62	104	91	4
Clark, Jerald	.267	52	101	12	27	4	1	5	11	5	24	0
#Cora, Joey	.270	51	100	12	27	3	0	0	2	6	9	8
Faries, Paul	.189	14	37	4	7	1	0	0	2	4	7	0
*Gwynn, Tony	.309	141	573	79	177	29	10	4	72	44	23	17
#Howard, Tom	.273	20	44	4	12	2	0	0	0	0	11	0
Jackson, Darrin	.257	58	113	10	29	3	0	3	9	5	24	3
*Lampkin, Tom	.222	26	63	4	14	0	1	1	4	4	9	0
*Lynn, Fred	.240	90	196	18	47	3	1	6	23	22	44	2
*Nelson, Rob	.000	5	5	0	0	0	0	0	0	0	4	0
*Pagliarulo, Mike	.254	128	398	29	101	23	2	7	38	39	66	1
Parent, Mark	.222	65	189	13	42	11	0	3	16	16	29	1
Reynolds, Ronn	.067	8	15	1	1	1	0	0	1	1	6	0
#Roberts, Bip	.309	149	556	104	172	36	3	9	44	55	65	46
Santiago, Benito	.270	100	344	42	93	8	5	11	53	27	55	5
*Stephenson, Phil	.209	103	182	26	38	9	1	4	19	30	43	2
#Templeton, Garry	.248	144	505	45	125	25	3	9	59	24	59	1
Williams, Eddie	.286	14	42	5	12	3	0	0	3	4	6	0

PITCHING	W	L	ERA	G	GS	CG	SV	IP	H	R	ER	BB	SO
Benes, Andy	10	11	3.60	32	31	2	0	192	177	87	77	69	140
*Clements, Pat	0	0	4.15	9	0	0	0	13	20	9	6	7	6
Davis, John	0	1	5.79	6	0	0	0	9	9	7	6	4	7
Dunne, Mike	0	3	5.65	10	6	0	0	29	28	21	18	17	15
Grant, Mark	1	1	4.85	26	0	0	0	39	47	23	21	19	29
*Hammaker, Atlee	0	4	4.66	9	1	0	0	19	16	11	10	6	6
Harris, Greg W.	8	8	2.30	73	0	0	9	117	92	35	30	49	97
*Hurst, Bruce	11	9	3.14	33	33	9	0	224	188	85	78	63	162
*Lefferts, Craig	7	5	2.52	56	0	0	23	79	68	26	22	22	60
*Lilliquist, Derek	3	3	4.33	16	7	1	0	60	61	29	29	23	29
*Rasmussen, Dennis	11	15	4.51	32	32	3	0	188	217	110	94	62	86
*Rodriguez, Rich	1	1	3.02	32	0	0	1	48	52	17	16	16	22
Schiraldi, Calvin	3	8	4.41	42	8	0	1	104	105	59	51	60	74
Show, Eric	6	8	5.76	39	12	0	1	106	131	74	68	41	55
Valdez, Rafael	0	1	11.12	3	0	0	0	6	11	7	7	2	3
Whitson, Ed	14	9	2.60	32	32	6	0	229	215	73	66	47	127

FIELDING

Catcher	PCT	G	PO	A	E
Cora	1.000	1	3	0	0
Lampkin	.971	20	92	10	3
Parent	.992	60	324	31	3
Reynolds	1.000	8	26	2	0
Santiago	.980	98	536	51	12

First Base	PCT	G	PO	A	E
Carter	.948	14	107	3	6
Ja. Clark	.994	110	855	69	6
Je. Clark	1.000	15	76	6	0
Stephenson	.997	60	345	36	1

Second Base	PCT	G	PO	A	E
Alomar	.976	137	311	392	17
Cora	.938	15	43	32	5
Faries	1.000	7	20	18	0
Roberts	.921	8	10	25	3

Third Base	PCT	G	PO	A	E
Faries	.875	1	1	6	1
Pagliarulo	.955	116	79	200	13

	PCT	G	PO	A	E
Roberts	.953	56	34	89	6
Williams	.897	13	5	21	3

Shortstop	PCT	G	PO	A	E
Alomar	.895	5	5	12	2
Cora	.833	21	13	17	6
Faries	.909	4	0	10	1
Roberts	.984	18	23	38	1
Templeton	.957	135	214	367	26

Outfield	PCT	G	PO	A	E
Abner	.991	62	108	1	1
Carter	.988	150	385	13	5
Je. Clark	.963	13	26	0	1
Gwynn	.985	141	327	11	5
Howard	.950	13	19	0	1
Jackson	.985	39	63	1	1
Lynn	1.000	55	92	1	0
Roberts	.983	75	162	8	3

SAN FRANCISCO

BATTING	AVG	G	AB	R	H	2B	3B	HR	RBI	BB	SO	SB
Anderson, Dave	.350	60	100	14	35	5	1	1	6	3	20	1
Bailey, Mark	.143	5	7	1	1	0	0	1	3	2	0	0
#Bass, Kevin	.252	61	214	25	54	9	1	7	32	14	26	2
Bathe, Bill	.229	52	48	3	11	0	1	3	12	7	12	0
Benjamin, Mike	.214	22	56	7	12	3	1	2	3	3	10	1
*Butler, Brett	.309	160	622	108	192	20	9	3	44	90	62	51
Carter, Gary	.254	92	244	24	62	10	0	9	27	25	31	1
*Clark, Will	.295	154	600	91	177	25	5	19	95	62	97	8
Decker, Steve	.296	15	54	5	16	2	0	3	8	1	10	0
*Kennedy, Terry	.277	107	303	25	84	22	0	2	26	31	38	1
*Kingery, Mike	.295	105	207	24	61	7	1	0	24	12	19	6
Komminsk, Brad	.200	8	5	2	1	0	0	0	0	1	2	0
*Laga, Mike	.185	23	27	4	5	1	0	2	4	1	7	0
*Leach, Rick	.293	78	174	24	51	13	0	2	16	21	20	0
*Leonard, Mark	.176	11	17	3	3	1	0	1	2	3	8	0
Litton, Greg	.245	93	204	17	50	9	1	1	24	11	45	1
Manwaring, Kirt	.154	8	13	0	2	0	1	0	1	0	3	0
Mitchell, Kevin	.290	140	524	90	152	24	2	35	93	58	87	4

San Francisco third baseman Matt Williams led National League hitters with 122 RBIs.

	AVG	G	AB	R	H	2B	3B	HR	RBI	BB	SO	SB
Parker, Rick	.243	54	107	19	26	5	0	2	14	10	15	6
Perezchica, Tony	.333	4	3	1	1	0	0	0	0	1	2	0
*Riles, Ernest	.200	92	155	22	31	2	1	8	21	26	26	0
#Santana, Andres	.000	6	2	0	0	0	0	0	1	0	0	0
Thompson, Robby	.245	144	498	67	122	22	3	15	56	34	96	14
#Uribe, Jose	.248	138	415	35	103	8	6	1	24	29	49	5
Williams, Matt	.277	159	617	87	171	27	2	33	122	33	138	7

PITCHING	W	L	ERA	G	GS	CG	SV	IP	H	R	ER	BB	SO
Bedrosian, Steve	9	9	4.20	68	0	0	17	79	72	40	37	44	43
Booker, Greg	0	0	13.50	2	0	0	0	2	7	3	3	0	1
Brantley, Jeff	5	3	1.56	55	0	0	19	87	77	18	15	33	61
Burkett, John	14	7	3.79	33	32	2	1	204	201	92	86	61	118
Camacho, Ernie	0	0	3.60	8	0	0	0	10	10	4	4	3	8
Dewey, Mark	1	1	2.78	14	0	0	0	23	22	7	7	5	11
Downs, Kelly	3	2	3.43	13	9	0	0	63	56	26	24	20	31
Garrelts, Scott	12	11	4.15	31	31	4	0	182	190	91	84	70	80
*Gunderson, Eric	1	2	5.49	7	4	0	0	20	24	14	12	11	14
*Hammaker, Atlee	4	5	4.28	25	6	0	0	67	69	33	32	21	28
*Knepper, Bob	3	3	5.68	12	7	0	0	44	56	28	28	19	24
LaCoss, Mike	6	4	3.94	13	12	1	0	78	75	37	34	39	39
McCament, Randy	0	0	3.00	3	0	0	0	6	8	2	2	5	5
*McClellan, Paul	0	1	11.74	4	1	0	0	8	14	10	10	6	2
McGaffigan, Andy	0	0	17.36	4	0	0	0	5	10	9	9	4	4
*Novoa, Rafael	0	1	6.75	7	2	0	1	19	21	14	14	13	14
O'Neal, Randy	1	0	3.83	26	0	0	0	47	58	23	20	18	30
Oliveras, Francisco	2	2	2.77	33	2	0	2	55	47	22	17	21	41
Quisenberry, Dan	0	1	13.50	5	0	0	0	7	13	12	10	3	2
Reuschel, Rick	3	6	3.93	15	13	0	1	87	102	40	38	31	49
Robinson, Don	10	7	4.57	26	25	4	0	158	173	84	80	41	78
Rodriguez, Rick	0	0	8.10	3	0	0	0	3	5	3	3	2	2
*Swan, Russ	0	1	3.86	2	1	0	0	2	6	4	1	4	1
*Thurmond, Mark	2	3	3.34	43	0	0	4	57	53	26	21	18	24
*Vosberg, Ed	1	1	5.55	18	0	0	0	24	21	16	15	12	12
*Wilson, Trevor	8	7	4.00	27	17	3	0	110	87	52	49	49	66

FIELDING

Catcher	PCT	G	PO	A	E
Bailey	1.000	1	3	0	0
Bathe	1.000	8	10	1	0
Carter	.992	80	323	31	3
Decker	.989	15	75	11	1
Kennedy	.991	103	390	38	4
Manwaring	1.000	8	22	3	0

First Base	PCT	G	PO	A	E
Anderson	1.000	3	9	0	0
Carter	1.000	3	25	0	0
Clark	.992	153	1455	120	12
Laga	1.000	10	33	5	0
Leach	1.000	7	37	2	0

Second Base	PCT	G	PO	A	E
Anderson	.964	13	7	20	1
Litton	1.000	18	19	25	0
Parker	.000	2	0	0	0
Perezchica	1.000	2	2	0	0
Riles	.974	24	28	48	2
Thompson	.989	142	286	441	8

Third Base	PCT	G	PO	A	E
Anderson	1.000	2	0	1	0
Litton	1.000	5	2	3	0

	PCT	G	PO	A	E
Parker	.500	1	1	0	1
Riles	1.000	10	4	8	0
Williams	.959	159	140	306	19

Shortstop	PCT	G	PO	A	E
Anderson	1.000	29	17	38	0
Benjamin	.988	21	30	53	1
Litton	1.000	7	9	9	0
Parker	1.000	1	0	2	0
Perezchica	.000	2	0	0	0
Riles	.986	26	21	49	1
Santana	1.000	3	2	1	0
Uribe	.965	134	182	373	20

Outfield	PCT	G	PO	A	E
Bass	.968	55	88	2	3
Butler	.986	159	420	4	6
Kingery	.978	95	126	6	3
Komminsk	1.000	7	3	0	0
Leach	.989	52	86	3	1
Leonard	1.000	7	10	0	0
Litton	.985	56	60	6	1
Mitchell	.971	138	295	9	9
Parker	.978	35	44	1	1

NLCS BOX SCORES

Game One: Pirates 4, Reds 3

PITTSBURGH	ab	r	h	bi	bb	so	CINCINNATI	ab	r	h	bi	bb	so
Backman 3b	2	0	0	0	1	1	Larkin ss	2	1	0	2	0	1
King ph-3b	2	0	0	0	0	1	Hatcher cf	3	0	0	0	0	2
Bell ss	3	0	0	1	1	1	Morris 1b	3	1	1	1	0	0
VanSlyke cf	4	0	1	1	0	2	Benzinger ph	1	0	1	0	0	0
Bonilla rf	4	0	1	0	0	1	Davis lf	3	1	1	0	1	1
Bonds lf	3	1	1	0	1	0	O'Neill rf	3	0	1	2	0	0
Bream 1b	3	1	2	2	1	0	Oester ph	1	0	0	0	0	0
LaValliere c	3	1	0	0	1	1	Bates pr	0	0	0	0	0	0
Lind 2b	4	0	1	1	0	1	Sabo 3b	4	0	1	0	0	2
Walk p	2	0	0	0	0	2	Reed c	3	0	0	0	0	1
Redus ph	1	1	1	0	0	0	Duncan 2b	3	0	0	0	0	2
Belinda p	0	0	0	0	0	0	Rijo p	2	0	0	0	0	1
Reynolds ph	1	0	0	0	0	1	Charlton p	0	0	0	0	0	0
Patterson p	0	0	0	0	0	0	Winningham ph	1	0	0	0	0	0
Power p	0	0	0	0	0	0	Dibble p	0	0	0	0	0	0
TOTALS	32	4	7	4	5	12	TOTALS	29	3	5	3	3	9

Pittsburgh . . . . 001 200 100—4
Cincinnati . . . . 300 000 000—3

E—Bonilla. DP—Cincinnati 1. LOB—Pittsburgh 6, Cincinnati 3. 2B—Van Slyke, Davis, O'Neill. 3B—Lind. HR—Bream. SB—Redus, Larkin. S—Hatcher.

Pittsburgh	IP	H	R	ER	BB	SO	Cincinnati	IP	H	R	ER	BB	SO
Walk W	6	4	3	3	2	5	Rijo	5⅓	4	3	3	3	8
Belinda	2	0	0	0	0	3	Charlton L	2⅔	3	1	1	2	1
Patterson	⅓	1	0	0	0	0	Dibble	1	0	0	0	0	3
Power	⅔	0	0	0	0	1							

T—2:51. A—52,911.

Game Two: Reds 2, Pirates 1

PITTSBURGH	ab	r	h	bi	bb	so	CINCINNATI	ab	r	h	bi	bb	so
Redus 1b	2	0	1	0	1	0	Larkin ss	3	1	1	0	1	0
Bream ph-1b	1	0	0	0	0	0	Winningham cf	4	1	2	0	0	1
Bell ss	3	0	2	0	1	0	O'Neill rf	4	0	2	2	0	1
VanSlyke cf	4	0	1	0	0	0	Davis lf	4	0	0	0	0	2
Bonilla rf-3b	4	0	1	0	0	0	Morris 1b	1	0	0	0	1	0
Bonds lf	4	0	0	0	0	1	Sabo 3b	3	0	0	0	0	1
King 3b	0	0	0	0	1	0	Oliver c	3	0	0	0	0	1
Reynolds rf	3	0	0	0	0	1	Duncan 2b	3	0	0	0	0	1
Slaught c	2	0	0	0	0	0	Browning p	2	0	0	0	0	1
Backman ph	1	0	0	0	0	0	Dibble p	1	0	0	0	0	1
LaValliere c	0	0	0	0	1	0	Myers p	0	0	0	0	0	0
Lind 2b	3	1	1	1	1	0							
Drabek p	3	0	0	0	0	1							
TOTALS	30	1	6	1	5	5	TOTALS	28	2	5	2	2	8

Pittsburgh . . . . 000 010 000—1
Cincinnati . . . . 100 010 00x—2

DP—Cincinnati 1. LOB—Pittsburgh 7, Cincinnati 5. 2B—Winningham, O'Neill. HR—Lind. SB—Larkin, Winningham, O'Neill.

Pittsburgh	IP	H	R	ER	BB	SO	Cincinnati	IP	H	R	ER	BB	SO
Drabek L	8	5	2	2	2	8	Browning W	6	6	1	1	3	3
							Dibble	1⅓	0	0	0	1	2
							Myers S	1⅔	0	0	0	1	0

HBP—Morris (by Drabek). T—2:38. A—54,456.

Game Three: Reds 6, Pirates 3

CINCINNATI	ab	r	h	bi	bb	so	PITTSBURGH	ab	r	h	bi	bb	so
Larkin ss	5	1	1	0	0	0	King 3b	5	0	1	0	0	3
Duncan 2b	5	1	3	4	0	0	Bell ss	5	1	2	0	0	1
Sabo 3b	5	0	1	0	0	2	VanSlyke cf	4	1	0	0	1	2
Davis lf	4	0	0	0	0	2	Bonilla rf	4	0	1	1	0	0
Braggs rf	4	0	1	0	0	0	Bonds lf	3	1	1	0	1	1
Benzinger 1b	4	1	0	0	0	0	Martinez 1b	4	0	1	1	0	1
Oliver c	4	1	2	0	0	0	Slaught c	2	0	1	0	2	0
Bates pr	0	0	0	0	0	0	Lind 2b	4	0	1	0	0	1
Reed c	0	0	0	0	0	0	Smith p	2	0	0	0	0	1
Hatcher cf	4	2	3	2	0	0	Landrum p	0	0	0	0	0	0
Jackson p	1	0	0	0	0	1	Redus ph	1	0	0	0	0	1
Dibble p	1	0	0	0	0	0	Smiley p	0	0	0	0	0	0
Charlton p	0	0	0	0	0	0	Reynolds ph	1	0	0	0	0	0
Morris ph	1	0	1	0	0	0	Belinda p	0	0	0	0	0	0
Myers p	0	0	0	0	0	0							
TOTALS	38	6	13	6	0	7	TOTALS	35	3	8	2	4	11

Cincinnati . . . . 020 030 001—6
Pittsburgh . . . . 000 200 010—3

E—Duncan. DP—Pittsburgh 1. LOB—Cincinnati 6, Pittsburgh 9. 2B—Hatcher, Bell, Martinez, Slaught, Lind. HR—Duncan, Hatcher. S—Jackson

Cincinnati	IP	H	R	ER	BB	SO	Pittsburgh	IP	H	R	ER	BB	SO
Jackson W	5⅓	7	2	2	3	4	Smith L	5	8	5	5	0	5
Dibble	1⅔	0	0	0	0	3	Landrum	1	0	0	0	0	1
Charlton	1	1	1	0	1	0	Smiley	2	2	0	0	0	1
Myers S	1	0	0	0	0	3	Belinda	1	3	1	1	0	1

T—2:51. A—46,611.

Game Four: Reds 5, Pirates 3

CINCINNATI	ab	r	h	bi	bb	so	PITTSBURGH	ab	r	h	bi	bb	so
Larkin ss	5	0	0	0	0	1	Backman 3b	4	1	1	0	0	1
Hatcher cf	4	0	0	0	0	0	Bell ss	4	1	1	0	1	0
O'Neill rf	4	1	3	1	0	0	VanSlyke cf	4	1	1	1	0	1
Davis lf	4	1	1	0	0	1	Bonilla rf	3	0	1	0	1	0
Morris 1b	4	2	3	0	0	0	Bonds lf	4	0	1	0	0	2
Sabo 3b	3	1	2	3	0	0	Bream 1b	3	0	1	1	1	1
Reed c	3	0	0	0	0	1	LaValliere c	3	0	0	0	1	0
Oliver c	1	0	0	0	0	0	Lind 2b	4	0	2	0	0	1
Duncan 2b	3	0	1	0	0	2	Walk p	2	0	0	0	0	2
Benzinger ph	0	0	0	0	1	0	Reynolds ph	0	0	0	0	1	0
Oester 2b	0	0	0	0	0	0	Power p	0	0	0	0	0	0
Rijo p	3	0	0	0	0	0	King ph	1	0	0	0	0	1
Myers p	0	0	0	0	0	0							
Quinones ph	0	0	0	1	0	0							
Dibble p	0	0	0	0	0	0							
TOTALS	34	5	10	5	1	5	TOTALS	32	3	8	3	4	10

Cincinnati . . . . 000 200 201—5
Pittsburgh . . . . 100 100 010—3

E—Larkin. DP—Cincinnati 1, Pittsburgh 1. LOB—Cincinnati 5, Pittsburgh 6. 2B—O'Neill, Morris, Backman, Bonilla, Bream. HR—O'Neill, Sabo, Bell. SB—Backman, Van Slyke, Bonds. SF—Quinones, Sabo.

Cincinnati	IP	H	R	ER	BB	SO	Pittsburgh	IP	H	R	ER	BB	SO
Rijo W	7	6	3	3	4	7	Walk L	7	7	4	4	0	3
Myers	1	2	0	0	1	0	Power	2	3	1	1	1	2
Dibble S	1	0	0	0	0	2							

Rijo pitched to 1 batter in 8th.
T—3:00. A—50,461.

Game Five: Pirates 3, Reds 2

CINCINNATI	ab	r	h	bi	bb	so	PITTSBURGH	ab	r	h	bi	bb	so
Larkin ss	4	1	2	1	0	0	Redus 1b	3	0	0	0	0	1
Winningham cf	2	0	0	1	1	0	Bream 1b	1	0	1	0	0	0
O'Neill rf	4	0	1	0	0	0	Bell ss	2	1	0	0	0	0
Davis lf	4	0	1	0	0	3	VanSlyke cf	4	1	2	1	0	1
Morris 1b	3	0	0	0	0	0	Bonilla 3b	3	0	0	0	1	0
Sabo 3b	3	0	1	0	1	0	Bonds lf	3	1	0	1	1	0
Oliver c	2	0	0	0	0	0	Reynolds rf	4	0	2	0	0	0
Oester ph	1	0	0	0	0	1	Slaught c	3	0	0	1	0	1
Reed c	0	0	0	0	0	0	Lind 2b	3	0	0	0	0	0
Duncan 2b	3	0	1	0	0	0	Drabek p	3	0	1	0	0	1
Browning p	1	0	0	0	0	0	Patterson p	0	0	0	0	0	0
Benzinger ph	1	0	1	0	0	0							
Mahler p	0	0	0	0	0	0							
Charlton p	0	0	0	0	0	0							
Quinones ph	1	1	0	0	0	0							
Scudder p	0	0	0	0	0	0							
TOTALS	30	2	7	2	2	5	TOTALS	29	3	6	3	3	4

Cincinnati . . . . 100 000 010—2
Pittsburgh . . . . 200 100 00x—3

E—Drabek. DP—Pittsburgh 2. LOB—Cincinnati 5, Pittsburgh 7. 2B—Larkin 2. 3B—Van Slyke. SB—Bonds, Reynolds. S—Morris. SF—Slaught, Winningham.

Cincinnati	IP	H	R	ER	BB	SO	Pittsburgh	IP	H	R	ER	BB	SO
Browning L	5	3	3	3	3	2	Drabek W	8⅓	7	2	1	1	5
Mahler	1⅔	2	0	0	0	0	Patterson S	⅔	0	0	0	1	0
Charlton	⅓	0	0	0	0	1							
Scudder	1	1	0	0	0	1							

HBP—Bell (by Browning). WP—Drabek. T—2:38. A—48,221.

Game Six: Reds 2, Pirates 1

PITTSBURGH	ab	r	h	bi	bb	so	CINCINNATI	ab	r	h	bi	bb	so
King 3b	2	0	0	0	0	0	Larkin ss	4	1	2	0	0	0
Reynolds ph-rf	1	0	0	0	1	0	Hatcher cf	4	0	2	0	0	0
Bell ss	3	0	0	0	1	0	O'Neill rf	2	0	1	0	1	0
VanSlyke cf	4	0	0	0	0	1	Quinones ph	1	0	1	1	0	0
Bonilla 3b-1b	3	0	0	1	0	0	Myers p	0	0	0	0	0	0
Bonds lf	1	1	0	0	3	1	Davis lf	4	0	1	0	0	0
Martinez 1b	4	0	1	1	0	0	Sabo 3b	4	0	0	0	0	0
Slaught c	4	0	0	0	0	2	Benzinger 1b	3	0	0	0	1	0
Lind 2b	3	0	0	0	0	0	Duncan 2b	3	0	1	0	0	1
Power p	1	0	0	0	0	1	Charlton p	0	0	0	0	0	0
Smith p	1	0	0	0	0	0	Braggs rf	1	0	0	0	0	0
Belinda p	0	0	0	0	0	0	Oliver c	4	0	0	0	0	1
Redus ph	1	0	0	0	0	1	Jackson p	2	0	0	0	0	1
Landrum p	0	0	0	0	0	0	Oester 2b	1	1	1	0	0	0
TOTALS	28	1	1	1	6	7	TOTALS	33	2	9	2	2	3

| Pittsburgh | | | | | | | | | 000 | 010 | 000—1 |
| Cincinnati | | | | | | | | | 100 | 000 | 10x—2 |

E—Reynolds, Bell, Slaught. LOB—Pittsburgh 6, Cincinnati 9. 2B—Martinez. SB—Larkin, Quinones.

Pittsburgh	IP	H	R	ER	BB	SO	Cincinnati	IP	H	R	ER	BB	SO
Power	2⅓	3	1	1	1	0	Jackson	6	1	1	1	4	4
Smith L	4	6	1	1	1	3	Charlton W	1	0	0	0	0	0
Belinda	⅔	0	0	0	0	0	Myers S	2	0	0	0	2	3
Landrum	1	0	0	0	0	0							

Jackson pitched to 2 batters in 7th.
T—2:57. A—56,079.

NLCS COMPOSITE BOX

PITTSBURGH

Player, Pos.	AVG	G	AB	R	H	2B	3B	HR	RBI	BB	SO	SB
Sid Bream, 1b	.500	4	8	1	4	1	0	1	3	2	3	0
Jay Bell, ss	.250	6	20	3	5	1	0	1	1	4	3	0
Gary Redus, ph-1b	.250	5	8	1	2	0	0	0	0	1	3	1
Carmelo Martinez, 1b	.250	2	8	0	2	2	0	0	2	0	1	0
Jose Lind, 2b	.238	6	21	1	5	1	1	1	2	1	4	0
Andy VanSlyke, cf	.208	6	24	3	5	1	1	0	3	1	7	1
R.J. Reynolds, ph-rf	.200	6	10	0	2	0	0	0	0	2	2	1
Bobby Bonilla, rf-3b	.190	6	21	0	4	1	0	0	1	3	1	0
Barry Bonds, lf	.167	6	18	4	3	0	0	0	1	6	5	2
Doug Drabek, p	.167	2	6	0	1	0	0	0	0	0	2	0
Wally Backman, 3b-ph	.143	3	7	1	1	1	0	0	0	1	3	1
Jeff King, 3b-ph	.100	5	10	0	1	0	0	0	1	5	0
Don Slaught, c	.091	4	11	0	1	1	0	0	1	2	3	0
Mike LaValliere, c	.000	3	6	1	0	0	0	0	0	3	1	0
Zane Smith, p	.000	2	3	0	0	0	0	0	0	0	1	0
Bob Walk, p	.000	2	4	0	0	0	0	0	0	0	1	0
Ted Power, p	.000	3	1	0	0	0	0	0	0	0	1	0
TOTALS	.194	6	186	15	36	9	2	3	14	27	49	6

Pitcher	W	L	ERA	G	GS	CG	SV	IP	H	R	ER	BB	SO
John Smiley	0	0	0.00	1	0	0	0	2	2	0	0	0	0
Bill Landrum	0	0	0.00	2	0	0	0	2	0	0	0	0	1
Bob Patterson	0	0	0.00	2	0	0	1	1	1	0	0	2	0
Doug Drabek	1	1	1.65	2	2	1	0	16⅓	12	4	3	3	13
Stan Belinda	0	0	2.45	3	0	0	0	3⅔	3	1	1	0	4
Ted Power	0	0	3.60	3	1	0	1	5	6	2	2	2	3
Bob Walk	1	1	4.85	2	2	0	0	13	11	7	7	2	8
Zane Smith	0	2	6.00	2	1	0	0	9	14	6	6	1	8
TOTALS	2	4	3.29	6	6	1	2	52	49	20	19	10	37

CINCINNATI

Player, Pos.	AVG	G	AB	R	H	2B	3B	HR	RBI	BB	SO	SB
Luis Quinones, ph	.500	3	2	1	1	0	0	0	2	0	0	1
Paul O'Neill, rf	.471	5	17	1	8	3	0	1	4	1	1	1
Hal Morris, 1b	.417	5	12	3	5	1	0	0	1	1	0	0
Todd Benzinger, 1b-ph	.333	5	9	0	3	0	0	0	2	0	0	0
Billy Hatcher, cf	.333	4	15	2	5	1	0	1	2	0	2	0
Ron Oester, 2b-ph	.333	4	3	1	1	0	0	0	0	1	0	0
Mariano Duncan, 2b	.300	6	20	1	6	0	0	1	4	0	8	0
Herm Winningham, ph-cf	.286	3	7	1	2	1	0	0	1	1	1	1
Barry Larkin, ss	.261	6	23	5	6	2	0	0	1	3	1	3
Chris Sabo, 3b	.227	6	22	1	5	0	0	1	3	1	4	0
Glenn Braggs, rf	.200	2	5	0	1	0	0	0	0	1	0	0
Eric Davis, lf	.174	6	23	2	4	1	0	2	1	9	0
Joe Oliver, c	.143	5	14	1	2	0	0	0	0	0	2	0
Tom Browning, p	.000	2	3	0	0	0	0	0	0	0	1	0
Rob Dibble, p	.000	4	2	0	0	0	0	0	0	0	1	0
Danny Jackson, p	.000	2	3	0	0	0	0	0	0	2	0	0
Jeff Reed, c	.000	4	7	0	0	0	0	0	0	1	0	0
Jose Rijo, p	.000	2	5	0	0	0	0	0	0	0	3	0
Billy Bates, pr	—	2	0	1	0	0	0	0	0	0	0	0
TOTALS	.255	6	192	20	49	9	0	4	20	10	37	6

Pitcher	W	L	ERA	G	GS	CG	SV	IP	H	R	ER	BB	SO
Rob Dibble	0	0	0.00	4	0	0	1	5	0	0	0	1	10
Rick Mahler	0	0	0.00	1	0	0	0	1⅓	2	0	0	0	0
Randy Myers	0	0	0.00	4	0	0	3	5⅔	2	0	0	3	7
Scott Scudder	0	0	0.00	1	0	0	0	1	1	0	0	0	0
Norm Charlton	1	1	1.80	4	0	0	0	5	4	2	1	3	3
Danny Jackson	1	0	2.38	2	2	0	0	11⅓	8	3	3	7	8
Tom Browning	1	1	3.27	2	2	0	0	11	9	4	4	6	6
Jose Rijo	1	0	4.38	2	2	0	0	12⅓	10	6	6	7	15
TOTALS	4	2	2.38	6	6	0	4	53	36	15	14	27	49

| Pittsburgh | 3 | 0 | 1 | | 6 | 2 | 0 | | 1 | 2 | 0 | | — | 15 |
| Cincinnati | 6 | 2 | 0 | | 2 | 4 | 0 | | 3 | 1 | 2 | | — | 20 |

E—Bonilla, Drabek, Reynolds, Bell, Slaught, Duncan, Larkin. DP—Pittsburgh 4, Cincinnati 3. LOB—Pittsburgh 41, Cincinnati 33. S—Jackson, Hatcher, Morris. SF—Slaught, Quinones, Sabo, Winningham. HBP—Morris (by Drabek), Bell (by Browning). WP—Drabek. Umpires—Jerry Crawford, Gerry Davis, John McSherry, Dutch Rennert, Paul Runge, Harry Wendelstedt.

THE MINOR LEAGUES

Triple-A Leagues

Double-A Leagues

Class A Leagues

Short-Season Class A

Rookie Leagues

MINOR LEAGUES
1990 IN REVIEW

Cash scramble: Attendance, franchise values skyrocket

By JON SCHER

The signs were unmistakable. The dollar signs, that is.

In 1990, the game, the minor league game, became a business. Clubs that used to change hands in handshake agreements now cost millions of dollars. Wealthy men wearing blazers bearing the family crest were lined up to purchase franchises in the Midwest League. Squabbles over minor league territorial rights were generating reams of paperwork and hundreds of billable hours for law firms.

It's a numbers game, and we're not talking about batting average and ERA. Some of the highlights of the minor leagues' 1990 annual report:

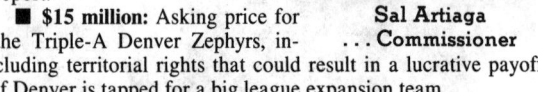

**Sal Artiaga
. . . Commissioner**

■ **$15 million:** Asking price for the Triple-A Denver Zephyrs, including territorial rights that could result in a lucrative payoff if Denver is tapped for a big league expansion team.

■ **$11.28 million:** Stadium referendum to raise money for a new ballpark for the Class A Durham Bulls. The referendum was defeated by voters, and the club was sold for a reported $4 million.

ORGANIZATION STANDINGS

	— 1990 —			1989	1988	1987
	W	L	Pct.	Pct.	Pct.	Pct.
Los Angeles (7) ...	450	310	.592	.545	.581	.499
Mets (7)	424	342	.554	.524	.514	.492
Cincinnati (6)	385	312	.552	.512	.540	.501
Milwaukee (6)	372	303	.551	.531	.553	.592
Minnesota (6)	375	316	.543	.528	.529	.450
Cleveland (6)	341	289	.541	.538	.534	.514
Montreal (6)	374	324	.536	.536	.551	.490
Texas (6)	366	325	.529	.541	.491	.436
Cubs (6)	369	344	.518	.482	.477	.533
Yankees (7)	435	410	.515	.559	.512	.524
Oakland (6)	352	338	.510	.504	.443	.504
Baltimore (5)	317	308	.507	.468	.515	.549
California (6)	349	340	.507	.468	.458	.464
Detroit (6)	356	347	.506	.498	.517	.461
Atlanta (8)	459	452	.504	.513	.484	.473
San Francisco (5) .	313	311	.502	.482	.526	.537
White Sox (6)	343	355	.491	.582	.527	.491
Pittsburgh (6)	343	364	.485	.490	.500	.542
Houston (6)	340	367	.481	.454	.506	.549
Kansas City (6)	336	364	.480	.507	.532	.493
Toronto (6)	339	368	.479	.464	.468	.511
Seattle (6)	325	368	.479	.496	.466	.472
St. Louis (8)	412	482	.461	.516	.508	.567
San Diego (7)	362	466	.437	.504	.548	.530
Philadelphia (6) ...	302	404	.428	.452	.443	.475
Boston (6)	298	399	.428	.433	.396	.445

Omaha's Tommy Hinzo tags out Rochester's Donell Nixon during action in Triple-A Classic.

■ **$11 million:** Offer to purchase the Triple-A Nashville Sounds. The offer was declined.

■ **$7.5 million:** Cost of a new stadium for the Triple-A Iowa Cubs. The project was approved by voters.

■ **$7 million:** Offer to purchase the Triple-A Portland Beavers. The offer was declined.

■ **$6.8 million:** Cost of Cohen Stadium, a 10,000-seat facility for the Double-A El Paso Diablos, which opened in June.

■ **$5.5 million:** Offer made by Japanese investors to purchase the Triple-A Vancouver Canadians. The offer was accepted.

■ **$4 million:** Price paid by California businessman Alan Levin for the Class A South Bend White Sox and the short-season Welland Pirates.

■ **$3.6 million:** Price paid by a subsidiary of the Suntory Corp., a Japanese firm, to purchase the Double-A Birmingham Barons. The franchise last changed hands in 1981—for $150,000.

More than 25 million tickets were sold (or at least distributed) to minor league baseball games in 1990, the most since 1949. Even taking into account the widespread padding of attendance figures, it seemed pretty obvious that minor league baseball's vital signs were good.

Major league owners certainly noticed. At the end of the year, the rules and agreements that bind the majors and minors were set to expire. Under the terms of the standard player development contract, major league clubs pay virtually all player salaries and offer other financial benefits to their minor league affiliates.

The system was drafted in the early '60s, when the minors were failing. Now, reasoning that minor league owners were getting rich at their expense, the majors proposed considerable changes. When negotiations began in July, representatives of Major League Baseball demanded more control over the affairs of the minor leagues, and proposed to eliminate the minor leagues' share of the majors' lucrative television package.

The National Association of Professional Baseball Leagues, the minors' governing body, rejected the changes, and a serious split seemed possible. The major leagues began drafting a plan to operate their own minor leagues in 1991 at spring training bases in Florida and Arizona. The minors were thinking about legal action and an appeal to the congressmen and senators whose constituents would be deprived of baseball.

The price of success, minor league owners have found, can be high.

Meanwhile, down on the field . . .

No one threw three no-hitters in 1990, the way Vancouver's Tom Drees did in '89, but two pitchers managed a feat that's nearly as rare.

White Sox slugger named top player

Frank Thomas may carry a big stick, but he doesn't speak softly.

Thomas, the Chicago White Sox' No. 1 pick in 1989, felt he didn't get a fair chance to make the team during the abbreviated 1990 major league spring training. He proved his point at Double-A Birmingham, batting .323 with 18 homers and 71 RBIs in the tough Southern League. He walked an unbelievable 112 times in 109 games.

Frank Thomas
. . . player of the year

"It's shocking, the level of respect I've gotten," Thomas said. "It's been ridiculous."

His exploits at Birmingham earned Thomas an Aug. 1 promotion to Chicago. Thomas also earned membership in an exclusive club, when he was named Baseball America's Minor League Player of the Year.

In the 10th year of the award, all nine recipients (Gregg Jefferies won twice) were playing in the major leagues. Thomas finished with a .330 average, seven homers and 31 RBIs in 60 games with Chicago.

Baseball America's Minor League Player of the Year
- 1981—Mike Marshall, 1b, Albuquerque (Dodgers)
- 1982—Ron Kittle, of, Edmonton (White Sox)
- 1983—Dwight Gooden, p, Lynchburg/Tidewater (Mets)
- 1984—Mike Bielecki, p, Hawaii (Pirates)
- 1985—Jose Canseco, of, Huntsville/Tacoma (A's)
- 1986—Gregg Jefferies, ss, Columbia/Lynchburg/Jackson (Mets)
- 1987—Gregg Jefferies, ss-3b, Jackson/Tidewater (Mets)
- 1988—Tom Gordon, p, Appleton/Memphis/Omaha (Royals)
- 1989—Sandy Alomar Jr., c, Las Vegas (Padres)
- 1990—Frank Thomas, 1b, Birmingham (White Sox)

Dodgers' Kennedy saluted

Many have vied for the chance to succeed Tommy Lasorda in the Dodgers organization, and many have fallen by the wayside. Kevin Kennedy could be the real thing.

In seven years as a minor league manager, Kennedy's teams have never finished lower than second. His lifetime record is 454-315 (.590). For leading the Triple-A Albuquerque Dukes to a 91-51 season and the 1990 Pacific Coast League championship, Kennedy was named Baseball America's Minor League Manager of the Year.

Kevin Kennedy
. . . top manager

"I know my situation," said Kennedy, 36. "I know I'm knocking at the door. But yet I respect Tommy Lasorda. He's been there, he deserves to be there. But I know when the opportunity arises that I'm going to be considered."

Baseball America's Minor League Manager of the Year
- 1981—Ed Nottle, Tacoma (A's)
- 1982—Eddie Haas, Richmond (Braves)
- 1983—Bill Dancy, Reading (Phillies)
- 1984—Sam Perlozzo, Jackson (Mets)
- 1985—Jim Lefebvre, Phoenix (Giants)
- 1986—Brad Fischer, Huntsville (A's)
- 1987—Dave Trembley, Harrisburg (Pirates)
- 1988—Joe Sparks, Indianapolis (Expos)
- 1989—Buck Showalter, Albany (Yankees)
- 1990—Kevin Kennedy, Albuquerque (Dodgers)

Twenty-game winners in 1990: Randy Marshall (Tigers), left, and Denny Neagle (Twins).

Randy Marshall and Denny Neagle each won 20 games, the first to reach that plateau in the U.S.-based minors since the legendary Blaise Ilsley in 1986.

When Marshall was in school at Eastern Michigan, he used to seek advice from Frank Tanana of the Tigers. Nothing unusual about that, right? Well, it seems Tanana didn't know Randy Marshall from Adam Peterson, so Marshall got around the introductions by participating in Tanana's call-in radio show.

"I'd phone in, tell Frank who I was and ask questions," Marshall said. "It was pretty neat."

In his third season as a member of the Tigers organization, Marshall evidently figured out how to apply his knowledge. He went 20-2 at Class A Fayetteville (13-0) and Lakeland (7-2) and staked his claim to a chance to eventually succeed Tanana, striking out 121 and walking 23 in 173 innings.

Neagle modeled himself after a different major leaguer. While at the University of Minnesota, Neagle often attended Minnesota Twins home games, studying the style of then-Twins ace Frankie "Sweet Music" Viola. Neagle taught himself Viola's best pitch, the circle-changeup.

"I got to see him pitch quite a bit," Neagle said. "I saw him throw the circle-change when the count was 3-1 and 3-0. The circle change is now my best pitch."

As Neagle compiled a 20-3 record at Class A Visalia (8-0) and Double-A Orlando (12-3), people began wondering if the Twins cloned Viola before they traded him. Actually, they simply had the foresight to make Neagle their third-round pick in 1989.

The top single-game pitching performance in 1990 came from an unlikely source: Charlie Rogers, the 16th and last player picked by the independent Miami Miracle in the June draft. Rogers didn't pitch much for the Class A club, but he finished the season on a high note, striking out 20 Baseball City Royals.

For the hitters, 1990 was a fairly routine year. With the exception of Bernard Gilkey, of course. Gilkey had a career in the third inning of an early-season game, banging out *three* hits for the Triple-A Louisville Redbirds against the Nashville Sounds. Gilkey supplied a three-run homer and two singles to fuel Louisville's 16-run inning, during which the Redbirds sent 21 men to the plate. They won the game 18-4.

"Everybody was laughing and having a good time," said Louisville's Ray Lankford, who belted a grand slam. "No, a great time."

In case you're wondering, Gilkey was the third minor leaguer to get three hits in an inning. In fact, Gene Rye of Waco (Texas) *homered* three times in an inning in 1930.

New champ in Alliance

It's hard to build a dynasty in the minor leagues, since the faces change so frequently and the best players don't stay long.

That's why it was so unusual when the Indianapolis Indians won four consecutive American Association pennants, beating the International League champion in the first two Triple-A Classics for good measure.

The dynasty fizzled quietly in 1990, as the Expos affiliate finished last in the Eastern Division. "I don't think it'll ever happen again," said Max Schumacher, Indianapolis president and general manager.

Despite the demise of the Indians, the Association continued to dominate the three-year-old Triple-A Alliance with the International League. Association teams won 52 percent of interleague games, and the Omaha Royals clobbered Rochester 4-1 to win the Classic.

A few more highlights and lowlights of minor league baseball, 1990:

■ The resurgent Los Angeles Dodgers organization led the minors with a .592 composite winning percentage. Triple-A Albuquerque, Class A Vero Beach and Rookie-level Great Falls

TRIPLE-A ALL-STAR GAME

Williams leads National stars, 8-5

Eddie Williams of the host Las Vegas Stars drove in a run with a sacrifice fly in the third inning, hit a leadoff double in the sixth and scored a run to help the National League affiliates to an 8-5 win over the American League affiliates in the third annual Triple-A All-Star Game. The NL won for the second year in a row.

It was an extraordinarily well-played game, despite scorching desert heat. Brilliant defensive plays were turned in by shortstops Luis Sojo of Syracuse, Jose Offerman of Albuquerque and Paul Faries of Las Vegas, third baseman Leo Gomez of Rochester, second baseman Craig Smajstrla of Tucson and outfielder Chito Martinez of Omaha. Juan Gonzalez of Oklahoma City blasted a colossal home run in the third inning to give the American League a short-lived 2-1 lead.

"I thought the game was super," said Syracuse's Bob Bailor, the AL manager. "There was power, gap shots, the defense was super. I would have paid to see it."

National 8, American 5

AMERICAN	ab	r	h	bi	bb	so	NATIONAL	ab	r	h	bi	bb	so
Sojo 2b-ss	5	1	4	0	0	0	Offerman ss	4	1	1	0	0	1
Segui 1b	3	0	1	0	0	0	Faries ss	1	0	0	0	0	1
Hare 1b	2	0	0	0	0	1	Gilkey lf	3	1	1	0	0	0
Whiten rf	1	0	1	0	0	0	Garcia cf	1	0	0	0	0	0
Martinez cf	4	0	0	0	0	1	Torve 1b	3	0	1	1	0	0
Gonzalez dh	5	2	2	2	0	1	Rivera 1b	1	0	0	0	0	0
Gomez 3b	2	0	1	0	1	1	Williams 3b	2	1	1	1	0	0
Redfield 3b	2	1	2	2	0	0	Carter 1b	1	0	0	0	0	0
Stevens lf	3	0	1	0	0	1	Hughes dh	4	1	1	0	0	1
Meulens lf	2	0	0	0	0	1	Miller rf	2	0	1	0	0	0
Hill cf-rf	2	1	0	0	1	1	Hansen ph-3b	2	1	1	1	0	0
Cockrell rf	2	0	0	0	0	1	Fletcher c	2	0	0	0	0	1
Willard c	1	0	1	0	1	0	Pappas c	1	1	1	0	1	0
McIntosh c	1	0	0	0	0	1	Huff cf	1	0	0	0	0	0
Dorsett c	1	0	0	0	0	0	Leonard ph-lf	2	1	2	2	0	0
Naehring ss	1	0	0	0	0	0	Small 2b	2	1	1	0	0	0
Haney 2b	2	0	1	1	0	0	Smajstrla 2b	2	0	1	1	0	0
TOTALS	39	5	14	5	3	9	TOTALS	35	8	12	6	1	4

American			002	100	002—5
National			013	002	02x—8

DP—National 1. LOB—American 11, National 5. 2B—Gonzalez, Stevens, Hughes, Pappas. 3B—Sojo, Leonard. HR—Gonzalez, Redfield. SB—Hughes, Miller. S—Haney. SF—Williams.

American	IP	H	R	ER	BB	SO	National	IP	H	R	ER	BB	SO
Chiamparino L	3	6	4	4	0	3	Taylor	2⅔	5	2	2	1	3
Mmahat	1	0	0	0	0	0	Gilmore W	2⅓	3	1	1	1	1
Bitker	1	0	0	0	0	0	Polley	2	3	0	0	1	1
Cook	1	4	2	2	0	0	Perez	1	2	0	0	0	2
Stottlemyre	1	0	0	0	0	0	Walsh	1	1	2	1	0	2
Dalton	1	2	2	2	1	1							

WP—Taylor. T—2:52. A—10,323.

CLASSIFICATION ALL-STARS

(Selected by Baseball America)

CLASS AAA

C—Tim McIntosh, Denver (American Association). **1B**—Tino Martinez, Calgary (Pacific Coast). **2B**—Paul Faries, Las Vegas (Pacific Coast). **3B**—Leo Gomez, Rochester (International). **SS**—Jose Offerman, Albuquerque (Pacific Coast). **OF**—Hensley Meulens, Columbus (International); Juan Gonzalez, Oklahoma City (American Association); Phil Plantier, Pawtucket (International). **DH**—Chris Hoiles, Rochester (International). **P**—Chris Hammond, Nashville (American Association); Dave Eiland, Columbus (International); Scott Chiamparino, Tacoma (Pacific Coast); Steve Adkins, Columbus (International); Dorn Taylor, Buffalo (American Association).

Player of the Year—Jose Offerman, Albuquerque (Pacific Coast).

Manager of the Year—Kevin Kennedy, Albuquerque (Pacific Coast).

CLASS AA

C—Greg Colbrunn, Jacksonville (Southern). **1B**—Jeff Conine, Memphis (Southern). **2B**—Williams Suero, Knoxville (Southern). **3B**—Jeff Bagwell, New Britain (Eastern). **SS**—Mark Lewis, Canton (Eastern). **OF**—Henry Rodriguez, San Antonio (Texas); Bernie Williams, Albany (Eastern); Mike Humphreys, Wichita (Texas). **DH**—Frank Thomas, Birmingham (Southern). **P**—Mike Gardiner, Williamsport (Eastern); Denny Neagle, Orlando (Southern); Brian Barnes, Jacksonville (Southern); Anthony Young, Jackson (Texas); Terry Bross, Jackson (Texas).

Player of the Year—Frank Thomas, Birmingham (Southern)

Manager of the Year—Jerry Manuel, Jacksonville (Southern)

CLASS A

C—Ivan Rodriguez, Charlotte (Florida State). **1B**—Ryan Klesko, Sumter (South Atlantic)-Durham (Carolina). **2B**—Tim Howard, Columbia (South Atlantic). **3B**—Frank Bolick, Stockton-San Bernardino (California); Gary Scott, Winston-Salem (Carolina). **SS**—Royce Clayton, San Jose (California). **OF**—Reggie Sanders, Cedar Rapids (Midwest); Darrell Sherman, Riverside (California); Kenny Lofton, Osceola (Florida State). **DH**—Nikco Riesgo, St. Lucie (Florida State). **P**—Randy Marshall, Fayetteville (South Atlantic)-Lakeland (Florida State); Rich Garces, Visalia (California); Frank Seminara, Prince William (Carolina); Alan Newman, Kenosha (Midwest)-Visalia (California); Tim Pugh, Charleston W.Va. (South Atlantic).

Player of the Year—Randy Marshall, Fayetteville (South Atlantic)-Lakeland (Florida State).

Manager of the Year—Felipe Alou, West Palm Beach (Florida State)

SHORT-SEASON

C—Eric Helfand, Southern Oregon (Northwest). **1B**—Paul Russo, Elizabethton (Appalachian). **2B**—Kevin Jordan, Oneonta (New York-Penn). **3B**—Jim Thome, Burlington (Appalachian). **SS**—Jon Shave, Butte (Pioneer). **OF**—K.C. Gillum, Billings (Pioneer); Mark Dalesandro, Boise (Northwest); Matt Mieske, Spokane (Northwest). **DH**—Andy Hartung, Geneva (New York-Penn). **P**—Hilly Hathaway, Boise (Northwest); Sam Militello, Oneonta (New York-Penn); Bruce Bensching, Spokane (Northwest); Tim Parker, Geneva (New York-Penn); Lance Painter, Spokane (Northwest).

Player of the Year—Matt Mieske, Spokane (Northwest).

Manager of the Year—Ray Smith, Elizabethton (Appalachian).

and Kissimmee won league championships, and six of the Dodgers' seven farm clubs were in the playoffs.

■ Minor league managers are usually secure from the turmoil that faces their brethren in the majors. Not in 1990. Three Triple-A managers felt the axe during the season: John Wockenfuss of Toledo (Tigers), Ed Nottle of Pawtucket (Red Sox) and Bob Molinaro of Colorado Springs (Indians), and Tommy Helms resigned from his position at Double-A Charlotte (Cubs).

The firing of Nottle, a flamboyant former Baseball America Minor League Manager of the Year, received the most attention. "I'm a lot like Tommy Lasorda, and I guess there isn't room

Expos named top organization

Recognizing their stockpile of talent, Baseball America named the Montreal Expos Organization of the Year in 1988. Then, in 1989, the Expos traded three top prospects to Seattle for Mark Langston, and failed to sign their No. 1 draft pick. Free agents Langston, Bryn Smith and Hubie Brooks hit the bricks in search of greener pastures.

In 1990, the Expos were back on top with a vengeance. They promoted 10 rookies to the major league roster, providing a transfusion of new blood that fueled the team to a surprising third-place finish in the National League East. Meanwhile, scouting director Gary Hughes conducted a strong draft, taking advantage of compensation picks for the lost free agents to select an unprecedented 10 players in the first two rounds.

For replenishing their stock of prospects while successfully integrating their rookies at the major league level, the Montreal Expos are Baseball America's 1990 Organization of the Year.

Baseball America's Organization of the Year

1982—Oakland A's	**1987**—Milwaukee Brewers
1983—New York Mets	**1988**—Montreal Expos
1984—New York Mets	**1989**—Texas Rangers
1985—Milwaukee Brewers	**1990**—Montreal Expos
1986—Milwaukee Brewers	

Bob Freitas Awards

The Baseball America/Bob Freitas Awards were launched in 1989 to honor minor league clubs for long-term success. The recipients have demonstrated consistently high standards, both in the ballpark and in the front office. Their facilities are comfortable, clean and well-run, and their franchises are profitable.

Baseball America/Bob Freitas Awards

Triple-A: Pawtucket Red Sox (International)
1989—Columbus Clippers (International)

Double-A: Arkansas Travelers (Texas)
1989—El Paso Diablos (Texas)

Class A: San Jose Giants (California)
1989—Durham Bulls (Carolina)

Short-Season: Salt Lake Trappers (Pioneer)
1989—Eugene Emeralds (Northwest)

in baseball for two Tommy Lasordas," said Nottle, a lounge singer during the offseason who often performed at charity affairs in Rhode Island.

■ After a 13-year quest to become Major League Baseball's first female umpire, Pam Postema was released by the Triple-A Alliance. Alliance commissioner Randy Mobley notified Postema before the season that neither the American League or the National League considered her a prospect. "For that reason, as has been the case with many others, she was released," Mobley said.

Postema, 35, was the second female umpire to reach Triple-A. She received highly-publicized spring-training tryouts by the NL in 1988 and '89.

Later in the year, Postema filed a sex-discrimination suit against baseball.

■ Department leaders:

Phil Plantier of Pawtucket led the minors with 33 homers ... Luis Lopez of Albuquerque hit for the highest batting average, .353 ... Tom Dodd of Triple-A Calgary (Mariners) led with 114 RBIs ... Tom Goodwin stole 82 bases for Class A Bakersfield and Double-A San Antonio (Dodgers) ... Jose Tolentino of Triple-A Tucson (Astros) hit safely in 30 consecutive games ... Rich Garces spelled relief for Class A

Buffalo cracked the million mark in attendance for the third year in a row, attracting 1,174,358 to Pilot Field.

Visalia and Double-A Orlando (Twins), compiling 36 saves . . . The lowest ERA belonged to Jeff Hoffman of Class A Greensboro (Yankees), 1.47 . . . Brian Barnes of Double-A Jacksonville (Expos) struck out 213 batters.

Around the minors

National Association president Sal Artiaga was named commissioner of minor league baseball. Artiaga has headed the National Association since 1988. No one had ever held the title of commissioner . . . The Rookie-level Elizabethton Twins won 20 consecutive games, the longest streak since the Salt Lake Trappers set a pro baseball record with 29 in a row in 1987 . . . Bob Richmond succeeded Jack Cain as president of the short-season Northwest League in September. Richmond will remain president of the Rookie-level Arizona League as well . . . Eighteen cities applied for two Triple-A expansion teams, which are expected to begin play in 1993. The franchises, costing at least $5 million each, will be awarded in mid-'91 . . . The Boardwalk and Baseball theme park, home of two Kansas City Royals farm teams, closed before the season. The amusement park, at the intersection of Interstate 4 and U.S. 27 southeast of Orlando, Fla., was dismantled, but the stadium and practice facilities continued operating. The Baseball City Royals (Florida State) announced a season-long attendance of 18,884—worst among all full-season clubs . . . The Philadelphia Phillies operated two farm clubs in the Rookie-level Appalachian League: the Martinsville Phillies and the Princeton Patriots. Officially, the Princeton club was a co-op, with a few players from other organizations. But that team finished 31-36, seven games *ahead* of Martinsville . . . In 1987, Steve Gasser was considered the game's best righthanded pitching prospect. Three years later, after a trade from the Twins to the Mets, Gasser was incapable of throwing the ball over the plate in A-ball. In his first outing of 1990 for Columbia, Gasser walked 11 of the 13 batters he faced. Gasser was released May 22, later signing with the Braves. He finished the year 0-3 with a 11.25 ERA, with 55 walks in 24 innings for Columbia and Sumter . . . In what was believed to be a first, a father-son umpire team worked five games together in the Northwest League. When Paul Schreiber's partner was reassigned before a series at Eugene, league president Jack Cain asked Schreiber's father, Harry, a

Rangers prospect dies

Ronaldo Romero, a 19-year-old pitcher in the Texas Rangers organization, collapsed and died in the dugout May 14 during a South Atlantic League game between the Gastonia Rangers and Fayetteville Generals.

Ronaldo Romero
... defective heart

Romero started and pitched the first two innings of the game, played at Fayetteville's J.P. Riddle Stadium. Between the second and third innings, with Fayetteville leading 7-0, Romero complained of a rapid heartbeat. The Gastonia trainer asked him to begin breathing deeply, a tactic that seemed to help. Romero flashed a smile. "I can still pitch," he said.

Those were his last words. The 6-foot-3, 220-pound right-hander collapsed and fell to the dugout floor. He was rushed to a nearby hospital, where he was pronounced dead. A medical examiner said Romero died from right ventricular cardiomyopathy, an enlargement and weakening of the heart wall.

Later, Texas Rangers officials discovered that Romero's father may have a similar heart condition. But doctors had noticed no abnormality during the player's annual spring physical, and Romero never mentioned any family medical problems.

"He was like a son," said Gastonia manager Orlando Gomez, "with a smile all the time on his face. He always worked hard. He wanted to be better."

Romero, a native of Barranquilla, Colombia, signed with the Rangers in 1987. He was just beginning to scratch his potential, going 2-1 with a 2.45 ERA and 21 strikeouts in 22 innings for Gastonia.

Romero was the first professional baseball player to die during a game since 1974. That year, Alfredo Edmead of the Salem Pirates (Carolina) received a fatal head injury in a collision with a teammate.

former NWL umpire who lived nearby, to step in. Later that week, under similar circumstances, umpire Steve Graley and his father, Hooks, worked a South Atlantic League series together in their hometown, Charleston, W.Va ... In September 1989, Hurricane Hugo tore apart College Park in Charleston, S.C., home of the Class A Charleston Rainbows. The park was repaired in time for the 1990 season, using $600,000 in insurance money and federal disaster-relief funds.

Quotes of the year

CHARLIE ESHBACH, Eastern League president, after the National Association voted 13-4 to change Sal Artiaga's title from president to commissioner of minor league baseball: "There's strong sentiment in my league for me to be named Pharaoh, but my wife doesn't want to be a handmaiden."

BILL MURRAY, director of operations in the major league commissioner's office, asked about low salaries for minor league players: "Quite frankly, we look at the National Association as a sort of apprentice-type arrangement. The real job is in the major leagues."

MARTY KUEHNERT, president of the Birmingham Barons (Southern), after the Alabama Department of Labor ordered the team to send its teenage batboys home at 9 p.m.: "Is the government telling us kids can't be at the ballpark? Would they rather have them roaming the streets? It's very stupid."

AMERICAN ASSOCIATION

Banner attendance year; Omaha takes league title

By GEORGE RORRER

It probably won't get much better than this for the American Association: In 1990, the eight Association clubs broke the 4 million mark in attendance with an all-time minor league record 4,061,717. Buffalo went over the one million home attendance mark for a record third straight time, drawing 1,174,358, and Nashville and Omaha set club records.

Chris Hammond
... 15-1, 2.17

After surviving a marathon Association championship series against Nashville, Omaha maintained the league's dominance of the Triple-A Alliance by beating Rochester of the International League 4 games to 1 in the Triple-A Classic.

Association clubs also regained their edge over IL clubs in regular-season play, 181 victories to 170.

Nashville's Chris Hammond became the first pitcher to lead the Association in victories (15), ERA (2.17) and strikeouts (149) since Herb Score did it for Indianapolis in 1954 with 22 wins, a 2.62 ERA and a whopping 330 strikeouts.

There was, however, uncertainty about the Association's future. Buffalo, Denver and Nashville were candidates for two

LEAGUE CHAMPIONS

Playoff Champions, Where Applicable

1990—Omaha	1957—Denver	1928—Indianapolis
1989—Indianapolis	1956—Denver	1927—Toledo
1988—Indianapolis	1955—Minneapolis	1926—Louisville
1987—Indianapolis	1954—Louisville	1925—Louisville
1986—Indianapolis	1953—Kansas City	1924—St. Paul
1985—Louisville	1952—Kansas City	1923—Kansas City
1984—Louisville	1951—Milwaukee	1922—St. Paul
1983—Denver	1950—Columbus	1921—Louisville
1982—Indianapolis	1949—Indianapolis	1920—St. Paul
1981—Denver	1948—St. Paul	1919—St. Paul
1980—Springfield	1947—Milwaukee	1918—Kansas City
1979—Evansville	1946—Louisville	1917—Indianapolis
1978—Omaha	1945—Louisville	1916—Louisville
1977—Denver	1944—Louisville	1915—Minneapolis
1976—Denver	1943—Columbus	1914—Milwaukee
1975—Evansville	1942—Columbus	1913—Milwaukee
1974—Tulsa	1941—Columbus	1912—Minneapolis
1973—Tulsa	1940—Louisville	1911—Minneapolis
1972—Evansville	1939—Louisville	1910—Minneapolis
1971—Denver	1938—Kansas City	1909—Louisville
1970—Omaha	1937—Columbus	1908—Indianapolis
1969—Omaha	1936—Milwaukee	1907—Columbus
1963-68—Did Not	1935—Minneapolis	1906—Columbus
Operate	1934—Columbus	1905—Columbus
1962—Louisville	1933—Columbus	1904—St. Paul
1961—Louisville	1932—Minneapolis	1903—St. Paul
1960—Louisville	1931—St. Paul	1902—Indianapolis
1959—Minneapolis	1930—Louisville	
1958—Minneapolis	1929—Kansas City	

Oklahoma City's Juan Gonzalez led Association hitters in homers and RBIs, and was named league MVP.

1993 National League expansion franchises, and the Association joined with the other two Triple-A leagues in making plans for expansion and realignment. Eighteen cities officially applied for Triple-A franchises in September.

"Our operators have done another great job," league president Randy Mobley said of the attendance boom. "It's something that's been a steamrolling effect since Louisville got things rolling a few years ago. Buffalo chimed in, and the others have continued to improve.

"We have a lot of irons in the fire with expansion and realignment a couple of years down the road, with our club in Denver saying it could be purchased for the right price and with three clubs applying for National League franchises.

"We are preparing as best we can for whatever happens."

Omaha subdues Nashville

Omaha, managed by Sal Rende, won its fourth Association title after losing in the championship series to Indianapolis in 1988 and '89. The Royals hadn't won the Association title in 12 years.

Nashville took its first Eastern Division title in a one-game playoff against Buffalo, winning 4-3 in 18 innings on Chris Jones' run-scoring double and seven innings of four-hit shutout relief pitching by Charlie Mitchell.

Omaha and Nashville split the first two games of the best-of-5 championship series in Omaha, then the Royals outlasted the Sounds 8-7 at Nashville in a 20-inning, six-hour, 25-minute marathon that ended at 3:50 a.m. CDT.

Nashville's Adam Casillas had sent the game into extra innings with a two-run homer with two out in the ninth, but Omaha took an 8-6 lead in the 20th on a throwing error by third baseman Denny Gonzalez and a run-scoring double by Russ Morman. Nashville scored in the bottom of the inning and had the winning run at second base, but Greg Everson struck out Skeeter Barnes to end it.

Nashville won game four 5-4, but Omaha took the title the following night with an 8-7 victory highlighted by first-inning home runs by Morman, Luis de los Santos and Chito Martinez. Keith Lockhart's grand slam for Nashville tied the score 6-6 in the sixth, but Morman's second homer of the game, a two-run shot, decided it.

Omaha's Gary Thurman, who batted .556 in the series, was named Most Valuable Player.

The Triple-A Classic wasn't nearly as thrilling. Omaha split the first two games with the Red Wings in Rochester, then won the next three games. Morman, who hit .571 with three homers and nine RBIs, was named the series' MVP.

"We've had three parties now, and each one has been sweeter," Morman said. "I don't think I could

Mark Ryal
. . . batting champ

have scripted this any better. Everything worked out. Not just for me, but for the club."

Omaha's victory over the International League champion continued the Association's dominance of the Triple-A Classic. Indianapolis, which finished last in the East in 1990, won it the first two years.

Ryal edges out Thurman

Buffalo veteran Mark Ryal won the league batting title at .334, getting enough at-bats to qualify and beat out Omaha's Thurman (.331) because of the Eastern Division playoff game.

Oklahoma City slugger Juan Gonzalez won the home run and RBI titles at age 20 with 29 and 101, respectively, and led in total bases with 252. He was also selected the league's top major league prospect in a Baseball America poll of managers.

1990 *FINAL STANDINGS*

East	W	L	Pct.	GB
Buffalo (Pirates)	85	61	.582	—
Nashville (Reds)..............	85	61	.582	—
Louisville (Cardinals)	74	72	.507	11
Indianapolis (Expos)	61	85	.418	24
West				
Omaha (Royals)	86	60	.589	—
Iowa (Cubs)	72	74	.493	14
Denver (Brewers)	68	78	.466	18
Oklahoma City (Rangers) ...	58	87	.400	27½

1990 *GENERAL INFORMATION*

Playoffs: Omaha defeated Nashville 3-2 in best-of-5 final for league championship; Omaha defeated Rochester (International) 4-1 in best-of-7 Triple-A Classic.

Regular-Season Attendance: Buffalo, 1,174,358; Louisville, 616,687; Nashville, 556,250; Denver, 433,880; Omaha, 341,129; Indianapolis, 314,264; Oklahoma City, 282,773; Iowa, 270,215.

Managers: Buffalo—Terry Collins; **Denver**—Dave Machemer; **Indianapolis**—Tim Johnson; **Iowa**—Jim Essian; **Louisville**—Gaylen Pitts; **Nashville**—Pete Mackanin; **Oklahoma City**—Steve Smith; **Omaha**—Sal Rende.

1990 Official All-Star Team: C—Tim McIntosh, Denver. **1B**—Orlando Merced, Buffalo. **2B**—Jeff Small, Iowa. **3B**—Joe Redfield, Denver. **SS**—Paul Zuvella, Omaha. **OF**—Bernard Gilkey, Louisville;

Juan Gonzalez, Oklahoma City; Ray Lankford, Louisville. **DH**—Mark Ryal, Buffalo. **RHP**—Dorn Taylor, Buffalo. **LHP**—Chris Hammond, Nashville. **Most Valuable Player**—Juan Gonzalez, Oklahoma City. **Most Valuable Pitcher**—Chris Hammond, Nashville. **Rookie of the Year**—Juan Gonzalez, Oklahoma City. **Manager of the Year**—Sal Rende, Omaha.

Top 10 Major League Prospects (by Baseball America): 1. Juan Gonzalez, of, Oklahoma City; 2. Chris Hammond, lhp, Nashville; 3. Ray Lankford, of, Louisville; 4. Ken Hill, rhp, Louisville; 5. Bernard Gilkey, of, Louisville; 6. Scott Scudder, rhp, Nashville; 7. Omar Olivares, rhp, Louisville; 8. Moises Alou, of, Buffalo/Indianapolis; 9. Mike York, rhp, Buffalo; 10. Derrick May, of, Iowa.

1990 BATTING, PITCHING STATS

CLUB BATTING

	AVG	G	AB	R	H	2B	3B	HR	BB	SO	SB
Iowa	.272	146	4757	642	1294	228	21	102	467	837	151
Denver	.271	146	4824	724	1309	241	58	118	490	816	108
Omaha	.268	146	4769	678	1279	190	56	97	511	973	170
Nashville	.262	147	4888	628	1280	241	33	88	448	776	130
Buffalo	.260	147	4963	621	1289	231	46	86	435	762	127
Indianapolis	.258	146	4810	573	1243	217	34	68	403	863	140
Oklahoma City	.252	145	4915	639	1238	264	48	96	499	978	116
Louisville	.250	146	4615	564	1156	202	47	54	519	707	122

CLUB PITCHING

	ERA	G	CG	SHO	SV	IP	H	R	ER	BB	SO
Buffalo	3.15	147	16	16	36	1322	1269	547	462	398	839
Nashville	3.23	147	22	17	34	1291	1146	553	463	498	879
Indianapolis	3.49	146	15	12	22	1262	1153	596	490	513	809
Omaha	3.50	146	11	14	48	1267	1223	555	493	517	899
Louisville	3.78	146	13	11	40	1256	1185	591	528	454	855
Iowa	4.34	146	10	5	33	1239	1309	694	598	570	900
Oklahoma City	4.40	145	10	5	25	1275	1432	747	623	477	838
Denver	5.16	146	10	7	40	1262	1460	839	723	493	866

INDIVIDUAL BATTING LEADERS
(Minimum 394 Plate Appearances)

	AVG	G	AB	R	H	2B	3B	HR	RBI	BB	SO	SB
*Ryal, Mark, Buffalo	.334	109	371	49	124	34	2	9	49	17	22	3
Thurman, Gary, Omaha	.331	98	381	65	126	14	8	0	26	31	68	39
*Carter, Steve, Buffalo	.303	120	426	62	129	19	12	8	45	25	61	10
Morman, Russ, Omaha	.298	121	436	67	130	14	9	13	81	51	78	21
*May, Derrick, Iowa	.296	119	459	55	136	27	1	8	69	23	50	5
Bierley, Brad, Iowa	.296	133	436	71	129	28	2	16	71	66	71	9
*Landrum, Cedric, Iowa	.296	123	372	71	110	10	4	0	24	43	63	46
Gilkey, Bernard, Lou	.295	132	499	83	147	26	8	3	46	75	49	45
#Smith, Greg, Iowa	.291	105	398	54	116	19	1	5	44	37	57	26
Moore, Billy, Denver	.288	120	416	74	120	30	4	18	68	56	77	6

INDIVIDUAL PITCHING LEADERS
(Minimum 117 Innings)

	W	L	ERA	G	GS	CG	SV	IP	H	R	ER	BB	SO
*Hammond, Chris, Nash	15	1	2.17	24	24	5	0	149	118	43	36	63	149
Fireovid, Steve, Ind	10	12	2.63	29	26	4	0	171	163	70	50	34	84
Olivares, Omar, Lou	10	11	2.82	23	23	5	0	159	127	58	50	59	88
Taylor, Dorn, Buffalo	14	6	2.91	30	29	5	0	195	170	74	63	51	112
Lemasters, Jim, Omaha	11	10	3.16	30	25	3	0	154	170	69	54	55	86
Gakeler, Dan, Ind	5	5	3.23	22	21	1	0	120	101	55	43	55	89
Hinkle, Mike, Lou	8	7	3.29	29	18	1	0	129	126	53	47	40	66
Anderson, Scott, Ind	12	10	3.31	27	25	6	0	182	166	74	67	61	116
Gross, Kip, Nash	12	7	3.33	40	11	2	3	127	113	54	47	47	62
Lopez, Rob, Nash	7	10	3.38	28	25	4	0	144	141	72	54	50	76

BUFFALO

BATTING	AVG	G	AB	R	H	2B	3B	HR	RBI	BB	SO	SB
Banister, Jeff, c-1b	.320	12	25	3	8	2	0	1	3	3	5	0
Bilardello, Dann, c	.286	52	154	19	44	8	1	5	26	7	20	0
Burdick, Kevin, 2b	.282	110	429	61	121	24	3	3	41	29	38	5
#Cangelosi, John, of	.348	24	89	17	31	2	2	0	7	12	8	15
*Carter, Steve, of	.303	120	426	62	129	19	12	8	45	25	61	10
Chamberlain, Wes, of	.250	123	416	43	104	24	2	6	52	34	58	14
#Cook, Jeff, of	.220	53	141	19	31	4	2	1	13	8	23	14
*Gainey, Ty, of-dh	.412	12	34	3	14	1	0	1	3	4	7	1
Garcia, Carlos, ss	.264	63	197	23	52	10	0	5	18	16	41	7
Kiefer, Steve, 3b-1b	.233	84	275	30	64	18	1	8	33	24	76	2
Little, Scott, of	.226	36	106	17	24	1	2	1	10	14	19	8
#Merced, Orlando, 1b-3b	.262	101	378	52	99	12	6	9	55	46	63	14
Moreno, Armando, 2b-3b	.273	92	286	39	78	20	1	10	30	47	43	2
Prince, Tom, c	.225	94	284	38	64	13	0	7	37	39	46	4
Richardson, Jeff, ss-2b	.207	66	164	15	34	4	0	1	15	14	21	1
Rossy, Rico, ss	.176	8	17	3	3	0	1	0	2	4	2	1
*Ryal, Mark, 1b-of	.334	109	371	49	124	34	2	9	49	17	22	3

	AVG	G	AB	R	H	2B	3B	HR	RBI	BB	SO	SB
Sheaffer, Danny, c-of	.243	55	144	23	35	7	0	2	19	11	14	4
Shields, Tommy, 3b-ss	.247	123	380	42	94	20	3	2	30	21	72	12
#Shines, Razor, 1b-dh	.170	42	112	8	19	1	1	2	15	22	19	0
*Steels, James, ph	.000	1	1	0	0	0	0	0	0	0	1	0
*Szekely, Joe, c	.000	2	4	1	0	0	0	0	0	1	0	0
#Yacopino, Ed, of	.250	27	72	7	18	1	0	0	4	2	13	1

PITCHING	W	L	ERA	G	GS	CG	SV	IP	H	R	ER	BB	SO
Bair, Doug	4	2	2.75	29	0	0	6	52	53	19	16	18	29
Belinda, Stan	3	1	1.90	15	0	0	5	24	20	8	5	8	25
*Dillard, Gordon	1	0	0.00	10	1	0	1	11	10	1	0	1	7
*Garcia, Miguel	0	2	5.25	9	1	0	0	12	12	9	7	4	6
*Hancock, Lee	0	0	0.00	1	0	0	0	0	0	0	0	1	0
Huismann, Mark	6	2	2.61	49	0	0	4	76	69	23	22	15	32
Kemp, Hugh	7	7	3.42	26	21	1	0	134	134	66	51	27	80
*Kipper, Bob	0	0	7.71	5	1	0	0	5	6	4	4	1	6
Kramer, Randy	6	1	2.57	18	12	0	3	74	55	29	21	33	58
Mason, Roger	3	5	2.10	29	2	0	3	77	78	21	18	25	45
Medvin, Scott	2	2	1.46	13	0	0	1	25	13	7	4	11	10
Minor, Blas	0	1	3.38	1	0	0	0	3	2	1	1	2	2
Neely, Jeff	1	0	4.15	6	0	0	1	9	5	4	4	4	5
Palacios, Vicente	13	7	3.43	28	28	5	0	184	173	77	70	53	137
Reed, Rick	7	4	3.46	15	15	2	0	91	82	37	35	21	63
*Reuss, Jerry	4	4	3.52	14	9	0	1	61	73	25	24	12	29
Roesler, Mike	0	3	4.29	24	0	0	0	42	50	25	20	17	19
Ross, Mark	6	8	2.02	47	0	0	11	71	73	23	16	12	36
*Samuels, Roger	0	0	3.60	5	0	0	0	5	6	2	2	1	4
Taylor, Dorn	14	6	2.91	30	29	5	0	195	170	74	63	51	112
Tibbs, Jay	0	0	3.00	2	1	0	0	3	3	1	1	2	1
*Tomlin, Randy	0	0	3.38	3	1	0	0	8	12	3	3	1	3
York, Mike	8	7	4.20	27	26	3	0	159	165	87	74	78	130

DENVER

BATTING	AVG	G	AB	R	H	2B	3B	HR	RBI	BB	SO	SB
Brantley, Mickey, of	.264	20	72	14	19	3	2	2	10	6	3	1
*Canale, George, 1b	.254	134	468	76	119	17	6	12	60	69	103	12
*Carrillo, Matias, of	.267	21	75	15	20	6	2	2	10	2	16	0
*Escalera, Ruben, of	.152	12	33	3	5	0	0	0	2	4	3	0
*Gantner, Jim, 2b-3b	.364	6	22	1	8	1	0	0	1	2	1	1
Higgins, Mark, of-dh	.283	107	361	55	102	21	1	16	65	32	68	1
Kmak, Joe, c	.232	28	95	12	22	3	0	1	10	4	16	1
#Mattox, Frank, 2b	.262	81	282	44	74	13	4	2	24	26	41	21
McIntosh, Tim, c	.288	116	416	72	120	21	3	18	74	26	59	6
Mitchell, Joe, dh-1b	.251	71	247	27	62	17	2	4	34	20	55	1
*Monico, Mario, of	.263	100	319	41	84	18	6	2	38	45	36	5
Moore, Billy, of	.288	120	416	74	120	30	4	18	68	56	77	6
Olander, Jim, of	.288	74	233	33	67	12	4	3	36	20	47	2
Pino, Rolando, 2b-ss	.200	6	5	3	1	1	0	0	0	2	0	0
Polidor, Gus, ss-2b	.303	46	165	17	50	8	0	1	16	4	19	3
Redfield, Joe, 3b	.274	137	525	87	144	23	10	17	71	57	76	34
Smith, D. L., ss	.275	94	295	35	81	6	6	5	38	24	34	3
*Spiers, Bill, ss	.316	11	38	6	12	0	0	1	7	10	8	1
#Sveum, Dale, 3b-1b	.289	57	218	25	63	17	2	2	26	20	49	1
Torricelli, Tim, c-3b	.212	17	33	6	7	1	0	1	5	3	5	0
Walters, Darryel, of	.244	100	287	45	70	16	4	10	45	36	77	5
*Xavier, Joe, 2b-ss	.224	38	107	12	24	5	1	0	6	11	15	1

PITCHING	W	L	ERA	G	GS	CG	SV	IP	H	R	ER	BB	SO
August, Don	7	7	6.75	22	22	3	0	124	164	98	93	27	67
Birkbeck, Mike	3	8	5.33	21	20	0	0	96	102	73	57	36	69
Capel, Mike	4	3	4.26	41	3	0	2	101	98	55	48	39	60
Davis, John	1	3	12.46	6	0	0	1	4	4	7	6	8	1
Easley, Logan	3	1	5.79	46	0	0	9	75	99	63	48	41	39
Edens, Tom	1	1	5.40	19	0	0	4	37	32	23	22	22	26
Filer, Tom	3	5	6.49	9	9	1	0	51	70	39	37	9	22
*Fossas, Tony	5	2	1.51	25	0	0	4	36	29	8	6	10	45
George, Chris	1	1	18.56	7	0	0	0	5	17	11	11	4	4
Gordon, Don	1	0	3.24	5	0	0	0	8	10	6	3	4	5
Henry, Doug	2	3	4.44	27	0	0	8	51	46	26	25	27	54
*Horton, Ricky	3	1	4.81	5	5	0	0	24	37	17	13	7	10
Hunter, Jim	6	8	4.69	20	20	2	0	117	138	76	61	45	57
*Lee, Mark	3	1	2.25	20	0	0	4	28	25	7	7	6	35
May, Scott	1	1	8.04	7	5	0	0	28	45	26	25	13	20
McGrath, Chuck	3	2	6.07	12	4	0	0	46	57	32	31	17	30
Navarro, Jaime	2	3	4.20	6	6	1	0	41	41	27	19	14	28
Peterek, Jeff	2	3	6.82	9	6	0	0	34	43	29	26	15	23
Powell, Dennis	4	4	3.61	11	11	2	0	62	63	34	25	21	46
*Puig, Ed	2	0	3.38	19	0	0	0	27	35	12	10	9	24
Robertson, Doug	2	3	4.44	21	0	0	0	26	27	18	13	21	20
Sadler, Alan	2	5	5.50	12	12	1	0	52	54	33	32	23	26
Sebra, Bob (23 Nash)	4	3	3.27	44	2	0	20	63	61	26	23	24	69
Thomas, Roy	2	1	5.23	7	2	0	0	21	28	14	12	7	13
Veres, Randy	1	6	5.19	16	7	0	2	50	60	36	29	27	36
Watkins, Tim	1	3	5.51	18	9	0	0	67	82	44	41	21	55
Wegman, Bill	1	0	3.29	3	3	0	0	14	10	5	5	7	14

INDIANAPOLIS

BATTING	AVG	G	AB	R	H	2B	3B	HR	RBI	BB	SO	SB
Alou, Moises, of (75 Buff) ..	.264	90	326	44	86	5	6	5	37	33	50	13
Beltre, Esteban, ss	.226	133	407	33	92	11	2	1	37	32	77	8
*Braun, Randy, 1b	.221	23	68	3	15	4	0	1	8	4	11	0
Bullock, Eric, of	.281	107	434	62	122	19	7	3	32	32	43	40
Castro, Jose, 3b	.163	19	49	1	8	1	0	1	4	7	13	0
Cucjen, Romy, 3b-ss	.271	73	240	32	65	10	3	3	26	32	42	3
Goff, Jerry, c-3b	.287	39	143	23	41	10	2	5	26	24	33	3
*Green, Otis, of-1b	.274	76	197	34	54	12	3	1	16	18	34	5
Grissom, Marquis, of	.182	5	22	3	4	0	0	2	3	0	5	1
*Hecht, Steve, 2b-of	.254	58	197	21	50	12	2	2	13	7	32	11
Houston, Mel, inf-of	.266	106	286	36	76	15	2	1	25	22	41	10
#Johnson, Wallace, 1b	.300	11	40	6	12	1	0	1	11	4	3	0
Leary, Rob, ph	.500	2	2	1	1	1	0	0	0	0	0	0
*Lowry, Dwight, c	.310	73	187	23	58	6	1	2	25	19	34	0
*Mack, Quinn, of	.276	121	392	55	108	25	2	7	53	25	46	11
Marquez, Edwin, c-of	.163	20	49	3	8	2	0	0	6	7	17	0
Paredes, Johnny, 2b	.261	94	322	46	84	7	1	3	17	42	38	20
Reyes, Gil, c	.233	89	309	22	72	14	1	9	45	24	79	2
Rivera, German, 1b-3b	.287	125	446	67	128	25	5	10	59	41	75	1
Roomes, Rolando, of	.232	53	198	22	46	5	1	7	31	9	61	11
Salazar, Angel, 3b-ss	.208	15	53	2	11	3	0	0	3	4	7	0
Santovenia, Nelson, c-3b ..	.318	11	44	3	14	2	0	1	10	1	7	0
*St.Laurent, Jim, of-dh	.241	10	29	3	7	0	0	0	4	2	6	0
*Steels, James, of-1b	.267	71	247	37	66	15	2	4	22	26	40	10
*Vanderwal, John, of-dh ...	.296	51	135	16	40	6	0	2	14	13	28	0
Wilson, Jim, 1b	.255	28	94	7	24	5	0	2	11	5	26	0

PITCHING	W	L	ERA	G	GS	CG	SV	IP	H	R	ER	BB	SO
Anderson, Scott	12	10	3.31	27	25	6	0	182	166	74	67	61	116
Bennett, Chris	2	7	4.89	23	0	0	3	35	36	24	19	24	15
Chambers, Travis	1	3	4.55	22	1	0	1	28	25	18	14	20	33
Costello, John	0	3	7.04	22	0	0	0	31	36	26	24	20	32
Davins, Jim	3	6	4.47	41	0	0	4	56	52	31	28	27	45
Dixon, Eddie	6	7	3.25	57	6	0	5	111	87	47	40	35	40
Farmer, Howard	7	9	3.89	26	26	4	0	148	150	84	64	48	99
Fireovid, Steve	10	12	2.63	29	26	4	0	171	163	70	50	34	84
*Frey, Steve	0	0	0.00	2	0	0	1	3	0	0	0	1	3
Gakeler, Dan	5	5	3.23	22	21	1	0	120	101	55	43	55	89
Galvez, Balvino	0	1	10.29	3	2	0	0	7	11	8	8	8	5
Hoover, John (24 OkC) ...	4	5	5.92	28	12	1	1	97	120	73	64	39	47
Malloy, Bob	2	2	3.78	23	1	0	6	33	31	15	14	8	31
*Marchok, Chris	1	2	2.28	23	0	0	0	24	20	7	6	10	17
Mohorcic, Dale	2	0	1.13	13	0	0	2	16	11	3	2	3	9
*Nabholz, Chris	0	6	4.83	10	10	0	0	63	66	38	34	28	44
*Olker, Joe	0	0	0.00	1	0	0	0	1	0	0	0	1	0
*Perez, Yorkis	1	1	2.31	9	0	0	0	12	8	5	3	6	8
Rojas, Mel	2	4	3.13	17	17	0	0	98	84	42	34	47	64
*Sauveur, Rich	2	2	1.93	14	7	0	0	56	45	14	12	25	24
*Straker, Les	0	0	0.00	3	1	0	0	7	1	2	0	3	7
Thompson, Rich	3	2	5.47	15	1	0	0	25	31	16	15	10	14

IOWA

BATTING	AVG	G	AB	R	H	2B	3B	HR	RBI	BB	SO	SB
Bafia, Bob, 3b-1b	.234	72	188	18	44	15	2	3	18	5	46	0
#Berryhill, Damon, c	.215	22	79	8	17	1	0	3	6	4	18	0
Bierley, Brad, of-3b	.296	133	436	71	129	28	2	16	71	66	71	9
#Guinn, Brian, inf-of	.270	123	318	50	86	15	3	8	50	48	55	9
Hearron, Jeff, c-1b	.235	78	153	14	36	7	0	4	19	9	41	0
*Landrum, Cedric, of	.296	123	372	71	110	10	4	0	24	43	63	46
*May, Derrick, of	.296	119	459	55	136	27	1	8	69	23	50	5
McClendon, Lloyd, 1b	.286	25	91	14	26	2	0	2	18	8	19	3
Pappas, Erik, c-of	.249	131	405	56	101	19	2	16	55	65	84	6
*Sheridan, Pat, of	.329	23	70	16	23	3	0	4	10	11	18	2
Small, Jeff, 2b	.287	125	457	50	131	26	3	4	47	13	61	5
#Smith, Greg, ss	.291	105	398	54	116	19	1	5	44	37	57	26
*Strange, Doug, 3b	.305	82	269	31	82	17	1	5	35	28	42	6
*Sullivan, Glenn, 1b-of ...	.103	28	68	5	7	3	0	0	8	4	10	2
*Varsho, Gary, of-1b	.301	63	229	35	69	9	0	7	33	25	35	18
*Villanueva, Hector, c-1b ..	.266	52	177	20	47	7	1	8	34	19	36	0
#Walker, Chico, of-dh	.360	32	114	30	41	7	1	6	19	25	17	9
Walton, Jerome, of	.188	4	16	3	3	0	0	1	1	2	4	0
Wrona, Bill, ss-2b	.216	74	190	19	41	7	0	0	13	18	28	4
Wrona, Rick, c	.226	58	146	16	33	4	0	2	15	10	35	0

PITCHING	W	L	ERA	G	GS	CG	SV	IP	H	R	ER	BB	SO
Blankenship, Kevin	10	9	3.42	27	27	1	0	163	175	79	62	78	101
Boskie, Shawn	4	2	3.18	8	8	1	0	51	46	22	18	21	51
*Bowden, Mark	0	0	0.82	11	0	0	0	11	6	1	1	4	8
Clay, Danny (19 Ind)	2	2	2.30	25	0	0	0	31	24	10	8	32	30
Clear, Mark	0	0	9.00	2	0	0	0	1	1	1	1	1	0
Coffman, Kevin	2	5	3.43	9	9	0	0	60	43	26	23	40	49
Damian, Len	4	3	4.38	23	5	0	0	51	59	30	25	20	26
*Harrison, Phil	4	6	4.77	29	10	0	1	66	61	42	35	43	58
Kallevig, Greg	4	10	5.67	19	16	0	0	94	118	73	59	36	35
*Kraemer, Joe	7	6	3.76	20	20	3	0	122	113	56	51	40	84

Bernard Gilkey ...45 SB

Cedric Landrum ...46 SB

Russ Morman 298-13-81

	W	L	ERA	G	GS	CG	SV	IP	H	R	ER	BB	SO
Lancaster, Les	0	1	4.08	6	0	0	1	18	20	10	8	5	15
Masters, Dave	1	4	12.30	9	8	0	0	26	42	36	36	32	22
Nunez, Jose	7	6	3.94	16	16	4	0	107	105	51	47	32	109
Pavlas, Dave	8	3	3.26	53	3	0	8	99	84	38	36	48	96
Pico, Jeff	0	0	5.79	1	1	0	0	5	7	3	3	0	1
Renfroe, Laddie	7	3	4.96	44	14	1	9	118	146	68	65	30	56
Ritter, Reggie	0	3	9.00	3	3	0	0	11	22	15	11	5	5
*Rosario, Dave	2	3	6.89	21	0	0	1	16	22	14	12	12	13
Slocumb, Heath	3	2	2.00	20	0	0	1	27	16	10	6	18	21
Sutcliffe, Rick	0	2	7.82	2	2	0	0	13	18	13	11	7	12
Wilkins, Dean	6	2	3.70	52	2	0	11	73	75	37	30	38	61
Wilmet, Paul	1	2	4.09	25	2	0	0	44	47	23	20	23	38
Zarranz, Fernando	1	0	6.75	5	0	0	0	7	5	6	5	10	3

LOUISVILLE

BATTING	AVG	G	AB	R	H	2B	3B	HR	RBI	BB	SO	SB
#Alicea, Luis, 3b	.348	25	92	10	32	6	3	0	10	5	12	0
Austin, Pat, of	.000	8	8	0	0	0	0	0	1	1	2	0
*Brewer, Rod, 1b	.251	144	514	60	129	15	5	12	83	54	62	0
#Crosby, Todd, 2b-3b	.294	97	255	37	75	8	0	4	24	37	32	3
Figueroa, Bien, ss	.240	128	396	41	95	18	2	0	39	24	37	5
Fox, Mike, c	.333	5	9	0	3	1	0	0	0	2	1	0
*Francona, Terry, of	.263	86	285	29	75	9	3	6	30	12	23	1
*Fulton, Ed, c	.240	36	100	9	24	5	2	2	14	8	16	2
Gilkey, Bernard, of	.295	132	499	83	147	26	8	3	46	75	49	45
Lankford, Ray, of	.260	132	473	61	123	25	8	10	72	72	81	30
*Maclin, Lonnie, of	.310	17	58	9	18	3	2	0	6	7	11	1
Martinez, Julian, 3b-ss	.213	94	267	34	57	17	0	2	23	38	51	1
*Mendez, Jesus, of-1b	.190	47	79	5	15	1	0	0	6	9	8	0
Nichols, Gary, c	.143	27	63	5	9	1	0	0	2	6	13	1
Nunez, Mauricio, of	.248	106	214	24	53	9	1	0	26	15	21	4
#Pena, Geronimo, 2b-ss	.249	118	390	65	97	24	6	6	35	69	116	24
Royer, Stan, 3b	.267	4	15	1	4	1	1	0	4	2	5	0
#Silver, Roy, dh-of	.248	88	226	30	56	11	2	0	21	23	17	1
Stephens, Ray, c	.221	98	294	20	65	8	1	3	27	27	74	0
Wilson, Craig, 2b-3b	.279	124	204	30	57	9	2	2	23	28	15	5

PITCHING	W	L	ERA	G	GS	CG	SV	IP	H	R	ER	BB	SO
*Alba, Gibson	2	4	5.09	9	9	1	0	41	36	25	23	21	41
Arnold, Scott	1	3	6.08	14	4	0	0	47	56	38	32	23	23
Camacho, Ernie	1	1	4.41	15	0	0	2	16	16	10	8	7	15
Carpenter, Cris	10	8	3.70	22	22	2	0	143	146	61	59	21	100
*Clarke, Stan	10	9	4.56	32	21	0	0	150	159	82	76	51	93
*Cormier, Rheal	1	1	2.25	4	4	0	0	24	18	8	6	3	9
Cox, Danny	0	3	15.55	4	3	0	0	11	22	20	19	10	6
*Francona, Terry	0	0	1.17	5	0	0	0	8	4	1	1	2	6
Grater, Mark	0	2	3.18	24	0	0	3	28	24	13	10	15	18
Heinkel, Don	0	1	10.38	1	1	0	0	4	3	5	5	1	2
Hill, Ken	6	1	1.79	12	12	2	0	85	47	20	17	27	104
Hilton, Howard	4	3	3.60	56	1	0	0	80	73	40	32	34	55
Hinkle, Mike	8	7	3.29	29	18	1	0	129	126	53	47	40	66
Kisten, Dale	0	0	6.75	9	0	0	0	13	15	10	10	8	10
*Mathews, Greg	0	2	9.22	4	4	0	0	14	18	15	14	12	6
Niedenfuer, Tom	0	0	2.45	5	0	0	2	7	5	2	2	4	7
Olivares, Omar	10	11	2.82	23	23	5	0	159	127	58	50	59	88
Osteen, Dave	5	2	3.42	13	10	0	0	71	74	29	27	26	34
Oyster, Jeff	0	0	4.50	2	0	0	0	2	2	1	1	2	1
*Parker, Steve (44 Iowa)	1	2	5.34	50	2	0	1	64	85	44	38	26	40
Perez, Mike	7	7	4.28	57	0	0	31	67	64	34	32	33	69
Potestio, Frank	0	1	10.13	2	2	0	0	5	10	7	6	6	2
*Richardson, Dave	0	0	1.69	5	0	0	0	5	1	1	1	1	2
*Sherrill, Tim	4	3	2.49	52	0	0	2	61	49	17	17	21	57
Stone, Brian	1	0	6.23	3	0	0	0	4	4	3	3	8	3
Tewksbury, Bob	3	2	2.43	6	6	2	0	41	41	15	11	3	22
*Trout, Steve	1	1	5.68	4	4	0	0	19	24	12	12	9	12

AA DEPARTMENT LEADERS

BATTING

R	Joe Redfield, Denver	87
H	Skeeter Barnes, Nash	156
TB	Juan Gonzalez, Okla. City	252
2B	Mark Ryal, Buffalo	34
3B	Steve Carter, Buffalo	12
HR	Juan Gonzalez, Okla. City	29
RBI	Juan Gonzalez, Okla. City	101
SH	Jim Olander, Denver	9
	Ray Stephens, Louisville	9
SF	Luis DeLosSantos, Omaha	12
BB	Bernard Gilkey, Lou	75
IBB	Mark Ryal, Buffalo	9
	Ray Lankford, Louisville	9
HBP	Geronimo Pena, Lou	18
SO	Chito Martinez, Omaha	129
SB	Cedric Landrum, Iowa	46
CS	Bernard Gilkey, Lou	32
OB%	Brad Bierley, Iowa	.392

PITCHING

G	Mike Perez, Louisville	57
	Eddie Dixon, Indianapolis	57
GS	Rodney Imes, Nashville	29
	Dorn Taylor, Buffalo	29
CG	Scott Anderson, Indianapolis	6
ShO	Chris Hammond, Nashville	3
Sv	Mike Perez, Louisville	31
W	Chris Hammond, Nashville	15
L	Mark Petkovsek, Okla. City	14
IP	Dorn Taylor, Buffalo	195
H	Mark Petkovsek, Okla. City	187
R	Mark Petkovsek, Okla. City	103
HR	Greg Kallevig, Iowa	20
	Stan Clarke, Louisville	20
BB	Mike York, Buffalo	78
	Kevin Blankenship, Iowa	78
HB	Dave Pavlas, Iowa	10
SO	Chris Hammond, Nash	149
WP	Three tied at	11
Bk	Ray Chadwick, Omaha	10

NASHVILLE

BATTING	AVG	G	AB	R	H	2B	3B	HR	RBI	BB	SO	SB
Barnes, Skeeter, of	.285	144	548	83	156	21	2	7	66	47	57	34
#Bates, Billy, 2b (25 Den)	.293	98	362	51	106	15	3	0	34	29	28	15
Benavides, Freddie, ss	.211	77	266	30	56	7	3	2	20	12	50	3
*Casillas, Adam, 1b-of	.320	7	25	3	8	3	0	0	1	8	3	0
Colvard, Benny, of	.267	14	30	1	8	0	0	0	2	1	6	0
Defrancesco, Tony, c	.278	13	36	4	10	2	0	0	5	1	9	1
*Garcia, Leo, of	.287	129	435	62	125	33	8	6	39	33	44	11
Gonzalez, Denny, 3b	.397	52	184	36	73	8	0	8	36	37	33	3
#Jefferson, Reggie, 1b	.270	37	126	24	34	11	2	5	23	14	30	1
Jones, Chris, of	.261	134	436	53	114	23	3	10	52	23	86	12
Lane, Brian, 3b	.193	48	161	17	31	6	0	1	20	18	48	3
Lee, Terry, of	.304	72	260	38	79	18	1	15	67	31	47	3
*Lockhart, Keith, 2b-ss	.260	126	431	48	112	25	4	9	63	51	74	8
*Lombardozzi, Chris, 3b-2b	.067	8	15	0	1	0	1	0	1	3	3	0
McGriff, Terry, c	.280	94	325	44	91	17	0	9	54	38	46	2
*Morris, Hal, of	.344	16	64	8	22	5	0	1	10	5	10	4
#Nelson, Jerome, of	.220	51	132	19	29	3	2	1	8	9	17	6
Noce, Paul, ss-2b	.218	100	293	46	64	10	2	2	18	28	63	18
Pearson, Kevin, 2b-ss	.236	38	110	8	26	4	0	2	15	7	11	3
#Scott, Donnie, c-1b	.226	78	243	18	55	12	3	0	21	24	30	0
#Tanner, Eddie, inf	.261	93	222	24	58	12	0	4	22	19	12	0

PITCHING	W	L	ERA	G	GS	CG	SV	IP	H	R	ER	BB	SO
Allen, Neil	0	0	6.60	12	0	0	1	15	22	12	11	6	10
*Birtsas, Tim	2	4	4.37	8	5	2	0	35	33	21	17	16	34
Brown, Keith	7	8	2.39	39	9	1	9	94	83	37	25	24	50
Gross, Kip	12	7	3.33	40	11	2	3	127	113	54	47	47	62
*Hammond, Chris	15	1	2.17	24	24	5	0	149	118	43	36	63	149
Hill, Milton	4	4	2.27	48	0	0	3	71	51	20	18	18	58
Imes, Rodney	10	8	3.71	29	29	3	0	170	175	82	70	68	97
*Jackson, Danny	1	0	0.00	2	2	0	0	11	9	0	0	4	3
*Lazor, Joe	0	1	7.90	11	0	0	0	14	14	12	12	11	9
Lopez, Rob	7	10	3.38	28	25	4	0	144	141	72	54	50	76
Mahler, Rick	0	1	2.45	1	1	0	0	7	6	2	2	3	5
*Minutelli, Gino	5	2	3.22	11	11	3	0	78	65	34	28	31	61
Mitchell, Charlie	6	3	3.25	40	0	0	3	80	76	33	29	13	58
Moore, Bobby	1	1	7.79	13	0	0	1	17	18	15	15	9	14
*Powell, Ross	0	0	3.38	3	0	0	0	3	1	1	1	0	4
Rijo, Jose	0	0	8.31	1	1	0	0	4	5	4	4	2	2
*Rodriguez, Rosario	0	1	10.38	5	0	0	0	4	4	5	5	3	1
Scudder, Scott	7	1	2.34	11	11	1	0	81	53	27	21	32	60
Vasquez, Luis	4	6	3.64	18	18	1	0	99	85	46	40	59	54
*Vierra, Joey	3	3	3.28	49	0	0	1	58	55	25	21	25	37

OKLAHOMA CITY

BATTING	AVG	G	AB	R	H	2B	3B	HR	RBI	BB	SO	SB
Allanson, Andy, c	.100	13	40	3	4	0	0	0	4	6	7	0
Berger, Mike, c-1b	.236	83	267	32	63	15	6	5	21	35	64	0
Buechele, Steve, 3b	.143	6	21	1	3	0	0	1	1	2	4	0
Capra, Nick, of	.277	122	451	80	125	26	3	5	45	68	61	35
Coolbaugh, Scott, 3b	.225	76	293	39	66	17	2	6	30	27	62	0
*Dodson, Pat, 1b	.217	23	69	4	15	2	0	1	9	9	13	0
Engle, Dave, 1b-dh	.241	16	54	6	13	6	1	1	7	6	6	0
#Espy, Cecil, of	.270	34	126	15	34	4	1	2	20	15	29	7
Fariss, Monty, ss	.302	62	225	30	68	12	3	4	31	34	48	1
Garman, Pat, 1b	.236	19	55	3	13	1	1	1	6	7	22	0
Gonzalez, Juan, of	.258	128	496	78	128	29	4	29	101	32	109	2
Green, Gary, ss	.234	55	167	19	39	11	0	4	25	22	43	1
#House, Bryan, 2b	.277	126	513	79	142	26	8	0	36	37	70	30

	AVG	G	AB	R	H	2B	3B	HR	RBI	BB	SO	SB
Kreuter, Chad, c	.223	92	291	41	65	17	1	7	35	52	80	0
Kunkel, Jeff, ss	.421	4	19	0	8	1	0	0	3	0	2	0
Loy, Darren, c	.222	3	9	2	2	1	0	0	2	1	2	0
Millay, Gar, of-1b	.257	104	327	39	84	16	2	3	42	38	53	4
Motley, Darryl, of-dh (33 Nash)	.266	100	350	42	93	18	2	3	38	31	67	8
Palmer, Dean, 3b-1b	.218	88	316	33	69	17	4	12	39	20	106	1
*Reimer, Kevin, dh-1b	.283	51	198	24	56	18	2	4	33	18	25	2
Russell, John, c	.409	6	22	7	9	4	0	2	6	2	3	0
#Tatis, Bernie, of	.189	55	175	23	33	4	2	3	17	18	36	11
Washington, Ron, inf	.238	101	357	37	85	15	6	1	23	5	60	7
Williams, Reggie, of	.274	50	164	16	45	7	0	3	19	22	23	7

PITCHING	W	L	ERA	G	GS	CG	SV	IP	H	R	ER	BB	SO
Alexander, Gerald	13	2	4.10	20	20	2	0	119	126	58	54	45	94
Arnsberg, Brad	0	4	5.16	14	3	0	2	30	35	19	17	10	17
*Barfield, John	1	6	3.53	19	3	0	1	43	44	21	17	21	25
*Bohanon, Brian	1	2	3.66	14	4	0	1	32	35	16	13	8	22
Bronkey, Jeff	2	0	4.35	28	0	0	0	52	58	28	25	28	18
Bryant, Phil	4	5	5.90	14	9	1	0	58	61	41	38	21	22
Castillo, Felipe	1	3	3.45	20	1	0	0	29	40	19	11	10	12
Cecena, Jose	0	0	6.52	9	0	0	0	10	11	7	7	4	9
*Daniel, Clay	0	0	3.68	5	0	0	0	7	6	4	3	1	6
Guzman, Jose	0	3	5.65	7	7	0	0	29	35	20	18	9	26
Hardy, Jack	5	4	2.34	53	0	0	4	88	81	29	23	25	78
*Hayward, Ray	5	9	5.16	18	17	1	0	89	92	55	51	49	61
Lankard, Steve	0	0	5.13	12	0	0	0	26	34	20	15	7	18
*Lynch, David	0	4	5.74	14	2	0	1	27	34	24	17	14	20
Mathews, Terry	2	7	3.69	12	11	1	0	71	81	39	29	15	36
McMurtry, Craig	1	1	2.70	6	5	0	0	27	31	15	8	21	19
Mielke, Gary	0	0	1.59	5	0	0	0	6	5	2	1	4	7
Miller, David	7	9	4.78	31	21	2	0	143	165	88	76	53	92
Petkovsek, Mark	7	14	5.25	28	28	2	0	151	187	103	88	42	81
Rosenthal, Wayne	3	4	3.00	42	0	0	14	48	40	24	16	18	39
Satzinger, Jeff	1	4	5.13	23	4	0	0	47	51	28	27	27	23
St.Claire, Randy	1	2	2.01	29	0	0	1	54	45	15	12	12	68

OMAHA

BATTING	AVG	G	AB	R	H	2B	3B	HR	RBI	BB	SO	SB
Brumfield, Jacob, of	.325	24	77	10	25	6	1	2	11	7	14	10
Burrell, Kevin, c	.219	65	201	22	44	6	0	5	28	9	52	3
*Castaneda, Nick, 1b-dh	.429	5	14	1	6	1	0	1	1	1	4	0
DelosSantos, Luis, 3b-1b	.280	135	521	55	146	23	1	5	74	34	82	2
Garber, Jeff, 3b	.000	1	1	0	0	0	0	0	0	0	1	0
*Hamelin, Bob, 1b-dh	.232	90	271	31	63	11	2	8	30	62	78	2
#Hinzo, Tommy, 2b-of	.243	35	111	16	27	5	1	0	9	2	22	6
#Loggins, Mike, of	.250	73	208	25	52	10	4	2	31	20	39	10
*Martinez, Chito, of	.264	122	364	59	96	12	8	21	67	54	129	6
Meacham, Bobby, 2b-ss	.225	114	329	50	74	13	5	3	35	49	84	9
Morman, Russ, 1b-of	.298	121	436	67	130	14	9	13	81	51	78	21
Palacios, Rey, 3b-c	.133	4	15	2	2	0	1	0	2	0	6	0
Pecota, Bill, 3b-2b	.302	29	116	30	35	6	0	4	13	17	17	11
Pulliam, Harvey, of	.268	123	436	72	117	18	5	16	72	49	82	9
*Reece, Thad, 3b-2b	.232	64	190	25	44	3	3	1	14	14	16	6
*Schulz, Jeff, of	.299	69	231	35	69	16	1	4	27	16	46	2
Shumpert, Terry, 2b	.255	39	153	24	39	6	4	2	12	14	28	18
Spehr, Tim, c	.225	102	307	42	69	10	2	6	34	41	88	5
Thurman, Gary, of	.331	98	381	65	126	14	8	0	26	31	68	39
Zuvella, Paul, ss	.283	111	407	47	115	16	1	5	41	38	39	11

PITCHING	W	L	ERA	G	GS	CG	SV	IP	H	R	ER	BB	SO
Appier, Kevin	2	0	1.50	3	3	0	0	18	15	3	3	3	17
Baller, Jay	3	6	3.24	52	0	0	20	75	69	35	27	33	68
*Campbell, Jim	2	2	1.32	4	4	1	0	27	25	4	4	10	19
Chadwick, Ray	7	11	5.00	42	16	1	2	131	125	79	73	63	102
Clark, Dera	8	3	3.73	17	17	0	0	92	82	40	38	44	66
Codiroli, Chris	1	1	5.63	4	4	0	0	16	19	10	10	9	9
Crawford, Steve	0	0	0.00	4	0	0	0	6	9	0	0	2	11
Dozier, Tom	2	1	5.63	4	2	0	0	16	14	11	10	10	7
Encarnacion, Luis	6	5	2.96	44	0	0	7	76	70	30	25	30	62
Everson, Greg	4	0	2.35	33	0	0	2	61	48	18	16	30	29
*Ferreira, Tony	6	6	3.78	33	17	1	1	138	143	61	58	52	79
*Filson, Pete	12	2	2.78	17	17	1	0	107	107	41	33	31	66
Johnston, Joel	0	0	0.00	2	0	0	0	3	1	0	0	1	3
Lemasters, Jim	11	10	3.16	30	25	3	0	154	170	69	54	55	86
*Magnante, Mike	2	5	4.11	13	13	2	0	77	72	39	35	25	56
McGaffigan, Andy	2	1	3.71	10	0	0	0	17	22	7	7	5	17
Moeller, Dennis	5	2	4.02	11	11	1	0	65	63	29	29	30	53
Smith, Daryl	6	2	3.09	11	10	0	0	64	59	25	22	32	56
Stottlemyre, Mel	2	1	1.51	29	0	0	13	42	26	9	7	11	33
Tresemer, Mike	1	1	9.00	11	0	0	0	16	29	16	16	4	13
*Walter, Gene	4	1	3.20	20	7	1	3	59	52	24	21	32	43
*Wilkinson, Bill	0	0	7.11	7	0	0	0	6	10	5	5	5	4

INTERNATIONAL LEAGUE

Big '90 season has IL looking at expansion

By PATTI SINGER

Before the 1990 season was complete, the International League had a blueprint for change.

The IL received expansion inquiries during the course of the season from Ottawa, Ontario; Springfield, Mass.; Dayton, Ohio and Grand Rapids, Mich. At its September meeting, the IL, along with the American Association and Pacific Coast League, received applications from several more cities.

With the National League committed to expanding in 1993, Triple-A baseball will be one of the beneficiaries. The IL was preparing for a decidedly new look over the next several years.

Even established clubs, concerned about the competition for

Leo Gomez
. . . .277-28-97

franchises, want to make things better. The New York Mets informed the Tidewater Tides that they want a new stadium or vast improvements at Met Park, or they would take the franchise elsewhere. The city of Norfolk, Va., was putting together a plan to keep the Mets in Tidewater.

Big gates in Columbus, Scranton

Led by 584,010 fans in Columbus and 545,844 more in

LEAGUE CHAMPIONS

Playoff Champions, Where Applicable
(Since 1900)

1990—Rochester	1959—Havana	1928—Rochester
1989—Richmond	1958—Montreal	1927—Buffalo
1988—Rochester	1957—Buffalo	1926—Toronto
1987—Columbus	1956—Rochester	1925—Baltimore
1986—Richmond	1955—Rochester	1924—Baltimore
1985—Tidewater	1954—Syracuse	1923—Baltimore
1984—Pawtucket	1953—Montreal	1922—Baltimore
1983—Tidewater	1952—Rochester	1921—Baltimore
1982—Richmond	1951—Montreal	1920—Baltimore
1981—Columbus	1950—Baltimore	1919—Baltimore
1980—Columbus	1949—Montreal	1918—Toronto
1979—Columbus	1948—Montreal	1917—Toronto
1978—Richmond	1947—Syracuse	1916—Buffalo
1977—Charleston	1946—Montreal	1915—Buffalo
1976—Syracuse	1945—Newark	1914—Providence
1975—Tidewater	1944—Baltimore	1913—Newark
1974—Rochester	1943—Syracuse	1912—Toronto
1973—Pawtucket	1942—Syracuse	1911—Rochester
1972—Tidewater	1941—Montreal	1910—Rochester
1971—Rochester	1940—Newark	1909—Rochester
1970—Syracuse	1939—Rochester	1908—Baltimore
1969—Syracuse	1938—Newark	1907—Toronto
1968—Jacksonville	1937—Newark	1906—Buffalo
1967—Toledo	1936—Buffalo	1905—Providence
1966—Toronto	1935—Syracuse	1904—Buffalo
1965—Toronto	1934—Toronto	1903—Jersey City
1964—Rochester	1933—Buffalo	1902—Toronto
1963—Indianapolis	1932—Newark	1901—Rochester
1962—Atlanta	1931—Rochester	1900—Providence
1961—Buffalo	1930—Rochester	
1960—Toronto	1929—Rochester	

Hensley Meulens led Columbus to first place in the IL's Western Division by slamming 26 homers and 96 RBIs.

Scranton/Wilkes-Barre, the International League drew 2,777,395 fans during 1990. Here's some of what they saw:

The Rochester Red Wings won their opening game of the season, and led the Eastern Division wire-to-wire. The Red Wings' 89 victories were the most in their 30-year affiliation with the Baltimore Orioles, and their highest total since 1953.

Columbus, after a brief scare from Tidewater, won the West. The Clippers went into Tidewater in a late-season series with a three-game lead, but won the series and never were threatened again.

The Red Wings won their second IL title in three years, beating the Clippers in the Governors' Cup playoffs, three games to two. After taking a 2-0 lead at home, the Red Wings lost the next two games in Columbus, setting up a winner-take-all fifth game. The Red Wings cleaned the table with a 5-1 victory, as Mickey Weston (11-1, 1.98 during the regular season) won for the second time in the series.

Tony Chance led Rochester in the series with a .389 average and seven RBIs, while Leo Gomez drilled three homers. Only 12,405 took in the five games.

Three managerial changes

For the second time in two seasons, a manager boarded the Columbus-New York shuttle. Stump Merrill went to the Yankees June 6, replacing Bucky Dent, who was fired.

Rick Down, who has made a career of being manager pro tem in Columbus, took over the Clippers, who at the time were in first place in the West. Down also replaced Dent in 1989.

Down said his job was to make sure he didn't mess up a good thing, and he didn't. The Clippers grew stronger, and won the West with an 87-59 record, eight games ahead of second-place Tidewater.

The Pawtucket Red Sox also lost their manager, but for a different reason. On June 27, the Boston Red Sox fired Ed Nottle, who in his fifth season was the dean of IL managers. The Red

Rochester's David Segui, left, won the IL batting title in 1990, while Syracuse's Mark Whiten was rated the top prospect.

Sox replaced Nottle with organization man Johnny Pesky, but the result was the same. Pawtucket, which hasn't made the playoffs since the old four-team format in 1986, finished last in the four-team East Division for the second straight season.

But the 1990 season had its moments for the Pawsox. They set an attendance record of 290,953 fans, who came to see prospects Mo Vaughn, Phil Plantier, Tim Naehring and Scott Cooper—some of the best young players Boston has provided in several seasons.

Toledo also changed managers, axing John Wockenfuss a month into the season. He was replaced by Detroit's minor league field coordinator, Tom Gamboa, who himself was fired at the end of the season.

Gold Stars to:

■ Thirty-six-year-old lefthander Dan Boone, who pitched the first Red Wings no-hitter in 16 seasons. Boone, a seventh-generation nephew of pioneer Daniel Boone, shut down the Syracuse Chiefs in the second game of doubleheader July 23.

Boone, discovered throwing a knuckleball for the Bradenton Explorers of the Senior Professional Baseball League by Orioles scout Birdie Tebbetts, finished second in the league with a 2.60 ERA, and he didn't get his first of nine starts until June 28. Boone, who had been out of baseball since 1984 and hadn't pitched in the majors since 1982, earned a promotion to Baltimore in September.

■ Scranton's Wally Ritchie, who had a no-hitter through the first seven innings of a regulation seven inning game, also against the Chiefs. He lost it in the eighth.

■ Syracuse first baseman Jim Eppard, who shook off a slump early in the season and won the batting title over Tidewater's Keith Hughes, .310 to .309.

■ Pawtucket's 20-year-old outfielder Phil Plantier, who won the home run title with 33, despite 147 strikeouts.

1990 FINAL STANDINGS

East	W	L	Pct.	GB
Rochester (Orioles)	89	56	.614	—
Scranton/Wilkes-Barre (Phillies) ..	68	78	.466	21½
Syracuse (Blue Jays)	62	83	.428	27
Pawtucket (Red Sox)	62	84	.425	27½
West				
Columbus (Yankees)	87	59	.596	—
Tidewater (Mets)	79	67	.541	8
Richmond (Braves)	71	74	.490	15½
Toledo (Tigers)..............	58	86	.403	28

Playoffs: Rochester defeated Columbus 3-2 in best-of-5 final for league championship; Omaha (American Association) defeated Rochester 4-1 in best-of-7 Triple-A Classic.

Regular-Season Attendance: Columbus, 584,010; Scranton, 545,844; Richmond, 427,552; Rochester, 331,927; Pawtucket, 290,953; Syracuse, 245,045; Tidewater, 193,055; Toledo, 159,009.

Managers: Columbus—Stump Merrill, Rick Down; **Pawtucket**—Ed Nottle, Johnny Pesky; **Richmond**—Jim Beauchamp; **Rochester**—Greg Biagini; **Scranton**—Bill Dancy; **Syracuse**—Bob Bailor; **Tidewater**—Steve Swisher; **Toledo**—John Wockenfuss, Tom Gamboa.

1990 Official All-Star Team: C—Brian Dorsett, Columbus. **1B**—David Segui, Rochester. **2B**—Luis Sojo, Syracuse. **3B**—Leo Gomez, Rochester. **SS**—Tim Naehring, Pawtucket. **OF**—Hensley Meulens, Columbus; Phil Plantier, Pawtucket; Mark Whiten, Syracuse. **DH**—Chris Hoiles, Rochester. **SP**—Dave Eiland, Columbus. **RP**—Todd Frohwirth, Scranton. **Most Valuable Player**—Hensley Meulens, Columbus. **Most Valuable Pitcher**—Dave Eiland, Columbus. **Rookie of the Year**—Phil Plantier, Pawtucket. **Manager of the Year**—Greg Biagini, Rochester.

Top 10 Major League Prospects (by Baseball America) 1. Mark Whiten, of, Syracuse; **2.** David Segui, 1b, Rochester; **3.** Hensley Meulens, of, Columbus; **4.** Steve Avery, lhp, Richmond; **5.** Travis Fryman, ss, Toledo; **6.** Leo Gomez, 3b, Rochester; **7.** Chris Hoiles, c, Rochester; **8.** Mo Vaughn, 1b, Pawtucket; **9.** Dave Eiland, rhp, Columbus; **10.** Jason Grimsley, rhp, Scranton.

1990 *BATTING, PITCHING STATS*

CLUB BATTING

	AVG	G	AB	R	H	2B	3B	HR	BB	SO	SB
Rochester	.273	145	4607	735	1259	216	38	109	610	872	104
Syracuse	.261	145	4709	569	1230	202	39	83	426	785	103
Columbus	.258	146	4695	710	1212	249	33	113	656	871	173
Tidewater	.256	146	4648	592	1191	205	24	65	530	701	99
Toledo	.254	144	4633	589	1178	241	30	94	472	789	104
Scranton/Wilkes-Barre	.251	146	4629	580	1163	184	36	90	524	936	95
Pawtucket	.249	146	4799	673	1194	243	23	165	535	1066	87
Richmond	.245	145	4669	559	1143	181	23	94	469	884	74

CLUB PITCHING

	ERA	G	CG	SHO	SV	IP	H	R	ER	BB	SO
Columbus	3.28	146	31	16	38	1256	1129	524	458	465	935
Tidewater	3.42	146	21	15	44	1231	1186	551	468	446	880
Richmond	3.62	145	16	7	41	1242	1197	576	500	521	825
Rochester	3.89	145	20	9	36	1214	1206	621	525	431	820
Syracuse	3.94	145	25	14	26	1224	1165	622	536	558	785
Scranton/Wilkes-Barre	4.10	146	8	5	39	1231	1096	641	560	575	862
Toledo	4.24	144	9	7	35	1220	1184	678	575	571	849
Pawtucket	4.65	146	20	4	31	1253	1318	741	648	507	775

INDIVIDUAL BATTING LEADERS
(Minimum 394 Plate Appearances)

	AVG	G	AB	R	H	2B	3B	HR	RBI	BB	SO	SB
*Eppard, Jim, Syr	.310	133	461	72	143	18	3	4	48	47	49	5
*Hughes, Keith, Tide	.309	117	379	77	117	24	5	10	53	57	58	7
*Torve, Kelvin, Tide	.303	115	402	62	122	25	1	11	76	56	43	9
*Vaughn, Mo, Paw	.295	108	386	62	114	26	1	22	72	44	87	3
*Azocar, Oscar, Col	.291	94	374	49	109	20	5	5	52	9	26	8
#Whiten, Mark, Syr	.290	104	390	65	113	19	4	14	48	37	72	14
Meulens, Hensley, Col	.285	136	480	81	137	20	5	26	96	66	132	6
Stanicek, Steve, Scr	.282	127	425	52	120	23	0	10	76	58	65	2
*Stone, Jeff, Paw	.280	112	393	51	110	28	1	8	41	31	84	25
#Miller, Keith, Scr	.280	143	508	82	142	27	2	11	74	57	87	12

INDIVIDUAL PITCHING LEADERS
(Minimum 117 Innings)

	W	L	ERA	G	GS	CG	SV	IP	H	R	ER	BB	SO
Marak, Paul, Rich	9	8	2.49	32	16	5	0	148	130	49	41	50	75
*Boone, Dan, Roch	11	5	2.60	47	9	3	8	121	96	44	35	30	65
Eiland, Dave, Col	16	5	2.87	27	26	11	0	175	155	63	56	32	96
*Adkins, Steve, Col	15	7	2.90	27	27	6	0	177	153	72	57	98	138
*Kilgus, Paul, Syr	6	8	2.94	20	17	7	0	126	116	47	41	39	75
Valera, Julio, Tide	10	10	3.02	24	24	9	0	158	146	66	53	39	133
Davidson, Bob, Col	5	8	3.37	40	12	2	5	128	134	58	48	25	69
Linton, Doug, Syr	10	10	3.40	26	26	8	0	177	154	77	67	67	113
*Polley, Dale, Rich	4	7	3.53	36	15	1	0	135	121	66	53	48	64
*Brown, Kevin, Tide	10	6	3.55	26	24	3	0	134	138	71	53	60	109

COLUMBUS

BATTING	AVG	G	AB	R	H	2B	3B	HR	RBI	BB	SO	SB
*Azocar, Oscar, of	.291	94	374	49	109	20	5	5	52	9	26	8
Blowers, Mike, 3b	.339	62	230	30	78	20	6	6	50	29	40	3
Brower, Bob, of	.230	66	204	41	47	5	1	2	27	30	38	34
Cerone, Rick, c	.091	4	11	0	1	0	0	0	1	2	1	0
Datz, Jeff, c	.238	28	63	4	15	4	0	0	10	5	9	0
Dorsett, Brian, c	.272	114	415	44	113	28	1	14	67	49	71	1
Fishel, John, of	.200	93	185	20	37	11	0	3	21	39	36	6
Green, Bobby, of	.000	1	2	0	0	0	0	0	0	0	0	0
Leyritz, Jim, 3b	.289	59	204	36	59	11	1	8	32	37	33	4
Lyden, Mitch, 1b	.224	41	147	18	33	8	0	7	20	7	34	0
*Maas, Jason, of-dh	.248	81	210	42	52	9	2	4	29	37	46	13
*Maas, Kevin, 1b-dh	.284	57	194	37	55	15	2	13	38	34	45	2
Meulens, Hensley, of-1b	.285	136	480	81	137	20	5	26	96	66	132	6
Ramos, John, c	.000	2	6	0	0	0	0	0	0	1	0	0
#Rodriguez, Carlos, ss	.273	71	220	31	60	12	0	0	16	30	8	3
*Sanders, Deion, of	.321	22	84	21	27	7	1	2	10	17	15	9
Sax, Dave, c	.249	73	205	18	51	9	0	4	19	32	38	2
Sepanek, Rob, 1b	.233	45	90	13	21	7	0	2	9	17	24	0
*Snider, Van, of	.235	127	409	61	96	26	0	15	49	35	118	7
Sparks, Don, 3b	.118	16	51	3	6	3	0	0	2	2	10	0
Stankiewicz, Andy, 2b-ss	.229	135	446	68	102	14	4	1	48	71	63	25
*Walewander, Jim, 2b-3b	.250	131	368	80	92	14	5	1	31	90	67	49
Wasinger, Mark, 3b-2b	.194	25	62	8	12	5	0	0	4	14	13	0
*Zeihen, Bob, of	.265	10	34	5	9	1	0	0	4	4	3	1

PITCHING	W	L	ERA	G	GS	CG	SV	IP	H	R	ER	BB	SO
*Adkins, Steve	15	7	2.90	27	27	6	0	177	153	72	57	98	138
Burns, Britt	0	1	12.00	1	1	0	0	3	5	4	4	3	3
Chapin, Darrin	0	1	7.27	6	0	0	2	9	10	8	7	6	8
Clayton, Royal	1	2	3.81	4	4	0	0	26	33	12	11	7	15
Davidson, Bob	5	8	3.37	40	12	2	5	128	134	58	48	25	69
Davis, Ron	0	1	4.76	10	0	0	1	11	6	6	6	6	6
Eiland, Dave	16	5	2.87	27	26	11	0	175	155	63	56	32	96
Green, John	0	0	0.00	2	0	0	0	3	2	0	0	1	0
Habyan, John	7	7	3.21	36	11	1	6	112	99	52	40	30	77
*Holcomb, Scott	0	0	0.00	2	0	0	0	2	2	3	0	0	0
Jones, Jimmy	5	2	2.34	11	11	3	0	73	46	20	19	35	78
Leiter, Mark	9	4	3.60	30	14	2	1	123	114	56	49	27	115
McCullers, Lance	0	0	0.00	3	0	0	0	3	0	0	0	2	2
Mills, Alan	3	3	3.38	17	0	0	6	29	22	11	11	14	30
*Mmahat, Kevin	11	5	3.76	20	20	1	0	115	99	52	48	61	81
Monteleone, Rich	4	4	2.24	38	0	0	9	64	51	17	16	23	60
*Pena, Hipolito	1	0	12.60	9	0	0	0	5	8	7	7	4	1
Smith, Mike	0	0	0.00	2	0	0	0	4	5	1	0	1	4
Smith, Willie	3	1	6.23	33	0	0	7	35	38	24	24	29	47
Taylor, Wade	6	4	2.19	14	14	4	0	99	91	25	24	30	57
Torres, Ricky	0	2	4.46	21	3	0	1	42	37	24	21	21	34

PAWTUCKET

BATTING	AVG	G	AB	R	H	2B	3B	HR	RBI	BB	SO	SB
*Cooper, Scott, 3b	.266	124	433	56	115	17	1	12	44	39	75	2
Flaherty, John, c	.227	99	317	35	72	18	0	4	32	24	43	1
Gonzalez, Angel, 2b-3b	.185	66	173	27	32	6	1	1	12	22	25	1
Kutcher, Randy, ss	.316	35	136	18	43	8	1	1	14	14	19	2
*Lancellotti, Rick, dh-1b	.223	127	430	63	96	15	1	20	61	61	105	1
Marshall, Mike, of	.304	6	23	5	7	0	0	2	4	3	3	0
Marzano, John, c	.320	26	75	16	24	4	1	2	8	11	9	6
#McDougal, Julius, ss-2b	.246	105	362	45	89	13	2	9	47	46	68	8
Naehring, Tim, ss-3b	.269	82	290	45	78	16	1	15	47	37	56	0
Pankovits, Jim, 2b-of	.231	122	468	64	108	26	3	9	52	49	87	13
Pina, Mickey, of	.223	123	421	49	94	26	2	9	47	44	118	15
*Plantier, Phil, of	.253	123	430	83	109	22	3	33	79	62	148	1
*Robidoux, Billy Jo, dh	.204	22	54	5	11	1	0	3	7	9	16	0
*Stone, Jeff, of-dh	.280	112	393	51	110	28	1	8	41	31	84	25
Tremblay, Gary, c	.210	44	105	15	22	5	1	4	13	12	26	0
*Vaughn, Mo, 1b	.295	108	386	62	114	26	1	22	72	44	87	3
Wade, Scott, of	.231	105	303	34	70	12	4	11	41	27	97	9

PITCHING	W	L	ERA	G	GS	CG	SV	IP	H	R	ER	BB	SO
*Bast, Steve	7	16	5.65	25	23	2	0	147	158	97	92	64	91
*Bolton, Tom	1	0	3.86	4	2	0	0	12	9	6	5	7	8
Curry, Steve	0	1	11.00	3	0	0	0	9	21	11	11	2	5
*Dalton, Mike	7	4	2.55	49	2	1	5	99	94	42	28	22	49
Dopson, John	2	1	4.91	5	5	0	0	22	28	12	12	8	13
Gray, Jeff	0	0	3.41	21	0	0	1	32	20	14	12	7	35
Guante, Cecilio	0	0	0.00	2	0	0	0	5	1	0	0	2	4
Hetzel, Eric	6	5	3.64	19	18	3	0	109	85	51	44	74	90
Irvine, Daryl	2	5	3.24	42	0	0	12	50	47	24	18	19	35
Johnson, Joe	6	7	5.16	29	27	2	1	171	213	107	98	35	70
Leister, John	2	10	5.78	19	17	2	1	95	114	65	61	39	47
Manzanillo, Josias	4	7	5.55	15	15	5	0	83	75	57	51	45	77
*Owen, Dave	3	2	4.71	6	6	2	0	42	40	23	22	19	26
Plympton, Jeff	1	0	0.00	11	0	0	3	17	10	0	0	11	11
*Rochford, Mike	3	3	2.70	9	8	1	0	43	36	19	13	13	31
Shikles, Larry	8	12	4.99	39	17	2	0	148	170	99	82	48	65

Phil Plantier
...33 homers

Dave Eiland
...16-5, 2.87

Todd Frohwirth
...21 saves

	W	L	ERA	G	GS	CG	SV	IP	H	R	ER	BB	SO
*Stewart, Tito	4	4	4.31	40	0	0	4	65	75	36	31	32	54
Trautwein, John	6	7	5.87	51	3	0	4	104	119	75	68	60	64

RICHMOND

BATTING	AVG	G	AB	R	H	2B	3B	HR	RBI	BB	SO	SB
Alva, John, 2b-ss	.249	99	341	38	85	12	2	1	23	19	68	0
Berroa, Geronimo, of	.269	135	499	56	134	17	2	12	80	34	89	4
Cabrera, Francisco, 1b ...	.227	35	132	12	30	3	1	7	20	7	23	2
Crabbe, Bruce, inf	.268	129	473	64	127	26	0	9	51	38	68	2
Denson, Drew, 1b	.231	90	295	25	68	4	1	7	29	26	57	0
Dowell, Ken, 2b	.200	36	80	7	16	2	1	0	7	17	13	0
#Hinzo, Tommy, 2b	.224	17	49	9	11	0	0	2	5	5	12	1
Hood, Dennis, of	.247	121	389	50	96	15	5	8	36	33	120	14
Hunter, Brian, of-1b	.197	43	137	13	27	4	0	5	16	18	37	2
Infante, Alex, 2b	.240	31	96	8	23	3	0	1	12	9	8	1
*Jones, Barry, of	.269	99	350	41	94	7	1	12	52	16	49	13
*Justice, Dave, of	.356	12	45	7	16	5	1	2	7	7	6	0
*Kremers, Jimmy, c	.232	63	190	25	44	8	0	6	24	35	47	1
Maldonado, Phil, c	.100	4	10	0	1	1	0	0	0	2	1	0
Mann, Kelly, c	.202	63	203	18	41	13	0	3	20	16	36	1
*Mizerock, John, c	.222	34	90	11	20	4	0	2	10	10	18	0
Morris, Rick, 3b	.111	17	27	0	3	0	0	0	1	2	8	0
Olson, Greg, c	.000	3	7	0	0	0	0	0	0	0	0	0
Rossy, Rico, ss	.232	107	380	58	88	13	0	4	32	69	43	13
*Taylor, Dwight, of	.255	39	106	17	27	1	2	1	11	9	20	4
*Tomberlin, Andy, of ...	.304	80	283	36	86	19	3	4	31	39	43	11
Tubbs, Greg, of	.217	11	23	3	5	0	0	0	1	11	6	0
Whited, Ed, 3b	.248	108	339	55	84	22	4	7	33	42	70	5

PITCHING	W	L	ERA	G	GS	CG	SV	IP	H	R	ER	BB	SO
*Alba, Gibson	1	3	3.25	12	2	0	0	28	9	12	10	19	19
*Avery, Steve	5	5	3.50	13	13	3	0	82	85	35	31	21	69
*Castillo, Tony	3	1	2.52	5	4	1	0	25	14	7	7	6	27
Czarnik, Chris	0	1	7.00	5	0	0	0	9	13	7	7	3	8
Freeman, Marvin (7 Scr) ..	3	4	4.18	9	9	1	0	47	45	25	22	28	43
*Gomez, Pat	1	1	8.80	4	4	0	0	15	19	16	15	10	8
Henry, Dwayne	1	1	2.33	13	0	0	2	27	12	7	7	16	36
Kerfeld, Charley	2	0	3.38	15	1	0	0	21	22	10	8	16	24
Laskey, Bill	6	4	2.79	49	1	0	14	87	83	32	27	29	60
*Lilliquist, Derek	4	0	2.57	5	1	0	0	35	31	11	10	11	24
Luecken, Rick	1	1	1.35	5	0	0	4	13	11	3	2	8	15
Marak, Paul	9	8	2.49	32	16	5	0	148	130	49	41	50	75
*Mercker, Kent	5	4	3.55	12	10	0	1	58	60	30	23	27	69
Nezelek, Andy	4	9	5.13	25	14	2	0	81	101	52	46	26	39
*Olwine, Ed	3	1	5.40	25	0	0	5	28	30	18	17	15	21
*Polley, Dale	4	7	3.53	36	15	1	0	135	121	66	53	48	64
Reynoso, Armando	3	1	2.25	4	3	0	0	24	26	7	6	7	15
Richards, Rusty	6	9	4.55	30	26	0	0	140	159	83	71	73	56
*Snyder, Brian	4	1	2.48	46	0	0	12	58	54	19	16	20	49
Taylor, Bill	0	0	0.00	2	0	0	0	3	4	0	0	0	0
Turner, Matt	2	3	3.86	22	1	0	2	42	44	20	18	16	36
*Upshaw, Lee	0	3	6.17	5	5	0	0	23	35	19	16	8	16
Ziem, Steve	0	0	3.60	7	0	0	1	10	13	4	4	5	7

ROCHESTER

BATTING	AVG	G	AB	R	H	2B	3B	HR	RBI	BB	SO	SB
#Bell, Juan, ss	.285	82	326	59	93	12	5	6	35	36	59	16
Brown, Marty, inf-of	.242	67	211	32	51	8	4	5	25	21	47	5
Chance, Tony, of	.269	130	454	55	122	17	4	14	75	41	115	14
#Contreras, Joaquin, of	.250	61	208	32	52	10	3	1	29	28	38	6
Dulin, Tim, 2b	.238	117	399	56	95	17	3	3	46	46	75	9
Eberle, Mike, c	.233	19	43	1	10	0	0	0	4	1	13	0
Gomez, Leo, 3b	.277	131	430	97	119	26	4	26	97	89	89	2
Harris, Walt, of	.154	4	13	1	2	0	0	0	1	2	1	1
Hithe, Victor, of	.274	71	164	20	45	7	2	0	15	16	41	5

	AVG	G	AB	R	H	2B	3B	HR	RBI	BB	SO	SB
Hoiles, Chris, c-dh	.348	74	247	52	86	20	1	18	56	44	48	4
*Horn, Sam, dh-1b	.414	17	58	16	24	3	0	9	26	9	13	0
Hulett, Tim, 2b	.372	14	43	10	16	2	1	2	4	11	7	0
Komminsk, Brad, of	.291	28	79	7	23	2	0	1	8	10	16	0
Lofton, Rodney, ss	.143	14	28	3	4	0	0	0	0	2	7	1
#McKnight, Jeff, of-ss	.280	100	339	56	95	21	3	7	45	41	58	7
Miller, Darrell, of-c	.204	21	54	2	11	1	0	0	5	7	13	1
Nixon, Donell, of	.247	85	291	54	72	3	4	2	26	42	55	21
*Padget, Chris, 1b-of	.279	74	240	33	67	15	1	6	43	18	30	0
#Segui, David, 1b	.336	86	307	55	103	28	0	2	51	45	28	5
Shamburg, Ken, 1b	.333	2	6	1	2	0	0	0	0	1	1	0
*Stanicek, Pete, 2b-1b	.174	28	86	13	15	3	0	0	6	12	12	0
Tackett, Jeff, c	.239	108	306	37	73	8	3	4	33	47	50	4
*Turner, Shane, of-inf	.282	86	209	29	59	7	0	1	19	25	41	3
*Walker, Greg, dh	.303	22	66	14	20	6	0	2	11	16	15	0

PITCHING	W	L	ERA	G	GS	CG	SV	IP	H	R	ER	BB	SO
Aldrich, Jay	4	1	5.37	30	1	0	3	54	72	38	32	7	34
Bautista, Jose	7	8	4.06	27	13	3	2	109	115	51	49	15	50
Bell, Eric	9	6	4.86	27	27	3	0	148	168	90	80	65	90
*Boone, Dan	11	5	2.60	47	9	3	8	121	96	44	35	30	65
DelaRosa, Francisco	0	0	0.00	2	0	0	1	9	4	0	0	1	1
*Hickey, Kevin	2	1	5.79	16	0	0	3	23	31	15	15	7	28
Holton, Brian	1	4	9.19	9	1	1	0	16	26	16	16	6	18
*Jones, Mike	2	3	6.00	8	5	0	0	30	36	23	20	14	27
Kelley, Anthony	1	0	5.14	2	1	0	0	7	4	4	4	6	2
*Linskey, Mike	7	9	3.58	19	18	2	0	111	116	60	44	28	54
McDonald, Ben	3	3	2.86	7	7	0	0	44	33	18	14	21	37
*McKeon, Joel	4	2	4.68	24	1	1	3	42	45	25	22	17	35
Mesa, Jose	1	2	2.42	4	4	0	0	26	21	11	7	12	23
Mitchell, John	5	0	1.57	8	7	3	0	46	39	9	8	9	15
Mussina, Mike	0	0	1.35	2	2	0	0	13	8	2	2	4	15
Schilling, Curt	4	4	3.92	15	14	1	0	87	95	46	38	25	83
Schwarz, Jeff	0	0	7.11	5	1	0	0	13	10	10	10	19	4
Smith, Mike	9	6	4.96	29	20	1	0	123	118	76	68	73	112
Stanhope, Chuck	1	0	4.09	4	0	0	0	11	7	5	5	4	5
Tirado, Aris	1	0	7.43	4	0	0	1	13	13	11	11	8	6
Weston, Mickey	11	1	1.98	29	12	2	6	109	93	36	24	22	58
Woodward, Rob	6	1	3.00	48	2	0	6	56	33	21	21	37	52

SCRANTON/WILKES-BARRE

BATTING	AVG	G	AB	R	H	2B	3B	HR	RBI	BB	SO	SB
*Adduci, Jim, of-1b	.244	121	353	30	86	11	1	6	40	17	89	2
Agostinelli, Sal, c	.203	71	182	12	37	2	1	0	15	22	20	6
*Bellino, Frank, dh	.167	9	18	0	3	0	0	0	2	1	5	0
*Ford, Curt, of	.221	56	194	28	43	5	3	5	12	23	39	14
Gibbons, John, c	.223	78	202	29	45	8	2	6	30	33	66	2
Heath, Kelly, 3b-of	.237	79	232	33	55	7	3	7	32	33	46	3
Infante, Kennedy, 3b	.229	40	131	12	30	4	0	2	10	6	14	0
*Jones, Ron, of-dh	.264	44	148	13	39	4	1	3	26	19	18	5
Jordan, Ricky, 1b	.279	27	104	8	29	1	0	2	11	5	18	0
*Knabenshue, Chris, of	.237	129	379	61	90	16	1	18	62	76	108	11
Legg, Greg, 3b-2b	.308	61	169	25	52	5	0	1	21	31	27	1
*Meadows, Louie, of	.273	48	172	29	47	6	2	4	18	21	36	12
#Miller, Keith, of-3b	.280	143	507	82	142	27	2	11	74	58	87	12
Morandini, Mickey, 2b	.260	139	503	76	131	24	10	1	31	60	90	16
Nieto, Tom, c	.223	37	112	9	25	2	0	2	15	8	36	0
Rayford, Floyd, dh-c	.152	19	33	0	5	2	0	0	6	3	5	0
Rosario, Victor, ss	.252	143	477	45	120	23	6	5	42	12	91	8
Stanicek, Steve, 1b-of	.282	127	425	52	120	23	0	10	76	58	65	2
Vatcher, Jim, of-3b	.254	55	181	30	46	12	4	5	22	32	33	1

PITCHING	W	L	ERA	G	GS	CG	SV	IP	H	R	ER	BB	SO
Boudreaux, Eric	1	2	9.45	8	1	0	0	13	23	16	14	8	9
Buonantony, Rich	0	0	5.40	8	0	0	0	12	11	8	7	11	10
DeJesus, Jose	1	4	3.38	10	10	1	0	56	41	30	21	39	45
Frohwirth, Todd	9	7	3.04	67	0	0	21	83	77	34	28	32	56
Grimsley, Jason	8	5	3.93	22	22	0	0	128	111	68	56	78	99
Greene, Tommy (19 Rich)	5	8	3.49	20	19	2	0	116	93	49	45	67	69
Madrid, Alex	3	8	4.65	16	15	0	0	93	91	52	48	40	56
Malone, Chuck	4	3	6.39	26	11	0	0	76	47	57	54	78	79
Mauser, Tim	5	7	3.66	16	16	4	0	98	75	48	40	34	54
*McElroy, Chuck	6	8	2.72	57	1	0	7	76	62	24	23	34	78
Moore, Brad	3	7	3.72	35	12	1	0	102	97	48	42	28	45
*Mulholland, Terry	0	1	3.00	1	1	0	0	6	9	4	2	2	2
Noles, Dickie	3	2	3.35	26	0	0	6	38	31	15	14	14	18
*Ritchie, Wally	4	3	4.15	20	13	1	0	82	75	46	38	28	47
Scanlan, Bob	8	11	4.85	23	23	1	0	130	128	79	70	59	74
Service, Scott	5	4	4.76	45	9	0	2	96	95	56	51	44	94
*Sharts, Steve	6	2	2.99	61	4	0	3	96	76	33	32	25	58

SYRACUSE

BATTING	AVG	G	AB	R	H	2B	3B	HR	RBI	BB	SO	SB
Bell, Derek, of	.261	109	402	57	105	13	5	7	56	23	75	21
DelaCruz, Hector, of-1b	.234	83	235	27	55	9	0	4	19	17	54	4
Diaz, Carlos, c	.203	77	251	18	51	10	0	1	19	17	51	2
*Ducey, Rob, of	.267	127	438	53	117	32	7	7	47	60	87	14

BATTING

R	Leo Gomez, Rochester . . 97
H	Jim Eppard, Syracuse . . 143
TB	Hensley Meulens, Col . . 245
2B	Torey Lovullo, Toledo . . . 38
3B	Mickey Morandini, Scr . . . 10
HR	Phil Plantier, Pawtucket . . 33
RBI	Leo Gomez, Rochester . . 97
SH	Jim Pankovits, Pawtucket 11
SF	Luis Sojo, Syracuse 9
BB	Jim Walewander, Col 90
IBB	Shawn Hare, Toledo 9
HBP	Jim Walewander, Col 11
SO	Phil Plantier, Pawtucket . 148
SB	Milt Cuyler, Toledo 52
CS	Milt Cuyler, Toledo 14
OB%	Jim Walewander, Col . . .408

PITCHING

G	Todd Frohwirth, Scranton . 67
GS	Scott Aldred, Toledo 29
CG	Dave Eiland, Columbus . . . 11
ShO	Three tied at 3
Sv	Todd Frohwirth, Scranton . 21
W	Dave Eiland, Columbus . . . 16
L	Steve Bast, Pawtucket . . . 16
IP	Doug Linton, Syracuse . . . 177
	Steve Adkins, Columbus . 177
H	Joe Johnson, Pawtucket . . 213
R	Joe Johnson, Pawtucket . . 107
HR	Joe Johnson, Pawtucket . . 24
BB	Steve Adkins, Columbus . . 98
HB	Joe Johnson, Pawtucket . . 10
SO	Manny Hernandez, Tide . 157
WP	Jason Grimsley, Scranton . 18
Bk	Steve Bast, Pawtucket . . . 12

BATTING	AVG	G	AB	R	H	2B	3B	HR	RBI	BB	SO	SB
*Dziadkowiec, Andy, c	.000	1	3	0	0	0	0	0	0	0	1	0
*Eppard, Jim, 1b	.310	133	461	72	143	18	3	4	48	47	49	5
Escobar, Jose, ss-2b	.270	79	252	16	68	6	2	0	17	18	35	3
Garrison, Webster, 2b	.198	37	101	12	20	5	1	0	14	20	0	
Munoz, Pedro, of-dh	.319	86	317	41	101	22	3	7	56	24	64	16
*Myers, Greg, c	.182	3	11	0	2	1	0	0	2	1	1	0
*Pederson, Stu, dh-of	.296	96	301	34	89	12	1	2	34	42	40	5
Rivers, Ken, c	.000	1	1	0	0	0	0	0	0	0	0	0
Runge, Paul, ss-3b	.233	119	391	45	91	11	3	6	31	59	67	3
Schunk, Jerry, 2b	.240	26	100	8	24	4	0	0	7	3	10	1
Sojo, Luis, 2b-ss	.296	75	297	39	88	12	3	6	25	14	23	10
Sprague, Ed, 3b	.239	142	519	60	124	23	5	20	75	31	100	4
*Szekely, Joe, c	.174	50	155	17	27	3	2	5	16	10	20	1
Virgil, Ozzie, c	.143	28	84	5	12	2	0	0	7	9	16	0
#Whiten, Mark, of	.290	104	390	65	113	19	4	14	48	37	72	14

PITCHING	W	L	ERA	G	GS	CG	SV	IP	H	R	ER	BB	SO
Blair, Willie	0	2	4.74	3	3	1	0	19	20	13	10	8	6
Blohm, Pete	0	1	7.20	4	0	0	0	5	5	7	4	3	4
*Boucher, Denis	8	5	3.85	17	17	2	0	108	100	52	46	37	80
Buchanan, Bob	5	3	3.52	24	6	1	5	64	63	32	25	25	21
Cummings, Steve	5	3	3.11	16	13	4	0	81	76	31	28	37	34
Gilles, Tom	3	3	2.14	43	0	0	5	71	58	21	16	21	44
Gozzo, Mauro	3	8	3.58	34	10	0	7	98	87	46	39	44	62
Jones, Chris	0	0	3.98	10	0	0	1	20	22	10	9	4	19
*Kilgus, Paul	6	8	2.94	20	17	7	0	126	116	47	41	39	75
*Leiter, Al	3	8	4.62	15	14	1	0	78	59	43	40	68	69
Linton, Doug	10	10	3.40	26	26	8	0	177	174	77	67	67	113
Loynd, Mike	4	8	3.68	24	8	0	1	86	68	39	35	34	65
Lysander, Rick	0	1	6.92	10	0	0	0	13	18	10	10	7	8
*MacDonald, Rob	0	2	5.40	9	0	0	2	8	4	5	5	9	6
Sanchez, Alex	5	9	5.71	22	22	1	0	112	111	77	71	79	65
*Shea, John	8	5	3.64	40	0	0	3	82	83	45	33	40	58
Wapnick, Steve	0	1	5.06	11	1	0	2	16	16	9	9	6	19
Williams, Woody	0	1	10.00	3	0	0	0	9	15	10	10	4	8
Wishnevski, Rob	2	5	6.66	9	8	0	0	49	65	40	36	23	28

TIDEWATER

BATTING	AVG	G	AB	R	H	2B	3B	HR	RBI	BB	SO	SB
Bogar, Tim, ss	.162	33	117	10	19	2	0	0	4	8	22	1
#Carr, Chuck, of	.259	20	81	13	21	5	1	0	8	4	12	6
*Cuevas, Angelo, of	.255	20	47	6	12	2	0	0	3	4	4	0
DeButch, Mike, ss-3b	.239	82	238	36	57	7	1	1	15	38	36	12
#Diaz, Alex, of-2b	.256	124	437	55	112	15	2	1	36	30	39	23
Diaz, Mario, ss	.317	29	104	15	33	8	0	1	9	6	6	1
*Freiling, Howie, 1b	.167	13	36	1	6	1	0	0	2	3	7	0
*Gardner, Jeff, 2b-ss	.270	138	463	55	125	11	1	0	33	84	33	1
Gonzalez, Denny, 3b	.274	65	212	27	58	13	1	3	29	37	37	1
Graves, Kenny, c	.250	3	8	0	2	0	0	0	0	0	3	0
*Hughes, Keith, of-1b	.309	117	379	77	117	24	5	10	53	57	58	7
Jelic, Chris, 3b-1b	.306	92	265	39	81	21	1	4	49	48	52	2
Kiefer, Steve, 3b-ss	.248	35	113	15	28	6	0	4	16	11	29	2
#Lara, Crucito, ss-3b	.143	21	49	4	7	1	0	0	1	1	11	0
Liddell, Dave, c	.212	73	189	16	40	5	0	2	15	21	51	0
*Lyons, Barry, c	.171	57	164	8	28	5	0	0	17	16	25	0
Mercado, Orlando, c	.264	24	72	5	19	4	0	1	10	7	11	0
#Monell, Johnny, dh-of	.182	13	33	3	6	0	0	0	4	2	5	1
Reed, Darren, of	.265	104	359	58	95	21	6	17	74	51	62	16
Roca, Gil, c	.230	24	61	4	14	1	0	0	5	1	3	0
Sanchez, Zoilo, of-dh	.282	110	312	33	88	19	0	6	39	27	55	2
Shipley, Craig, ph	.000	4	3	1	0	0	0	0	0	0	1	0
*Thornton, Lou, of	.227	109	379	40	86	9	4	4	38	10	51	13
*Torve, Kelvin, 1b-of	.303	115	402	62	122	25	1	11	76	56	43	9

PITCHING	W	L	ERA	G	GS	CG	SV	IP	H	R	ER	BB	SO
*Barton, Shawn	0	0	5.82	16	0	0	0	22	27	17	14	10	23
*Brown, Kevin	10	6	3.55	26	24	3	0	134	138	71	53	60	109
Childress, Rocky	7	5	3.45	27	3	0	4	63	54	26	24	23	37
*Givens, Brian	4	6	4.12	15	15	0	0	83	99	45	38	39	53
*Glynn, Ed	0	0	0.00	1	0	0	0	1	2	0	0	0	1
Hernandez, Manny	12	11	3.79	27	27	6	0	173	170	79	73	54	157
Innis, Jeff	5	2	1.71	40	0	0	19	53	34	11	10	17	42
Machado, Julio	0	1	1.69	16	0	0	8	21	16	7	4	8	24
Mejia, Cesar	6	3	4.96	18	15	0	0	82	87	53	45	42	40
*Musselman, Jeff	4	3	3.51	10	10	1	0	56	60	24	22	16	31
Nielsen, Scott	1	4	4.24	17	1	0	3	40	41	23	19	14	12
Plummer, Dale	2	2	3.25	17	4	0	1	52	46	21	19	23	28
*Samuels, Roger	3	3	2.83	35	1	0	2	41	39	15	13	13	29
*Schourek, Pete	1	0	2.57	2	2	1	0	14	9	4	4	5	14
Sisk, Doug	5	1	2.81	8	6	0	0	42	39	16	13	10	20
Soff, Ray	6	4	2.38	31	12	1	0	110	90	31	29	32	63
Trautwein, Dave	1	5	3.80	51	0	0	6	71	75	35	30	35	49
Valera, Julio	10	10	3.02	24	24	9	0	158	146	66	53	39	133
Vasquez, Aguedo	1	0	4.91	3	0	0	1	4	4	2	2	4	3
Whitehurst, Wally	1	0	2.00	2	2	0	0	9	7	2	2	1	10

TOLEDO

BATTING	AVG	G	AB	R	H	2B	3B	HR	RBI	BB	SO	SB
*Allaire, Karl, ss	.244	33	82	10	20	5	1	0	4	6	13	1
*Alvarez, Chris, 1b	.182	4	11	0	2	0	0	0	0	2	4	0
Clark, Phil, dh-c	.227	75	207	15	47	14	1	2	22	14	35	1
#Cuyler, Milt, of	.258	124	461	77	119	11	8	2	42	60	77	52
Davis, Jody, c	.125	3	8	1	1	0	0	0	0	0	0	0
DeCillis, Dean, 2b	.286	31	77	8	22	4	0	0	9	8	7	0
*Freeman, Lavel, of	.214	89	280	37	60	9	1	5	26	24	84	5
Fryman, Travis, ss	.257	87	327	38	84	22	2	10	53	17	59	4
*Hare, Shawn, of-dh	.254	127	429	53	109	25	4	9	55	49	77	9
#Leiper, Tim, of-3b	.293	74	249	26	73	14	1	2	34	27	21	2
Lindeman, Jim, 1b-of	.227	109	374	48	85	17	2	12	50	26	83	2
*Livingstone, Scott, 3b	.272	103	345	44	94	19	0	6	36	22	40	1
Lombardozzi, Steve, ss-2b ..	.248	62	210	31	52	11	3	6	23	19	30	1
#Lovullo, Torey, 2b-3b	.270	141	486	71	131	38	1	14	58	61	74	4
*Lusader, Scott, of	.250	76	268	35	67	12	1	4	25	34	51	15
Michel, Domingo, 1b-dh ...	.269	110	327	35	88	14	4	7	51	46	59	4
#Ouellette, Phil, c	.245	99	274	30	67	12	1	8	33	40	40	1
Rowland, Rich, c	.260	62	192	28	50	12	0	7	22	15	33	2
#Shelby, John, of	.316	5	19	2	6	1	0	0	1	2	1	0
#Wiley, Craig, c	.167	3	6	0	1	1	0	0	1	0	1	0

PITCHING	W	L	ERA	G	GS	CG	SV	IP	H	R	ER	BB	SO
*Aldred, Scott	6	15	4.90	29	29	2	0	158	145	93	86	81	133
Burtt, Dennis	2	6	5.18	17	6	0	0	49	50	29	28	16	33
Cooper, David	1	1	9.00	7	0	0	0	7	11	8	7	7	6
*DuBois, Brian	5	4	2.71	13	10	2	0	70	67	27	21	26	47
Hansen, Mike	5	7	4.76	15	13	1	0	76	89	47	40	24	52
Holman, Shawn	2	1	7.52	17	0	0	0	20	27	22	17	14	10
Kinzer, Matt	0	3	2.50	15	0	0	8	18	15	7	5	8	25
Link, Bobby	1	1	2.78	25	0	0	8	32	29	15	10	19	19
Lugo, Urbano	2	2	3.93	29	6	1	1	66	56	30	29	27	43
Nosek, Randy	5	8	5.19	22	19	0	0	109	112	70	63	66	55
Parker, Clay (3 Col)	2	5	3.33	9	9	2	0	54	58	23	20	13	34
*Ramos, Jose	0	1	4.22	31	0	0	1	32	40	19	15	14	16
Rightnowar, Ron	4	5	4.74	28	0	0	6	38	46	24	20	10	28
Ritz, Kevin	3	6	5.22	20	18	0	0	90	93	68	52	59	57
Rivera, Lino	0	3	3.07	18	0	0	1	29	27	12	10	13	23
Schwabe, Mike	6	5	3.83	51	2	0	5	108	112	58	46	22	69
*Searcy, Steve	10	5	2.92	17	17	2	0	105	71	40	34	52	105
Stone, Eric	2	4	3.95	36	7	0	4	68	52	35	30	63	57
*Vesling, Don	3	6	4.36	35	11	0	1	109	105	61	53	44	51

PACIFIC COAST LEAGUE

Dukes dominate PCL in every department

By MIKE KLIS

Every Duke had his day. Day after day after day.

Add it up and the Albuquerque Dukes finished with one great 1990 season. They won the Pacific Coast League Southern Division first-half title by nine games. They needed no down-to-the-wire dramatics to clinch the second-half title. After slipping by the Colorado Springs Sky Sox, 3-2 in the first-round playoffs, Albuquerque swept Edmonton, 3-0 in the PCL championship series.

The Dukes were champs for the fifth time in 11 seasons.

The keys to Albuquerque's success? Start with its phenomenal performance at Albuquerque Sports Stadium, where the Dukes posted a 52-18 home record.

Albuquerque's whack-and-run offense created havoc to

Tino Martinez
. . . .320-17-93

opposing pitchers and defenses. The Dukes hit a PCL-high .307 and made up for a lack of power (a league-low 71 homers) by swiping a club-record 195 bases.

Offerman: league MVP

Igniting the Dukes' offense was Jose Offerman, a 21-year-

LEAGUE CHAMPIONS

Playoff Champions, Where Applicable

1990—Albuquerque	1961—Tacoma	1931—San Fran.
1989—Vancouver	1960—Spokane	1930—Hollywood
1988—Las Vegas	1959—Salt Lake City	1929—Hollywood
1987—Albuquerque	1958—Phoenix	1928—San Fran.
1986—Las Vegas	1957—San Fran.	1927—Oakland
1985—Vancouver	1956—Los Angeles	1926—Los Angeles
1984—Edmonton	1955—Seattle	1925—San Fran.
1983—Portland	1954—San Diego	1924—Seattle
1982—Albuquerque	1953—Hollywood	1923—San Fran.
1981—Albuquerque	1952—Hollywood	1922—San Fran.
1980—Albuquerque	1951—Seattle	1921—Los Angeles
1979—Salt Lake City	1950—Oakland	1920—Vernon
1978—*Tacoma	1949—Hollywood	1919—Vernon
*Albuquerque	1948—Oakland	1918—Los Angeles
1977—Phoenix	1947—Los Angeles	1917—San Fran.
1976—Hawaii	1946—San Fran.	1916—Los Angeles
1975—Hawaii	1945—San Fran.	1915—San Fran.
1974—Spokane	1944—San Fran.	1914—Portland
1973—Spokane	1943—San Fran.	1913—Portland
1972—Albuquerque	1942—Seattle	1912—Oakland
1971—Salt Lake City	1941—Seattle	1911—Portland
1970—Spokane	1940—Seattle	1910—Portland
1969—Tacoma	1939—Sacramento	1909—San Fran.
1968—Tulsa	1938—Sacramento	1908—Los Angeles
1967—San Diego	1937—San Diego	1907—Los Angeles
1966—Seattle	1936—Portland	1906—Portland
1965—Okla. City	1935—San Fran.	1905—Los Angeles
1964—San Diego	1934—Los Angeles	1904—Tacoma
1963—Okla. City	1933—Los Angeles	1903—Los Angeles
1962—San Diego	1932—Portland	*co-champions

Albuquerque shortstop Jose Offerman hit .326 and stole a PCL-leading 60 bases.

old, switch-hitting shortstop. A leadoff batter, Offerman hit .326, drew 71 walks, stole a PCL-high 60 bases and scored 104 runs before earning a promotion to Los Angeles after 117 games. Offerman was named the PCL's Most Valuable Player.

There were plenty of Dukes behind Offerman to keep him running. Luis Lopez, the Dukes' DH-first baseman, won the PCL batting crown at .353 and drove in 81 runs. His teammate, Butch Davis, finished second in the batting race at .342 and had 85 RBIs. Center fielder Michael Huff (.325, 84 RBIs) and third baseman Dave Hansen (.316, 92 RBIs, league-high 90 walks) were PCL all stars.

The pitching staff wasn't too shabby either. The strength lied in the bullpen, where Duke relievers posted a club-record 45 saves. Albuquerque's top three relievers—Darren Holmes, Dave Walsh and Mike Christopher—combined for a 24-3 record, 33 saves and 1.81 ERA. Jeff Bittiger (15-6), the PCL's winningest pitcher, anchored the rotation that also featured the likes of Jim Neidlinger, John Wetteland and Mike Maddux.

Bringing this team together was Kevin Kennedy, Baseball America's minor-league manager of the year. Kennedy-managed teams have never finished lower than second since he took up the occupation in 1984.

Second winning season

Albuquerque was not the only PCL team to have a good year in 1990. Edmonton, which had enjoyed just one winning season since the franchise began in 1981, added its second in 1990 with a 78-63 overall mark. The Trappers finished with the PCL's best second-half record at 47-25 and won the Northern Division championship by defeating first-half Northern Division champ Tacoma, 3-2.

Tacoma's Tigers boasted the PCL's most formidable rotation with Scott Chiamparino (13-9), Ed Wojna (10-5), Ray Young (14-7) and Dave Veres (11-8). Bullpen stopper Joe Bitker broke a 13-year-old PCL record by posting 26 saves.

Calgary (66-77) was one of several teams that didn't meet expectations, but the Cannons did have the league's best 1-2 punch in rookie first baseman Tino Martinez and veteran DH Tom Dodd. Dodd led the PCL with 114 RBIs and Martinez was second with 93.

Brito leads in homers—again

The PCL home-run title went to Portland's Bernardo Brito, who led a minor league in homers for the fifth time. The veteran DH finished with 25 homers, including 19 during a six-week tear in July and August.

Perhaps, no individual achievement topped Jose Tolentino's 30-game hitting streak—the best in all of professional baseball in 1990. Tucson's left-handed hitting left fielder hit .413 with 11 homers, 11 doubles and two triples during the streak that ran from July 27-Sept. 1.

Las Vegas didn't have much to brag about, unless you count the 1990 Triple-A All Star Game at Cashman Field, won by National League-affiliated teams, 8-5. The Stars finished with the PCL's worst record at 58-86. They did post the league's only no-hitter as Mike Dunne, pitching on a rehab assignment, blanked Portland, 2-0 on May 6.

It was a big year for transactions. And we're not just talking players. Three clubs—Edmonton, Vancouver and Tacoma—were all sold. Price tags ran from $4.8 million to $5.5 million. Those clubs will stay put for the 1991 season.

But no one enjoyed 1990 more than the Albuquerque Dukes. They even won the attendance race, overcoming a team-record nine rainouts to draw a PCL-high 324,046 in just 59 dates (5,492 average).

1990 FINAL STANDINGS

FIRST HALF

North	W	L	Pct.	GB
Tacoma (Athletics)	43	27	.614	—
Vancouver (White Sox)	42	27	.609	½
Calgary (Mariners)	37	35	.514	7
Edmonton (Angels)	31	38	.449	11½
Portland (Twins)	23	47	.329	20

South	W	L	Pct.	GB
Albuquerque (Dodgers)	46	25	.648	—
Colorado Springs (Indians)	37	34	.521	9
Phoenix (Giants)	35	33	.515	9½
Tucson (Astros)	29	43	.403	17½
Las Vegas (Padres)	29	43	.403	17½

SECOND HALF

North	W	L	Pct.	GB
Edmonton (Angels)	47	25	.653	—
Portland (Twins)	33	36	.478	12½
Vancouver (White Sox)	32	40	.444	15
Tacoma (Athletics)	32	40	.444	15
Calgary (Mariners)	29	42	.408	17½

South	W	L	Pct.	GB
Albuquerque (Dodgers)	45	26	.634	—
Tucson (Astros)	42	28	.600	2½
Colorado Springs (Indians)	39	33	.542	6½
Las Vegas (Padres)	29	43	.403	16½
Phoenix (Giants)	28	43	.394	17

OVERALL

	W	L	Pct.	GB
Albuquerque (Dodgers)	91	51	.641	—
Edmonton (Angels)	78	63	.553	12½
Colorado Springs (Indians)	76	67	.531	15½
Tacoma (Athletics)	75	67	.528	16
Vancouver (White Sox)	74	67	.525	16½
Tucson (Astros)	71	71	.500	20
Calgary (Mariners)	66	77	.462	25½
Phoenix (Giants)	63	76	.453	26½
Portland (Twins)	56	83	.403	33½
Las Vegas (Padres)	58	86	.403	34

Playoffs: Edmonton defeated Tacoma 3-2 in best-of-5 semifinal; Albuquerque defeated Colorado Springs 3-2 in best-of-5 semifinal; Albuquerque defeated Edmonton 3-0 in best-of-5 final for league championship.

Regular-Season Attendance: Albuquerque, 324,046; Las Vegas, 312,522; Calgary, 312,416; Tacoma, 309,210; Vancouver, 281,540; Phoenix, 248,660; Tucson, 238,629; Edmonton, 229,307; Colorado Springs, 201,642; Portland, 150,054.

Managers: Albuquerque—Kevin Kennedy; **Calgary**—Tom Jones; **Colorado Springs**—Bob Molinaro, Charlie Manuel; **Edmonton**—Max Oliveras; **Las Vegas**—Pat Kelly; **Phoenix**—Duane Espy; **Portland**—Jim Shellenback; **Tacoma**—Brad Fischer; **Tucson**—Bob Skinner; **Vancouver**—Marv Foley.

1990 Official All-Star Team: C—Jerry Willard, Vancouver. **1B**—Tino Martinez, Calgary. **2B**—Todd Haney, Calgary. **3B**—Dave Hansen, Albuquerque. **SS**—Jose Offerman, Albuquerque. **OF**—Mark Leonard, Phoenix; Mike Huff, Albuquerque; Butch Davis, Albuquerque. **DH**—Tom Dodd, Calgary. **RHP**—Scott Chiamparino, Tacoma. **LHP**—Grady Hall, Vancouver. **RP**—Joe Bitker, Tacoma. **Most Valuable Player**—Jose Offerman, Albuquerque. **Manager of the Year**—Kevin Kennedy, Albuquerque.

Top 10 Major League Prospects (by Baseball America): 1. Jose Offerman, ss, Albuquerque; **2.** Tino Martinez, 1b, Calgary; **3.** Lee Stevens, 1b-of, Edmonton; **4.** Scott Chiamparino, rhp, Tacoma; **5.** Rafael Valdez, rhp, Las Vegas; **6.** Dave Hansen, 3b, Albuquerque; **7.** Mark Leonard, of, Phoenix; **8.** Thomas Howard, of, Las Vegas; **9.** Karl Rhodes, of, Tucson; **10.** Ray Young, rhp, Tacoma.

1990 *BATTING, PITCHING STATS*

CLUB BATTING

	AVG	G	AB	R	H	2B	3B	HR	BB	SO	SB
Albuquerque	.307	142	4692	813	1441	244	51	71	572	614	195
Colorado Springs	.292	143	4689	832	1369	272	45	113	633	764	124
Tucson	.281	142	4755	768	1335	263	58	80	571	835	103
Calgary	.279	143	4698	737	1312	242	40	97	508	749	122
Las Vegas	.279	144	4872	753	1357	234	49	112	623	913	157
Edmonton	.277	141	4779	738	1324	274	48	98	584	847	124
Phoenix	.272	139	4659	671	1267	229	60	89	537	883	115
Tacoma	.265	142	4628	695	1228	248	42	89	541	890	124
Vancouver	.260	141	4574	661	1189	223	43	77	573	746	127
Portland	.254	139	4514	591	1148	241	33	105	499	811	83

CLUB PITCHING

	ERA	G	CG	SHO	SV	IP	H	R	ER	BB	SO
Edmonton	3.97	141	17	4	41	1240	1338	652	547	481	802
Vancouver	4.03	141	20	8	31	1209	1157	628	542	575	807
Albuquerque	4.25	142	13	7	45	1201	1211	658	567	544	966
Tacoma	4.27	142	10	11	34	1206	1184	661	572	607	833
Portland	4.55	139	10	6	25	1184	1227	713	599	610	849
Phoenix	4.67	139	10	5	33	1198	1367	731	621	497	667
Colorado Springs	4.76	143	19	9	38	1207	1347	758	638	526	789
Tucson	5.00	142	13	3	34	1222	1378	779	679	589	727
Calgary	5.31	143	9	4	34	1207	1310	803	712	589	772
Las Vegas	5.51	144	10	5	28	1245	1451	876	763	623	850

INDIVIDUAL BATTING LEADERS
(Minimum 389 Plate Appearances)

	AVG	G	AB	R	H	2B	3B	HR	RBI	BB	SO	SB
Lopez, Luis, Alb	.353	128	448	65	158	23	2	11	81	47	49	3
Davis, Butch, Alb	.342	124	480	87	164	31	9	10	85	24	53	25
Haney, Todd, Cal	.339	108	419	81	142	15	6	1	36	37	38	16
*Leonard, Mark, Phx	.333	109	390	76	130	22	2	19	82	76	81	6
#Howard, Thomas, LV	.328	89	341	58	112	26	8	5	51	44	63	27
#Offerman, Jose, Alb	.326	117	454	104	148	16	11	0	56	71	81	60
Huff, Mike, Alb	.325	138	474	99	154	28	11	7	84	82	68	27
Cockrell, Alan, CS	.323	119	375	77	121	24	5	17	71	50	73	6
Powell, Alonzo, Port	.322	107	376	56	121	25	3	8	62	40	79	23
*Martinez, Tino, Cal	.320	128	453	83	145	28	1	17	93	74	37	8

INDIVIDUAL PITCHING LEADERS
(Minimum 115 Innings)

	W	L	ERA	G	GS	CG	SV	IP	H	R	ER	BB	SO
Cook, Mike, Port	6	8	3.20	19	19	2	0	115	105	54	41	59	63
Chiamparino, Scott, Tac	13	9	3.28	26	26	4	0	173	174	79	63	72	110
Clark, Terry, Tucson	11	4	3.54	29	22	3	1	155	172	73	61	41	80
Melendez, Jose, Cal	11	4	3.90	45	10	1	2	125	119	61	54	44	95
Lewis, Scott, Edm	13	11	3.90	27	27	6	0	178	198	90	77	35	124
Wojna, Ed, Tacoma	10	5	3.99	24	23	3	0	142	121	71	63	55	99

	W	L	ERA	G	GS	CG	SV	IP	H	R	ER	BB	SO
Heredia, Gil, Phx	9	7	4.10	29	19	0	1	147	159	81	67	37	75
Bittiger, Jeff, Alb	15	6	4.15	28	26	2	0	154	162	78	71	62	125
Young, Ray, Tacoma	14	7	4.20	28	27	1	0	165	155	87	77	105	137
*Hall, Grady, Van	13	8	4.24	28	28	4	0	185	185	100	87	89	106

ALBUQUERQUE

BATTING	AVG	G	AB	R	H	2B	3B	HR	RBI	BB	SO	SB
Bean, Billy, of	.295	129	427	85	126	26	5	7	67	69	63	16
*Brown, Adam, c	.364	5	11	2	4	0	0	0	1	0	1	0
Davis, Butch, of-dh	.342	124	480	87	164	31	9	10	85	24	53	25
*Fletcher, Darrin, c	.291	105	350	58	102	23	1	13	65	40	37	1
Garbey, Barbaro, dh	.000	1	4	0	0	0	0	0	0	0	1	0
*Gibson, Kirk, of-dh	.429	5	14	6	6	2	0	1	4	4	3	1
Hansen, Dave, 3b	.316	135	487	90	154	20	3	11	92	90	54	9
Henley, Dan, 2b	.305	87	243	40	74	12	0	2	31	24	35	4
Hernandez, Carlos, c	.315	52	143	11	45	8	1	0	16	8	25	2
Hoffman, Glenn, ss	.302	24	63	7	19	3	1	0	10	2	9	1
Huff, Mike, of	.325	138	474	99	154	28	11	7	84	82	68	27
*Kirby, Wayne, of	.278	119	342	56	95	14	5	0	30	28	36	29
Lopez, Luis, 1b-dh	.353	128	448	65	158	23	2	11	81	47	49	3
Mangham, Eric, of	.111	6	9	1	1	0	0	0	0	0	0	0
*McConnell, Walt, 3b	.204	34	49	5	10	2	0	0	5	6	4	0
*Offerman, Jose, ss	.326	117	454	104	148	16	11	0	56	71	81	60
*Traxler, Brian, 1b	.277	98	318	43	88	20	0	7	53	39	39	4
#Vizcaino, Jose, 2b-ss ...	.279	81	276	46	77	10	2	2	38	30	33	13

PITCHING	W	L	ERA	G	GS	CG	SV	IP	H	R	ER	BB	SO
Bittiger, Jeff	15	6	4.15	28	26	2	0	154	162	78	71	62	125
Christopher, Mike	6	1	1.97	54	0	0	8	69	62	20	15	23	47
*Davis, Steve	7	8	4.31	31	18	2	0	129	145	81	62	44	76
Deleon, Luis	0	0	13.50	1	0	0	0	1	4	2	2	1	2
Fischer, Jeff	0	0	6.00	3	0	0	0	3	3	2	2	1	4
Hartley, Mike	0	0	0.00	3	0	0	2	3	3	0	0	2	3
Hartsock, Jeff	3	3	6.22	11	10	0	0	46	62	38	32	30	33
Holmes, Darren	12	6	3.11	56	0	0	13	93	78	34	32	39	99
*Madden, Morris	6	4	4.78	31	13	1	0	92	86	55	49	68	99
Maddux, Mike	8	5	4.25	20	19	2	0	108	122	59	51	32	85
Mayberry, Greg	4	7	5.66	32	12	0	0	95	106	69	60	36	76
*Munoz, Mike	4	1	4.25	49	0	0	6	59	65	33	28	19	40
Neidlinger, Jim	8	5	4.29	20	18	4	0	120	129	70	57	34	81
Scott, Tim	2	1	4.20	17	0	0	1	15	14	9	7	14	15
Springer, Dennis	0	0	5.68	2	2	0	0	6	10	4	4	7	2
*Walsh, Dave	6	0	2.61	47	0	0	12	62	50	21	18	31	66
*Wells, Terry	8	6	4.62	24	19	1	1	115	83	64	59	87	86
Wetteland, John	2	2	5.59	8	5	1	0	29	27	19	18	13	26

CALGARY

BATTING	AVG	G	AB	R	H	2B	3B	HR	RBI	BB	SO	SB
Brantley, Mickey, of	.233	29	103	17	24	3	0	1	8	8	12	3
#Brumley, Mike, ss	.321	8	28	4	9	1	0	0	1	1	3	3
*Brundage, Dave, of	.304	92	309	63	94	22	3	3	48	60	60	8
Buhner, Jay, dh-of	.206	13	34	6	7	1	0	2	5	7	11	0
Close, Casey, of	.270	128	463	71	125	30	4	12	69	34	76	15
#Cochrane, Dave, of-inf ...	.275	69	262	43	72	14	4	8	36	23	62	2
Diaz, Mario, 3b-ss	.333	32	105	10	35	5	1	1	19	1	8	0
DiMascio, Dan, dh-c	.357	14	42	4	15	3	1	0	2	4	7	0
Dodd, Tom, dh	.281	135	501	71	141	31	3	16	114	42	101	6
#Fulton, Greg, 3b-of	.291	22	55	11	16	5	0	0	4	7	6	0
Giles, Brian, ss-2b	.262	38	122	28	32	8	0	5	19	23	33	5
Haney, Todd, 2b	.339	108	419	81	142	15	6	1	36	37	38	16
Jurak, Ed, 3b-of	.255	114	353	47	90	17	2	7	52	54	56	5
*Martinez, Tino, 1b	.320	128	453	83	145	28	1	17	93	74	37	8
McGuire, Bill, c	.229	118	358	47	82	12	2	7	46	33	69	4
Miller, Darrell, c-of	.297	59	172	25	51	5	2	3	26	11	31	4
Morales, Rich, c	.000	2	7	0	0	0	0	0	0	0	1	0
#Murray, Steve, 2b-ss	.292	22	65	8	19	1	0	0	6	5	15	3
Schaefer, Jeff, ss-3b	.241	49	170	24	41	9	2	0	19	18	15	8
Sinatro, Matt, c	.300	9	20	1	6	0	0	1	2	2	3	0
Turang, Brian, 2b	.222	3	9	1	2	0	0	0	1	2	4	0
Vizquel, Omar, ss	.233	48	150	18	35	6	2	0	8	13	10	4
*Weaver, Jim, of	.257	120	354	43	91	23	3	7	42	41	69	20
#Williams, Ted, of	.266	43	143	30	38	3	4	6	20	8	22	9

PITCHING	W	L	ERA	G	GS	CG	SV	IP	H	R	ER	BB	SO
Bankhead, Scott	0	1	6.43	2	2	0	0	7	9	5	5	3	7
*Blasucci, Tony	1	2	4.80	15	0	0	1	30	25	17	16	16	33
Burba, Dave	10	6	4.67	31	18	1	2	114	124	64	59	45	47
*Clark, Bryan	4	3	3.95	18	10	0	0	57	55	40	25	29	27
DeLucia, Rich	2	2	3.62	5	5	1	0	32	30	17	13	12	23
*Givens, Brian	0	1	12.71	2	2	0	0	7	8	8	8	4	4
Harris, Gene	3	0	2.35	6	0	0	2	8	7	2	2	4	6
*Helton, Keith	6	7	5.80	60	1	0	6	81	88	59	52	51	68
Lazorko, Jack	4	8	5.18	31	13	1	2	115	129	74	66	43	79
*Lovelace, Vance	5	5	3.47	56	0	0	6	70	64	33	27	44	60
Medvin, Scott	1	3	4.97	43	0	0	11	51	47	30	28	24	31
Melendez, Jose	11	4	3.90	45	10	1	2	125	119	61	54	44	95
Pacillo, Pat	5	4	5.20	32	13	0	0	90	91	65	52	64	66

PITCHING	W	L	ERA	G	GS	CG	SV	IP	H	R	ER	BB	SO
Rice, Pat	1	1	6.35	15	2	0	2	28	34	21	20	13	27
Shaw, Theo	6	9	5.62	23	23	2	0	130	141	86	81	56	50
*Swan, Russ	3	6	4.45	11	11	0	0	57	69	35	28	27	35
Taylor, Terry	0	7	9.97	25	14	0	0	71	96	84	79	61	71
*Vandeberg, Ed	1	0	8.27	10	0	0	0	16	29	17	15	8	10
Walker, Mike	5	11	5.35	25	24	3	0	145	176	92	86	45	64

COLORADO SPRINGS

BATTING	AVG	G	AB	R	H	2B	3B	HR	RBI	BB	SO	SB
*Allred, Beau, of	.278	115	378	79	105	23	6	13	74	60	54	6
#Baerga, Carlos, 3b	.380	12	50	11	19	2	1	1	11	5	4	1
Belle, Albert, of	.344	24	96	16	33	3	1	5	19	5	16	4
#Castillo, Juan, 2b-ss	.284	113	345	56	98	8	4	1	33	42	56	16
*Cockrell, Alan, of (6 Port)	.323	119	375	77	121	24	5	17	71	50	73	6
*Cole, Alex, of (90 LV)	.308	104	390	71	120	9	4	0	31	55	69	38
*Gainey, Ty, of	.237	19	38	7	9	3	0	1	8	6	8	0
Gerhart, Ken, of	.000	4	7	1	0	0	0	0	0	1	4	0
Hearn, Ed, c	.288	17	52	7	15	3	0	1	8	0	6	0
#Jefferson, Stan, of	.345	33	119	27	41	9	3	3	17	20	22	8
Lewis, Mark, ss	.306	34	124	16	38	8	1	1	21	9	13	2
*Magallanes, Ever, ss-2b	.308	125	377	60	116	17	3	1	63	43	49	3
Magrann, Tom, c	.276	88	228	36	63	16	0	2	39	33	30	1
Manto, Jeff, 3b-1b	.297	96	316	73	94	27	1	18	82	78	65	10
#McLemore, Mark, 2b-ss (9 Edm)	.269	23	93	15	25	4	0	1	10	17	18	5
Medina, Luis, dh	.272	94	320	58	87	15	0	18	53	33	68	7
Melendez, Francisco, 1b	.294	34	102	15	30	6	1	4	18	12	14	0
*Neel, Troy, 1b-dh	.281	98	288	39	81	15	0	6	50	43	52	5
Sullivan, Marc, c	.313	12	32	4	10	3	0	1	7	4	6	0
Swain, Rob, 3b-2b	.244	18	41	5	10	3	1	0	3	4	9	0
*Taylor, Dwight, of	.179	13	28	3	5	2	0	1	1	2	3	1
#Ward, Turner, of	.299	133	495	89	148	24	9	6	65	72	70	22
Webster, Casey, 3b	.218	27	78	12	17	7	0	0	12	15	13	3
*Wetherby, Jeff, of-1b	.313	96	268	48	84	23	0	5	42	41	51	6

PITCHING	W	L	ERA	G	GS	CG	SV	IP	H	R	ER	BB	SO
*Bearse, Kevin	11	9	5.00	25	24	6	0	146	170	92	81	49	79
Browning, Mike (3 Tuc)	1	1	2.63	8	0	0	0	14	9	4	4	5	8
Collins, Allen	0	0	0.00	1	0	0	0	2	0	0	0	1	1
*Curtis, Mike	2	2	4.55	19	6	0	1	55	66	33	28	17	33
Edwards, Jeff	1	1	5.00	4	4	0	0	18	25	11	10	11	16
*Kaiser, Jeff	2	2	2.93	25	0	0	3	43	36	16	14	22	46
*Lambert, Reese (31 Tac)	3	3	6.12	36	0	0	0	57	71	40	39	30	35
McMichael, Greg	2	3	5.80	12	12	1	0	59	72	45	38	30	34
Nichols, Rod	12	9	5.13	22	22	4	0	133	160	84	76	48	74
Nipper, Al	5	5	4.74	17	16	1	0	89	80	53	47	56	47
Olin, Steve	3	1	0.66	14	0	0	2	27	18	9	2	15	30
Robertson, Doug	1	2	5.76	31	0	0	12	30	33	21	19	35	28
Seanez, Rudy	1	4	6.75	12	0	0	1	12	15	10	9	10	7
Shaw, Jeff	10	3	4.29	17	16	4	0	99	98	54	47	52	55
Sisk, Doug	1	0	7.04	8	0	0	0	8	8	6	5	7	
Skalski, Joe	5	7	5.73	21	17	1	0	99	129	76	63	21	81
*Valdez, Efrain	4	2	3.81	46	1	0	6	76	72	38	32	30	52
Valdez, Sergio	4	3	5.19	7	7	2	0	43	55	29	25	13	33
Walker, Mike	2	7	5.58	18	12	0	1	79	96	62	49	36	50
Ward, Colby	4	3	2.00	43	0	0	9	63	45	23	14	30	56
Willis, Carl	5	3	6.39	41	6	0	2	99	136	80	70	32	42

EDMONTON

BATTING	AVG	G	AB	R	H	2B	3B	HR	RBI	BB	SO	SB
Aguayo, Luis, 2b-1b	.286	23	77	12	22	7	1	2	14	6	7	1
Alfonzo, Edgar, ss	.182	4	11	1	2	0	0	0	1	0	0	0
*Allaire, Karl, ss	.254	44	122	16	31	6	2	0	14	16	18	3
#Amaro, Ruben, of	.289	82	318	53	92	15	4	3	32	40	43	32
Anderson, Kent, 2b-3b	.271	18	59	10	16	6	1	0	7	8	8	1
Coachman, Pete, dh-3b	.291	111	419	78	122	15	2	5	51	74	49	27
Cron, Chris, 1b-3b	.287	104	401	54	115	31	0	17	75	28	92	7
Davis, Doug, c-1b	.247	53	162	18	40	12	0	2	23	25	31	0
Davis, Mark, of	.368	35	133	30	49	10	5	9	34	17	23	7
*DeAngelis, Steve, dh-of	.299	61	224	34	67	8	2	4	30	16	39	3
DiSarcina, Gary, ss	.212	97	330	46	70	12	2	4	37	25	46	5
*Grunhard, Dan, of	.301	126	462	69	139	27	4	6	58	59	78	7
*Howell, Jack, 3b-dh	.333	20	75	14	25	7	1	2	15	7	13	3
Knapp, Mike, c-1b	.205	12	39	3	8	0	1	0	4	4	6	0
McCollom, Jim, dh-1b	.292	6	24	6	7	1	1	0	3	3	3	1
Nichols, Howard, 3b-1b	.118	5	17	0	2	1	0	0	1	3	4	0
Orton, John, c	.241	50	174	29	42	8	0	6	26	19	63	4
Peters, Reed, of	.232	51	181	16	42	9	1	2	22	19	29	2
Rood, Nelson, 2b-ss	.077	18	26	4	2	0	0	0	1	6	5	0
Rose, Bobby, 2b-3b	.283	134	502	84	142	27	10	9	68	56	83	6
Schofield, Dick, ss	.389	5	18	4	7	1	0	1	4	3	4	0
Schu, Rick, 1b-3b	.300	18	60	8	18	7	0	1	8	6	3	0
*Sconiers, Daryl, 1b	.333	2	6	1	2	1	0	0	2	2	1	0
*Skurla, John, of (1 Phx)	.229	43	144	20	33	7	2	3	21	15	28	0
*Stevens, Lee, of-1b	.293	90	338	57	99	31	2	16	66	55	83	1
Tingley, Ron, c	.267	54	172	27	46	9	2	5	23	21	39	1
Wasinger, Mark, 3b-1b	.277	68	195	31	54	10	1	1	30	38	28	9
#White, Devon, of	.364	14	55	9	20	4	4	0	6	7	12	4

PCL *TOP PERFORMERS*

Luis Lopez
... top hitter

Bernardo Brito
... homer leader

Dave Hansen
... .316-11-92

PITCHING	W	L	ERA	G	GS	CG	SV	IP	H	R	ER	BB	SO
*Abbott, Kyle	1	0	14.81	3	3	0	0	10	26	18	17	4	14
*Bailes, Scott	0	1	6.00	9	3	0	0	18	21	13	12	8	12
Beasley, Chris	12	9	4.49	28	27	5	0	176	201	107	88	70	108
Bockus, Randy	0	0	0.00	2	0	0	1	4	3	0	0	2	2
Buckels, Gary	2	7	4.57	53	0	0	10	67	66	38	34	32	61
Burcham, Tim	9	10	4.57	27	26	3	0	158	182	94	80	69	97
Clear, Mark	1	0	3.07	12	0	0	2	15	14	5	5	8	21
*Corbett, Sherman	3	1	3.50	47	1	0	3	69	64	31	27	25	44
Erb, Mike	4	4	4.26	16	14	0	0	82	90	46	39	60	45
Fetters, Mike	1	1	0.99	5	5	1	0	27	22	9	3	13	26
Fraser, Willie	1	0	3.14	3	3	0	0	14	11	8	5	6	12
Grahe, Joe	3	0	1.35	5	5	2	0	40	35	10	6	11	21
Heathcock, Jeff	1	3	7.52	8	4	0	0	26	42	23	22	6	11
Lewis, Scott	13	11	3.90	27	27	6	0	178	198	90	77	35	124
Meeks, Tim	0	1	12.27	4	0	0	0	4	12	7	5	2	4
Montalvo, Rafael	1	5	2.74	48	0	0	9	85	76	33	26	22	42
Monteleone, Rich	1	0	1.93	5	1	0	1	14	7	3	3	4	9
Ohnoutka, Brian (10 LV)	1	4	4.96	12	3	0	1	33	41	21	18	15	20
Richardson, Jeff	5	0	1.86	38	0	0	10	48	46	17	10	27	31
Tolliver, Fred	8	2	3.99	13	12	0	0	68	71	34	30	28	45
Trudeau, Kevin	5	2	4.12	22	8	0	1	74	87	41	34	34	35
*Young, Cliff	7	4	2.42	30	0	0	4	52	45	15	14	10	30

LAS VEGAS

BATTING	AVG	G	AB	R	H	2B	3B	HR	RBI	BB	SO	SB
Basso, Mike, c	.193	50	150	5	29	5	0	1	12	16	20	1
Clark, Jerald, 1b-of	.304	40	161	30	49	7	4	12	32	5	35	2
Conley, Greg, c	.333	2	6	1	2	0	0	0	1	0	2	0
#Cora, Joey, ss-2b	.351	51	211	41	74	13	9	0	24	29	16	15
Faries, Paul, 2b-ss	.312	137	552	109	172	29	3	5	64	75	60	48
#Gieseke, Mark, of-1b	.227	5	22	2	5	1	0	0	2	2	2	0
*Higgins, Kevin, c	.269	9	26	4	7	1	1	0	3	4	3	0
Hillemann, Charles, of	.243	91	300	36	73	11	3	3	25	23	63	3
#Howard, Thomas, of	.328	89	341	58	112	26	8	5	51	44	63	27
Humphreys, Mike, of	.238	12	42	7	10	1	0	2	6	4	11	1
Jackson, Darrin, of	.276	29	98	14	27	4	0	5	15	9	21	3
*Lampkin, Tom, c (69 LV)	.224	70	201	32	45	7	5	1	18	19	20	7
Levasseur, Tom, ss	.218	90	257	35	56	10	3	5	37	36	37	7
#Mota, Jose, ss-of	.300	92	247	44	74	4	4	4	21	42	35	2
*Nelson, Rob, 1b-dh	.264	112	390	56	103	18	1	20	90	68	129	1
*Newson, Warren, of-dh	.304	123	404	80	123	20	3	13	58	83	110	13
Reynolds, Ronn, c	.255	81	247	35	63	17	0	9	41	25	62	0
Santiago, Benito, c-dh	.300	6	20	5	6	2	0	1	3	1	3	0
*Sherman, Darrell, of	.000	4	12	1	0	0	0	0	1	1	2	1
Springer, Steve, 2b-3b (73 CS)	.272	95	324	46	88	26	5	8	52	24	67	6
Walters, Dan, c	.255	53	184	19	47	9	0	3	26	13	24	0
Williams, Eddie, 3b	.316	93	348	59	110	29	2	17	75	42	47	0
*Yurtin, Jeff, 3b-of	.260	102	334	39	87	15	4	5	49	39	52	1

PITCHING	W	L	ERA	G	GS	CG	SV	IP	H	R	ER	BB	SO
Bones, Ricky	2	1	3.47	5	5	0	0	36	45	17	14	10	25
*Clements, Pat	4	3	6.05	26	13	1	0	86	106	68	58	34	57
Davis, John	2	4	4.34	18	11	1	1	75	68	40	36	43	68
Dunne, Mike	1	2	3.21	4	4	1	0	28	20	12	10	10	12
Gilmore, Terry	13	7	5.13	42	18	3	6	154	182	96	88	41	122
Lewis, Jim	5	6	4.55	59	1	0	5	93	109	60	47	46	54
Lynch, Joe	5	8	5.22	58	0	0	2	88	121	59	51	31	44
Maysey, Matt	6	10	5.62	26	25	1	0	139	155	97	86	88	72
Murphy, Dan	4	7	5.81	27	10	1	3	69	74	54	45	56	60
*Nolte, Eric	2	11	8.58	33	18	1	0	123	187	130	117	49	79
*Peters, Steve	0	2	7.52	47	0	0	2	41	49	35	34	39	32
Quinzer, Paul	0	0	3.24	5	0	0	0	8	8	3	3	2	5
*Roberts, Pete	1	3	5.40	12	4	1	0	37	40	24	22	14	29
*Rodriguez, Rich	3	4	3.51	27	2	0	8	59	50	24	23	22	46
Sierra, Candy	2	1	5.59	15	0	0	0	19	25	12	12	10	16
Smithberg, Roger	2	7	6.95	13	13	0	0	66	91	63	51	39	30

	W	L	ERA	G	GS	CG	SV	IP	H	R	ER	BB	SO
Valdez, Rafael	4	7	4.92	17	17	0	0	86	82	58	47	65	79

PHOENIX

BATTING	AVG	G	AB	R	H	2B	3B	HR	RBI	BB	SO	SB
#Bailey, Mark, c-1b	.223	57	175	19	39	4	0	7	28	28	31	2
#Bass, Kevin, of-dh	.242	8	33	2	8	2	0	0	4	0	4	1
Bathe, Bill, dh	.286	18	56	9	16	5	0	1	9	6	7	0
Beauchamp, Kash, of	.281	55	121	12	34	4	2	1	15	7	21	2
Benjamin, Mike, ss	.251	118	419	61	105	21	7	5	39	25	89	13
*Brady, Brian, of-1b	.254	102	303	36	77	11	3	3	32	48	68	3
#Carter, Jeff, 2b-of	.292	121	435	80	127	21	9	2	63	63	81	28
Colbert, Craig, 3b-c	.280	111	400	41	112	22	2	8	47	31	80	4
*Green, Otis, of	.273	8	22	4	6	2	0	0	0	1	7	0
Hinshaw, George, of-dh	.272	90	294	29	80	11	4	6	49	18	57	2
Jackson, Chuck, 3b-of	.289	74	273	47	79	18	4	0	26	33	28	3
Johnson, Erik, 2b-3b	.000	2	3	0	0	0	0	0	0	1	1	0
*Kingery, Mike, of	.240	35	100	12	24	9	2	1	16	18	15	2
*Laga, Mike, 1b	.298	89	309	63	92	18	3	22	71	42	62	0
*Leonard, Mark, of-dh	.333	109	390	76	130	22	2	19	82	76	81	6
Litton, Greg, of-3b	.273	6	22	3	6	1	0	0	4	2	7	0
Manwaring, Kirt, c	.235	74	247	20	58	10	2	3	14	24	34	0
McNamara, Jim, c	.450	6	20	2	9	0	0	0	1	3	4	0
*Owens, Mark, c	.143	11	21	4	3	0	0	0	1	2	7	0
Parker, Rick, 3b-of	.335	44	173	38	58	7	4	1	18	22	25	18
Perezchica, Tony, 2b-ss	.268	105	392	55	105	22	6	9	49	34	76	8
*Ritchie, Gregg, of	.237	105	342	53	81	13	10	1	28	50	74	23

PITCHING	W	L	ERA	G	GS	CG	SV	IP	H	R	ER	BB	SO
Aldrich, Jay	0	0	4.32	8	1	0	0	17	19	8	8	2	9
Beck, Rod	4	7	4.93	12	12	2	0	77	100	51	42	18	43
*Bonilla, George	2	1	5.09	36	0	0	0	41	38	24	23	19	26
Booker, Greg	2	4	4.58	49	0	0	10	73	83	46	37	36	29
Bordi, Rich	0	0	3.86	4	0	0	0	9	10	5	4	2	4
Burkett, John	2	1	2.74	3	3	2	0	23	18	8	7	3	9
Camacho, Ernie	1	0	1.80	13	0	0	4	15	12	4	3	11	17
Dewey, Mark	2	3	2.67	19	0	0	8	30	26	14	9	10	27
Downs, Kelly	0	0	1.80	1	1	0	0	5	5	3	1	0	4
Eave, Gary (1 Cal)	3	3	7.82	11	11	0	0	51	63	47	44	40	27
*Gunderson, Eric	5	7	8.23	16	16	0	0	82	137	87	75	46	41
Heredia, Gil	9	7	4.10	29	19	0	1	147	159	81	67	37	75
*Hickerson, Bryan	0	4	5.50	14	4	0	0	34	48	25	21	16	26
*Knepper, Bob	1	2	3.65	4	4	0	0	25	21	14	10	9	13
McCament, Randy	3	3	3.79	46	0	0	6	78	99	40	33	32	32
McClellan, Paul	7	16	5.17	28	27	1	0	172	192	112	99	78	102
Mead, Timber	0	2	5.23	22	0	0	1	41	49	26	24	14	19
Meier, Kevin	5	3	4.35	13	13	0	0	68	82	41	33	21	25
O'Neal, Randy	5	0	2.97	7	6	2	0	39	34	14	13	8	25
Rodriguez, Rick	4	2	4.75	14	4	1	0	42	36	24	22	22	21
*Vosberg, Ed	1	3	2.65	24	0	0	3	34	36	14	10	16	28
*Wilson, Trevor	5	5	3.82	11	10	2	0	66	63	31	28	44	45

PORTLAND

BATTING	AVG	G	AB	R	H	2B	3B	HR	RBI	BB	SO	SB
Baine, Tom, of-dh	.241	26	83	11	20	3	0	2	7	13	11	2
#Baker, Doug, Inf-of	.216	91	301	46	65	15	2	3	18	41	61	6
Brito, Bernardo, dh-of	.282	113	376	48	106	26	3	25	79	27	102	1
*Bruett, J.T., of	.235	10	34	8	8	2	0	0	3	11	4	2
*Bush, Randy, dh-of	.222	3	9	2	2	2	0	0	1	3	1	0
*Dalena, Pete, 1b (56 Van)	.254	99	355	39	90	19	4	2	42	30	42	2
*Delima, Rafael, of	.202	61	188	23	38	6	2	1	19	18	18	6
*Hale, Chip, 2b	.280	130	479	71	134	24	2	3	40	68	57	6
Jacas, David, of	.231	112	350	57	81	18	4	7	26	30	60	18
Jorgensen, Terry, 3b	.259	123	440	43	114	28	3	10	50	44	83	0
*Lanoux, Marty, dh	.187	28	75	5	14	5	0	1	10	11	7	0
Laudner, Tim, c-dh	.000	9	29	2	0	0	0	0	0	3	9	0
Leius, Scott, ss	.229	103	353	34	81	13	5	2	23	35	66	5
Manrique, Fred, ph	1.000	1	1	0	1	0	0	0	1	0	0	0
Munoz, Pedro, of	.318	30	110	19	35	4	0	5	21	15	18	8
Naveda, Ed, of-1b	.231	78	255	28	59	11	3	2	28	32	19	2
Nelson, Jaime, c	.253	76	217	25	55	9	0	4	24	15	31	0
Parks, Derek, c	.177	76	231	27	41	8	1	11	27	18	56	0
Powell, Alonzo, of	.322	107	376	56	121	25	3	8	62	40	79	23
Rodriguez, Victor, dh-1b	.282	12	39	4	11	1	0	1	2	2	5	0
Siwa, Joe, c	.190	6	21	1	4	1	0	0	1	0	5	0
*Sorrento, Paul, 1b	.302	102	354	59	107	27	1	19	72	64	95	3

PITCHING	W	L	ERA	G	GS	CG	SV	IP	H	R	ER	BB	SO
Abbott, Paul	5	14	4.56	23	23	4	0	128	110	75	65	82	129
Bangtson, Pat	6	7	5.55	29	12	0	1	105	130	76	65	53	64
*Casian, Larry	9	9	4.48	37	23	1	0	157	171	90	78	59	89
Cook, Mike	6	8	3.20	19	19	2	0	115	105	54	41	59	63
Delkus, Pete	5	3	4.18	19	0	0	4	90	109	48	42	21	35
Dyer, Mike	0	1	34.71	2	2	0	0	2	6	10	9	9	0
*Guthrie, Mark	1	3	2.98	9	8	1	0	42	47	19	14	12	39
Johnson, Greg	3	0	4.50	15	0	0	1	26	27	20	13	14	24
Lind, Orlando	0	3	5.06	7	0	0	0	16	18	9	9	9	14
*Mason, Mike	0	0	0.00	3	0	0	0	3	4	2	0	3	1
Oliveras, Francisco	3	4	2.90	11	6	1	1	62	44	23	20	22	56

BATTING

R	Paul Faries, Las Vegas	109
H	Paul Faries, Las Vegas	172
TB	Butch Davis, Alb	243
2B	Rich Amaral, Vancouver	39
3B	Kevin Ward, Tacoma	14
HR	Bernardo Brito, Portland	25
RBI	Tom Dodd, Calgary	114
SH	Bill McGuire, Calgary	11
	Juan Castillo, Colo. Spr	11
SF	Butch Davis, Alb	11
BB	Dave Hansen, Alb	90
IBB	Tino Martinez, Calgary	11
	Lee Stevens, Edmonton	11
HBP	Kevin Ward, Tacoma	14
SO	Mike Simms, Tucson	135
SB	Jose Offerman, Alb	60
CS	Jose Offerman, Alb	19
	Alex Cole, Colo. Spr./LV	19
OB%	Jeff Manto, Colo. Spr	.446

PITCHING

G	Pete Delkus, Portland	65
GS	Randy Hennis, Tucson	28
	Grady Hall, Vancouver	28
CG	Kevin Bearse, Colo. Spr	6
	Scott Lewis, Edmonton	6
ShO	Four tied at	2
Sv	Joe Bitker, Tacoma	26
W	Jeff Bittiger, Albuquerque	15
L	Paul McClellan, Phoenix	16
IP	Grady Hall, Vancouver	185
H	Chris Beasley, Edmonton	201
R	Eric Nolte, Las Vegas	130
HR	Charles Scott, Colo. Spr./Port	23
BB	Ray Young, Tacoma	105
HB	Chris Beasley, Edmonton	16
SO	Ray Young, Tacoma	137
WP	Terry Wells, Albuquerque	17
Bk	Ray Young, Tacoma	16

	W	L	ERA	G	GS	CG	SV	IP	H	R	ER	BB	SO
Pittman, Park	0	1	6.99	28	0	0	6	28	28	24	22	34	22
Redding, Mike	0	1	11.57	1	1	0	0	2	6	4	3	1	1
Savage, Jack	1	2	1.31	16	0	0	3	21	17	8	3	11	25
Scott, Charles (3 CS)	7	11	4.59	32	21	0	1	157	170	87	80	66	130
*Wayne, Gary	2	4	3.41	22	0	0	5	32	29	14	12	13	30
Weber, Weston (35 Tac)	5	2	5.42	39	3	0	1	73	79	54	44	48	42
*Williams, Jimmy	4	6	5.04	51	3	0	3	84	73	64	47	74	62
Yett, Rich	4	6	6.17	22	20	1	0	101	117	72	69	60	58

TACOMA

BATTING	AVG	G	AB	R	H	2B	3B	HR	RBI	BB	SO	SB
Afenir, Troy, c	.249	88	289	44	72	14	2	15	47	30	81	1
Arndt, Larry, 3b-1b	.251	121	438	59	110	17	5	2	59	38	87	16
Blankenship, Lance, 2b-of	.258	24	93	18	24	7	1	1	9	14	16	7
Bordick, Mike, ss	.227	111	348	49	79	16	1	2	30	46	40	3
Brosius, Scott, 2b	.143	3	7	2	1	0	1	0	0	1	3	0
*Casey, Tim, of	.189	48	106	15	20	5	1	2	7	17	35	0
Dietrick, Pat, of	.200	13	30	3	6	2	0	0	1	3	10	0
*Fields, Bruce, dh-of	.280	87	336	46	94	18	2	2	34	36	62	8
#Fox, Eric, of	.276	62	221	37	61	9	2	4	34	20	34	8
Hemond, Scott, 2b-c	.243	72	218	32	53	11	0	8	35	24	52	10
Howard, Steve, of	.270	97	330	55	89	18	4	10	45	42	100	17
Howitt, Dann, 1b-of	.265	118	437	58	116	30	1	11	69	38	95	4
*Jennings, Doug, of-1b	.346	60	208	32	72	19	1	6	30	31	36	4
#Johnson, Wallace, dh-1b	.333	6	18	5	6	1	1	0	2	3	1	0
Lewis, Darren, of	.291	60	247	32	72	5	2	2	26	16	35	16
McGinnis, Russ, c-1b	.248	110	359	57	89	19	1	13	77	75	70	2
Mercedes, Henry, c-dh	.194	12	31	3	6	1	0	0	2	3	7	0
Pedrique, Al, Inf	.261	123	380	54	99	16	2	0	46	49	37	3
Scott, Dick, 2b	.308	21	26	2	8	2	0	0	3	3	5	0
*Shockey, Scott, 1b	.279	13	43	1	12	4	1	0	7	0	7	0
#Vice, Darryl, 2b-dh	.400	7	10	3	4	1	0	0	1	7	2	1
Ward, Kevin, of	.297	123	421	83	125	30	14	10	60	44	72	24
Witmeyer, Ron, 1b	.290	10	31	5	9	2	0	1	7	1	3	0

PITCHING	W	L	ERA	G	GS	CG	SV	IP	H	R	ER	BB	SO
*Allison, Dana	0	0	0.00	2	0	0	0	1	1	0	0	1	2
*Ariola, Tony	0	1	5.51	6	2	0	0	16	24	14	10	2	6
Bitker, Joe	2	3	3.20	48	0	0	26	56	51	22	20	20	52
Chiamparino, Scott	13	9	3.28	26	26	4	0	173	174	79	63	72	110
Chitren, Steve	0	0	0.00	1	0	0	0	1	1	0	0	0	2
Corsi, Jim	0	0	1.50	5	0	0	0	9	9	2	1	1	3
Law, Joe	2	5	6.16	17	11	0	1	61	66	43	42	42	46
*Leiper, Dave	0	1	5.82	6	0	0	2	17	19	12	11	9	8
*McCoy, Tim	0	5	8.46	8	5	0	0	22	26	24	21	18	8
Miller, Russ	0	1	8.31	4	1	0	0	9	7	8	8	12	3
Norris, Mike	0	1	3.72	3	2	0	0	10	7	4	4	2	5
*Otto, Dave	0	0	4.50	2	0	0	0	2	3	1	1	1	2
*Raczka, Mike (4 LV)	7	5	4.28	46	2	0	2	67	59	37	32	44	61
Shaver, Jeff	0	4	5.76	19	6	0	2	45	54	33	29	26	42
Slusarski, Joe	4	2	3.40	9	9	0	0	56	54	24	21	22	37
Strebeck, Ricky	0	0	0.00	3	0	0	0	3	3	0	0	2	0
Veres, Dave	11	8	4.69	32	23	2	1	152	136	90	79	88	88
Walton, Bruce	5	5	3.11	46	5	0	7	98	103	42	34	23	67
Wojna, Ed	10	5	3.99	24	23	3	0	142	121	71	63	55	99
Young, Ray	14	7	4.20	28	27	1	0	165	155	87	77	105	137

TUCSON

BATTING	AVG	G	AB	R	H	2B	3B	HR	RBI	BB	SO	SB
*Anthony, Eric, of	.286	40	161	28	46	10	2	6	26	17	41	8
*Baldwin, Jeff, of	.135	19	37	4	5	0	0	0	5	7	11	0
Brown, Todd, of	.400	8	20	2	8	0	0	0	2	1	5	0

	AVG	G	AB	R	H	2B	3B	HR	RBI	BB	SO	SB
#Candaele, Casey, 2b	.214	7	28	2	6	1	0	0	2	3	2	1
Colombino, Carlo, 3b	.252	81	290	31	73	7	3	4	40	10	35	3
Davidson, Mark, of	.335	56	182	35	61	13	1	6	46	22	35	5
Dean, Kevin, of	.257	13	35	5	9	1	0	0	5	4	12	0
#Harris, Rusty, ss	.294	44	126	24	37	7	3	0	8	7	19	2
Hubbard, Trent, 2b-3b	.222	12	27	5	6	2	2	0	2	3	6	1
#Kellner, Frank, ss	.300	19	60	13	18	1	0	0	7	15	6	1
Marquez, Edwin, c	.339	18	56	12	19	2	2	1	10	6	7	1
*Meadows, Louie, of	.298	25	84	16	25	3	3	3	18	18	8	6
Mikulik, Joe, of	.331	62	175	31	58	11	2	1	29	13	17	3
Nichols, Carl, c-of	.253	58	170	24	43	11	0	4	33	30	39	1
Olander, Jim, of	.235	33	98	12	23	8	2	1	12	14	24	0
Ortiz, Javier, of	.352	49	179	36	63	16	2	5	39	22	36	2
Ortiz, Joe, c	.250	7	12	1	3	0	0	0	3	0	2	0
#Renteria, Ed, 3b-ss	.291	35	110	15	32	2	0	1	12	7	14	2
*Rhodes, Karl, of	.275	107	385	68	106	24	11	3	59	47	75	24
*Rohde, Dave, 2b-ss	.353	47	170	42	60	10	2	0	20	40	20	5
Sanchez, Pedro, ss	.183	73	202	29	37	5	3	0	15	20	45	13
Servais, Scott, c	.218	89	303	37	66	11	3	5	37	18	61	0
Simms, Mike, of	.273	124	421	75	115	34	5	13	72	74	135	3
*Smajstrla, Craig, 2b-3b	.313	124	473	86	148	25	4	2	42	58	36	8
*Spilman, Harry, dh	.268	77	190	11	51	13	1	4	42	16	27	0
*Strange, Doug, 3b	.224	37	98	7	22	3	0	0	7	8	23	0
*Tolentino, Jose, of-1b	.308	116	377	69	116	32	3	21	78	48	44	0
#Young, Gerald, of	.333	49	183	37	61	7	4	0	24	40	18	14

PITCHING	W	L	ERA	G	GS	CG	SV	IP	H	R	ER	BB	SO
Bowen, Ryan	1	3	9.35	10	7	0	0	35	41	36	36	38	29
Brennan, William	8	7	4.73	41	8	2	0	110	104	68	58	89	88
*Buchanan, Bob	0	0	5.54	9	0	0	1	13	13	8	8	9	8
Cano, Jose	2	5	7.09	10	10	1	0	46	61	43	36	24	19
Clancy, Jim	3	2	2.98	10	5	0	0	42	48	17	14	9	34
Clark, Terry	11	4	3.54	29	22	3	1	155	172	73	61	41	80
Eichhorn, Dave	2	4	3.38	28	0	0	3	48	55	24	18	16	13
Fisher, Brian	8	8	6.80	30	13	0	6	87	113	72	66	36	47
Hennis, Randy	10	8	4.41	28	28	3	0	159	153	87	78	92	101
Heredia, Hector	2	2	5.27	34	0	0	3	56	66	36	33	21	47
*Ilsley, Blaise	2	1	6.46	20	6	1	2	63	87	50	45	24	39
Kile, Darryl	5	10	6.64	26	23	1	0	123	147	97	91	68	77
Meyer, Brian	5	7	2.97	64	0	0	15	100	91	43	33	38	54
*Normand, Guy	2	0	7.71	4	0	0	0	5	3	4	4	5	1
*Reuss, Jerry	0	0	15.19	5	0	0	0	5	18	14	9	2	3
St.Claire, Randy	4	3	5.46	23	0	0	0	31	45	22	19	21	16
*Thurmond, Mark	0	0	3.27	9	0	0	1	11	11	4	4	1	6
Tunnell, Lee	6	7	4.78	33	20	2	2	124	144	76	66	48	59
*Walter, Gene	0	0	0.00	3	0	0	0	3	4	3	0	3	4

VANCOUVER

BATTING	AVG	G	AB	R	H	2B	3B	HR	RBI	BB	SO	SB
Amaral, Rich, ss-3b	.301	130	462	87	139	39	5	4	56	88	68	20
Campbell, Darrin, 3b	.143	2	7	0	1	0	0	0	0	0	1	0
*Gaither, Horace, ss	.000	1	3	0	0	0	0	0	0	0	1	0
Grebeck, Craig, ss-3b	.195	12	41	8	8	0	0	1	3	6	7	1
*Hill, Orsino, of	.284	106	366	61	104	20	3	11	60	55	86	5
#Lawton, Marcus, of	.252	122	417	48	105	22	9	2	43	36	50	16
#Martin, Norberto, 2b	.266	130	508	77	135	20	4	3	45	27	63	10
McCray, Rod, of	.226	19	53	7	12	4	2	0	6	10	20	4
McPhail, Marlin, 3b-of	.288	109	386	50	111	23	5	8	60	35	59	6
#Penigar, C.L., of-dh	.211	90	289	40	61	16	6	6	46	41	74	13
*Pledger, Kinnis, ph	.000	1	1	0	0	0	0	0	0	0	0	0
#Sambo, Ramon, of	.250	102	324	46	81	3	3	0	31	54	59	30
#Smith, Keith, ss	.236	85	259	36	61	7	0	1	24	28	39	4
Trafton, Todd, 1b	.188	42	117	10	22	2	0	2	15	18	27	4
Wakamatsu, Don, c	.262	62	187	20	49	10	0	3	13	13	35	2
*Willard, Jerry, c	.279	121	380	66	106	21	0	20	76	85	60	2
Williams, Dana, of	.196	32	107	16	21	6	0	1	4	6	14	2
Woodson, Tracy, 3b-1b	.267	131	480	70	128	22	5	17	81	50	70	6

PITCHING	W	L	ERA	G	GS	CG	SV	IP	H	R	ER	BB	SO
*Alvarez, Wilson	7	7	6.00	17	15	1	0	75	91	54	50	51	35
Campbell, Mike	4	5	5.83	21	8	0	0	66	76	45	43	30	50
Cedeno, Vinicio	0	1	3.38	4	0	0	0	8	5	3	3	7	8
Davino, Mike	0	0	0.00	1	0	0	0	1	0	0	0	1	1
*Drees, Tom	8	5	3.98	17	16	4	0	97	94	49	43	51	63
Garcia, Ramon	0	0	0.00	1	0	0	0	1	2	0	0	0	1
*Hall, Grady	13	8	4.24	28	28	4	0	185	185	100	87	89	106
Hernandez, Roberto	3	5	2.84	11	11	3	0	79	73	33	25	26	49
Hillegas, Shawn	5	3	1.74	36	0	0	9	67	49	22	13	15	52
Kutzler, Jerry	5	7	4.20	19	19	2	0	114	124	64	53	34	73
*Manzanillo, Ravelo	7	3	3.61	38	6	0	4	92	74	41	37	60	64
Menendez, Tony	2	5	3.72	24	9	2	0	73	63	34	30	28	48
Pawlowski, John	7	7	4.76	30	14	1	2	117	125	68	62	64	67
Peterson, Adam	4	1	2.09	6	6	3	0	43	26	11	10	15	30
*Rosenberg, Steve	6	5	3.57	40	7	0	8	88	66	43	35	44	74
*Scheid, Rich	2	2	3.20	20	2	0	0	39	37	19	14	24	38
Segura, Jose	1	3	5.10	40	0	0	8	55	49	34	31	35	47
Stephens, Ron	0	0	7.36	3	0	0	0	4	9	4	3	0	1

EASTERN LEAGUE

Given up for dead, London rallies to win EL crown

By PHIL BOWMAN

"Going, going . . . "

That was the newspaper headline that greeted the London Tigers when they returned from Canton, down 2-0 in their best-of-5 Eastern League playoff semifinal.

The Tigers were going all right—to New Britain for the title series. The Tigers won three in a row against Canton at Labatt Park to stay alive. They had an easier time in the championship series, sweeping the Britsox, 3-0. It was the first time the Detroit organization ever had a championship team in the Eastern League, although Glens Falls won regular-season titles in 1981 and in 1988.

Luis Mercedes
. . . top hitter

The Tigers' crown ended Albany's domination. The Yankees won the regular-season title with a 79-60 mark, but were denied their third EL crown in a row when they were eliminated in the semi-finals, 3-2, by fourth-place New Britain.

Albany finished first, despite an early season managerial shift. When Rick Down was promoted to Columbus, to replace Stump Merrill who was asked to step in for fired Bucky Dent at the helm of the New York Yankees, Down was replaced by Dan Radison, the Yankees organization hitting instructor.

The race for playoff spots was exciting. Just 11½ games separated the top six teams. In 1989, Albany finished first, 19 games ahead of second-place Harrisburg.

The champion Tigers had plenty of heroes.

Rico Brogna, Detroit's first baseman of the future, led the

LEAGUE CHAMPIONS

Playoff Champions, Where Applicable

1990—London	1966—Elmira	1943—Elmira
1989—Albany	1965—Pittsfield	1942—Scranton
1988—Albany	1964—Elmira	1941—Elmira
1987—Harrisburg	1963—Charleston	1940—Binghamton
1986—Vermont	1962—Elmira	1939—Scranton
1985—Vermont	1961—Springfield	1938—Elmira
1984—Vermont	1960—*Williamsport	1937—Elmira
1983—New Britain	—*Springfield	1936—Scranton
1982—West Haven	1959—Springfield	1935—Binghamton
1981—Bristol	1958—Binghamton	1934—Williamsport
1980—Holyoke	1957—Reading	1933—Binghamton
1979—West Haven	1956—Schenectady	1932—Wilkes-Barre
1978—Bristol	1955—Allentown	1931—Harrisburg
1977—West Haven	1954—Albany	1930—Wilkes-Barre
1976—West Haven	1953—Binghamton	1929—Binghamton
1975—Bristol	1952—Binghamton	1928—Harrisburg
1974—Thetford Mines	1951—Scranton	1927—Harrisburg
1973—Reading	1950—Wilkes-Barre	1926—Scranton
1972—West Haven	1949—Binghamton	1925—*York
1971—Elmira	1948—Scranton	—*Williamsport
1970—Waterbury	1947—Utica	1924—Williamsport
1969—York	1946—Scranton	1923—Williamsport
1968—Reading	1945—Albany	
1967—Binghamton	1944—Binghamton	*co-champions

Canton shortstop Mark Lewis hit .272 with 10 homers and was named the EL's top major league prospect.

league with 21 home runs and tied for the lead with 77 RBIs. Righthander Rusty Meacham led the league with 15 victories, while Dave Haas and Mike Wilkins chipped in with 13 wins apiece.

Second-year skipper Chris Chambliss was named the league's manager of the year for guiding his team to a 76-63 record.

Mercedes wins bat title

The Eastern League had many big-name prospects during the 1990 season. Canton shortstop Mark Lewis was named the league's top prospect after hitting .272 with 10 homers and 60 RBIs before earning a promotion to Class AAA Colorado Springs in early August.

If you were looking for pure hitters, try Hagerstown's Luis Mercedes and New Britain's Jeff Bagwell. Mercedes edged Bagwell for the batting title—.334 to .333.

Mercedes claimed his second consecutive crown. He won the Carolina League title in 1989 with a .309 mark. Bagwell, in his first full professional season, led the league most of the year, but slipped at the end. He was traded to the Houston Astros organization with three days left in the regular season in a deal that brought the parent Red Sox veteran pitcher Larry Andersen.

Bagwell did manage to lead the league in hits and was tied for the lead in doubles. He also was named the league's MVP.

Hagerstown's Pat Austin was the only other hitter in the league to top the .300 mark. He hit .307.

Strong pitching

Why were there only three hitters with better than .300 averages?

Pitching, pitching and more pitching.

Williamsport righthander Mike Gardiner was named the league's pitcher of the year. He was 12-8 with a 1.90 ERA, pitching for seventh-place Williamsport. Harrisburg's Randy Tomlin was the league's best lefthander. He was 9-6 with a 2.28 ERA before joining the National League East champion Pittsburgh Pirates.

**Mike Gardiner
. . . ERA leader**

Gardiner and Tomlin weren't the only pitchers to reach "The Show" in 1990. Canton's Charles Nagy (13-8, 2.52) got the call, as did Hagerstown's Anthony Telford (10-2, 1.97 ERA).

Kevin Morton, considered Boston's top pitching prospect, pitched a seven-inning perfect game against Reading late in the season.

Harrisburg sets pace

The Eastern League set an all-time attendance record as 1,369,589 fans passed through the turnstiles 1990. Harrisburg led the league with 223,533 fans. Reading, Canton and Albany also drew more than 200,000.

Perhaps the most amazing numbers were posted by Reading. The Phillies drew 204,240 despite finishing in last place. The Phillies drew more than 15,000 for their final three-game home series of the season.

Williamsport was last in the league with 76,921 fans. Marvin Goldklang sold the franchise to CD&M Associates during the season. The franchise was expected to move to Binghamton, N.Y., for the 1991 season.

1990 FINAL STANDINGS

	W	L	Pct.	GB
Albany (Yankees)	79	60	.568	—
London (Tigers)	76	63	.547	3
Canton-Akron (Indians)	76	64	.543	3½
New Britain (Red Sox)	72	67	.518	7
Harrisburg (Pirates)	69	69	.500	9½
Hagerstown (Orioles)	67	71	.486	11½
Williamsport (Mariners)	61	79	.436	18½
Reading (Phillies)	55	82	.401	23

1990 GENERAL INFORMATION

Playoffs: New Britain defeated Albany 3-2 in best-of-5 semifinal; London defeated Canton 3-2 in best-of-5 semifinal; London defeated New Britain 3-0 in best-of-5 final for league championship.

Regular-Season Attendance: Harrisburg, 223,503; Reading, 204,240; Albany, 203,423; Canton, 203,096; Hagerstown, 167,725; London, 167,664; New Britain, 123,017; Williamsport, 76,921.

Managers: Albany—Rick Down, Dan Radison; **Canton**—Ken Bolek; **Hagerstown**—Jerry Narron; **Harrisburg**—Marc Bombard; **London**—Chris Chambliss; **New Britain**—Butch Hobson; **Reading**—Don McCormack; **Williamsport**—Rich Morales.

1990 Official All-Star Team: C—Mitch Lyden, Albany. 1B—Rico Brogna, London; 2B—Pat Kelly, Albany. 3B—Jeff Bagwell, New Britain. SS—Mark Lewis, Canton. UTIL INF—Gary Alexander, Reading. OF—Scott Meadows, Hagerstown; Bernie Williams, Albany; Luis Mercedes, Hagerstown. DH—Jeff Grotewold, Reading. RHP—Mike Gardiner, Williamsport. LHP—Randy Tomlin, Harrisburg. RP—Darrin Chapin, Albany. **Most Valuable Player**—Jeff Bagwell, New Britain. **Pitcher**

of the Year—Mike Gardiner, Williamsport. **Manager of the Year—** Chris Chambliss, London.

Top 10 Major League Prospects (by Baseball America): 1. Mark Lewis, ss, Canton; **2.** Bernie Williams, of, Albany; **3.** Rico Brogna, 1b, London; **4.** Jeff Bagwell, 3b, New Britain; **5.** Mike Gardiner, rhp, Williamsport; **6.** Carlos Garcia, ss, Harrisburg; **7.** Charles Nagy, rhp, Canton; **8.** Luis Mercedes, of, Hagerstown; **9.** Mike Mussina, rhp, Hagerstown; **10.** Pat Kelly, 2b, Albany.

1990 BATTING, PITCHING STATS

CLUB BATTING

	AVG	G	AB	R	H	2B	3B	HR	BB	SO	SB
Hagerstown	.267	138	4504	566	1202	188	33	52	450	776	144
Albany	.262	139	4449	620	1166	233	30	84	486	836	117
Harrisburg	.258	138	4539	531	1169	182	30	39	366	746	109
London	.251	139	4550	549	1144	174	25	71	432	755	89
Canton	.245	140	4459	556	1091	185	30	69	437	787	108
New Britain	.241	139	4433	506	1068	219	33	31	523	752	52
Williamsport	.236	140	4472	467	1057	174	21	47	380	810	104
Reading	.235	137	4299	474	1012	188	13	77	360	859	82

CLUB PITCHING

	ERA	G	CG	SHO	IP	H	R	ER	BB	SO
New Britain	3.17	139	19	16	38	1193	1133	519	420	390	809
Hagerstown	3.17	138	14	14	38	1183	1088	513	416	435	867
Harrisburg	3.20	138	22	13	33	1176	1091	526	418	390	710
London	3.26	139	23	16	33	1202	1125	526	435	431	840
Williamsport	3.30	140	17	8	26	1193	1137	526	437	366	785
Canton	3.33	140	26	13	32	1201	1145	546	444	435	818
Albany	3.48	139	19	13	36	1165	1068	533	451	534	731
Reading	3.73	137	12	11	33	1139	1122	578	472	453	761

INDIVIDUAL BATTING LEADERS
(Minimum 378 Plate Appearances)

	AVG	G	AB	R	H	2B	3B	HR	RBI	BB	SO	SB
Mercedes, Luis, Hag	.334	108	416	71	139	12	4	3	37	34	70	38
Bagwell, Jeff, NB	.333	136	481	63	160	34	7	4	61	73	57	5
Austin, Pat, Hag	.307	97	375	53	115	10	6	0	34	31	30	22
*Twardoski, Mike, NB	.293	127	413	72	121	34	3	1	46	95	46	4
Meadows, Scott, Hag	.293	138	495	60	145	29	3	6	75	66	70	9
#Yacopino, Ed, Harr	.290	96	362	39	105	19	4	4	49	26	57	5
Wehner, John, Harr	.288	138	511	71	147	27	1	4	62	40	51	24
*Williams, Bernie, Alb	.281	134	466	91	131	28	5	8	54	98	97	39
#Peguero, Julio, Read	.277	107	423	40	117	14	9	1	28	31	54	8
Batiste, Kim, Read	.276	125	486	57	134	14	4	6	33	13	73	28

INDIVIDUAL PITCHING LEADERS
(Minimum 112 Innings)

	W	L	ERA	G	GS	CG	SV	IP	H	R	ER	BB	SO
Gardiner, Mike, Will	12	8	1.90	26	26	5	0	180	136	47	38	29	149
DelaRosa, Francisco, Hag	9	5	2.06	23	20	2	0	131	97	34	30	51	105
DeLucia, Rich, Will	6	6	2.11	18	18	2	0	115	92	30	27	30	76
*Tomlin, Randy, Harr	9	6	2.28	19	18	4	0	126	101	43	32	34	92
Wilson, Gary, Read	7	12	2.38	33	21	3	2	151	140	64	40	39	70
Wilkins, Mike, London	13	5	2.42	25	25	6	0	175	156	57	47	47	91
Nagy, Charles, Canton	13	8	2.52	23	23	9	0	175	132	62	49	39	99
*Owen, Dave, NB	7	9	2.93	20	20	4	0	132	123	54	43	48	88
Haas, David, London	13	8	2.99	27	27	3	0	178	151	64	59	74	116
Tracy, Jim, Harr	14	8	3.00	25	23	5	1	153	143	63	51	37	106

ALBANY

BATTING	AVG	G	AB	R	H	2B	3B	HR	RBI	BB	SO	SB
#DeJardin, Bobby, ss	.263	103	388	52	102	21	0	1	27	43	75	12
Dickerson, Bobby, inf	.220	58	182	20	40	8	2	1	17	7	29	0
Hailey, Freddie, of-dh	.261	31	92	7	24	7	0	1	14	7	14	0
Kelly, Pat, 2b	.270	126	418	67	113	19	6	8	44	37	79	32
Livesey, Jeff, c-dh	.158	9	19	0	3	0	0	0	1	1	7	0
Lyden, Mitch, c-1b	.296	85	311	55	92	22	1	17	63	24	67	1
Masse, Billy, of-dh	.188	31	96	12	18	1	0	3	8	22	20	0
*Phillips, Vince, of	.241	117	402	49	97	20	5	2	46	36	67	6
Ramos, John, c-dh	.314	84	287	38	90	20	1	4	46	36	39	1
Rodriguez, Carlos, ss	.280	18	75	10	21	4	0	0	7	2	1	1
Silvestri, Dave, ss	.286	2	7	0	2	0	0	0	2	0	1	0
*Skeels, Andy, c	.270	75	215	18	58	7	0	1	21	23	29	1
Sparks, Don, 3b	.266	112	418	48	111	20	5	4	52	33	70	2
*Sparks, Greg, 1b	.246	129	455	66	112	24	1	19	77	42	119	0
Turgeon, Dave, 3b	.179	12	28	1	5	1	0	0	1	2	4	0
#Williams, Bernie, of	.281	134	466	91	131	28	5	8	54	98	97	39
Williams, Gerald, of	.250	96	324	61	81	17	2	13	58	35	74	18
*Zeihen, Bob, of-dh	.248	92	266	32	66	14	2	2	25	38	43	3

PITCHING	W	L	ERA	G	GS	CG	SV	IP	H	R	ER	BB	SO
Bond, Daven	6	2	2.76	35	2	0	0	65	71	27	20	20	41
Chapin, Darrin	3	2	2.53	43	0	0	21	53	43	20	16	21	61
Clayton, Royal	10	9	3.18	21	21	6	0	142	149	58	50	43	68
Cook, Andy	12	8	3.45	24	24	5	0	157	146	69	60	52	53
Draper, Mike	2	2	6.44	8	8	0	0	43	51	34	31	19	15

New Britain third baseman Jeff Bagwell lost the EL bat title to Luis Mercedes by a single point, .334 to .333.

	W	L	ERA	G	GS	CG	SV	IP	H	R	ER	BB	SO
*Garcia, Victor	3	4	2.12	16	9	1	1	72	49	26	17	39	42
Gogolewski, Doug	1	3	13.81	5	5	0	0	14	17	24	22	19	21
*Holcomb, Scott	0	0	14.09	6	0	0	0	8	10	14	12	15	9
*Howard, Chris	0	0	14.40	2	0	0	0	5	9	8	8	7	2
*Johnson, Jeff	4	3	1.63	9	9	3	0	61	44	14	11	15	41
Kamieniecki, Scott	10	9	3.20	22	21	3	0	132	113	55	47	61	99
Manon, Ramon	1	2	5.96	9	3	0	0	26	24	19	17	29	21
Newell, Tom	4	4	4.79	22	8	0	0	62	54	42	33	53	34
Popplewell, Tom	8	2	4.08	14	12	0	0	64	56	31	29	36	34
*Rub, Jerry	3	0	4.45	22	0	0	0	32	43	21	16	31	37
Smith, Mike (Mississippi) .	0	1	2.91	10	1	0	0	22	24	7	7	10	16
Smith, Willie	1	1	0.00	9	0	0	4	9	6	1	0	5	12
Stanford, Don	4	2	2.15	56	1	0	10	88	68	21	21	24	65
Taylor, Wade	6	4	2.88	12	12	1	0	84	71	30	27	18	44
Torres, Ricky	1	2	2.36	9	3	0	0	26	20	12	7	17	16

CANTON

BATTING	AVG	G	AB	R	H	2B	3B	HR	RBI	BB	SO	SB
*Allison, Jamie, of	.187	50	123	4	23	3	1	0	10	10	25	4
Belle, Albert, dh	.250	9	32	4	8	1	0	0	3	3	7	0
Blackwell, Barry, c	.266	23	64	7	17	4	0	1	7	5	16	0
*Epley, Daren, 1b	.261	119	403	50	105	21	1	6	37	39	63	6
Ferretti, Sam, 3b-2b	.258	129	434	58	112	15	1	1	43	35	51	10
#Foster, Lindsay, ss	.244	13	41	7	10	0	0	0	4	0	7	1
#Francois, Manny, 2b	.175	62	143	20	25	8	0	2	12	18	35	3
Hearn, Ed, c	.270	29	89	14	24	4	0	2	11	5	16	0
Jackson, Leverne, of	.234	104	346	32	81	12	2	5	46	33	65	6
*Kesselmark, Joe, of	.114	27	79	9	9	1	0	0	3	11	6	1
Lewis, Mark, ss	.272	102	390	55	106	19	3	10	60	23	49	8
*Liebert, Allen, c	.243	114	362	32	88	17	1	9	45	39	89	1
*Melendez, Francisco, dh-1b .	.244	41	131	13	32	2	1	2	16	15	22	0
Mota, Carlos, c	.048	8	21	1	1	1	0	0	1	1	4	0
*Orsag, Jim, dh-of	.260	65	181	26	47	10	1	7	28	27	57	12
*Ramos, Ken, of	.329	19	73	12	24	2	2	0	11	8	10	2
*Sabino, Miguel, of	.270	65	230	37	62	2	5	2	19	22	41	10
Swain, Rob, 2b-3b	.239	79	222	24	53	13	2	2	21	31	41	3
#Tatis, Bernie, of-3b	.272	69	272	53	74	16	5	5	33	27	46	25

	AVG	G	AB	R	H	2B	3B	HR	RBI	BB	SO	SB
Tatum, Jim, 3b-1b	.179	30	106	6	19	6	0	2	11	6	19	1
*Taylor, Dwight, pr	.000	1	0	1	0	0	0	0	0	0	0	0
Webster, Casey, 3b	.153	27	85	12	13	2	1	1	3	17	13	0
Wine, Robbie, c	.206	19	63	3	13	2	0	1	6	6	15	2
#Young, Delwyn, dh	.250	49	176	23	44	10	1	4	23	13	38	7
Zambrano, Roberto, of	.257	115	393	53	101	14	3	7	44	43	52	6

PITCHING	W	L	ERA	G	GS	CG	SV	IP	H	R	ER	BB	SO
Borgatti, Mike (19 Hag)	1	4	4.65	28	0	0	0	62	86	40	32	26	33
*Bowden, Mark	0	1	3.38	2	0	0	0	3	4	2	1	1	0
Bruske, Jim	9	3	3.28	32	13	3	0	118	118	53	43	42	62
Collins, Allen	2	5	4.25	37	3	0	2	72	70	51	34	39	46
*Curtis, Mike	5	4	2.95	13	13	1	0	79	72	34	26	23	73
DiPoto, Jerry	1	0	2.57	3	2	0	0	14	15	5	4	4	12
Egloff, Bruce	3	2	1.98	34	0	0	15	55	44	16	12	15	53
Farrell, John	1	1	7.20	2	2	0	0	10	13	8	8	2	5
*Fassero, Jeff	5	4	2.80	61	0	0	6	64	66	24	20	24	61
Ferlenda, Greg	1	0	7.15	9	0	0	1	11	17	12	9	5	7
Heinkel, Don	1	1	2.25	5	4	0	0	28	21	8	7	14	15
Keliipuleole, Carl	5	9	4.22	27	19	0	1	107	113	56	50	60	59
Kramer, Tom	6	3	3.00	12	10	2	0	72	67	25	24	14	46
McMichael, Greg	2	3	3.35	13	4	0	0	43	39	17	15	17	19
*Mutis, Jeff	11	10	3.16	26	26	7	0	165	178	73	58	44	94
Nagy, Charles	13	8	2.52	23	23	9	0	175	132	62	49	39	99
Roscoe, Greg	6	7	3.78	20	20	4	0	119	115	63	50	41	106
Seanez, Rudy	1	0	2.16	15	0	0	5	17	9	4	4	12	27
Soper, Mike	2	1	3.92	16	0	0	1	21	16	10	9	14	20
Spagnola, Glenn	1	0	5.87	4	0	0	0	8	4	5	5	5	2
Walker, Mike	1	0	0.00	1	1	0	0	7	4	0	0	4	3

HAGERSTOWN

BATTING	AVG	G	AB	R	H	2B	3B	HR	RBI	BB	SO	SB
*Anderson, Brady, dh-of	.382	9	34	8	13	0	2	1	5	5	5	2
Austin, Pat, 2b	.307	97	375	53	115	10	6	0	34	31	30	22
Berlin, Randy, ss-3b	.118	6	17	2	2	0	0	0	1	1	7	1
*Bettendorf, Dave, dh	.211	23	71	5	15	1	1	3	10	8	12	0
Brown, Don, of	.173	28	52	3	9	0	0	0	1	9	16	2
#Buford, Don, 2b	.196	50	163	28	32	4	1	1	6	18	25	12
Devereaux, Mike, of	.250	4	20	4	5	3	0	0	3	0	1	0
Eberle, Mike, c	.250	39	124	10	31	8	0	1	10	8	36	0
Faulkner, Craig, c-1b	.249	104	370	36	92	18	0	5	44	22	75	0
Gutierrez, Ricky, ss	.234	20	64	4	15	0	1	0	6	3	8	2
Harris, Walt, of	.167	8	24	0	4	0	0	0	2	5	5	0
Hayden, Paris, of	.233	47	129	16	30	5	0	2	8	6	30	1
Hithe, Victor, of	.270	27	100	24	27	4	1	2	11	19	25	11
*Horn, Sam, dh	.261	7	23	2	6	2	0	1	3	6	5	0
Latmore, Bobby, 3b-ss	.259	132	479	52	124	19	2	9	64	21	80	7
Lofton, Rodney, ss	.272	89	294	35	80	7	2	0	34	23	50	24
Lundblade, Rick, 1b-dh	.259	18	58	9	15	3	0	2	8	10	10	1
Meadows, Scott, of	.293	138	495	60	145	29	3	6	75	66	70	9
Mercedes, Luis, of-dh	.334	108	416	71	139	12	4	3	37	34	70	38
Robbins, Doug, c-1b	.242	102	322	43	78	16	2	2	38	56	51	2
Shamburg, Ken, 1b-3b	.276	72	272	29	75	19	5	2	42	18	37	2
Simonds, Dan, c	.206	11	34	2	7	1	0	0	1	1	4	0
#Stanicek, Pete, 2b-dh	.241	33	112	10	27	0	1	0	6	21	17	2
*Turner, Shane, ss	.237	10	38	5	9	1	0	0	1	0	10	1
Voigt, Jack, of	.256	126	418	55	107	26	2	12	70	59	97	5

PITCHING	W	L	ERA	G	GS	CG	SV	IP	H	R	ER	BB	SO
Burdick, Stacey	8	9	3.93	20	16	2	0	92	81	48	40	43	81
*Cavers, Mike	2	10	5.64	32	12	0	1	97	110	69	61	44	63
Culkar, Steve	0	0	6.35	2	0	0	1	4	4	5	4	5	2
Delarosa, Francisco	9	5	2.06	23	20	2	0	131	97	42	30	51	105
Jones, Stacy	1	6	5.13	19	0	0	2	40	46	27	23	11	41
Kinzer, Matt	0	1	0.00	3	0	0	1	4	0	1	0	2	3
*Linskey, Mike	7	1	1.47	8	7	0	0	55	40	16	9	14	40
McDonald, Ben	0	1	6.55	3	3	0	0	11	11	8	8	3	15
*McKeon, Joel	0	1	2.10	22	0	0	7	34	31	10	8	11	29
Mesa, Jose	5	5	3.42	15	15	3	0	79	77	35	30	30	72
Miller, Dave	4	5	2.81	24	7	0	7	83	80	34	26	22	37
Mussina, Mike	3	0	1.49	7	7	2	0	42	34	10	7	7	40
*Myers, Chris	6	11	3.44	21	21	1	0	110	108	53	42	56	74
Peraza, Oswald	0	0	1.93	2	0	0	0	14	3	3	3	3	4
*Rhodes, Arthur	3	4	3.73	12	12	0	0	72	62	32	30	39	60
Sander, Mike	5	6	2.48	38	2	0	7	102	99	42	28	27	55
Telford, Anthony	10	2	1.97	14	13	3	0	96	80	26	21	25	73
Thorpe, Paul	3	2	4.05	46	1	0	12	66	66	31	30	29	49

HARRISBURG

BATTING	AVG	G	AB	R	H	2B	3B	HR	RBI	BB	SO	SB
Alou, Moises, of	.295	36	132	19	39	12	2	3	22	16	21	7
Banister, Jeff, c-1b	.269	101	368	43	99	13	0	10	57	23	71	2
Barczi, Scott, c	.197	86	264	35	52	7	1	0	17	35	53	1
#Cook, Jeff, of	.186	13	43	5	8	0	0	1	1	5	4	3
Crowley, Terry, 2b-dh	.253	123	471	54	119	18	2	4	52	33	54	7
#Edge, Greg, ss-2b	.214	50	187	18	40	3	0	0	13	22	10	2

London's slugging first baseman Rico Brogna celebrates one of his league high 21 homers.

	AVG	G	AB	R	H	2B	3B	HR	RBI	BB	SO	SB
Garcia, Carlos, ss	.277	65	242	36	67	11	2	5	25	16	36	12
Harris, Robert, of	.226	79	239	28	54	6	0	2	18	13	60	11
Huyler, Mike, ss	.246	36	114	14	28	5	0	0	5	4	18	1
Jewett, Trent, c	.156	15	45	4	7	0	0	0	3	4	22	0
#Longmire, Tony, of	.297	24	91	9	27	6	0	1	13	7	11	5
*Merejo, Domingo, of	.231	36	117	11	27	4	0	0	6	5	28	2
*Osborne, Jeffrey, 1b-dh ...	.241	84	266	28	64	15	2	1	34	27	52	0
Pennye, Darwin, of	.156	11	32	2	5	2	0	0	4	4	10	2
Perez, Julio, 2b-ss	.232	63	194	20	45	6	1	1	23	7	27	3
Tubbs, Greg, of	.282	54	213	35	60	6	5	3	21	23	35	8
Vizcaino, Junior, 1b	.254	84	236	20	60	8	1	0	23	27	73	6
Wehner, John, 3b	.288	138	511	71	147	27	1	4	62	40	51	24
#Yacopino, Ed, of	.290	96	362	39	105	19	4	4	49	26	57	5

PITCHING	W	L	ERA	G	GS	CG	SV	IP	H	R	ER	BB	SO
Adams, Steve	7	8	3.84	26	21	5	2	138	151	67	59	39	40
Ausanio, Joe	3	2	1.83	43	0	0	15	54	36	15	11	16	50
Czajkowski, Jim	0	0	4.30	9	0	0	0	15	17	7	7	6	6
*Garcia, Miguel	8	10	3.98	21	20	0	0	131	143	76	58	38	52
*Hancock, Lee (7 Will) ...	9	9	3.22	27	26	3	0	165	145	71	59	77	92
Miller, Paul	2	1	2.19	5	5	2	0	37	27	9	9	10	11
Minor, Blas	6	4	3.06	38	6	0	5	94	81	41	32	29	98
Murphy, Pete	3	2	2.86	28	3	0	1	63	63	29	20	20	35
Neely, Jeff	4	4	1.78	40	0	0	9	66	49	22	13	18	62
Richardson, Keith	0	6	5.11	8	8	0	0	37	40	25	21	21	22
Roesler, Mike	2	1	4.56	10	0	0	0	24	29	14	12	6	11
*Tomlin, Randy	9	6	2.28	19	18	4	0	126	101	43	32	34	92
Tracy, Jim	14	8	3.00	25	23	5	1	153	143	63	51	37	106
Webb, Ben	5	10	3.59	28	15	3	0	120	105	64	48	59	60

LONDON

BATTING	AVG	G	AB	R	H	2B	3B	HR	RBI	BB	SO	SB
Aldrich, Tom, dh-1b	.136	9	22	4	3	2	0	0	4	5	6	0
*Alvarez, Chris, 3b	.200	60	180	23	36	4	0	3	20	41	21	1
Balthazar, Doyle, c	.282	36	117	15	33	3	3	2	19	13	21	0
Baxter, Jim, c	.237	13	38	6	9	1	0	1	4	5	5	0
Beyeler, Arnie, 2b	.247	103	388	48	96	5	2	0	26	33	57	5
*Brogna, Rico, 1b	.262	137	488	70	128	21	3	21	77	50	100	1
Cabrera, Basilio, of	.231	78	308	31	71	9	3	3	25	14	66	15
Decillis, Dean, ss	.280	72	264	27	74	19	1	3	29	17	21	5
#Frazier, Lou, of-2b	.219	81	242	29	53	4	1	0	15	27	52	20
Galindo, Luis, ss-3b	.225	108	374	36	84	6	2	1	28	40	44	0
Green, Steve, of	.238	47	143	18	34	6	1	1	15	13	33	0
Hurst, Jody, of	.257	44	152	26	39	10	1	4	13	20	46	6

BATTING

R	Bernie Williams, Albany	91
H	Jeff Bagwell, New Britain	160
TB	Jeff Bagwell, New Britain	220
2B	Mike Twardoski, NB	34
	Jeff Bagwell, New Britain	34
3B	Julio Peguero, Reading	9
HR	Rico Brogna, London	21
RBI	Greg Sparks, Albany	77
	Rico Brogna, London	77
SH	Dave Milstein, NB	12
SF	Jack Voigt, Hagerstown	11
BB	Bernie Williams, Albany	98
IBB	Jeff Bagwell, New Britain	12
HBP	Casey Waller, Reading	10
	Bobby DeJardin, Albany	10
SO	Greg Sparks, Albany	118
SB	Bernie Williams, Albany	39
CS	Bernie Williams, Albany	18
OB%	Mike Twardoski, NB	.424

PITCHING

G	Jeff Fassero, Canton	61
GS	David Haas, London	27
CG	Charles Nagy, Canton	9
	Rusty Meacham, London	9
ShO	Four tied at	3
Sv	Darrin Chapin, Albany	21
W	Rusty Meacham, London	15
L	Kevin Morton, New Britain	14
IP	Mike Gardiner, Will	180
H	Jeff Mutis, Canton	178
R	Kevin Morton, New Britain	86
HR	Three tied at	13
BB	David Holdridge, Reading	79
HB	Kevin Morton, New Britain	14
SO	Mike Gardiner, Will	149
WP	Dana Ridenour, Will	15
Bk	Don Stanford, Albany	6
	Greg Roscoe, Canton	6

BATTING	AVG	G	AB	R	H	2B	3B	HR	RBI	BB	SO	SB
Ingram, Riccardo, of	.255	92	271	27	69	10	2	0	26	27	49	3
#Leiper, Tim, of-3b	.301	48	166	30	50	7	0	2	20	26	14	8
Marigny, Ron, 3b-2b	.251	72	255	28	64	9	1	2	19	19	30	1
Pegues, Steve, of	.271	126	483	48	131	22	5	8	63	12	59	17
Rowland, Rich, c	.286	47	161	22	46	10	0	8	30	20	33	1
*Toale, John, dh-c	.257	108	354	44	91	16	0	11	48	34	71	1
#Wiley, Craig, c	.225	49	142	16	32	8	0	2	12	16	26	3

PITCHING	W	L	ERA	G	GS	CG	SV	IP	H	R	ER	BB	SO
Desilva, John	5	6	3.84	14	14	1	0	89	87	47	38	27	76
Haas, David	13	8	2.99	27	27	3	0	178	151	64	59	74	116
Hansen, Mike	5	6	2.17	13	13	3	0	91	80	32	22	16	63
Holman, Shawn	0	3	6.10	28	0	0	8	31	35	26	21	15	26
Jones, Mike	7	9	3.57	25	21	1	0	126	140	72	50	39	81
Kiely, John	3	0	1.76	46	0	0	12	77	62	17	15	42	52
Knudsen, Kurt	2	1	2.08	15	0	0	1	26	15	6	6	11	26
Lumley, Mike	0	2	6.42	15	2	0	0	34	38	33	24	27	28
Meacham, Rusty	15	9	3.13	26	26	9	0	178	161	70	62	36	123
*Ramos, Jose	5	2	3.12	16	6	1	0	52	50	21	18	19	25
Richards, Dave	6	6	4.28	45	0	0	8	55	61	27	26	35	74
Rightnowar, Ron	2	2	3.25	23	0	0	4	44	40	20	16	9	33
Wilkins, Mike	13	5	2.42	25	25	6	0	175	156	57	47	47	91
*Williams, Ken	0	4	6.18	22	5	0	0	44	45	34	30	31	24

NEW BRITAIN

BATTING	AVG	G	AB	R	H	2B	3B	HR	RBI	BB	SO	SB
Bagwell, Jeff, 3b	.333	136	481	63	160	34	7	4	61	73	57	5
Byrd, James, 2b	.200	2	5	1	1	1	0	0	0	0	1	0
*Degifico, Vinnie, dh-1b	.249	120	377	46	94	18	3	3	54	62	72	2
Delgado, Alex, ss	.056	7	18	3	1	1	0	0	0	2	5	0
#Housie, Wayne, of	.274	30	113	13	31	8	3	1	12	6	33	7
Kelly, Mike, of	.256	123	430	40	110	17	3	2	46	41	62	1
#McDougal, Julius, ss	.200	12	40	3	8	1	1	5	5	0	10	1
Milstien, Dave, 2b	.215	115	376	31	81	12	0	0	24	23	44	6
Paris, Juan, of	.212	74	179	29	38	6	1	1	12	11	27	2
Pratt, Todd, dh-c	.231	70	195	15	45	14	1	2	22	18	56	0
Randle, Randy, ss-2b	.214	111	384	62	82	8	4	2	24	47	86	10
*Twardoski, Mike, 1b	.293	127	413	72	121	34	3	1	46	95	46	4
Valentin, John, ss	.218	94	312	20	68	18	1	2	31	25	46	1
Wedge, Eric, c	.227	103	339	36	77	13	1	5	47	50	54	1
*Weidie, Stuart, of	.174	76	219	22	38	6	4	3	20	29	66	2
Wilson, Craig, c	.165	37	91	5	15	2	0	2	10	5	22	0
Zupcic, Bob, of	.213	132	461	45	98	26	1	2	41	36	65	10

PITCHING	W	L	ERA	G	GS	CG	SV	IP	H	R	ER	BB	SO
Carista, Mike	3	1	5.60	17	1	0	0	35	43	24	22	12	21
Conroy, Brian	0	1	6.00	1	1	0	0	6	7	4	4	1	3
Davis, Freddie	0	0	2.08	23	0	0	4	35	30	8	8	6	21
*Fischer, Tom	13	10	4.19	27	26	3	0	163	166	89	76	64	116
Florence, Don	6	4	3.50	34	4	0	1	80	85	37	31	26	39
Kuzniar, Paul	0	0	0.00	3	0	0	0	3	3	1	0	3	3
Livernois, Derek	9	2	1.98	15	14	1	0	96	80	24	21	31	67
Manzanillo, Josias	4	4	3.41	12	12	2	0	74	66	34	28	37	51
*Morton, Kevin	8	14	3.81	26	26	7	0	163	151	86	69	48	131
*O'Neill, Dan (2 London)	7	0	0.72	35	0	0	11	63	36	7	5	13	49
Owen, Dave	7	9	2.93	20	20	4	0	132	123	54	43	48	88
Plympton, Jeff	3	4	2.67	37	0	0	13	64	62	31	19	16	55
Quantrill, Paul	7	11	3.53	22	22	1	0	133	148	65	52	23	53
Sanders, Al	2	1	2.55	6	6	0	0	35	31	12	10	11	30
*Stewart, Tito	1	2	1.42	7	0	0	1	13	11	5	2	3	7

	W	L	ERA	G	GS	CG	SV	IP	H	R	ER	BB	SO
*Taylor, Scott	0	2	1.65	5	5	1	0	27	23	8	5	13	27
Walters, Dave	2	2	3.13	43	2	0	8	75	72	32	26	38	50

READING

BATTING	AVG	G	AB	R	H	2B	3B	HR	RBI	BB	SO	SB
Agostinelli, Sal, c	.000	5	9	0	0	0	0	0	0	0	2	0
Alexander, Gary, 1b-of ..	.255	129	428	73	109	29	0	19	60	74	99	1
Batiste, Kim, ss	.276	125	486	57	134	14	4	6	33	13	73	28
*Bellino, Frank, of	.258	115	403	46	104	23	2	7	57	39	77	0
*Brumfield, Harvey, of	.119	14	59	3	7	1	1	0	0	2	16	2
Calvert, Chris, of	.067	7	15	2	1	1	0	0	1	0	3	1
Fitzgerald, Mike, 1b-dh ..	.236	53	174	17	41	7	0	8	20	6	47	0
Foley, Marty, 2b-3b	.146	53	144	12	21	3	0	0	9	14	31	3
*Grotewold, Jeff, 1b-c	.269	127	412	56	111	33	1	15	72	62	83	2
Holyfield, Vince, of	.201	97	323	36	65	11	1	9	28	21	96	17
Infante, Kennedy, 3b	.248	36	125	8	31	4	0	2	6	4	15	1
*Kirkpatrick, Steve, of ...	.243	107	346	51	84	8	0	19	42	43	12	
Lindsey, Doug, c	.173	107	323	16	56	11	0	1	32	26	78	2
Lozinski, Tony, c	.087	10	23	0	2	1	0	0	0	0	8	0
Marsh, Tom, of	.258	41	132	13	34	6	1	1	10	8	27	5
Muratti, Rafael, of	.115	9	26	2	3	0	0	0	1	5	6	0
#Peguero, Julio, of (104 Harr)	.277	107	423	40	117	14	9	1	28	31	54	8
Posey, John, c	.300	5	10	0	3	0	0	0	1	0	1	0
#Robertson, Rod, 2b-ss ...	.206	51	189	16	39	3	0	1	12	6	26	7
Scarsone, Steve, 2b-ss ..	.265	74	245	26	65	12	1	3	23	14	63	0
#Waller, Casey, 3b	.242	67	236	24	57	11	2	3	24	15	32	1
Williams, Cary, of	.246	49	179	16	44	10	0	2	18	7	32	0

PITCHING	W	L	ERA	G	GS	CG	SV	IP	H	R	ER	BB	SO
Ashby, Andy	10	7	3.42	23	23	4	0	140	134	65	53	48	94
Ayrault, Bob	4	6	2.30	44	9	0	10	109	77	33	28	34	84
Backs, Jason	1	0	1.50	1	1	0	0	6	6	1	1	3	5
Borland, Toby	4	1	1.44	14	0	0	0	25	16	6	4	11	26
Boudreaux, Eric	3	4	4.13	35	5	0	0	85	111	52	39	29	43
Brantley, Cliff	4	9	4.55	17	17	0	0	87	93	51	44	39	69
Buonantony, Rich	1	2	7.24	9	0	0	0	14	13	11	11	12	10
Carreno, Amalio	4	13	3.66	25	23	3	1	128	137	62	52	47	86
*Christopher, Fred	0	0	3.27	6	0	0	1	11	11	4	4	2	10
Holdridge, David	8	12	4.58	24	24	1	0	128	114	74	65	79	78
Magee, Warren	2	3	5.36	19	2	0	0	45	46	30	27	34	36
Mauser, Tim	3	4	3.30	8	8	1	0	46	35	20	17	15	40
McLarnan, John	0	2	6.64	13	0	0	2	20	18	16	15	8	15
Moore, Brad	1	0	0.00	1	1	0	0	2	1	0	0	1	4
Ontiveros, Steve	0	2	9.00	2	0	0	0	6	7	6	6	2	8
Shelton, Mike	0	1	13.94	5	1	0	0	10	22	17	16	9	5
*Sims, Mark	0	1	3.41	54	0	0	13	69	79	32	26	16	41
Stevens, Matt	3	3	2.84	25	0	0	4	44	43	23	14	20	34
Wilson, Gary	7	12	2.44	33	21	3	2	151	140	64	41	39	70

WILLIAMSPORT

BATTING	AVG	G	AB	R	H	2B	3B	HR	RBI	BB	SO	SB
Alfredson, Tom, of	.235	35	119	15	28	3	3	3	12	13	18	0
Barbara, Dan, c	.400	2	5	0	2	0	0	0	0	1	3	2
*Bowie, Jim, 1b	.274	128	446	45	122	18	0	5	48	51	47	0
*Brundage, Dave, of	.333	31	99	19	33	4	0	1	9	31	13	9
Clark, Isaiah, of-3b	.254	80	279	29	71	13	0	1	28	8	28	12
Gonzalez, Ruben, 1b	.190	7	21	0	4	1	0	0	4	6	5	0
Haney, Todd, 2b	.500	1	2	0	1	1	0	0	0	1	0	0
Hooper, Jeff, dh-c	.217	78	249	20	54	11	0	7	36	12	67	0
Howard, Chris, c	.237	118	401	48	95	19	1	5	49	37	91	3
King, Bryan, ss	.188	54	144	14	27	3	1	0	4	22	18	7
*Kosco, Dru, of-dh	.195	96	267	19	52	11	0	1	25	23	58	1
Lennon, Pat, of-3b	.293	49	167	24	49	6	4	5	22	10	37	10
Letterio, Shane, 2b	.251	120	450	42	113	18	3	2	34	31	69	3
*McDonald, Mike, of	.239	124	452	46	108	19	3	5	34	30	92	5
#Merchant, Mark, of	.179	44	156	16	28	5	0	0	10	14	36	7
Pennington, Ken, 3b-dh ..	.260	134	461	59	120	14	4	7	51	43	66	3
Razook, Mark, inf-of	.171	88	258	19	44	10	0	2	15	22	65	2
Smith, Jack, ss	.190	67	174	14	33	7	0	2	14	11	37	1
#Williams, Ted, of	.227	81	321	37	73	11	2	1	18	14	59	34

PITCHING	W	L	ERA	G	GS	CG	SV	IP	H	R	ER	BB	SO
Balabon, Rick	3	4	3.27	13	13	1	0	77	76	35	28	18	62
*Blasucci, Tony	2	0	3.60	28	0	0	3	35	26	16	14	14	34
Blueberg, Jim	9	11	3.83	25	25	4	0	153	161	81	65	42	82
DeLucia, Rich	6	6	2.11	18	18	2	0	115	92	30	27	30	76
Evers, Troy	4	12	3.69	28	23	4	0	156	152	74	64	48	66
*Figueroa, Fernando	2	10	3.96	37	4	0	4	61	65	34	27	21	32
Gardiner, Mike	12	8	1.90	26	26	5	0	180	136	47	38	29	149
Goff, Mike	0	0	2.45	2	0	0	0	4	3	1	1	1	5
*Hensley, Chuck	0	2	3.63	15	0	0	0	22	20	12	9	13	16
*Jones, Dennis	1	1	9.90	4	1	0	0	10	11	11	11	6	4
Nelson, Jeff	1	4	6.44	10	10	0	0	43	65	35	31	18	14
Newlin, Jim	1	1	3.49	20	0	0	0	39	45	22	15	15	23
Rice, Pat	4	4	3.98	25	8	0	0	72	77	36	32	24	58
Ridenour, Dana	4	7	2.86	45	2	1	6	79	75	31	25	41	70
Rojas, Ricky	8	6	3.39	43	3	0	11	85	83	37	32	16	57
Wooden, Mark	1	1	2.30	10	0	0	2	16	11	4	4	5	8

SOUTHERN LEAGUE

Rain, no-hitters highlight '90 campaign

By RUBIN GRANT

The year of the no-hitter wasn't just a happening in the major leagues. A record five no-hitters were thrown in the Southern League during the 1990 season, including two by Knoxville pitchers.

The Blue Jays' Rob Wishnevski no-hit Charlotte June 4 and two months later teammate Pete Blohm no-hit Greenville. Jacksonville's Kent Bottenfield, Charlotte's Frank Castillo and Orlando's Johnny Ard also threw no-hitters.

Jeff Conine
....320-15-95

Bottenfield's was the only one to go a full nine innings. Blohm's came in a six-inning, rain-shortened game, while the others were seven-inning gems in the first game of doubleheaders. The five no-hitters eclipsed the league's previous high of four in a season, set in 1971 and matched in 1978.

Chicks pluck first title

Neither rain, nor, well, more rain, could keep the Memphis Chicks from winning their first Southern League championship in 1990.

Tied 1-1 with Orlando in their best-of-5 championship series, the Chicks and SunRays endured two consecutive rainouts before Memphis went on to win the title in five games. The clincher came on the last day that the playoffs could be completed under National Association guidelines. Another rainout and the teams

LEAGUE CHAMPIONS

Playoff Champions, Where Applicable

1990—Memphis	1962—Macon	1929—Knoxville
1989—Birmingham	1961—Asheville	1928—Asheville
1988—Chattanooga	1960—Savannah	1927—Greenville
1987—Birmingham	1959—Gastonia	1926—Greenville
1986—Columbus	1958—Macon	1925—Spartanburg
1985—Huntsville	1957—Charlotte	1924—Augusta
1984—Charlotte	1956—Jacksonville	1923—Charlotte
1983—Birmingham	1955—Augusta	1922—Charleston
1982—Nashville	1954—Savannah	1921—Columbia
1981—Orlando	1953—Savannah	1920—Columbia
1980—Charlotte	1952—Montgomery	1919—Columbia
1979—Nashville	1951—Montgomery	1918—Did Not
1978—Knoxville	1950—Macon	Operate
1977—Montgomery	1949—Macon	1917—Columbia
1976—Montgomery	1948—Greenville	1916—Augusta
1975—Montgomery	1947—Savannah	1915—Columbus
1974—Knoxville	1946—Augusta	1914—Savannah
1973—Montgomery	1943-45—Did Not	1913—Savannah
1972—Montgomery	Operate	1912—Jacksonville
1971—Did Not	1942—Macon	1911—Columbus
Operate	1941—Columbia	1910—Columbus
1970—Columbus	1940—Columbus	1909—Chattanooga
1969—Charlotte	1939—Augusta	1908—Jacksonville
1968—Asheville	1938—Macon	1907—Charleston
1967—Birmingham	1937—Savannah	1906—Savannah
1966—Mobile	1936—Columbus	1905—Macon
1965—Columbus	1931-35—Did Not	1904—Macon
1964—Lynchburg	Operate	
1963—Augusta	1930—Greenville	

Jacksonville lefthander **Brian Barnes** led all minor leaguers in strikeouts in 1990, with 213 in 201 innings.

would have been declared co-champions.

In the decisive fifth game, third baseman Sean Berry hit a two-run homer to cap a four-run sixth inning and propel the Chicks to a 5-3 victory. League MVP Jeff Conine and Jorge Pedre also hit home runs for Memphis. Reliever Victor Cole got the win, his third in three playoff appearances and Carlos Maldonado earned his third save in the series.

The SL championship series went to a deciding fifth game for the first time since 1985 when Huntsville defeated Charlotte. The Chicks, who had the best record (44-28) in the league in the first half, rebounded after slumping to 29-43 in the second half.

"I'm happy," Memphis manager Jeff Cox said. "You can't win division championships and league championships without talented players. We have a talented bunch of ballplayers who made nothing but strides this season. This is the best team I've been a part of in 17 years of professional baseball."

More pitching feats

Orlando lefthander Denny Neagle became the first pitcher in the minors to win 20 games since 1986. Neagle (20-3) was 8-0 at Class A Visalia (California) and went 12-3 after being promoted to Orlando. Another pitcher, Detroit farmhand Randy Marshall, also went on to win 20 games in 1990.

Jacksonville lefthander Brian Barnes, who was voted the league's most outstanding pitcher, became only the fifth pitcher in league history to record more than 200 strikeouts, and just the second since 1973. Barnes, the nation's top collegiate strikeout artist in 1989, finished the season with 213 strikeouts.

Conine, the Barbarian/Destroyer

Conine, a former 58th-round draft choice, was voted the league's MVP. The Memphis first baseman hit .372 in the first half, leading the Chicks to a first-half divisional title and was in the running for a possible Triple Crown. He slumped in the second half, but still finished third in the league in batting (.320) and was second in RBIs (95).

Chattanooga's Adam Casillas won his second straight batting

title with a .336 average. Casillas led the Midwest League with a .321 average in 1989.

Columbus' Luis Gonzalez homered on the final day of the season to tie Jacksonville's Terrel Hansen for the home-run title with 24. The 24 homers were the lowest total to lead the league since 1977 when a trio of players led the league with 17.

One of the more remarkable feats during the 1990 season was Columbus' Willie Ansley hitting back-to-back, inside-the-park home runs in a game against Huntsville. Birmingham designated hitter Matt Stark, who sat out the entire '89 season while recovering from shoulder surgery, won the league RBI crown with 109, which tied a modern Barons' record.

Charlotte's Rusty Crockett set a league record for being hit by pitches. He was plunked 32 times, doubling the old record of 16 set in 1966. Crockett's 32 HBPs were only 12 fewer than his walks (44). He was not a big target at 5-foot-7, 150 pounds. Hansen, who was hit 24 times, also surpassed the previous ker-plunk mark.

Something foggy going on

Birmingham and Knoxville were fogged out Aug. 2 when their landlocked game was called after seven innings with the score tied 4-4. The game was delayed 55 minutes before it was called.

1990 *FINAL STANDINGS*

FIRST HALF

East	W	L	Pct.	GB
Orlando (Twins)	42	30	.583	—
Jacksonville (Expos)	38	33	.571	3½
Columbus (Astros)	33	39	.458	9
Charlotte (Cubs)	32	40	.444	10
Greenville (Braves)	28	44	.389	14

West	W	L	Pct.	GB
Memphis (Royals)	44	28	.611	—
Huntsville (Athletics)	41	31	.569	3
Birmingham (White Sox)	37	34	.521	6½
Chattanooga (Reds)	35	36	.493	8½
Knoxville (Blue Jays)	28	43	.394	15½

SECOND HALF

East	W	L	Pct.	GB
Jacksonville (Expos)	46	27	.630	—
Orlando (Twins)	43	29	.597	2½
Columbus (Astros)	34	38	.472	11½
Charlotte (Cubs)	33	39	.458	12½
Greenville (Braves)	29	43	.403	16½

West	W	L	Pct.	GB
Birmingham (White Sox)	40	33	.548	—
Knoxville (Blue Jays)	39	34	.534	1
Huntsville (Athletics)	38	34	.528	1½
Chattanooga (Reds)	31	42	.425	9
Memphis (Royals)	29	43	.403	10½

OVERALL

	W	L	Pct.	GB
Orlando (Twins)	85	59	.590	—
Jacksonville (Expos)	84	60	.583	1
Huntsville (Athletics)	79	65	.549	6
Birmingham (White Sox)	77	67	.535	8
Memphis (Royals)	73	71	.507	12
Columbus (Astros)	67	77	.465	18
Knoxville (Blue Jays)	67	77	.465	18
Chattanooga (Reds)	66	78	.458	19
Charlotte (Cubs)	65	79	.451	20
Greenville (Braves)	57	87	.396	28

Playoffs: Orlando defeated Jacksonville 3-1 in best-of-5 semifinal; Memphis defeated Birmingham 3-1 in best-of-5 semifinal; Memphis defeated Orlando 3-2 in best-of-5 final to win league championship.

Regular-Season Attendance: Charlotte, 271,302; Birmingham, 256,227; Jacksonville, 244,404; Huntsville, 228,821; Greenville, 204,929; Memphis, 193,758; Orlando, 147,070; Chattanooga, 135,825; Columbus, 94,265; Knoxville, 82,676.

Managers: Birmingham—Ken Berry; **Charlotte**—Tommy Helms, Jay Loviglio; **Chattanooga**—Jim Tracy; **Columbus**—Rick Sweet; **Greenville**—Buddy Bailey; **Huntsville**—Jeff Newman; **Jacksonville**—Jerry Manuel; **Knoxville**—John Stearns; **Memphis**—Jeff Cox; **Orlando**—Ron Gardenhire.

1990 Official All-Star Team: C—Greg Colbrunn, Jacksonville. **1B**—Jeff Conine, Memphis. **2B**—Williams Suero, Knoxville. **3B**—Sean Berry, Memphis. **SS**—Eddie Zosky, Knoxville. **UTIL INF**—Scott Brosius, Huntsville; Frank Thomas, Birmingham. **OF**—Terrel Hanson, Jacksonville; Adam Casillas, Chattanooga; Brian McRae, Memphis; Bobby Moore, Memphis. **DH**—Matt Stark, Birmingham. **RHP**—Scott Erickson, Orlando. **LHP**—Brian Barnes, Jacksonville. **RP**—Steve Chitren, Huntsville. **Most Valuable Player**—Jeff Conine, Memphis. **Most Outstanding Pitcher**—Brian Barnes, Jacksonville. **Best Hustler**—Rusty Crockett, Charlotte. **Manager of the Year**—Ron Gardenhire, Orlando; Jerry Manuel, Jacksonville.

Top 10 Major League Prospects (by Baseball America): 1. Frank Thomas, 1b, Birmingham; **2.** Jeff Conine, 1b, Memphis; **3.** Eddie Zosky, ss, Knoxville; **4.** Brian Barnes, lhp, Jacksonville; **5.** Scott Erickson, rhp, Orlando; **6.** Darren Lewis, of, Huntsville; **7.** Chuck Knoblauch, 2b, Orlando; **8.** Williams Suero, 2b, Knoxville; **9.** Greg Colbrunn, c, Jacksonville; **10.** Denny Neagle, lhp, Orlando.

1990 *BATTING, PITCHING STATS*

CLUB BATTING

	AVG	G	AB	R	H	2B	3B	HR	BB	SO	SB
Birmingham	.271	145	4767	771	1292	251	37	93	675	923	144
Memphis	.266	144	4750	721	1264	207	46	74	603	740	165
Knoxville	.260	145	4751	615	1234	212	44	100	436	944	148
Chattanooga	.257	144	4711	642	1209	235	34	77	590	828	94
Orlando	.254	144	4678	685	1189	218	31	73	635	762	129
Huntsville	.252	144	4746	678	1197	216	23	111	592	876	86
Columbus	.251	144	4712	645	1181	188	43	116	535	1095	178
Jacksonville	.249	144	4792	665	1195	227	34	106	515	947	113
Greenville	.237	144	4710	575	1117	187	21	81	570	896	103
Charlotte	.234	144	4624	583	1080	201	20	107	475	823	109

CLUB PITCHING

	ERA	G	CG	SHO	SV	IP	H	R	ER	BB	SO
Jacksonville	3.17	144	13	15	47	1268	1058	557	447	544	1000
Orlando	3.35	144	17	8	47	1239	1114	582	461	501	860
Memphis	3.65	144	11	7	37	1246	1172	625	505	555	872
Charlotte	3.71	144	14	9	35	1243	1208	642	513	567	909
Columbus	3.86	144	9	13	31	1251	1247	676	536	546	916
Huntsville	3.96	144	10	4	47	1260	1228	681	554	514	852
Knoxville	4.15	145	10	12	36	1253	1143	673	578	675	928
Birmingham	4.18	145	8	5	37	1242	1239	717	577	550	811
Greenville	4.35	144	5	10	36	1246	1316	722	603	575	836
Chattanooga	4.55	144	20	4	37	1226	1233	705	620	599	850

INDIVIDUAL BATTING LEADERS
(Minimum 389 Plate Appearances)

	AVG	G	AB	R	H	2B	3B	HR	RBI	BB	SO	SB
*Casillas, Adam, Chat	.336	123	378	56	127	27	1	3	64	76	29	2
Thomas, Frank, Birm	.323	109	353	85	114	27	5	18	71	112	74	7
Conine, Jeff, Memphis	.320	137	487	89	156	37	8	15	95	94	88	21
Stark, Matt, Birmingham	.309	129	453	69	140	26	0	14	109	85	52	3
Cole, Stu, Memphis	.308	113	357	61	110	18	2	1	49	55	55	20
Moore, Bobby, Memphis	.303	112	422	93	128	20	6	2	36	56	32	27
Colbrunn, Greg, Jax	.301	125	458	57	138	29	1	13	76	38	78	1
Brosius, Scott, Hunt	.296	142	547	94	162	39	2	23	88	81	81	12
Magallanes, Willie, Birm	.292	123	459	72	134	24	3	16	65	41	139	10
Berry, Sean, Memphis	.292	135	487	73	142	25	4	14	77	44	89	19

INDIVIDUAL PITCHING LEADERS
(Minimum 115 Innings)

	W	L	ERA	G	GS	CG	SV	IP	H	R	ER	BB	SO
Carter, Jeff, Jax	8	3	1.84	52	7	2	15	117	90	36	24	33	76
Wagner, Hector, Memphis	12	4	2.03	40	11	1	1	133	114	37	30	41	63
*Neagle, Denny, Orlando	12	3	2.45	17	17	4	0	121	94	40	33	31	94

	W	L	ERA	G	GS	CG	SV	IP	H	R	ER	BB	SO
*Simons, Doug, Orlando ...	15	12	2.54	29	28	5	0	188	160	76	53	43	109
*Barnes, Brian, Jax	13	7	2.77	29	28	3	0	201	144	78	62	87	213
Hentgen, Pat, Knox	9	5	3.05	28	26	0	0	153	121	57	52	68	142
Williams, Woody, Knox ...	7	9	3.14	42	12	0	5	126	111	55	44	39	74
Brito, Mario, Jax	9	7	3.19	18	18	1	0	116	100	57	41	34	49
Schock, Will, Hunt	11	7	3.22	29	28	2	0	179	164	84	64	57	100
Centala, Scott, Memphis ..	11	8	3.22	25	25	1	0	142	131	57	51	66	116

BIRMINGHAM

BATTING	AVG	G	AB	R	H	2B	3B	HR	RBI	BB	SO	SB
Alfredson, Tom, of	.255	51	157	23	40	9	0	4	28	23	47	1
Bernhardt, Cesar, 2b	.279	142	574	96	160	26	9	6	82	46	53	30
Brown, Kurt, c	.269	82	253	38	68	8	0	4	43	19	47	8
Busby, Wayne, ss	.262	102	386	46	101	27	4	2	43	37	91	16
#Caceres, Ed, ss-3b	.262	62	214	31	56	5	1	0	17	15	26	7
Campbell, Darrin, c	.182	3	11	0	2	0	0	0	0	1	3	0
*Gaither, Horace, 3b-ss	.121	16	33	5	4	0	0	0	2	4	9	0
*Garcia, Cornelio, of	.343	25	67	9	23	6	0	0	6	12	16	3
*Lee, Derek, of	.255	126	411	68	105	21	3	7	75	71	93	14
Magallanes, Willie, of	.292	123	459	72	134	24	3	16	65	41	139	10
McCray, Rodney, of	.197	60	188	36	37	2	2	1	16	36	42	25
Merullo, Matt, c-1b	.291	102	378	57	110	26	1	8	50	34	49	2
Ocasio, Javier, 2b-of	.000	2	6	0	0	0	0	0	0	0	2	1
*Roth, Greg, 3b	.196	57	179	34	35	8	1	2	16	41	40	4
Smith, Ed, 3b	.247	72	247	22	61	14	3	1	23	22	49	2
Stark, Matt, dh	.309	129	453	69	140	26	0	14	109	85	52	3
*Tedder, Scott, 1b-of	.333	2	3	1	1	0	0	0	2	2	1	0
Thomas, Frank, 1b	.323	109	353	85	114	27	5	18	71	112	74	7
Trafton, Todd, 1b-of	.259	35	116	21	30	5	1	5	26	18	28	0
*Waggoner, Aubrey, of	.257	81	276	57	71	17	4	5	32	56	60	11

PITCHING	W	L	ERA	G	GS	CG	SV	IP	H	R	ER	BB	SO
*Alvarez, Wilson	5	1	4.27	7	7	1	0	46	44	24	22	25	36
Cedeno, Vinicio	2	1	3.13	20	2	0	0	37	40	17	13	17	26
Cortes, Argenis	0	0	6.55	8	0	0	0	11	13	8	8	10	9
DelaCruz, Carlos	1	7	7.55	13	12	1	0	54	64	55	45	36	30
Drahman, Brian	6	4	4.08	50	1	0	17	90	90	50	41	24	72
Fernandez, Alex	3	0	1.08	4	4	0	0	25	20	7	3	6	27
*Groom, Buddy	6	8	5.07	20	20	0	0	115	135	81	65	48	66
*Hall, Todd	3	1	4.19	33	2	0	0	69	62	35	32	36	43
Hasler, Curt	9	6	3.27	23	19	1	0	124	118	61	45	33	58
Hernandez, Roberto	8	5	3.67	17	17	1	0	108	103	57	44	43	62
Hudek, John	6	6	4.58	42	10	0	4	92	84	59	47	52	67
Kennedy, Bo	11	12	4.73	30	30	3	0	175	175	118	92	89	121
Perschke, Greg	3	1	2.60	4	4	1	0	28	20	9	8	6	18
*Resnikoff, Rob	1	0	7.91	14	0	0	0	19	24	17	17	11	16
Reynolds, Dave	4	4	3.09	31	1	0	5	76	80	29	26	28	48
*Scheid, Rich	2	1	2.22	25	0	0	4	45	37	17	11	21	37
Stephens, Ron	7	10	3.65	39	16	0	7	123	122	65	50	61	74
Ventura, Jose	0	0	32.40	1	0	0	0	1	4	4	4	6	0

CHARLOTTE

BATTING	AVG	G	AB	R	H	2B	3B	HR	RBI	BB	SO	SB
Arias, Alex, ss	.246	119	419	55	103	16	3	4	38	42	53	12
Bafia, Bob, dh-1b	.253	28	91	13	23	6	0	3	12	6	13	2
Bell, Lenny, 1b	.155	32	84	7	13	4	1	1	6	5	32	1
Canan, Dick, 3b-of	.233	123	404	38	94	17	3	6	40	26	83	9
Crockett, Rusty, 2b	.243	133	403	65	98	18	2	6	34	44	50	19
Duffy, Darrin, 2b-ss	.241	108	319	48	77	18	1	3	23	50	62	4
Garcia, Butch, of-1b	.212	63	198	23	42	11	0	8	38	19	30	1
*Grayum, Richie, of	.237	113	316	38	75	8	0	10	35	31	64	6
#Griffin, Ty, 3b-of	.209	78	249	34	52	9	1	8	27	57	55	7
#Hannon, Phil, of	.205	98	190	22	39	4	2	2	18	22	47	13
Posey, John, c	.194	26	72	5	14	1	0	2	11	4	6	2
Rivera, Pablo, of	.136	36	81	7	11	3	1	0	7	6	12	1
#Roberson, Kevin, of	.244	31	119	14	29	6	2	5	16	8	25	2
Scott, Gary, 3b	.308	35	143	21	44	9	0	4	17	7	17	3
*Stefero, John, c-1b	.190	57	126	9	24	5	1	1	15	10	28	0
*Sullivan, Glenn, 1b	.254	100	335	50	85	20	1	5	34	35	77	7
#Walker, Chico, of	.265	88	310	49	82	15	1	12	45	44	72	10
*Wilkins, Rick, c	.227	127	449	48	102	18	1	17	71	43	95	4
Williams, Dana, of	.294	50	180	23	53	12	0	7	19	4	8	6

PITCHING	W	L	ERA	G	GS	CG	SV	IP	H	R	ER	BB	SO
Bullinger, Jim	3	4	5.11	9	9	0	0	44	42	30	25	18	33
Castillo, Frank	6	6	3.88	18	18	4	0	111	113	54	48	27	112
Coffman, Kevin	7	3	2.03	14	14	5	0	93	77	28	21	54	84
Damian, Len	1	2	6.11	7	1	0	0	18	24	12	12	3	12
Davis, Braz	1	2	9.28	4	3	0	0	11	16	13	11	14	3
*Dickson, Lance	2	1	0.38	3	3	1	0	24	13	1	1	3	28
*Harrison, Phil	5	3	3.48	9	9	0	0	54	49	25	21	31	41
Kallevig, Greg	2	2	3.54	15	0	0	1	28	23	12	11	9	14
Kazmierczak, Bill	6	9	4.37	18	16	1	0	91	89	58	44	46	66
Lopez, Marcos	1	7	3.96	15	11	0	0	84	97	47	37	17	46
Mount, Chuck	11	9	4.15	40	20	2	0	154	154	97	71	93	77
Mullino, Ray	3	4	4.52	39	7	0	1	96	98	63	48	35	70
Robinson, Brett	5	6	3.99	21	13	0	0	95	111	47	42	36	56

Orlando's Denny Neagle, left, was one of two 20-game winners in minors; Birmingham's Frank Thomas led minors in on-base percentage.

	W	L	ERA	G	GS	CG	SV	IP	H	R	ER	BB	SO
*Rodriguez, Gabby	0	1	13.50	3	0	0	0	3	4	8	4	5	2
*Rosario, David	1	1	2.55	28	0	0	4	35	26	12	10	19	42
Slocumb, Heath	3	1	2.15	43	0	0	12	50	50	20	12	32	37
*Sodders, Mike	1	9	4.64	15	14	0	0	85	89	50	44	46	57
Strauss, Julio	2	1	3.45	24	0	0	2	44	39	21	17	21	44
*Stroud, Derek	2	5	3.58	12	6	1	2	38	28	19	15	26	32
Zarranz, Fernando	3	3	2.09	51	0	0	13	82	64	24	19	31	51

CHATTANOOGA

BATTING	AVG	G	AB	R	H	2B	3B	HR	RBI	BB	SO	SB
Benavides, Freddie, ss	.259	55	197	20	51	10	1	1	28	11	25	4
*Branson, Jeff, 2b-ss	.210	63	233	19	49	9	1	2	29	13	48	3
Bryant, Scott, of	.313	44	131	23	41	10	3	6	30	22	28	1
*Casillas, Adam, 1b-of	.336	123	378	56	127	27	1	3	64	76	29	2
Colvard, Benny, of	.288	97	326	49	94	24	3	13	56	25	69	5
Defrancesco, Tony, c	.253	70	217	24	55	8	2	2	15	15	53	1
*Finley, Brian, of	.192	116	343	46	66	8	3	0	25	71	46	9
Forney, Jeff, of	.278	122	356	57	99	29	3	9	44	76	86	10
*Hayden, Alan, of	.266	93	241	40	64	9	3	0	15	21	27	24
Lane, Brian, 3b	.239	79	293	41	70	13	2	6	51	37	73	2
Lee, Terry, 1b	.327	43	156	25	51	8	1	8	20	20	27	4
Lonigro, Greg, ss-2b	.256	106	347	40	89	22	0	6	38	25	29	3
#Nelson, Jerome, of	.282	69	252	46	71	10	4	5	29	40	27	14
Pearson, Kevin, ss-1b	.317	60	227	31	72	12	2	5	29	14	21	0
Rosario, Melvin, c	.207	66	179	19	37	6	0	4	22	23	44	1
Sellner, Scott, 2b-3b	.267	129	446	71	119	20	3	2	49	65	69	7
*Sepanek, Rob, 1b	.230	17	61	11	14	1	0	3	8	8	10	1
Sutko, Glenn, c	.167	53	174	12	29	7	1	2	11	8	66	1

PITCHING	W	L	ERA	G	GS	CG	SV	IP	H	R	ER	BB	SO
Banning, Doug	9	10	4.48	31	26	1	0	165	181	96	82	56	77
Bruno, Joe	1	1	5.93	20	0	0	1	27	25	18	18	19	19
Dodd, Bill	3	0	2.85	32	0	0	2	47	35	16	15	24	27
Foster, Steve	5	10	5.34	50	0	0	20	59	69	38	35	33	52
*Grovom, Carl	1	3	10.35	9	4	0	0	20	28	23	23	13	15
*Henry, Butch	8	8	4.21	24	22	2	0	143	151	74	67	58	95
Jeffery, Scott	3	6	4.10	31	9	3	0	90	91	48	41	34	70
Kaiser, Keith	9	11	5.74	33	28	1	0	171	166	122	109	109	123
*Lazor, Joe	6	5	3.53	31	8	1	2	92	71	39	36	55	80
*Minutelli, Gino	9	5	3.99	17	17	5	0	108	106	52	48	46	75
Moscrey, Mike	2	3	5.62	41	0	0	5	58	72	47	36	40	41
*Powell, Ross	8	14	3.55	29	27	6	0	185	172	89	73	57	132
*Rodriguez, Rosario	2	2	4.36	36	2	1	7	54	52	29	26	48	39
Watson, Steve	0	0	9.00	1	1	0	0	3	7	6	3	2	2

COLUMBUS

BATTING	AVG	G	AB	R	H	2B	3B	HR	RBI	BB	SO	SB
Acta, Manny, 3b	.239	41	109	15	26	4	0	1	10	5	24	0
Ansley, Willie, of	.255	120	415	69	106	9	7	9	37	54	121	33
*Anthony, Eric, of-dh	.167	4	12	2	2	0	0	1	3	3	4	0
*Baldwin, Jeff, of	.316	77	250	43	79	11	1	7	37	33	36	0
*Casey, Tim, of-dh	.175	37	80	9	14	1	0	3	9	15	28	1
Cedeno, Andujar, ss	.240	132	495	57	119	21	11	19	64	33	135	6
Cooper, Gary, dh-of	.263	54	160	29	42	7	0	8	30	30	30	1
Davis, Glenn, 1b	.297	12	37	3	11	0	0	1	8	2	9	1
Dean, Kevin, of	.288	22	73	8	21	7	0	0	11	16	19	4
Eusebio, Tony, c	.283	92	318	36	90	18	0	4	37	21	80	6
*Gonzalez, Luis, 1b-3b	.265	138	495	86	131	30	6	24	89	54	100	27
#Harris, Rusty, 3b	.245	64	208	42	51	5	3	0	19	49	29	8
#Hubbard, Trent, 2b-of	.251	95	335	39	84	14	4	4	35	37	51	17
#Hunter, Bert, of	.233	133	443	56	103	12	4	9	39	65	136	36

	AVG	G	AB	R	H	2B	3B	HR	RBI	BB	SO	SB
Jenkins, Bernard, of	.228	51	162	19	37	6	2	5	20	20	45	6
Lombardozzi, Steve, 2b-ss	.200	6	20	1	4	0	0	1	2	0	2	1
Makarewicz, Scott, c	.235	28	85	5	20	1	0	2	11	11	13	0
Mikulik, Joe, of	.258	46	120	17	31	3	2	4	20	16	22	8
Mota, Andy, 2b	.286	111	413	59	118	21	1	11	62	28	81	17
Nyssen, Dan, of	.218	18	55	4	12	5	0	1	6	4	10	1
Ortiz, Joe, c	.152	42	112	13	17	2	1	2	11	9	29	0
Renteria, Ed, 3b-ss	.257	62	179	22	46	10	1	0	19	21	27	6

PITCHING	W	L	ERA	G	GS	CG	SV	IP	H	R	ER	BB	SO
Allen, Harold	7	9	3.71	22	22	0	0	114	98	59	47	70	78
Bauer, Pete	0	4	2.52	34	0	0	3	50	37	15	14	21	42
Bond, Daven	0	3	6.40	27	0	0	6	32	44	25	23	19	21
Bowen, Ryan	8	4	3.74	18	18	2	0	113	103	59	47	49	109
Browning, Mike	3	3	2.59	16	0	0	4	24	22	10	7	3	14
Cano, Jose	1	0	0.63	7	5	0	0	14	11	3	1	8	12
Costello, Fred	0	5	4.17	35	5	0	7	45	54	31	21	23	39
*Credeur, Todd	1	1	3.52	11	3	0	0	23	17	21	9	20	16
Eichhorn, Dave	3	1	0.57	10	0	0	1	16	14	3	1	2	3
*Hartgraves, Dean	8	8	4.70	33	14	0	0	100	108	66	52	48	64
*Ilsley, Blaise	6	4	1.94	12	12	3	0	84	70	26	18	13	70
Juden, Jeff	1	3	5.37	11	11	0	0	52	55	36	31	42	40
*Normand, Guy	0	0	2.70	3	0	0	0	3	3	1	1	3	4
*Osuna, Al	7	5	3.38	60	0	0	6	69	57	30	26	33	82
Ponte, Edward	1	2	3.00	18	0	0	0	33	32	14	11	17	30
*Reuss, Jerry	1	0	1.66	10	0	0	0	22	23	4	4	1	10
Reynolds, Shane	9	10	4.81	29	27	2	0	155	181	104	83	70	92
Sheehan, John	0	1	4.50	8	4	0	0	22	23	12	11	16	18
Simon, Rich	5	2	3.32	49	1	0	2	87	88	41	32	34	59
Tafoya, Dennis	0	5	6.75	31	0	0	2	40	55	36	30	18	21
*Trice, Wally	6	7	4.02	33	22	2	0	152	153	80	68	33	91

GREENVILLE

BATTING	AVG	G	AB	R	H	2B	3B	HR	RBI	BB	SO	SB
Alva, John, ss	.161	15	62	6	10	2	0	0	5	3	6	0
#Batiste, Kevin, of	.232	99	340	44	79	13	1	4	31	40	94	14
*Bell, Mike, 1b	.291	106	405	50	118	24	2	6	42	41	63	10
Carter, Dennis, of	.075	14	40	3	3	1	0	1	5	3	13	0
#Casarotti, Rich, 2b-dh	.226	113	367	39	83	10	2	5	42	32	74	3
Castilla, Vinny, ss	.235	46	170	20	40	5	1	4	16	13	23	4
Champion, Brian, 1b	.265	34	102	10	27	5	0	1	7	18	12	2
Deak, Brian, c	.218	66	188	24	41	13	0	3	26	43	47	2
Dean, Kevin, of	.193	22	57	6	11	5	1	0	3	19	15	2
Hall, Lamar, ss	.214	32	103	11	22	5	0	0	7	4	17	3
Hunter, Brian, of	.241	88	320	45	77	13	1	14	55	43	62	3
#Jose, Manny, of	.234	68	239	25	56	6	3	5	22	17	46	13
Kowitz, Brian, of	.132	20	68	4	9	0	0	0	4	8	10	1
Maldonado, Phil, c-1b	.182	8	22	2	4	1	0	0	1	2	2	0
Maloney, Rich, ss-3b	.205	59	161	26	33	2	1	0	16	33	14	1
Mann, Kelly, c	.316	50	155	25	49	13	0	7	27	32	22	6
*Martin, Al, of	.242	133	455	64	110	17	4	11	50	43	101	20
*Mizerock, John, c	.250	2	4	1	1	1	0	0	0	1	1	0
Morris, Rick, 3b-2b	.242	75	198	29	48	9	1	0	19	36	30	1
#Olmeda, Jose, ss	.125	2	8	1	1	0	0	0	0	1	3	0
Pino, Rolando, ss	.207	12	29	0	6	3	0	0	2	6	4	0
Plumb, David, c	.192	68	177	17	34	5	0	2	14	12	35	0
Redington, Tom, 3b	.252	124	409	55	103	13	1	12	52	63	69	2
Rossy, Rico, ss	.190	5	21	4	4	1	0	0	0	1	2	0
Snover, Dan, 2b	.294	15	34	4	10	3	0	0	4	2	3	1
*Tomberlin, Andy, of	.311	60	196	31	61	9	1	4	25	20	35	9
*Whitt, Ernie, c	.333	4	12	1	4	1	0	0	0	2	1	0
*Xavier, Joe, 2b	.238	64	189	41	45	5	0	1	17	16	39	3

PITCHING	W	L	ERA	G	GS	CG	SV	IP	H	R	ER	BB	SO
Barton, Shawn	0	1	8.10	15	0	0	1	17	24	15	15	9	8
*Boltz, Brian	9	10	3.73	28	28	0	0	159	157	80	66	56	98
Czarnik, Chris	4	4	2.98	21	4	0	1	57	53	28	19	27	31
Del Rosario, Maximo	7	7	4.12	60	2	0	1	116	128	72	53	42	67
*Diez, Scott	0	0	2.89	11	0	0	0	9	10	3	3	6	7
*Gomez, Pat	6	8	4.49	23	21	0	0	124	126	75	62	71	94
*Johnson, Judd	5	10	4.11	28	24	3	1	149	159	75	68	43	59
Johnson, Lee	0	4	3.31	9	5	0	1	35	38	21	13	18	24
*Kilner, John	0	3	2.75	28	0	0	15	36	24	11	11	28	28
*Leibrandt, Charlie	1	0	0.00	2	2	0	0	13	5	4	0	5	12
Rivera, Ben	1	4	6.58	13	13	0	0	52	68	40	38	26	32
Satzinger, Jeff	1	2	4.02	29	0	0	1	40	32	20	18	22	45
Smith, Pete	0	0	0.00	2	2	0	0	3	1	0	0	0	2
*Stanton, Mike	0	1	1.59	4	4	0	0	6	7	1	1	3	4
*Stockam, Doug	1	4	5.21	34	0	0	2	47	59	29	27	21	33
Turner, Matt	6	4	2.66	40	0	0	8	68	59	24	20	29	60
*Upshaw, Mike	6	12	4.42	22	21	1	0	128	148	77	63	64	59
Watson, Preston	3	1	8.44	11	0	0	0	16	25	17	15	11	8
Weems, Danny	3	2	6.75	24	0	0	1	63	73	53	47	37	43
Wendell, Turk	4	9	5.74	36	13	1	2	91	105	70	58	48	85
Wohlers, Mark	0	1	4.02	14	0	0	6	16	14	7	7	14	20

BATTING

R	Jarvis Brown, Orlando . .	104
H	Scott Brosius, Huntsville	162
TB	Scott Brosius, Huntsville	274
2B	Scott Brosius, Huntsville .	39
3B	Andujar Cedeno, Col	11
HR	Terrel Hansen, Jax	24
	Luis Gonzalez, Col	24
RBI	Matt Stark, Birmingham .	109
SH	Three tied at	14
SF	Luis Gonzalez, Columbus	12
	Matt Stark, Birmingham . .	12
BB	Frank Thomas, Birm . . .	112
IBB	Luis Gonzalez, Columbus .	9
	Tony Brown, Huntsville . . .	9
HBP	Rusty Crockett, Charlotte .	32
SO	Tom Quinlan, Knoxville .	157
SB	Paul Rodgers, Knoxville .	41
CS	Williams Suero, Knoxville	21
OB%	Frank Thomas, Birm . . .	.487

PITCHING

G	Three tied at	60
GS	Jimmy Rogers, Knoxville . .	30
	Bo Kennedy, Birmingham .	30
CG	Richie LeBlanc, Memphis . .	6
	Ross Powell, Chattanooga .	6
ShO	Blaise Ilsley, Columbus	3
	Pete Blohm, Knoxville	3
Sv	Steve Chitren, Huntsville .	27
W	Doug Simons, Orlando . . .	15
L	Nate Cromwell, Knoxville .	14
	Ross Powell, Chattanooga .	14
IP	Brian Barnes, Jax	201
H	Shane Reynolds, Col . . .	182
R	Keith Kaiser, Chat	122
HR	Keith Kaiser, Chat	21
	Richie LeBlanc, Memphis .	21
BB	Keith Kaiser, Chat	109
HB	Keith Kaiser, Chat	12
SO	Brian Barnes, Jax	213
WP	Juan Guzman, Knoxville . .	21
Bk	Gino Minutelli, Chat	13

HUNTSVILLE

BATTING	AVG	G	AB	R	H	2B	3B	HR	RBI	BB	SO	SB
Borrelli, Dean, c	.179	27	78	7	14	4	1	1	3	5	20	0
Brito, Jorge, c	.268	57	164	17	44	6	1	2	20	30	49	0
Brosius, Scott, ss-2b	.296	142	547	94	162	39	2	23	88	81	81	12
*Brown, Tony, of-dh	.290	127	445	74	129	29	1	10	60	67	96	4
Buccheri, James, 2b-of . . .	.209	84	278	39	58	2	1	0	22	40	38	15
Canseco, Ozzie, of	.225	97	325	50	73	21	0	20	67	47	103	2
Carcione, Tom, c	.194	24	62	6	12	0	1	0	9	13	12	1
Coomer, Ron, 2b-1b	.222	66	194	22	43	7	0	3	27	21	40	3
Kating, Jim, of	.227	72	220	37	50	11	2	2	20	31	34	1
Kuld, Pete, c	.220	57	168	23	37	8	1	7	23	14	57	2
Lewis, Darren, of	.296	71	284	52	84	11	3	3	23	36	28	21
Matos, Fransisco, ss	.228	45	180	18	41	3	3	0	12	9	18	7
Ralston, Bob, 2b	.147	36	109	5	16	1	0	0	5	5	11	1
Robinson, Martese, 1b	.265	104	366	43	97	13	2	6	50	34	66	5
Royer, Stan, 3b	.258	137	527	69	136	29	3	14	89	43	113	4
#Simmons, Nelson, dh-of . . .	.256	123	453	70	116	19	1	15	55	62	64	0
Wilson, Tack, of	.220	83	255	34	56	9	1	0	16	39	30	9
*Witmeyer, Ron, 1b	.319	27	91	18	29	4	0	5	18	15	16	0

PITCHING	W	L	ERA	G	GS	CG	SV	IP	H	R	ER	BB	SO
*Allison, Dana	7	1	2.39	35	0	0	2	53	52	14	14	6	38
Berg, Rich	3	3	3.93	33	0	0	4	50	51	27	22	31	21
Briscoe, John	0	0	13.50	3	0	0	0	5	9	7	7	7	7
*Chavez, Sam	4	4	6.70	18	5	0	0	47	58	38	35	21	34
Chitren, Steve	2	4	1.68	48	0	0	27	54	32	18	10	22	61
Eskew, Dan	14	3	3.34	25	25	0	0	148	133	62	55	60	128
Garcia, Apolinar	5	1	3.50	7	7	2	0	54	45	24	21	18	29
Green, Daryl	1	0	6.41	13	0	0	2	27	31	20	19	12	23
*Grott, Matt	0	0	2.87	10	0	0	1	16	8	5	5	10	12
*Guzman, Johnny	5	6	3.58	16	16	0	0	106	89	52	42	54	63
*Harris, Ray	4	4	4.31	12	12	1	0	71	75	47	34	25	44
Harris, Reggie	0	2	3.03	5	5	0	0	30	26	12	10	16	34
Kracl, Darin	4	6	7.12	12	10	1	0	54	72	50	43	26	31
*MacLeod, Kevin	0	2	5.14	6	3	0	0	21	27	17	12	11	9
*McCoy, Tim	1	1	2.70	6	1	0	0	13	18	8	4	4	17
Schock, Will	11	7	3.22	29	28	2	0	179	164	84	64	57	100
Slusarski, Joe	6	8	4.47	17	17	2	0	109	114	65	54	35	75
Stancel, Mark	5	8	4.39	46	4	0	7	96	102	59	47	47	51
Strebeck, Rick	1	1	5.02	12	0	0	2	14	13	8	8	6	7
*Veilleux, Brian	1	0	3.27	11	0	0	1	11	13	4	4	3	4
*Wernig, Pat	5	4	3.27	19	11	2	1	96	86	50	35	36	59

JACKSONVILLE

BATTING	AVG	G	AB	R	H	2B	3B	HR	RBI	BB	SO	SB
#Barberie, Bret, 2b	.260	133	431	71	112	18	3	7	56	86	64	20
Cianfrocco, Archi, 1b-3b . .	.219	62	196	18	43	10	0	5	29	12	45	0
Colbrunn, Greg, c	.301	125	458	57	138	29	1	13	76	38	78	1
Cordero, Will, ss	.234	131	444	63	104	18	4	7	40	56	122	9
*Faulk, Jim, of	.258	52	190	40	49	3	1	2	12	38	39	19
#Fulton, Greg, 1b-3b	.278	11	36	4	10	1	0	1	4	4	4	0
Hansen, Terrel, of	.260	123	420	72	109	26	2	24	83	43	88	3
Hernandez, Cesar, of	.239	118	393	58	94	21	7	10	50	18	75	17
#Kosco, Bryn, 3b	.248	33	113	7	28	8	0	0	15	11	23	0
Marquez, Edwin, 1b-of	.122	17	49	5	6	1	0	0	4	3	19	0
Munoz, Omer, inf	.254	70	197	19	50	5	0	1	18	5	18	3
Natal, Rob, c	.246	62	171	23	42	7	1	7	25	14	42	0
*Penn, Trevor, 1b-of	.222	104	316	43	70	11	3	7	34	39	60	7

Matt Stark ...109 RBIs | **Luis Gonzalez** ...24 homers | **Adam Casillas** ...top hitter

	AVG	G	AB	R	H	2B	3B	HR	RBI	BB	SO	SB
*Rodriguez, Boi, 3b-1b	.281	105	367	50	103	22	5	9	58	45	81	2
#Santana, Miguel, of	.221	92	303	56	67	4	3	1	10	27	35	21
Stairs, Matt, 3b-of	.254	79	280	26	71	17	0	3	34	22	43	5
*Vanderwal, John, of	.303	77	277	45	84	25	3	8	40	39	46	6

PITCHING	W	L	ERA	G	GS	CG	SV	IP	H	R	ER	BB	SO
*Barnes, Brian	13	7	2.77	29	28	3	0	201	144	78	62	87	213
Bennett, Chris	3	4	3.24	37	0	0	9	50	45	23	18	13	45
Bottenfield, Kent	12	10	3.41	29	28	2	0	169	158	72	64	67	121
Brito, Mario	9	7	3.19	18	18	1	0	116	100	57	41	34	49
Carter, Jeff	8	3	1.84	52	7	2	15	117	90	36	24	33	76
Davins, Jim	0	0	4.50	3	0	0	0	6	2	4	3	3	7
Galvez, Balvino	0	0	6.75	1	1	0	0	4	6	4	3	1	3
*Haney, Chris	1	0	0.00	1	1	0	0	6	6	0	0	4	5
Jones, Al	1	3	4.79	5	3	0	0	21	30	18	11	6	12
Lewis, Richie	0	0	1.26	11	0	0	5	14	7	2	2	5	14
Malloy, Bob	4	1	3.32	8	5	1	0	43	34	17	16	16	25
*Marchok, Chris	0	2	2.86	25	0	0	3	28	26	12	9	16	27
Masters, Dave	0	2	3.46	20	4	0	0	42	28	22	16	44	49
*Nabholz, Chris	7	2	3.03	11	11	0	0	74	62	28	25	27	77
*Perez, Yorkis	2	2	6.00	28	2	0	1	42	36	34	28	34	39
Peters, Tim	0	0	4.50	2	0	0	0	2	3	1	1	2	1
Piatt, Doug	5	1	2.20	35	0	0	6	49	30	17	12	29	51
Rivera, Hector	6	6	3.60	18	18	2	0	105	93	46	42	44	60
Schmidt, Dave	0	1	4.50	3	2	0	0	6	4	3	3	0	4
Sossamon, Tim	0	0	3.95	7	0	0	1	14	19	8	6	5	17
Wainhouse, David	7	7	4.33	17	16	2	0	96	97	59	46	47	59
*Winston, Darrin	6	2	2.14	47	0	0	7	63	38	16	15	28	45

KNOXVILLE

BATTING	AVG	G	AB	R	H	2B	3B	HR	RBI	BB	SO	SB
*Dziadkowiec, Andy, c	.221	38	122	7	27	3	0	0	12	11	20	2
*Jeter, Shawn, of	.273	131	461	66	126	25	2	4	43	39	95	25
Knorr, Randy, c-dh	.276	116	392	51	108	12	1	13	64	31	83	0
*Maksudian, Mike, of-c	.287	121	422	51	121	22	5	8	55	50	66	6
Martinez, Domingo, 1b-dh	.257	128	463	53	119	20	3	17	66	51	81	2
Monzon, Jose, c	.333	1	3	1	1	0	0	0	0	0	0	0
Morrison, Brian, ph	.000	1	1	0	0	0	0	0	0	0	1	0
Nunez, Bernie, of	.233	105	313	30	73	11	5	2	39	16	67	10
Quinlan, Tom, 3b	.258	141	481	70	124	24	6	15	51	49	157	8
Rodgers, Paul, of	.228	142	482	64	110	15	4	4	35	49	84	41
Schunk, Jerry, ss-of	.288	85	274	32	79	13	1	3	31	9	25	8
Suero, Williams, 2b	.263	133	483	80	127	29	7	16	60	78	78	40
Taylor, Mike, 2b	.133	12	15	2	2	0	0	0	2	2	6	1
Yan, Julian, 1b-dh	.244	113	389	55	95	18	3	15	48	25	108	2
Zosky, Eddie, ss	.271	115	450	53	122	20	7	3	45	26	73	3

PITCHING	W	L	ERA	G	GS	CG	SV	IP	H	R	ER	BB	SO
Blohm, Pete	5	5	4.50	30	12	3	2	108	101	58	54	37	53
*Cromwell, Nate	5	14	5.56	27	23	2	0	121	119	85	75	91	79
Guzman, Juan	11	9	4.24	37	21	0	1	157	145	84	74	80	138
Hall, Darren	3	5	4.86	28	0	0	1	33	29	23	18	33	28
Hentgen, Pat	9	5	3.05	28	26	0	0	153	121	57	52	68	142
*Horsman, Vince	2	1	4.63	8	0	0	0	12	11	7	6	5	10
Jones, Chris	4	4	5.25	35	0	0	0	74	78	49	43	38	50
Jones, Dennis	0	1	6.94	9	4	0	1	23	14	22	18	35	33
*MacDonald, Bob	1	2	1.89	36	0	0	15	57	37	17	12	29	54
Martinez, Domingo	0	0	3.00	3	0	0	0	3	5	1	1	0	3
Rauth, Chris	0	1	6.75	8	0	0	0	17	23	16	13	6	10
Rogers, Jimmy	9	12	4.47	31	30	2	0	173	179	98	86	104	113
Sanders, Earl	4	4	4.75	37	0	0	2	61	63	41	32	57	39
Timlin, Mike	1	2	1.73	17	0	0	8	26	20	6	5	7	21
Williams, Woody	7	9	3.14	42	16	0	5	126	111	55	44	39	74
Wishnevski, Rob	6	3	3.83	20	17	1	1	106	84	54	45	39	74

MEMPHIS

BATTING	AVG	G	AB	R	H	2B	3B	HR	RBI	BB	SO	SB
*Alborano, Pete, of-dh	.255	81	259	33	66	8	1	2	35	32	31	0
Berry, Sean, 3b	.292	135	487	73	142	25	4	14	77	44	89	19
Cole, Stu, ss-2b	.308	113	357	61	110	18	2	1	49	55	55	20
Conine, Jeff, 1b	.320	137	487	89	156	37	8	15	95	94	88	21
*Dunbar, Tommy, of-1b	.203	95	290	44	59	7	3	5	42	33	31	9
#Hinzo, Tommy, 2b-ss (27 Gvl)	.223	45	121	15	27	3	3	1	14	14	21	6
#Howard, David, ss	.250	116	384	41	96	10	4	5	44	39	74	15
*Koslofski, Kevin, of	.213	118	367	52	78	11	5	3	32	54	89	12
*Ladnier, Deric, dh	.143	2	7	0	1	1	0	0	1	1	2	0
Laureano, Francisco, 2b	.241	108	320	44	77	14	2	4	36	57	51	7
*Mayne, Brent, c-dh	.267	115	412	48	110	16	3	2	61	52	51	5
*McRae, Brian, of	.268	116	470	78	126	24	6	10	64	44	65	21
Moore, Bobby, of	.303	112	422	93	128	20	6	2	36	56	32	27
Pedre, Jorge, c-dh	.258	99	360	55	93	14	1	9	54	27	47	6
Reese, Kyle, c	.103	16	29	1	3	1	0	0	1	0	15	0
#Wright, George, of	.216	18	51	6	11	0	0	2	5	11	11	0

PITCHING	W	L	ERA	G	GS	CG	SV	IP	H	R	ER	BB	SO
*Campbell, Jim	5	5	2.44	40	12	0	0	100	78	38	27	32	79
Centala, Scott	11	8	3.22	25	25	1	0	142	131	57	51	66	116
Codiroli, Chris	1	1	8.10	4	3	0	0	13	16	12	12	10	13
Cole, Victor	3	8	4.35	46	6	0	4	108	91	61	52	70	102
Cruz, Andres	8	12	3.67	28	28	3	0	162	173	90	66	47	76
Everson, Greg	3	3	2.43	24	0	0	2	41	33	14	11	13	28
Hudson, Jim	1	3	6.48	4	4	0	0	17	23	15	12	10	5
Johnston, Joel	0	0	6.75	4	3	0	0	7	5	9	5	16	6
LeBlanc, Richie	12	10	3.81	30	29	6	0	182	175	95	77	70	94
Maldonado, Carlos	4	5	2.91	55	0	0	20	77	61	29	25	37	77
McCormack, Brian	1	1	6.10	28	7	0	2	62	74	48	42	41	46
*Moeller, Dennis	7	6	6.25	14	14	0	0	68	79	55	47	30	42
Nelson, Doug	1	1	2.93	6	1	0	0	15	16	5	5	3	8
Parnell, Mark	1	1	3.72	17	0	0	1	29	24	13	12	17	28
*Pierce, Ed	0	0	0.00	1	0	0	0	1	0	0	0	1	1
*Sanchez, Israel	1	2	3.10	15	0	0	6	29	21	11	10	8	32
Schaefer, Chris	0	0	0.00	1	1	0	0	3	2	0	0	3	1
Smith, Daryl	2	1	3.17	21	0	0	1	48	46	27	17	23	48
Vaughn, Randy	0	0	12.46	4	0	0	0	4	6	6	6	9	4
Wagner, Hector	12	4	2.03	40	11	1	1	133	114	37	30	41	63

ORLANDO

BATTING	AVG	G	AB	R	H	2B	3B	HR	RBI	BB	SO	SB
Brown, Jarvis, of	.260	135	527	104	137	22	7	14	57	80	79	33
Eccles, John, dh-c	.185	62	178	16	33	9	0	2	10	24	66	0
Gilbert, Shawn, ss	.254	123	433	68	110	18	2	4	44	61	69	31
Knoblauch, Chuck, 2b	.289	118	432	74	125	23	6	2	53	63	31	23
Marzan, Jose, 1b	.230	77	200	22	46	5	0	1	16	35	27	0
*Morgan, Kenny, of	.247	136	462	54	114	21	7	13	62	59	85	11
Naveda, Ed, of-3b	.347	28	98	10	34	7	0	1	19	12	8	0
*Olmstead, Reed, 1b	.266	102	335	43	89	11	3	8	65	33	64	0
*Ortiz, Ray, of	.257	71	265	41	68	16	0	9	49	27	57	1
*Randle, Mike, of	.234	102	342	56	80	10	3	2	36	31	46	16
Reboulet, Jeff, inf	.230	97	287	43	66	12	2	2	28	57	37	10
*Resetar, Gary, dh-c	.278	95	299	41	83	15	1	4	44	41	42	0
*Richardson, A.J., dh	.250	1	4	0	1	0	0	0	1	0	2	0
Valdez, Frank, 3b	.233	111	361	44	84	18	0	3	38	44	92	4
Webster, Lenny, c	.262	126	455	69	119	31	0	8	71	68	57	0

PITCHING	W	L	ERA	G	GS	CG	SV	IP	H	R	ER	BB	SO
Ard, Johnny	12	9	3.79	29	29	4	0	180	167	90	76	85	101
Banks, Willie	7	9	3.93	28	28	1	0	163	161	93	71	98	114
Erickson, Scott	8	3	3.03	15	15	3	0	101	75	38	34	24	69
Garces, Richard	2	1	2.08	15	0	0	8	17	17	4	4	14	22
Hull, Jeffrey	0	0	27.00	1	0	0	0	0	1	2	1	1	1
Johnson, Greg	3	3	2.93	43	0	0	19	43	39	21	14	15	42
Lind, Orlando	6	4	4.41	25	13	0	4	88	88	47	43	39	82
Meyer, Basil	4	4	4.33	55	0	0	3	71	66	46	34	40	58
*Muh, Steve	2	1	4.04	9	8	0	0	42	47	21	19	21	23
*Neagle, Denny	12	3	2.45	17	17	4	0	121	94	40	33	31	94
Redding, Mike	5	2	2.81	34	5	0	1	74	60	32	23	37	44
*Simons, Doug	15	12	2.54	29	28	5	0	188	160	76	53	43	109
*Stowell, Steve	1	3	4.39	60	0	0	6	53	54	33	26	33	36
Wassenaar, Rob	8	5	2.98	52	1	0	6	97	85	39	32	20	65

TEXAS LEAGUE

Perseverence pays off as Captains win title

By TED BAKAMJIAN

The Shreveport Captains had developed postseason futility into an art.

In four consecutive seasons from 1986-89, the Captains qualified for the Texas League Eastern Division playoffs, but not once in those years did they reach the league championship series, let alone win the title.

Henry Rodriguez ... MVP

Shreveport qualified for postseason play again in 1990 by winning the first-half Eastern Division title. But because the Captains fell to third place in the second half and finished with a 65-68 overall record—only the sixth-best in the eight-team league—it appeared likely their postseason woes would continue.

But manager Bill Evers' club swept a pitching-rich Jackson team at home in the best-of-3 divisional playoff, then downed Western Division-champion San Antonio—which posted the league's best regular-season record, 78-56—in six games in the best-of-7 championship series.

The Captains, a farm team of the San Francisco Giants, became the first team with a losing regular-season record to win the league title since Arkansas did it in 1977, when the

LEAGUE CHAMPIONS

Playoff Champions, Where Applicable

1990—Shreveport	1960—Tulsa	1927—Wichita Falls
1989—Arkansas	1959—Austin	1926—Dallas
1988—Tulsa	1958—Corp. Christi	1925—Ft. Worth
1987—Wichita	1957—Houston	1924—Ft. Worth
1986—El Paso	1956—Houston	1923—Ft. Worth
1985—Jackson	1955—Shreveport	1922—Ft. Worth
1984—Jackson	1954—Houston	1921—Ft. Worth
1983—Beaumont	1953—Dallas	1920—Ft. Worth
1982—Tulsa	1952—Shreveport	1919—Shreveport
1981—Jackson	1951—Houston	1918—Dallas
1980—Arkansas	1950—San Antonio	1917—Dallas
1979—Arkansas	1949—Tulsa	1916—Waco
1978—El Paso	1948—Ft. Worth	1915—Waco
1977—Arkansas	1947—Houston	1914—*Houston
1976—Amarillo	1946—Dallas	—*Waco
1975—*Lafayette	1943-45—Did Not	1913—Houston
—*Midland	Operate	1912—Houston
1974—Victoria	1942—Shreveport	1911—Austin
1973—Memphis	1941—Dallas	1910—*Dallas
1972—El Paso	1940—Houston	—*Houston
1971—Did Not	1939—Ft. Worth	1909—Houston
Operate	1938—Beaumont	1908—San Antonio
1970—Albuquerque	1937—Ft. Worth	1907—Austin
1969—Memphis	1936—Tulsa	1906—Cleburne
1968—El Paso	1935—Okla. City	1905—Ft. Worth
1967—Albuquerque	1934—Galveston	1904—Corsicana
1966—Arkansas	1933—San Antonio	1903—Dallas
1965—Albuquerque	1932—Beaumont	1902—Corsicana
1964—San Antonio	1931—Houston	1900-01—Did Not
1963—Tulsa	1930—Ft. Worth	Operate
1962—Tulsa	1929—Dallas	
1961—San Antonio	1928—Houston	*co-champions

San Antonio's Eric Karros led the Texas League with a .352 average, and the minors with 179 hits and 45 doubles.

league reinstituted the split-season format. Shreveport won its first TL title since 1955.

Rafael Novoa and two relievers combined on a three-hitter as Shreveport won 6-0 in the opener of the title series, but San Antonio won the next two games at Shreveport. That left the Captains needing to win three games at San Antonio.

Eric Gunderson pitched eight shutout innings and struck out 12 as the Captains won 3-1 in Game 6 to eliminate the Missions, who had reached the finals by beating El Paso 2-1 in the Western Division playoff.

Dodgers, Mets most talented

The league's most highly regarded prospects were concentrated on the two teams Shreveport beat in the postseason to win the championship.

TL pitcher of the year Anthony Young, a righthander who went 15-3 with a 1.65 ERA, headed an outstanding Jackson staff that also included lefthander Pete Schourek (11-4, 3.04), righthander Mike Miller (7-7, 2.91) and 6-foot-9 righthander Terry Bross, who led the league with 28 saves.

San Antonio had the most dynamic offensive club. Henry Rodriguez, a lefthanded-hitting outfielder, was the league's Most Valuable Player. He batted .291 for the Missions and led the league in home runs (28) and RBIs (109).

Eric Karros, a righthanded-hitting first baseman, won the batting championship with a .352 average. He also had a minor-league high 45 doubles.

New park at El Paso

After several delays, El Paso's new ballpark, Cohen Stadium, finally opened on June 13. The $6.8 million, 10,000-seat stadium replaced Dudley Field, which had been in use since 1924.

Cohen Stadium, named after brothers Sid and Andy Cohen,

who were major-league players and El Paso civic leaders, remained under construction even after play had begun there. Clubhouses weren't ready for use until just before the end of the season. Prior to that, players had to dress elsewhere and ride buses to the ballpark.

El Paso beat Wichita 6-2 before 6,212 fans in the first game played at Cohen Stadium, but the night was filled with misadventure. The Wichita team bus overheated en route to the ballpark, forcing a half-hour delay in the start. During the game Wichita manager Steve Lubratich and a player were ejected, and umpires had trouble deciding where to send them until finally dispatching them to the team bus.

The game was delayed again in the eighth inning when a bank of lights went out. Then in the ninth, El Paso mayor Suzie Azar was struck with a foul ball. She was not hurt.

During the final 2½ months of the season, it was evident that several bugs needed to be worked out of the new facility. During one game, the automatic sprinkler system was activated unexpectedly, and players in the field got soaked.

Midland changes hands

The Midland franchise was sold midway through the 1990 season by Rick Holtzman to New York attorney Miles Prentice and Arizona League president Bob Richmond.

During the season, it became evident that the Jackson franchise and the New York Mets would sever their 16-year association because the city had dragged its feet on making much-needed improvements to Smith-Wills Stadium.

Jackson owner Con Maloney, who had looked into relocating the franchise, said he planned to obtain a new affiliation and operate the franchise in Jackson again in 1991.

1990 FINAL STANDINGS

FIRST HALF

East	W	L	Pct.	GB
Shreveport (Giants)	34	31	.523	—
Jackson (Mets)	35	32	.522	—
Tulsa (Rangers)	34	32	.515	½
Arkansas (Cardinals)	27	40	.403	8

West	W	L	Pct.	GB
El Paso (Brewers)	39	29	.574	—
Wichita (Padres)	37	29	.561	1
San Antonio (Dodgers)	35	31	.530	3
Midland (Angels)	25	42	.373	13½

SECOND HALF

East	W	L	Pct.	GB
Jackson (Mets)	38	30	.559	—
Tulsa (Rangers)	34	36	.486	5
Shreveport (Giants)	31	37	.456	7
Arkansas (Cardinals)	29	40	.420	9½

West	W	L	Pct.	GB
San Antonio (Dodgers)	43	25	.632	—
El Paso (Brewers)	38	29	.567	4½
Midland (Angels)	31	38	.449	12½
Wichita (Padres)	30	39	.435	13½

OVERALL

	W	L	Pct.	GB
San Antonio (Dodgers)	78	56	.582	—
El Paso (Brewers)	77	58	.570	1½
Jackson (Mets)	73	62	.541	5½
Tulsa (Rangers)	68	68	.500	11
Wichita (Padres)	67	68	.496	11½
Shreveport (Giants)	65	68	.489	12½
Arkansas (Cardinals)	56	80	.412	23
Midland (Angels)	56	80	.412	23

Playoffs: Shreveport defeated Jackson 2-0 in best-of-3 semifinal; San Antonio defeated El Paso 2-1 in best-of-3 semifinal; Shreveport defeated San Antonio 4-2 in best-of-7 final for league championship.

Regular-Season Attendance: Arkansas, 256,074; Tulsa, 226,461; Wichita, 218,109; Shreveport, 204,872; El Paso, 201,068; San Antonio, 180,931; Midland, 168,742; Jackson, 124,142.

Managers: Arkansas—Dave Bialas; **El Paso**—Dave Huppert; **Jackson**—Clint Hurdle; **Midland**—Eddie Rodriguez; **San Antonio**—John Shoemaker; **Shreveport**—Bill Evers; **Tulsa**—Tommy Thompson; **Wichita**—Steve Lubratich.

1990 Official All-Star Team: C—Steve Decker, Shreveport; Bill Haselman, Tulsa. **1B**—Eric Karros, San Antonio. **2B**—Dean Kelley, Wichita. **3B**—Steve Finken, San Antonio. **SS**—Charlie Montoya, El Paso. **UTIL INF**—Dave Patterson, Shreveport. **OF**—Henry Rodriguez, San Antonio; Tom Goodwin, San Antonio; Mike Humphreys, Wichita. **DH**—Jesus Alfaro, El Paso. **P**—Anthony Young, Jackson; Pete Schourek, Jackson; Terry Bross, Jackson; Mike James, San Antonio; Ricky Bones, Wichita. **Most Valuable Player**—Henry Rodriguez, San Antonio. **Pitcher of the Year**—Anthony Young, Jackson. **Manager of the Year**—Clint Hurdle, Jackson.

Top 10 Major League Prospects (by Baseball America): 1. Anthony Young, rhp, Jackson; **2.** Henry Rodriguez, of, San Antonio; **3.** Eric Karros, 1b, San Antonio; **4.** Pete Schourek, lhp, Jackson; **5.** Tom Goodwin, of, San Antonio; **6.** Terry Bross, rhp, Jackson; **7.** Kevin Belcher, of, Tulsa; **8.** Todd Hundley, c, Jackson; **9.** Steve Decker, c, Shreveport; **10.** Chris George, rhp, El Paso.

1990 *BATTING, PITCHING STATS*

CLUB BATTING

	AVG	G	AB	R	H	2B	3B	HR	BB	SO	SB
Midland	.281	137	4793	709	1346	231	43	108	443	797	144
San Antonio	.277	134	4579	669	1267	210	41	88	467	789	153
Tulsa	.275	136	4487	624	1232	218	51	96	424	903	121
Wichita	.274	136	4604	683	1262	226	29	94	491	746	187
El Paso	.272	135	4622	653	1259	200	41	62	530	757	132
Shreveport	.253	133	4352	538	1099	182	39	76	417	778	128
Jackson	.250	135	4366	515	1094	204	42	54	518	919	173
Arkansas	.246	136	4247	503	1043	203	40	51	473	842	121

CLUB PITCHING

	ERA	G	CG	SHO	SV	IP	H	R	ER	BB	SO
Jackson	3.15	135	10	16	42	1188	1082	499	416	396	748
Shreveport	3.16	133	11	12	31	1158	1125	496	406	388	871
San Antonio	3.30	134	10	7	40	1196	1104	544	438	479	815
El Paso	3.99	135	8	4	43	1198	1254	613	531	483	837
Tulsa	4.11	136	12	6	35	1155	1136	620	527	592	820
Arkansas	4.22	136	19	12	27	1126	1168	650	528	454	817
Wichita	4.48	136	10	4	28	1178	1276	684	586	414	794
Midland	5.31	137	5	3	24	1202	1456	827	711	556	832

INDIVIDUAL BATTING LEADERS
(Minimum 367 Plate Appearances)

	AVG	G	AB	R	H	2B	3B	HR	RBI	BB	SO	SB
Karros, Eric, SA	.352	131	509	90	179	45	2	18	78	57	80	8
Haselman, Bill, Tulsa	.319	120	430	68	137	39	2	18	80	43	96	3
Rohrmeier, Dan, Tulsa	.305	119	453	76	138	24	7	10	62	37	51	14
Brooks, Jerry, SA	.302	106	391	52	118	19	0	9	58	26	39	5
Alfaro, Jesus, El Paso	.301	129	485	80	146	29	4	16	88	68	81	0
*Maurer, Rob, Tulsa	.300	104	367	55	110	31	4	21	78	54	112	4
*David, Greg, Wichita	.299	112	402	55	120	30	1	13	59	38	90	3
*Lee, Wiley, Midland	.297	102	377	70	112	15	6	8	38	27	66	45
Belcher, Kevin, Tulsa	.293	110	423	66	124	17	7	11	43	55	88	29
Decker, Steve, Shreve	.293	116	403	52	118	22	1	15	80	40	64	3

INDIVIDUAL PITCHING LEADERS
(Minimum 109 Innings)

	W	L	ERA	G	GS	CG	SV	IP	H	R	ER	BB	SO
Young, Anthony, Jackson	15	3	1.65	23	23	3	0	158	116	38	29	52	95
Cinnella, Doug, Jackson	8	3	2.27	40	8	0	2	111	105	33	28	41	69
Lienhard, Steve, Shreve	5	7	2.50	48	6	1	5	115	109	42	32	35	68
Miller, Mike, Jackson	7	7	2.91	22	21	3	0	139	113	54	45	32	95
Hostetler, Tom, Shreve	8	8	3.04	23	22	1	0	130	119	55	44	40	112
*Schourek, Pete, Jackson	11	4	3.04	19	19	1	0	124	109	53	42	39	94
Springer, Dennis, SA	8	6	3.31	24	24	3	0	163	147	76	60	73	77
James, Mike, SA	11	4	3.32	26	26	3	0	157	144	73	58	78	97
Opperman, Dan, SA	12	8	3.41	27	27	3	0	156	153	75	59	62	96
Bones, Ricky, Wichita	6	4	3.48	21	21	2	0	137	138	66	53	45	96

ARKANSAS

BATTING	AVG	G	AB	R	H	2B	3B	HR	RBI	BB	SO	SB
Abreu, Frank, ss-2b	.273	11	22	1	6	2	0	0	1	3	4	0
#Alicea, Luis, 2b	.286	14	49	11	14	3	1	0	4	7	8	2
#Carmona, Greg, ss	.232	114	319	29	74	3	3	0	20	74	82	20
*Carter, Eddie, of	.188	10	16	0	3	1	0	0	2	0	3	0
Christian, Ric, of	.235	111	336	55	79	18	3	1	20	23	92	343
Elliot, Terry, of	.000	2	1	0	0	0	0	0	0	0	0	0
Fanning, Steve, 2b-ss	.225	126	404	50	91	23	4	4	34	59	91	0
*Fernandez, Joey, 1b	.271	123	402	62	109	22	2	14	63	59	55	8
*Fernandez, Jose, c	.169	55	177	13	30	5	1	4	25	14	65	0
Fitzgerald, Mike, 1b-dh	.240	41	129	13	31	4	0	4	16	12	32	0
*Fulton, Ed, c	.264	48	148	24	39	9	1	3	25	19	26	0
Hall, Joe, of-3b	.271	115	399	44	108	13	4	4	44	35	41	21
Jordan, Brian, of	.160	16	50	4	8	1	0	0	0	0	11	0
*Maclin, Lonnie, of	.311	74	264	32	82	15	5	2	25	19	35	11
Melvin, Scott, 3b-1b	.273	74	154	17	42	11	0	0	17	23	20	0
Nichols, Scott, c-of	.157	43	108	7	17	0	0	0	10	19	33	1
Redman, Tim, c	.304	9	23	0	7	2	0	0	4	2	3	0
Ross, Mike, 3b-2b	.251	128	435	55	109	34	2	8	56	39	93	1
*Thoutsis, Paul, of	.282	101	266	25	75	15	5	5	37	12	37	0
White, Charlie, of	.251	118	390	53	98	14	9	2	26	41	65	22

PITCHING	W	L	ERA	G	GS	CG	SV	IP	H	R	ER	BB	SO
*Alleyne, Isaac	1	4	5.86	20	7	0	0	51	61	42	33	33	43
Arnold, Scott	1	0	2.63	4	4	0	0	24	21	11	7	7	15
*Burgos, John	2	3	2.77	6	6	0	0	39	37	13	12	10	15
Clark, Mark	5	11	3.82	19	19	5	0	115	111	56	49	37	87
*Cormier, Rheal	5	12	5.04	22	21	3	0	121	133	81	68	30	102
Cox, Danny	1	0	1.29	1	1	1	0	7	3	1	1	1	3
Ericks, John	1	2	9.39	4	4	1	0	15	17	19	16	19	19
Grater, Mark	2	0	2.86	29	0	0	17	44	31	18	14	18	43
Hoffman, Rick	0	2	3.66	4	4	0	0	20	21	13	8	12	16
Kisten, Dale	2	3	3.25	45	0	0	3	53	46	29	19	21	40
*Lepley, John	6	4	2.62	59	0	0	4	79	70	36	23	36	61
Majer, Steffen	0	2	10.22	3	3	0	0	12	19	15	14	8	4
*Mathews, Greg	0	1	2.57	1	1	0	0	7	4	2	2	1	4
*Milchin, Mike	6	8	4.31	17	17	4	0	102	103	62	49	47	75
Osteen, Dave	5	5	3.01	13	13	4	0	84	77	32	28	21	51
Ozuna, Gab	3	2	3.30	54	0	0	0	71	82	36	26	26	61
Picota, Len	10	8	4.57	26	24	0	0	138	159	84	70	57	71
Pierson, Larry	3	4	5.48	21	6	0	0	48	68	30	29	12	21
Smith, Ken	0	0	10.80	3	0	0	0	3	7	4	4	1	2
Stone, Brian	1	1	3.90	7	6	0	0	28	22	14	12	23	27
Thoutsis, Paul	0	0	9.00	3	0	0	0	3	4	3	3	2	2
Vargas, Jose	1	4	6.75	15	0	0	3	21	27	18	16	13	21
Weese, Dean	1	3	5.22	19	0	0	0	40	43	28	23	17	34

EL PASO

BATTING	AVG	G	AB	R	H	2B	3B	HR	RBI	BB	SO	SB
Alfaro, Jesus, dh-inf	.301	129	485	80	146	29	4	16	88	68	81	0
Ashley, Shon, of	.261	122	429	53	112	23	3	11	67	55	91	6
Cooper, Craig, 1b	.282	130	493	73	139	34	3	11	63	61	89	1
*Dixon, Dee, of	.286	127	535	81	153	17	6	6	61	40	80	53
#Edge, Greg, ss-3b	.180	57	167	17	30	0	0	0	12	12	9	8
*Escalera, Ruben, of	.281	112	402	54	113	15	6	2	56	46	73	6
*Guerrero, Sandy, 2b-3b	.248	118	452	45	112	21	5	2	45	32	48	6
Hannahs, Mitch, 2b	.331	37	121	20	40	9	0	2	24	16	14	4
*Heffernan, Bert, c	.279	110	390	49	109	18	2	1	42	60	68	6
Kappesser, Bob, c	.222	14	36	3	8	0	0	0	2	1	7	0
Kmak, Joe, c	.284	35	109	8	31	3	2	2	11	7	22	0
*Lombardozzi, Chris, 2b-3b	.250	34	100	15	25	1	1	1	7	11	16	1
#Mattox, Frank, 2b	.244	12	41	5	10	1	1	1	6	11	4	2
Montoyo, Charlie, ss	.289	94	322	71	93	15	3	3	44	72	43	9
*Skeete, Rafel, of	.278	109	367	57	102	6	4	1	28	19	72	28
Webster, Casey, 3b	.209	50	172	22	36	7	1	3	18	19	39	2

PITCHING	W	L	ERA	G	GS	CG	SV	IP	H	R	ER	BB	SO
Austin, Jim	11	3	2.44	38	3	0	6	92	91	36	25	26	77
Chapman, Mark	3	4	3.92	42	1	0	3	87	87	42	38	42	76
Eldred, Cal	5	4	4.49	19	19	0	0	110	126	61	55	47	93
*Elvira, Narciso	0	2	4.50	4	4	0	0	18	17	11	9	6	12
Fleming, Keith	3	1	7.03	18	0	0	0	32	42	30	25	14	21
Fortugno, Tim	2	3	3.14	12	2	0	2	29	23	12	10	22	24
Freeland, Dean	10	8	4.01	26	26	2	0	157	145	74	70	74	94
*Garces, Robinson	2	4	3.56	19	0	0	1	56	47	24	22	22	52
George, Chris	8	3	1.78	39	0	0	13	56	41	16	11	20	38
Henry, Doug	1	0	2.93	15	0	0	9	31	31	13	10	11	25
Hunter, Jim	6	3	3.92	9	9	2	0	62	64	31	27	15	37
Ignasiak, Mike	6	3	4.35	15	15	1	0	83	96	45	40	34	39
May, Scott	6	4	3.79	22	13	2	0	100	113	48	42	38	85
McGrath, Chuck	3	3	3.48	13	12	1	0	78	89	39	30	27	32
*Miglio, John	2	0	4.02	8	0	0	1	16	16	8	7	6	10
Monson, Steve	6	9	6.33	22	20	0	0	108	125	87	76	49	61
*Puig, Ed	1	0	1.14	19	0	0	0	24	18	3	3	11	24
Sparks, Steve	1	2	6.53	7	6	0	0	30	43	24	22	15	17
Watkins, Tim	1	2	2.17	5	5	0	0	29	35	7	7	3	19

Tom Goodwin
...60 SB

Terry Bross
...28 saves

Steve Decker
...293-15-80

JACKSON

BATTING	AVG	G	AB	R	H	2B	3B	HR	RBI	BB	SO	SB
Baez, Kevin, ss	.233	106	326	29	76	11	0	2	29	38	44	3
Brown, Don, of	.138	15	29	3	4	0	0	0	1	4	13	4
#Carr, Chuck, of	.258	93	361	60	93	19	9	3	24	43	77	48
*Cuevas, Angelo, of	.234	77	222	32	52	13	2	3	24	42	29	3
*Davis, Steve, of	.215	81	228	26	49	11	4	2	18	19	79	11
Dellicarri, Joe, 2b-ss	.275	49	120	18	33	7	3	1	9	15	35	2
*Donnels, Chris, 3b	.272	130	419	66	114	24	0	12	63	111	80	10
Dozier, D.J., of	.324	29	102	20	33	5	7	2	23	16	28	3
*Freiling, Howie, 1b-dh	.264	74	197	21	52	7	3	2	29	25	37	1
Gonzalez, Javier, c	.175	45	137	16	24	4	0	4	15	13	44	0
Graves, Kenny, c	.167	4	12	0	2	1	0	0	3	0	2	0
#Hartmann, Reid, of	.200	8	20	4	4	1	0	1	1	2	6	1
Hernandez, Rudy, 2b	.242	123	443	63	107	14	5	0	30	41	61	32
#Hundley, Todd, c	.265	81	279	27	74	12	2	1	35	34	44	5
*Jimenez, Al, 1b	.280	123	421	50	118	33	2	6	61	37	72	4
#Lara, Crucito, ss-2b	.196	61	163	11	32	2	0	1	10	9	45	1
McDaniel, Terry, of	.286	67	234	34	67	14	2	5	37	31	70	19
Morrisette, Jim, of-3b	.220	16	50	3	11	1	0	1	6	3	14	2
Navarro, Tito, ss	.182	3	11	0	2	1	0	0	1	2	2	0
Roca, Gil, c	.267	8	30	4	8	1	0	0	3	2	0	0
Roseboro, Jaime, of	.275	93	349	53	96	19	2	7	44	24	45	23
#Zinter, Alan, c	.200	6	20	2	4	1	0	0	1	3	11	1

PITCHING	W	L	ERA	G	GS	CG	SV	IP	H	R	ER	BB	SO
Bross, Terry	3	4	2.64	58	0	0	28	72	46	21	21	40	51
Bumgarner, Jeff	0	2	4.50	3	0	0	0	8	11	5	4	2	4
Cinnella, Doug	6	3	2.27	40	8	0	2	111	105	33	28	41	69
*Diez, Scott	0	0	13.50	1	0	0	0	3	4	4	4	1	0
*Douma, Todd	0	0	3.00	1	1	0	0	6	3	2	2	3	5
*Elli, Rocky	3	6	4.54	17	15	1	0	75	74	43	38	34	52
*Gideon, Ron	0	0	7.47	9	0	0	0	16	19	14	13	6	10
Hernandez, Manny	1	0	3.00	1	1	0	0	6	6	2	2	1	1
*Hillman, Eric	6	5	3.93	15	15	0	0	89	92	42	39	30	61
Kline, Doug	6	8	3.94	31	14	1	1	110	119	55	48	31	79
Larose, Steve	1	3	3.90	19	0	0	1	28	36	20	12	15	18
Miller, Mike	7	7	2.91	22	21	3	0	139	113	54	45	32	95
Nivens, Toby	6	8	3.86	18	18	1	0	103	115	54	44	19	36
Perez, Vladimir	2	1	2.20	26	0	0	0	49	42	16	12	19	33
Plummer, Dale	1	1	2.00	4	0	0	0	9	5	2	2	3	3
*Schourek, Pete	11	4	3.04	19	19	1	0	124	109	53	42	39	94
Vasquez, Aguedo	5	7	3.36	53	0	0	10	78	64	39	29	27	41
Young, Anthony	15	3	1.65	23	23	3	0	158	116	38	29	52	94

MIDLAND

BATTING	AVG	G	AB	R	H	2B	3B	HR	RBI	BB	SO	SB
Aguayo, Luis, 3b-2b	.317	50	186	28	59	10	0	10	35	20	30	5
Alfonzo, Edgar, 2b-ss	.298	37	121	20	36	4	1	1	9	8	18	1
#Amaro, Ruben, of	.357	57	224	50	80	15	6	4	38	29	23	10
Aylward, Jim, 3b	.263	69	274	36	72	13	2	4	27	17	23	1
Barns, Jeff, ss-c	.287	58	178	17	51	7	0	2	24	7	18	3
Cerny, Scott, 2b	.250	116	440	58	110	12	1	2	50	43	41	5
Davis, Doug, c	.304	42	148	22	45	8	5	3	18	9	32	1
Davis, Kevin, ss	.264	59	201	28	53	7	2	6	26	14	45	8
Davis, Mark, of	.266	92	353	66	94	16	1	12	41	48	96	16
*DeAngelis, Steve, of-dh	.336	56	217	37	73	24	2	9	53	23	31	3
Doran, Mark, of	.286	38	147	25	42	7	1	4	14	20	25	4
Flora, Kevin, ss-2b	.228	71	232	35	53	17	5	5	32	23	54	11
Hall, Andy, c	.107	7	28	2	3	0	0	1	1	0	12	0
Howie, Mark, 1b	.291	113	453	55	132	22	0	6	58	30	43	4
Knapp, Mike, c	.259	57	193	16	50	8	2	2	21	16	29	1
*Lee, Wiley, dh-of	.297	102	377	70	112	15	6	8	38	27	65	45
#Monell, Johnny, of-dh	.262	32	126	12	33	5	1	3	19	11	15	5
Nichols, Howard, 3b-dh	.330	57	224	38	74	10	1	12	44	25	42	0
Peters, Reed, of	.280	69	236	41	66	8	4	6	34	32	24	14

	AVG	G	AB	R	H	2B	3B	HR	RBI	BB	SO	SB
Salmon, Tim, of	.268	27	97	17	26	3	1	3	16	18	38	1
*Sconiers, Daryl, 1b	.323	8	31	7	10	1	0	1	5	6	6	1
*Skurla, John, of	.268	32	127	17	34	9	3	3	16	9	34	3
*Sturdivant, Dave, c	.218	32	101	6	22	5	0	1	9	5	26	1
*Taylor, Terry, 3b	.125	4	16	0	2	2	0	0	4	1	8	0
Wagner, Dan, of	.196	19	56	4	11	2	1	0	6	2	17	1
Zayas, Carlos, c	.429	2	7	2	3	1	0	0	1	1	2	0

PITCHING	W	L	ERA	G	GS	CG	SV	IP	H	R	ER	BB	SO
*Abbott, Kyle	6	9	4.14	24	24	2	0	128	124	75	59	73	91
*Acosta, Clemente	1	0	1.50	2	2	0	0	12	15	4	2	4	6
Bockus, Randy	2	0	2.08	7	4	0	0	30	27	9	7	7	8
Butcher, Tim	3	7	6.21	35	8	0	0	87	109	68	60	55	84
Carter, Glenn	3	8	5.87	20	20	1	0	103	132	84	67	46	66
Cliburn, Stu	0	0	1.80	5	0	0	1	10	10	2	2	4	5
Erb, Mike	1	1	5.17	6	6	0	0	31	39	20	18	24	25
Grahe, Joe	7	5	5.29	18	18	1	0	119	145	75	70	34	58
*Hamilton, Carl	3	8	7.39	20	20	0	0	91	116	82	75	56	62
Holzemer, Mark	1	7	5.26	15	15	1	0	77	92	55	45	41	54
*Hook, Mike	0	1	9.35	7	0	0	0	9	9	9	9	7	10
Martinez, David	6	6	5.17	34	0	0	0	71	95	47	41	30	74
Meeks, Tim	7	4	4.74	35	6	0	6	74	86	40	39	28	53
Merejo, Luis	1	3	7.13	29	0	0	1	48	66	44	38	20	27
Merriman, Brett	1	0	2.25	2	0	0	0	4	7	1	1	0	1
Minton, Greg	0	0	0.00	4	0	0	0	6	3	0	0	1	1
Moore, Robert	4	1	4.95	20	1	0	0	56	55	31	31	18	40
Trudeau, Kevin	2	2	5.26	19	2	0	1	53	68	35	31	12	29
Vann, Brandy	2	5	4.13	32	0	0	7	52	59	26	24	27	43
Vidmar, Don	1	6	7.51	11	11	0	0	44	67	45	37	18	20
Zappelli, Mark	3	4	4.40	35	0	0	6	45	57	28	22	14	35

SAN ANTONIO

BATTING	AVG	G	AB	R	H	2B	3B	HR	RBI	BB	SO	SB
Bournigal, Rafael, ss-2b	.211	69	194	20	41	4	2	0	14	8	25	2
Brooks, Jerry, of	.302	106	391	52	118	20	4	9	58	26	39	5
Brown, Adam, dh	.300	43	120	13	36	9	1	2	21	11	27	1
*Carr, Ernie, 3b	.260	72	146	13	38	5	1	2	21	15	23	0
Castillo, Braulio, of	.228	75	241	34	55	11	3	3	24	14	72	11
*Dostal, Bruce, of	.260	53	127	16	33	3	4	0	16	18	29	10
Finken, Steve, 3b	.284	120	395	68	112	25	3	13	66	82	98	22
Goodwin, Tom, of	.278	102	428	76	119	15	4	0	28	38	72	60
Karros, Eric, 1b	.352	131	509	90	180	45	2	18	78	57	79	8
Martinez, Luis, ss	.277	109	383	60	106	12	0	4	37	37	46	4
Pye, Eddie, 2b	.248	119	455	67	113	18	7	2	44	45	68	19
#Rice, Lance, c	.241	79	245	25	59	11	2	0	35	24	47	3
*Rodriguez, Henry, of	.291	129	495	82	144	22	9	28	109	61	66	5
Rojas, Homar, c	.282	82	241	29	68	10	2	5	36	24	34	0
Valdez, Mica, 1b	.220	18	41	5	9	1	0	0	3	1	11	0
*White, Mike, dh	.391	13	46	10	18	1	1	1	14	3	1	3

PITCHING	W	L	ERA	G	GS	CG	SV	IP	H	R	ER	BB	SO
Bustillos, Albert	0	1	6.48	5	0	0	0	8	8	6	6	5	6
Campbell, Kevin	2	6	2.33	49	0	0	8	81	67	29	21	25	84
Coleman, Dale	1	1	3.90	14	0	0	3	28	30	14	12	8	16
Hartsock, Jeff	6	4	3.93	16	16	0	0	94	88	42	41	42	68
Hershiser, Gordie	0	0	1.13	3	0	0	0	8	5	1	1	2	7
James, Mike	11	4	3.32	26	26	3	0	157	144	73	58	78	97
Marquez, Isidrio	3	1	4.86	13	0	0	0	21	20	10	9	8	15
McAndrew, Jamie	7	3	1.93	12	12	0	0	79	68	28	17	32	50
Opperman, Dan	12	8	3.41	27	27	3	0	156	153	75	59	62	96
Pitz, Mike	4	4	4.12	26	9	1	0	87	82	45	40	16	56
*Poole, Jim	6	7	2.40	54	0	0	16	64	55	31	17	27	77
Scott, Tim	3	3	2.85	30	0	0	7	47	35	17	15	14	52
Shinall, Zak	6	3	3.55	20	15	0	0	91	93	44	36	41	43
Springer, Dennis	8	6	3.31	24	24	3	0	163	147	76	60	73	77
*Terrill, James	1	1	3.52	3	0	0	0	15	15	8	6	2	5
Vanzytveld, Jeff	0	1	1.66	8	2	0	1	22	16	6	4	13	9
*Wray, James	8	3	3.71	45	0	0	4	78	75	34	32	30	56

SHREVEPORT

BATTING	AVG	G	AB	R	H	2B	3B	HR	RBI	BB	SO	SB
*Aldrete, Rich, 1b-of	.228	123	434	43	99	21	2	2	46	37	56	7
Beauchamp, Kash, of	.319	38	141	15	45	11	0	5	18	8	16	7
Cooper, Jamie, of	.231	126	471	56	109	17	6	6	30	17	136	25
Decker, Steve, c	.293	116	403	52	118	22	1	15	80	39	64	3
Ealy, Tom, of	.257	103	276	25	71	9	2	6	23	28	60	2
Guerrero, Juan, 2b	.241	118	390	55	94	21	1	16	47	26	74	4
Ham, Mike, c	.205	19	39	3	8	1	0	0	2	3	13	1
*Hecht, Steve, of-inf	.300	64	200	37	60	12	7	2	27	13	15	12
Johnson, Erik, ss-3b	.222	91	270	35	60	6	0	1	15	22	38	6
#Jones, Jimmy, 3b-2b	.241	19	29	1	7	1	0	0	1	7	4	2
*McNamara, Jim, c	.241	28	79	2	19	7	0	0	13	7	9	0
Nelson, Rick, of-1b	.176	17	34	4	6	2	0	1	2	4	9	0
*Owens, Mark, 3b-c	.216	55	125	5	27	4	0	2	13	25	28	2
Patterson, Dave, 3b-1b	.286	126	423	52	121	18	5	3	54	58	69	5
#Santana, Andres, ss	.292	92	336	50	98	5	4	0	24	31	41	32
Strijek, Randy, ss	.111	17	27	2	3	0	0	0	0	1	13	0

Jackson's Anthony Young led the Texas League in wins (15) and ERA (1.85), and was voted the top prospect.

	AVG	G	AB	R	H	2B	3B	HR	RBI	BB	SO	SB
Westbrooks, Elanis, of	.208	31	48	11	10	1	0	0	0	6	11	2
*Wood, Ted, of	.265	131	456	81	121	22	11	17	72	74	76	17

PITCHING	W	L	ERA	G	GS	CG	SV	IP	H	R	ER	BB	SO
Beck, Rod	10	3	2.23	14	14	2	0	93	85	26	23	17	71
*Bonilla, George	0	1	4.00	9	0	0	0	9	12	4	4	2	12
Carter, Larry	1	0	3.50	5	4	0	0	18	15	7	7	4	12
*Connolly, Steve	2	5	3.19	50	0	0	2	59	61	24	21	20	50
Dewey, Mark	1	5	1.88	33	0	0	13	38	37	11	8	10	23
*Estes, Joel	0	0	5.79	9	0	0	0	14	20	10	9	5	9
*Gunderson, Eric	2	2	3.25	8	8	1	0	53	51	24	19	17	44
*Hickerson, Bryan	3	6	4.23	27	6	0	1	66	71	37	31	26	63
Hostetler, Tom	5	8	3.04	23	22	1	0	130	119	55	44	40	112
Lienhard, Steve	5	7	2.50	48	6	1	5	115	109	42	32	35	68
Mead, Timber	2	2	2.25	16	0	0	2	28	19	9	7	6	23
Meier, Kevin	6	5	3.08	14	14	1	0	88	91	32	30	21	61
*Novoa, Rafael	5	4	2.64	11	10	2	0	72	60	21	21	25	65
*Pena, Jim	10	7	3.69	25	24	1	0	139	138	70	57	57	101
Potestio, Frank	1	1	5.06	12	0	0	0	27	31	17	15	8	19
Reed, Steve	3	1	1.64	45	0	0	8	60	53	20	11	20	59
*Remlinger, Mike	9	11	3.90	25	25	2	0	148	149	82	64	72	75

TULSA

BATTING	AVG	G	AB	R	H	2B	3B	HR	RBI	BB	SO	SB
Alyea, Brant, dh	.150	6	20	1	3	2	0	0	2	0	6	0
Belcher, Kevin, of-dh ...	.293	110	423	66	124	18	7	11	43	55	88	29
#Burgos, Paco, 3b-2b ...	.257	126	470	60	121	17	7	5	41	18	48	9
#Colon, Cris, ss	.244	65	234	24	57	9	1	3	29	5	37	6
Fariss, Monty, ss	.299	71	244	45	73	15	6	7	34	36	60	8
Garman, Pat, 3b	.360	7	25	5	9	2	1	1	4	1	4	0
Garner, Darrin, 2b	.250	107	348	50	87	7	3	1	24	62	71	20
Green, David, dh-of	.286	16	49	4	14	2	0	0	8	4	10	0
Harris, Donald, of	.160	64	213	16	34	5	1	1	15	7	69	7
Haselman, Bill, c	.319	120	430	68	137	39	2	18	80	44	96	3
Iavarone, Greg, c	.267	32	90	10	24	5	0	0	9	14	28	2
*Maurer, Rob, 1b	.300	104	367	55	110	31	4	21	78	54	112	4
Palmer, Dean, 3b	.292	7	24	4	7	0	1	3	9	4	10	0
*Peltier, Dan, of	.279	117	448	66	125	21	4	11	57	40	67	10
Postier, Paul, 3b-1b	.236	89	301	27	71	8	1	0	33	12	55	2
Rohrmeier, Dan, of-dh ...	.305	119	453	76	138	24	7	10	62	37	51	14
Scruggs, Tony, of	.344	53	195	28	67	5	6	4	37	14	50	4
Threadgill, George, of ..	.208	41	149	19	31	8	0	0	11	16	39	3

BATTING

R	Mike Humphreys, Wichita 92
H	Eric Karros, San Antonio 179
TB	Eric Karros, San Antonio 282
2B	Eric Karros, San Antonio . 45
3B	Ted Wood, Shreveport 11
HR	Henry Rodriguez, SA 28
RBI	Henry Rodriguez, SA . . . 109
SH	Jamie Cooper, Shrev . . . 13
	Paco Burgos, Tulsa 13
SF	Henry Rodriguez, SA 14
BB	Chris Donnels, SA 111
IBB	Angelo Cuevas, Jackson . 10
HBP	Luis Martinez, SA 9
	Ruben Amaro, Midland . . 9
SO	Jamie Cooper, Shrev . . . 136
SB	Tom Goodwin, SA 60
CS	Will Taylor, Wichita 29
OB%	Charlie Montoyo, EP 428

PITCHING

G	John Lepley, Arkansas . . . 59
GS	Dan Opperman, SA 27
CG	Mark Clark, Arkansas . . . 5
ShO	Dave Osteen, Arkansas . . . 3
Sv	Terry Bross, Jackson 28
W	Anthony Young, Jackson . 15
L	Rheal Cormier, Arkansas . 12
	A.J. Sager, Wichita 12
IP	Dennis Springer, SA 163
H	A.J. Sager, Wichita 200
R	A.J. Sager, Wichita 105
HR	Jeremy Hernandez, Wich . 18
BB	Eric McCray, Tulsa 83
HB	Mike Taylor, Tulsa 10
SO	Tom Hostetler, Shrev . . . 112
WP	Dean Freeland, El Paso . . 19
Bk	Tim Meeks, Midland 7

PITCHING

	W	L	ERA	G	GS	CG	SV	IP	H	R	ER	BB	SO
Allen, Steve	8	4	3.83	54	0	0	5	89	97	43	38	42	84
Bryant, Phil	6	4	3.38	19	7	1	1	69	75	35	26	17	36
Castillo, Felipe	6	1	2.35	20	0	0	1	46	41	13	12	26	39
Compres, Fidel	0	1	6.10	6	0	0	0	10	12	10	7	11	9
Cunningham, Everett	7	2	4.35	17	12	1	0	79	75	42	38	49	47
Guzman, Jose	0	0	6.00	1	1	0	0	3	3	2	2	0	2
Hoover, John	2	1	3.42	4	4	0	0	24	29	12	9	11	18
Hurst, Jonathan	0	2	9.47	8	3	0	0	26	29	30	27	17	23
Hvizda, Jim	1	3	3.77	32	0	0	9	43	50	20	18	11	24
*Lynch, Dave	4	4	3.81	21	6	0	5	59	60	25	25	21	37
Mathews, Terry	5	7	4.27	14	14	4	0	86	88	50	41	36	48
*McCray, Eric	8	7	4.21	25	25	1	0	141	142	79	66	82	98
Nen, Robb	0	5	5.06	7	7	0	0	27	23	20	15	21	21
Pavlik, Roger	6	5	2.33	16	16	2	0	100	66	29	26	71	91
Postier, Paul	0	0	1.35	5	0	0	0	7	4	1	1	2	2
Reed, Bobby	2	1	2.79	5	5	1	0	29	31	12	9	11	14
Rockman, Marv	1	2	3.79	24	0	0	4	38	46	20	16	13	23
Rosenthal, Wayne	2	2	2.40	12	0	0	4	15	9	6	4	9	18
*Shaw, Cedric	4	5	6.86	14	12	0	0	63	72	51	48	44	41
Shiflett, Chris	0	1	3.00	13	0	0	4	27	24	12	9	9	26
*Smith, Dan	3	2	3.76	7	7	0	0	38	27	16	16	16	32
Taylor, Mike	1	6	5.79	33	9	2	2	98	108	69	63	47	59
Thomas, Mitch	2	3	3.35	8	0	0	0	38	25	23	14	26	28

WICHITA

BATTING

	AVG	G	AB	R	H	2B	3B	HR	RBI	BB	SO	SB
*Cisarik, Brian, of-1b	.267	118	434	84	116	13	1	2	37	71	63	45
*David, Greg, 3b	.299	112	402	55	119	30	1	13	59	38	91	3
#Dewey, Todd, c	.269	10	26	2	7	2	0	0	2	3	4	0
*Higgins, Kevin, c	.358	52	187	24	67	7	1	1	23	16	8	5
Hillemann, Charlie, of	.296	19	71	16	21	3	1	3	12	14	16	7
Humphreys, Mike, of	.276	116	421	92	116	21	4	17	79	67	79	38
*Kelley, Dean, 2b	.271	124	468	71	127	24	5	10	59	34	54	9
Lutticken, Bob, c	.250	49	152	14	38	5	0	4	20	10	27	2
McWilliam, Tim, of	.284	112	401	54	114	17	1	5	63	35	42	8
Repoz, Craig, 3b-of	.213	59	141	23	30	9	0	4	15	26	40	3
Staton, Dave, 1b	.305	45	164	26	50	11	0	6	31	22	36	0
#Taylor, Will, of	.266	102	414	57	110	18	7	4	31	37	78	51
#Valentin, Jose, ss	.278	11	36	4	10	2	0	0	2	5	7	2
Velasquez, Guillermo, 1b-dh	.271	105	377	48	102	21	2	12	72	35	66	0
Villanueva, Juan, ss	.240	105	359	43	86	11	2	4	38	22	63	4
#Wallace, Tim, ss-2b	.317	77	224	29	71	17	4	1	31	23	23	7
Walters, Dan, c	.296	58	199	25	59	12	0	7	40	21	21	0

PITCHING

	W	L	ERA	G	GS	CG	SV	IP	H	R	ER	BB	SO
Bones, Ricky	6	4	3.48	21	21	2	0	137	138	66	53	45	96
Brocail, Doug	2	2	4.33	12	9	0	0	52	53	30	25	24	27
Chavez, Rafael	6	5	4.18	46	1	0	9	84	85	46	39	16	47
*DiMichele, Frank	4	5	6.27	46	1	0	2	66	95	60	46	34	60
*Hansen, Todd	6	3	4.67	27	8	0	0	94	103	49	49	37	52
Hernandez, Jeremy	7	6	4.53	26	26	1	0	155	163	92	78	50	101
*Holsman, Rich	7	6	4.20	46	0	0	6	71	81	39	33	30	85
Loubier, Steve	1	4	6.68	15	3	0	0	34	42	36	25	18	20
*Martinez, Pedro	6	10	4.80	24	23	2	0	129	139	83	69	70	88
Quinzer, Paul	2	4	4.56	31	2	0	2	73	75	42	37	24	43
*Roberts, Pete	9	6	3.76	18	16	3	0	103	107	49	43	27	63
Sager, A.J.	11	12	5.48	26	26	2	0	154	200	105	94	29	79
Wood, Brian	2	4	2.73	44	0	0	11	69	61	26	21	32	70

CALIFORNIA LEAGUE

Stockton reasserts place at head of class

By MAUREEN DELANY

After years of watching regular season success crumble in the playoffs, Stockton won its first California League title in four years in 1990.

Stockton had the best record in the Cal League in the decade of the '80s and made it to the league championship series the previous two years, but the Ports

were swept each time. In 1990, they squeaked past the Bakersfield Dodgers in five games.

"I think it was a matter of some excellent pitching from the bullpen, coupled with timely hitting," Stockton manager Chris Bando said. "Our veteran players came through."

Stockton survived one of the longest games in league history, a 4-3 loss in 22 innings to the defending champion Dodgers in Game One.

Frank Bolick
... 102 RBIs

The game was tied, 3-3, after nine innings and remained deadlocked after 21 innings. League president Joe Gagliardi suspended the game at 1:27 a.m. Stockton had chances to win the game in the 20th and 21st innings, but runners were thrown out at the plate on double plays each time.

The game continued the next night, and Bakersfield scored two runs in the top of the 22nd to pull out a 5-4 victory. Stockton won the regular game, 4-3, later that night to knot the series. The Ports won the series three nights later, 8-6, scoring three runs in the top of the ninth.

Reno enjoys rare winning season

Stockton ran away with the first half title in the Northern Division to earn a berth in post-season play. In the second half, the Reno Silver Sox jumped on top early, but by late July fell several games behind eventual champion San Jose, and never

LEAGUE CHAMPIONS

Playoff Champions, Where Applicable

1990—Stockton	1972—Modesto	1954—Modesto
1989—Bakersfield	1971—Visalia	1953—San Jose
1988—Riverside	1970—Bakersfield	1952—Fresno
1987—Fresno	1969—Stockton	1951—Santa Barb.
1986—Stockton	1968—Fresno	1950—Modesto
1985—Fresno	1967—San Jose	1949—San Jose
1984—Modesto	1966—Modesto	1948—Santa Barb.
1983—Redwood	1965—Stockton	1947—Stockton
1982—Modesto	1964—Fresno	1946—Stockton
1981—Lodi	1963—Stockton	1943-45—Did Not
1980—Stockton	1962—San Jose	Operate
1979—San Jose	1961—Reno	1942—Santa Barb.
1978—Visalia	1960—Reno	1941—Santa Barb.
1977—Lodi	1959—Modesto	1916-40—Did Not
1976—Reno	1958—Fresno	Operate
1975—Reno	1957—Salinas	1915—Modesto
1974—Fresno	1956—Fresno	1914—Fresno
1973—Lodi	1955—Fresno	

San Bernardino righthander Roger Salkeld, one of the Cal League's top prospects, went 11-5 with a 3.40 ERA.

recovered. Still, the Silver Sox became the first independent team in years to finish with a winning record (71-68) overall.

Visalia won both the first- and second-half Southern Division titles, and finished with the best overall record in the league. But the Oaks stumbled in the playoffs. Visalia's ace, George Tsamis (17-4), lost two post-season games as Bakersfield defeated Visalia, 3-2, in the Southern Division playoffs.

A crippling setback for the Oaks came in early August when closer Rich Garces was promoted to Double-A Orlando. Garces, a 19-year-old Venezuelan, saved 28 games for Visalia—two short of tying a league record—and then added eight more saves at Orlando.

Two-team player named MVP

San Bernardino third baseman Frank Bolick, who began the year in Stockton and was part of an early season trade involving Milwaukee and Seattle, was selected the league's MVP. Bolick led the league with 102 RBIs, but fell short of a triple crown by batting .324—seven points behind Reno's Tom Eiterman—and hitting 18 home runs.

Veteran Reno outfielder Ken Whitfield slugged three home runs in the final week of the season to pull ahead of Bakersfield DH Brett Magnusson in the home run race. Whitfield hit 24 homers. Magnusson finished with 23, but missed the last two weeks of the regular season with a hand injury.

Bakersfield second baseman Matt Howard proved to be one of the steadiest infielders in the league. Howard made just six errors in 691 total chances for a league-record .991 fielding percentage. Howard led all second basemen in doubles plays (107), assists (432) and total chances.

San Bernardino Spirit center fielder Tow Maynard led the league with 80 stolen bases—the highest mark in 1990 for a player in one league. Tom Goodwin, who started the season at Bakersfield, stole a total of 82 bases, but only 22 at Bakersfield before being promoted in May to Double-A San Antonio, where he had 60 more. Stockton's Pat Listach finished with 78 steals, fourth best in the minor leagues.

San Jose righthander Dan Rambo was named the league's pitcher of the year. Rambo (12-2) edged Tsamis for the ERA crown with a mark of 2.19, after pitching an inning of scoreless relief in the Giants' final series. Teammate Kevin Rogers led the league with 186 strikeouts.

1990 FINAL STANDINGS

FIRST HALF

North	W	L	Pct.	GB
Stockton (Brewers)	47	23	.671	—
Reno (Independent)	33	35	.485	13
San Jose (Giants)	33	38	.465	14½
Modesto (Athletics)	28	42	.400	19
Salinas (Independent)	22	47	.319	24½

South	W	L	Pct.	GB
Visalia (Twins)	48	22	.686	—
Bakersfield (Dodgers)	40	31	.563	8½
San Bernardino (Mariners)	39	32	.549	9½
Riverside (Padres)	35	36	.493	13½
Palm Springs (Angels)	26	45	.366	22½

SECOND HALF

North	W	L	Pct.	GB
San Jose (Giants)	41	30	.577	—
Reno (Independent)	38	33	.535	3
Stockton (Brewers)	35	36	.493	6
Modesto (Athletics)	31	40	.437	10
Salinas (Independent)	25	46	.352	16

South	W	L	Pct.	GB
Visalia (Twins)	42	29	.592	—
Bakersfield (Dodgers)	40	31	.563	2
San Bernardino (Mariners)	38	33	.535	4
Palm Springs (Angels)	36	35	.507	6
Riverside (Padres)	29	42	.408	13

OVERALL

	W	L	Pct.	GB
Visalia (Twins)	90	51	.638	—
Stockton (Brewers)	82	59	.582	8
Bakersfield (Dodgers)	80	62	.563	10½
San Bernardino (Mariners)	77	65	.542	13½
San Jose (Giants)	74	68	.521	16½
Reno (Independent)	71	68	.511	18
Riverside (Padres)	64	78	.451	26½
Palm Springs (Angels)	62	80	.437	28½
Modesto (Athletics)	59	82	.418	31
Salinas (Independent)	47	93	.336	42½

1990 GENERAL INFORMATION

Playoffs: Stockton defeated San Jose 3-1 in best-of-5 semifinal; Bakersfield defeated Visalia 3-2 in best-of-5 semifinal; Stockton defeated Bakersfield 3-2 in best-of-5 final for league championship.

Regular-Season Attendance: San Bernardino, 190,890; Bakersfield, 142,280; San Jose, 108,478; Reno, 87,048; Stockton, 85,436; Riverside, 82,420; Visalia, 78,212; Palm Springs, 76,462; Modesto, 62,089; Salinas, 33,465.

Managers: Bakersfield—Tom Beyers; **Modesto**—Ted Kubiak; **Palm Springs**—Nate Oliver; **Reno**—Mike Brown; **Riverside**—Bruce Bochy; **Salinas**—Hide Koga; **San Bernardino**—Keith Bodie; **San**

Jose—Tom Spencer; **Stockton**—Chris Bando; **Visalia**—Scott Ullger.

1990 Official All-Star Team: C—Bryan Baar, Bakersfield. **1B**—Bo Dodson, Stockton. **2B**—John Patterson, San Jose. **3B**—Frank Bolick, Stockton/San Bernardino. **SS**—Royce Clayton, San Jose. **OF**—Darrell Sherman, Riverside; Tom Eiterman, Reno; J.T. Bruett, Visalia. **DH**—Brett Magnusson, Bakersfield. **P**—Dan Rambo, San Jose; Richard Garces, Visalia; George Tsamis, Visalia; Jason Brosnan, Bakersfield; Chris Johnson, Stockton; Jamie McAndrew, Bakersfield. **Most Valuable Player**—Frank Bolick, Stockton/San Bernardino. **Pitcher of the Year**—Dan Rambo, San Jose. **Rookie of the Year**—Dave Staton, Riverside. **Manager of the Year**—Scott Ullger, Visalia.

Top 10 Major League Prospects (by Baseball America): 1. Rich Garces, rhp, Visalia; **2.** Royce Clayton, ss, San Jose; 3. Roger Salkeld, rhp, San Bernardino; **4.** Jason Brosnan, lhp, Bakersfield; **5.** Dave Staton, 3b-1b, Riverside; **6.** Dan Rambo, rhp, San Jose; **7.** Bo Dodson, 1b, Stockton; **8.** Dave Nilsson, c, Stockton; **9.** Bryan Baar, c, Bakersfield; **10.** Frank Bolick, 3b, Stockton/San Bernardino.

1990 BATTING, PITCHING STATS

CLUB BATTING

	AVG	G	AB	R	H	2B	3B	HR	BB	SO	SB
Reno	.282	139	4716	816	1330	208	47	97	566	884	120
Visalia	.279	141	4776	724	1331	209	39	71	596	821	126
San Bernardino	.276	142	4829	803	1333	212	33	118	548	1030	202
Bakersfield	.263	142	4774	730	1256	241	30	107	522	1011	191
San Jose	.262	142	4788	766	1254	177	48	72	606	976	159
Riverside	.254	142	4619	608	1172	172	40	54	573	955	205
Palm Springs	.251	142	4715	609	1185	196	42	40	466	1098	110
Modesto	.250	142	4696	625	1172	203	27	92	536	1036	140
Stockton	.247	141	4409	691	1087	169	45	67	604	953	182
Salinas	.243	140	4535	565	1103	163	32	60	525	1019	152

CLUB PITCHING

	ERA	G	CG	SHO	SV	IP	H	R	ER	BB	SO
Visalia	3.36	141	16	20	49	1228	1112	568	459	530	1101
Bakersfield	3.87	142	4	8	46	1235	1225	661	531	600	1043
Stockton	3.88	141	13	13	47	1203	1148	611	518	512	1013
San Jose	3.89	142	8	8	36	1246	1135	688	539	571	999
Modesto	3.97	141	6	4	34	1227	1150	684	542	610	940
Riverside	4.12	142	7	5	35	1226	1358	709	561	459	904
San Bernardino	4.18	142	15	7	36	1249	1210	746	580	667	1198
Palm Springs	4.21	142	7	3	29	1233	1266	705	577	525	761
Salinas	4.63	140	28	3	19	1202	1321	770	618	498	944
Reno	4.71	139	13	6	34	1202	1298	795	629	570	880

INDIVIDUAL BATTING LEADERS
(Minimum 383 Plate Appearances)

	AVG	G	AB	R	H	2B	3B	HR	RBI	BB	SO	SB
Eiterman, Tom, Reno	.331	121	471	92	156	19	6	7	73	55	73	6
#Bolick, Frank, Stock-SB	.324	128	441	100	143	33	5	18	102	91	86	8
*Harper, Milt, Reno	.317	91	322	69	102	23	2	20	73	62	58	0
Magnusson, Brett, Bak	.311	121	434	92	135	34	2	23	85	73	104	5
Buckley, Troy, Vis	.307	117	404	69	124	24	4	5	64	43	58	5
*Bruett, J.T., Vis	.307	123	437	86	134	15	3	1	33	101	60	50
Chimelis, Joel, Mod	.303	131	531	87	161	26	10	4	70	49	56	30
#Patterson, John, SJ	.302	131	530	91	160	23	6	4	66	46	74	29
*Dejardin, Brad, Reno	.297	114	387	66	115	17	1	6	54	38	89	15
Turang, Brian, SB	.296	132	487	86	144	25	5	12	69	67	98	25

INDIVIDUAL PITCHING LEADERS
(Minimum 114 Innings)

	W	L	ERA	G	GS	CG	SV	IP	H	R	ER	BB	SO
Rambo, Dan, San Jose	12	2	2.19	26	17	2	1	144	104	47	35	42	142
*Tsamis, George, Vis	17	4	2.21	26	26	4	0	184	168	62	45	61	145
*Wiese, Phil, Visalia	10	4	2.52	20	19	2	0	118	109	43	33	44	95
Johnson, Chris, Stock	13	6	2.98	23	23	1	0	142	121	56	47	54	112
Davis, Rick, Riv	10	9	3.04	26	26	0	0	163	175	72	55	44	122
Woodson, Kerry, SB	8	6	3.10	27	23	1	0	137	111	62	47	83	131
*Brosnan, Jason, Bak	12	4	3.11	26	25	0	0	136	113	63	47	91	157
Mahomes, Pat, Vis	11	11	3.30	28	28	5	0	185	136	77	68	118	178
Salkeld, Roger, SB	11	5	3.40	25	25	2	0	153	140	77	58	83	167
Trombley, Mike, Vis	14	6	3.43	27	25	3	0	176	163	79	67	50	164

BAKERSFIELD

BATTING	AVG	G	AB	R	H	2B	3B	HR	RBI	BB	SO	SB
Ashley, Billy, of	.218	99	331	48	72	13	1	9	40	25	135	17
Baar, Bryan, c	.285	111	389	53	111	23	1	20	71	34	114	1
Barker, Tim, ss	.271	125	443	83	120	22	6	8	63	71	117	33
#Beals, Bryan, 2b-3b	.125	13	24	3	3	1	0	0	3	6	5	5
Beard, Garrett, c-3b	.200	5	15	2	3	2	1	0	3	1	2	0
*Deutsch, John, 1b	.255	120	415	62	106	20	0	10	74	73	77	3
#Forrester, Gary, ss	.153	48	111	9	17	5	0	1	12	8	25	1
*Goodwin, Tom, of	.291	32	134	24	39	6	2	0	13	11	22	22

	AVG	G	AB	R	H	2B	3B	HR	RBI	BB	SO	SB
*Griffin, Mark, of	.275	106	429	77	118	14	4	3	32	39	70	33
Howard, Matt, 2b	.261	137	551	75	144	22	3	1	54	37	39	47
*Lewis, Alan, 3b	.304	96	329	56	100	20	4	6	49	43	42	4
Lott, Billy, of	.203	38	133	11	27	1	1	2	14	6	46	3
Magnusson, Brett, dh-of	.311	121	434	92	135	34	2	23	85	73	104	5
McMurray, Brock, of	.290	66	238	41	69	20	2	7	35	28	58	3
*Morrow, Chris, of	.240	95	325	37	78	17	2	5	40	20	53	8
#Munoz, Jose, 3b	.179	14	39	3	7	1	0	0	6	6	7	2
O'Donnell, Steve, 3b-1b	.243	68	230	32	56	12	1	9	36	25	59	4
Teel, Garrett, c	.208	42	101	13	21	1	0	2	6	10	17	0
Valdez, Amilcar, 1b-dh	.291	40	93	9	30	7	0	1	14	9	18	0

PITCHING	W	L	ERA	G	GS	CG	SV	IP	H	R	ER	BB	SO
Aase, Don	0	0	1.00	6	6	0	0	9	6	1	1	2	4
Astacio, Pedro	5	2	2.77	10	7	1	0	52	46	22	16	15	34
*Bishop, Craig	0	1	9.00	5	1	0	0	7	9	10	7	9	6
Braase, John	3	3	4.84	29	1	0	2	67	83	44	36	17	58
*Brosnan, Jason	12	4	3.11	26	25	0	0	136	113	63	47	91	157
Coleman, Dale	1	6	4.61	39	0	0	16	55	50	33	28	26	52
*Crane, Rich	3	3	3.42	33	8	0	1	92	99	43	35	42	75
Delahoya, Javier	4	1	5.95	9	7	0	0	39	50	30	26	24	37
Forrester, Gary	0	0	18.00	2	0	0	0	2	5	4	4	2	2
Frame, Mike	1	3	4.50	31	1	0	4	46	47	27	23	30	26
Gott, Jim	0	0	2.77	7	3	0	0	13	13	5	4	4	16
Helmick, Tony	6	6	3.73	34	9	0	4	113	110	56	47	51	110
*Humber, Frank	6	5	3.47	57	0	0	13	70	68	30	27	32	44
Jones, Kiki	3	3	3.48	9	8	0	0	44	33	20	17	23	38
Knapp, John	8	2	5.15	12	11	1	0	72	93	45	41	18	36
McAndrew, Jamie	10	3	2.27	14	14	1	0	95	88	31	24	29	82
Mesa, Baltazar	0	1	9.49	5	2	0	0	12	12	15	13	12	6
Parisotto, Barry	3	4	3.93	13	8	1	0	53	59	41	23	28	42
*Perry, Pat	0	0	3.60	3	3	0	0	5	3	3	2	1	7
Potthoff, Mike	0	0	3.00	7	2	0	1	15	17	6	5	10	15
Robinson, Napoleon	7	4	3.11	45	4	0	4	101	94	47	35	48	81
Sampson, Mike	3	4	4.96	12	10	0	0	53	46	36	29	45	37
*Searage, Ray	1	2	3.21	10	5	0	0	14	8	5	5	8	17
Tapia, Jose	1	2	3.93	13	6	0	0	34	31	21	15	17	21
Tatis, Fausto	3	3	5.97	18	1	0	1	32	38	21	21	16	36

MODESTO

BATTING	AVG	G	AB	R	H	2B	3B	HR	RBI	BB	SO	SB
Booker, Eric, of	.320	8	25	4	8	1	0	0	5	1	5	2
Borrelli, Dean, c	.230	52	148	22	34	9	1	1	11	25	25	0
Buccheri, James, 2b-of	.280	36	125	27	35	4	1	0	7	25	16	15
Carcione, Tom, c	.231	66	195	22	45	5	0	5	25	29	47	0
Chimelis, Joel, ss (85 Reno)	.303	131	531	87	161	26	10	4	70	49	56	30
Conte, Mike, of	.243	73	268	31	65	14	1	6	37	35	50	6
Correia, Ron, 2b-3b	.244	87	246	27	60	6	3	0	16	22	41	4
*Hendley, Brett, c-1b	.184	67	201	26	37	8	1	6	27	37	68	3
#Hernandez, Carlos, 2b-ss	.143	15	42	5	6	1	0	0	3	5	17	1
Hosey, Dwayne, of	.294	113	453	77	133	21	5	16	61	50	70	30
Kennedy, Michael, c	.119	14	42	1	5	0	0	0	1	4	15	0
Lofthus, Kevin, dh	.200	23	80	6	16	4	0	1	10	5	34	1
Matos, Francisco, ss	.274	83	321	46	88	12	1	1	20	15	65	26
Messerly, Mike, of-1b	.241	113	353	49	85	22	1	4	33	53	86	3
Ortiz, Joe, c-1b	.333	7	6	0	2	0	0	0	0	0	4	2
Paquette, Craig, 3b	.238	130	495	65	118	23	4	15	59	47	123	8
Parry, Bob, of-dh	.252	80	282	38	71	14	2	8	42	32	46	3
*Shockey, Scott, 1b-of	.325	51	200	32	65	13	0	9	50	13	48	1
#Thomas, Keith, of	.223	62	215	24	48	7	0	4	21	14	65	16
Vannaman, Tim, of	.200	57	190	18	38	5	0	1	19	18	52	7
#Vice, Darryl, 2b	.277	59	202	25	56	3	1	3	25	26	40	1
*Waggoner, James, 2b-ss	.163	35	86	13	14	3	0	0	5	21	25	1
*Witmeyer, Ron, 1b	.234	92	333	38	78	14	5	10	45	41	74	0

PITCHING	W	L	ERA	G	GS	CG	SV	IP	H	R	ER	BB	SO
*Allison, Dana	0	0	2.33	10	0	0	0	13	9	5	3	3	19
Briscoe, John	3	6	4.59	29	12	1	4	86	72	50	44	52	66
*Chavez, Sam (1 Reno)	5	2	3.94	10	10	1	0	59	61	30	26	23	48
Erwin, Scott	6	11	4.32	25	25	2	0	131	122	89	63	78	128
Garcia, Apolinar	3	11	3.59	20	20	1	0	123	113	63	49	41	96
Green, Daryl (20 Reno)	3	2	3.06	26	2	0	2	50	47	24	17	23	49
*Grott, Matthew	2	0	2.04	12	0	0	4	18	10	7	4	14	28
*Guzman, Johnny	7	4	1.91	13	13	1	0	85	67	25	18	23	58
Hill, Freddie	0	0	10.80	2	0	0	0	2	4	2	2	2	1
Lardizabal, Ruben	3	10	4.36	26	18	0	0	130	138	76	63	52	70
Lawson, James	3	5	4.61	23	2	0	2	53	40	33	27	39	39
*Leiper, Dave	1	0	0.00	3	0	0	0	9	2	1	0	1	6
Love, Will	1	1	4.90	37	2	0	2	68	71	46	37	50	60
McCoy, Tim	1	1	1.74	11	1	0	2	21	9	4	4	9	23
*Miller, Rick	2	3	3.24	10	1	0	1	25	22	13	9	11	20
Patrick, Bronswell	3	7	5.18	14	14	0	0	75	92	58	43	32	37
Peck, Steve	4	2	4.14	30	2	0	0	59	58	29	27	28	46
Pena, Pedro	3	7	3.75	12	12	0	0	72	66	37	30	37	43
Phoenix, Steve	4	1	4.58	6	6	0	0	37	43	21	19	16	23
Rose, Bill	0	0	1.29	6	0	0	0	14	14	5	2	6	10

	W	L	ERA	G	GS	CG	SV	IP	H	R	ER	BB	SO
Shaver, Jeff	0	1	9.00	1	1	0	0	4	7	5	4	3	1
Smith, Todd	2	5	4.43	41	0	0	4	65	62	40	32	48	65
Strebeck, Ricky	2	1	3.05	14	0	0	4	21	12	7	7	10	13
Taylor, Bill	4	1	3.51	22	0	0	2	33	29	15	13	19	29
*Zancanaro, David	1	2	6.23	4	2	0	0	13	13	9	9	14	7

PALM SPRINGS

BATTING	AVG	G	AB	R	H	2B	3B	HR	RBI	BB	SO	SB
Alfonzo, Edgar, dh-inf	.276	57	203	44	56	4	2	2	12	30	37	5
Aylward, Jim, 3b-1b	.347	59	219	38	76	14	1	4	31	22	16	2
Barbara, Don, 1b	.291	66	220	22	64	8	0	4	39	24	27	1
Carr, Terence, of	.151	52	159	23	24	2	2	0	12	24	48	4
Davis, Kevin, ss	.254	30	126	11	32	6	0	0	16	6	32	5
Dominguez, Frank, dh-c	.251	56	199	16	50	15	1	0	19	10	32	1
Doran, Mark, of	.364	15	55	16	20	4	0	3	10	10	11	3
*Edmonds, Jim, of	.293	91	314	36	92	18	6	3	56	27	75	5
Kelso, Jeff, dh-of	.167	14	42	4	7	1	0	0	2	2	25	1
Kipila, Jeff, 3b-1b	.241	72	253	29	61	12	5	3	30	34	75	6
Ledinsky, Ray, of	.267	55	180	20	48	3	1	3	29	11	37	2
#McLemore, Mark, 2b	.273	6	22	3	6	0	0	0	2	3	7	0
*Musolino, Mike, c	.140	20	43	4	6	1	0	0	3	8	8	0
Nelson, Rick, of	.224	40	143	17	32	7	1	6	22	11	52	1
Nichols, Howard, 1b	.373	21	75	17	28	6	0	1	11	8	17	0
Oberdank, Jeff, inf-of	.236	116	428	56	101	17	5	0	42	29	66	12
Parker, Richard, c	.176	71	199	21	35	6	5	1	16	13	58	3
Partrick, Dave, of	.169	44	154	14	26	5	3	0	5	3	72	8
*Perez, Beban, of	.298	76	228	30	68	9	2	0	27	16	55	1
*Phillips, J.R., 1b	.198	46	162	14	32	4	1	1	15	10	58	3
Ramirez, Fausto, ss	.224	51	156	20	35	4	2	0	14	10	24	4
Renfroe, Randy, c	.164	28	55	9	9	0	0	2	7	5	13	2
#Romero, Charlie, of	.220	29	100	6	22	2	0	0	3	6	25	3
Salmon, Tim, of	.288	36	118	19	34	6	0	2	21	21	44	11
Schroeder, Bill, c	.333	6	12	2	4	1	0	0	1	1	3	0
Shepperd, Richard, of	.162	26	68	8	11	0	0	0	2	8	13	2
*Sturdivant, Dave, c	.207	30	87	4	18	1	0	0	5	14	18	0
*Taylor, Terry, 2b	.293	124	434	66	127	26	5	4	53	69	109	10
#Wallace, Tim, ss	.233	35	116	18	27	7	0	0	4	17	12	11
Zayas, Carlos, c	.242	20	62	7	15	6	0	1	7	3	15	0

PITCHING	W	L	ERA	G	GS	CG	SV	IP	H	R	ER	BB	SO
*Acosta, Clemente	10	10	4.40	29	26	2	0	160	182	97	78	40	93
Archibald, Dan	1	1	4.80	9	0	0	0	15	18	8	8	4	7
Cliburn, Stu	2	1	4.07	16	0	0	6	24	29	11	11	5	23
Cobb, Marvin	4	1	4.75	32	0	0	2	47	50	30	25	31	31
*Dunn, Stephen	4	4	5.28	28	1	0	0	90	112	62	53	35	49
Fritz, John	8	7	4.19	31	21	1	0	131	131	80	61	75	64
Hillman, Stewart	0	1	13.06	4	1	0	0	10	15	15	15	2	5
*James, Todd	3	3	4.37	12	12	1	0	70	63	36	34	38	44
Kelso, Jeff	0	0	4.50	1	0	0	0	2	2	1	1	2	1
Loubier, Steve	0	1	5.40	9	1	0	0	17	14	10	10	13	14
Martinez, Dave	0	6	4.72	12	9	0	0	55	59	32	29	16	37
*McClure, Bob	0	0	0.00	2	1	0	0	3	0	0	0	1	6
Meeks, Tim	1	0	0.00	6	0	0	1	10	5	0	0	2	12
Merejo, Luis	5	3	2.54	25	0	0	4	39	37	11	11	12	18
Merriman, Brett	3	10	3.75	24	16	0	0	101	106	60	42	55	53
*Neal, Dave	2	1	5.27	10	3	0	0	27	24	18	16	21	22
Pardo, Larry	9	10	4.10	25	24	1	0	138	137	77	63	57	78
*Search, Mike	1	0	4.13	24	0	0	0	28	38	21	13	21	13
Shull, Mike	0	6	6.99	15	3	0	0	28	33	32	22	14	26
Tolliver, Fred	0	1	2.87	7	1	0	0	16	15	5	5	6	5
Vann, Brandy	1	0	2.05	28	0	0	8	26	17	8	6	12	29
Vidmar, Don	5	10	3.43	17	17	2	0	113	105	51	43	29	60
*Warrecker, Willy	3	3	3.49	37	0	0	2	57	52	29	22	24	45
Zappelli, Mark	0	1	2.45	21	0	0	6	22	17	7	6	9	25

RENO

BATTING	AVG	G	AB	R	H	2B	3B	HR	RBI	BB	SO	SB
Blackwell, Barry, c	.286	32	98	18	28	6	0	7	20	8	23	0
*Charbonnet, Mark, of	.074	9	27	1	2	0	0	1	0	5	0	0
*DeJardin, Brad, of	.297	114	387	66	115	17	1	6	54	38	89	15
#Donahue, Timo, 2b	.264	103	352	68	93	16	3	5	45	50	69	19
*Easley, Mike, 1b-2b	.263	124	438	86	115	16	5	6	46	90	69	10
Eiterman, Tom, of-dh	.331	121	471	92	156	19	6	7	73	55	73	6
*Ferran, Alex, of	.208	46	125	14	26	4	1	0	8	18	28	2
Firova, Dan, c	.262	57	183	17	48	7	0	2	21	14	34	3
Garcia, Santiago, ss-2b	.194	14	36	6	7	2	0	0	2	1	8	0
*Harper, Milt, 1b-c	.317	91	322	69	102	23	2	20	73	62	58	0
Johnson, Dodd, of	.330	29	103	27	34	5	2	3	21	19	18	0
Lachmann, Tom, c	.533	6	15	5	8	1	0	1	9	4	2	0
McDonald, Chad, 3b	.353	34	119	21	42	7	0	2	29	22	24	0
Mota, Carlos, c	.276	85	275	42	76	14	2	3	32	19	50	14
Nalls, Gary, of	.214	72	192	26	41	7	0	3	25	23	43	7
Pough, Clyde, 3b	.151	16	53	1	8	0	1	0	2	6	18	0
Sarbaugh, Mike, 3b-ss	.291	121	454	78	132	22	7	6	67	46	76	14
Swain, Rob, 2b-ss	.077	4	13	1	1	0	0	1	1	1	5	0
Whitfield, Ken, of-dh	.281	112	437	82	123	21	4	24	90	36	108	7
Wong, Kaha, of-3b	.294	83	238	36	70	9	2	2	36	20	44	3

Rich Garces
... top prospect

Darrell Sherman
... 74 steals

Tom Eiterman
... .331-7-73

PITCHING	W	L	ERA	G	GS	CG	SV	IP	H	R	ER	BB	SO
*Alexander, Chuck	0	1	11.57	1	1	0	0	5	5	6	6	6	5
Anderson, Dave	4	1	3.90	27	4	0	0	58	60	30	25	25	56
*Bickler, Dave	0	0	9.00	1	0	0	0	1	1	1	1	2	1
Caraballo, Felix	2	0	9.68	17	4	0	0	31	45	35	33	20	22
Clark, Garry	6	2	4.87	23	11	3	0	92	97	57	50	24	55
Cole, Chris	5	5	3.72	14	12	3	0	85	90	51	35	27	49
*Dwyer, Vince	0	0	4.05	5	0	0	0	7	10	5	3	2	5
Guthrie, Joe	0	1	4.26	5	0	0	0	6	6	7	3	4	6
*Hurst, James	4	11	5.47	25	21	1	1	132	165	102	80	68	90
*Langley, Lee	6	1	4.46	42	0	0	2	77	83	43	38	57	84
*Ortiz, Angel	7	6	4.27	16	16	0	0	91	108	67	43	52	68
Palmer, David	1	0	3.38	3	3	0	0	11	8	4	4	8	10
Paxton, Greg	2	3	7.56	6	6	0	0	25	33	25	21	10	22
Pettiford, Cecil	12	9	4.75	24	24	2	0	142	151	91	75	62	87
Powers, Tad	5	6	3.88	54	0	0	8	107	114	59	46	41	82
Rauth, Chris	2	7	6.12	14	12	2	0	75	101	58	51	34	40
Shepherd, Keith	1	4	5.40	5	5	0	0	25	22	25	15	18	16
Soper, Mike	2	3	1.81	43	0	0	21	45	24	11	9	17	46
Wertz, Bill	1	3	6.60	17	9	0	0	61	61	58	45	52	52
Whitney, Jeff	4	3	4.54	17	7	2	1	67	65	40	34	15	31

RIVERSIDE

BATTING	AVG	G	AB	R	H	2B	3B	HR	RBI	BB	SO	SB
Ayala, Adan, c	.228	44	114	8	26	5	1	0	16	21	34	3
#Bethea, Steve, ss-3b	.171	104	315	38	54	9	3	0	21	57	105	13
Bigham, Scott, 2b	.244	117	409	46	100	13	3	0	37	38	68	13
#Dewey, Todd, c	.300	26	80	12	24	6	1	0	6	14	19	2
Dombrowski, Bob, 3b-2b	.208	85	259	20	54	10	3	1	33	17	57	6
#Farmer, Reggie, of	.255	118	411	54	105	15	8	5	42	47	113	25
#Gieseke, Mark, of-1b	.270	128	482	59	130	26	2	4	60	51	93	5
#Harris, Vince, of	.282	69	245	44	69	4	1	0	21	35	35	40
Hendricks, Steve, 1b-of	.289	128	484	59	140	27	7	11	90	32	77	10
*Higgins, Kevin, c	.301	49	176	27	53	5	1	2	18	27	15	0
#Lopez, Luis, ss	.370	14	46	5	17	3	1	1	4	3	3	4
McGee, Tony, c	.209	80	235	23	49	7	0	0	30	29	61	0
Meury, Bill, ss	.173	49	150	16	26	2	0	1	8	13	38	1
*Sherman, Darrell, of	.290	131	483	97	140	10	4	0	35	89	51	74
Smith, Greg, of-dh	.221	117	393	44	87	14	4	9	51	48	107	5
Staton, Dave, 3b-1b	.290	92	335	56	97	16	1	20	64	52	78	4

PITCHING	W	L	ERA	G	GS	CG	SV	IP	H	R	ER	BB	SO
*Beckett, Robbie	2	1	7.02	3	3	0	0	17	18	13	13	11	11
*Bryand, Renay	7	2	5.30	47	6	0	0	88	128	66	52	31	68
Davis, Rick	10	9	3.04	26	26	0	0	163	175	72	55	44	122
Deville, Dan	3	2	4.67	42	1	0	2	81	89	49	42	32	74
Estrada, Jay	0	1	2.70	13	0	0	0	17	11	5	5	5	12
*Harrison, Brian	5	2	1.19	37	0	0	18	45	31	9	6	20	55
Haslock, Chris	2	4	4.91	43	1	0	3	81	75	47	44	38	86
*Knox, Kerry	11	12	3.66	27	27	3	0	180	188	97	73	49	111
Lane, Heath	5	7	4.93	32	11	0	1	100	117	72	55	58	55
Lifgren, Kelly	6	14	4.55	27	27	3	0	164	195	107	83	68	113
Marx, Bill	0	1	7.00	2	2	0	0	9	8	7	7	6	2
*Reed, Billy	0	2	3.57	4	2	0	0	18	18	10	7	16	10
Reichle, Darrin	0	2	6.19	6	6	0	0	16	19	13	11	13	15
Sierra, Candy	3	4	2.14	38	0	0	11	67	63	32	16	17	71
Smithberg, Roger	1	2	4.15	3	3	0	0	13	12	7	6	2	5
Thomas, Royal	9	13	4.72	27	27	1	0	166	209	103	87	49	93

SALINAS

BATTING	AVG	G	AB	R	H	2B	3B	HR	RBI	BB	SO	SB
*Alegre, Paul, of	.130	14	23	1	3	1	0	1	4	1	13	0
Allanson, Andy, c	.291	36	127	21	37	6	1	3	19	19	22	6
Barton, Shawn, 2b (16 Reno)	.275	104	338	41	93	11	3	1	37	34	31	12
Beeler, Pete, c	.200	15	45	1	9	1	0	0	4	1	6	0
Carlson, Bill, 1b-3b	.261	139	487	72	127	21	4	12	59	73	97	15

	AVG	G	AB	R	H	2B	3B	HR	RBI	BB	SO	SB
#Craig, Rodney, of	.000	6	14	1	0	0	0	0	1	5	2	2
Deiley, Lou, c	.205	32	83	12	17	0	0	2	8	10	21	0
*Durham, Leon, dh-1b	.228	36	114	20	26	5	1	8	26	19	25	0
*Hahn, Brent, 3b-c	.221	123	348	30	77	8	1	0	33	36	58	4
#Housie, Wayne, of	.270	92	367	51	99	20	6	5	49	22	72	27
Jaster, Scott, of	.264	59	212	23	56	10	1	5	29	22	38	3
#Jose, Manny, of	.304	48	207	39	63	8	3	3	25	17	54	19
Kohno, Takayuki, 3b	1.000	2	1	1	1	0	0	0	1	0	0	0
Landphere, Ed, of	.172	18	58	2	10	0	0	1	6	10	19	0
*Mannion, Greg, of	.227	7	22	2	5	0	0	0	0	3	9	2
Meredith, Steve, of	.237	15	38	3	9	0	0	0	2	5	9	2
*Nishusima, Takayuki, of	.269	31	78	15	21	4	2	0	7	14	30	4
Ohtsuka, Don, c	.225	60	178	12	40	5	0	1	12	20	40	1
*Palma, Brian, of-dh	.313	55	166	24	52	7	2	2	18	22	34	7
*Paul, Corey, of	.226	89	230	34	52	8	2	4	28	42	83	10
Peguero, Jerry, ss	.175	45	154	9	27	3	0	1	11	9	31	4
Perea, Mike, ss	.139	18	36	3	5	0	0	0	2	0	12	0
Rowe, Pete, ph	.000	1	1	0	0	0	0	0	0	0	0	0
Shevlin, Jim, 3b	.167	19	54	4	9	0	0	0	2	12	7	0
Tashiro, Hiroyuki, 3b	.125	24	48	3	6	2	0	0	2	4	26	0
#Thompson, Sean, of-2b	.157	62	115	14	18	0	0	0	5	11	31	2
#West, Hassan, of	.111	7	9	1	1	0	0	0	0	2	4	0
*Yamanouchi, Kenichi, 1b-dh	.204	118	338	36	69	15	4	5	31	34	125	2
Yanagita, Shikato, ss-2b	.270	139	463	65	125	21	1	2	45	61	83	13
#Young, Delwyn, of	.248	45	153	20	38	4	1	4	16	14	35	16
#Young, Selwyn, 2b-of	.238	20	63	7	15	3	0	0	1	6	7	1

PITCHING	W	L	ERA	G	GS	CG	SV	IP	H	R	ER	BB	SO
Arola, Bruce	2	0	3.05	18	2	0	0	38	33	20	13	15	17
Barton, Shawn	1	0	1.29	3	0	0	0	7	1	1	2	2	
Carrasco, Carlos	5	14	5.22	26	25	4	0	153	174	112	89	66	107
*Emoto, Kouichi	7	4	3.07	54	0	0	6	82	81	36	28	38	72
Gardey, Rudy	0	0	2.70	3	0	0	0	7	6	2	2	3	6
*Howe, Steve	0	1	2.12	10	6	0	0	17	19	8	4	5	14
Leslie, Reggie	5	3	3.89	19	2	0	2	35	39	18	15	24	28
Maye, Steve	10	14	3.74	30	27	14	0	185	195	102	77	66	114
Murakami, Seiichi	3	5	4.54	25	8	1	0	83	77	48	42	33	69
Myers, Don	3	7	3.77	30	5	1	3	72	83	42	30	18	61
*Ohtsuka, Ken	5	10	4.82	31	23	4	1	151	188	94	81	44	121
Page, Greg	0	2	7.31	11	0	0	0	16	30	18	13	6	11
Reilley, John	1	8	5.09	19	14	1	0	81	66	57	46	55	90
Sasaki, Shigeki	3	14	6.02	34	16	2	0	123	140	98	82	75	86
Stewart, John	0	1	3.86	11	0	0	0	16	20	9	7	5	22
Tanoue, Keisaburo	0	0	4.58	10	1	0	0	18	19	9	9	3	8
Uchiyama, Kenichi	3	10	5.92	37	11	1	6	111	141	88	73	32	111
Velasquez, Ray	0	0	3.72	6	0	0	1	10	6	5	4	6	7

SAN BERNARDINO

BATTING	AVG	G	AB	R	H	2B	3B	HR	RBI	BB	SO	SB
Arguelles, Fernando, c	.249	82	257	28	64	7	0	3	32	36	60	5
#Bolick, Frank, 3b (50 Stock)	.324	128	441	100	143	33	5	18	102	91	86	8
Clark, Isaiah, 3b-ss	.323	62	251	51	81	15	2	12	45	19	20	4
Del Pozo, Roberto, of	.252	76	214	29	54	8	1	1	17	30	63	7
Gonzalez, Ruben, 1b-dh	.336	44	140	27	47	5	1	5	26	27	24	1
Hoffman, Joe, c	.114	13	35	2	4	0	0	0	2	2	11	0
Jones, Bobby, of	.312	82	308	55	96	13	1	14	59	34	77	7
*Keitges, Jeff, 1b	.276	124	420	53	116	26	0	9	60	39	85	3
Kingwood, Tyrone, of	.310	26	84	18	26	6	0	4	14	8	14	3
Lennon, Patrick, 3b-of	.288	44	163	29	47	6	2	8	30	15	51	6
Magallanes, Bobby, ss	.187	56	193	26	36	4	0	3	21	24	52	1
Manahan, Anthony, ss	.318	51	198	46	63	10	2	7	30	24	35	8
Maynard, Tow, of	.236	127	488	92	115	10	7	3	25	63	116	80
#Merchant, Mark, of-dh	.314	29	102	22	32	3	0	4	19	20	34	8
Morales, Rich, c-of	.232	34	62	6	19	4	0	0	12	3	14	0
Nava, Lipso, ss	.174	7	23	1	4	1	0	0	1	0	9	0
Pirkl, Greg, c-dh	.295	58	207	37	61	10	0	5	28	13	34	3
Seda, Israel, ss	.300	3	10	1	3	1	0	0	2	0	1	0
Smith, David, of	.269	54	119	14	32	4	2	1	11	4	33	3
#Stargell, Tim, 2b-of	.262	136	545	84	143	22	3	17	96	29	93	20
Turang, Brian, 2b-of	.296	132	487	86	144	25	5	12	67	69	98	25
#Vizquel, Omar, ss	.250	6	28	5	7	0	0	0	3	3	1	1
Williams, Ray, dh-of	.239	78	197	30	47	8	3	0	24	33	51	14

PITCHING	W	L	ERA	G	GS	CG	SV	IP	H	R	ER	BB	SO
*Bennett, Jim	0	0	1.69	4	0	0	0	5	6	2	1	1	2
*Cummings, John	2	4	4.20	7	7	1	0	41	47	27	19	20	30
DeLucia, Rich	4	1	2.05	5	5	1	0	31	19	9	7	3	35
Evans, David	14	9	4.18	26	26	4	0	155	135	83	72	74	143
*Felix, Nick	0	3	6.68	37	2	0	0	66	78	58	49	42	67
*Fleming, Dave	7	3	2.60	12	12	4	0	80	64	29	23	30	77
*Furcal, Manuel	7	8	4.65	35	14	1	2	108	106	75	56	41	98
Goff, Mike	0	1	1.93	3	0	0	0	5	6	2	1	2	4
Green, Derek	0	0	12.60	5	0	0	0	10	16	17	14	12	11
Jones, Calvin	5	3	2.96	53	0	0	9	67	43	32	22	54	94
*McDonald, David	0	0	5.27	9	0	0	0	14	18	13	8	9	10
Newlin, Jim	1	5	3.60	36	0	0	12	45	35	24	18	21	56

BATTING

R Pat Listach, Stockton . . . 116
H Joel Chimelis, Modesto . 161
TB Brett Magnusson, Bak . . 242
2B Brett Magnusson, Bak . . . 34
3B Tim Raley, Stockton 14
HR Ken Whitfield, Reno 24
RBI Frank Bolick, Sto/SB . . . 102
SH Shikato Yanagita, Salinas 22
SF Ken Jackson, Stockton . . 13
    Frank Bolick, Sto/SB 13
BB Pat Listach, Stockton . . . 105
IBB Jeff Keitges, SB 12
HBP Adell Davenport, SJ. 16
SO Steve Hosey, San Jose . 139
SB Ellerton Maynard, SB. . . . 80
CS Ellerton Maynard, SB. . . . 32
OB% J.T. Bruett, Visalia 439

PITCHING

G Johnny Wiggs, SB 64
GS Pat Mahomes, Visalia 28
CG Steve Maye, Salinas 14
ShO George Tsamis, Visalia 3
Sv Rich Garces, Visalia 28
W George Tsamis, Visalia . . 17
L Four tied at 14
IP Steve Maye, Salinas . . . 185
    Pat Mahomes, Visalia . . . 185
H Royal Thomas, Riverside 209
R Carlos Carrasco, Salinas 112
HR James Hurst, Reno 19
BB Pat Mahomes, Visalia . . . 118
HB Kerry Woodson, SB. 12
SO Kevin Rogers, San Jose . 186
WP Chris Fye, San Jose 22
Bk Dave Anderson, Reno 6
    Shigeki Sasaki, Salinas 6

	W	L	ERA	G	GS	CG	SV	IP	H	R	ER	BB	SO
Pitcher, Scott	3	1	5.04	36	7	0	3	75	82	55	42	47	66
Salkeld, Roger	11	5	3.40	25	25	2	0	153	140	77	58	83	167
Sheehan, John	0	2	6.19	22	0	0	2	36	43	32	25	25	19
Taylor, Scott	8	8	5.41	34	21	1	1	126	148	100	76	69	86
*Wiggs, Johnny	7	6	3.95	64	0	0	8	93	112	48	41	48	97
Woodson, Kerry	8	6	3.10	27	23	1	0	137	111	62	47	83	131

SAN JOSE

BATTING	AVG	G	AB	R	H	2B	3B	HR	RBI	BB	SO	SB
#Bass, Kevin, of	.364	6	22	2	8	1	0	0	4	0	1	1
*Brady, Pat, of	.212	54	151	22	32	5	1	1	17	24	32	2
Brauning, Jeff, 3b-ss	.278	99	331	63	92	8	3	3	45	34	38	17
Cala, Craig, of-dh	.227	48	88	12	20	5	0	0	9	7	30	0
*Carey, Frank, 3b-2b	.282	27	85	21	24	3	1	0	11	15	25	2
Christopherson, Eric, c . . .	.174	7	23	4	4	0	0	0	1	3	6	0
Clayton, Royce, ss	.267	123	460	80	123	15	10	7	71	68	98	33
Crowe, Ron, 3b-1b	.333	19	57	11	19	1	0	0	12	8	7	0
Davenport, Adell, 1b	.251	132	495	76	124	20	5	17	66	46	108	3
*Davis, Mike, of	.088	9	34	2	3	0	0	0	1	7	7	0
Fernandez, Dan, c	.263	36	76	19	20	2	0	1	14	13	21	0
Ham, Mike, c	.500	5	8	2	4	1	0	0	0	0	1	0
Hosey, Steve, of	.232	139	479	85	111	13	6	16	78	71	139	16
#Jones, Dan, 3b-ss	.224	53	156	20	35	3	3	0	14	24	48	6
*Lewis, Dan, of-dh	.292	116	415	58	121	23	3	14	93	61	78	7
*McNamara, Jim, c-1b	.203	53	158	20	32	2	2	1	22	18	30	1
Miller, Roger, c	.571	3	7	1	4	0	0	0	2	1	0	0
Nes Smith, John, ph	.000	1	1	0	0	0	0	0	0	0	1	0
#Patterson, John, 2b	.302	131	530	91	160	23	6	4	66	46	74	29
#Shaw, Kerry, 3b-1b	.223	83	211	25	47	8	0	0	22	36	38	5
Smiley, Reuben, of	.266	135	455	78	121	9	5	3	48	40	105	25
Tucker, Scooter, c-dh	.280	123	439	59	123	28	2	5	71	71	69	9
Westbrooks, Elanis, of	.252	48	103	14	26	7	1	0	9	13	18	3

PITCHING	W	L	ERA	G	GS	CG	SV	IP	H	R	ER	BB	SO
Brock, Don	0	2	6.23	9	1	0	0	17	19	13	12	11	11
Dour, Brian	6	6	4.03	25	24	1	0	127	133	85	57	41	77
Downs, Kelly	0	1	1.80	1	1	0	0	5	5	2	1	0	3
*Estes, Joel	2	2	2.60	33	0	0	4	52	53	20	15	8	42
Foley, Jim	4	5	4.82	27	12	0	2	93	88	54	50	61	85
*Fye, Chris	7	11	5.47	43	15	1	0	127	120	90	77	75	84
Gustafson, Ed	0	0	0.00	2	0	0	0	3	2	0	0	0	4
*Hancock, Chris	0	0	1.17	1	1	0	0	8	7	1	1	4	7
*Herring, Vince	2	4	3.41	35	0	0	2	71	61	34	27	42	63
Johnson, Dom	5	8	5.40	25	19	2	0	100	89	72	60	72	61
Lacoss, Mike	1	0	1.50	1	1	0	0	6	5	1	1	0	6
Mead, Timber	1	0	0.00	2	1	0	0	10	8	1	0	5	9
*Meyers, Paul	2	3	4.78	8	8	0	0	38	36	26	20	22	20
Myers, Jim	5	8	3.21	60	0	0	25	84	80	44	30	34	61
O'Neal, Randy	0	0	3.00	1	1	0	0	3	4	1	1	0	2
Oliveras, Francisco	0	0	2.45	1	1	0	0	4	4	2	1	1	3
Potestio, Frank	3	0	4.55	6	4	0	0	30	24	18	15	14	21
Rambo, Dan	12	2	2.19	26	17	2	1	144	104	47	35	42	142
Robinson, Don	1	0	3.86	2	2	0	0	5	4	3	2	1	8
*Rogers, Kevin	14	5	3.61	28	26	1	0	172	143	86	69	68	186
Sharko, Gary	6	5	3.28	44	3	0	0	96	97	49	35	36	60
Taylor, Rob	3	2	7.08	13	0	0	2	20	24	19	16	15	18
Vuz, John	0	4	4.08	5	5	1	0	29	23	20	13	19	26

STOCKTON

BATTING	AVG	G	AB	R	H	2B	3B	HR	RBI	BB	SO	SB
*Butcher, Arthur, of	.125	3	8	1	1	0	0	0	0	0	4	1
Cassels, Chris, of-1b	.284	93	299	42	85	17	2	9	50	27	64	0

	AVG	G	AB	R	H	2B	3B	HR	RBI	BB	SO	SB
Diaz, Remigio, ss	.216	84	231	25	50	3	0	0	28	24	37	3
Diaz, Steve, ss	.000	12	13	0	0	0	0	0	0	1	7	0
*Dodson, Bo, 1b	.273	120	363	70	99	16	4	6	46	73	103	1
Esquer, Dave, ss (29 PS) ..	.213	48	141	16	30	2	0	0	16	16	25	4
Finn, John, of	.207	95	290	48	60	4	0	1	23	52	50	29
Guerrero, Mike, ss-3b	.250	105	320	36	80	5	5	1	36	24	54	14
Hailey, Fred, of	.176	33	74	5	13	1	0	0	2	18	13	2
Jackson, Ken, c	.231	84	273	37	63	18	3	5	55	17	65	8
Jaha, John, dh	.262	26	84	12	22	5	0	4	19	18	25	0
Kappesser, Bob, c	.184	63	147	17	27	2	1	0	12	15	39	2
Listach, Pat, 2b	.272	139	503	116	137	21	6	2	39	105	122	78
*Love, Sylvester, of	.183	46	131	21	24	7	4	1	15	21	32	8
*Nilsson, Dave, c	.290	107	359	70	104	22	3	7	47	43	36	6
*O'Leary, Troy, of	.500	2	6	1	3	1	0	0	0	2	1	0
*Raley, Tim, of-dh	.256	124	399	54	102	12	14	10	71	51	71	6
Sass, James, of	.235	111	281	41	66	8	1	0	27	41	79	15
Stiner, Rick, c	.159	58	126	10	20	1	1	1	14	15	48	0
Tatum, Jim, 3b-1b	.262	70	260	41	68	16	0	12	59	13	49	4
Vargas, Trinidad, ss	.000	5	15	0	0	0	0	0	0	1	7	0

PITCHING	W	L	ERA	G	GS	CG	SV	IP	H	R	ER	BB	SO
Cangemi, Jamie	3	7	3.01	62	1	0	6	99	86	41	33	52	102
*Carmody, Kevin	5	3	5.16	49	0	0	1	84	90	60	48	35	58
Carter, Larry	0	0	15.00	1	1	0	0	3	5	5	5	2	2
Czajkowski, Jim	0	0	0.00	2	0	0	1	3	1	0	0	2	2
DelaRosa, Domingo	0	0	9.00	2	0	0	0	2	1	2	2	3	2
Eldred, Cal	4	2	1.62	7	7	3	0	50	31	12	9	19	75
Enriquez, Martin	1	0	3.24	8	0	0	0	8	13	6	3	6	9
Fitzgerald, Dave	10	10	6.02	34	24	1	0	129	146	102	86	56	87
Guilbe, Victor	0	0	11.25	4	0	0	0	4	10	7	5	4	2
Hamilton, Scott	4	4	3.51	38	9	0	0	85	88	42	33	38	73
Henry, Doug	1	0	1.13	4	0	0	1	8	4	1	1	3	13
Ignasiak, Mike	3	1	3.94	6	6	1	0	32	18	14	14	17	23
Johnson, Chris	13	6	2.98	23	23	1	0	142	121	56	47	54	112
Kiefer, Mark	5	2	3.30	11	10	0	0	60	65	23	22	17	37
Krippner, Curt	0	1	22.50	2	0	0	0	2	5	5	5	1	1
*Lee, Mark	1	0	2.35	5	0	0	1	8	5	2	2	3	7
McGrath, Chuck	0	0	2.25	1	1	0	0	4	3	1	1	1	3
*Miranda, Angel	9	4	2.66	52	9	2	24	108	75	37	32	49	138
Perez, Leo	1	1	3.97	6	5	0	0	23	24	11	10	5	23
Sandoval, Guillermo	8	5	4.08	34	16	0	0	124	131	63	56	54	79
Schwarz, Jeff	3	3	4.79	19	8	0	2	56	59	36	30	36	59
Sparks, Steve	10	7	3.69	19	19	5	0	129	136	63	53	31	77
Uribe, Juan	1	3	4.62	31	2	0	11	39	32	23	20	24	28

VISALIA

BATTING	AVG	G	AB	R	H	2B	3B	HR	RBI	BB	SO	SB
*Bruett, J.T., of	.307	123	437	86	134	15	3	1	33	101	60	50
Buckley, Troy, c-dh	.307	117	404	69	124	24	4	5	64	43	58	5
Capellan, Carlos, 2b-of ...	.284	105	415	54	118	13	2	1	50	13	33	9
Cedeno, Ramon, of	.281	91	313	44	88	20	6	6	45	13	71	1
*Cohen, John, of	.302	49	169	20	51	10	0	2	27	8	35	0
#Fraticelli, Carl, 3b-of ...	.111	11	18	0	2	0	0	0	2	5	0
#Garcia, Jose, 3b	.274	137	486	68	133	29	4	10	71	56	68	10
House, Mike, of-dh	.266	88	308	47	82	8	0	10	42	38	83	1
*Kvasnicka, Jay, of	.232	114	384	63	89	18	6	6	43	56	83	32
*Logan, Todd, c-dh	.287	108	352	60	101	18	2	12	62	72	70	2
*Masteller, Dan, 1b	.281	135	473	71	133	20	5	4	73	81	76	2
#McCreary, Bob, ss	.284	139	503	72	143	12	4	1	45	58	88	3
Milene, Jeff, c	.109	22	46	5	5	1	0	0	1	6	19	0
*Ortiz, Ray, of-dh	.315	62	235	43	74	15	1	13	53	26	47	1
Raabe, Brian, 2b	.246	42	138	11	34	3	2	0	17	10	9	5
Segui, Daniel, 3b	.211	33	95	11	20	3	0	0	5	13	16	0

PITCHING	W	L	ERA	G	GS	CG	SV	IP	H	R	ER	BB	SO
Aspray, Mike	2	2	3.46	19	0	0	3	42	41	20	16	8	30
Best, Jayson	1	1	5.87	4	3	0	0	15	16	14	10	16	13
Fine, Tom	0	0	5.06	3	0	0	1	5	3	3	3	6	4
Garces, Richard	2	2	1.81	47	0	0	28	55	33	14	11	16	75
Krol, David	4	3	5.94	28	10	0	1	67	71	48	44	42	42
Lipson, Marc	1	0	1.64	17	0	0	12	22	21	5	4	6	15
Mahomes, Pat	11	11	3.30	28	28	5	0	185	136	77	68	118	178
*Muh, Steve	5	3	3.96	12	12	2	0	84	80	40	37	38	54
*Neagle, Denny	8	0	1.43	10	10	0	0	63	39	13	10	16	92
*Newman, Alan	3	1	2.23	5	5	0	0	36	29	15	9	22	42
Russo, Pat	0	3	5.59	17	0	0	0	29	34	29	18	22	26
Swanson, Chad	6	7	4.99	39	0	0	3	79	90	55	44	37	68
Trombley, Mike	14	6	3.43	27	25	3	0	176	163	79	67	50	164
*Tsamis, George	17	4	2.21	26	26	4	0	184	168	62	45	61	145
White, Fred	6	4	5.45	37	3	0	1	66	77	51	40	28	57
*Wiese, Phil	10	4	2.52	20	19	2	0	118	109	43	33	44	95

CAROLINA LEAGUE

Star-spangled season for second-year Keys

By DEAN GYORGY

Years from now, when fans of the Frederick Keys look back, they'll want to say they were there in 1990. It was a magical year for all associated with the team.

The second-year franchise began the season with a new home, $5-million Harry Grove Stadium. They drew a franchise-record number of fans, 277,802, second-best in the league. And on the field, the Baltimore Orioles' affiliate won both Northern Division half-titles by a healthy margin.

But the real excitement came in the championship series against Kinston. In Game One, the Keys scored six times in the ninth inning for a 6-4 win. They emerged with a 1-0, 11-inning victory in Game

Gary Scott
...MVP

Three. And in the deciding Game Five, the Keys battled back from a 5-0 deficit, helped by a three-run, sixth-inning homer by Tim Holland. The Keys held on for a 6-5 victory and their first Carolina League championship.

"It was quite a season," Keys broadcaster Matt Hicks said. "People will talk about this for a long time."

Runners-up

Postseason participants got to go home a few days early in 1990. There was no need for divisional playoffs, as the Kinston Indians, like Frederick in the North, won both halves of the Southern Division.

The Indians had a good year under first-year manager Brian Graham, posting the league's best overall record at 88-47 (.652). Ken Ramos, the league's leading hitter at .345, opened the season with the Indians, but some late arrivals gave the club a big push down the stretch.

Tim Costo, Cleveland's No. 1 draft pick in June, made his professional debut in Kinston. After a move to first base from shortstop, Costo went on to hit .316 with four homers and 42 RBIs.

LEAGUE CHAMPIONS

Playoff Champions, Where Applicable

1990—Frederick	1974—Salem	1958—Burlington
1989—Pr. William	1973—Win.-Salem	1957—Durham
1988—Kinston	1972—Salem	1956—Fayetteville
1987—Salem	1971—Peninsula	1955—Danville
1986—Win.-Salem	1970—Win.-Salem	1954—Fayetteville
1985—Win.-Salem	1969—Raleigh-Dur.	1953—Danville
1984—Lynchburg	1968—High Pt.-Th.	1952—Reidsville
1983—Lynchburg	1967—Durham	1951—Win.-Salem
1982—Alexandria	1966—Rocky Mount	1950—Win.-Salem
1981—Hagerstown	1965—Tidewater	1949—Burlington
1980—Peninsula	1964—Win.-Salem	1948—Martinsville
1979—Win.-Salem	1963—Wilson	1947—Raleigh
1978—Lynchburg	1962—Kinston	1946—Raleigh
1977—Peninsula	1961—Wilson	1945—Danville
1976—Win.-Salem	1960—Greensboro	
1975—Rocky Mount	1959—Wilson	

Prince William righthander Frank Seminara led CL in wins (16) and ERA (1.90).

Righthander Oscar Munoz, who went 15-2 with the University of Miami and was a fifth-round pick of the Indians, left the New York-Penn League in late July and went 7-0 for Kinston down the stretch. And third baseman Jim Thome, the No. 1-rated prospect in the Appalachian League, left triple-crown-type numbers in Burlington and hit .308 in 117 at-bats with Kinston.

Winston-Salem now knows what the 1981 Cincinnati Reds felt like. The Spirits had the second-best overall record, 10 games ahead of eventual-champions Frederick, but failed to make the playoffs.

The Spirits did have the league MVP, however. Third baseman Gary Scott, the Cubs' second-round pick in 1989, hit .295 with 12 homers and 70 RBIs for the Spirits before a Double-A call-up in late July.

Turnstiles keep turning

Durham did it again at the gate in 1990. For the third year in a row, the Bulls set an all-time Class A attendance mark, this time topping the 300,000 plateau. With 300,499, Durham outdrew all 26 Double-A and 12 Triple-A teams.

Bulls owner Miles Wolff, who elected to sell the club to a Raleigh, N.C. broadcasting executive at the conclusion of the season, never dreamt that big when he revived the Bulls in 1980.

"I thought the maximum we could ever draw was 100,000," Wolff said. "I thought 70,000-100,000 would be good, and I would leave after three years . . . but it just kept growing."

The rest of the league prospered as well. Every team bettered their attendance of 1989.

The most dramatic increase in attendance, although the total was still by far the lowest in the league, took place in Hampton, Va. The Peninsula Pilots went from 20,059 in 1989 to 70,647 in 1990. The biggest factor for the jump was a working agreement with the Seattle Mariners. After operating as a co-op for two seasons, the fans finally had a team to identify with.

CL clippings

Durham's Chris Czarnik tossed a seven-inning no-hitter against Winston-Salem on May 24. With the game tied, he left after surrendering a hit in the eighth and received no decision . . . Peninsula's Rick Balabon no-hit Frederick 4-0 on June 16 . . . Salem catcher Mandy Romero led the league in RBIs with 90 . . . Prince William's Frank Seminara won the ERA title with an impressive 16-8, 1.90 ledger . . . Durham outfielder Popeye Cole stole second, third and home in the same inning against Prince William . . . The Lynchburg Red Sox broke the league strikeout record, as its hitters went down 1,197 times . . . Red Sox third baseman Chris Whitehead was married in a home-plate ceremony at Lynchburg's City Stadium in late June . . . Prince William reliever Mike Gardella tied the league save record with 30 . . . The Boston Red Sox No. 1 draft pick in 1989, Greg Blosser, hit 12 second-half home runs for Lynchburg and led the league with 18. He was selected the league's top prospect in a Baseball America poll of managers.

1990 FINAL STANDINGS

FIRST HALF

North	W	L	Pct.	GB
Frederick (Orioles)	39	31	.557	—
Prince William (Yankees) ...	33	37	.471	6
Lynchburg (Red Sox)	33	37	.471	6
Salem (Pirates)	25	45	.357	14

South	W	L	Pct.	GB
Kinston (Indians)	46	24	.657	—
Winston-Salem (Cubs)	45	25	.643	1
Durham (Braves)	37	33	.529	9
Peninsula (Mariners)........	22	48	.314	24

SECOND HALF

North	W	L	Pct.	GB
Frederick (Orioles)	35	31	.530	—
Prince William (Yankees) ...	31	38	.449	5½
Salem (Pirates)	30	39	.435	6½
Lynchburg (Red Sox)	25	43	.368	11

South	W	L	Pct.	GB
Kinston (Indians)	42	23	.646	—
Winston-Salem (Cubs)	41	29	.586	3½
Peninsula (Mariners)........	35	35	.500	9½
Durham (Braves)	34	35	.493	10

OVERALL

	W	L	Pct.	GB
Kinston (Indians)	88	47	.652	—
Winston-Salem (Cubs)	86	54	.614	4½
Frederick (Orioles)	74	62	.544	14½
Durham (Braves)	71	68	.511	19
Prince William (Yankees) ...	64	75	.460	26
Lynchburg (Red Sox)	58	80	.420	31½
Peninsula (Mariners)........	57	83	.407	33½
Salem (Pirates)	55	84	.396	35

1990 GENERAL INFORMATION

Playoffs: Frederick defeated Kinston 3-2 in best-of-5 final for league championship.

Regular-Season Attendance: Durham, 300,499; Frederick, 277,802; Prince William, 210,262; Salem, 126,121; Kinston, 106,219; Winston-

Salem, 102,558; Lynchburg, 92,607; Peninsula, 70,647.

Managers: Durham—Grady Little; **Frederick**—Wally Moon; **Kinston**—Brian Graham; **Lynchburg**—Gary Allenson; **Peninsula**—Jim Nettles; **Prince William**—Gary Denbo; **Salem**—Stan Cliburn; **Winston-Salem**—Brad Mills.

1990 Official All-Star Team: C—Mandy Romero, Salem. **1B**—J.T. Snow, Prince William. **2B**—Rouglas Odor, Kinston. **3B**—Gary Scott, Winston-Salem. **SS**—Ricky Gutierrez, Frederick. **UTIL INF**—Bruce Schreiber, Salem. **OF**—Greg Blosser, Lynchburg; Keith Mitchell, Durham; Ken Ramos, Kinston. **UTIL OF**—Nolan Lane, Kinston. **DH**—Doug Welch, Winston-Salem. **SP**—Frank Seminara, Prince William. **RP**—Mike Gardella, Prince William. **Most Valuable Player**—Gary Scott, Winston-Salem. **Pitcher of the Year**—Frank Seminara, Prince William. **Manager of the Year**—Wally Moon, Frederick.

Top 10 Major League Prospects (by Baseball America): 1. Greg Blosser, of, Lynchburg; **2.** Ryan Klesko, 1b, Durham; **3.** Gary Scott, 3b, Winston-Salem; **4.** Tim Costo, 1b, Kinston; **5.** Russ Davis, 3b, Prince William; **6.** Ricky Gutierrez, ss, Frederick; **7.** Keith Mitchell, of, Durham; **8.** Sherman Obando, of, Prince William; **9.** Mike Gardella, lhp, Prince William; **10.** Ty Kovach, rhp, Kinston.

1990 BATTING, PITCHING STATS

CLUB BATTING

	AVG	G	AB	R	H	2B	3B	HR	BB	SO	SB
Kinston	.270	135	4527	697	1222	198	40	67	522	914	171
Frederick	.268	136	4553	612	1221	225	32	50	440	801	93
Winston-Salem	.260	140	4692	674	1219	194	32	83	538	888	147
Salem	.255	139	4695	633	1199	205	47	98	524	1054	114
Durham	.254	139	4672	605	1189	212	33	78	523	764	114
Prince William	.246	139	4544	554	1119	222	37	60	447	916	114
Peninsula	.234	140	4497	507	1051	149	22	51	468	967	142
Lynchburg	.232	138	4538	549	1052	176	27	91	524	1198	99

CLUB PITCHING

	ERA	G	CG	SHO	SV	IP	H	R	ER	BB	SO
Kinston	3.04	135	9	11	43	1190	1033	509	402	481	1011
Frederick	3.13	136	17	16	27	1180	1068	517	410	449	981
Winston-Salem	3.24	140	21	10	44	1235	1166	540	445	483	960
Prince William	3.42	139	9	15	34	1188	1108	533	451	497	963
Durham	3.65	139	9	9	36	1234	1158	622	500	500	995
Peninsula	3.79	140	13	9	29	1198	1193	631	504	495	847
Lynchburg	4.26	138	14	11	29	1201	1236	678	568	489	885
Salem	4.80	139	15	8	25	1215	1310	801	648	592	860

INDIVIDUAL BATTING LEADERS
(Minimum 378 Plate Appearances)

	AVG	G	AB	R	H	2B	3B	HR	RBI	BB	SO	SB
*Ramos, Ken, Kinston	.345	96	339	71	117	16	6	0	31	48	34	18
Welch, Doug, W-S	.320	107	363	58	116	20	3	11	68	29	65	1
Holland, Tim, Fred	.302	115	424	63	128	26	4	8	68	38	75	6
*Levis, Jesse, Kinston	.296	107	382	63	113	18	3	7	64	64	42	4
Scott, Gary, W-S	.295	102	380	63	112	22	0	12	70	29	66	17
Mitchell, Keith, Durham	.294	129	456	81	134	24	3	6	48	92	48	18
Cole, Popeye, Durham	.293	118	389	64	114	11	4	2	40	27	52	24
#Romero, Armando, Salem	.291	124	460	62	134	31	3	17	90	55	68	0
Schreiber, Bruce, Salem	.290	134	552	71	160	24	5	4	48	33	109	6
Pennye, Darwin, Salem	.284	104	405	51	115	27	4	10	52	23	74	15

INDIVIDUAL PITCHING LEADERS
(Minimum 112 Innings)

	W	L	ERA	G	GS	CG	SV	IP	H	R	ER	BB	SO
Seminara, Frank, Pw	16	8	1.90	25	25	4	0	170	136	51	36	52	132
*Czarkowski, Mark, Pen	8	6	2.32	21	16	3	0	116	128	50	30	34	40
Watson, Preston, Durham	10	6	2.42	34	16	2	3	137	101	51	37	60	122
Miller, Paul, Salem	8	6	2.45	22	22	5	0	151	145	58	41	33	83
Kovach, Ty, Kinston	12	3	2.56	18	18	2	0	123	78	46	35	53	90
Salles, John, W-S	14	5	2.58	25	25	4	0	171	160	59	49	48	100
Oquist, Mike, Fred	9	8	2.81	25	25	3	0	166	134	64	52	48	170
Kerr, Zachary, Fred	14	7	2.94	26	26	5	0	178	160	64	58	56	129
Estrada, Pete, Lynch	7	7	3.05	25	25	2	0	153	153	71	52	55	88
Wright, Skipper, Durham	6	7	3.16	50	1	0	8	117	101	46	41	34	100

DURHAM

BATTING	AVG	G	AB	R	H	2B	3B	HR	RBI	BB	SO	SB
#Alicea, Edwin, 3b-of	.278	113	370	55	103	28	0	13	49	68	79	14
*Brust, Dave, 3b-c	.175	86	228	18	40	6	0	7	23	15	49	1
*Campbell, D.C., of	.219	108	338	44	74	15	5	6	37	47	61	21
*Castleberry, Kevin, 2b	.242	119	372	59	90	18	4	7	27	23	64	15
Champion, Brian, 1b-dh	.263	93	334	36	88	18	1	6	55	34	58	4
Cole, Popeye, of	.293	118	389	64	114	11	4	2	40	27	52	24

Lynchburg's Greg Blosser, named the league's top prospect, had a CL-high 18 homers.

	AVG	G	AB	R	H	2B	3B	HR	RBI	BB	SO	SB
Cuevas, Johnny, c	.255	66	192	12	49	5	1	0	16	8	30	0
Deak, Brian, c	.188	43	133	14	25	3	1	3	16	23	41	2
#Dewey, Todd, c-3b	.167	7	18	1	3	2	0	0	0	4	2	0
Harring, Ken, 2b-3b	.211	96	251	19	53	13	1	1	20	12	34	3
*Klesko, Ryan, 1b-dh	.274	77	292	40	80	16	1	7	47	32	53	10
Maldonado, Phil, c-1b	.215	48	130	7	28	3	0	0	11	8	19	1
Maloney, Rich, ss	.300	47	160	23	48	7	2	2	12	19	18	2
Mitchell, Keith, of	.294	129	456	81	134	24	3	6	48	92	48	18
#Mordecai, Mike, ss	.280	72	271	42	76	11	7	3	36	42	45	10
Perez, Eduardo, c	.237	31	93	9	22	1	0	3	10	1	12	0
*Robles, Josman, 1b-dh . . .	.236	32	89	10	21	5	0	3	14	9	18	0
*Ross, Sean, dh	.272	21	81	9	22	4	0	2	13	3	15	4
Snover, Dan, 3b2b-2b	.215	23	65	11	14	4	0	1	6	3	3	0
*Todd, Theron, of	.255	126	408	49	104	18	3	6	50	53	62	9

PITCHING	W	L	ERA	G	GS	CG	SV	IP	H	R	ER	BB	SO
*Borbon, Pedro	4	5	5.43	11	11	0	0	61	73	40	37	16	37
*Byerly, Rod	2	2	3.33	26	0	0	1	27	29	16	10	8	18
Cummings, Brian	2	5	5.40	14	13	1	0	63	69	42	38	27	50
Czarnik, Chris	5	1	1.15	17	5	0	2	55	33	11	7	17	39
*Diez, Scott	2	1	5.34	20	0	0	2	30	36	20	18	16	17
*Hailey, Roger	3	5	5.11	11	11	1	0	56	57	40	32	26	48
Johnson, Lee	4	4	3.59	29	8	0	3	85	71	38	34	47	73
*Karasinski, Dave	2	1	5.23	24	1	0	4	31	40	25	18	8	24
Longuil, Rich	2	2	3.27	11	0	0	0	22	21	12	8	15	15
Mathews, Eddie	1	0	11.37	6	0	0	1	6	11	10	8	2	7
Minchey, Nate	4	11	3.79	25	24	2	0	133	143	75	56	46	100
Nied, David	1	1	3.83	10	10	0	0	42	38	19	18	14	27
Richey, Rodney	7	1	2.75	42	0	0	10	59	46	21	18	39	72
Rivera, Ben	5	3	3.60	16	13	1	1	75	69	41	30	33	64
*Smith, Chad	0	2	3.86	4	3	0	0	19	17	10	8	5	8
Taylor, Bill	0	0	3.24	5	0	0	0	8	8	3	3	1	10
Tilmon, Pat	6	5	3.90	38	7	0	1	102	105	54	44	37	104
Vazquez, Marcos	4	2	3.79	12	11	1	0	57	60	33	24	29	28
Watson, Preston	10	6	2.42	34	16	2	3	137	101	51	37	60	122
Weems, Danny	0	1	4.05	6	0	0	0	7	5	5	3	5	6
Wendell, Turk	1	3	1.86	6	5	1	0	39	24	10	8	15	26
Wright, Skipper	6	7	3.16	50	1	0	8	117	101	46	41	34	100

FREDERICK

BATTING	AVG	G	AB	R	H	2B	3B	HR	RBI	BB	SO	SB
*Anderson, Brady, dh-of ...	.429	2	7	2	3	1	0	0	3	1	1	0
Beasley, Tony, 2b ...	.251	124	399	57	100	14	6	1	31	30	68	10
Berthel, Daniel, of ...	.267	110	363	58	97	18	2	3	35	33	61	8
*Brooks, Brian, Pr ...	.000	7	0	1	0	0	0	0	0	0	0	0
Devereaux, Mike, of ...	.500	2	8	3	4	0	0	1	3	1	2	1
#Fowler, John, dh ...	.077	7	13	1	1	1	0	0	1	0	7	0
#Gilbert, Roy, of ...	.253	125	471	81	119	26	3	2	48	55	56	22
Gutierrez, Ricky, ss ...	.275	112	425	54	117	16	4	1	46	38	59	12
Harms, Tom, of ...	.100	3	10	0	1	0	0	0	0	2	6	0
Hayden, Paris, of ...	.296	22	54	7	16	1	1	0	6	3	12	1
Hedge, Pat, of ...	.227	67	172	22	39	3	0	3	12	14	45	4
Hildreth, Brad, inf ...	.091	5	11	1	1	1	0	0	1	0	4	0
Holland, Tim, of-3b ...	.302	115	424	63	128	26	4	8	68	38	75	5
Horowitz, Ed, c ...	.315	55	149	18	47	9	0	2	19	13	34	1
Kessinger, Keith, ss-2b ...	.152	64	145	18	22	4	0	0	8	20	36	0
Kingwood, Tyrone, of ...	.335	90	334	47	112	21	0	7	52	30	48	13
Lehman, Mike, c ...	.260	105	346	37	90	20	2	5	42	44	69	7
Lewis, T.R., dh ...	.325	22	80	12	26	4	3	1	11	11	11	5
Lofton, Rodney, dh ...	.556	2	9	1	5	1	0	0	2	0	1	2
Reynolds, Doug, c-dh ...	.246	55	126	14	31	5	0	3	13	18	44	0
*Richardson, Mike, 1b ...	.234	110	334	33	78	13	1	3	33	29	66	0
*Rose, Pete, 3b ...	.232	97	323	32	75	14	2	1	41	26	33	0
Shamburg, Ken, dh-1b ...	.321	66	243	35	78	20	2	7	54	31	38	1
Stiegele, Rob, 2b-3b ...	.217	10	23	2	5	2	0	0	4	3		0
Wearing, Mel, 1b ...	.329	22	79	13	26	5	2	2	14	9	19	0

PITCHING	W	L	ERA	G	GS	CG	SV	IP	H	R	ER	BB	SO
*Brooks, Brian ...	0	0	12.46	3	0	0	0	4	5	9	6	8	7
Bumgarner, Jeff ...	6	6	3.09	17	15	1	0	96	101	42	33	47	67
Deutsch, Mike ...	4	0	4.39	23	4	1	0	68	75	39	33	32	42
Jones, Stacy ...	1	2	3.38	15	0	0	2	27	31	13	10	7	24
Kerr, Zachary ...	14	7	2.94	26	26	5	0	178	160	64	58	56	129
*Leinen, Pat ...	6	6	3.00	14	14	0	0	87	81	36	29	37	45
Mondile, Steve ...	5	4	3.53	32	1	0	3	66	69	35	26	26	27
*O'Donoghue, John ...	0	1	4.50	1	1	0	0	4	5	2	2	0	3
Oquist, Mike ...	9	8	2.81	25	25	3	0	166	134	64	52	48	170
Peraza, Oswald ...	0	2	3.33	7	7	0	0	24	19	14	9	12	28
*Rhodes, Arthur ...	4	6	2.12	13	4	0	0	81	62	25	19	21	103
Ricci, Chuck ...	7	12	4.41	26	18	2	0	122	126	79	60	47	94
Riddle, David ...	2	3	2.34	25	1	0	1	50	45	19	13	26	28
Schullstrom, Erik ...	2	0	3.46	2	2	0	0	13	9	5	5	6	8
Slomkowski, Rich ...	0	0	6.00	26	0	0	3	33	41	22	22	16	24
Stephan, Todd ...	8	2	1.32	42	1	0	17	82	47	17	12	32	102
Telford, Anthony ...	4	2	1.68	8	8	1	0	54	35	15	10	11	49
Williams, Jeff ...	2	1	4.68	16	0	0	1	25	23	17	13	17	31

KINSTON

BATTING	AVG	G	AB	R	H	2B	3B	HR	RBI	BB	SO	SB
*Allison, Jamie, of ...	.281	49	171	34	48	6	2	5	25	20	34	5
Bautista, Ramon, 2b ...	.235	84	260	40	61	12	1	0	20	25	81	12
Costo, Tim, 1b-ss ...	.316	56	206	34	65	13	1	4	42	23	47	4
*Dejardin, Brad, 1b ...	.000	0	0	0	0	0	0	0	0	1	0	0
Eiterman, Tom, dh-of ...	.364	2	11	1	4	0	0	1	4	0	2	0
Falkner, Rick, of ...	.242	61	157	13	38	5	1	3	15	20	34	0
#Foster, Lindsay, ss-3b ...	.280	91	329	46	92	10	1	0	28	23	46	35
Gilmore, Matt, ss ...	.143	9	28	2	4	0	0	0	0	0	11	1
Gomez, Fabio, 3b-of ...	.247	121	430	72	106	18	8	8	52	53	91	13
Johnson, Brian, c ...	.242	80	269	30	65	17	1	9	43	23	83	5
Lane, Nolan, of ...	.253	123	435	66	110	21	5	8	73	36	105	25
*Levis, Jesse, c-dh ...	.296	107	382	63	113	18	3	7	64	64	42	4
*Miller, Billy, of-dh ...	.167	19	42	3	7	1	0	0	7	8	6	0
Odor, Rouglas, 2b-ss ...	.261	114	445	64	116	21	1	2	42	42	99	30
*Orsag, Jim, 1b-dh ...	.296	47	169	39	50	7	2	5	34	24	45	7
*Ramos, Ken, of ...	.345	96	339	71	117	16	6	0	31	48	34	18
*Sanders, Tracy, of ...	.438	10	32	6	14	3	3	0	9	7	6	1
Sarbaugh, Mike, 3b-2b ...	.375	2	8	2	3	0	0	1	3	2	1	0
*Tepper, Marc, 1b ...	.276	108	373	54	103	17	2	5	55	33	56	5
*Thome, Jim, 3b ...	.308	33	117	19	36	4	1	4	16	24	26	4
Verdugo, Mando, dh ...	.154	20	52	4	8	1	0	1	7	7	16	1
Williams, Danny, c-dh ...	.176	28	68	8	12	1	0	1	10	10	13	0
Zambrano, Eddie, of ...	.245	63	204	26	50	7	2	3	30	29	36	1

PITCHING	W	L	ERA	G	GS	CG	SV	IP	H	R	ER	BB	SO
Borgatti, Mike ...	1	1	6.75	7	0	0	1	13	16	11	10	7	13
*Bryant, Shawn ...	1	1	5.19	2	2	0	0	9	10	6	5	7	13
Cole, Chris ...	1	3	5.00	7	6	0	0	36	53	26	20	15	23
Dipoto, Jerry ...	11	4	3.78	24	24	1	0	145	129	75	61	77	143
*Ellis, Tim ...	1	1	3.20	9	2	0	0	20	21	14	7	12	7
Ferlenda, Greg ...	0	2	1.22	46	0	0	23	52	23	10	7	18	60
Gonzales, Mike ...	1	0	4.06	14	0	0	1	31	37	18	14	15	11
*Gonzales, Todd ...	11	4	3.14	19	17	0	0	92	81	41	32	35	61
Howard, Chris ...	1	1	2.45	8	0	0	0	15	21	5	4	6	16
*Kiser, Garland ...	5	3	1.71	55	0	0	9	95	81	25	18	27	82
Kovach, Ty ...	12	3	2.56	18	18	2	0	123	78	46	35	53	90
Kramer, Tommy ...	7	4	2.85	16	16	2	0	98	82	34	31	29	96

Ken Ramos
...top hitter

Mike Gardella
...30 saves

Russ Davis
...37 doubles

	W	L	ERA	G	GS	CG	SV	IP	H	R	ER	BB	SO
Leskanic, Curtis	6	5	3.68	14	14	2	0	73	61	34	30	30	71
Morgan, Scott	1	1	1.32	12	1	0	1	34	21	7	5	16	37
Munoz, Oscar	7	0	2.39	9	9	2	0	64	43	18	17	18	55
Neill, Scott	8	3	2.74	41	0	0	0	82	80	34	25	27	67
Oliveras, David	1	0	5.40	4	4	0	0	15	11	13	9	17	17
Person, Robert	1	0	2.70	4	3	0	0	17	17	6	5	9	7
Peters, Tim	2	1	1.96	12	0	0	1	23	19	7	5	7	27
*Pinder, Chris	7	4	3.29	29	13	0	3	98	104	50	36	28	68
Poehl, Mike	0	1	7.50	4	0	0	0	12	11	10	10	6	7
*Tepper, Marc	0	0	4.50	1	0	0	0	2	2	1	1	2	2
Vespe, Will	3	5	3.29	18	2	0	4	41	31	18	15	19	36

LYNCHBURG

BATTING	AVG	G	AB	R	H	2B	3B	HR	RBI	BB	SO	SB
*Blosser, Greg, of-dh	.282	119	447	63	126	23	1	18	62	55	99	5
Byrd, James, ss	.225	131	511	59	115	20	1	8	45	38	139	24
Dorante, Lou, c	.213	14	47	7	10	2	1	0	3	8	11	1
Flaherty, John, c	.000	1	4	0	0	0	0	0	1	0	1	0
Hanks, Chris, dh	.286	56	161	20	46	14	0	3	16	9	38	4
*Leach, Chris, of	.194	97	279	36	54	3	1	4	22	55	87	3
*Luis, Joe, c	.169	26	65	4	11	1	0	0	7	4	15	0
*Malzone, John, 3b	.257	65	187	18	48	4	1	2	15	27	63	3
Monegro, Miguel, 2b-3b	.262	69	183	18	48	10	0	0	18	13	43	0
Perozo, Ender, of	.230	73	222	12	51	10	4	3	26	17	68	4
Powers, Scott, 2b	.238	122	433	54	103	13	2	2	36	59	99	7
#Rivers, Mickey, of	.216	113	408	42	88	13	7	3	39	8	102	22
Spencer, John, of	.250	7	16	4	4	2	0	0	4	2	4	0
#Tatum, Willie, dh-1b	.223	93	319	38	71	16	1	9	35	38	69	14
*Wallin, Les, 1b	.234	114	389	56	91	17	1	15	50	48	95	1
#Weidie, Stu, of	.146	26	96	10	14	1	0	1	7	14	32	1
Whitehead, Chris, 3b-of	.210	117	377	50	79	13	3	7	33	71	164	7
Williams, Paul, c	.236	113	394	58	93	14	4	16	64	58	69	3

PITCHING	W	L	ERA	G	GS	CG	SV	IP	H	R	ER	BB	SO
Abril, Odie	0	1	7.36	2	0	0	0	4	9	4	3	1	3
*Brown, Paul	4	7	5.17	27	11	0	1	92	96	64	53	56	77
Conroy, Brian	10	12	3.53	26	26	8	0	186	160	84	73	51	147
Davis, Freddie	3	2	2.70	35	0	0	15	47	43	17	14	11	29
Estrada, Pete	7	7	3.05	25	25	2	0	153	153	71	52	55	88
*Landry, Howard	7	8	5.00	28	20	0	1	122	146	76	68	49	84
Powers, Terry	0	7	4.45	11	10	0	0	55	60	40	27	28	27
Pratts, Tato	6	1	6.64	29	0	0	0	62	73	51	46	34	23
Ryan, Ken	6	14	5.13	28	28	3	0	161	182	104	92	82	109
Scott, Rennie	6	8	3.87	57	0	0	11	91	93	44	39	29	90
Stange, Tim	0	3	5.97	33	0	0	1	57	62	40	38	23	31
*Taylor, Scott	5	6	2.73	13	13	1	0	89	76	36	27	30	120
Uhrhan, Kevin	4	4	4.21	29	5	0	1	77	77	45	36	38	53

PENINSULA

BATTING	AVG	G	AB	R	H	2B	3B	HR	RBI	BB	SO	SB
#Bailey, Lash, 1b-dh	.211	102	342	40	72	10	0	7	33	43	100	3
Barbara, Dan, c-dh	.279	79	247	27	69	6	0	0	17	37	62	3
Boone, Bret, 2b	.267	74	255	42	68	13	2	8	38	47	57	5
Brakebill, Mark, 3b	.178	50	157	15	28	6	1	0	13	8	53	1
Campanis, Jim, c	.250	112	364	47	91	22	0	14	60	40	76	3
Holley, Bobby, of-ss	.258	85	306	35	79	15	1	8	43	33	46	4
King, Bryan, ss	.231	70	260	37	60	6	3	0	28	32	31	13
Pezzoni, Ron, of	.267	109	408	47	109	15	4	2	42	23	59	26
Pilkinton, Lem, 1b-3b	.239	114	394	37	94	13	4	3	43	54	104	3
Raasch, Glen, c-dh	.000	5	12	1	0	0	0	0	0	2	7	0
#Robles, Jorge, 3b-ss	.252	98	345	34	87	9	1	0	27	38	23	18
*Saetre, Damon, of	.216	110	352	36	76	8	2	1	32	42	66	8
Santana, Ruben, ss-2b	.213	26	80	3	17	1	0	0	5	1	22	6
Tavarez, Jesus, of	.237	108	379	39	90	10	1	0	32	20	79	40
Thomas, Delvin, 2b-of	.194	84	258	28	50	7	1	4	19	14	81	3

BATTING

R	Greg Sims, Salem	91
H	Bruce Schreiber, Salem	160
TB	Armando Romero, Sal	222
2B	Russ Davis, Pr. William	37
3B	Fabio Gomez, Kinston	8
	Tim Hines, Salem	8
HR	Greg Blosser, Lynchburg	18
RBI	Armando Romero, Sal	90
SH	Tony Beasley, Frederick	12
SF	Tim Costo, Kinston	8
	Doug Welch, W-S	8
BB	Greg Sims, Salem	111
IBB	John Jensen, W-S	8
HBP	Jim Campanis, Peninsula	18
SO	Chris Whitehead, Lynch	164
SB	Fernando Ramsey, W-S	43
CS	Roy Gilbert, Frederick	20
OB%	Ken Ramos, Kinston	.426

PITCHING

G	Mike Gardella, Pr. William	62
GS	Three tied at	28
CG	Brian Conroy, Lynchburg	8
ShO	Brian Conroy, Lynchburg	4
Sv	Mike Gardella, Pr. William	30
W	Frank Seminara, PW	16
L	Three tied at	14
IP	Tim Wakefield, Salem	190
H	Tim Wakefield, Salem	187
R	Steve Buckholz, Salem	110
HR	Tim Wakefield, Salem	24
BB	Tim Wakefield, Salem	85
HB	Steve Buckholz, Salem	13
SO	Mike Oquist, Frederick	170
WP	Mike Pomeranz, Salem	24
Bk	Jeff Darwin, Peninsula	9

	AVG	G	AB	R	H	2B	3B	HR	RBI	BB	SO	SB
*Thomas, Kelvin, of	.194	104	278	32	54	7	2	4	20	26	78	4
Williams, Landon, 2b	.119	23	59	6	7	1	0	0	1	8	23	2

PITCHING	W	L	ERA	G	GS	CG	SV	IP	H	R	ER	BB	SO
Balabon, Rick	7	4	2.65	14	14	4	0	102	73	35	30	24	107
*Czarkowski, Mark	8	6	2.32	21	16	3	0	116	128	50	30	34	40
Darwin, Jeff	8	14	4.01	25	25	1	0	150	153	86	67	57	89
*Duke, Kyle	0	8	7.79	14	12	0	0	54	78	54	47	36	36
Garcia, Marcos	3	7	4.31	36	7	0	1	100	113	54	48	45	89
*Gordon, Anthony	0	3	5.02	25	3	0	0	43	40	37	24	48	45
Gutierrez, Jim	11	13	3.44	28	28	4	0	186	171	82	71	41	95
*King, Kevin	4	2	4.46	7	7	0	0	36	42	23	18	13	20
Lodgek, Scott	1	6	4.44	12	8	0	0	47	54	26	23	21	27
Loe, Darin	4	5	3.25	46	3	0	5	89	81	33	32	39	76
Mullins, Ron	2	5	5.57	35	3	0	1	74	84	61	46	53	66
Nelson, Jeff	2	2	3.15	18	7	1	6	60	47	21	21	25	49
Poissant, Rod	1	2	1.47	26	0	0	9	31	24	10	5	18	26
*Rivas, Oscar	1	3	4.46	34	0	0	5	42	50	33	21	13	42
Rivera, Randy	5	3	3.23	17	7	0	2	61	54	25	22	25	37

PRINCE WILLIAM

BATTING	AVG	G	AB	R	H	2B	3B	HR	RBI	BB	SO	SB
Ausmus, Brad, c	.236	107	364	46	86	12	2	0	27	32	73	2
Blackwell, Juan, 2b	.241	27	79	10	19	2	0	0	6	1	24	2
Bridges, Jason, of	.210	58	157	16	33	9	1	0	10	8	28	4
Davis, Russ, 3b	.249	137	510	55	127	37	3	16	71	37	136	3
Erhardt, Herb, dh-c	.210	43	105	5	22	3	0	2	12	11	26	0
Hernandez, Enrique, dh-c	.250	107	360	39	90	20	2	6	47	40	68	0
*Howell, Dave, of	.220	104	337	36	74	12	1	3	24	59	63	1
Knoblauh, Jay, of	.221	38	131	17	29	6	0	2	9	10	23	5
Obando, Sherman, of	.267	121	439	67	117	24	6	10	67	42	85	5
#Oster, Paul, of	.239	96	327	39	78	13	4	4	34	17	53	3
Rodriguez, Andres, 2b-ss	.241	33	79	9	19	2	0	0	7	2	19	2
Silvestri, Dave, ss	.258	131	465	74	120	30	7	5	56	77	90	37
#Snow, J.T., 1b	.256	138	520	57	133	25	1	8	72	46	65	2
*Viera, John, of	.243	68	235	33	57	6	4	4	26	36	59	27
*Weeks, Tom, 1b	.211	9	19	0	4	1	0	0	3	1	3	0
#Zazueta, Mauricio, 2b	.266	122	417	51	111	20	6	0	36	28	81	21

PITCHING	W	L	ERA	G	GS	CG	SV	IP	H	R	ER	BB	SO
*Canestro, Art	7	7	4.34	29	10	0	0	83	85	47	40	33	46
Draper, Mike	0	2	6.35	5	4	1	0	23	31	20	16	9	8
*Gardella, Mike	4	3	2.01	62	0	0	30	72	61	18	16	31	86
Gilbert, Brent	0	1	3.49	13	1	0	0	28	29	12	11	10	22
Greer, Ken	1	0	2.35	1	1	0	0	8	7	2	2	2	7
Hartzog, Cullen	5	6	3.75	18	18	1	0	106	101	48	44	57	100
Marris, Mark	0	1	6.38	7	5	0	0	24	26	21	17	8	13
Martel, Ed	8	13	4.08	25	25	2	0	143	134	77	65	65	95
Moody, James	3	2	2.35	54	0	0	3	88	67	25	23	31	103
*Nielsen, Gerald	7	12	3.92	26	26	1	0	152	149	76	66	79	119
Polak, Rich	3	6	2.69	44	1	0	1	77	75	30	23	25	61
Prybylinski, Bruce	1	2	3.92	9	1	0	0	21	17	9	9	4	20
Ralph, Curtis	4	3	3.15	43	0	0	0	80	69	30	28	40	75
Seminara, Frank	16	8	1.90	25	25	4	0	170	136	51	36	52	132
Wiley, Jim	5	9	4.34	22	22	0	0	114	121	67	55	51	76

SALEM

BATTING	AVG	G	AB	R	H	2B	3B	HR	RBI	BB	SO	SB
Antigua, Felix, c-dh	.194	30	108	9	21	2	0	0	7	7	16	0
#Bailey, Rob, 2b-ss	.181	74	227	28	41	6	2	1	19	25	71	12
*Brewington, Mike, of-1b	.237	21	76	11	18	4	1	2	12	10	14	0
Caraballo, Nelson, c	.000	1	1	0	0	0	0	0	0	0	0	0

	AVG	G	AB	R	H	2B	3B	HR	RBI	BB	SO	SB
Estep, Chris, of	.214	110	350	52	75	13	2	17	53	58	126	9
*Greene, Willie, ss	.183	17	60	9	11	1	1	3	9	7	18	0
*Hines, Tim, 1b-c	.279	106	380	44	106	17	8	11	55	28	72	3
*Holmes, Bill, 1b-of	.000	6	11	0	0	0	0	0	0	0	3	0
Huyler, Mike, ss	.296	67	247	23	73	9	2	2	30	10	40	6
Manahan, Austin, 3b	.279	41	154	22	43	6	2	4	24	11	51	8
McNabb, Glen, 2b	.267	49	146	21	39	5	0	0	13	19	21	3
*Merejo, Domingo, of-dh	.283	82	290	37	82	12	6	9	56	23	50	1
Morrison, Brian, dh-of	.183	18	60	4	11	2	0	0	3	5	25	1
Pennye, Darwin, of	.284	104	405	51	115	27	4	10	52	23	74	15
Raisanen, Keith, dh-1b	.120	19	50	7	6	2	0	0	3	10	22	0
Rodriguez, Roman, ss	.183	24	82	6	15	4	0	0	7	6	17	0
#Romero, Armando, c-dh	.291	124	466	62	134	31	3	17	90	55	68	0
Schreiber, Bruce, 3b-2b	.290	134	552	71	160	24	5	4	48	33	109	6
Shelton, Ben, 1b	.206	109	320	44	66	10	2	10	36	55	116	1
#Sims, Greg, of	.245	128	466	91	114	16	6	5	46	111	104	31
*Trusky, Ken, of	.304	43	148	24	45	10	2	0	9	21	20	7
Williams, Flavio, 2b	.230	47	100	16	23	4	1	2	8	7	17	1

PITCHING	W	L	ERA	G	GS	CG	SV	IP	H	R	ER	BB	SO
*Bird, Dave	3	1	2.93	8	0	0	0	15	13	9	5	10	27
Buckholz, Steve	8	10	6.01	32	22	3	0	138	168	110	92	75	64
Czajkowski, Jim	1	1	2.57	18	0	0	6	28	17	10	8	11	26
Deller, Tom	1	2	4.43	16	0	0	3	22	26	17	11	18	19
Duncan, Chip	6	4	5.21	37	3	2	1	85	105	61	49	48	95
Fansler, Stan	0	5	4.26	10	10	0	0	51	44	29	24	23	35
Felix, Antonio	0	3	7.54	8	3	0	0	23	23	21	19	19	17
*Honeywell, Brent	2	2	6.65	22	0	0	0	43	60	39	32	23	21
*Latham, John	1	4	6.46	8	8	0	0	39	51	39	28	24	25
McDowell, Tim	6	9	3.82	32	11	0	2	113	114	62	48	56	90
Miller, Paul	8	6	2.45	22	22	5	0	151	145	58	41	33	83
Murphy, Pete	0	2	5.59	3	3	0	0	19	22	15	12	8	12
Neely, Jeff	0	1	2.45	6	0	0	2	7	5	2	2	3	11
*Pomeranz, Mike	3	7	6.90	35	3	0	1	59	68	58	45	54	43
Richardson, Keith	3	3	3.82	9	9	3	0	66	64	34	28	19	50
*Schlopy, Butch	1	4	4.07	16	6	0	0	49	55	31	22	18	25
*Underwood, Bobby	1	4	6.80	10	7	0	0	41	52	38	31	24	26
Wagner, Paul	0	1	5.00	11	4	0	2	36	39	22	20	17	28
Wakefield, Tim	10	14	4.73	28	28	2	0	190	187	109	100	85	127
Williams, Roger	0	0	8.59	10	0	0	0	15	24	18	14	8	12
Zimmerman, Mike	1	1	5.96	19	0	0	8	26	28	19	17	16	24

WINSTON-SALEM

BATTING	AVG	G	AB	R	H	2B	3B	HR	RBI	BB	SO	SB
Adames, Juan, 2b-3b	.167	36	54	5	9	1	1	0	4	6	10	1
Bell, Lenny, 1b-3b	.250	51	176	20	44	12	2	4	27	17	55	2
#Blair, Paul, 2b	.278	118	425	48	118	11	3	1	36	53	62	11
Castellano, Pete, 3b	.197	19	66	6	13	0	0	1	8	10	11	1
Craig, Dale, c	.181	56	127	15	23	1	0	2	9	17	34	1
#Griffin, Ty, of	.217	33	120	18	26	8	1	1	10	28	39	8
*Jensen, John, of	.246	126	403	59	99	17	4	12	67	77	95	4
Moore, Timothy, 2b	.200	4	5	0	1	0	0	0	0	0	2	0
Murphy, Jim, of	.246	23	69	7	17	2	1	1	11	1	17	2
*Paulino, Elvin, 1b	.262	109	409	69	107	23	2	14	63	49	66	5
Posey, John, c	.254	27	71	10	18	3	0	0	4	17	4	0
Ramsey, Fernando, of	.255	124	428	52	109	12	4	5	48	19	50	43
#Roberson, Kevin, of	.268	85	313	49	84	23	3	5	45	25	70	7
Scott, Gary, 3b	.295	102	380	63	112	22	0	12	70	29	66	17
Simonds, Dan, c	.156	27	64	5	10	0	0	0	2	4	4	0
Smith, Tracy, ss-3b	.243	68	144	19	35	5	1	1	21	11	33	7
Taylor, Scott, c	.276	64	203	25	56	8	0	0	25	18	23	0
Welch, Doug, dh	.320	107	363	58	116	20	3	11	68	20	65	1
White, Billy, ss	.269	134	505	85	136	15	2	5	54	70	108	25
*Williams, Eddie, of-dh	.234	114	367	61	86	11	5	8	34	58	73	12

PITCHING	W	L	ERA	G	GS	CG	SV	IP	H	R	ER	BB	SO
Bullinger, Jim	7	6	3.70	14	13	3	0	90	81	43	37	46	85
Caballero, Ed	4	3	3.28	9	9	0	0	49	49	25	18	15	29
Davis, Braz	9	9	3.91	26	18	3	1	127	118	71	55	46	109
DiBartolomeo, Steve	5	4	3.50	41	4	2	12	108	101	54	42	48	73
Eddings, Jay	2	3	3.89	29	0	0	12	42	38	19	18	8	34
Gardner, John	5	4	3.53	34	2	0	5	87	70	40	34	55	97
*Jaques, Eric	0	0	3.86	2	0	0	0	2	5	1	1	1	0
Jones, Shannon	7	5	3.22	18	17	1	0	101	99	44	36	28	107
Kazmierczak, Bill	3	4	3.25	8	8	0	0	53	68	20	19	26	32
Lopez, Marcos	8	3	2.54	15	15	4	0	110	110	40	31	18	66
Massicotte, Jeff	1	0	3.38	6	0	0	0	8	8	5	3	4	7
Melvin, Bill	8	3	3.41	30	14	1	0	119	107	51	45	71	88
Rasp, Ronnie	0	0	12.27	4	0	0	0	4	8	5	5	1	3
Robinson, Brett	0	1	1.04	2	1	1	0	9	8	1	1	1	5
Salles, John	14	5	2.58	25	25	4	0	171	160	59	49	48	100
Smith, Tracy	0	0	0.00	3	0	0	0	5	1	0	0	1	3
*Sodders, Mike	7	1	2.06	12	12	2	0	74	57	20	17	25	43
Strauss, Julio	1	1	1.93	25	0	0	11	28	24	8	6	6	25
*Stroud, Derek	5	1	3.35	34	0	0	3	40	37	18	15	26	47
Taylor, Aaron	0	0	0.00	1	0	0	0	2	1	0	0	2	0
Willis, Travis	0	1	20.77	2	2	0	0	4	13	12	10	3	2

FLORIDA STATE LEAGUE

Dodgers emerge through back door to win title

By DAVID JONES

It was the year of the improbable comeback in the Florida State League in 1990.

Start with the Vero Beach Dodgers, who spent April trying to stay out of the cellar in the league's Eastern Division, then used September for a championship run. The Dodgers finished with the best second-place record in the league's three divisions in the second half of the 1990 season and qualified for post-season play as a wild card team.

Nikco Riesgo
...MVP

They beat St. Lucie, the other wild card entry, in three games to advance to the semi-final round. Next up was defending league champion Charlotte, and the Dodgers again prevailed, 2-1.

The obstacle the Dodgers faced in the championship round, however, was West Palm Beach, owners of the best record (92-40) among full-season clubs in Organized Baseball in 1990.

The Expos blasted Vero Beach in the opener, 7-2, but the Dodgers came back with a pair of 2-1 wins to claim the title. Dodgers second baseman Eric Young faked a bunt then punched the ball past a drawn-in infield for the winning hit in the ninth inning of the deciding game.

Expos settle for second

West Palm Beach had to settle for a consolation prize, despite winning at a season-long .697 clip and winning the Eastern Division in both halves. Felipe Alou was selected the league's manager of the year.

One of the primary reasons for the Expos success was pitcher

LEAGUE CHAMPIONS

Playoff Champions, Where Applicable

1990—Vero Beach	1968—Orlando	1946—Orlando
1989—Charlotte	1967—St. Petersburg	1942-45—Did Not
1988—St. Lucie	1966—Leesburg	Operate
1987—Ft. Lauderdale	1965—Ft. Lauderdale	1941—Leesburg
1986—St. Petersburg	1964—Ft. Lauderdale	1940—Orlando
1985—Ft. Myers	1963—Sarasota	1939—Sanford
1984—Ft. Lauderdale	1962—Ft. Lauderdale	1938—Gainesville
1983—Vero Beach	1961—Tampa	1937—Gainesville
1982—Ft. Lauderdale	1960—Palatka	1936—St. Augustine
1981—Daytona Beach	1959—St. Petersburg	1928-35—Did Not
1980—Ft. Lauderdale	1958—St. Petersburg	Operate
1979—Winter Haven	1957—Tampa	1927—Orlando
1978—Miami	1956—Cocoa	1926—Sanford
1977—Lakeland	1955—Orlando	1925—Tampa
1976—Lakeland	1954—Lakeland	1924—Lakeland
1975—St. Petersburg	1953—Daytona Bch.	1923—Orlando
1974—W. Palm Bch.	1952—Palatka	1922—St. Petersburg
1973—St. Petersburg	1951—DeLand	1921—Orlando
1972—Miami	1950—DeLand	1920—Tampa
1971—Miami	1949—St. Augustine	1919—*Sanford
1970—Miami	1948—Daytona Bch.	*Orlando
1969—Miami	1947—Gainesville	*co-champions

Former **NFL** running back D.J. Dozier enjoyed an all-star **FSL** season, hitting .297 with 13 homers.

Chris Pollack, who missed the entire 1989 season because of rotator cuff surgery. Pollack came back to post a 13-2 record.

Dunedin started the year as the hottest team in minor league baseball. The D-Jays broke FSL marks for wins in the first half (53-14) and winning percentage (.791).

Miami showed the biggest attendance gain. The Miracle, playing in nearby Pompano Beach, drew 43,157 fans—compared to a league-worst 14,972 the previous season.

The Miracle, struggling to field a competitive team but finding no support from major league clubs in their never-ending search for player help, took advantage of a rule which allows non-affiliated Class A clubs to enter the June amateur draft. Beginning with the fourth round, the Miracle picked 16 players, signed 15 of them, and paid out close to $250,000 in bonuses.

They showed marked improvement in the second half, posting a 29-39 record compared to 15-54 in the first half. That didn't keep Mike Easler around, who quit as the team's manager in August.

Riesgo selected MVP

St. Lucie's Nikco Riesgo started the year as a 23-year-old question mark. He ended it as the league's most valuable player and near triple crown winner, hitting .298 with 14 homers, 98 RBIs and 46 steals. The New York Mets then traded Riesgo to Philadelphia and the first baseman found himself in Triple-A by the end of the 1990 season.

At Charlotte, Barry Manuel was a pitcher with a fastball in the mid-90s who had struggled in three years of pro ball. Manuel went to Texas Rangers officials and asked for a shot at being a full-time reliever again. He had been an All-American in that role at Louisiana State.

Manuel went on to collect 37 saves in 56 games, shattering the old league mark of 33, set by Aguedo Vasquez of Baseball City in 1988.

Around the league

Perhaps the player who caused the biggest stir in the FSL in 1990 was D.J. Dozier, an athlete known more for his football talents as a Minnesota Vikings running back. Dozier shook off the rust from not playing baseball in several years and played well enough for St. Lucie to earn a promotion to Class AA in late season ... Jacob Brumfield of Baseball City had a tremendous year, winning the batting title with a .336 mark despite being released briefly during spring training ... Kenny Lofton, an athlete known more for his basketball talents at Arizona, hit .331 to finish second in the batting race and stole 62 bases ... In a season of new faces, it was an old, familiar one who accomplished the most amazing of feats. In his 27th season as a minor league manager, Lakeland's John Lipon collected his 2,000th win.

1990 FINAL STANDINGS

FIRST HALF

East	W	L	Pct.	GB
West Palm Beach (Expos)	49	19	.721	—
Vero Beach (Dodgers)	41	27	.603	8
St. Lucie (Mets)	39	29	.574	10
Ft. Lauderdale (Yankees)	33	36	.478	16½
Miami (Independent)	15	54	.217	34½

Central	W	L	Pct.	GB
Lakeland (Tigers)	44	24	.647	—
Osceola (Astros)	36	34	.523	9
Baseball City (Royals)	29	41	.414	16
Winter Haven (Red Sox)	16	54	.229	29

West	W	L	Pct.	GB
Dunedin (Blue Jays)	53	14	.791	—
Charlotte (Rangers)	44	24	.647	9½
St. Petersburg (Cards)	30	35	.462	22
Sarasota (White Sox)	27	42	.391	27
Clearwater (Phillies)	23	46	.333	31

SECOND HALF

East	W	L	Pct.	GB
West Palm Beach (Expos)	43	21	.672	—
Vero Beach (Dodgers)	38	29	.567	6½
St. Lucie (Mets)	37	29	.561	7
Miami (Independent)	29	39	.426	16
Ft. Lauderdale (Yankees)	29	39	.426	16

Central	W	L	Pct.	GB
Lakeland (Tigers)	39	25	.609	—
Osceola (Astros)	36	32	.529	5
Baseball City (Royals)	31	37	.456	10
Winter Haven (Red Sox)	24	40	.375	15

West	W	L	Pct.	GB
Charlotte (Rangers)	41	29	.586	—
Sarasota (White Sox)	36	33	.522	4½
Dunedin (Blue Jays)	31	38	.449	9½
St. Petersburg (Cards)	30	39	.435	10½
Clearwater (Phillies)	27	41	.397	13

OVERALL

	W	L	Pct.	GB
West Palm Beach (Expos)	92	40	.697	—
Lakeland (Tigers)	83	49	.629	9
Dunedin (Blue Jays)	84	52	.618	10
Charlotte (Rangers)	85	53	.616	10
Vero Beach (Dodgers)	79	56	.585	14½
St. Lucie (Mets)	76	58	.567	17
Osceola (Astros)	72	66	.522	23
Sarasota (White Sox)	63	75	.457	32
Ft. Lauderdale (Yankees)	62	75	.453	32½
St. Petersburg (Cards)	60	74	.448	33
Baseball City (Royals)	60	78	.435	35
Clearwater (Phillies)	50	87	.365	44½
Miami (Independent)	44	93	.321	50½
Winter Haven (Red Sox)	40	94	.299	53

Playoffs: Vero Beach defeated St. Lucie 2-1 in best-of-3 quarterfinal; Charlotte defeated Dunedin 2-0 in best-of-3 quarterfinal; West Palm Beach defeated Lakeland 2-1 in best-of-3 semifinal; Vero Beach defeated Charlotte 2-1 in best-of-3 semifinal; Vero Beach defeated West Palm Beach 2-1 in best-of-3 final to win league championship.

Regular-Season Attendance: St. Petersburg, 190,146; Charlotte, 122,478; Vero Beach, 94,832; Clearwater, 91,040; West Palm Beach, 83,673; St. Lucie, 65,597; Dunedin, 65,348; Lakeland, 57,967; Sarasota, 51,775; Osceola, 46,421; Miami, 43,580; Ft. Lauderdale, 34,826; Winter Haven, 23,008; Baseball City, 18,884.

Managers: Baseball City—Brian Poldberg; **Charlotte**—Bobby Jones; **Clearwater**—Lee Elia; **Dunedin**—Dennis Holmberg; **Ft. Lauderdale**—Mike Hart; **Lakeland**—John Lipon; **Miami**—Mike Easler, Freddi Gonzalez. **Osceola**—Sal Butera; **St. Lucie**—Tim Blackwell; **St. Petersburg**—Joe Pettini; **Sarasota**—Tony Franklin; **Vero Beach**—Joe Alvarez; **West Palm Beach**—Felipe Alou; **Winter Haven**—Dave Holt.

1990 Official All-Star Team: C—Ivan Rodriguez, Charlotte; Jason Townley, Dunedin. **1B**—Nikco Riesgo, St. Lucie. **2B**—Jeff Kent, Dunedin. **3B**—Fred Samson, Charlotte. **SS**—Keith Kimberlin, Lakeland. **UTIL INF**—Javier Ocasio, Sarasota. **OF**—D.J. Dozier, St. Lucie; Kenny Lofton, Osceola; Jacob Brumfield, Baseball City. **UTIL OF**—Juan DeLaRosa, Dunedin. **DH**—Greg O'Halloran, Dunedin. **RHP**—John Johnstone, St. Lucie; Ramon Taveras, Vero Beach. **LHP**—Anthony Ward, Dunedin; Chris Pollack, West Palm Beach. **RP**—Barry Manuel, Charlotte; Larry Stanford, Ft. Lauderdale. **Most Valuable Player**—Nikco Riesgo, St. Lucie. **Manager of the Year**—Felipe Alou, West Palm Beach.

Top 10 Major League Prospects (by Baseball America): 1. Ivan Rodriguez, c, Charlotte; **2.** Jeff Juden, rhp, Osceola; **3.** Denis Boucher, lhp, Dunedin; **4.** Nikco Riesgo, 1b, St. Lucie; **5.** Kenny Lofton, of, Osceola; **6.** Jeff Kent, 2b, Dunedin; **7.** Ivan Cruz, 1b, Lakeland; **8.** Mike Timlin, rhp, Dunedin; **9.** John Johnstone, rhp, St. Lucie; **10.** D.J. Dozier, of, St. Lucie.

CLUB BATTING

	AVG	G	AB	R	H	2B	3B	HR	BB	SO	SB
Vero Beach	.266	136	4406	673	1173	219	31	60	522	746	307
Dunedin	.256	136	4548	639	1163	203	46	92	454	966	111
Charlotte	.252	138	4480	581	1130	183	52	30	539	855	127
Lakeland	.252	133	4239	559	1067	161	45	35	485	757	123
West Palm Beach	.251	132	4359	597	1096	167	44	36	509	764	172
St. Lucie	.250	134	4253	641	1063	154	43	59	533	1000	273
Osceola	.246	138	4496	603	1106	151	55	36	587	942	207
Ft. Lauderdale	.246	137	4387	537	1078	199	37	47	490	866	150
Baseball City	.243	138	4437	542	1079	148	35	26	434	820	234
Sarasota	.241	138	4488	536	1080	155	38	32	561	912	145
St. Petersburg	.239	134	4366	515	1044	164	38	31	512	774	120
Clearwater	.235	137	4419	476	1037	161	45	26	422	775	111
Miami	.227	137	4349	437	987	163	25	33	505	1038	156
Winter Haven	.222	134	4367	439	970	156	33	34	432	1016	168

CLUB PITCHING

	ERA	G	CG	SHO	SV	IP	H	R	ER	BB	SO
Charlotte	2.34	138	10	20	51	1201	860	404	313	492	982
Lakeland	2.50	133	9	21	40	1143	983	406	317	388	932
West Palm Beach	2.63	132	5	17	59	1166	1055	428	341	423	840
Dunedin	3.16	136	5	15	41	1203	1037	511	423	482	966
St. Lucie	3.29	134	25	8	33	1145	1063	531	419	421	808
Osceola	3.32	138	6	7	33	1213	1047	576	447	586	947
St. Petersburg	3.35	134	10	11	30	1184	1107	527	441	439	842
Sarasota	3.40	138	12	9	33	1208	1135	575	456	460	898
Vero Beach	3.43	136	15	16	36	1164	1048	532	444	525	859
Clearwater	3.58	137	14	4	26	1160	1085	595	462	536	830
Winter Haven	4.07	134	10	9	23	1162	1129	658	525	530	777
Ft. Lauderdale	4.10	137	12	3	19	1177	1177	654	532	491	851
Baseball City	4.29	138	4	3	37	1169	1146	675	557	606	837
Miami	4.50	137	16	7	18	1157	1201	703	578	606	862

INDIVIDUAL BATTING LEADERS
(Minimum 378 Plate Appearances)

	AVG	G	AB	R	H	2B	3B	HR	RBI	BB	SO	SB
Brumfield, Jacob, BC	.336	109	372	66	125	24	3	0	40	60	44	47
*Lofton, Kenny, Osc	.331	124	481	98	159	15	5	2	35	61	77	62
Vargas, Hector, FtL	.308	117	429	48	132	20	9	0	61	30	68	21
Riesgo, Nikco, StL	.298	131	456	93	136	35	3	14	94	74	77	46

	AVG	G	AB	R	H	2B	3B	HR	RBI	BB	SO	SB
Barron, Anthony, VB	.297	111	344	58	102	21	3	6	60	30	82	42
Massarelli, John, Osc	.295	120	396	55	117	8	3	2	50	41	73	54
#Munoz, Jose, VB	.295	113	397	57	117	18	3	2	47	34	43	28
Townley, Jason, Dun	.292	119	397	58	116	22	1	11	63	41	82	1
Ocasio, Javier, Sar	.292	127	497	65	145	13	3	1	45	55	67	45
#Zinter, Alan, StL	.291	98	333	63	97	19	6	7	63	54	70	8

INDIVIDUAL PITCHING LEADERS
(Minimum 112 Innings)

	W	L	ERA	G	GS	CG	SV	IP	H	R	ER	BB	SO
Brown, Rob, Char	8	5	1.90	40	4	0	4	119	73	33	25	40	102
Freed, Dan, WPB	12	8	2.00	26	25	1	0	171	188	63	38	32	98
*Pollack, Chris, WPB	13	2	2.05	24	24	0	0	140	111	38	32	62	91
Compres, Fidel, Char	9	2	2.24	22	16	2	1	117	89	38	29	43	69
Johnstone, John, StL	15	6	2.24	25	25	0	0	173	145	53	43	60	120
Sanders, Al, WH	7	7	2.30	31	11	3	0	113	95	37	29	35	113
Sommer, David, WPB	11	4	2.37	29	19	1	0	133	89	43	35	64	126
Krumm, Todd, Lake	7	9	2.41	25	24	6	1	146	135	48	39	49	112
*Terrill, Jim, VB	12	4	2.53	23	21	1	0	132	117	44	37	35	80
Gohr, Greg, Lake	13	5	2.62	25	25	0	0	138	125	52	40	50	90

BASEBALL CITY

BATTING	AVG	G	AB	R	H	2B	3B	HR	RBI	BB	SO	SB
#Andrews, Jay, of	.278	21	79	5	22	1	1	0	4	3	17	4
*Beall, Mike, 1b-dh	.201	64	204	20	41	5	1	1	24	31	26	0
Bridges-Clements, Tony, 2b-dh	.257	63	214	32	55	3	1	1	14	20	40	11
Brumfield, Jacob, of	.336	109	372	66	125	24	3	0	40	60	44	47
Collins, Sean, 2b-of	.238	85	256	36	61	8	2	1	30	40	40	31
Deleon, Huascar, c	.206	12	34	2	7	3	0	0	4	3	10	0
Dyer, Linton, c	.196	42	92	15	18	1	0	0	6	19	27	4
Garber, Jeff, 3b-2b	.215	129	446	53	96	12	2	6	46	53	96	17
Garibaldo, Chris, ss	.205	93	303	27	62	8	2	0	20	16	33	4
Gonzalez, David, ss	.206	20	68	8	14	3	0	0	4	4	16	6
Griesser, Grant, c-1b	.248	44	129	10	32	3	0	1	9	14	24	2
Holley, Bobby, dh-3b	.205	27	88	16	18	5	0	3	14	15	20	1
#Indriago, Juan, 2b-3b	.135	19	37	8	5	0	1	0	0	11	12	1
Koenig, Gary, c	.229	89	275	23	63	11	0	0	22	14	68	0
*Long, Kevin, of-1b	.282	85	308	53	87	17	5	2	33	32	28	22
Moser, Ricky, 3b-2b	.146	12	41	3	6	0	0	0	3	3	15	0
Robinson, Darryl, 1b-3b ...	.262	115	409	38	107	9	3	2	65	17	33	7
Schreiner, John, 1b	.161	8	31	2	5	0	0	1	3	1	8	0
*Walker, Hugh, of	.244	128	463	51	113	15	6	4	54	32	107	28
Watkins, Daren, of	.250	120	448	53	112	18	5	2	48	31	134	40
Wright, Don, of	.250	20	48	7	12	1	1	2	11	9	11	1

PITCHING	W	L	ERA	G	GS	CG	SV	IP	H	R	ER	BB	SO
Alicano, Pedro	3	3	4.13	20	0	0	1	48	51	27	22	21	28
Berumen, Andres	3	5	4.30	9	9	1	0	44	30	27	21	28	35
Brucato, Bob	0	1	14.54	4	0	0	0	4	8	7	7	3	2
Chrisman, Jim	0	0	4.50	2	0	0	0	4	4	2	2	1	4
Drohan, Bill	1	5	8.54	7	7	0	0	33	48	38	31	22	16
Dunn, Bubba	4	3	3.86	19	7	0	0	68	43	36	29	44	55
Harvey, Greg	5	1	2.04	7	7	0	0	40	27	14	9	19	29
Harwell, Dave	1	2	7.04	13	1	0	0	15	15	16	12	29	14
Hoeme, Steve	2	2	3.30	33	1	0	0	60	49	28	22	40	51
Hopper, Brad	10	10	4.13	30	18	0	2	137	138	71	63	55	72
Hudson, Jim	9	5	3.16	16	15	0	0	103	105	43	36	22	50
Johnston, Joel	2	4	4.88	31	7	1	7	55	36	37	30	49	60
*Magee, Byron	2	5	6.24	32	4	0	1	62	71	50	43	52	25
McCormick, John	1	4	7.00	11	3	0	1	36	52	35	28	25	33
Nelson, Doug	0	0	4.50	1	1	0	0	2	3	1	1	0	2
Otto, Steve	5	6	3.83	24	16	2	1	106	119	52	45	25	60
Parnell, Mark	2	2	1.86	36	0	0	17	39	24	9	8	15	40
Pichardo, Hipolito	1	6	3.80	11	10	0	0	45	47	28	19	25	40
*Pierce, Ben	1	1	5.19	18	2	0	2	35	33	25	20	23	38
*Pierce, Ed	3	1	3.24	37	0	0	5	50	49	21	18	32	53
*Sanchez, Israel	1	1	1.08	7	1	0	0	17	18	8	2	1	17
Shaw, Kevin	0	4	5.70	10	8	0	0	30	32	20	19	14	6
Vaughn, Randy	3	6	4.08	21	21	0	0	121	124	65	55	48	91
*Webster, Mike	1	1	8.36	7	0	0	0	14	13	13	13	10	15

CHARLOTTE

BATTING	AVG	G	AB	R	H	2B	3B	HR	RBI	BB	SO	SB
#Crespo, Mike, c	.135	23	52	3	7	0	1	0	0	5	14	0
*Cronk, Doug, 1b	.186	106	322	30	60	15	8	4	47	57	91	0
Douglas, Arthur, of	.286	3	7	0	2	0	0	0	0	0	3	1
Frye, Jeff, 2b	.272	131	503	77	137	16	7	0	50	80	66	29
*Hays, Daren, of	.226	70	186	19	42	5	1	3	27	20	34	2
Hernandez, Jose, ss	.255	121	388	43	99	14	7	1	44	50	122	11
Law, Travis, of	.198	58	182	21	36	5	3	0	9	24	31	7
Losa, Bill, c-dh	.264	22	53	7	14	3	0	0	9	9	15	0
McCoy, Trey, of-dh	.231	45	160	19	37	11	0	3	18	23	35	0
Morris, Rod, of	.255	120	436	66	111	11	4	2	45	42	66	18
Niethammer, Darren, 1b-c ..	.276	72	214	31	59	5	0	0	20	28	24	3
*Oller, Jeff, 3b-dh	.275	104	327	37	90	17	1	1	39	43	67	3
Peel, Jack, of	.229	87	271	43	62	14	4	2	8	40	43	4
Rodriguez, Ivan, c	.287	109	408	48	117	17	7	2	55	12	50	1

	AVG	G	AB	R	H	2B	3B	HR	RBI	BB	SO	SB
Sable, Luke, 3b-2b	.267	67	206	24	55	5	5	0	23	23	30	18
Samson, Fred, 3b-ss	.286	104	350	60	100	21	1	5	38	51	68	12
Swain, Thayer, of	.245	105	322	44	79	19	4	0	25	42	73	15
Threadgill, George, of	.238	20	63	5	15	3	1	1	9	9	13	2
Williams, Reggie, of	.267	7	30	4	8	2	0	0	2	1	10	1

PITCHING	W	L	ERA	G	GS	CG	SV	IP	H	R	ER	BB	SO
Alexander, Gerald	6	1	0.63	7	7	0	0	43	24	7	3	14	39
Arner, Mike	3	3	2.97	12	12	0	0	79	56	26	26	17	72
Brown, Rob	8	5	1.90	40	4	0	4	119	73	33	25	40	102
Cecena, Jose	3	2	2.03	20	0	0	0	31	24	7	7	13	35
Compres, Fidel	9	2	2.24	22	16	2	1	117	89	38	29	43	69
Cunningham, Everett	6	3	2.15	11	11	2	0	75	50	25	18	28	57
*Gore, Bryan	9	4	2.19	23	15	0	0	111	82	36	27	29	60
Guzman, Jose	0	1	2.16	2	2	0	0	8	10	3	2	4	7
Hurst, Jonathan	0	1	2.19	6	0	0	0	12	8	3	3	5	8
Hvizda, Jim	3	0	1.57	13	0	0	4	29	18	5	5	8	18
MacNeil, Tim (10 Miami)	1	4	6.00	17	6	0	0	48	53	39	32	30	40
Manuel, Barry	1	5	2.88	57	0	0	36	56	39	23	18	30	60
Nen, Robb	1	4	3.69	11	11	1	0	54	44	28	22	36	38
Pavlik, Roger	5	3	2.44	11	11	1	0	66	50	21	18	40	76
Perez, David	6	4	3.35	14	14	0	0	83	63	35	31	28	83
*Reitzel, Mike (13 Miami)	5	9	3.71	26	15	1	3	104	111	61	43	45	64
*Romero, Brian	7	2	1.70	12	12	2	0	74	45	19	14	24	72
Rowley, Steve	0	4	5.32	5	5	0	0	24	19	16	14	21	7
Russell, Jeff	0	1	0.00	1	0	0	0	0	1	1	1	0	0
*Shaw, Cedric	5	3	1.59	11	11	1	0	68	48	18	12	27	69
Spencer, Kyle	8	2	1.52	43	0	0	3	83	50	28	14	52	78
Stafford, Tim	1	0	1.50	1	1	0	0	6	4	1	1	3	3

CLEARWATER

BATTING	AVG	G	AB	R	H	2B	3B	HR	RBI	BB	SO	SB
Adams, Brian, c	.179	23	67	3	12	2	0	0	8	1	6	0
*Barragan, Jimmy, 1b	.209	13	43	6	9	3	0	0	3	10	4	0
Brown, Dana, of	.256	96	363	55	93	9	5	0	28	40	47	30
*Cummings, Brian, 1b-dh	.243	103	341	21	83	11	2	3	32	21	34	6
*Hayes, Von, dh-of	.167	2	6	0	1	1	0	0	0	2	1	0
Hulse, Jeff, c	.221	69	213	20	47	10	4	0	14	28	56	0
Infante, Kennedy, dh-3b	.293	42	171	21	46	11	2	2	22	8	11	1
Lozinski, Tony, c	.246	36	122	11	30	2	0	0	10	12	25	0
*McDevitt, Terry, ss-2b	.189	53	111	10	21	2	0	1	13	16	25	1
Millette, Joe, ss	.183	108	295	31	54	5	0	0	18	29	53	4
Paulsen, Troy, 2b	.198	54	167	11	33	3	0	0	9	16	21	1
#Robertson, Rod, ss-2b	.216	58	204	17	44	7	1	2	21	18	30	8
#Rosado, Ed, c	.171	63	170	14	29	3	2	0	14	10	30	2
Scarsone, Steve, 2b	.275	59	211	20	58	9	5	3	23	19	57	3
Tenhunfeld, Joe, of-dh	.191	74	204	22	39	9	2	0	13	11	69	1
Trevino, Tony, 1b-3b	.258	133	465	60	120	20	5	4	62	65	85	2
*Urbon, Joe, of	.257	60	191	21	49	8	2	0	16	19	35	2
#Ventress, Leroy, of	.193	39	140	24	27	2	0	0	9	26	30	12
#Waller, Casey, 3b	.284	59	208	29	59	14	4	8	31	18	31	4
Williams, Cary, of	.261	63	245	20	64	12	3	1	21	7	33	2
Woodruff, Pat, of	.240	135	496	60	119	18	8	2	49	46	92	32

PITCHING	W	L	ERA	G	GS	CG	SV	IP	H	R	ER	BB	SO
Backs, Jason	5	7	3.75	15	15	4	0	96	80	46	40	40	62
Borland, Toby	1	2	2.26	44	0	0	5	60	44	21	15	35	44
Brantley, Cliff	1	4	2.94	8	8	2	0	49	44	20	16	17	37
*Carter, Andy	4	14	4.88	26	26	2	0	131	121	82	71	69	90
*Christopher, Fred	1	3	5.68	32	1	0	2	52	54	35	33	40	56
Dell, Tim	2	6	5.46	16	9	0	0	56	68	41	34	18	41
Elam, Todd	2	4	3.14	32	7	1	1	80	64	37	28	49	61
Fletcher, Paul	5	8	3.38	20	18	2	1	117	104	56	44	49	104
Fynan, Kevin	0	2	4.26	9	0	0	0	13	16	7	6	1	9
Gunderson, Greg	0	1	7.80	10	0	0	0	15	26	14	13	8	7
*Langley, Lee	0	0	2.25	9	0	0	0	12	11	9	3	9	9
Lindsey, Darrell	10	9	3.43	26	26	1	0	155	166	76	59	53	73
Madrid, Alex	1	1	0.95	5	2	1	0	19	15	3	2	7	16
Martin, John	0	0	0.00	1	0	0	0	1	1	0	0	0	1
*McCarthy, Greg	1	3	3.47	42	1	0	5	60	47	33	23	38	67
Ontiveros, Steve	0	0	2.35	3	3	0	0	8	4	2	2	3	2
Patterson, Jeff	3	6	2.96	11	11	0	0	67	63	34	22	22	28
Randall, Mark	2	3	8.31	16	0	0	3	17	19	17	16	9	10
Stevens, Matt	1	1	0.75	10	0	0	1	12	4	1	1	4	11
Sullivan, Mike	2	1	1.23	13	0	0	3	15	8	2	2	4	16
*Tabaka, Jeff	5	2	3.03	8	5	0	0	36	39	17	12	18	23
Wells, Bob	0	2	4.91	6	1	0	1	15	17	9	8	6	11
*Wiegandt, Scott	4	8	2.62	33	4	0	4	76	70	33	22	37	52

DUNEDIN

BATTING	AVG	G	AB	R	H	2B	3B	HR	RBI	BB	SO	SB
*Beacom, Chris, 1b-3b	.227	84	238	26	54	14	4	2	24	17	52	0
#Cedeno, Domingo, ss	.221	124	493	64	109	12	10	7	61	48	127	10
DelaRosa, Juan, of	.257	131	529	57	136	19	8	10	76	19	98	9
*Giannelli, Ray, 1b-3b	.288	118	416	64	120	18	1	18	57	66	56	5
*Hodge, Tim, of	.244	91	291	30	71	14	2	3	30	37	90	5
Irish, Jeff, c	.200	10	15	2	3	0	0	0	1	4	5	0

	AVG	G	AB	R	H	2B	3B	HR	RBI	BB	SO	SB
Kent, Jeff, 2b	.277	132	447	72	124	32	2	16	60	53	98	17
Miller, Scott, 2b-ss	.214	17	42	2	9	0	0	0	5	2	7	0
Monzon, Jose, c-dh	.303	30	76	11	23	5	1	0	7	10	19	1
*O'Halloran, Greg, dh-c	.284	121	465	70	132	26	4	11	75	37	70	2
Provence, Todd, 3b-of	.197	19	61	10	12	3	1	1	6	3	22	2
Taveras, Marcos, of	.258	41	62	16	16	2	1	2	6	7	15	2
Taylor, Mike, 3b-2b	.237	69	169	29	40	7	0	0	14	32	37	8
Thompson, Ryan, of	.231	117	438	56	101	15	5	6	37	20	100	18
Townley, Jason, c	.292	119	397	58	116	22	1	11	63	41	82	1
Young, Mark, of-3b	.237	117	409	72	97	14	6	5	38	58	88	31

PITCHING	W	L	ERA	G	GS	CG	SV	IP	H	R	ER	BB	SO
*Aylmer, Bob	1	1	1.69	8	0	0	0	16	14	6	3	4	8
Blohm, Pete	1	0	1.29	2	0	0	1	7	5	1	1	0	6
*Boucher, Denis	7	0	0.75	9	9	2	0	60	45	8	5	8	62
Brown, Tim	2	3	4.43	36	0	0	1	67	76	41	33	18	55
Cross, Jesse	13	7	3.29	28	18	0	0	139	100	54	51	70	126
DePastino, Rich	6	3	5.02	22	14	0	0	84	85	54	47	57	72
*Horsman, Vince	4	7	3.24	28	0	0	1	50	53	21	18	15	41
*Jordan, Ricardo	0	2	2.38	13	2	0	0	23	15	9	6	19	16
*Key, Jimmy	2	0	2.50	3	3	0	0	18	21	7	5	3	14
*Leiter, Al	0	0	2.63	6	6	0	0	24	18	8	7	12	14
Martin, Gregg	2	1	3.77	12	0	0	0	14	10	7	6	11	16
Rudolph, Blaine	3	0	3.11	35	5	0	4	81	71	37	28	45	62
Silverstein, Al	7	5	2.26	45	0	0	6	76	52	28	19	34	70
Timlin, Mike	7	2	1.43	42	0	0	22	50	36	11	8	16	46
Trlicek, Rick	5	8	3.73	26	26	0	0	154	128	74	64	72	125
*Ward, Anthony	14	6	2.83	27	26	1	0	181	150	63	57	39	137
Weathers, Dave	10	7	3.70	27	27	2	0	158	158	82	65	59	96

FT. LAUDERDALE

BATTING	AVG	G	AB	R	H	2B	3B	HR	RBI	BB	SO	SB
Barnwell, Rich, of	.274	71	274	54	75	15	5	4	20	32	62	24
*Brown, Todd, dh-3b	.247	56	146	10	36	8	0	0	16	22	32	3
*Cortes, Hernan, 1b	.303	84	277	46	84	21	2	1	25	51	51	1
*Devereaux, Todd, 1b-of	.237	102	346	36	82	17	1	1	33	42	53	6
Dulom, Kirk, 3b-of	.172	76	204	16	35	8	1	2	24	33	46	1
Ehrhard, Rod, c	.197	78	254	27	50	7	2	5	18	30	68	7
*Erhardt, Herb, c-1b	.250	36	116	8	29	4	0	2	12	16	20	0
Knoblauh, Jay, of	.288	96	361	54	104	18	2	8	48	30	59	26
Livesey, Jeff, c	.176	45	148	11	26	6	0	4	15	15	55	0
Masse, Billy, of	.274	68	230	42	63	15	0	6	33	33	28	9
*Nelloms, Skip, of	.236	120	407	44	96	16	5	2	47	46	88	14
#Noriega, Rey, 2b-ss	.226	84	305	52	69	17	4	3	28	35	85	7
Pimentel, Ed, 2b-3b	.192	115	355	36	68	10	1	1	38	30	57	10
Turgeon, Dave, 3b-1b	.211	98	331	28	70	13	0	1	30	29	42	1
Vargas, Hector, ss	.308	117	429	48	132	20	9	0	61	30	68	22
Williams, Gerald, of	.289	50	204	25	59	4	5	7	43	16	52	19

PITCHING	W	L	ERA	G	GS	CG	SV	IP	H	R	ER	BB	SO
Brubaker, John	4	5	5.74	40	1	0	2	78	103	61	50	47	35
*Burns, Britt	1	2	10.80	4	3	1	0	10	16	14	12	7	3
Draper, Mike	9	1	2.25	14	14	1	0	96	80	30	24	22	52
*Garcia, Victor	1	4	2.36	20	3	0	1	50	45	16	13	22	56
*Gietzen, Peter	0	2	6.80	23	4	0	0	48	62	49	36	32	37
Gogolewski, Doug	5	9	4.67	16	16	2	0	89	87	58	46	50	88
Green, John	1	0	1.04	5	0	0	1	9	7	3	1	4	2
Greer, Ken	4	9	5.44	38	5	0	1	89	115	64	54	33	55
Johnson, Jeff	6	8	3.65	17	17	1	0	104	101	55	42	25	84
*Malone, Todd	0	5	5.45	8	7	1	0	36	46	26	22	29	29
Manon, Ramon	2	3	5.86	11	5	0	0	35	39	26	23	23	40
Marris, Mark	5	7	5.36	27	11	0	1	87	93	57	52	59	43
Newell, Tom	0	3	5.67	7	7	0	0	33	32	22	21	19	22
Ohlms, Mark	8	8	3.43	21	19	1	0	115	103	57	44	15	104
Perez, Pascual	0	0	6.00	1	1	0	0	3	3	2	2	1	1
Popplewell, Tom	6	5	2.23	15	15	3	0	101	82	38	25	23	59
*Rub, Jerry	1	1	6.23	15	0	0	2	22	26	15	15	10	16
*Seiler, Stuart	0	0	0.56	8	0	0	0	16	13	1	1	6	15
Smith, Shad	0	0	0.00	1	0	0	0	3	2	0	0	2	1
Stanford, Larry	3	1	1.31	57	0	0	29	62	42	15	9	18	60
*Tucker, Steve	6	2	4.15	21	9	2	2	78	77	41	36	43	49

LAKELAND

BATTING	AVG	G	AB	R	H	2B	3B	HR	RBI	BB	SO	SB
Albright, Eric, c	.202	70	203	34	41	9	0	1	23	41	42	4
Aldrich, Tom, dh-1b	.266	92	305	26	81	22	0	1	37	47	63	3
Anglero, Jose, 3b-ss (28 BC)	.244	66	176	24	43	3	4	0	15	12	19	11
Balthazar, Doyle, c	.259	43	147	17	38	5	3	1	20	9	25	3
Cole, Mark, 2b	.230	105	369	43	85	10	4	0	33	31	63	10
*Cornelius, Brian, of	.238	34	122	17	29	5	2	1	15	6	15	1
*Cruz, Ivan, 1b	.285	118	414	61	118	23	2	11	73	49	71	8
Gillette, Mike, c	.143	23	63	10	9	2	0	1	8	9	24	1
Goodale, Jeff, of	.244	107	308	40	75	14	4	1	31	49	76	4
Hurst, Jody, of	.301	75	286	38	86	12	5	10	47	25	50	19
#Kimberlin, Keith, ss	.260	122	419	56	109	16	5	0	35	54	68	16
Marigny, Ron, 3b-ss	.251	55	203	26	51	5	2	1	18	25	22	6
Martin, Darryl, of	.246	110	354	48	87	8	8	3	41	36	63	19

Ivan Rodriguez ... top prospect | Jacob Brumfield ... bat champion | Kenny Lofton ... .331, 62 SB

	AVG	G	AB	R	H	2B	3B	HR	RBI	BB	SO	SB
*Raley, Dan, dh-1b	.226	10	31	1	7	1	0	0	3	3	6	0
#Reimink, Robert, 3b-2b	.222	112	388	52	86	8	3	2	41	47	80	6
Spann, Tookie, of	.194	23	72	11	14	3	1	0	3	11	22	1
#Tresh, Mickey, of-inf	.268	122	471	69	126	16	4	2	49	37	59	19

PITCHING	W	L	ERA	G	GS	CG	SV	IP	H	R	ER	BB	SO
*Alcantara, Francisco	0	0	0.00	2	0	0	0	2	1	0	0	0	0
*Berrios, Hector	2	2	1.80	21	0	0	0	45	36	14	9	14	42
*Cook, Ron	2	2	1.90	43	2	0	5	76	56	21	16	30	59
DeSilva, John	8	1	1.48	14	14	0	0	91	54	18	15	25	113
Doherty, John	5	1	1.10	30	0	0	10	41	33	7	5	5	23
Ettles, Mark	5	5	3.31	45	0	0	3	68	63	34	25	16	62
Ferm, Ed	6	7	4.46	18	18	0	0	81	80	57	40	58	60
Gohr, Greg	13	5	2.62	25	25	0	0	138	125	52	40	50	90
*Hursey, Darren	5	5	3.12	25	13	0	1	89	101	41	31	26	59
Knudsen, Kurt	5	0	2.28	14	8	0	3	67	42	18	17	22	70
Krumm, Todd	7	9	2.41	25	24	6	1	146	135	48	39	49	112
Lira, Felipe	0	0	5.40	1	0	0	0	2	3	1	1	3	4
Lumley, Mike	5	4	2.38	13	9	1	2	4	56	22	17	22	47
*Marshall, Randy	7	2	3.00	13	13	2	0	72	71	29	24	14	40
Rivera, Lino	1	0	0.41	36	0	0	14	44	31	3	2	12	38
Torres, Leonardo	2	0	2.60	12	0	0	0	17	15	7	5	10	16
Willis, Marty	10	6	2.65	34	7	0	1	99	80	33	29	30	96

MIAMI

BATTING	AVG	G	AB	R	H	2B	3B	HR	RBI	BB	SO	SB
*Alegre, Paul, of	.250	3	4	0	1	1	0	0	0	1	3	0
*Bargman, Robert, dh-1b	.067	5	15	1	1	0	0	0	2	3	9	0
*Beaulac, Joe, 1b	.158	17	38	3	6	0	0	0	2	9	13	0
Bible, Mike, of	.231	14	26	1	6	0	0	0	1	2	9	1
#Boyce, Tommy, of-dh	.206	53	136	15	28	5	1	4	9	20	36	3
Bradbury, Miah, c	.210	50	157	10	33	8	0	1	12	16	25	0
Burnett, Joe, of	.179	12	28	3	5	0	0	1	5	12	2
*Carey, Paul, of	.327	49	153	23	50	5	3	4	20	43	39	4
D'Alexander, Greg, 3b	.218	63	220	17	48	8	0	0	24	20	43	2
#Durkin, Marty, of-2b	.256	109	360	52	92	16	6	5	29	36	83	20
Garcia, Librado, of	.177	30	79	8	14	0	1	1	5	5	24	4
Garczyk, Eddie, 2b	.184	38	76	13	14	0	0	0	2	9	20	5
*Giordano, Marc, of-dh	.224	122	343	31	77	10	0	2	38	71	94	7
*Gomez, Pierre, 2b-ss	.000	7	4	2	0	0	0	0	0	2	2	2
Gutierrez, Jackie, ss-2b	.220	121	381	39	84	15	2	1	35	40	63	8
Hall, Lamar, 3b-ss	.294	39	143	15	42	6	2	0	14	8	24	8
Hudson, Lance, of	.189	27	95	11	18	4	1	1	11	13	19	7
*Kidd, Dennis, of	.246	102	349	46	86	10	5	0	25	26	92	25
Landrum, Tito, of	.152	26	66	4	10	2	0	0	2	1	12	0
Lansing, Mike, ss	.242	61	207	20	50	5	2	2	11	29	35	15
McKinley, Tim, c	.149	26	47	4	7	2	0	0	0	13	13	0
Miller, Bill, c-of	.169	73	183	17	31	9	0	4	10	12	73	2
Morris, Angel, of	.255	37	110	10	28	7	0	1	17	14	18	2
Raffo, Tom, 1b	.258	67	225	16	58	13	0	3	30	24	46	1
Rigsby, Tim, 2b-ss	.232	54	164	19	38	6	1	0	14	14	43	4
Sardinha, Eddie, 3b-2b	.176	13	34	2	6	0	0	0	1	1	8	0
*Shelton, Harry, of	.254	107	346	34	88	15	0	0	26	24	68	26
Taylor, Dave, of	.154	9	13	0	2	0	0	0	0	2	7	1
Varni, Pat, 2b-3b	.129	50	93	11	12	5	0	1	9	16	27	3
Weinheimer, Wayne, 1b-of	.204	71	206	17	42	8	1	3	22	22	67	3

PITCHING	W	L	ERA	G	GS	CG	SV	IP	H	R	ER	BB	SO
Alexander, Dave	0	2	6.29	16	0	0	0	24	25	19	17	15	17
Boyle, Bob	1	0	14.29	4	0	0	0	6	14	10	9	4	0
*Cakora, Matt	1	3	3.56	45	3	1	2	73	78	36	29	30	48
*Daniel, Clay	6	5	2.65	15	10	4	0	75	68	24	22	13	44
Delgado, Tim	0	1	5.59	4	2	0	0	10	13	6	6	5	4
Ericson, Mike	2	2	4.00	25	1	0	1	36	33	16	16	19	27
Gregory, Brad	4	7	4.12	16	13	1	0	79	96	52	36	24	57

	W	L	ERA	G	GS	CG	SV	IP	H	R	ER	BB	SO
Kelley, Anthony	5	8	4.58	30	19	0	0	132	145	81	67	58	90
Kerfut, George	8	6	3.82	45	13	2	1	125	107	60	53	68	93
Lugo, Angel	0	6	6.99	19	6	1	0	48	58	42	37	30	14
Magria, Javier	1	1	9.79	19	0	0	2	27	29	30	29	28	34
Michno, Tom	5	9	3.83	31	10	3	2	102	79	37	32	58	78
Olson, Dan	0	1	15.00	1	1	0	0	3	7	7	5	5	1
Pascual, Jorge	2	10	4.76	37	12	0	6	98	102	67	52	63	84
Ponder, Kevin	4	2	3.89	15	7	0	2	44	57	30	19	9	44
*Rogers, Charlie	2	5	2.63	14	10	2	1	72	57	26	21	49	64
*Sauveur, Rich	0	4	3.32	11	6	1	0	41	41	16	15	17	34
*Smith, Chad	1	7	7.02	22	5	0	1	41	58	42	32	30	34
*Williams, Kenny	0	3	7.03	13	3	1	0	24	24	22	19	25	18

OSCEOLA

BATTING	AVG	G	AB	R	H	2B	3B	HR	RBI	BB	SO	SB
Acta, Manny, 1b-3b	.206	44	126	12	26	3	0	0	2	15	17	2
Angotti, Don, c-1b	.143	24	35	2	5	2	0	0	1	3	17	0
Beams, Mike, of	.253	126	419	62	106	21	4	9	50	62	96	15
Cooper, Gary, dh-of	.154	8	26	4	4	4	0	0	2	3	3	0
*Cruz, Ruben, ph	.000	1	1	0	0	0	0	0	0	0	0	0
Dean, Kevin, dh	.223	28	94	13	21	2	2	1	22	21	32	9
Foster, Bryan, ss	.218	35	110	15	24	1	0	0	4	11	34	2
Henderson, David, 2b-ss	.184	86	250	43	46	7	0	2	23	39	63	10
#Kellner, Frank, ss-2b	.247	109	369	43	91	9	7	0	34	65	65	14
*Lamphere, Larry, 2b	.186	74	167	28	31	7	0	0	22	30	35	11
Lewis, Mica, 2b	.195	43	118	15	23	3	3	1	12	23	42	6
*Lofton, Kenny, of	.331	124	481	98	159	15	5	2	35	61	57	62
Madsen, Lance, 3b	.244	135	488	62	119	23	11	6	62	59	131	7
Makarewicz, Scott, c	.277	94	343	35	95	12	2	4	49	21	62	0
Massarelli, John, c-dh	.295	120	396	55	117	8	3	2	50	41	73	54
Nyssen, Dan, of	.233	112	417	48	97	13	8	7	66	44	61	6
Ortiz, Joe, 1b	.146	19	48	3	7	2	0	0	4	3	9	0
*Prager, Howard, 1b	.248	99	331	44	82	11	4	1	45	61	49	2
#Reed, Toncie, of	.191	89	277	21	53	8	6	1	26	25	76	7

PITCHING	W	L	ERA	G	GS	CG	SV	IP	H	R	ER	BB	SO
Bauer, Pete	4	1	1.55	24	0	0	10	29	18	6	5	11	32
Black, Scott	1	0	3.48	13	0	0	0	21	21	8	8	10	9
Dovey, Troy	0	0	5.23	6	0	0	0	10	13	6	6	8	7
Dunnum, Rick	5	1	2.80	51	2	0	5	113	83	45	35	44	113
Griffiths, Brian	5	10	4.81	28	23	0	0	129	129	88	69	75	79
Hyson, Cole	6	12	4.01	26	26	0	0	141	130	76	63	70	92
Jones, Todd	12	10	3.51	27	27	1	0	151	124	81	59	109	106
Juden, Jeff	10	1	2.27	15	15	2	0	91	72	37	23	42	85
Luckham, Ken	6	12	4.14	27	27	1	0	150	158	88	69	90	89
*Mallicoat, Rob	0	0	0.00	3	0	0	0	12	8	2	0	9	10
Ponte, Ed	1	3	2.83	32	0	0	4	57	36	23	18	28	67
*Rambo, Matt	5	8	3.09	25	15	2	0	105	97	50	36	38	91
Rodriguez, Gabriel	12	5	1.68	51	0	0	10	91	57	21	17	25	89
Tafoya, Dennis	1	3	4.91	22	0	0	2	44	53	27	24	8	24
*Windes, Rodney	4	0	1.98	44	0	0	2	68	48	18	15	19	54

ST. LUCIE

BATTING	AVG	G	AB	R	H	2B	3B	HR	RBI	BB	SO	SB
Brown, Don, of	.148	22	61	13	9	1	0	0	4	18	17	9
*Burnitz, Jeromy, of	.156	11	32	6	5	1	0	0	3	7	12	1
#Butterfield, Chris, 3b-c	.197	118	386	50	76	10	5	4	36	64	128	21
Carroll, Kevin, c	.000	6	7	1	0	0	0	0	1	1	4	0
Castillo, Alberto, c	.364	3	11	4	4	0	0	1	3	1	1	0
Davis, Brian, of-dh	.176	5	17	2	3	0	0	0	2	2	4	1
Dellicarri, Joe, ss	.206	40	126	16	26	1	2	0	13	17	34	5
Dozier, D.J., of	.297	93	317	65	94	11	3	13	57	45	76	33
Graves, Kenny, c	.213	42	122	11	26	3	1	1	15	8	32	1
#Hartmann, Reid, 2b-ss	.227	31	97	10	22	2	0	1	10	12	23	1
Henderson, Derek, ss	.207	59	184	16	38	2	2	0	26	15	34	7
Kelly, Jimy, ss	.250	30	104	12	26	4	0	0	6	10	23	3
#May, Lee, of	.253	124	447	70	113	17	6	0	35	46	122	52
McBride, Loy, of	.249	81	297	43	74	11	8	1	37	27	60	30
Morrisette, Jim, of-3b	.268	89	313	53	84	13	1	8	48	33	78	16
Olah, Bob, 1b-dh	.257	84	288	29	74	10	0	5	45	19	54	1
Perozo, Ender, of	.500	1	2	1	1	1	0	0	0	0	1	0
Riesgo, Nikco, 1b-dh	.298	131	456	93	136	35	3	14	94	74	77	46
Saunders, Doug, 2b	.225	115	408	52	92	8	4	1	43	43	96	24
Young, Derrick, of	.257	79	245	40	63	5	2	3	30	37	54	14
#Zinter, Alan, c	.291	98	333	63	97	19	6	7	63	54	70	8

PITCHING	W	L	ERA	G	GS	CG	SV	IP	H	R	ER	BB	SO
Brady, Mike	2	4	4.67	38	0	0	8	44	45	28	23	33	42
Corbin, Archie	7	8	2.97	20	18	3	0	118	97	47	39	59	105
Furmanik, Dan	6	6	4.21	22	9	0	2	73	71	43	34	30	45
Hansell, Greg (21 WH)	9	14	3.35	27	27	2	0	153	129	85	57	79	95
Harriger, Denny	5	3	3.52	27	7	1	2	72	73	36	28	20	47
*Hill, Chris	9	8	3.19	27	25	2	1	150	149	77	53	69	82
*Hillman, Eric	2	0	0.67	4	3	0	0	27	15	2	2	8	23
Johnson, Paul	0	1	5.60	22	0	0	3	35	46	29	22	10	20
Johnstone, John	15	6	2.24	25	25	9	0	173	145	53	43	60	120
Larose, Steve	1	1	3.57	17	0	0	7	18	16	9	7	10	13

BATTING

R	Eric Young, Vero Beach	101
H	Kenny Lofton, Osceola	159
TB	Nikco Riesgo, St. Lucie	219
2B	Nikco Riesgo, St. Lucie	35
3B	Lance Madsen, Osceola	11
HR	Ray Giannelli, Dunedin	18
RBI	Nikco Riesgo, St. Lucie	94
SH	Keith Kimberlin, Lakeland	21
SF	Hector Vargas, Ft. Laud	11
BB	Kinnis Pledger, Sarasota	94
IBB	Rex Peters, Vero Beach	11
HBP	Mike Beams, Osceola	12
	Javier Ocasio, Sarasota	12
SO	Daren Watkins, BC	134
	Kinnis Pledger, Sarasota	134
SB	Eric Young, Vero Beach	75
CS	Javier Ocasio, Sarasota	27
OB%	Jacob Brumfield, BC	.429

PITCHING

G	David Grimes, St. Pete	58
GS	Four tied at	27
CG	John Johnstone, St. Lucie	9
ShO	Todd Krumm, Lakeland	4
Sv	Barry Manuel, Charlotte	36
W	John Johnstone, Lakeland	15
L	Three tied at	14
IP	Anthony Ward, Dunedin	181
H	Dan Freed, WPB	188
R	Brian Griffiths, Osceola	88
	Ken Luckham, Osceola	88
HR	Ramon Garcia, Sarasota	10
BB	Todd Jones, Osceola	109
HB	Al Silverstein, Dunedin	17
SO	Anthony Ward, Dunedin	137
WP	Bill Bene, Vero Beach	23
Bk	Charlie Rogers, Miami	14

	W	L	ERA	G	GS	CG	SV	IP	H	R	ER	BB	SO
Mejia, Cesar	1	1	10.61	2	2	0	0	9	13	12	11	3	4
Newton, Steve	2	1	5.19	31	1	0	1	68	77	44	39	34	48
Perez, Vlad	2	2	3.44	19	0	0	5	37	34	15	14	20	41
Reich, Andy	0	0	20.25	2	0	0	0	3	8	6	6	2	1
Rogers, Bryan	9	8	3.09	29	19	5	4	149	127	66	51	26	96
*Schourek, Pete	4	1	0.97	5	5	2	0	37	29	4	4	8	28
Telgheder, Dave	9	4	3.00	14	14	3	0	96	84	38	32	14	77

ST. PETERSBURG

BATTING	AVG	G	AB	R	H	2B	3B	HR	RBI	BB	SO	SB
Abreu, Frank, 3b-ss	.276	86	293	30	81	10	2	0	27	21	49	6
#Alicea, Luis, dh-2b	.232	29	95	14	22	1	4	0	12	20	14	9
Belbru, Juan, of	.000	4	5	1	0	0	0	0	1	1	0	0
*Carter, Ed, of	.230	47	135	17	31	6	0	0	13	15	15	6
Cromer, Tripp, ss	.216	121	408	53	88	12	5	5	38	46	78	7
Deloach, Bobby, of	.238	123	466	54	111	24	7	9	58	23	98	9
*Federico, Joe, 1b	.162	31	99	6	16	2	0	0	9	10	24	0
Ferguson, Jim, 3b	.333	6	3	2	1	0	0	0	0	2	0	0
*Fernandez, Jose, c	.254	42	138	12	35	10	0	1	19	34	39	0
Fielitz, Bill, c	.077	7	13	0	1	0	0	0	0	1	5	0
Fiore, Mike, 3b-of	.271	118	436	57	118	24	2	5	56	53	36	19
Graham, Steve, of	.257	80	276	27	71	11	3	0	26	20	41	10
#Grier, Antron, of	.244	98	352	37	86	8	2	0	26	27	66	15
*Hernandez, Henry, 1b-dh	.157	41	121	6	19	2	0	0	7	25	36	5
Jordan, Brian, of	.167	9	30	3	5	0	1	0	1	2	11	0
Kindred, Vince, of	.181	55	155	18	28	5	1	0	11	17	30	3
*Maclin, Lonnie, of	.387	31	119	18	46	6	3	2	17	11	12	6
*Martinez, Luis, dh-of	.311	19	74	14	23	3	2	0	9	3	6	3
Redman, Tim, c	.242	79	236	21	57	4	0	2	22	23	44	4
Sellick, John, 1b	.197	110	370	49	73	20	2	9	44	59	105	7
#Shireman, Jeff, 2b-3b	.255	123	415	61	106	10	1	0	37	87	34	11
Thomas, Orlando, c	.250	23	48	4	12	3	1	0	5	10	19	0
Trujillo, Jose, 2b	.177	28	79	11	14	3	0	0	8	2	12	0

PITCHING	W	L	ERA	G	GS	CG	SV	IP	H	R	ER	BB	SO
*Burgos, John	7	4	3.11	19	14	0	0	93	77	37	32	36	67
Clark, Mark	3	2	3.05	10	10	1	0	62	63	33	21	14	58
Duvall, Brad	0	0	1.80	1	1	0	0	5	5	2	1	0	0
Ericks, John	2	1	1.57	4	4	0	0	23	16	5	4	6	25
*Green, Don	2	2	2.79	35	0	0	0	58	52	19	18	38	43
Grimes, David	2	6	2.28	58	0	0	2	83	60	25	21	25	58
*Hitt, Daniel	1	3	3.51	27	0	0	0	41	44	19	16	18	16
Hoffman, Rich	6	8	3.61	23	19	2	0	120	122	58	48	47	60
Keller, Clyde	0	1	3.78	15	0	0	6	17	16	11	7	3	16
Lata, Tim	1	5	4.97	8	8	3	0	51	52	30	28	22	27
Majer, Steffen	2	3	1.52	14	0	0	0	59	47	11	10	20	45
Meamber, Tim	0	2	5.87	6	0	0	0	8	11	8	5	1	10
*Milchin, Mike	6	1	2.77	11	11	1	0	68	57	25	21	20	66
Pacheco, Al	0	3	11.81	5	4	0	0	11	14	20	14	22	4
Plemel, Lee	3	3	3.02	10	9	1	0	63	66	25	21	10	42
*Richardson, Dave	4	1	2.11	47	0	0	1	64	38	18	15	13	51
Satterfield, Cory	1	8	6.12	17	10	0	0	60	70	45	41	22	38
Shackle, Rick	3	4	2.40	8	8	1	0	45	41	19	12	15	30
Smith, Ken	3	6	6.75	17	5	0	0	37	50	28	28	20	21
Tolbert, Mark	2	3	6.85	5	5	0	0	24	30	21	18	12	14
Vargas, Jose	4	6	3.35	38	0	0	12	54	51	24	20	25	46
Weese, Dean	2	2	2.52	20	0	0	9	25	17	7	7	13	27
Wiseman, Dennis	1	0	2.63	17	17	1	0	113	108	37	33	36	75

SARASOTA

BATTING	AVG	G	AB	R	H	2B	3B	HR	RBI	BB	SO	SB
Alvarez, Clemente, c	.160	37	119	9	19	4	1	1	9	8	24	0
Busby, Wayne, ss-3b	.186	23	70	11	13	3	0	0	6	6	7	2

	AVG	G	AB	R	H	2B	3B	HR	RBI	BB	SO	SB
Campbell, Darrin, c	.235	93	319	26	75	10	1	4	37	26	67	4
*Chasey, Mark, 1b	.263	116	400	56	105	18	6	3	52	64	111	8
#Coleman, Ken, 2b-3b	.249	65	225	23	56	6	1	1	22	14	30	14
Cruz, Bernardo, ss	.314	12	35	7	11	0	1	0	0	4	4	1
*Gaither, Horace, ss-3b	.179	75	240	16	43	6	1	0	14	7	42	3
*Gonzalez, Cliff, of	.239	109	348	35	83	10	3	3	40	40	44	7
Hornacek, Jay, dh-c	.143	17	35	1	5	1	0	1	2	5	8	0
*Lukachyk, Rob, of-3b	.243	118	428	56	104	23	9	4	36	31	88	17
*McGough, Greg, c	.190	9	21	2	4	1	0	0	1	2	5	0
Ocasio, Javier, 2b-ss	.292	127	497	65	145	13	3	1	45	55	67	45
Payton, Ray, dh-of	.260	95	285	26	74	14	1	5	38	32	68	1
*Pledger, Kinnis, of	.248	131	460	72	114	18	4	3	40	94	134	26
*Roth, Greg, 3b	.210	62	186	33	39	7	2	1	17	56	53	1
Singley, Joe, c (17 Miami)	.178	44	118	7	21	5	0	1	6	11	35	1
Smith, Ed, 3b-1b	.192	63	239	22	46	10	3	4	23	11	61	0
Sullivan, Carl, of	.207	34	116	7	24	3	0	0	8	8	24	3
*Tedder, Scott, of-1b	.283	121	381	65	108	6	2	0	47	90	46	13
Tejada, Alex, 3b-ss	.083	5	12	0	1	0	0	0	1	1	5	0

PITCHING	W	L	ERA	G	GS	CG	SV	IP	H	R	ER	BB	SO
*Dabney, Fred	6	7	5.20	24	21	1	0	126	146	82	73	57	77
Davino, Mike	8	9	3.91	46	13	1	6	124	128	63	54	55	101
Fernandez, Alex	1	1	1.84	2	2	0	0	15	8	4	3	3	23
*Forrester, Tom	0	1	2.95	20	0	0	0	21	11	8	7	11	14
*Galvan, Mike	2	2	3.19	39	0	0	5	73	67	33	26	33	62
Garcia, Ramon	9	14	3.95	26	26	1	0	157	155	84	69	45	130
Gennings, Brian	0	0	7.90	8	0	0	0	14	15	15	12	10	5
Keyser, Brian	6	7	3.66	38	10	2	2	116	107	54	47	40	83
King, Eric	1	0	2.25	2	2	0	0	8	8	4	2	2	5
Merigliano, Frank	3	11	3.76	21	21	1	0	122	130	64	51	44	85
Middaugh, Scott	4	3	1.54	22	4	2	1	70	46	17	12	26	46
Perschke, Greg	7	3	1.21	42	10	2	9	111	83	32	15	29	107
*Resnikoff, Rob	4	6	2.11	45	0	0	10	60	44	18	14	17	59
Smith, Roosevelt	0	2	4.05	4	2	0	0	13	16	10	6	13	7
Ventura, Jose	12	8	3.39	25	25	2	0	162	153	79	61	69	85
Wickman, Rob	0	1	1.98	2	2	0	0	14	17	7	3	4	8

VERO BEACH

BATTING	AVG	G	AB	R	H	2B	3B	HR	RBI	BB	SO	SB
Alvarez, Jorge, 2b-ss	.289	124	454	56	131	19	5	1	48	31	58	31
Barron, Anthony, of	.297	111	344	58	102	21	3	6	60	30	82	42
Beard, Garrett, 1b-c	.250	6	16	1	4	1	0	0	3	2	2	0
Boddie, Eric, of	.236	80	144	21	34	3	1	1	15	22	38	3
*Collier, Anthony, of	.276	115	380	58	105	21	1	4	59	57	74	14
*Dostal, Bruce, of	.302	58	192	43	58	9	2	6	29	24	20	31
Ebel, Dino, ss	.167	96	198	26	33	6	0	0	12	14	33	5
Galle, Mike, 3b	.095	9	21	2	2	0	0	0	4	2	5	0
Gonzalez, Freddy, of-1b	.299	107	335	49	100	17	6	13	51	27	85	28
Gonzalez, Pete, c	.217	90	198	31	43	12	0	2	21	42	40	2
*Gorman, Dirk, of	.167	6	6	0	1	0	0	0	1	1	1	0
*Griffin, Mark, of	.189	31	106	12	20	2	1	0	6	11	14	16
*Lewis, Alan, 3b	.354	15	48	6	17	3	0	0	8	8	2	0
Marabell, Scott, of	.265	89	226	38	60	19	2	8	42	22	56	5
#Munoz, Jose, ss-3b	.295	113	397	57	117	18	3	2	47	34	43	28
#Peters, Rex, 1b	.267	129	408	65	109	19	0	9	72	88	50	15
Piazza, Michael, c-1b	.250	88	272	27	68	20	0	6	45	11	68	0
Teel, Garrett, c	.000	8	14	1	0	0	0	0	1	6	4	0
*Wismer, Michael, 3b	.198	61	187	19	37	6	0	0	15	21	36	9
Young, Eric, 2b-dh	.287	127	460	101	132	23	7	2	50	69	35	76

PITCHING	W	L	ERA	G	GS	CG	SV	IP	H	R	ER	BB	SO
Astacio, Pedro	1	5	6.32	8	8	0	0	47	54	39	33	23	41
Bene, Bill	1	10	6.99	17	14	0	0	57	49	55	44	96	34
Biberdorf, Cam	6	4	2.00	48	0	0	25	67	51	17	15	20	87
Brady, Mike	0	0	2.65	9	0	0	1	17	11	6	5	8	13
Bustillos, Albert	11	5	3.04	22	20	2	0	136	131	50	46	45	89
Calhoun, Ray	7	1	2.81	31	0	0	2	58	51	20	18	23	34
Delahoya, Javier	1	2	5.57	4	4	0	0	21	14	14	13	20	22
*Enno, Clayton	1	2	2.68	29	3	0	2	50	49	20	15	26	29
Fischer, Jeff	1	2	4.09	5	5	1	0	22	24	10	10	1	18
*Fletcher, Bob	1	2	5.31	32	0	0	3	35	40	25	20	21	26
Knapp, John	3	5	3.31	18	9	1	1	73	64	37	27	25	48
*Nina, Robin	0	0	7.20	7	0	0	0	10	12	8	8	5	4
Patrick, Tim	0	3	6.23	4	4	0	0	22	29	18	15	10	11
Perez, Pedro	1	1	6.75	15	0	0	1	31	42	33	23	26	29
Taveras, Ramon	13	7	3.11	26	26	5	0	165	143	67	57	65	116
Terrill, Jim	12	4	2.53	23	21	1	0	132	117	44	37	35	80
Treadwell, Jody	9	1	1.79	16	8	2	1	80	59	17	16	22	80
Vanzytveld, Jeff	6	1	1.38	17	7	3	0	65	40	12	10	17	51
Wengert, William	5	1	3.86	22	7	0	0	75	66	40	32	36	47

WEST PALM BEACH

BATTING	AVG	G	AB	R	H	2B	3B	HR	RBI	BB	SO	SB
#Boddie, Rod, of	.266	90	334	49	89	12	4	0	41	35	50	14
*Faulk, Jim, of-dh	.315	70	254	52	80	12	3	3	31	30	47	33
*Fletcher, Rob, 2b-3b	.260	103	393	59	102	15	6	1	32	32	42	22

BATTING	AVG	G	AB	R	H	2B	3B	HR	RBI	BB	SO	SB
Foster, Kevin, 3b	.167	3	6	0	1	0	1	0	2	1	1	0
#Fulton, Greg, 3b-1b	.260	44	169	27	44	10	6	3	39	11	25	3
Gonzalez, Eddie, dh-1b	.084	32	83	8	7	3	0	1	5	10	23	0
Grace, Mike, 3b	.143	5	14	0	2	0	0	0	1	3	1	0
Hargis, Dan, c	.226	13	31	1	7	3	0	0	2	1	11	1
Lake, Ken, of	.245	103	306	39	75	8	6	7	52	35	76	8
Laker, Tim, c	.000	2	3	0	0	0	0	0	0	0	1	0
Martin, Chris, ss	.279	59	222	31	62	17	1	3	31	27	37	7
Mason, Rob, c	.148	26	61	5	9	0	0	0	5	3	20	0
*Mayo, Todd, of	.261	108	375	54	98	6	1	0	28	52	39	9
Mello, John, 3b-2b	.212	87	312	39	66	15	2	6	43	29	64	8
Rodriguez, Abimael, ss	.111	4	9	0	1	0	0	0	1	4	2	0
*Sanchez, Perry, c	.143	2	7	1	1	0	0	0	0	0	1	0
#Santangelo, F.P., ss-of	.277	116	394	63	109	19	2	0	38	51	49	22
*Siddall, Joe, c	.223	106	349	29	78	12	1	0	32	20	55	6
#Smith, Joel, of-dh	.203	52	177	18	36	4	1	2	20	14	58	14
Stairs, Matt, 3b-ss	.339	55	183	30	62	9	3	3	30	41	19	15
*Terris, Adam, 1b	.250	108	352	53	88	14	1	5	48	56	60	0
Weimerskirch, Mike, of	.282	22	71	13	20	3	0	0	4	8	11	1
Williams, Fred, dh-2b	.232	82	254	26	59	5	6	2	29	46	72	9

PITCHING	W	L	ERA	G	GS	CG	SV	IP	H	R	ER	BB	SO
*Ciaglo, Paul	0	0	18.00	1	0	0	0	1	2	2	2	1	2
Collins, Stacey	3	0	2.35	16	8	0	0	57	53	20	15	17	33
Cornelius, Reid	2	3	3.38	11	11	0	0	56	54	25	21	25	47
Davis, Bret	4	0	3.29	43	0	0	11	66	57	25	24	25	49
Freed, Dan	12	8	2.00	26	25	1	0	171	188	63	38	32	98
Kerrigan, Rob	10	2	3.46	51	0	0	11	83	79	33	32	23	70
Lewis, Richie	0	1	3.00	10	0	0	2	15	12	8	5	11	14
Logan, Joe	1	0	1.88	6	1	0	0	14	13	5	3	5	10
Piatt, Doug	4	1	0.99	21	0	0	9	27	12	6	3	16	41
*Pollack, Chris	13	2	2.05	24	24	0	0	140	111	38	32	62	91
Reyes, Rafael	5	4	4.74	16	10	0	1	57	58	32	30	32	47
*Shehan, Brian	0	0	3.00	2	0	0	0	3	6	1	1	2	2
Sommer, David	11	4	2.37	29	19	1	0	133	89	43	35	64	126
Thoden, John	3	5	3.30	13	10	1	1	71	73	31	26	14	40
Tuss, Jeff	6	3	2.11	29	0	0	1	47	34	16	11	25	28
Wainhouse, David	6	3	2.11	12	12	2	0	77	68	28	18	34	58
Wenrick, John	4	1	3.62	21	0	0	4	37	40	16	15	8	22
Young, Pete	8	3	2.47	39	12	0	19	109	106	36	30	27	62

WINTER HAVEN

BATTING	AVG	G	AB	R	H	2B	3B	HR	RBI	BB	SO	SB
#Bethea, Scott, ss	.429	5	14	0	6	0	0	0	1	2	2	0
Chick, Bruce, of	.227	37	128	10	29	2	0	4	11	23	4	
Colon, Felix, Inf	.196	89	275	21	54	14	2	6	25	38	80	1
Delgado, Alex, ss-3b	.224	89	303	37	68	9	2	1	25	37	36	10
Dixon, Colin, 3b-1b	.246	117	414	35	102	19	0	6	39	31	64	4
Dukes, Willie, of	.186	24	70	6	13	5	0	1	8	8	30	1
Fagnant, Ray, c	.179	47	95	7	17	4	1	0	11	5	23	1
*Fox, Blane, dh-of	.222	65	212	23	47	6	5	1	17	18	30	9
*Friedman, Jason, 1b	.160	50	163	12	26	5	0	1	11	16	26	1
#Graham, Greg, ss-2b	.051	15	39	0	2	0	0	0	1	2	16	0
Jenkins, Garrett, of	.244	63	209	32	51	10	2	0	13	28	69	40
Matilla, Pedro, c	.193	118	353	28	68	12	0	3	34	42	77	1
McNeely, Jeff, of	.161	16	62	4	10	0	0	0	3	3	19	7
Michael, Steve, 1b	.211	102	318	41	67	10	2	9	43	30	110	4
Moore, Bart, 2b	.205	82	185	18	38	3	1	0	10	27	46	35
Moore, Boo, of	.255	123	431	46	110	19	7	4	33	32	99	17
Morrison, Jim, of	.238	75	227	26	54	3	4	2	16	41	68	15
Munoz, Lou, ss-2b	.129	32	70	6	9	3	0	0	5	4	18	0
*Norris, Bill, 3b	.189	28	95	8	18	2	0	0	11	9	21	0
Villalobos, Gary, 2b-ss	.271	88	291	33	79	14	3	0	19	9	53	5
Witherspoon, Rich, of	.179	34	106	16	19	2	1	2	6	16	34	7
Zambrano, Jose, of	.270	88	307	30	83	14	3	4	32	23	72	6

PITCHING	W	L	ERA	G	GS	CG	SV	IP	H	R	ER	BB	SO
Allen, Tracy	0	2	6.00	18	0	0	1	36	35	29	24	28	31
Burgo, Dale	3	1	1.33	4	4	1	0	27	18	6	4	7	12
Crouch, Matt	0	0	4.50	3	3	0	0	6	3	3	3	2	8
Davis, Freddie	1	0	1.08	3	0	0	0	8	6	1	1	1	8
Delgado, Richard	0	1	4.67	12	0	0	0	17	28	17	9	10	11
*Dennison, Jim	0	0	12.19	4	0	0	0	10	18	16	14	7	5
Hoy, Peter	2	10	3.56	52	3	0	7	109	110	54	43	30	48
Kane, Tom	2	5	3.72	34	0	0	5	68	58	32	28	27	65
Kite, Dan	1	10	7.57	15	14	0	0	52	49	53	44	60	45
Miller, Todd	0	1	11.25	1	1	0	0	4	7	5	5	3	2
*Mosley, Tony	1	4	6.16	29	1	0	1	61	73	50	42	38	49
Painter, Gary	1	3	3.80	4	4	0	0	21	17	9	9	12	15
Quantrill, Paul	2	5	4.14	7	7	1	0	46	46	24	21	6	14
Richardson, Ronnie	0	8	4.34	34	6	0	7	83	87	48	40	42	51
*Riley, Ed	4	9	3.11	31	24	0	0	159	152	79	55	64	106
Rush, Andy	5	12	4.08	30	23	2	2	154	139	86	70	58	88
Sanders, Al	7	7	2.30	31	11	3	0	113	95	37	29	35	113
Thompson, Mike	4	6	4.82	15	12	1	0	71	93	46	38	36	27

MIDWEST LEAGUE

Angels look to heavens to win Midwest title

By CURT RALLO

In a season in which there was plenty of . . . "un-heavenly" ruckus raised, it might have been appropriate that Quad City's Angels raised a Midwest League pennant in 1990.

Quad City rolled to a second-half title in the Southern Division and then staged a series of electrifying triumphs to stand tall in the playoffs.

Cedar Rapids had finished with the league's best overall record, a full 10 games better than Quad City, but the Angels dispatched the Reds in the semi-finals, winning two straight games.

South Bend, the 1989 league champion, captured the Northern Division crown with a two-game sweep of Madison.

Quad City's Marcus Moore, a winner in nine of his last 10 regular season starts, maintained his torrid

**Scott Cepicky
. . . bat champ**

pace in the playoffs. Moore handcuffed South Bend in Game One of the championship series, as the Angels won 6-2.

South Bend exploded for a 10-2 triumph in Game Two, but the Angels' used a couple of late rallies to wrap up the best-of-5 series. Quad City wiped out a 5-0 South Bend lead for a 6-5 triumph in Game Three, then wrapped the series up with a 3-2 win in 13 innings in the deciding game.

Jim Aylward, who did not play for Quad City during the regular season, delivered the game winning hit in the 13th for the Angels. White Sox manager Rick Patterson felt that a 'ringer' delivered the Angels their rings.

"I feel bad we got beat by a guy who didn't play in the Midwest League in the regular season," said Patterson. "I feel bad for our kids who played here all year long."

Aylward hit .268 at Double-A Midland and .344 at Class A Palm Springs. He was put on the Quad City roster on the final day of the regular season, with an injured player taken off to make room for him.

"Why do we have to have our rosters set Aug. 15?" asked

LEAGUE CHAMPIONS

Playoff Champions, Where Applicable

1990—Quad City	1975—Waterloo	1960—Waterloo
1989—South Bend	1974—Danville	1959—Waterloo
1988—Cedar Rapids	1973—Wis. Rapids	1958—Waterloo
1987—Kenosha	1972—Appleton	1957—Decatur
1986—Waterloo	1971—Quad City	1956—Paris
1985—Kenosha	1970—Quincy	1955—Dubuque
1984—Appleton	1969—Appleton	1954—Danville
1983—Appleton	1968—Quad City	1953—Decatur
1982—Appleton	1967—Appleton	1952—Decatur
1981—Wausau	1966—Fox Cities	1951—Danville
1980—Waterloo	1965—Burlington	1950—Centralia
1979—Quad City	1964—Fox Cities	1949—Paducah
1978—Appleton	1963—Clinton	1948—West Franfort
1977—Burlington	1962—Dubuque	1947—Belleville
1976—Waterloo	1961—Quincy	

Rich Tunison	Alan Newman	Rafael Novoa
. . . .300-8-86	. . . ERA leader	. . . 9-2, 2.40

Patterson. "I don't blame the Angels. I fault the league."

The tarp incident

South Bend was the site of a caper that turned foul during the regular season.

Five members of the Wausau Timbers—catcher Jim Roso, infielder Brad Hildreth, and pitchers John Boothby, Jim Dedrick and Kip Yaughn—illegally entered Coveleski Stadium on the night of Aug. 12, after a game between the Sox and Timbers had been postponed.

Hoping for a postponement of the following night's game and a quick getaway out of town, the players removed the tarp from the Coveleski infield during a downpour. But the South Bend grounds crew discovered the soaked field the next morning and managed to get it in playing shape for a doubleheader that night.

That's when matters took a turn for the worse. South Bend starting pitching Lenny Brutcher, who led the team in victories, hurt his knee when he slipped on the wet grass attempting to field a bunt. Brutcher was lost for the rest of the season and the playoffs.

South Bend policemen checked into the tarp removal, and discovered that the players had taken a cab from their hotel to the darkened stadium. Police were prepared to arrest the players between games of the doubleheader, but Patterson intervened. The players admitted their guilt and no charges were filed.

The Midwest League handled the situation by suspending the players and fining them. Wausau's parent team, the Baltimore Orioles, also fined the players, and released Boothby. The players were suspended for the rest of the season and 10 games into the 1991 season.

Just passing through

The two players who attracted the most media attention in the Midwest League in 1990 were two who spent the least time in it.

Todd Van Poppel and Lance Dickson, No. 1 draft picks of the Oakland A's and Chicago Cubs' respectively, created a stir with brief appearances in the league.

Van Poppel, who had signed a $1.2 million contract, was treated with kid gloves by the A's during his time in Madison. He was shielded from the press and long bus trips.

Dickson made his mark in a two-week period in the league. He struck out 17 batters in a seven-inning appearance against Madison, then shortly thereafter found himself in Double-A and the majors.

Cedar Rapids outfielder Reggie Sanders stayed around all season and was selected the league's top prospect. He hit .285 with 17 homers and 40 stolen bases.

South Bend first baseman Scott Cepicky, a former University

of Wisconsin punter, emerged from a five-man pack to win the batting crown with a .312 average.

Only two no-hitters were thrown in the league, by two of the most unlikely pitchers. Neither was a solo, nine-inning effort.

Appleton's John Conner had an ERA of more than 9.00 as a relief pitcher, when the Foxes moved him to the starting rotation. He pitched the first seven innings of a no-hitter against Wausau, with Jay Smith completing the final two innings.

Tim Nedin of Kenosha took the mound Aug. 21 against Burlington with a 2-12 record. The Braves had beaten Kenosha six times in six attempts earlier in the season, but Nedin prevented a sweep with a seven-inning no-hitter.

1990 *FINAL STANDINGS*

FIRST HALF

North	W	L	Pct.	GB
Madison (Athletics)	40	28	.588	—
South Bend (White Sox)	35	31	.530	4
Beloit (Brewers)	35	32	.522	4½
Rockford (Expos)	34	34	.500	6
Kenosha (Twins)	29	39	.426	11
Appleton (Royals)	26	37	.413	11½
Wausau (Orioles)	23	45	.338	17

South	W	L	Pct.	GB
Cedar Rapids (Reds)	45	21	.682	—
Burlington (Braves)	42	26	.623	3½
Clinton (Giants)	40	25	.615	4½
Quad City (Angels)..........	36	34	.514	11
Springfield (Cards)	32	38	.457	15
Peoria (Cubs)	27	41	.397	19
Waterloo (Padres)	26	40	.394	19

SECOND HALF

North	W	L	Pct.	GB
South Bend (White Sox)	42	26	.618	—
Beloit (Brewers)	37	31	.544	5
Appleton (Royals)	36	34	.514	7
Madison (Athletics)	34	33	.507	7½
Kenosha (Twins)	32	38	.457	11
Wausau (Orioles)	26	42	.382	16
Rockford (Expos)	22	46	.324	20

South	W	L	Pct.	GB
Quad City (Angels)..........	45	25	.643	—
Cedar Rapids (Reds)	43	25	.632	1
Clinton (Giants)	36	33	.522	8½
Burlington (Braves)	35	33	.515	9
Waterloo (Padres)	34	36	.486	11
Springfield (Cards)	31	38	.449	13½
Peoria (Cubs)	28	41	.406	16½

OVERALL

	W	L	Pct.	GB
Cedar Rapids (Reds)	88	46	.657	—
Quad City (Angels)..........	81	59	.579	10
South Bend (White Sox)	77	57	.575	11
Burlington (Braves)	78	59	.569	11½
Clinton (Giants)	76	58	.567	12
Madison (Athletics)	74	61	.548	14½
Beloit (Brewers)	72	63	.533	16½
Appleton (Royals)	62	71	.466	25½
Springfield (Cards)	63	76	.453	27½
Kenosha (Twins)	61	77	.442	29
Waterloo (Padres)	60	76	.441	29
Rockford (Expos)	56	80	.412	33
Peoria (Cubs)	55	82	.401	24½
Wausau (Orioles)	49	87	.360	40

Playoffs: South Bend defeated Madison 2-0 in best-of-3 semifinal; Quad City defeated Cedar Rapids 2-0 in best-of-3 semifinal; Quad City defeated South Bend 3-1 in best-of-5 final for league championship.

Regular-Season Attendance: South Bend, 212,485; Quad City, 204,889; Peoria, 195,671; Springfield, 161,271; Rockford, 140,864; Cedar Rapids, 121,340; Beloit, 95,876; Appleton, 84,396; Madison, 82,490; Waterloo, 82,451; Burlington, 81,230; Clinton, 75,325; Wausau, 56,434; Kenosha, 53,373.

Managers: Appleton—Joe Breeden; **Beloit**—Bob Derksen; **Burlington**—Jim Saul; **Cedar Rapids**—Dave Miley; **Clinton**—Jack Mull; **Kenosha**—Steve Liddle; **Madison**—Casey Parsons; **Peoria**—Greg Mahlberg; **Quad City**—Don Long; **Rockford**—Mike Quade; **South Bend**—Rick Patterson; **Springfield**—Keith Champion; **Waterloo**—Bryan Little; **Wausau**—Mike Young.

1990 Official All-Star Team: C—Eddie Taubensee, Cedar Rapids. **1B**—Rich Tunison, Appleton. **2B**—Chad Curtis, Quad City. **3B**—John Byington, Beloit. **SS**—Damion Easley, Quad City. **OF**—Reggie Sanders, Cedar Rapids; Troy O'Leary, Beloit; Scott Bryant, Cedar Rapids. **DH**—Fred Cooley, Madison. **RHP**—Darin Kracl, Madison. **LHP**—Alan Newman, Kenosha. **RHRP**—Clyde Keller, Springfield. **LHRP**—Mike Hook, Quad City. **Most Valuable Player**—Reggie Sanders, Cedar Rapids. **Manager of the Year**—Don Long, Quad City.

Top 10 Major League Prospects (by Baseball America): 1. Reggie Sanders, of, Cedar Rapids; **2.** Scott Bryant, of, Cedar Rapids; **3.** Rafael Novoa, lhp, Clinton; **4.** Alan Newman, lhp, Kenosha; **5.** Lance Dickson, lhp, Peoria; **6.** Rich Tunison, 1b, Appleton; **7.** Ramon Caraballo, ss, Burlington; **8.** Javy Lopez, c, Burlington; **9.** Troy O'Leary, of, Beloit; **10.** Damion Easley, ss, Quad City.

1990 *BATTING, PITCHING STATS*

CLUB BATTING

	AVG	G	AB	R	H	2B	3B	HR	BB	SO	SB
South Bend	.262	134	4235	611	1109	195	40	50	483	946	154
Cedar Rapids	.251	134	4293	574	1079	200	22	94	522	825	141
Quad City	.249	140	4376	660	1093	208	18	88	553	956	171
Burlington	.249	137	4452	646	1110	185	35	79	528	863	122
Beloit	.246	135	4253	595	1046	202	18	72	492	999	128
Peoria	.245	137	4509	532	1105	200	39	57	412	943	91
Clinton	.239	134	4291	563	1027	165	33	53	492	813	194
Waterloo	.235	136	4318	533	1014	181	28	47	515	1050	141
Madison	.235	135	4311	602	1012	166	28	82	529	1151	144
Appleton	.235	133	4235	564	994	162	38	37	509	929	173
Springfield	.234	139	4519	549	1059	177	20	57	545	1031	69
Kenosha	.230	138	4329	521	997	174	22	59	489	1055	194
Wausau	.227	136	4313	461	981	148	24	64	451	883	114
Rockford	.226	136	4339	525	982	187	34	42	523	1063	122

CLUB PITCHING

	ERA	G	CG	SHO	SV	IP	H	R	ER	BB	SO
Cedar Rapids	2.66	134	26	18	47	1144	917	430	338	418	1035
Clinton	2.77	134	12	17	38	1148	904	452	354	529	1108
Quad City	2.90	140	21	17	33	1169	1026	525	377	550	1049
Beloit	3.09	135	10	9	38	1144	1015	563	393	533	1109
Kenosha	3.27	138	15	14	33	1173	1034	545	426	503	995
South Bend	3.32	134	15	14	40	1146	984	568	422	588	927
Madison	3.33	135	13	14	30	1155	1027	567	427	507	871
Burlington	3.34	137	27	14	27	1174	1113	570	436	444	905
Appleton	3.63	133	6	14	33	1132	1034	557	456	505	916
Waterloo	3.65	136	15	15	29	1161	1049	559	471	479	766
Peoria	3.69	137	22	10	24	1168	1079	595	479	410	987
Rockford	3.68	136	9	6	33	1151	1103	614	471	523	932
Springfield	3.93	139	9	10	39	1205	1217	668	526	451	877
Wausau	4.37	136	9	4	26	1153	1106	723	560	604	1032

INDIVIDUAL BATTING LEADERS

(Minimum 378 Plate Appearances)

	AVG	G	AB	R	H	2B	3B	HR	RBI	BB	SO	SB
Cepicky, Scott, SB	.312	128	462	65	144	30	5	7	77	55	72	12
Curtis, Chad, QC	.307	135	492	87	151	28	1	14	65	57	78	63
#McCoy, Brent, Bur	.304	125	461	80	140	23	1	5	70	58	75	17
#Tunison, Rich, Appleton	.300	129	490	69	147	21	6	8	86	39	115	32
*O'Leary, Troy, Beloit	.298	118	436	73	130	29	1	6	62	41	90	12
*Dunn, Steve, Kenosha	.297	130	478	48	142	29	1	10	72	49	104	13
#Caraballo, Ramon, Bur	.290	102	390	83	113	18	14	7	55	49	69	41
*James, Joey, Clinton	.289	125	450	58	130	25	4	18	76	34	67	3
Grace, Mike, Rockford	.287	107	366	41	105	20	2	3	42	44	56	7
Sanders, Reggie, CR	.285	127	466	89	133	21	4	17	63	59	97	40

INDIVIDUAL PITCHING LEADERS
(Minimum 112 Innings)

	W	L	ERA	G	GS	CG	SV	IP	H	R	ER	BB	SO
*Newman, Alan, Kenosha ..	10	4	1.64	22	22	5	0	154	95	41	28	78	158
Turek, Joe, CR	13	6	2.34	25	25	4	0	169	131	54	44	61	154
Carter, Larry, Beloit	7	9	2.54	21	19	3	0	128	118	50	36	41	78
*Martinez, Fili, QC	12	7	2.57	26	26	7	0	171	128	66	49	79	195
Rapp, Pat, Clinton	14	10	2.64	27	26	4	0	167	132	60	49	79	132
McKeon, Brian, Waterloo .	11	11	2.70	28	25	1	0	180	152	66	54	34	141
King, Steve, QC	9	9	2.70	31	20	3	0	160	139	64	48	69	162
Sanford, Mo, CR	13	4	2.74	25	25	2	0	158	112	50	48	55	180
Brutcher, Len, SB	11	4	2.74	22	22	4	0	128	87	49	39	77	118
*Galindez, Luis, Waterloo .	10	7	2.78	26	26	2	0	149	122	61	46	75	99

APPLETON

BATTING

	AVG	G	AB	R	H	2B	3B	HR	RBI	BB	SO	SB
Caraballo, Gary, 3b	.214	123	406	37	87	14	3	6	50	39	62	6
Cole, Butch, of	.232	34	112	16	26	2	2	0	10	5	14	3
Collins, Sean, 2b	.226	22	53	9	12	0	0	1	4	15	12	11
*Darter, Keith, of	.244	46	131	9	32	5	1	0	7	11	21	4
Garcia, Francisco, of	.111	7	18	2	2	0	0	0	0	2	7	1
Garibaldo, Chris, ss	.125	7	16	1	2	0	0	0	2	1	4	0
Gerald, Ed, of	.216	45	125	22	27	4	1	0	6	17	45	4
Gilcrist, John, of	.252	129	472	82	119	16	9	5	60	44	78	24
Griesser, Grant, c	.236	35	89	9	21	4	0	1	12	13	18	1
Hernandez, Arnie, of	.159	44	113	19	18	2	0	1	7	5	35	4
King, David, dh-1b	.266	90	316	34	84	23	0	8	64	22	72	1
Miranda, Giovanni, 2b	.227	55	141	15	32	1	2	0	7	16	26	4
#Moore, Kerwin, of	.222	128	451	93	100	17	7	2	36	111	139	57
#Russell, Fred, ss	.264	122	401	48	106	22	4	2	45	46	103	12
Ryan, Colin, c	.165	86	242	27	40	7	0	0	18	36	68	2
*Solseth, Dave, dh-c	.212	94	273	22	58	15	2	3	35	38	31	1
*Stillwell, Rod, 2b-ss	.213	92	240	31	51	5	1	0	16	27	47	1
#Tunison, Rich, 1b	.300	129	490	69	147	21	6	8	86	39	115	32
#Vazquez, Pedro, 2b	.211	66	128	17	27	4	0	0	9	18	28	0
#Young, Don, of	.167	6	18	2	3	0	0	0	3	3	4	1

PITCHING

	W	L	ERA	G	GS	CG	SV	IP	H	R	ER	BB	SO
Ahern, Brian	2	9	5.12	12	11	1	0	63	85	46	36	22	38
*Baez, Francisco	1	7	5.44	10	10	0	0	46	56	40	28	25	28
*Baldwin, Kirk	0	1	3.07	9	0	0	0	15	14	7	5	13	14
Chrisman, Jim	3	1	6.16	11	0	0	0	19	24	14	13	12	16
Conner, John	5	8	4.21	30	12	0	0	113	115	59	53	52	70
Gross, John	3	4	3.36	13	13	0	0	67	61	28	25	22	65
Hoeme, Steve	1	1	3.86	7	0	0	0	12	10	5	5	8	15
Jacobs, Jake	7	6	3.47	25	18	2	1	127	117	59	49	46	105
Karchner, Matt	2	7	4.82	27	11	1	0	71	70	42	38	31	58
*Lindsey, Don	2	2	7.47	21	3	0	0	37	53	38	31	27	31
Milton, Herb	4	5	3.13	22	20	0	0	112	75	47	39	84	80
Schaefer, Chris	6	2	1.71	13	12	1	0	79	63	18	15	18	68
Shifflett, Steve	6	5	2.94	57	0	0	10	83	67	35	27	28	40
Smith, Jim	1	1	3.16	35	0	0	4	68	47	30	24	37	85
Talbert, Lou	11	6	3.50	24	19	1	0	123	107	55	48	55	110
*Walter, Gene	1	0	1.00	2	2	0	0	9	3	1	1	1	8
Wiley, Skip	7	6	2.30	57	0	0	8	82	63	31	21	22	82

BELOIT

BATTING

	AVG	G	AB	R	H	2B	3B	HR	RBI	BB	SO	SB
*Butcher, Arthur, of	.258	75	213	21	55	14	1	5	33	7	42	10
Byington, John, 3b-ss	.263	127	438	75	115	23	1	17	89	49	68	2
Charpia, Rusty, 2b-3b	.000	4	2	0	0	0	0	0	0	1	0	1
*Clark, Tim, of	.260	67	219	27	57	13	1	4	44	31	45	3
Cornell, Daren, ss	.204	39	108	12	22	4	0	0	14	8	40	0
#Diggs, Tony, of	.000	2	4	0	0	0	0	0	0	0	0	0
*Edwards, Todd, dh-of	.303	21	66	5	20	2	0	0	4	11	20	4
Esquer, Dave, ss	.305	19	59	8	18	1	0	0	3	4	9	2
*Gantner, Jim, dh-2b	.379	9	29	10	11	1	0	2	6	7	1	2
Garcia, Librado, of	.136	42	81	10	11	0	1	2	10	5	37	2
*Glenn, Leon, 1b	.193	65	202	19	39	4	3	5	29	20	93	10
#Haugen, Troy, 2b-ss	.226	109	363	48	82	15	2	0	26	78	93	4
Knabenshue, Jeff, of	.177	23	62	8	11	0	1	0	6	7	16	2
*Marrero, Oreste, 1b-dh ...	.275	119	400	59	110	25	1	16	55	45	107	4
Marrero, Vilato, 3b-c	.271	87	255	37	69	13	1	5	24	24	34	3
Molitor, Paul, dh	.500	1	4	1	2	0	0	1	1	0	0	0
*O'Leary, Troy, of	.298	118	436	73	130	29	1	6	62	41	90	12
#Reynoso, Henry, 2b	.223	94	260	37	58	6	2	0	13	21	64	27
#Robertson, Bill, of	.220	38	118	14	26	7	0	1	8	20	26	3
Smith, Rob, of	.270	96	318	57	86	21	2	4	44	39	61	8
Snyder, Randy, c	.201	101	319	43	64	17	0	4	29	30	71	7
*White, Darrin, c-of	.166	82	217	23	36	4	1	0	12	37	65	11
#Wrona, Dave, ss	.300	24	80	7	24	3	0	0	8	7	17	2

PITCHING

	W	L	ERA	G	GS	CG	SV	IP	H	R	ER	BB	SO
Andrzejewski, Joe	6	9	5.61	24	19	1	0	79	57	67	49	97	81
Archer, Kurt	5	0	1.53	11	0	0	0	29	24	11	5	9	27
Bosio, Chris	0	0	3.00	1	1	0	0	3	4	2	1	1	2
Carter, Larry	7	9	2.54	21	19	3	0	128	118	50	36	41	78

Cedar Rapids outfielder Reggie Sanders was the Midwest League's MVP and No. 1 prospect.

	W	L	ERA	G	GS	CG	SV	IP	H	R	ER	BB	SO
Correa, Ramser	3	0	2.19	4	4	0	0	25	24	8	6	9	30
Crim, Chuck	0	0	4.50	1	1	0	0	2	3	2	1	0	0
Czajkowski, Jim	2	0	1.65	21	0	0	11	27	16	7	5	8	37
DelaRosa, Domingo	1	1	3.98	8	0	0	0	20	28	16	9	11	17
Drake, Sam	2	4	5.37	13	13	0	0	57	60	44	34	38	63
*Elvira, Narciso	3	2	2.35	8	7	0	1	38	37	16	10	9	45
Fleming, Keith	6	2	1.95	31	1	0	8	74	60	23	16	17	85
*Fortugno, Tim	8	4	1.56	31	0	0	7	63	38	16	11	38	106
*Garces, Robinson	3	2	2.65	15	1	0	2	37	29	11	11	12	57
Kimball, Scott	5	8	2.88	22	18	4	2	128	134	65	41	46	79
Knabenshue, Jeff	0	0	27.00	1	0	0	0	1	2	4	3	3	0
*Krueger, Bill	1	0	1.50	1	1	0	0	6	4	1	1	0	4
Landry, Greg	3	2	2.68	8	8	0	0	40	35	18	12	27	29
Marrero, Vilato	0	0	3.27	3	0	0	0	11	11	4	4	4	3
McGraw, Tom	7	3	1.93	12	12	1	0	70	49	33	15	34	61
Miller, Pat	0	2	5.66	4	3	0	0	21	26	15	13	7	20
Muscat, Scott	4	6	3.89	20	10	1	0	76	65	46	33	44	51
*Nieves, Juan	2	3	3.99	7	7	0	0	29	29	17	13	6	22
Snyder, Brett	1	4	3.32	30	7	0	3	81	78	45	30	38	86
Vancho, Bob	2	2	2.99	32	2	0	4	84	71	35	28	26	108
Wegman, Bill	0	0	0.00	1	1	0	0	2	1	0	0	1	2
*Wheeler, Brad	0	0	10.13	3	0	0	0	5	8	7	6	4	8

BURLINGTON

BATTING	AVG	G	AB	R	H	2B	3B	HR	RBI	BB	SO	SB
Apolinario, Oswaldo, 2b	.211	42	133	16	28	2	1	0	7	6	32	6
Baldwin, Tony, of	.212	84	264	41	56	7	1	8	40	52	60	9
*Blanks, Daryl, of	.203	48	133	8	27	2	1	1	11	11	20	1
#Caraballo, Ramon, ss	.290	102	390	83	113	18	14	7	55	49	68	41
Clark, Jeff, of	.257	96	288	47	74	4	2	0	27	51	38	9
Ellis, Paul, dh	.000	1	2	0	0	0	0	0	0	0	2	0
*Gardner, Glen, 1b	.260	137	489	64	127	30	2	8	61	60	47	3
Gillis, Tim, 3b	.256	131	464	66	119	28	2	12	61	41	98	4
Harper, Greg, c	.000	9	16	0	0	0	0	0	0	1	8	0
Lopez, Javy, c	.265	116	422	48	112	11	3	11	55	14	84	0
Marze, Dickey, of	.204	86	221	32	45	6	2	4	22	27	75	11
#McCoy, Brent, dh-ss	.304	125	461	80	140	23	1	5	71	58	75	17

BATTING	AVG	G	AB	R	H	2B	3B	HR	RBI	BB	SO	SB
Morrison, Brian, of	.242	69	240	29	58	14	1	14	50	26	76	0
#Olmeda, Jose, ss-2b	.259	27	112	6	29	3	0	0	7	8	17	1
Reis, Paul, 2b	.227	111	379	67	86	8	4	1	40	81	60	11
*Simmons, Randy, of	.230	106	361	50	83	21	1	8	42	32	79	9
Swail, Steve, c	.147	33	75	9	11	2	0	0	3	10	24	0
Zeller, William, c	.667	5	3	0	2	0	0	0	1	1	0	0

PITCHING	W	L	ERA	G	GS	CG	SV	IP	H	R	ER	BB	SO
Borbon, Pedro	11	3	1.47	14	14	6	0	98	73	25	16	23	76
Bruck, Tom	9	6	4.15	19	18	1	0	104	89	65	48	66	81
*Byerly, Rod	0	1	1.93	14	0	0	0	9	5	3	2	3	8
Calderone, Jeff	4	7	3.38	46	0	0	3	83	74	42	31	38	75
*Deleon, Roberto	3	1	2.45	26	0	0	1	29	31	9	8	11	16
Grove, Scott	5	6	3.40	20	18	2	1	109	112	53	41	29	68
*Kelly, Kevin	3	1	4.65	34	7	0	1	79	85	60	41	55	74
Murray, Matt	11	7	3.26	26	26	6	0	163	139	72	59	61	134
Nied, Dave	5	3	2.25	10	9	1	0	64	55	21	16	10	66
Reis, Dave	5	7	3.38	44	0	0	17	67	62	33	25	34	45
Ritter, Darren	6	10	3.78	25	25	6	0	157	172	80	66	53	108
Roy, Walt	7	0	2.60	34	0	0	4	69	74	26	20	11	62
Slomkowski, Rick	1	0	4.76	5	0	0	0	11	9	7	6	8	7
Valle, Tony	2	2	4.06	12	7	0	0	44	44	24	20	22	42
Vazquez, Marcos	6	5	3.81	15	13	5	0	87	89	50	37	20	41

CEDAR RAPIDS

BATTING	AVG	G	AB	R	H	2B	3B	HR	RBI	BB	SO	SB
Allen, Rick, 3b	.233	121	390	47	91	19	1	8	46	37	65	7
Beeler, Pete, 1b-c	.274	79	277	28	76	10	0	7	42	28	58	3
*Branson, Jeff, ss	.251	62	239	37	60	13	4	6	24	24	44	11
Bryant, Scott, of-1b	.264	67	212	40	56	10	3	14	48	50	47	6
Cudjo, Lavell, of	.127	30	79	10	10	3	0	0	2	15	21	2
Dombrowski, Bob, 2b	.095	10	21	4	2	0	0	0	0	4	7	0
*Gillum, K.C., of	.375	4	16	3	6	1	0	0	2	1	3	0
*Hollis, Jack, of-dh	.309	49	149	21	46	10	0	4	19	21	33	6
#Javier, Vicente, 2b-ss	.193	62	135	14	26	3	2	1	15	13	33	1
Jones, Motor-Boat, of	.251	59	215	41	54	12	1	2	23	33	39	14
Kremblas, Frank, 2b-c	.252	92	266	18	67	13	0	5	26	23	54	2
#Krumback, Mark, of-3b	.236	122	440	59	104	14	2	3	29	64	73	17
*Lombardozzi, Chris, 2b-3b	.272	47	169	11	46	6	1	1	25	18	20	8
Mulvaney, Mike, 1b	.259	101	367	42	95	27	0	8	47	26	43	5
Nichols, Brian, c	.286	7	14	3	4	1	0	0	3	1	4	0
Rush, Eddie, ss	.267	57	172	23	46	5	0	0	10	25	22	1
Sanders, Reggie, of	.285	127	466	89	133	21	4	17	63	59	97	40
Schiel, Rob, 2b-ss (29 Ken)	.179	67	195	20	35	6	0	3	12	20	58	4
Sutko, Glenn, c-dh	.300	4	10	0	3	0	0	0	0	0	2	0
*Taubensee, Eddie, c	.259	122	417	57	108	21	1	16	62	51	98	11
Terzarial, Tony, of-dh	.190	44	116	15	22	6	3	1	11	18	33	4

PITCHING	W	L	ERA	G	GS	CG	SV	IP	H	R	ER	BB	SO
Anderson, Mike	10	5	3.38	23	23	2	0	138	134	67	52	62	101
Ayala, Bobby	3	2	3.38	18	7	3	1	53	40	24	20	18	59
Borcherding, Mark	6	3	1.45	21	9	1	3	75	59	24	12	20	49
Economy, Scott	0	0	3.68	4	0	0	0	7	9	3	3	4	14
Garcia, Victor	8	3	1.52	49	0	0	15	71	36	15	12	18	106
*Grovom, Carl	4	1	3.94	8	4	0	0	32	32	14	14	16	20
Hester, Steve	0	1	1.50	1	1	0	0	6	9	4	1	0	3
Jeffery, Scott	6	1	1.38	9	9	6	0	72	45	15	11	11	56
*King, Doug	3	6	3.71	32	0	0	2	51	49	31	21	23	45
Leslie, Reggie	0	0	4.26	6	0	0	0	6	6	3	3	4	7
Manon, Ramon	5	0	4.54	19	0	0	1	40	43	21	20	7	14
Marsh, Quinn	0	0	0.00	2	0	0	0	2	2	0	0	2	1
McAuliffe, Dave	6	1	1.97	41	0	0	26	50	34	13	11	25	40
*McCarthy, Steve	0	1	0.75	8	0	0	0	12	8	6	1	6	11
Risley, Bill	8	9	2.81	22	22	7	0	138	99	51	43	68	123
Rodgers, Darrell	3	2	3.42	9	9	1	0	50	55	27	19	13	37
Sanford, Mo	13	4	2.74	25	25	2	0	158	112	50	48	55	180
Spradlin, Jerry	0	1	3.00	5	0	0	0	12	13	8	4	5	5
Turek, Joe	13	6	2.34	25	25	4	0	169	131	54	44	61	154

CLINTON

BATTING	AVG	G	AB	R	H	2B	3B	HR	RBI	BB	SO	SB
Ahrens, Kelly, c	.178	21	45	4	8	1	0	0	3	4	16	1
Bellinger, Clay, ss	.217	109	383	52	83	17	4	10	48	27	102	13
*Bonner, Jeff, of	.214	78	196	30	42	10	2	0	20	27	34	13
*Borgogno, Mate, 2b	.120	10	25	0	3	0	0	0	0	3	7	1
Brady, Pat, of-dh	.224	49	156	23	35	6	1	2	20	23	25	2
*Carey, Frank, 2b	.296	66	213	31	63	5	3	2	32	28	54	8
Crowe, Ron, 3b-1b	.280	101	332	56	93	20	4	7	42	36	50	6
Davis, Courtney, of	.210	38	119	11	25	1	0	3	15	16	45	13
Grahovac, Mike, c	.147	33	102	8	15	5	0	0	3	5	33	1
*James, Joey, 1b-dh	.289	125	450	58	130	25	4	18	76	34	67	3
Johnson, Randy, of	.222	32	81	12	18	4	1	0	10	27	22	3
Kasper, Kevin, ss-2b	.210	102	314	43	66	8	0	1	25	50	54	21
*McFarlin, Jason, of	.227	129	475	68	108	9	5	0	31	48	79	73
Miller, Roger, c	.257	111	319	31	82	11	1	3	41	28	49	5
Palyan, Vince, of	.262	95	290	42	76	7	2	0	35	41	35	12

	AVG	G	AB	R	H	2B	3B	HR	RBI	BB	SO	SB
*Pattin, Jon, 1b-c	.135	46	111	6	15	3	0	0	10	14	27	1
Rolen, Steve, 3b	.237	77	257	31	61	14	3	3	36	20	51	6
Vollmer, Gus, dh-of	.230	67	200	25	46	9	1	3	23	35	25	2
*Weber, Pete, of	.271	31	107	17	29	6	2	1	15	17	26	7
Young, Jason, 2b	.252	37	115	15	29	4	0	0	6	10	31	7

PITCHING	W	L	ERA	G	GS	CG	SV	IP	H	R	ER	BB	SO
*Aleys, Max	2	3	3.77	25	4	0	3	60	52	30	25	37	49
Brummett, Greg	2	2	3.51	6	4	0	0	26	18	14	10	9	22
*Callahan, Steve	2	4	2.25	41	0	0	2	64	52	25	16	25	47
Ebert, Scott	1	2	5.92	10	5	0	0	24	19	20	16	37	14
Flanagan, Daniel	0	2	2.86	25	0	0	3	35	33	12	11	10	25
Foley, Jim	1	0	3.77	7	0	0	0	14	12	8	6	10	10
Gustafson, Ed	7	1	1.81	40	1	0	12	84	50	23	17	32	123
*Hancock, Chris	11	3	2.28	18	17	2	0	111	78	33	28	43	123
Hanselman, Carl	9	10	3.23	25	24	2	0	145	120	71	52	75	128
*Hernandez, Marino	1	2	4.17	15	1	0	0	37	33	19	17	25	27
Huisman, Rick	6	5	2.05	14	13	0	0	79	56	19	18	33	103
Huslig, Jim	4	4	2.55	12	12	0	0	74	51	24	21	34	62
*Novoa, Rafael	9	2	2.40	15	14	3	0	98	73	32	26	30	113
Rapp, Pat	14	10	2.64	27	26	4	0	167	132	60	49	79	132
Taylor, Rob	5	2	1.53	31	0	0	17	35	29	13	6	16	42
Whatley, Fred	1	1	3.66	4	3	0	0	20	14	10	8	8	22

KENOSHA

BATTING	AVG	G	AB	R	H	2B	3B	HR	RBI	BB	SO	SB
Cordova, Marty, of	.216	81	269	35	58	7	5	7	25	28	73	6
Delanuez, Rex, of-dh	.245	72	253	35	62	16	2	5	35	42	49	20
Delarwelle, Chris, dh	.298	66	252	31	75	15	1	4	45	21	24	6
*Dunn, Steve, 1b	.297	130	478	48	142	29	1	10	72	49	105	13
Gentile, Randy, 3b-of	.209	80	258	28	54	12	0	7	34	22	84	3
Gross, Deryk, of	.204	59	167	22	34	5	0	1	17	14	47	10
Hoerner, Troy, of	.148	25	88	7	13	4	0	2	3	6	39	1
Lewis, Mica, ss-ss	.227	64	238	33	54	9	1	4	14	25	73	20
Lloyd, Mike, 2b-3b	.266	83	267	41	71	4	0	1	26	36	50	28
Mathiot, Mike, 2b-of	.184	48	158	22	29	10	0	1	15	19	47	3
Meares, Pat, 3b	.239	52	197	26	47	10	2	4	22	25	45	2
Milene, Jeff, c	.000	2	1	0	0	0	0	0	0	1	0	0
#Morris, Steve, of	.235	105	349	59	82	13	3	0	29	65	74	41
#Mota, Willie, c	.181	80	265	20	48	8	2	0	20	18	39	0
#Nunez, Alex, ss	.197	117	365	42	72	4	1	0	21	32	105	20
Owens, Jay, of	.236	66	216	31	51	9	2	5	30	39	59	15
Pichardo, Francisco, of	.188	45	133	10	25	2	1	1	9	12	38	3
Roskom, Bryan, of-1b	.191	28	89	6	17	2	0	2	4	8	21	2
Siwa, Joe, c	.246	67	211	17	52	13	1	3	25	17	54	0

PITCHING	W	L	ERA	G	GS	CG	SV	IP	H	R	ER	BB	SO
Best, Jayson	8	6	3.56	19	19	1	0	94	67	45	37	59	98
Diaz, Sandy	1	5	4.86	14	7	0	0	46	47	30	25	27	35
*Harrington, Jody	3	4	1.74	22	1	0	1	47	26	13	9	29	36
Hoppe, Dennis	1	3	4.10	4	4	1	0	26	29	14	12	8	12
Krol, Dave	0	2	1.84	5	0	0	1	15	9	4	3	2	15
Lindaman, Chad	1	2	3.10	16	0	0	1	20	17	8	7	11	19
Lipson, Marc	1	4	2.53	47	0	0	20	53	38	19	15	17	34
Misuraca, Mike	9	9	3.33	26	26	1	0	167	164	81	62	57	116
Musselwhite, Darren	6	5	3.13	42	1	0	3	72	64	31	25	15	63
*Nedin, Tim	3	13	3.39	27	22	3	0	141	131	74	53	63	144
*Newman, Alan	10	4	1.64	22	22	5	0	154	95	41	28	78	158
*Pulido, Carlos	5	5	2.34	56	0	0	6	62	55	21	16	36	70
Robles, Scott	3	5	4.75	34	8	0	1	89	105	57	47	27	70
Roskom, Bryan	1	0	0.00	1	1	0	0	6	3	0	0	3	3
Swope, Mark	6	1	4.58	16	10	1	0	71	69	41	36	30	52
Thelen, Jeff	3	9	4.80	28	17	3	0	105	111	64	56	39	64

MADISON

BATTING	AVG	G	AB	R	H	2B	3B	HR	RBI	BB	SO	SB
Abbott, Kurt, ss-2b	.232	104	362	38	84	18	0	0	28	47	74	21
Armas, Marcos, 3b-1b	.238	75	260	32	62	13	0	7	33	10	80	3
*Beck, Wynn, dh-c	.264	102	330	41	87	13	1	8	51	46	66	0
Campa, Eric, ss-3b	.255	29	102	11	26	1	0	0	8	4	19	0
Conte, Mike, 3b-of	.173	55	173	24	30	2	1	4	16	21	38	4
Cooley, Fred, 1b-dh	.259	101	363	50	94	18	1	22	66	29	112	1
#Dattola, Kevin, of	.324	25	102	12	33	0	2	1	9	7	10	11
*Henry, Scott, 3b-c	.239	46	134	21	32	6	1	1	15	32	22	0
Lydy, Scott, of	.190	54	174	33	33	6	2	4	19	25	62	7
McCormick, Glenn, dh-3b	.163	19	49	6	8	2	0	0	5	11	17	0
Mercedes, Henry, c	.227	90	282	29	64	13	2	3	37	30	100	6
Osinski, Glenn, 2b-3b	.249	54	213	32	53	13	1	2	26	16	49	9
Parry, Bob, of	.125	2	8	1	1	0	0	0	0	0	3	0
*Shockey, Scott, 1b-of	.261	71	253	45	66	16	2	10	43	26	60	2
Simmons, Enoch, of	.184	117	359	47	66	10	1	3	29	47	98	17
#Tamarez, Carlos, ss-2b	.146	17	41	6	6	1	0	0	3	5	21	0
#Thomas, Keith, of	.211	44	142	21	30	3	1	3	20	10	42	12
#Tinsley, Lee, of	.251	132	482	88	121	14	12	12	59	78	175	44
Tredway, Ed, c	.211	42	90	9	19	2	0	0	8	3	23	1
#Vice, Darryl, 2b	.235	65	196	28	46	7	0	0	12	39	45	1

	AVG	G	AB	R	H	2B	3B	HR	RBI	BB	SO	SB
*Waggoner, Jim, 3b-ss	.246	39	114	16	28	3	0	1	8	26	18	4
Weaver, Trent, ss	.293	22	75	10	22	4	1	1	11	14	16	1

PITCHING	W	L	ERA	G	GS	CG	SV	IP	H	R	ER	BB	SO
Brimhall, Brad	0	1	8.06	11	3	0	0	22	29	23	20	20	18
Cormier, Russ	3	0	2.06	8	8	2	0	52	34	17	12	17	38
Deleon, Gerbacio	4	6	4.78	15	15	0	0	81	108	64	43	26	46
Gibbs, Jim	2	0	4.05	18	0	0	7	20	16	10	9	20	24
*Grott, Matt	2	0	0.36	22	0	0	12	25	15	5	1	14	36
Gulledge, Hugh	3	6	3.74	19	13	1	0	79	78	38	33	36	54
Kracl, Darin	10	2	1.98	14	14	4	0	100	73	39	22	37	58
*Kuhn, Chad	5	4	3.18	21	7	0	0	65	60	30	23	26	37
Latter, Dave	6	8	2.53	43	1	0	1	78	52	29	22	34	77
Lawson, Jim	0	0	19.85	7	0	0	0	11	29	28	25	9	8
Martinez, Rey	0	0	4.70	6	0	0	0	8	11	6	4	4	6
Mejia, Leandro	6	2	1.92	20	5	0	0	66	52	19	14	21	42
*Mohler, Mike	1	1	3.41	42	2	0	1	63	56	34	24	32	72
*Osteen, Gavin	10	10	3.10	27	27	1	0	154	126	69	53	80	120
Patrick, Bronswell	3	7	3.60	13	12	3	0	80	88	44	32	19	40
Peck, Steve	2	2	5.24	5	4	0	0	22	24	15	13	9	14
Peek, Tim	5	3	2.70	39	0	0	7	57	41	19	17	10	70
Pena, Pedro	5	4	2.68	14	14	2	0	84	63	31	25	41	48
Sudbury, Craig	4	2	4.62	7	6	0	0	37	32	23	19	29	18
Taylor, Bill	1	2	3.26	19	1	0	2	30	27	12	11	11	23
Van Poppel, Todd	2	1	3.95	3	3	0	0	14	8	11	6	10	17

PEORIA

BATTING	AVG	G	AB	R	H	2B	3B	HR	RBI	BB	SO	SB
Adames, Juan, 2b	.091	8	22	2	2	0	0	0	1	2	3	2
#Berryhill, Damon, c ...	.385	7	26	10	10	2	0	3	8	3	6	0
Cancel, Danny, of	.164	40	110	11	18	1	0	0	5	13	38	4
Castellano, Pedro, 3b ..	.276	117	417	61	115	27	4	2	44	63	73	7
Cole, Marvin, 2b	.250	60	236	25	59	9	1	1	20	14	10	2
Cunningham, Earl, of ...	.216	78	269	24	58	9	0	5	26	13	108	2
*Ebright, Chris, of-dh	.234	107	338	41	79	15	3	11	41	41	67	2
Erdman, Brad, c	.193	37	119	9	23	3	0	0	4	12	42	0
Francisco, Rene, of	.237	75	228	29	54	5	3	0	19	21	49	4
*Franco, Matt, 1b	.282	123	443	52	125	33	2	6	65	43	39	4
Mundy, Rick, c-1b	.236	43	123	16	29	8	1	1	14	14	32	0
Murphy, Jim, of	.260	58	200	31	52	8	0	2	16	20	49	8
Paynter, Bill, c	.115	19	52	2	6	1	0	0	2	1	13	0
Robinson, Jim, c	.224	26	67	4	15	3	0	0	8	10	8	0
Simonds, Dan, c	.318	19	66	8	21	5	0	0	4	3	7	1
Smith, Woody, dh-2b	.230	89	318	31	73	15	6	4	40	10	73	2
St. Peter, Bill, ss	.250	121	448	52	112	23	4	12	56	41	107	6
Torres, Paul, 1b-dh	.244	36	123	18	30	4	1	5	18	13	33	1
#Walbeck, Matt, c	.227	25	66	2	15	1	0	0	5	5	7	1
Washington, Kraig, of-of	.249	98	366	39	91	9	3	0	26	28	34	15
Weinheimer, Wayne, 1b ..	.292	8	24	3	7	2	0	0	2	3	8	0
#Williams, Jerrone, of	.248	124	448	62	111	17	11	5	43	39	137	30

PITCHING	W	L	ERA	G	GS	CG	SV	IP	H	R	ER	BB	SO
Bradford, Troy	2	6	4.47	8	8	1	0	52	51	30	26	19	35
*Dickson, Lance	3	1	1.51	5	5	1	0	36	22	9	6	11	54
Doss, Jason	2	6	4.64	18	13	1	0	78	77	47	40	37	71
*Duenas, Tony	0	0	9.00	1	0	0	0	1	1	1	1	0	0
Eddings, Jay	0	3	5.25	8	0	0	1	12	23	8	7	1	7
Gelb, Jac	2	6	5.14	23	5	0	0	63	60	41	36	26	56
Gomez, Henry	7	12	4.06	30	29	2	0	175	165	92	79	55	138
Hirsch, Jeff	0	3	3.97	10	0	0	1	11	11	6	5	5	11
Hollins, Jessie	0	0	5.59	5	0	0	0	10	12	9	6	5	8
*Jaques, Eric	6	6	3.33	52	0	0	12	68	57	36	25	18	73
Lutz, Chris	12	9	2.90	25	25	6	0	167	132	62	54	45	168
Mann, Thomas	1	0	1.65	9	1	0	1	16	19	3	3	7	11
Mullino, Ray	0	0	4.15	6	0	0	1	9	10	5	4	4	9
Rasp, Ronnie	2	2	3.77	26	0	0	3	43	49	26	18	15	30
Swartzbaugh, Dave	8	11	3.82	29	29	5	0	170	147	88	72	89	128
Sweeney, Jim	0	3	3.52	35	0	0	2	61	62	36	24	19	54
Willis, Travis	10	11	3.26	31	22	6	0	163	152	78	59	41	93
Young, Mark	0	3	3.31	24	0	0	3	33	29	16	12	11	40

QUAD CITY

BATTING	AVG	G	AB	R	H	2B	3B	HR	RBI	BB	SO	SB
*Billmeyer, Mickey, c ...	.269	77	234	30	63	14	0	5	33	28	36	1
Curtis, Chad, 2b-of	.307	135	492	87	151	28	1	14	65	57	78	64
#DelaRosa, Cesar, 2b-3b .	.236	23	72	7	17	3	0	0	6	3	18	1
Easley, Damion, ss	.274	103	365	59	100	19	3	10	56	41	60	25
*Gay, Jeff, dh-c	.241	81	278	26	67	16	0	6	34	13	47	0
Gonzales, Larry, c-dh ..	.307	99	309	44	95	16	1	8	75	36	56	2
Hirtensteiner, Rick, of	.220	87	259	36	57	12	0	4	24	26	78	10
#Jones, Bobby, of	.236	108	351	40	83	20	6	8	47	37	94	6
Kapano, Corey, 3b	.244	106	352	57	86	18	1	9	51	48	89	4
Martinez, Ray, 3b-ss ...	.225	105	306	47	69	10	0	9	40	58	82	4
Minnis, Billy, ss-2b ...	.333	3	9	2	3	1	0	0	2	0	3	0
*Ortegon, Ronnie, 1b ...	.224	134	442	73	99	17	4	3	49	68	87	9
Rodriguez, Edgal, of ...	.242	118	388	49	94	17	3	5	49	43	80	6
#Specyalski, Brian, 3b-ss	.067	6	15	1	1	1	0	0	0	0	4	0

MWL DEPARTMENT LEADERS

BATTING

R	Kerwin Moore, Appleton	93
H	Chad Curtis, Quad City	151
TB	Chad Curtis, Quad City	223
2B	Matt Franco, Peoria	33
3B	Ramon Caraballo, Bur	14
HR	Fred Cooley, Madison	22
RBI	John Byington, Beloit	89
SH	Alex Nunez, Kenosha	11
SF	Brent McCoy, Burlington	10
BB	Kerwin Moore, Appleton	111
IBB	Steve Dunn, Kenosha	8
HBP	Steve Morris, Kenosha	18
SO	Lee Tinsley, Madison	175
SB	Jason McFarlin, Clinton	72
CS	J.D. Noland, Waterloo	24
OB%	Chad Curtis, Quad City	.390

PITCHING

G	Chris Gorton, Springfield	59
GS	Dave Swartzbaugh, Peoria	29
	Henry Gomez, Peoria	29
CG	Three tied at	7
ShO	Brian McKeon, Waterloo	5
Sv	Dave McAuliffe, CR	26
	Clyde Keller, Springfield	26
W	Marcus Moore, Quad City	16
L	Steve Whitehead, Rockford	14
	Jose Lebron, Waterloo	14
IP	Brian McKeon, Waterloo	180
H	Jose Lebron, Waterloo	177
R	Henry Gomez, Peoria	92
HR	Jose Lebron, Waterloo	17
BB	Brad Pennington, Wau	121
HB	Travis Willis, Peoria	14
SO	Fili Martinez, Quad City	195
WP	John Conner, Appleton	20
	Joe Andrzejewski, Beloit	20
Bk	Steve King, Quad City	10
	Tom Infante, Springfield	10

	AVG	G	AB	R	H	2B	3B	HR	RBI	BB	SO	SB
Threadgill, Chris, of	.167	45	108	17	18	2	1	2	7	22	35	0
*Threadgill, Henry, 2b	.216	74	204	34	44	3	2	2	20	29	49	15
#Williams, Kent, of	.000	1	3	1	0	0	0	0	0	0	1	2	0
#Williams, Reggie, of	.243	58	189	50	46	11	2	3	12	39	60	24

PITCHING	W	L	ERA	G	GS	CG	SV	IP	H	R	ER	BB	SO
Adams, Dave	3	5	4.97	12	10	1	0	51	59	36	28	22	41
Archibald, Dan	0	0	3.52	14	0	0	0	23	21	12	9	11	11
Bennett, Erik	7	7	2.99	18	18	3	0	108	91	48	36	37	100
Castillo, Roberto	3	6	2.40	17	11	2	0	83	75	31	22	28	50
Craven, Britt	2	1	2.90	15	6	1	0	59	56	33	19	18	43
Haffner, Les	5	1	2.33	45	0	0	10	58	46	18	15	21	27
Helm, Wayne	1	1	4.00	4	1	0	0	9	8	6	4	8	8
Heredia, Julian	0	0	3.86	5	0	0	0	7	5	6	3	6	10
Hillman, Stewart	2	6	3.38	24	11	1	1	91	88	45	34	34	69
*Hook, Mike	6	3	1.89	30	0	0	7	38	18	10	8	22	66
King, Steve	9	9	2.70	31	20	3	0	160	139	64	48	69	162
Marchese, John	3	1	1.98	35	0	0	12	50	38	15	11	32	40
Martin, Justin	2	0	0.73	8	0	0	1	12	9	3	1	7	15
*Martinez, Fili	12	7	2.57	26	26	7	0	171	128	66	49	79	195
*Montoya, Norm	3	1	3.14	4	4	1	0	29	30	12	10	6	13
Moore, Marcus	16	5	3.31	27	27	2	0	160	150	83	59	106	160
*Neal, Dave	2	6	5.43	14	10	0	0	53	66	46	32	36	34
Refnes, Todd	3	1	2.41	9	5	1	0	34	43	16	9	15	22
*Vegely, Bruce	3	4	2.28	37	1	0	3	71	59	26	18	30	56

ROCKFORD

BATTING	AVG	G	AB	R	H	2B	3B	HR	RBI	BB	SO	SB
Cramer, Bill, 1b-c	.158	66	183	15	29	8	0	0	12	17	40	0
Davison, Scott, ss	.215	127	441	52	95	13	7	1	48	60	115	22
#Elder, Isaac, of	.227	89	216	43	49	13	1	2	15	34	72	21
Grace, Mike, 3b-1b	.287	107	366	41	105	20	2	3	42	44	56	7
*Greene, Willie, ss	.400	11	35	4	14	3	0	0	2	6	7	2
Hudson, Deryk, 3b-1b	.207	111	376	38	78	12	0	4	41	41	96	1
Kaub, Keith, 1b	.200	42	130	9	26	3	0	3	13	5	43	0
*Krause, Ron, 2b	.215	115	344	53	74	9	2	1	28	84	96	12
Laker, Tim, c	.221	120	425	46	94	18	3	7	57	32	83	7
Leary, Rob, c-1b	.243	34	70	9	17	3	0	1	7	10	15	1
Malinowski, Chris, 3b-of	.258	21	66	4	17	2	2	0	7	5	8	2
Ramirez, J.D., dh-2b	.259	119	432	56	112	21	5	2	51	53	58	6
*Ramsey, Jeff, of	.159	48	132	10	21	2	1	0	3	9	52	1
Ricker, Troy, of	.195	55	185	24	36	7	1	3	11	19	60	11
*Rodriguez, Buen, of-1b	.212	95	231	33	49	13	2	3	23	20	76	8
*Smith, Charlie, of	.223	81	251	38	56	13	3	4	38	39	64	16
Woods, Tyrone, of	.242	123	455	50	110	27	5	8	46	45	121	5

PITCHING	W	L	ERA	G	GS	CG	SV	IP	H	R	ER	BB	SO
Batista, Miguel	0	1	8.76	3	2	0	0	12	16	13	12	5	7
Bochtler, Doug	9	12	3.50	25	25	1	0	139	142	82	54	54	109
Bushing, Chris	3	6	3.28	46	0	0	12	80	62	38	29	38	99
Eddy, Jim	7	7	3.48	34	8	0	4	114	119	52	44	38	80
*Haney, Chris	2	4	2.21	8	8	3	0	53	40	15	13	6	45
Howze, Ben	2	7	6.28	19	14	0	0	72	83	58	50	48	31
*Kilgo, Rusty	4	4	2.23	45	0	0	9	89	62	26	22	20	85
Logan, Joe	10	2	2.63	18	15	2	0	89	83	36	26	36	67
Martinez, Martin	8	11	4.65	27	26	1	0	134	151	86	69	63	91
Regira, Gary	0	4	4.23	28	3	0	0	62	53	39	29	54	62
*Sullivan, Brian	2	0	2.31	13	0	0	2	23	16	7	6	6	20
Thoden, John	4	3	2.28	12	12	1	0	75	71	33	19	14	73

	W	L	ERA	G	GS	CG	SV	IP	H	R	ER	BB	SO
Whitehead, Steve	2	14	5.47	23	22	1	0	110	117	87	67	81	77
Wilkinson, Brian	3	5	2.77	42	1	0	6	78	67	30	24	49	76

SOUTH BEND

BATTING	AVG	G	AB	R	H	2B	3B	HR	RBI	BB	SO	SB
Alvarez, Clemente, c	.236	48	127	14	30	5	0	2	12	20	38	2
Cepicky, Scott, 1b-dh	.312	128	462	65	144	30	5	7	77	55	72	12
Eatinger, Mike, 2b	.264	129	477	63	126	29	3	4	57	36	63	16
Hairston, John, of-dh	.238	98	252	48	60	15	4	4	33	33	100	8
Harris, Keith, of	.209	15	43	4	9	0	3	0	2	3	14	3
Ingram, Jeff, c-dh	.286	61	168	22	48	3	2	4	22	15	32	3
Kobza, Greg, c-1b	.268	97	284	37	76	18	3	5	51	58	83	3
Kroeger, J.T., c	.250	9	16	0	4	1	0	0	2	3	5	0
*Plemmons, Ron, of	.263	129	438	89	115	21	5	7	51	86	71	22
Ramos, Jorge, ss-3b	.165	51	121	19	20	2	1	1	9	10	34	5
Singley, Joe, c	.262	24	61	9	16	2	1	1	4	5	19	1
Sullivan, Carl, of	.276	62	210	29	58	13	2	4	35	19	46	5
Tatarian, Dean, ss-3b	.295	38	112	19	33	3	1	0	10	16	31	9
Tejada, Alex, ss	.175	23	57	6	10	1	0	0	2	5	12	8
Tejada, Leo, ss	.243	83	243	28	59	7	2	0	17	10	44	4
Teter, Craig, of	.262	27	61	4	16	3	0	0	8	1	24	2
Walker, Dennis, 3b	.210	125	410	53	86	14	3	4	44	28	119	5
Wolak, Jerry, of	.278	121	352	48	98	17	0	1	28	37	68	11
*Zaksek, John, of	.286	93	322	52	92	11	4	5	38	39	69	20

PITCHING	W	L	ERA	G	GS	CG	SV	IP	H	R	ER	BB	SO
Bolton, Rod	5	1	1.94	7	7	3	0	51	34	14	11	12	50
Brutcher, Len	11	4	2.74	22	22	4	0	128	97	48	39	77	118
Campos, Frank	1	0	9.39	13	1	0	1	15	19	17	16	16	13
*Forrester, Tom	0	0	4.66	13	0	0	5	10	7	6	5	13	8
Gennings, Brian	1	1	3.77	11	0	0	4	14	13	13	6	11	7
Gorman, Dave	1	1	1.88	7	0	0	0	14	14	5	3	6	8
*Johnson, Earnie	5	3	2.09	27	0	0	3	60	50	20	14	23	52
*Long, Rich	1	5	4.35	27	7	0	0	70	75	41	34	36	56
Matznick, Danny	10	7	3.48	26	25	0	0	122	100	58	47	82	127
Mitchener, Mike	6	6	4.40	34	8	0	1	86	82	50	42	51	40
Mongiello, Mike	6	6	3.30	38	15	3	13	106	98	55	39	54	89
Ruffin, Johnny	7	6	4.17	24	24	0	0	123	117	86	57	82	92
Schrenk, Steve	7	6	2.95	20	14	2	0	104	79	44	34	25	92
Stevens, Scott	6	8	2.47	50	0	0	12	102	82	45	28	31	81
Thoma, Scott	1	0	6.35	7	0	0	0	6	8	4	6	9
Vanderwel, Bill	0	0	3.00	9	1	0	0	12	9	7	4	15	9
Van Winkle, David	2	1	5.18	29	1	0	1	57	62	36	33	34	27
Wickman, Bob	7	2	1.38	9	9	3	0	65	50	16	10	16	50

SPRINGFIELD

BATTING	AVG	G	AB	R	H	2B	3B	HR	RBI	BB	SO	SB
#Andujar, Juan, ss	.213	105	366	32	78	13	2	3	30	23	109	9
Bell, David, of	.143	55	84	11	12	3	0	0	4	9	31	1
Berlin, Randy, 3b-ss	.234	51	128	15	30	6	0	0	9	13	34	1
#Campas, Mike, 3b-2b	.242	121	392	52	95	15	0	8	46	62	96	1
*Carter, Ed, of	.233	7	30	4	7	0	1	0	2	1	5	2
*Clemens, Troy, dh	.272	105	316	37	86	16	2	2	40	30	44	0
*Ellis, Paul, c-1b	.235	50	183	18	43	5	0	5	25	26	34	0
*Federico, Joe, 1b	.242	90	293	44	71	19	2	8	37	39	82	2
Fielitz, Bill, c	.174	13	23	1	4	1	0	0	0	6	8	0
*Hernandez, Henry, 1b	.234	41	128	14	30	3	0	5	26	14	29	0
Herrera, Ezequiel, of	.265	123	490	56	130	14	4	0	42	35	99	11
Keating, Mike, ss	.136	10	22	1	3	1	0	0	0	0	7	0
Kindred, Vince, of	.280	38	125	22	35	6	1	3	20	21	31	7
*Kraft, Mike, of	.241	109	349	34	84	16	2	3	36	50	77	1
Landinez, Carlos, 2b-ss ...	.120	60	133	22	16	3	0	1	7	12	39	5
Langiotti, Fred, c	.219	98	306	31	67	9	0	4	34	47	50	0
#Martinez, Luis, of-1b	.267	105	382	58	102	12	4	10	54	40	50	7
Rittman, Alvin, 3b-2b	.175	81	183	23	32	8	1	2	16	21	62	1
Savinon, Odalis, of	.169	55	136	12	23	2	0	0	8	13	39	2
*Thomas, John, of	.250	39	152	19	38	11	0	1	12	10	36	3
Thomas, Orlando, c	.140	19	43	2	6	0	0	0	2	16	17	1
Thompson, Kourtney, of-dh	.182	6	22	1	4	2	0	0	1	3	9	1
Trujillo, Jose, 2b	.270	75	233	39	63	12	1	2	25	54	43	14

PITCHING	W	L	ERA	G	GS	CG	SV	IP	H	R	ER	BB	SO
*Botkin, Alan	0	4	6.17	6	5	0	0	23	27	23	16	12	20
Cimorelli, Frank	4	8	4.56	41	15	1	0	120	125	80	61	41	86
*Corona, John	5	1	3.71	54	0	0	1	68	68	36	28	29	58
Cox, Danny	0	0	0.00	1	1	0	0	5	1	0	0	0	3
*Eversgerd, Bryan	6	8	4.14	20	15	2	0	104	123	60	48	26	55
*Gewecke, Steve	3	5	3.61	38	13	0	0	105	103	52	42	38	79
Gorton, Chris	5	7	1.18	59	0	0	12	76	65	23	10	30	83
Hensley, Mike	2	1	5.48	5	4	0	0	21	21	14	13	12	15
Infante, Tom	3	5	5.35	50	0	0	0	72	94	59	43	32	41
Keller, Clyde	3	3	1.87	44	0	0	26	53	30	13	11	15	58
Lata, Tim	10	5	3.62	19	19	1	0	124	122	68	49	36	75
Meamber, Tim	5	11	5.59	26	18	1	0	113	143	84	70	39	83
Smith, Mark	4	2	3.96	8	8	0	0	52	50	25	23	15	34
*Spiller, Derron	0	2	12.27	3	3	0	0	11	20	16	15	9	3
Tolbert, Mark	4	1	3.24	6	5	1	0	33	40	13	12	9	21

	W	L	ERA	G	GS	CG	SV	IP	H	R	ER	BB	SO
*Weber, Ron	5	10	3.47	29	23	1	0	158	133	71	61	88	121
Wiseman, Dennis	4	3	2.71	10	10	2	0	63	49	25	19	16	41

WATERLOO

BATTING	AVG	G	AB	R	H	2B	3B	HR	RBI	BB	SO	SB
Billingsley, Rod, c	.043	18	23	1	1	0	0	0	2	2	10	0
Colon, David, of	.216	85	268	23	58	18	1	2	32	33	61	3
Conley, Greg, c	.209	82	239	20	50	7	0	1	12	17	90	2
*David, Greg, 3b	.000	1	1	0	0	0	0	0	0	1	0	0
Doyle, Tom, 1b-dh	.220	120	413	37	91	14	1	3	36	27	80	1
Gill, Steven, of	.264	56	197	24	52	5	2	1	19	22	34	3
Holbert, Ray, ss	.204	133	411	51	84	10	1	3	39	51	117	16
Martin, Steve, 3b	.251	122	398	64	100	21	4	9	48	57	118	31
Noland, J.D., of	.246	125	456	75	112	20	6	4	51	71	84	48
Rupp, Terry, dh-1b	.249	105	358	30	89	18	0	6	51	33	120	2
Sanchez, Osvaldo, of ...	.266	122	448	62	119	23	5	14	67	52	112	13
Toole, Matt, 3b-2b	.207	71	174	13	36	6	2	0	11	10	42	1
*Verstandig, Mark, c	.207	81	188	34	39	6	2	1	12	57	32	0
Whalen, Steve, of-dh ...	.234	93	273	24	64	9	2	2	33	23	46	2
Witkowski, Matt, 2b	.253	128	470	75	119	24	2	1	55	59	104	19

PITCHING	W	L	ERA	G	GS	CG	SV	IP	H	R	ER	BB	SO
Embry, Todd	0	5	7.25	29	8	0	4	63	68	56	51	56	40
Florie, Bryce	4	5	4.39	14	14	1	0	66	60	37	32	37	38
*Galindez, Luis	10	7	2.78	26	26	2	0	149	122	61	46	75	99
Hart, Jeff	3	4	2.63	46	0	0	5	65	57	24	19	26	49
Hays, Robert	0	1	4.03	12	0	0	0	22	23	11	10	12	17
*Hoyer, Brad	7	4	2.28	51	1	0	6	91	58	26	23	40	61
Lebron, Jose	7	14	4.18	26	26	3	0	164	177	89	76	61	93
Lewis, Tony	2	4	4.98	47	0	0	12	65	71	46	36	22	36
McKeon, Brian	11	11	2.70	28	25	7	0	180	152	66	54	34	141
Morton, Ron	8	11	3.45	44	8	1	2	125	114	54	48	16	89
*Reed, Billy	6	8	3.75	23	21	1	0	130	100	66	54	76	70
Sanders, Scott	2	2	4.86	7	7	0	0	37	43	21	20	21	29
Verstandig, Mark	0	0	3.60	5	0	0	0	5	4	2	2	3	4

WAUSAU

BATTING	AVG	G	AB	R	H	2B	3B	HR	RBI	BB	SO	SB
Alexander, Manny, ss	.178	44	152	16	27	3	1	0	11	12	41	8
Asencio, Matires, ss-2b ...	.111	19	36	1	4	0	0	0	2	3	12	0
*Bautista, Hector, of	.223	32	94	11	21	5	1	3	13	8	13	0
Benitez, Christian, 2b ...	.229	75	205	16	47	2	1	1	6	20	33	9
#Buford, Damon, of	.300	41	160	31	48	7	2	1	14	21	32	15
Cairo, Sergio, of	.240	111	333	31	80	8	4	3	29	25	49	12
Davis, Bo, of	.164	28	61	5	10	2	1	0	1	3	26	1
Devares, Cesar, c	.199	56	171	7	34	4	1	3	19	7	28	2
DiMarco, Steve, 3b	.138	18	65	4	9	1	0	1	3	5	15	2
#Fowler, John, dh-of	.224	70	223	25	50	16	1	5	25	16	53	6
Fuller, Paul, c-dh	.234	55	175	21	41	9	0	2	26	26	30	3
Godin, Steve, of	.248	48	145	14	36	6	0	3	13	18	32	4
*Hicks, Aman, of	.208	99	289	36	60	11	4	0	12	29	60	12
Hildreth, Brad, ss-3b	.239	87	268	23	64	7	0	4	18	24	36	4
Kessinger, Keith, ss-2b ...	.216	37	134	17	29	8	0	0	9	6	23	1
Lamitola, Mike, 2b	.180	42	122	11	22	1	1	0	6	5	21	1
*Lee, Keith, of	.079	16	38	0	3	0	0	0	0	1	10	0
Lewis, T.R., 3b-of	.285	115	404	60	115	24	2	8	45	46	64	10
*Miller, Brent, 1b	.301	19	83	9	25	7	0	1	8	2	18	2
Nicosia, Steve, of	.141	31	71	3	10	0	0	0	2	6	20	2
Roso, Jimmy, c-of	.242	97	298	24	72	9	0	4	30	29	62	2
*Schmidt, Keith, of	.153	32	85	7	13	1	1	3	12	8	37	1
Shingledecker, Gary, 3b ..	.243	24	74	10	18	4	1	1	6	8	4	0
*Tyler, Brad, ss-2b	.232	57	190	31	44	4	3	2	24	44	45	11
Wearing, Melvin, 1b	.256	105	336	45	86	9	0	18	56	72	101	6
#Zaun, Greg, c	.130	37	100	3	13	0	1	1	7	7	17	0

PITCHING	W	L	ERA	G	GS	CG	SV	IP	H	R	ER	BB	SO
*Anderson, Matt	1	3	4.43	18	2	0	0	43	49	31	21	24	39
Boothby, John	3	1	6.75	25	0	0	0	45	48	39	34	36	30
Dedrick, James	0	1	2.70	3	1	0	0	10	6	4	3	4	8
*Hale, Shane	3	4	4.79	12	9	1	0	56	47	34	30	39	57
Heiden, Shawn	2	4	5.02	19	2	0	6	29	29	17	16	27	37
*Leinen, Pat	3	9	3.54	13	13	3	0	81	73	42	32	25	73
Marett, John	1	0	5.88	14	0	0	0	26	40	27	17	8	14
*Martin, Tom	2	3	2.48	9	9	0	0	40	31	25	11	27	45
Medina, Victor	0	2	3.38	16	0	0	2	19	16	8	7	6	16
*Mercedes, Juan	0	2	4.64	6	4	0	0	21	22	16	11	14	14
*Moore, Daryl	4	6	2.47	36	0	0	12	55	41	26	15	17	72
Paveloff, Dave	2	3	2.98	28	1	0	1	57	51	29	19	20	44
*Pennington, Brad	4	9	5.18	32	18	1	0	106	81	89	61	121	142
Riddle, Dave	3	1	3.21	19	0	0	4	48	42	18	17	12	35
Schullstrom, Erik	0	2	4.66	5	5	0	0	19	20	12	10	7	21
*Smith, Rick	1	0	15.26	6	0	0	0	8	16	18	13	9	6
Taylor, Tom	3	11	5.27	23	20	1	0	111	103	74	65	62	78
Teixeira, Joe	1	0	9.53	7	0	0	0	11	22	15	12	4	7
*Unrein, Todd	1	1	2.03	23	1	0	0	31	30	12	7	15	24
Wheatcroft, Rob	6	12	3.91	27	22	3	0	152	149	78	66	50	115
*Williams, Steve	7	9	4.25	26	19	0	1	133	144	77	63	48	106
Yaughn, Kip	2	4	5.29	10	10	0	0	51	46	32	30	29	47

SOUTH ATLANTIC LEAGUE

Best talent, but Mets let title slip away

By GENE SAPAKOFF

It didn't seem fair: the Columbia Mets had the South Atlantic League's three top hitters (Tim Howard, Brook Fordyce, Tito Navarro), some of its best pitchers, the SAL's fastest player (Pat Howell), its top major-league prospect (Navarro) and its best manager (Bill Stein, by a vote of his peers).

To rub it in, the Columbia players could brag that living in the only league city home to a major university (U. of South Carolina) meant there were more coeds than in, say, Gastonia. You can imagine the envy from Charleston, S.C., to Charleston, W.Va., especially after the Mets steam-rolled their way to a first-half Southern Division title and, eventually, the league's best overall regular-season record.

Tim Howard
. . . leading hitter

But darned if Charleston, W.Va., didn't win its first SAL championship—without even having to face Columbia. The Wheelers won 19 of their last 22 regular-season games to run away with the Northern Division second-half title, then gave up only four runs in five postseason games—a 2-0 sweep of Fayetteville in the Northern Division playoffs and a 3-0 sweep of Savannah in the championship series.

Star pitcher Tim Pugh, a former Oklahoma State righthander who went 15-6 with a 1.88 ERA and 154 strikeouts in the regular season, had a shutout in each series, including a four-hitter in the 6-0 title-clincher played before a crowd of 4,500 at Charleston's Watt Powell Park.

Calling Frank Tanana

Batters around the South Atlantic League were awfully glad Randy Marshall and Dave "Gator" Telgheder did not stick around past the all-star break. Both pitchers earned promotions with terrific numbers and baffling, if not overpowering, command.

Marshall was 13-0 with a 1.33 ERA for Fayetteville with

LEAGUE CHAMPIONS

Playoff Champions, Where Applicable

1990—Charleston, WV	1977—Gastonia	1964—Salisbury
1989—Augusta	1976—Greenwood	1963—Greenville
1988—Spartanburg	1975—Spartanburg	1962—Statesville
1987—Myrtle Beach	1974—Gastonia	1961—Shelby
1986—Columbia	1973—Spartanburg	1960—Salisbury
1985—Florence	1972—Spartanburg	1953-59—Did Not
1984—Asheville	1971—Greenwood	Operate
1983—Gastonia	1970—Greenville	1952—Shelby
1982—Greensboro	1969—Greenwood	1951—Shelby
1981—Greensboro	1968—Greenwood	1950—Lenoir
1980—Greensboro	1967—Spartanburg	1949—Ruthrfrd Co.
1979—Greenwood	1966—Spartanburg	1948—Lincolnton
1978—Greenwood	1965—Rock Hill	

NOTE: League known as Western Carolina League from 1948 through 1962 and as Western Carolinas League through 1979.

Sumter first baseman Ryan Klesko hit .368 in a half season in the SAL.

81 strikeouts and nine walks in 102 innings. The lefty gave part of the credit for his success to Detroit Tigers pitcher Frank Tanana, for providing professional advice on a radio call-in show while Marshall was at Eastern Michigan.

"I'd phone in, tell Frank who I was and ask questions," Marshall said. "It was pretty neat."

All Telgheder did in the first half for Columbia was go 9-3 with a 1.54 ERA. A righthander, he fanned 81 batters and walked 10 in 99 innings.

Gastonia's Bobby Reed had an even shorter SAL stay. Fresh out of Mississippi State, the righthander threw 33 shutout innings and earned a quick promotion to Double-A Tulsa.

Another standout pitcher: Greensboro southpaw Sterling Hitchcock (12-12, 2.91), who followed a no-hitter with a complete-game, three-hit shutout and later pitched back-to-back shutouts. Twice, Hitchcock took a no-hitter into the sixth inning of what became a loss.

Myrtle Beach righthander Mike Ogliaruso (14-9, 2.52) was the MVP of the SAL all-star game for giving up three hits in four innings of an 8-0 Southern Division win.

McGraw suits up again

For the second year in a row, former big-league closer Tug McGraw made an SAL appearance, again as a favor to his buddy, Gastonia president Roman Gabriel. Danny Jackson, on a rehab trip to Charleston, W.Va., in August, gave up two runs in three innings against Spartanburg.

Neither McGraw nor Jackson, however, could match the interest generated when actress Julia Roberts took a break from filming "Sleeping With The Enemy" to attend a Spartanburg Phillies game with a cast party estimated at 50.

Charleston, S.C., took its lumps from Hurricane Hugo in the offseason and then again after College Park was repaired; The Rainbows' 1-12 start and an 18-game losing streak in the second-half led to the worst overall record in the league, 46-96.

Asheville shortstop Orlando Miller, whom the Houston Astros obtained in a March deal with the New York Yankees, hit .313 with four homers and 62 RBIs. Sumter catcher Tyler Houston, the second player picked in the 1989 draft, struggled early but showed improvement on offense and defense in the second half and wound up batting .210 with 13 home runs with 56 RBIs.

Howell, Columbia's center fielder, stole 80 bases. The league record is 145, set by Vince Coleman at Macon in 1983.

1990 FINAL STANDINGS

FIRST HALF

North	W	L	Pct.	GB
Fayetteville (Tigers)	46	26	.639	—
Gastonia (Rangers)	44	28	.611	2
Spartanburg (Phillies)	37	34	.521	8½
Charleston, W.Va. (Reds) ...	30	41	.423	15½
Greensboro (Yankees)......	29	43	.403	17
Asheville (Astros)	28	43	.394	17½

South	W	L	Pct.	GB
Columbia (Mets)	46	26	.639	—
Augusta (Pirates)	41	30	.477	4½
Myrtle Beach (Blue Jays) ...	39	31	.557	6
Sumter (Braves)	38	34	.528	8
Savannah (Cardinals).......	30	41	.423	15½
Charleston, S.C. (Padres) ...	20	51	.282	25½

SECOND HALF

North	W	L	Pct.	GB
Charleston, W.Va. (Reds) ...	47	25	.653	—
Gastonia (Rangers)	38	33	.535	8½
Asheville (Astros)	38	34	.528	9
Fayetteville (Tigers)	36	35	.507	10½
Greensboro (Yankees)......	30	42	.417	17
Spartanburg (Phillies)	26	44	.371	20

South	W	L	Pct.	GB
Savannah (Cardinals).......	43	27	.614	—
Myrtle Beach (Blue Jays) ...	38	32	.543	5
Columbia (Mets)	37	34	.521	6½
Sumter (Braves)	35	35	.500	8
Augusta (Pirates)	32	40	.444	12
Charleston, S.C. (Padres) ...	26	45	.366	17½

OVERALL

	W	L	Pct.	GB
Columbia (Mets)	83	60	.580	—
Gastonia (Rangers)	82	61	.573	1
Fayetteville (Tigers)	82	61	.573	1
Myrtle Beach (Blue Jays) ...	77	63	.550	4½
Charleston, W.Va. (Reds) ...	77	66	.538	6
Savannah (Cardinals).......	73	68	.518	9
Sumter (Braves)	73	69	.514	9½
Augusta (Pirates)	73	70	.510	10
Asheville (Astros)	66	77	.462	17
Spartanburg (Phillies)	63	78	.447	19
Greensboro (Yankees)......	59	85	.410	24½
Charleston, S.C. (Padres) ...	46	96	.324	36½

Playoffs: Charleston, W.Va. defeated Fayetteville 2-0 in best-of-3 semifinal; Savannah defeated Columbia 2-0 in best-of-3 semifinal; Charleston, W.Va. defeated Savannah 3-0 in best-of-5 final to win league championship.

Regular-Season Attendance: Greensboro, 153,232; Charleston, W.Va., 152,359; Augusta, 125,105; Asheville, 101,193; Columbia, 99,385; Fayetteville, 95,040; Savannah, 94,686; Charleston, S.C., 76,133; Myrtle Beach, 71,598; Gastonia, 48,767; Spartanburg, 45,104; Sumter, 37,412.

Managers: Asheville—Frank Cacciatore; **Augusta**—Lee Driggers; **Charleston, S.C.**—Jack Krol; **Charleston, W.Va.**—Jim Lett; **Columbia**—Bill Stein; **Fayetteville**—Gene Roof; **Gastonia**—Orlando Gomez; **Greensboro**—Brian Butterfield; **Myrtle Beach**—Mike Fischlin; **Savannah**—Rick Colbert; **Spartanburg**—Mel Roberts; **Sumter**—Ned Yost.

1990 Official All-Star Team: C—Brook Fordyce, Columbia. **1B**—Ryan Klesko, Sumter. **2B**—David Hajek, Asheville. **3B**—Tim Howard, Columbia. **SS**—Tito Navarro, Columbia. **UTIL INF**—Austin Manahan, Augusta. **OF**—Scott Pose, Charleston, W.Va.; Pat Howell, Columbia; Tony Scruggs, Gastonia. **UTIL OF**—Shawn Holtzclaw, Myrtle Beach. **DH**—Mike Burton, Gastonia. **RHP**—Tim Pugh, Charleston, W.Va. **LHP**—Randy Marshall, Fayetteville. **Most Valuable Player**—Tim Howard, Columbia. **Most Outstanding Pitcher**—Randy Marshall, Fayetteville. **Most Outstanding Prospect**—Ryan Klesko, Sumter. **Manager of the Year**—Bill Stein, Columbia.

Top 10 Major League Prospects (by Baseball America): 1. Tito Navarro, ss, Columbia; 2. Ryan Klesko, 1b, Sumter; 3. Willie Greene, ss, Augusta; 4. Tim Pugh, rhp, Charleston, W.Va.; 5. Brook Fordyce, c, Columbia; 6. Tim Howard, 2b-3b, Columbia; 7. Sterling Hitchcock, lhp, Greensboro; 8. Mike Ogliaruso, rhp, Myrtle Beach; 9. Pat Howell, of, Columbia; 10. Orlando Miller, ss, Asheville.

1990 *BATTING, PITCHING STATS*

CLUB BATTING

	AVG	G	AB	R	H	2B	3B	HR	BB	SO	SB
Columbia	.277	143	4916	732	1362	211	42	67	431	908	248
Augusta	.263	143	4835	683	1272	174	52	44	596	948	134
Asheville	.260	143	4665	638	1215	218	32	63	481	960	207
Charleston-WV	.252	143	4600	657	1157	200	32	30	629	772	157
Gastonia	.245	143	4661	627	1143	212	23	86	512	954	152
Myrtle Beach	.244	140	4545	610	1109	190	23	97	478	1024	89
Sumter	.240	143	4603	607	1106	186	40	69	579	894	147
Fayetteville	.234	143	4584	601	1072	153	36	44	582	921	80
Spartanburg	.232	141	4664	530	1084	155	32	42	477	905	74
Greensboro	.227	143	4657	547	1058	180	28	55	566	1077	166
Savannah	.227	141	4577	552	1038	164	23	63	462	898	169
Charleston-SC	.223	142	4601	473	1026	156	31	44	459	958	102

CLUB PITCHING

	ERA	G	CG	SHO	SV	IP	H	R	ER	BB	SO
Gastonia	2.83	143	9	16	41	1241	1053	511	390	573	1085
Sumter	3.04	142	15	13	34	1231	1086	529	416	443	890
Myrtle Beach	3.12	140	6	8	48	1206	1115	548	418	483	1031
Charleston-WV	3.14	143	19	10	37	1220	1057	528	425	526	912
Columbia	3.25	143	25	14	36	1251	1216	603	452	449	858
Fayetteville	3.27	143	15	14	38	1237	1111	552	449	472	886
Spartanburg	3.28	141	8	7	30	1225	1126	573	447	430	1024
Savannah	3.42	141	6	4	37	1240	1113	619	471	578	927
Greensboro	3.52	144	7	12	25	1254	1081	670	491	564	1051
Augusta	3.70	143	7	9	34	1245	1233	663	512	576	1006
Asheville	3.98	143	15	11	34	1220	1156	699	540	642	867
Charleston-SC	4.34	142	17	6	26	1208	1295	762	582	516	682

INDIVIDUAL BATTING LEADERS
(Minimum 389 Plate Appearances)

	AVG	G	AB	R	H	2B	3B	HR	RBI	BB	SO	SB
#Howard, Tim, Col	.323	128	505	80	163	18	11	10	89	46	44	30
Fordyce, Brook, Col	.315	104	372	45	117	29	1	10	54	39	42	4
Navarro, Tito, Col	.314	136	497	86	156	25	4	0	54	69	55	50
Hajek, David, Ashe	.313	135	498	86	156	28	0	6	60	61	50	43
Miller, Orlando, Ashe	.313	121	438	60	137	29	6	4	62	25	52	12
Manahan, Austin, Aug	.302	94	378	59	114	12	10	7	52	46	105	26
Rivers, Ken, MB	.299	100	358	51	107	18	2	12	67	31	61	1
*Pose, Scott, Char-WV	.298	135	480	106	143	13	5	0	46	114	56	49
Ratliff, Daryl, Aug	.295	122	417	70	123	11	6	1	55	67	62	24
#Nieves, Melvin, Sumter	.283	126	459	60	130	24	7	9	59	53	125	10

INDIVIDUAL PITCHING LEADERS

(Minimum 115 Innings)

	W	L	ERA	G	GS	CG	SV	IP	H	R	ER	BB	SO
Hoffman, Jeff, Gboro	8	3	1.47	47	1	0	1	116	86	43	19	40	93
Pugh, Tim, Char-WV	15	6	1.88	27	27	8	0	177	142	58	37	56	153
*Hailey, Roger, Sumter	10	1	1.94	17	17	4	0	120	66	31	26	46	126
*Blumberg, Rob, MB	13	4	2.16	25	23	1	0	129	101	43	31	68	128
Ogliaruso, Mike, MB	14	9	2.52	26	26	6	0	164	132	57	46	61	158
Garcia, Mike, Fay	12	8	2.55	28	28	6	0	180	152	69	51	41	113
Gardner, Chris, Ashe	5	10	2.62	23	23	3	0	134	102	57	39	69	81
Small, Aaron, MB	9	9	2.80	27	27	1	0	148	150	72	46	56	96
Dorn, Chris, Col	9	11	2.81	27	19	6	1	144	140	67	45	49	69
Buckley, Travis, Gas	12	6	2.84	27	26	3	0	162	149	66	51	61	149

ASHEVILLE

BATTING	AVG	G	AB	R	H	2B	3B	HR	RBI	BB	SO	SB
Berry, Perry, 2b	.223	61	202	26	45	11	1	2	19	26	44	4
Beuerlein, Ed, c-dh	.299	54	187	21	56	11	1	0	25	11	47	1
*Curtis, Craig, 1b	.228	119	360	65	82	7	3	17	51	75	91	33
Dallas, Gershon, of	.278	124	468	48	130	20	1	3	55	19	75	17
Encarnacion, Juan, of	.202	104	341	32	69	12	3	7	44	24	108	9
Hajek, David, 2b-ss	.313	135	498	86	156	28	0	6	60	61	50	43
*Holum, Brett, c-3b	.221	33	77	8	17	2	0	0	4	18	0	
Hunter, Brian, of	.250	127	444	84	111	14	6	0	16	60	72	45
*Johnson, Luther, of	.253	110	344	44	87	21	5	8	61	48	92	12
Lucin, T.J., c	.198	34	91	13	18	4	0	5	9	8	34	0
McCray, Justin, inf	.287	61	178	16	51	8	0	2	25	7	47	4
Miller, Orlando, ss	.313	121	438	60	137	29	6	4	62	25	52	12
Pineda, Jorge, of-dh	.198	37	106	13	21	3	2	2	9	11	25	2
Quijada, Ed, 3b	.228	119	356	43	81	16	2	2	36	59	84	5
#Santana, Jose, of	.243	31	70	6	17	2	0	0	5	2	16	2
Scott, Kevin, c	.274	129	460	66	126	29	2	5	79	37	93	17
#Valentin, Ed, 2b	.244	15	45	7	11	1	0	0	7	4	12	1

PITCHING	W	L	ERA	G	GS	CG	SV	IP	H	R	ER	BB	SO
August, Sam	3	0	2.25	5	4	0	0	20	17	6	5	6	17
Brown, Duane	0	1	7.82	3	2	0	0	13	17	13	11	7	8
Dovey, Troy	9	7	4.18	33	15	1	2	113	94	65	52	75	100
Gardner, Chris	5	10	2.62	23	23	3	0	134	102	57	39	69	81
Gonzales, Ben	3	4	2.35	53	0	0	18	73	50	25	19	44	66
*Gutierrez, Anthony	7	7	4.62	41	12	0	0	101	91	66	52	74	88
McDowell, Mike	4	3	5.13	41	2	0	1	86	84	64	49	79	60
Munoz, Julio	3	2	2.35	9	9	0	0	38	31	15	10	17	16
Perez, Francisco	6	4	5.35	36	8	1	1	99	115	81	59	46	77
*Rinaldi, Kevin	0	0	7.62	7	0	0	0	13	20	14	11	7	7
Rivas, Limbert	2	3	2.79	33	0	0	5	42	39	14	13	20	30
*Rosario, Eliezel	8	15	3.50	30	26	4	0	175	173	95	68	49	94
Small, Mark	3	4	4.15	34	0	0	6	52	54	36	24	37	34
Wall, Donnie	6	8	5.18	28	22	1	1	132	149	87	76	47	111
Wheeler, Ken	7	9	3.45	21	20	5	0	125	116	57	48	60	76

AUGUSTA

BATTING	AVG	G	AB	R	H	2B	3B	HR	RBI	BB	SO	SB
Antigua, Felix, c	.286	78	290	36	83	14	0	1	41	18	21	0
Aude, Rich, 1b-3b	.234	128	475	48	111	23	1	6	61	41	133	4
#Bailey, Rob, ss-2b	.237	36	131	26	31	3	3	0	10	18	37	15
*Brewington, Mike, of-1b ...	.310	60	213	33	66	8	6	1	36	37	51	12
Calder, Joe, ph	.000	1	0	0	0	0	0	0	0	1	0	0
*Curley, Tim, of	.230	64	213	28	49	9	2	3	25	38	41	3
Delossantos, Alberto, dh-of ...	.348	52	207	26	72	8	4	0	26	7	23	3
Green, Tom, of	.223	38	121	18	27	1	2	1	13	15	28	5
*Greene, Willie, ss	.258	86	291	59	75	12	4	11	47	61	58	7
*Holmes, Bill, dh-1b	.291	40	134	13	39	8	0	2	30	14	11	0
#Howard, Dave, dh-1b	.192	27	78	16	15	4	0	2	8	19	24	0
Johnson, Deron, 1b-of	.179	30	78	11	14	2	0	2	14	13	21	1
*Johnson, Mark, 1b	.250	43	144	12	36	7	0	0	19	24	18	4
Manahan, Austin, 3b-2b ...	.302	94	378	59	114	12	10	7	52	46	105	26
Nixon, Jason, c	.077	6	13	3	1	1	0	0	0	4	6	0
Pennyfeather, William, of ..	.262	122	465	69	122	14	4	4	48	23	85	21
Peterson, Robert, c	.159	23	69	8	11	1	1	0	6	11	20	0
Ratliff, Daryl, of	.295	122	417	70	123	11	6	1	55	67	62	24
Rodriguez, Hector, ss	.263	30	114	10	30	2	1	1	13	5	24	0
Rodriguez, Roman, ss-2b ...	.275	99	364	38	100	14	3	2	37	27	61	3
*Seymour, Winston, 1b	.182	12	33	5	6	2	0	0	3	8	8	0
Sondrini, Joe, 2b	.203	28	79	14	16	2	1	0	4	7	17	0
Torres, Jessie, c	.243	51	148	20	36	6	0	0	14	33	39	0
*Trusky, Ken, of	.272	79	294	52	80	9	3	0	28	52	35	5
#Ufret, Ricardo, 2b	.174	33	86	7	15	1	1	0	6	8	20	1

PITCHING	W	L	ERA	G	GS	CG	SV	IP	H	R	ER	BB	SO
Arvesen, Scott	8	11	4.32	28	28	2	0	158	186	89	76	54	102
*Bird, David	4	4	2.09	44	5	0	15	86	72	24	20	35	114
Dooley, Marvin	0	0	2.70	4	0	0	0	3	6	8	1	3	2
Fajardo, Hector	2	2	3.86	7	7	0	0	40	41	18	17	15	28
Futrell, Mark	0	1	2.25	3	0	0	0	4	5	2	1	3	1
*Honeywell, Brent	4	1	1.15	13	0	0	4	16	9	4	2	8	8
*Latham, John	3	2	4.39	28	6	0	2	66	64	42	32	55	61

Brook Fordyce	Austin Manahan	Tito Navarro
... .315 hitter	... .302, 28 SB	...No. 1 prospect

	W	L	ERA	G	GS	CG	SV	IP	H	R	ER	BB	SO
Martinez, Ramon	3	2	5.26	35	2	0	0	77	103	56	45	34	40
Masters, Wayne	2	1	3.18	37	0	0	5	68	62	34	24	24	55
Mooney, Troy	3	3	4.64	10	8	0	0	43	40	27	22	30	18
Parkinson, Eric	6	13	4.50	31	26	0	0	138	139	93	69	78	127
Redmond, Andre	0	2	13.50	4	0	0	0	5	6	9	7	5	3
Rychel, Kevin	10	4	4.12	27	23	0	0	129	127	79	59	87	105
Santiago, Delvy	9	10	3.42	31	19	3	2	145	137	69	55	37	101
*Underwood, Bobby	3	1	3.12	10	10	0	0	58	45	23	20	23	52
Wagner, Paul	7	7	2.75	35	1	0	4	72	71	30	22	30	71
*Watson, Dave	4	4	2.30	23	8	2	1	86	76	31	22	31	75
*Way, Ronald	5	2	3.08	24	0	0	1	50	41	24	17	21	42

CHARLESTON, S.C.

BATTING	AVG	G	AB	R	H	2B	3B	HR	RBI	BB	SO	SB
*Arredondo, Roberto, 1b	.249	136	490	50	122	19	4	4	48	24	87	2
*Barton, Jeff, of	.230	84	304	27	70	10	2	4	39	28	39	1
*Beck, Brian, of	.231	127	438	39	101	20	3	11	50	33	111	2
Bream, Scott, ss	.071	4	14	2	1	0	0	0	0	4	7	1
Brooks, Monte, of-3b	.249	113	414	55	103	20	4	0	38	48	81	30
Bruno, Julio, ss	.227	19	75	11	17	1	1	0	5	1	21	0
Coleman, Rico, of	.175	107	303	27	53	10	0	1	14	24	66	9
Curnow, Rob, c	.196	63	194	11	38	4	0	1	13	16	35	1
Decareau, Tom, of	.125	10	24	2	3	0	1	0	0	6	13	0
*Diaz, Tony, dh-3b	.230	113	404	40	93	15	1	4	42	53	64	1
*Gonzalez, Paul, 3b	.242	69	231	30	56	7	3	11	32	37	62	0
Henderson, Lee, c	.210	87	305	22	64	8	0	0	18	22	71	3
Lopez, Pedro, c-dh	.198	32	101	9	20	2	0	0	5	7	18	0
#Martinez, Pablo, ss-2b	.221	136	453	51	100	12	6	0	33	41	104	16
Mateo, Jose, 2b	.161	20	62	6	10	0	0	1	1	5	19	1
*Parsons, Will, 2b	.174	56	195	21	34	5	1	0	11	31	25	3
Pueschner, Craig, of	.241	94	344	41	83	11	2	6	41	43	77	29
Weaver, Trent, ss-2b	.232	75	250	28	58	12	3	1	26	36	58	3

PITCHING	W	L	ERA	G	GS	CG	SV	IP	H	R	ER	BB	SO
Banks, Lance	7	1	2.82	48	0	0	2	99	92	45	31	43	43
*Bennett, Jim	5	15	3.06	23	23	6	0	150	172	75	51	27	75
Cunningham, Troy	4	11	4.33	40	15	2	1	152	188	92	73	55	77
Curnow, Rob	0	0	4.50	4	0	0	0	6	7	3	3	2	4
*Ellis, Tim	1	2	7.90	3	3	0	0	14	16	12	12	12	3
Embry, Todd	1	0	1.38	2	2	1	0	13	8	2	2	7	15
*Garside, Russ	0	2	11.25	2	2	0	0	8	15	10	10	0	5
Guzman, Pete	1	1	4.10	28	2	0	1	77	86	45	34	29	38
Johnson, Bill	3	14	6.81	25	20	1	0	104	113	102	79	90	84
Marx, Bill	3	4	3.48	32	2	0	4	75	71	38	29	28	34
*Murdock, Joe	0	1	6.10	5	0	0	1	10	13	10	7	4	4
*Pickett, Danny	1	0	3.72	7	0	0	0	19	22	14	8	13	9
*Santiago, Rafael	8	15	3.68	25	23	3	0	147	143	82	60	50	94
Thompson, Charlie	4	17	4.73	26	26	1	0	148	166	110	78	58	56
Thompson, Squeezer	0	3	17.00	11	5	0	0	18	20	40	34	46	6
Worrell, Tim	5	8	4.64	20	19	3	0	111	120	65	57	28	68
Zinter, Ed	3	2	2.20	45	0	0	17	57	43	17	14	23	65

CHARLESTON, W.V.

BATTING	AVG	G	AB	R	H	2B	3B	HR	RBI	BB	SO	SB
Arland, Mark, of	.125	13	24	2	3	1	0	0	2	3	11	2
#Baxter, Dave, of	.133	9	15	2	2	0	0	0	0	2	3	1
Berry, Mark, 1b	.286	14	35	7	10	4	0	0	5	7	2	0
Bustamante, Rafael, inf	.255	89	318	40	81	10	2	0	38	42	52	3
Carr, Terry, of	.247	54	186	28	46	7	2	1	21	18	38	5
Cox, Darron, c	.253	103	367	53	93	11	3	1	44	40	75	14
Fuller, Jon, dh-c	.241	67	224	34	54	12	1	5	33	34	38	1
Gill, Chris, 2b	.251	126	462	69	116	22	0	0	40	53	51	16
*Gillum, K.C., of	.234	18	64	10	15	4	1	1	5	8	18	2
Hoffman, Trevor, ss-3b	.212	103	278	41	59	10	1	0	23	38	53	3
*Hollis, Jack, of-dh	.221	49	140	13	31	3	0	0	17	19	29	3

	AVG	G	AB	R	H	2B	3B	HR	RBI	BB	SO	SB
#Jones, Kevin, 3b-dh	.083	6	12	2	1	1	0	0	0	3	7	0
Jones, Motor-Boat, of	.253	71	261	36	66	19	4	2	46	32	41	3
Nichols, Brian, c-dh	.181	21	72	7	13	2	0	0	11	10	11	0
Perozo, Dan, of	.279	106	337	39	94	11	2	4	43	29	69	17
*Pose, Scott, of	.298	135	480	106	143	13	5	0	46	114	56	49
*Riggs, Kevin, 2b	.250	2	4	0	1	0	0	0	1	0	1	0
Rush, Ed, ss	.214	68	229	29	49	10	0	1	26	30	22	0
Velez, Noel, 3b	.222	54	180	15	40	8	1	1	12	17	44	3
Vondran, Steve, 3b-1b	.269	75	275	30	74	19	2	1	47	29	37	1
*Walker, Bernie, of	.324	51	170	39	55	9	6	7	39	45	52	16
*Watson, Todd, 1b	.235	105	353	39	83	15	1	2	44	43	45	2
Wilson, Dan, c	.248	32	113	16	28	9	1	2	17	13	17	0
Wright, Benny, ss	.000	2	1	0	0	0	0	0	0	0	0	0

PITCHING	W	L	ERA	G	GS	CG	SV	IP	H	R	ER	BB	SO
Ayala, Bobby	6	1	2.43	21	4	2	2	74	48	23	20	21	73
Borcherding, Mark	0	4	5.02	6	0	0	0	14	16	12	8	10	5
Cecil, Tim	7	5	3.76	29	17	1	0	115	121	59	48	45	67
Culberson, Calvain	5	5	3.08	14	14	0	0	79	62	32	27	32	57
Doty, Sean	3	1	0.82	19	0	0	4	44	23	6	4	22	30
*Duff, Scott	1	0	1.42	3	0	0	0	6	5	1	1	5	5
Hook, Chris	6	5	4.07	30	16	0	0	119	117	65	54	62	87
*Jackson, Danny	0	0	6.00	1	1	0	0	3	2	2	2	1	2
*King, Doug	0	1	5.06	11	0	0	1	11	12	6	6	5	10
*Malley, Mike	1	0	2.74	7	3	0	0	23	12	10	7	16	19
*McCarthy, Steve	2	3	2.61	29	0	0	10	38	32	14	11	21	31
Nieves, Ernie	1	3	3.60	20	0	0	2	25	19	14	10	16	21
Plemmons, Scott	6	6	3.48	18	18	1	0	109	90	50	42	50	92
Pugh, Tim	15	6	1.93	27	27	8	0	177	142	58	38	56	153
Ray, John	14	7	2.93	30	20	3	0	154	147	60	50	48	81
Satre, Jason	6	12	4.73	24	22	3	0	116	99	70	61	75	105
Spradlin, Jerry	3	4	2.54	43	1	1	17	74	74	23	21	17	39
Wilburn, Trey	1	3	3.49	23	0	0	1	39	36	23	15	24	35

COLUMBIA

BATTING	AVG	G	AB	R	H	2B	3B	HR	RBI	BB	SO	SB
Buhe, Tim, 2b-ss	.385	8	13	1	5	1	0	0	1	3	2	0
Cameron, Stanton, of-dh ..	.298	87	302	57	90	19	1	15	57	52	68	3
Carroll, Kevin, c	.145	31	83	7	12	3	0	1	6	10	26	0
Castillo, Alberto, c	.233	30	103	8	24	4	3	1	14	10	21	1
Davis, Brian, of	.273	111	388	60	106	13	4	3	32	19	101	27
*Davis, Nick, 1b-dh	.176	10	34	2	6	2	0	0	2	1	19	1
Diaz, Alberto, 2b	.270	106	363	41	98	10	2	1	32	14	47	17
Fordyce, Brook, c	.315	104	372	45	117	29	1	10	54	39	42	4
Harris, James, 1b-3b	.282	122	451	60	127	23	3	1	64	33	54	4
#Hartmann, Reid, 3b-ss ...	.215	39	107	16	23	6	1	1	9	13	28	2
*Hoffner, Jamie, dh-1b	.298	86	309	42	92	14	0	1	37	13	46	3
#Howard, Tim, 3b-2b	.323	128	505	80	163	18	11	10	89	46	44	30
#Howell, Pat, of	.264	135	573	98	151	15	5	1	37	22	111	79
McClinton, Tim, 3b-of	.204	54	147	20	30	3	1	1	19	19	38	7
Navarro, Tito, ss	.314	136	497	86	156	25	4	0	54	69	55	50
*Pride, Curtis, of	.267	53	191	38	51	4	4	6	25	21	45	11
Scott, Phil, ss-2b	.224	21	58	6	13	0	0	0	6	8	11	0
Thomas, Mark, of	.233	110	420	65	98	22	2	15	70	39	150	9

PITCHING	W	L	ERA	G	GS	CG	SV	IP	H	R	ER	BB	SO
Butler, Chris	7	2	2.70	15	11	1	0	80	75	33	24	29	70
Dorn, Chris	9	11	2.81	27	19	6	1	144	140	67	45	49	69
Emm, Art	4	4	4.95	39	2	0	1	73	86	54	40	33	47
Freitas, Mike	5	2	2.44	13	9	0	0	70	60	27	19	14	47
Furmanik, Dan	3	3	2.48	8	8	1	0	54	50	20	15	10	27
Johnson, Paul	1	1	2.88	16	0	0	1	25	39	13	8	7	19
*Langbehn, Greg	13	11	3.31	26	25	7	0	174	165	84	64	59	132
*McCann, Joe	13	5	3.29	25	23	1	0	142	149	64	52	38	83
Parker, Jarrod	0	0	13.50	4	1	0	0	10	20	21	15	7	5
Reich, Andy	3	6	4.07	26	10	0	3	84	93	55	38	31	47
Richmond, Ryan	1	5	4.96	22	7	0	2	65	79	50	36	29	34
Sample, Deron	6	2	1.99	46	2	0	18	81	48	20	18	46	84
Telgheder, David	9	3	1.54	14	13	5	0	99	79	22	17	10	81
Valle, Tony	0	0	6.98	11	0	0	0	19	27	15	15	11	13
Vasquez, Julian	1	4	2.17	25	0	0	9	29	28	15	7	17	37
Vitko, Joe	8	1	2.49	16	12	4	1	90	70	29	25	30	72

FAYETTEVILLE

BATTING	AVG	G	AB	R	H	2B	3B	HR	RBI	BB	SO	SB
Caines, Arturo, of	.217	59	189	29	41	12	0	4	30	20	48	4
*Cornelius, Brian, of	.305	94	331	51	101	16	11	4	58	33	40	3
Gillette, Mike, c	.161	62	199	16	32	4	0	0	10	30	47	4
Hall, Chris, 3b	.000	2	6	1	0	0	0	0	0	1	3	1
*Hoffman, Hunter, dh	.130	9	23	4	3	0	0	1	1	4	10	0
#Howard, Ron, 2b	.210	121	362	56	76	16	1	2	31	65	70	19
Keating, Dave, of	.212	25	66	6	14	2	3	0	7	4	18	1
#Maldonado, Carlos, 3b-2b ..	.137	43	117	10	16	0	0	0	5	5	29	0
#McKeon, Kasey, dh-3b	.183	104	290	28	53	5	1	1	18	30	73	2
McNamara, Dennis, of	.230	48	161	17	37	3	1	0	11	19	24	1
*Pedersen, Don, dh-of	.200	15	30	4	6	0	0	2	2	6	10	0
Pemberton, Rudy, of	.278	127	454	59	126	14	5	6	61	42	91	12

BATTING

R	Scott Pose, Char-WV	..106
H	Tim Howard, Columbia	. 163
TB	Tim Howard, Columbia	. 233
2B	Mike Burton, Gastonia	... 35
3B	Brian Cornelius, Fay	... 11
	Tim Howard, Columbia	... 11
HR	Cliff Brannon, Savannah	. 18
RBI	Tim Howard, Columbia	.. 89
SH	Ed Ortega, Spartanburg	. 20
SF	David Hajek, Asheville	... 10
BB	Scott Pose, Char-WV	. 114
IBB	Scott Pose, Char-WV	... 8
HBP	Jim Ferguson, Savannah	18
SO	Mark Thomas, Columbia	149
SB	Pat Howell, Columbia	. 79
CS	David Hajek, Asheville	... 24
OB%	Scott Pose, Char-WV	.. .435

PITCHING

G	Ernie Baker, Savannah	... 70
GS	Luis Faccio, Savannah	... 29
CG	Tim Pugh, Charleston, WV	. 8
ShO	Sterling Hitchcock, Green	.. 5
Sv	Jeff Braley, Fayetteville	. 27
W	Tim Pugh, Char-WV	... 15
L	Charlie Thompson, Char-SC	17
IP	Mike Garcia, Fayetteville	. 180
H	Troy Cunningham, Char-SC	188
R	Charlie Thompson, Char-SC	110
HR	Donnie Wall, Asheville	... 18
BB	Carl Randle, Gastonia	... 105
HB	Luis Faccio, Savannah	... 18
SO	Sterling Hitchcock, Green	171
WP	Steve Gasser, Col/Sumter	27
Bk	Rafael Quirico, Green	 10

	AVG	G	AB	R	H	2B	3B	HR	RBI	BB	SO	SB
*Pesavento, Pat, ss	.280	132	457	82	128	10	2	0	35	84	49	12
*Rendina, Mike, 1b	.255	137	475	59	121	23	3	11	77	76	90	4
#Sawkiw, Warren, of-2b ..	.257	59	210	31	54	6	1	0	18	30	35	4
Sellers, Rick, c-dh	.230	130	430	49	99	13	4	7	57	61	102	5
Tagliaferri, Gino, 3b	.212	58	179	24	38	8	1	4	18	22	74	0
Torres, Freddy, 3b-ss	.204	106	304	42	62	3	3	0	29	21	32	2
Walker, Duane, of	.224	72	214	26	48	13	1	1	19	15	54	6
*Wilson, Brad, dh-c	.195	29	87	7	17	5	0	2	10	14	22	0

PITCHING	W	L	ERA	G	GS	CG	SV	IP	H	R	ER	BB	SO
Braley, Jeff	9	3	1.87	57	0	0	27	87	69	25	18	43	69
Doherty, John	1	0	5.79	7	0	0	1	9	17	12	6	1	6
Ferm, Ed	0	3	4.02	3	3	0	0	16	17	7	7	11	13
Garcia, Mike	12	8	2.55	28	28	6	0	180	152	69	51	41	113
*Gonzales, Frank	10	6	3.02	25	25	0	0	143	123	54	48	66	101
Guzman, Jose	3	3	6.30	26	0	0	0	64	75	50	45	33	32
Herrmann, Tim	0	4	6.75	7	7	0	0	29	34	24	22	10	18
Ingram, Linty	8	7	3.97	32	21	2	0	143	141	75	63	50	101
Koller, Mike	2	2	3.06	9	9	0	0	47	38	20	16	20	33
Leimeister, Eric	1	1	3.54	26	0	0	1	41	35	17	16	16	38
Link, Robert	1	0	1.04	6	0	0	3	9	4	2	1	3	12
*Marshall, Randy	13	0	1.33	14	14	5	0	102	64	17	15	9	81
Neidinger, Joe	4	8	4.47	18	18	2	0	105	117	60	52	24	43
*Pierce, Ben	1	3	4.40	7	1	0	1	14	14	7	7	10	13
Pinto, Gustavo	0	0	3.15	16	0	0	0	20	14	9	7	12	17
*Rodriguez, Eddy	1	1	3.38	7	2	0	0	19	14	7	7	14	22
Rountree, Brian	0	1	13.50	6	0	0	0	5	9	10	7	5	3
*Seibert, Mac	0	0	3.60	7	0	0	2	10	9	4	4	5	5
Shea, Kurt	1	3	4.08	17	1	0	0	29	24	18	13	22	24
Stefany, Marino	6	5	2.01	40	0	0	1	62	42	25	14	29	48
Stokes, Randy	0	0	0.00	1	0	0	3	3	1	0	0	2	2
Torres, Leo	5	1	2.04	30	1	0	3	62	57	16	14	24	60
Wolf, Steve	4	2	3.82	8	7	0	0	38	41	24	16	21	32

GASTONIA

BATTING	AVG	G	AB	R	H	2B	3B	HR	RBI	BB	SO	SB
Burton, Mike, 1b	.272	135	486	75	132	35	2	17	80	59	79	3
Clinton, Jim, ss-2b	.202	60	124	13	25	5	1	0	7	13	34	3
#Colon, Cris, ss	.321	38	140	23	45	2	4	4	16	4	24	7
Eklund, Troy, of	.236	99	305	41	72	11	0	6	32	28	47	8
Harris, Donald, of	.208	58	221	27	46	10	0	3	13	14	63	15
Hernandez, Tom, dh-c	.200	17	35	2	7	0	0	0	3	2	9	0
*Lewis, Joe, dh-c	.235	32	81	7	19	2	1	0	9	6	15	2
*Marshall, Randy, dh-1b ...	.249	122	433	53	108	24	2	12	62	57	78	6
McCoy, Trey, of-dh	.338	24	80	13	27	6	0	4	11	12	12	1
Micheu, Buddy, c	.219	71	192	20	42	9	1	5	20	17	50	3
Morrow, Timmie, of	.206	105	378	55	78	10	2	7	34	33	99	19
Newkirk, Craig, 3b-2b	.268	135	467	73	125	23	0	5	46	63	81	16
Oliva, Jose, ss-3b	.209	120	387	43	81	25	1	10	52	26	104	9
Powell, Ken, of	.233	103	322	31	75	8	4	2	37	37	83	17
Scruggs, Tony, of	.307	75	274	50	84	16	0	8	48	26	57	20
Turco, Frank, ss	.125	5	8	2	1	0	0	0	0	1	1	0
*Wardlow, Joey, 2b	.245	122	396	48	97	12	2	1	42	75	51	9
Winford, Barry, c	.238	96	332	51	79	14	3	2	24	39	67	14

PITCHING	W	L	ERA	G	GS	CG	SV	IP	H	R	ER	BB	SO
Arner, Mike	8	2	2.03	14	14	1	0	89	74	25	20	16	86
*Asche, Scott	3	1	3.59	34	1	0	2	58	55	28	23	24	60
Bickhardt, Eric	8	6	3.14	50	0	0	4	80	67	34	28	35	82
Buckley, Travis	12	6	2.84	27	26	3	0	162	149	66	51	61	149
Burton, Mike	0	0	11.57	2	0	0	0	5	11	6	6	4	1
*Eischen, Joey	3	7	2.70	17	14	0	0	73	51	36	22	40	69
Evans, Brian	3	3	1.09	57	0	0	17	74	57	13	9	27	64
Franklin, Jay	4	7	3.10	28	12	0	1	93	92	50	32	47	64

	W	L	ERA	G	GS	CG	SV	IP	H	R	ER	BB	SO
Graves, John	3	5	2.01	33	0	0	13	44	34	17	10	20	53
*Holcomb, Lou	1	1	4.33	15	1	0	0	27	31	16	13	18	16
Hurst, Jonathan	8	1	2.64	15	7	0	1	61	48	21	18	19	49
*McGraw, Tug	0	0	5.40	1	1	0	0	5	6	3	3	2	1
*Oliver, Darren	0	0	13.50	1	1	0	0	2	1	3	3	4	2
Phillips, Brad	0	1	6.85	12	1	0	0	22	24	18	17	11	18
Randle, Carl	8	9	4.19	29	27	2	0	148	113	79	69	105	121
Reed, Bobby	3	1	0.00	8	5	1	1	38	16	1	0	9	26
*Romero, Brian	9	2	1.48	15	15	1	0	91	74	17	15	35	87
Romero, Ronaldo	2	1	2.45	11	2	0	0	22	17	13	6	14	21
Rowley, Steve	6	3	2.55	13	13	1	0	82	66	36	23	46	78
Stafford, Tim	0	3	3.96	4	3	0	0	25	27	14	11	8	12
*Steiner, Brian	0	0	1.38	21	0	0	0	26	25	6	4	17	23
Wells, Tim	1	2	5.27	10	0	0	0	14	15	9	8	12	7

GREENSBORO

BATTING	AVG	G	AB	R	H	2B	3B	HR	RBI	BB	SO	SB
Broderick, Sean, inf-of ..	.126	31	87	5	11	1	0	1	4	4	23	0
*Fox, Andy, 3b	.218	134	455	68	99	19	4	9	55	92	132	26
Garland, Tim, of	.213	77	258	25	55	6	1	1	12	21	73	15
Gilliam, Sean, of	.200	131	476	42	95	25	3	9	45	18	132	11
Hill, Lew, of	.196	83	270	28	53	11	0	6	25	41	83	19
*Jarvis, John, dh-c	.247	60	170	20	42	6	3	3	18	7	50	1
*Jimenez, Ramon, 1b	.279	143	537	73	150	29	7	10	75	64	109	23
Johnson, Brian, c	.238	137	496	58	118	15	0	7	51	57	65	4
Rhodes, Mike, of	.213	31	89	12	19	4	1	1	16	16	21	3
*Robertson, Jason, of ...	.250	133	496	71	124	22	5	6	44	67	110	21
Rodriguez, Andres, of ...	.241	56	216	22	52	2	1	0	14	11	36	6
Romano, Scott, 2b-3b ...	.201	58	189	17	38	8	0	0	11	23	43	12
Sanchez, Dan, 2b-ss ...	.218	49	142	11	31	2	0	0	9	14	32	4
*Smith, Tom, 2b	.209	24	67	7	14	3	0	0	5	7	20	2
*Turner, Brian, of	.203	37	118	14	24	5	1	0	5	16	29	3
#Van Scoyoc, Aaron, ss-2b .	.222	108	347	47	77	11	1	1	23	60	62	3
Walker, Larry, c-dh	.230	79	244	27	56	11	1	1	25	48	57	11

PITCHING	W	L	ERA	G	GS	CG	SV	IP	H	R	ER	BB	SO
Batchelor, Richard	2	2	1.58	27	0	0	8	51	39	15	9	14	38
*Haller, Jim	2	6	2.99	52	0	0	14	72	66	31	24	28	58
*Hitchcock, Sterling	12	12	2.91	27	27	6	0	173	122	68	56	60	171
Hoffman, Jeff	8	3	1.47	47	1	0	1	116	86	43	19	40	93
Hutton, Mark	1	10	6.31	21	19	0	0	81	77	78	57	62	72
Johnston, Dan	5	5	2.51	46	0	0	0	100	80	44	28	32	66
Juarbe, Ken	2	3	4.34	16	3	0	0	37	40	28	18	17	33
*Malone, Todd	4	3	4.86	17	6	0	1	46	45	32	25	26	44
Mauldin, James	2	2	4.56	13	0	0	0	24	23	14	12	11	23
Munoz, Roberto	5	12	3.73	25	24	0	0	133	134	70	55	58	100
Perez, Cesar	0	0	3.15	13	0	0	0	20	18	13	7	12	27
*Quirico, Rafael	2	6	5.00	13	13	1	0	72	74	60	40	30	52
Rhodes, Ricky	7	10	3.73	27	27	0	0	154	121	75	64	95	147
Smith, Shad	4	7	3.60	16	13	0	0	85	69	41	34	32	54
Springer, Russ	2	3	3.67	10	10	0	0	56	51	33	23	31	51
*Tucker, Steve	1	1	5.52	11	1	0	1	29	37	23	18	12	21

MYRTLE BEACH

BATTING	AVG	G	AB	R	H	2B	3B	HR	RBI	BB	SO	SB
*Abare, Bill, 1b	.251	118	391	49	98	19	0	10	44	59	121	1
Brooks, Eric, c	.263	68	213	26	56	8	0	3	23	44	34	1
*Holifield, Rick, of	.201	99	279	37	56	9	2	3	18	28	88	13
Holtzclaw, Shawn, of	.252	133	476	63	120	28	1	14	72	52	123	1
Jaime, Juan, c	.197	66	203	14	40	4	1	4	21	14	34	1
Mengel, Brad, 3b	.273	115	403	50	110	17	1	5	47	36	80	4
#Mercedes, Hector, ss ...	.196	98	326	37	64	11	0	4	24	14	77	7
Miller, Scott, 3b-ss	.249	96	313	41	78	18	0	4	32	44	44	5
Mobley, Anton, of	.181	52	177	20	32	1	0	6	13	11	78	1
Montalvo, Rob, ss-2b ...	.200	45	125	15	25	1	0	0	11	9	14	2
Parese, Bill, 2b	.237	121	439	67	104	16	5	5	47	60	73	16
Perez, Robert, of	.292	21	72	8	21	2	0	1	10	3	9	2
Provence, Todd, of-1b ...	.236	98	330	55	78	15	2	10	38	43	117	12
Rivers, Ken, dh-c	.299	100	358	51	107	18	2	12	67	31	61	1
*Wilson, Nigel, of	.273	110	440	77	120	23	9	16	62	30	71	22

PITCHING	W	L	ERA	G	GS	CG	SV	IP	H	R	ER	BB	SO
Bicknell, Greg	5	4	3.65	34	15	0	0	121	118	63	49	45	89
*Blumberg, Rob	13	4	2.16	25	23	1	0	129	101	43	31	68	128
Bradley, Eric	2	4	3.31	46	0	0	8	73	80	34	27	30	58
Brown, Daren	11	7	4.11	25	25	0	0	142	155	81	65	51	120
Hutson, Scott	0	2	4.85	13	1	0	2	26	21	15	14	13	25
Kizziah, Daren	6	6	3.47	35	6	1	4	99	103	56	38	35	48
*Kulina, Kenny	3	3	4.60	28	0	0	3	47	50	30	24	20	40
*Lloyd, Graeme	5	2	2.72	19	6	0	6	50	51	20	15	16	42
Mandia, John	0	1	0.64	9	0	0	4	14	6	1	1	4	5
Martin, Gregg	2	4	2.39	37	0	0	16	49	22	16	13	34	71
Menhart, Paul	3	0	0.59	5	4	1	0	31	18	5	2	5	18
Nowak, Rich	1	2	2.33	5	5	0	0	27	17	8	7	12	21
Ogliaruso, Mike	14	9	2.52	26	26	2	0	164	132	57	46	61	158
*Olivares, Jose	0	1	3.86	8	0	0	0	12	13	6	5	7	5
Small, Aaron	9	9	2.80	27	27	1	0	148	150	72	46	56	96
Wanish, John	3	5	4.24	35	2	0	6	74	78	41	35	37	69

SAVANNAH

BATTING	AVG	G	AB	R	H	2B	3B	HR	RBI	BB	SO	SB
Banton, Scott, of	.229	106	306	45	70	11	0	2	23	49	53	14
Beanblossom, Brad, ss	.240	60	208	28	50	10	0	4	27	17	20	12
*Beasley, Andrew, c	.180	32	89	7	16	3	0	0	9	9	26	0
Brannon, Cliff, of	.247	132	445	70	110	21	0	18	65	51	109	7
Calzado, Johnny, 1b-dh	.239	109	331	34	79	8	2	6	38	32	74	4
Coleman, Paul, of	.209	104	340	33	71	12	4	6	35	23	66	9
Duran, Ignacio, 3b	.209	127	412	42	86	14	2	2	31	24	95	10
Ferguson, Jim, ss-3b	.217	113	300	46	65	11	1	1	14	63	39	11
Fielitz, Bill, c	.063	5	16	1	1	0	1	0	2	2	7	0
*Gryskevich, Larry, 1b	.240	100	329	22	79	15	0	7	32	16	75	5
Keating, Mike, ss	.125	42	88	8	11	1	0	0	4	12	20	2
*Lewis, Anthony, of	.254	128	465	55	118	22	4	8	49	24	79	10
Martinez, Nicio, 2b-ss	.189	61	106	13	20	4	0	1	7	9	38	1
Ochs, Tony, of	.248	102	331	43	82	10	3	3	36	42	65	13
Ozuna, Mateo, 2b	.236	121	449	65	106	8	2	2	29	37	42	66
Spivey, Jim, c	.000	6	9	0	0	0	0	0	0	0	3	0
Tahan, Kevin, dh-1b	.222	106	302	36	67	11	4	3	40	44	66	5
*Turvey, Joe, c	.137	27	51	4	7	3	0	0	1	8	21	0

PITCHING	W	L	ERA	G	GS	CG	SV	IP	H	R	ER	BB	SO
Arias, Jose	1	5	6.34	20	11	0	0	60	59	50	42	58	41
Baker, Ernie	6	3	2.03	70	0	0	1	93	76	34	21	21	59
Betances, Marcos	0	4	5.79	7	5	0	0	23	31	21	15	18	15
Brannon, Cliff	0	0	2.84	6	0	0	0	6	5	2	2	5	7
*Cassidy, David	9	5	1.94	18	17	3	0	111	99	32	24	24	56
*Dixon, Steve	7	3	1.94	64	0	0	8	84	59	34	18	38	93
Duvall, Brad	2	3	2.13	7	7	0	0	38	32	19	9	19	23
Espinal, Willie	7	2	2.63	46	0	0	13	62	50	22	18	27	48
Faccio, Luis	8	11	3.88	29	29	1	0	165	153	95	71	84	169
Fletcher, Dennis	3	6	3.49	66	0	0	15	80	76	36	31	32	74
Gaston, Russ	3	10	4.61	31	17	0	0	121	100	74	62	86	88
*Green, Don	1	0	1.46	12	0	0	0	12	13	3	2	2	11
Hurst, Bill	2	1	3.41	7	7	0	0	32	22	17	12	27	14
*Nielsen, Kevin	1	4	7.36	7	6	0	0	22	34	23	18	12	20
*Osborne, Donovan	2	2	2.61	6	6	1	0	41	40	20	12	7	28
Pacheco, Al	8	6	3.90	22	18	0	0	99	86	47	43	53	45
*Sells, George	2	0	1.11	4	4	0	0	24	14	4	3	17	17
Shackle, Rick	8	2	2.71	17	11	1	0	86	81	35	26	14	70
Tolbert, Mark	3	1	4.13	29	3	0	0	76	77	44	35	29	48

SPARTANBURG

BATTING	AVG	G	AB	R	H	2B	3B	HR	RBI	BB	SO	SB
Adams, Brian, c	.220	40	118	9	26	8	1	0	9	13	22	0
Bennett, Al, of	.345	16	58	8	20	6	1	1	6	1	16	2
Brown, Dana, of	.291	34	134	27	39	6	1	0	15	22	18	10
Churchill, Tim, 1b	.252	93	337	38	85	10	2	2	49	21	33	0
*Current, Matt, c	.211	68	194	20	41	2	0	1	14	28	30	0
Escobar, John, 3b-ss	.232	126	466	42	108	10	3	2	31	37	76	9
*Estevez, Carlos, dh-1b	.243	53	189	21	46	11	1	7	27	20	53	0
Hamburg, Charles, c	.194	35	98	10	19	7	0	0	7	23	24	0
*Hardgrove, Tom, 1b-dh	.205	92	308	27	63	13	1	5	47	50	87	0
Linares, Antonio, of	.268	72	276	27	74	13	3	0	37	11	38	5
Lowery, Josh, ss	.213	59	207	17	44	5	3	2	16	20	34	2
Marsh, Tom, dh-c	.280	24	75	14	21	2	1	4	15	8	21	5
*Ortega, Ed, 2b	.237	130	518	61	123	9	2	0	30	43	61	11
Perez, Eulogio, ss	.187	22	75	6	14	3	1	0	3	7	24	0
Santa Cruz, Nick, 3b	.233	12	30	2	7	0	0	0	3	3	10	0
*Shannon, Dan, of	.156	58	167	15	26	5	0	2	14	19	47	1
*Sirak, Ken, 3b-ss	.213	53	164	20	35	5	2	0	13	20	40	0
*Taylor, Sam, of	.308	75	289	46	89	13	5	5	36	24	30	10
Thomas, Corey, of-ss	.234	92	321	53	75	10	1	5	26	48	82	11
*Urbon, Joe, of	.258	63	233	30	60	8	3	3	23	20	34	7
*Valencia, Gil, of-dh	.155	37	116	17	18	1	0	0	4	19	28	0
Welch, Dan, of	.175	86	291	20	51	8	1	3	24	20	97	1

PITCHING	W	L	ERA	G	GS	CG	SV	IP	H	R	ER	BB	SO
Backs, Jason	3	2	6.43	11	1	0	0	21	15	18	15	18	18
Baur, Albert	1	3	2.77	12	0	0	1	26	27	13	8	8	15
Bratlien, Erik	5	7	3.77	23	11	2	0	100	102	45	42	19	66
Elliott, Donnie	4	8	3.50	20	20	0	0	105	101	52	41	46	109
Fletcher, Paul	2	4	3.28	9	9	1	0	49	46	24	18	18	53
*Gaddy, Bob	9	7	3.33	30	19	0	2	140	107	65	52	67	143
Goedhart, Darrell	8	10	4.43	29	28	1	0	150	162	96	74	62	92
Goergen, Todd	7	8	3.30	19	18	0	0	104	117	49	38	12	73
Gray, Elliott	1	1	1.23	3	3	1	0	22	16	6	3	2	22
Gunderson, Greg	0	1	2.06	38	0	0	3	70	53	21	16	18	58
Kent, Troy	2	6	3.01	18	12	1	1	84	75	41	28	30	75
*Limbach, Chris	7	4	2.37	42	0	0	4	87	72	29	23	33	91
Randall, Mark	2	3	2.44	32	1	0	7	66	55	26	18	21	60
Shannon, Dan	1	1	21.60	4	0	0	0	3	9	8	8	7	1
Stevens, Matt	0	2	2.17	14	0	0	2	29	24	12	7	10	31
Sullivan, Mike	4	3	4.50	22	0	0	0	36	39	19	18	17	28
Wells, Bob	5	8	2.87	20	19	2	0	113	94	47	36	40	73
*Wiegandt, Scott	2	0	0.98	10	0	0	2	18	12	2	2	2	17

SUMTER

BATTING	AVG	G	AB	R	H	2B	3B	HR	RBI	BB	SO	SB
Anderson, Tony, dh	.000	7	20	0	0	0	0	0	0	2	5	0
*Burton, Chris, of-dh	.167	6	18	3	3	1	0	0	0	1	3	1
Castilla, Vinicio, ss	.268	93	339	47	91	15	2	9	53	28	54	2
*Giovanola, Ed, 2b	.244	35	119	20	29	4	0	0	8	34	17	8
Hall, Lamar, ss	.000	1	1	0	0	0	0	0	0	0	0	0
Heath, Lee, of	.207	126	455	59	94	9	5	2	25	39	112	35
*Houston, Tyler, c	.210	117	442	58	93	14	3	13	56	49	101	6
Kelly, Pat, 3b-2b	.222	121	437	57	97	12	2	1	44	61	65	23
*Klesko, Ryan, 1b	.368	63	231	41	85	15	1	10	38	31	30	13
Kupsey, John, 3b	.216	68	213	22	46	9	0	4	20	25	60	2
Lopez, Fred, c-dh	.224	53	152	19	34	7	0	1	13	40	37	0
Martin, Gene, of	.232	79	271	45	63	13	6	2	19	30	61	7
Mendez, Miguel, 3b-dh	.111	3	9	2	1	0	0	0	1	2	3	1
#Nieves, Melvin, of	.283	126	459	60	130	24	7	9	59	53	125	10
Noreen, Keith, dh-3b	.234	16	47	5	11	4	0	0	6	10	11	2
#Olmeda, Jose, 2b	.253	103	367	60	93	14	6	7	40	55	49	17
Perez, Ed, c-1b	.179	41	123	11	22	7	1	3	17	14	18	0
Roa, Hector, ss	.217	24	92	5	20	4	1	0	7	4	12	1
*Robles, Josman, 1b	.246	71	236	31	58	12	2	5	35	27	46	3
Santoya, Cristobal, ss	.212	20	66	5	14	1	0	0	4	6	9	1
*Sims, Dan, dh-of	.185	58	151	15	28	8	1	0	11	31	19	6
*Tarasco, Tony, of	.265	107	355	42	94	13	3	3	37	37	57	9

PITCHING	W	L	ERA	G	GS	CG	SV	IP	H	R	ER	BB	SO
Brown, Tab	5	7	3.49	23	22	3	0	137	149	71	53	43	69
Burlingame, Dennis	1	3	2.27	12	12	0	0	36	36	14	9	6	20
Cronin, Jeff	2	1	2.27	6	6	1	0	40	36	13	10	12	14
Cummings, Brian	1	0	4.00	7	0	0	1	9	10	4	4	4	6
Gabriele, Mike	0	0	8.16	11	0	0	0	14	24	18	13	11	8
Gasser, Steve	0	3	11.25	11	6	0	0	24	13	31	30	55	23
Haeberle, Kevin	8	10	3.02	23	21	2	0	131	119	57	44	48	73
*Hailey, Roger	10	1	2.02	17	17	4	0	120	66	31	27	46	126
Jewett, Earl	6	5	2.40	27	12	2	0	109	89	43	29	39	72
*Karasinski, Dave	1	3	2.05	23	0	0	0	26	27	9	6	12	21
Lemon, Don	1	2	6.33	4	4	0	0	21	29	20	15	5	3
Mathews, Eddie	1	0	0.00	4	0	0	0	5	3	0	0	1	4
Newman, Tom	0	0	1.64	8	0	0	0	11	9	2	2	4	11
Schafer, Bill	4	6	3.09	39	1	0	1	87	59	36	30	39	69
Shifflett, Matt	0	2	8.10	15	1	0	0	27	29	26	24	16	21
Sottile, Shaun	8	7	2.49	40	4	0	4	101	94	36	28	23	71
Steinmetz, Earl	11	8	3.42	25	24	2	0	145	148	67	55	34	105
Strange, Don	4	1	0.66	46	0	0	24	54	34	6	4	12	53
*Thomas, Ron	4	4	3.97	16	11	1	0	68	79	37	30	22	29
Weems, Danny	1	2	2.41	10	0	0	0	19	10	8	5	12	14
Wohlers, Mark	5	4	1.88	37	2	0	5	53	27	13	11	20	85

NEW YORK-PENN LEAGUE

Oneonta takes sixth league title in 12 years

By PETER CONRADI

Ho-hum. Another summer, another championship for the Oneonta Yankees.

The Yanks captured their 11th New York-Penn League title in 1990, disposing of the Erie Sailors 2-1 in the best-of-3 final. It was Oneonta's second crown in three years, sixth since 1979.

"They were one heck of a ball team," said Pat Daugherty, manager of the '89 champion Jamestown Expos, who were eliminated in the semifinals by Erie. "They had good pitching, guys who could hit, and they played good defense. They could do it all."

Indeed. The Yankees' 2.60 team ERA led the NY-P; they were third overall in hitting with a .259 average.

**Robbie Katzaroff
. . . top hitter**

The Yankees only real competition in the regular season came from the Geneva Cubs, who took the McNamara West pennant with a 51-26 mark. Oneonta was 52-26 in the East. Since both held first place almost all season, a thrilling playoff was in the making.

It didn't happen.

The Yankees, who entered the playoffs on a three-game losing streak, shook out the cobwebs and easily ousted the Cubs in two straight.

"We hit the hot switch," said Oneonta manager Trey Hillman. "A lull like we had can be dangerous, but we had the ability to come out of it."

In the Stedler Division, the hard-hitting Sailors took the pennant with a 44-33 record and swept Jamestown to enter the finals.

Youth prevails

The championship series featured an interesting matchup of veterans against rookies. The Sailors, who operated as an

LEAGUE CHAMPIONS

Playoff Champions, Where Applicable

1990—Oneonta	1972—Niagara Falls	1954—Corning
1989—Jamestown	1971—Oneonta	1953—Jamestown
1988—Oneonta	1970—Auburn	1952—Jamestown
1987—Geneva	1969—Oneonta	1951—Hornell
1986—St. Catharines	1968—Oneonta	1950—Olean
1985—Oneonta	1967—Auburn	1949—Bradford
1984—Little Falls	1966—Auburn	1948—Lockport
1983—Utica	1965—Binghamton	1947—Jamestown
1982—Niagara Falls	1964—Auburn	1946—*Jamestown
1981—Oneonta	1963—Batavia	—*Batavia
1980—Oneonta	1962—Auburn	1945—Batavia
1979—Oneonta	1961—Olean	1944—Jamestown
1978—Geneva	1960—Wellsville	1943—Wellsville
1977—Oneonta	1959—Wellsville	1942—Jamestown
1976—Elmira	1958—Geneva	1941—Bradford
1975—Newark	1957—Erie	1940—Olean
1974—Oneonta	1956—Wellsville	1939—Olean
1973—Auburn	1955—Hamilton	*co-champions

Oneonta's Dutch shortstop Robert Eenhoorn, a defensive genius, was rated the NYP's top prospect.

independent franchise, had a lineup of older, experienced players, most of whom had been cast aside by other organizations. The Yanks were a typical NY-P club, stocked primarily with June draft choices.

In the end, youth and sheer talent prevailed.

After splitting Games 1 and 2—Oneonta took the opener, 1-0, and Erie the second, 2-0—the Yanks unleashed their power in Game 3 for an 11-2 victory.

It was fitting that all-star righthander Sam Militello was the winner in Game 3. He was the league's most dominant pitcher in 1990. Working 89 innings, Militello compiled an 8-2 record, had a league-leading 119 strikeouts and 1.22 ERA, second in the league.

Dickson shoots to top

The NY-P was chalk-full of big league prospects. The quickest ascent was that of pitcher Lance Dickson, the No. 1 draft pick of the Cubs. Dickson started the season in Geneva and finished it in Chicago.

Other first-rounders who spent time in the NY-P included pitchers Kurt Miller (Welland) and Donovan Osborne (Hamilton), outfielder Jeromy Burnitz (Pittsfield) and pitcher Steve Karsay (St. Catharines).

Another high-profile player was St. Catharines pitcher Scott Burrell, better known for his exploits on the basketball court than the baseball diamond.

Burrell was taken in the first round of the 1989 draft by the Seattle Mariners, but turned down a six-figure bonus to play basketball at the University of Connecticut. The Toronto Blue Jays selected him in the fifth round in 1990, signed him, promised to let him return to school, and dispatched him to St. Catharines.

Burrell ran hot and cold in his pro debut season, finishing at 1-5 with a 5.86 ERA.

1990 FINAL STANDINGS

McNamara East	W	L	Pct.	GB
Oneonta (Yankees)	52	26	.667	—
Watertown (Indians).........	43	34	.558	8½
Pittsfield (Mets).............	43	34	.558	8½
Utica (White Sox)	31	47	.397	21
McNamara West				
Geneva (Cubs).............	51	26	.662	—
Batavia (Phillies)	41	35	.539	9½
Elmira (Red Sox)	32	45	.416	19
Auburn (Astros)	31	46	.403	20
Stedler				
Erie (Independent)	44	33	.571	—
Jamestown (Expos)	41	36	.532	3
Welland (Pirates)	36	42	.462	8½
Niagara Falls (Tigers)	35	42	.455	9
Hamilton (Cardinals)	30	46	.395	13½
St. Catharines (Blue Jays) ..	29	47	.382	14½

1990 GENERAL INFORMATION

Playoffs: Oneonta defeated Geneva 2-0 in best-of-3 semifinal; Erie defeated Jamestown 2-0 in best-of-3 semifinal; Oneonta defeated Erie 2-1 in best-of-3 final to win league championship.

Regular-Season Attendance: Pittsfield, 101,110; Hamilton, 74,744; Elmira, 66,204; Erie, 61,606; Oneonta, 58,742; Niagara Falls, 56,157; Utica, 52,074; Watertown, 51,992; Auburn, 45,475; Batavia, 39,257; Welland, 37,331; Jamestown, 35,364; Geneva, 35,032; St. Catharines, 29,742.

Managers: Auburn—Ricky Peters; **Batavia**—Dave Cash, Ramon Aviles; **Elmira**—Mike Verdi; **Erie**—Mal Fichman; **Geneva**—Bill Hayes; **Hamilton**—Luis Melendez; **Jamestown**—Pat Daugherty; **Niagara Falls**—Juan Lopez; **Oneonta**—Trey Hillman; **Pittsfield**—Jim Eschen; **St. Catharines**—Doug Ault; **Utica**—Tommy Thompson; **Watertown**—Jim Gabella; **Welland**—Jim Mallon.

1990 Official All-Star Team: C—Carlos Delgado, St. Catharines; Rob Fitzpatrick, Jamestown. **1B**—Mike Brown, Welland. **2B**—Kevin Jordan, Oneonta. **3B**—Mike Songini, Erie. **SS**—Andy Postema, Erie. **UTIL INF**—Robert Eenhoorn, Oneonta. **OF**—Robbie Katzaroff, Jamestown; Jeff McNeely, Elmira; Jalal Leach, Oneonta; Scott Bullett, Welland. **DH**—Andrew Hartung, Geneva. **RHP**—Jessie Hollins, Geneva; Sam Militello, Oneonta. **LHP**—Kirt Ojala, Oneonta; Alan Botkin, Hamilton. **Manager of the Year**—Trey Hillman, Oneonta.

Top 10 Major League Prospects (by Baseball America): 1. Robert Eenhoorn, ss, Oneonta; **2.** Steve Karsay, rhp, St. Catharines; **3.** Kurt Miller, rhp, Welland; **4.** Carlos Delgado, c, St. Catharines; **5.** Jeff McNeely, of, Elmira; **6.** Sam Militello, rhp, Oneonta; **7.** Jessie Hollins, rhp, Geneva; **8.** Jeff Barry, of, Jamestown; **9.** Scott Bullett, of, Welland; **10.** Jeromy Burnitz, of, Pittsfield.

1990 BATTING PITCHING STATS

CLUB BATTING

	AVG	G	AB	R	H	2B	3B	HR	BB	SO	SB
Erie	.266	78	2547	435	676	117	21	69	352	521	37
Pittsfield	.260	77	2473	379	643	95	30	27	356	504	129
Oneonta	.259	78	2440	363	632	85	24	20	355	501	165
Geneva	.257	77	2487	421	638	121	17	50	382	564	73
Jamestown	.251	77	2519	320	633	104	22	34	279	570	107
Welland	.248	78	2560	366	634	104	16	30	292	569	138
Auburn	.246	78	2553	345	629	106	21	29	263	652	129
Watertown	.244	78	2590	369	632	102	31	32	311	570	113
Batavia	.240	76	2467	369	592	102	20	48	341	602	118
St. Catharines	.234	76	2359	254	552	80	10	34	285	600	74
Elmira	.229	77	2442	315	560	74	18	23	287	582	133
Utica	.226	78	2487	313	561	80	15	18	338	700	128
Hamilton	.223	77	2478	287	552	81	5	41	252	596	71
Niagara Falls	.213	77	2365	295	504	82	8	31	333	571	94

CLUB PITCHING

	ERA	G	CG	SHO	SV	IP	H	R	ER	BB	SO
Oneonta	2.62	78	8	9	19	657	541	266	191	306	669
Geneva	2.88	77	6	10	25	659	550	283	211	299	677

	ERA	G	CG	SHO	SV	IP	H	R	ER	BB	SO
Watertown	2.89	78	8	6	20	685	608	303	220	275	593
Jamestown	3.09	77	9	3	19	656	605	319	225	307	580
Batavia	3.37	76	6	7	24	662	615	328	248	211	452
St. Catharines	3.52	76	1	3	17	633	577	317	248	292	584
Pittsfield	3.63	77	8	9	15	657	604	346	265	329	573
Utica	3.65	77	9	4	10	669	617	372	271	365	484
Hamilton	3.67	77	7	7	22	657	607	330	268	309	538
Welland	3.71	78	2	4	17	671	586	375	277	425	670
Erie	3.75	78	7	1	23	660	639	373	275	257	620
Elmira	3.85	77	16	3	13	659	617	379	282	296	515
Niagara Falls	4.34	77	8	9	19	642	627	388	310	315	533
Auburn	4.68	78	3	2	12	662	647	452	344	440	614

INDIVIDUAL BATTING LEADERS
(Minimum 211 Plate Appearances)

	AVG	G	AB	R	H	2B	3B	HR	RBI	BB	SO	SB
*Katzaroff, Robbie, Jam	.364	74	294	57	107	15	7	1	20	29	18	34
Postema, Andy, Erie	.345	75	261	53	90	18	2	3	39	37	33	0
Jordan, Kevin, Oneonta	.333	73	276	47	92	13	7	4	54	23	31	19
Hartung, Andy, Geneva	.331	74	263	48	87	19	2	11	70	45	55	1
*Songini, Mike, Erie	.321	78	280	61	90	12	2	8	51	39	30	2
#Barry, Jeff, Jamestown	.315	51	197	30	62	6	1	4	23	17	25	25
McNeely, Jeff, Elmira	.313	73	246	41	77	4	5	6	37	40	60	39
*Lambert, Layne, Auburn	.303	66	218	33	66	9	4	4	37	30	50	4
*Bullett, Scott, Welland	.302	74	255	46	77	11	4	3	33	13	50	30
*Burnitz, Jeromy, Pitt	.301	51	173	37	52	6	5	6	22	45	39	12

INDIVIDUAL PITCHING LEADERS
(Minimum 62 Innings)

	W	L	ERA	G	CG	CG	SV	IP	H	R	ER	BB	SO
*Ryan, Bobby, Watertown	5	3	0.73	27	0	0	9	62	47	11	5	20	69
Militello, Sam, Oneonta	8	2	1.22	13	13	3	0	89	53	14	12	24	119
Parker, Tim, Geneva	6	0	1.53	12	12	1	0	77	61	22	13	28	81
*Botkin, Alan, Hamilton	7	4	1.55	13	13	4	0	87	65	26	15	26	72
Hodges, Darren, Oneonta	6	3	1.67	14	14	1	0	86	81	30	16	24	85
*Douma, Todd, Pittsfield	5	4	2.14	15	11	2	0	84	60	25	20	26	84
*Ojala, Kirt, Oneonta	7	2	2.16	14	14	1	0	79	75	28	19	43	87
Warren, Brian, NF	2	6	2.17	12	10	1	0	62	53	20	15	15	62
Mikkelson, Linc, Erie	7	5	2.34	14	14	2	0	88	69	36	23	36	83
Barreiro, Effrain, Auburn	2	4	2.44	20	8	0	1	66	50	38	18	39	51

AUBURN

BATTING	AVG	G	AB	R	H	2B	3B	HR	RBI	BB	SO	SB
Ball, Jeff, 3b	.289	70	263	40	76	18	1	5	38	22	35	20
Delpiano, Marc, 2b	.250	13	20	2	5	0	0	0	3	2	7	0
Flores, Jose, ss	.183	42	109	13	20	2	0	0	6	18	16	3
Gilmore, Tony, c	.217	33	106	9	23	8	0	0	7	6	23	3
Gumbs, Lincoln, ss-3b	.182	15	33	3	6	0	0	0	0	5	11	1
Hatcher, Chris, of-dh	.247	72	259	37	64	10	0	9	45	27	86	8
Hurlbutt, Bob, c	.176	42	131	6	23	3	0	2	18	5	53	1
Jones, Marty, of	.200	30	50	9	10	0	2	2	6	5	24	3
*Lambert, Layne, ss-2b	.303	66	218	33	66	9	4	4	37	30	50	4
McCumiskey, Steve, c	.143	18	28	4	4	1	0	0	3	3	10	0
Montgomery, Ray, of-1b	.233	61	193	19	45	8	1	0	13	23	32	12
Mota, Gary, of	.258	69	248	39	64	12	4	3	19	26	74	12
Roman, Vince, of-dh	.269	64	193	42	52	6	5	1	15	14	40	27
Smith, Bryan, of	.211	62	199	27	42	5	1	0	15	29	58	9
Smith, Lance, c	.291	16	55	9	16	5	0	1	6	5	15	2
*Thompson, Fletcher, 2b	.286	59	199	35	57	8	3	0	21	37	45	19
Veit, Steve, 1b	.225	67	249	18	56	11	0	2	29	6	73	5

PITCHING	W	L	ERA	G	GS	CG	SV	IP	H	R	ER	BB	SO
Allen, David	0	1	4.02	14	0	0	3	16	16	8	7	2	19
Barreiro, Effrain	2	4	2.44	20	8	0	1	66	50	38	18	39	51
Brown, Duane	2	2	3.00	6	6	0	0	36	29	17	12	15	22
Hampton, Mark	3	5	6.93	13	13	1	0	51	51	46	39	43	27
*Hurta, Bob	1	4	4.31	15	5	0	4	31	21	19	15	29	41
Irwin, Michael	1	6	8.46	22	1	0	0	45	48	48	42	43	28
Ketchen, Doug	6	5	3.40	19	12	1	0	93	81	43	35	40	76
Martinez, Juan	0	0	5.40	1	0	0	0	2	1	2	1	2	1
*Powers, Steve	0	5	6.06	16	5	0	0	49	63	44	33	28	51
Reed, Dennis	6	4	4.52	25	0	0	0	68	78	42	34	49	83
*Rinaldi, Kevin	1	1	6.23	7	0	0	0	13	13	12	9	12	15
*Scott, Tyrone	5	5	4.52	13	13	0	0	88	93	59	44	63	78
*Stiteler, Mark	0	1	14.21	3	2	0	0	6	10	11	10	8	4
*Wall, Jason	0	1	5.23	12	0	0	2	10	10	8	6	9	10
Williams, Brian	0	0	4.05	3	3	0	0	7	6	5	3	6	7
Wilson, David	4	2	2.70	22	8	1	2	77	65	35	23	43	97

BATAVIA

BATTING	AVG	G	AB	R	H	2B	3B	HR	RBI	BB	SO	SB
#Bieser, Steve, of	.231	54	160	36	37	11	1	0	12	26	28	13
Cruz, Ismael, 2b-3b	.252	45	139	17	35	1	1	0	12	12	19	23	6
#Hartwig, Rob, of	.331	50	157	26	52	6	2	0	12	26	17	14
#Jackson, Jeff, of	.198	63	227	30	45	11	3	3	22	30	80	12
Judson, Erik, 3b	.258	55	178	29	46	13	3	2	23	23	57	8
Morgan, Gary, of-dh	.182	15	33	4	6	0	0	0	2	5	3	3

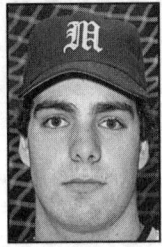

Andy Hartung
... RBI leader

Sam Militello
... 8-2, 1.22

Jeff McNeely
... .313, 39 SB

	AVG	G	AB	R	H	2B	3B	HR	RBI	BB	SO	SB
*Neitzel, R.A., 2b-3b	.266	62	218	40	58	7	0	1	27	36	37	17
Nuneviller, Tom, of	.232	71	259	36	60	10	0	9	31	30	45	15
*Owens, Mike, 1b-dh	.264	61	220	37	58	12	3	12	49	19	75	9
Pena, Porfirio, c	.170	15	47	3	8	2	0	2	9	2	16	0
Perez, Eulogio, ss	.187	37	91	7	17	1	0	1	9	6	34	3
Ridenour, Ryan, c-dh	.235	32	85	5	20	5	1	1	9	9	18	1
#Ryan, Sean, dh-1b	.273	73	231	54	63	11	1	16	53	66	52	5
#Savage, Jim, ss	.241	55	162	22	39	6	2	0	15	22	19	3
#Smith, Willie, c	.186	30	70	5	13	2	1	0	6	7	29	2
Tewell, Terrance, c	.193	33	109	11	21	3	1	1	12	9	38	2
*Valencia, Gil, of	.177	26	79	7	14	1	1	0	7	6	29	5

PITCHING	W	L	ERA	G	GS	CG	SV	IP	H	R	ER	BB	SO
Baur, Al	4	0	2.28	13	0	0	5	24	15	7	6	7	23
Gray, Elliott	5	3	2.89	11	11	2	0	65	67	29	21	13	46
Hill, Eric	2	4	4.02	10	8	2	1	54	49	27	24	10	34
Hurst, Charlie	4	3	2.73	14	14	1	0	82	81	38	25	23	54
*Ingram, John	0	1	2.18	12	0	0	3	21	15	6	5	9	21
Jones, Tom	2	4	4.92	19	6	0	0	60	71	48	33	26	31
Lovdal, Stewart	2	4	3.59	19	3	0	0	48	37	24	19	20	26
McGovern, Steve	4	4	5.02	14	11	0	0	61	76	41	34	14	31
Montgomery, Mike	4	5	5.56	21	3	0	1	45	45	33	28	22	31
Parris, Steve	7	1	2.64	14	14	0	0	82	70	34	24	22	50
*Ross, Dave	3	1	2.20	26	3	0	3	49	30	17	12	25	49
Slaughter, Garland	1	2	1.90	7	3	0	0	24	20	7	5	6	11
Williams, Mike	2	3	2.30	27	0	0	11	47	39	17	12	13	42

ELMIRA

BATTING	AVG	G	AB	R	H	2B	3B	HR	RBI	BB	SO	SB
*Alvarez, Dave, 1b	.195	37	77	4	15	5	0	1	11	6	16	1
#Berni, Denny, c-1b	.207	45	140	12	29	6	0	2	22	15	36	1
Brown, Randy, ss	.236	74	212	27	50	4	0	1	8	17	47	18
Davis, Tim, 2b-ss	.236	59	161	16	38	9	1	0	16	16	18	1
#Demus, Joe, c	.244	51	119	13	29	3	0	0	7	9	31	2
Dukes, Willie, dh-of	.213	63	178	24	38	3	1	5	25	25	67	12
Friedman, Jason, 1b	.239	67	213	25	51	16	0	0	23	26	28	3
*Graham, Tim, of	.203	70	212	25	43	5	3	0	22	19	64	7
Grant, Larry, 3b	.271	76	262	41	71	9	2	6	33	30	69	11
Lammon, John, c	.186	30	70	8	13	3	0	1	11	6	12	2
Limoncelli, Jeff, 2b-3b	.218	69	197	23	43	2	1	0	11	35	34	2
Lora, Jose, of	.212	67	184	35	39	2	4	1	0	20	44	22
Malave, Jose, of	.138	13	29	4	4	1	0	0	3	2	12	1
McNeely, Jeff, of	.313	73	246	41	77	4	5	6	37	40	60	39
Wardwell, Shea, of	.146	54	137	16	20	2	1	1	11	12	42	5

PITCHING	W	L	ERA	G	GS	CG	SV	IP	H	R	ER	BB	SO
Alvarez, Dave	0	0	9.00	4	0	0	0	4	2	7	4	6	1
Davis, Chris	1	3	5.14	15	9	0	1	56	59	35	32	25	41
*Dennison, Jim	7	4	3.11	15	14	4	0	93	73	43	32	37	72
Finnvold, Gar	5	5	3.13	15	15	5	0	95	91	43	33	22	89
Konopki, Mark	0	0	5.40	4	0	0	0	3	8	2	2	1	5
Locker, John	3	4	6.03	20	4	0	0	37	30	30	25	37	22
*Mitchelson, Mark	3	3	3.86	10	8	2	0	49	49	31	21	23	31
*Plantenberg, Erik	2	3	4.02	16	5	0	1	40	44	26	18	19	36
Ring, Dave	0	6	7.24	15	2	1	2	27	23	28	22	17	28
Santa Maria, Silverio	1	5	3.97	28	2	0	3	59	53	33	26	33	41
*Santiago, Cedric	1	1	4.93	15	5	1	0	35	43	27	19	12	33
Smith, Tim	4	6	3.68	23	2	2	5	66	62	33	27	25	52
Young, Brian	5	5	2.28	16	11	1	1	83	71	38	21	29	59

ERIE

BATTING	AVG	G	AB	R	H	2B	3B	HR	RBI	BB	SO	SB
*Boyce, Joe, 2b	.183	68	186	31	34	4	0	5	28	42	41	5
*Cerny, Mark, of	.200	2	5	0	1	0	0	0	0	0	3	0
*Cook, Stan, of	.255	70	212	29	54	9	6	7	40	23	37	7

	AVG	G	AB	R	H	2B	3B	HR	RBI	BB	SO	SB
*Daniels, Gary, of-dh	.258	41	124	23	32	4	4	0	14	25	24	2
*Echols, Tracy, of	.263	40	137	20	36	5	0	3	14	17	29	4
Floyd, D.J., c	.247	65	185	24	46	9	1	5	27	26	50	0
Holland, Mike, 2b-ss	.194	24	36	7	7	1	0	1	3	1	14	2
*Kemper, Robbie, 1b	.234	62	175	30	41	9	0	9	23	15	36	0
MacMillan, Darrell, dh-c ...	.261	38	115	12	30	4	1	2	17	10	15	0
Mitchell, Tommy, 3b-1b ...	.239	70	230	48	55	17	1	11	38	54	70	3
Postema, Andy, ss	.345	61	261	53	90	18	2	3	39	37	33	0
*Reimsnyder, Brian, of	.000	8	5	0	0	0	0	0	1	5	2	0
Rodriguez, Ruben, of	.267	63	243	48	65	6	3	2	18	24	54	10
Roebuck, Joe, of	.310	61	174	32	54	12	1	9	45	19	53	0
Sanderson, Shaun, c	.128	25	39	2	5	1	0	1	4	2	4	0
*Songini, Mike, 3b-dh	.321	78	280	61	90	12	2	8	51	39	29	2
*Stacey, Al, 1b	.309	44	55	3	17	1	0	0	6	5	11	1
Turco, Frank, 2b	.217	29	83	12	18	5	0	3	9	8	16	1
Varni, Pat, 2b	.500	3	2	0	1	0	0	0	0	0	0	0

PITCHING	W	L	ERA	G	GS	CG	SV	IP	H	R	ER	BB	SO
*Currie, Brian	6	3	4.06	18	11	0	0	69	78	41	31	19	66
Golden, Brian	1	2	7.39	20	1	0	1	28	29	27	23	17	37
Golmont, Van	7	4	3.14	14	14	1	0	80	68	36	28	35	58
*Jockish, Mike	3	2	3.38	29	0	0	0	21	12	10	8	21	24
Larson, Mike	1	2	14.81	10	0	0	0	10	23	26	17	8	5
Lomeli, Mike	5	3	3.70	15	12	0	0	73	81	37	30	17	49
Marte, Roberto	0	0	1.69	5	1	0	0	11	7	3	2	7	7
McCutcheon, Greg	1	0	3.27	10	6	0	0	33	40	24	12	8	38
Mikkelson, Linc	7	5	2.34	14	14	2	0	88	69	36	23	36	83
Rizza, Jerry	0	1	6.38	18	1	0	0	24	30	22	17	15	14
Santana, Ernesto	0	1	3.98	11	0	0	0	20	24	16	9	17	14
*Tafoya, Rod	1	2	12.34	3	3	0	0	12	21	20	16	5	8
Voit, David	5	6	1.97	41	0	0	3	59	40	20	13	31	87
*Woide, Steve	5	3	3.19	15	15	4	0	93	88	44	32	13	90
Wurm, Garry	2	0	2.20	35	0	0	19	41	29	10	10	12	42

GENEVA

BATTING	AVG	G	AB	R	H	2B	3B	HR	RBI	BB	SO	SB
Benitez, Luis, 2b	.167	2	6	0	1	0	0	0	0	0	1	0
Biasucci, Joe, 2b-ss	.298	51	168	29	50	8	2	4	29	16	43	4
Cancel, Victor, of	.286	67	203	38	58	7	2	0	23	48	47	13
Coffey, Stephen, ss	.191	67	209	21	40	4	2	0	21	24	58	8
*Dauphin, Phil, of	.236	73	233	47	55	8	1	12	47	51	45	8
DeRicco, John, 1b	.240	63	196	40	47	9	1	3	27	44	39	2
*Diaz, German, 3b	.254	61	209	39	53	11	2	3	19	36	44	6
Erdman, Brad, c	.225	34	111	12	25	4	0	0	15	11	31	2
#Fiacco, Charlie, 2b-3b ...	.251	60	223	41	56	8	2	4	25	36	39	5
Hartung, Andy, dh-3b	.331	74	263	48	87	19	2	11	70	45	55	1
Huff, Brad, c	.279	39	122	22	34	8	0	0	14	7	20	4
Medina, Ricardo, 1b	.222	41	90	11	20	5	0	2	8	15	10	4
Paynter, Billy, c	.224	29	76	8	17	3	0	1	6	4	27	0
Torres, Paul, of	.266	77	271	46	72	24	1	10	45	39	72	9
White, Clinton, of	.208	35	106	19	22	3	2	0	12	6	33	7
Wilson, Brian, ss	1.000	1	1	0	1	0	0	0	0	1	0	0

PITCHING	W	L	ERA	G	GS	CG	SV	IP	H	R	ER	BB	SO
Bradford, Troy	5	0	1.79	7	7	1	0	45	27	9	9	14	54
Cheetham, Sean	1	1	8.64	2	2	0	0	8	8	9	8	4	7
Correa, Amilcar	5	3	2.05	21	1	0	1	53	29	18	12	31	58
Delgado, Tim	1	1	2.80	17	2	0	4	45	43	19	14	14	37
*Dickson, Lance	2	1	0.53	3	3	0	0	17	5	1	1	4	29
Doss, Jason	3	3	3.27	9	8	1	0	44	36	19	16	23	39
Gelb, Jac	2	1	3.56	23	0	0	9	30	28	15	12	19	43
Godfrey, Tyson	1	0	0.00	1	0	0	0	3	2	0	0	2	3
Hollins, Jessie	10	3	2.77	17	16	1	0	97	87	49	30	49	115
Kessler, Greg	2	4	2.74	18	8	0	0	62	60	27	19	18	38
Kirk, Chuck	4	2	3.44	14	7	2	3	55	48	24	21	10	48
Parker, Tim	6	0	1.53	12	12	1	0	77	61	22	13	28	81
*Porcelli, Joe	3	2	4.57	31	2	0	1	45	46	29	23	35	47
*Rodriguez, Gabby	1	1	0.38	15	0	0	7	24	14	2	1	8	21
Smalls, Roberto	4	4	4.85	10	9	0	0	39	38	25	21	26	42
Stanley, Karl	1	0	7.20	7	0	0	0	10	14	9	8	12	10
Young, Michael	0	0	0.00	1	0	0	0	1	1	0	0	0	2

HAMILTON

BATTING	AVG	G	AB	R	H	2B	3B	HR	RBI	BB	SO	SB
Alesio, Chris, of	.217	39	83	5	18	2	0	0	10	3	7	2
*Beasley, Andy, c-1b	.175	16	57	4	10	2	0	1	9	2	16	0
Belbru, Juan, of	.267	72	251	40	67	9	2	10	34	29	61	10
*Bradshaw, Terry, of	.234	68	235	37	55	6	1	3	13	24	60	15
Cooper, Gary, 3b-1b	.180	65	211	19	38	6	0	4	16	22	59	3
Eldridge, Rod, 1b	.255	55	200	22	51	8	0	4	24	10	38	3
*Ellis, Paul, dh-c	.310	15	58	8	18	4	0	3	18	6	13	0
*Fayne, Jeff, of-dh	.250	58	176	20	44	5	0	6	26	20	45	1
Gonzalez, Rich, of	.255	40	137	13	35	2	0	1	7	11	17	4
Lowe, Chris, of	.188	9	16	2	3	0	0	1	2	9	0	
MacArthur, Mark, 2b-3b ...	.131	47	137	19	18	3	2	3	8	18	49	4
Perez, Ozzie, ss	.184	61	179	25	33	6	0	2	14	36	41	7
Pimentel, Wander, ss	.188	69	192	15	36	7	0	0	12	15	32	3

BATTING

R	Mike Songini, Erie	61
H	Robbie Katzaroff, Jam	107
TB	Andy Hartung, Gen	143
2B	Paul Torres, Geneva	23
3B	Kevin Jordan, Oneonta	7
	Robbie Katzaroff, Jam	7
HR	Sean Ryan, Batavia	16
RBI	Andy Hartung, Gen	70
SH	Wally Heckel, St. Cath	10
SF	Tim McClinton, Pittsfield	6
BB	Sean Ryan, Batavia	66
IBB	Layne Lambert, Auburn	6
	Danny Rogers, NF	6
HBP	Paul Torres, Geneva	10
SO	Anton Mobley, St. Cath	90
SB	Jeff McNeely, Elmira	39
CS	Shawn Scott, St. Cath	19
OB%	Jeromy Burnitz, Pitt	.444

PITCHING

G	Dave Voit, Erie	41
GS	Jessie Hollins, Geneva	16
CG	Gar Finnvold, Elmira	5
ShO	Alan Botkin, Hamilton	3
Sv	Garry Wurm, Erie	19
W	Three tied at	10
L	Three tied at	8
IP	Bill Wertz, Watertown	101
	John Smith, Utica	100
R	Rolando Caridad, Utica	60
HR	Alex Pacheco, Welland	11
BB	Tyrone Scott, Auburn	63
HB	Michael Irwin, Auburn	16
SO	Sam Militello, Oneonta	119
WP	Jessie Hollins, Geneva	21
Bk	Rafael Quirico, Oneonta	9

	AVG	G	AB	R	H	2B	3B	HR	RBI	BB	SO	SB
#Rodriguez, Ahmed, 2b-ss	.216	56	190	17	41	5	0	0	9	17	59	8
Ronan, Marc, c-1b	.228	56	167	14	38	6	0	1	15	15	37	1
*Thomas, John, of	.271	33	118	20	32	8	0	3	14	15	30	9
*Turvey, Joe, c	.206	27	68	7	14	2	0	0	6	7	22	1

PITCHING	W	L	ERA	G	GS	CG	SV	IP	H	R	ER	BB	SO
Alesio, Chris	0	0	6.00	3	0	0	1	6	3	4	4	4	2
Arias, Jose	2	3	3.95	10	9	0	0	55	58	32	24	25	39
Bailey, Roy	4	6	3.98	16	15	1	1	84	91	46	37	45	48
Betances, Marcos	4	7	3.70	18	12	2	0	83	71	43	34	31	60
Boss, David	1	5	4.84	11	5	0	0	35	39	22	19	14	27
*Botkin, Alan	7	4	1.55	13	13	4	0	87	65	26	15	26	68
*Fusco, Tom	4	0	2.98	24	2	0	1	45	27	16	15	43	44
*MacLeod, Kevin	1	1	1.47	29	0	0	3	43	24	8	7	27	44
Newby, Mike	3	1	2.73	24	0	0	2	33	27	12	10	8	32
*Osborne, Donovan	0	2	3.60	4	4	0	0	20	21	8	8	5	14
Rupkey, Rick	1	2	7.82	17	1	0	0	38	57	38	33	19	19
Salvoir, Troy	0	4	2.72	29	1	0	14	40	38	16	12	13	50
*Sells, George	1	3	5.40	6	5	0	0	25	17	16	15	19	37
Smith, Mark	2	4	4.05	7	5	0	0	33	33	15	15	13	34
Tolbert, Mark	0	0	6.00	1	0	0	0	3	2	2	2	0	2
*Urbani, Tom	0	4	6.15	5	5	0	0	26	33	26	18	15	17

JAMESTOWN

BATTING	AVG	G	AB	R	H	2B	3B	HR	RBI	BB	SO	SB
#Barry, Jeff, of	.315	51	197	30	62	6	1	4	23	17	25	25
Ciesla, Ted, 2b	.239	62	222	28	53	9	0	4	25	25	48	5
Fitzpatrick, Rob, c-dh	.268	62	209	23	56	14	0	6	34	28	53	1
Friedland, Mike, 3b-ss	.226	66	226	22	51	8	2	4	28	29	77	7
Hargis, Dan, c-dh	.164	47	159	11	26	7	0	1	10	16	44	2
Hirsch, Chris, c	.278	25	72	9	20	3	0	0	6	10	14	0
*Horne, Tyrone, dh-of	.304	7	23	1	7	2	1	0	5	4	5	3
*Katzaroff, Robbie, of	.364	74	294	57	107	15	7	1	20	29	18	34
*Marabella, Tony, 2b	.300	3	10	2	3	1	0	0	1	0	1	0
Matos, Domingo, 3b	.203	47	153	13	31	3	1	4	18	8	41	0
Murray, Glen, of	.224	53	165	20	37	8	4	1	14	21	43	12
Nyman, Jerry, of	.151	33	93	10	14	1	0	0	4	6	28	2
Rodriguez, Abimael, ss	.189	65	190	27	36	3	0	0	13	34	52	2
Samples, William, of	.246	59	183	22	45	6	4	1	13	13	48	13
*Tsitouris, Mark, 1b-dh	.246	46	142	20	35	7	1	4	17	15	29	0
*Wilstead, Randy, 1b	.272	54	180	24	49	11	1	4	21	25	44	1

PITCHING	W	L	ERA	G	GS	CG	SV	IP	H	R	ER	BB	SO
Aucoin, Derek	1	3	4.46	8	8	1	0	36	28	20	18	18	27
*Baxter, Bob	5	4	3.87	13	13	2	0	74	85	44	32	25	67
*Brewer, Billy	2	4	2.93	11	2	0	1	28	23	10	9	13	37
Diaz, Ralph	4	3	3.02	24	4	0	4	42	33	18	14	15	39
Grewal, Ranbir	0	3	2.72	19	1	0	3	36	28	15	11	22	30
*Haney, Chris	3	0	0.96	6	5	0	1	28	17	3	3	10	26
*Kotch, Darrin	5	1	2.14	18	2	1	0	55	42	20	13	20	53
Long, Steve	4	2	1.37	22	0	0	2	39	26	15	6	24	35
Mathile, Mike	4	4	2.50	14	14	1	0	90	95	40	25	28	54
Moya, Felix	6	2	2.54	14	14	3	0	89	83	32	25	26	78
Norris, Joe	3	7	5.20	13	13	1	0	62	63	48	36	43	72
*Polasek, John	2	3	1.89	25	0	0	8	33	17	7	7	16	35
Ricker, Troy	3	0	4.11	17	1	0	0	35	31	24	16	39	21
Turner, Brandon	0	0	6.75	3	0	0	0	5	11	7	4	3	4
Wessel, Troy	1	0	18.00	3	0	0	0	3	5	6	6	5	2

NIAGARA FALLS

BATTING	AVG	G	AB	R	H	2B	3B	HR	RBI	BB	SO	SB
Caines, Art, of-dh	.203	49	148	19	30	9	0	1	13	18	42	3
Debrand, Genaro, c	.143	17	49	7	7	2	1	0	3	3	8	0

	AVG	G	AB	R	H	2B	3B	HR	RBI	BB	SO	SB
*Jordan, Adrian, of	.213	31	89	13	19	2	1	0	5	12	14	2
Kimbler, Doug, ss	.192	59	177	21	34	10	1	2	18	26	42	11
Kirt, Tim, of	.213	63	169	20	36	3	0	1	12	23	28	4
Mastropietro, Dave, of . . .	.187	32	107	14	20	1	0	4	7	19	38	6
Mauro, Mike, inf	.000	11	11	0	0	0	0	0	0	1	4	0
McNamara, Denny, of	.222	10	36	6	8	0	1	0	3	3	6	2
Mendenhall, Kirk, ss-2b . . .	.249	63	217	28	54	9	0	0	15	36	29	16
Moccia, Mario, 1b-dh . . .	.143	10	28	2	4	1	0	0	1	1	8	0
*O'Neal, Kelley, 2b	.240	53	192	28	46	6	1	3	11	17	33	9
Radachowsky, Gregg, c . . .	.192	45	99	15	19	4	0	3	12	24	26	5
*Rogers, Danny, 1b	.204	71	226	29	46	9	0	10	38	42	86	8
Sadler, Sean, c-dh	.251	62	207	21	52	8	0	0	25	22	51	2
Saltzgaber, Brian, of	.225	53	178	23	40	6	1	2	20	31	24	17
#Sawkiw, Warren, dh-2b . . .	.400	7	20	7	8	1	1	0	4	15	3	2
Tagliaferri, Gino, 3b-of . . .	.177	74	243	24	43	4	1	4	26	24	88	4
*Voutour, Jim, dh-c	.191	20	47	6	9	2	0	1	2	6	15	2
Weinberg, Michael, of-dh . .	.238	40	122	12	29	5	0	0	16	10	26	1

PITCHING	W	L	ERA	G	GS	CG	SV	IP	H	R	ER	BB	SO
*Alcantara, Francisco	0	1	1.70	24	0	0	10	48	34	14	9	18	57
*Coppeta, Greg	5	7	3.21	14	14	3	0	73	61	34	26	24	44
Drell, Tom	2	7	4.01	14	14	3	0	83	87	44	37	24	53
Fazekas, Rob	6	6	5.55	14	14	1	0	71	79	53	44	27	58
Keon, Kevin	4	3	6.47	21	2	0	3	49	55	39	35	27	37
Leimeister, Eric	0	1	1.17	4	0	0	1	8	4	2	1	3	12
*Marcero, Doug	0	0	7.36	2	2	0	0	7	8	7	6	7	3
Nelson, Brian	0	0	14.58	12	0	0	0	17	16	30	27	34	9
*Pierce, Ben	0	0	2.79	3	0	0	0	10	8	4	3	5	8
Pinto, Gustavo	2	3	4.11	18	4	0	1	46	48	28	21	26	35
Rightnowar, Ron	1	0	0.00	1	1	1	0	7	4	1	0	1	9
*Rodriguez, Eddy	0	0	3.68	3	0	0	0	7	3	3	3	3	7
Schubert, Brian	3	1	3.48	6	6	0	0	31	35	14	12	7	25
Shea, Kurt	0	4	12.79	6	2	0	0	19	33	33	27	24	14
Thigpen, Arthur	1	1	7.36	8	1	0	0	18	25	19	15	13	11
Turri, Shawn	0	1	4.66	6	1	0	0	10	8	6	5	7	10
Undorf, Bob	4	1	3.35	22	0	0	4	40	34	19	15	22	38
Warren, Brian	2	6	2.17	12	10	1	0	62	53	26	15	15	62
Wolf, Steve	5	0	0.55	6	0	0	0	33	22	5	2	14	39

ONEONTA

BATTING	AVG	G	AB	R	H	2B	3B	HR	RBI	BB	SO	SB
Blackwell, Juan, 3b-ss	.263	5	19	1	5	1	0	0	2	1	7	2
#Carvajal, Jovino, of	.287	52	171	19	49	3	1	0	18	7	37	15
*Deller, Bob, of	.243	54	169	33	41	7	1	1	22	42	33	16
Demetre, Doug, c-dh	.204	20	49	5	10	2	0	1	12	15	15	0
Eenhoorn, Robert, ss	.268	57	220	30	59	9	3	2	18	18	29	11
Gallardo, Luis, c	.284	40	141	27	40	7	1	4	25	9	34	1
Hankins, Mike, inf	.271	50	166	20	45	4	0	0	18	30	27	11
Jordan, Kevin, 2b	.333	73	276	47	92	13	7	4	54	23	31	19
Lantrip, Rick, 3b	.183	70	230	31	42	5	4	3	33	48	81	7
*Leach, Jalal, of	.288	69	257	41	74	7	1	2	18	37	52	33
*Lohry, Adin, c	.197	44	137	14	27	1	2	0	14	20	28	5
Romano, Scott, of	.242	57	178	30	43	8	2	1	19	30	38	18
#Strickland, Dedrick, of-dh . .	.245	59	200	37	49	5	1	2	18	39	41	20
*Turner, Brian, 1b	.247	69	227	28	56	13	1	0	24	36	48	7

PITCHING	W	L	ERA	G	GS	CG	SV	IP	H	R	ER	BB	SO
*Dunbar, Matt	1	4	4.15	19	2	0	0	30	32	23	14	24	24
Faw, Bryan	0	0	9.00	1	0	0	0	3	6	3	3	2	2
Frazier, Ron	6	2	2.46	13	13	0	0	80	67	32	22	33	67
Hodges, Darren	6	3	1.67	14	14	1	0	86	81	30	16	24	85
*Malone, Todd	3	0	1.95	9	3	2	0	28	15	9	7	14	36
Militello, Sam	8	2	1.22	13	13	3	0	89	53	14	12	24	119
Morphy, Pat	3	5	3.02	25	2	0	0	60	56	32	20	26	56
*Ojala, Kirt	7	2	2.16	14	14	1	0	79	75	28	19	43	87
Perez, Cesar	2	2	3.14	28	0	0	2	29	21	12	10	17	33
*Perry, Steve	6	1	4.64	20	3	0	1	43	38	29	22	38	42
*Quirico, Rafael	6	3	3.21	14	14	1	0	87	69	38	31	39	69
Siberz, Bo	3	2	3.32	35	0	0	16	41	27	16	15	22	48

PITTSFIELD

BATTING	AVG	G	AB	R	H	2B	3B	HR	RBI	BB	SO	SB
#Allison, Tom, 2b-ss	.250	59	160	35	40	4	2	1	15	25	31	10
Arredondo, Joe, 3b-1b	.276	58	170	21	47	9	2	0	12	17	21	2
Buhe, Tim, 2b-ss	.262	66	206	39	54	11	2	2	36	35	33	12
Burnitz, Jeromy, of	.301	51	173	37	52	6	5	6	22	45	39	12
Castillo, Alberto, c	.219	58	187	19	41	8	1	4	24	26	35	3
*Davis, Nicky, 1b	.263	73	247	34	65	11	2	6	48	35	67	10
Dunn, Brian, c-dh	.301	31	83	8	25	6	1	1	7	10	10	3
Guzik, Robbie, of	.192	67	208	26	40	5	5	1	17	16	68	4
#King, Jason, ss	.245	51	143	27	35	2	1	0	9	30	17	3
#Kinyoun, Travis, c	.263	16	38	6	10	2	0	1	8	3	6	2
McClinton, Tim, 3b-of	.284	73	257	35	73	8	3	1	36	37	57	18
Minnifield, Wallace, of	.260	19	50	3	13	2	0	0	1	3	13	1
Perozo, Ender, of-dh	.342	32	111	15	38	6	1	2	18	16	19	4
Rudolph, Mason, c-of	.192	8	26	4	5	2	0	0	2	2	6	0
*Sciortino, Mike, p-1b	.286	31	7	0	2	0	0	0	1	0	0	0

	AVG	G	AB	R	H	2B	3B	HR	RBI	BB	SO	SB
Scott, Philip, ss-2b	.246	24	61	7	15	2	0	0	4	8	9	2
*Thornton, Eric, of	.228	51	114	20	26	4	2	0	6	4	16	11
Washington, Kyle, of	.267	63	225	42	60	7	3	2	23	44	53	32

PITCHING	W	L	ERA	G	GS	SV	IP	H	R	ER	BB	SO
Castillo, Juan	5	8	4.73	16	14	0	70	64	52	37	58	65
Coffee, Ken	2	0	3.57	6	1	0	23	21	12	9	9	17
*Douma, Todd	5	4	2.14	15	11	2	84	60	25	20	26	84
*Fidler, Andy	1	2	5.17	10	9	1	47	50	35	27	37	38
Freitas, Mike	1	0	3.86	5	0	0	9	7	4	4	4	8
Parker, Jarrod	0	1	1.80	4	1	0	5	5	1	1	5	4
Scheffler, Jim	4	2	2.16	27	0	9	42	27	13	10	22	32
*Sciortino, John	0	0	8.20	16	0	1	26	42	34	24	20	22
*Thomas, Mike	3	3	2.67	28	3	0	64	51	23	19	29	80
Thomas, Steve	3	1	4.78	19	8	0	53	62	37	28	30	53
Vazquez, Ed	10	2	2.41	18	14	3	101	84	36	27	23	49
Walker, Pete	5	7	4.16	16	13	1	90	74	43	37	46	73
Wilson, Tom	4	4	3.71	21	3	1	53	57	25	22	20	48

ST. CATHARINES

BATTING	AVG	G	AB	R	H	2B	3B	HR	RBI	BB	SO	SB
Ambrosio, Ciro, ss-dh	.245	68	216	23	53	12	2	0	22	43	51	7
Carlton, Drew, 3b-1b	.248	71	254	26	63	11	1	6	24	25	72	4
Delgado, Carlos, c	.281	67	228	30	64	13	0	6	39	35	65	2
*Harmes, Kris, c	.500	3	10	1	5	0	0	0	1	0	2	0
*Heckel, Wally, 2b	.204	73	196	30	40	2	0	0	10	33	64	7
Hudik, Matthew, 2b	.148	18	27	4	4	2	0	0	1	2	2	1
Irish, Jeff, c	.135	16	37	2	5	0	0	0	8	11	1	1
Marquez, Edgar, of-dh	.176	36	102	6	18	3	0	2	7	10	39	4
#Mobley, Anton, of	.184	66	212	26	39	4	2	7	25	27	91	4
Montalvo, Robert, ss	.183	38	115	11	21	2	0	0	5	21	16	1
Perez, Robert, of	.261	52	207	21	54	10	2	5	25	8	34	7
Querecuto, Juan, inf	.200	9	20	0	4	1	0	0	2	2	4	0
Rojas, Wilberto, 1b	.231	63	212	21	49	2	1	4	19	20	57	1
#Scott, Shawn, of	.284	75	278	29	79	10	2	1	14	30	53	31
Tollison, David, 3b	.214	42	154	14	33	6	0	2	14	13	25	2
*Yorro, Jacinto, of	.231	28	91	10	21	2	0	1	12	8	14	1

PITCHING	W	L	ERA	G	GS	CG	SV	IP	H	R	ER	BB	SO
*Aylmer, Bob	1	2	3.68	12	0	0	2	15	18	9	6	4	11
Brow, Scott	3	1	2.27	9	7	0	0	40	34	18	10	11	39
Burrell, Scott	1	4	5.86	7	7	0	0	28	29	20	18	15	24
Filter, Rusty	0	2	4.50	19	0	0	2	22	28	13	11	7	21
*Flener, Huck	4	3	3.36	14	7	0	1	62	45	29	23	33	46
Ganote, John	3	0	2.73	18	0	0	4	30	26	9	9	7	33
Karsay, Steve	1	1	0.79	5	5	0	0	23	11	4	2	12	25
Kower, Frank	0	1	2.84	15	0	0	2	32	38	14	10	11	17
Mandia, Sam	1	1	2.70	8	0	0	2	17	12	6	5	8	25
*Marcon, Dave	3	5	3.61	16	4	0	2	52	53	27	21	12	44
Menhart, Paul	0	5	4.05	8	8	0	0	40	34	27	18	19	38
Nellenbach, Rod	0	0	3.52	5	0	0	1	8	8	4	3	0	10
*Rhea, Allen	2	4	3.22	16	4	0	0	45	49	18	16	13	42
*Singer, Tom	2	3	4.66	13	4	0	1	39	38	24	20	23	44
Steed, Ricky	3	6	3.07	14	14	0	0	73	58	32	25	39	72
*Taylor, Michael	4	6	3.88	14	14	1	0	72	66	35	31	49	54
Watson, Matt	1	3	4.70	16	2	0	0	38	30	28	20	20	39

UTICA

BATTING	AVG	G	AB	R	H	2B	3B	HR	RBI	BB	SO	SB
Bradish, Michael, 1b-of	.240	59	183	20	44	7	0	1	18	21	32	2
*Coughlin, Kevin, of-1b	.274	68	215	37	59	4	5	0	16	27	41	17
Garcia, Manny, of	.211	29	76	12	16	2	2	1	6	9	27	4
Ingram, Jeff, c	.228	29	92	5	21	3	1	0	10	1	25	2
Martin, Todd, ss-3b	.157	43	121	11	19	1	0	0	11	13	39	4
Monzon, Dan, 2b	.243	64	214	36	52	14	0	3	27	39	44	14
#Nunez, Rogelio, c	.267	35	90	11	24	1	2	1	11	5	24	5
Ochoa, Rafael, of	.192	61	167	18	32	5	0	0	17	20	71	12
Perkins, Ron, c-dh	.130	19	46	3	6	1	0	0	2	10	17	0
*Randazzo, Mike, of	.250	24	56	6	14	1	0	0	4	4	4	3
Sanders, Adam, inf	.164	50	122	12	20	6	0	0	4	18	46	6
Solimine, Joe, c-dh	.200	53	140	12	28	7	1	1	20	18	48	3
Sparrow, Chris, 1b	.281	53	153	17	43	7	2	4	22	19	39	1
Strange, Keith, 3b-dh	.277	68	206	28	57	8	2	4	34	52	49	5
Tatarian, Dean, 3b	.262	18	65	11	17	0	0	2	8	8	16	1
Teter, Craig, of	.138	35	94	8	13	2	0	1	6	6	45	3
Valrie, Kerry, of	.188	42	149	14	28	4	1	0	10	8	46	12
#Williams, Barry, of	.209	59	129	19	27	3	1	0	8	32	41	16
Wilson, Brandon, ss	.248	53	165	31	41	2	0	0	14	28	45	16

PITCHING	W	L	ERA	G	GS	CG	SV	IP	H	R	ER	BB	SO
*Altaffer, Todd	0	2	6.26	13	2	0	1	23	25	27	16	15	24
Bolton, Rod	5	1	0.41	6	6	1	0	44	27	4	2	11	45
Campos, Frank	3	1	3.00	19	6	1	0	60	41	27	20	47	37
Caridad, Rolando	4	8	4.43	14	14	1	0	89	91	61	44	40	62
Dinuzzo, Jeff	1	3	5.35	18	3	0	0	34	54	25	20	15	28
Dorsey, Lee	0	0	81.00	2	0	0	0	1	5	6	6	7	0
Fruge, Chris	2	4	3.21	25	0	0	5	34	20	13	12	29	33

	W	L	ERA	G	GS	CG	SV	IP	H	R	ER	BB	SO
Gorman, Dave	4	8	3.29	17	10	1	1	79	62	39	29	41	47
Hoey, Andrew	1	1	4.13	12	1	0	1	24	25	13	11	13	15
*Hotz, Todd	0	4	6.55	27	1	0	0	34	33	28	25	23	25
Hulme, Pat	0	0	5.40	4	0	0	0	3	4	4	2	7	4
Jenkins, Jonathan	2	3	3.04	14	6	2	0	50	42	20	17	21	44
Smith, John	5	5	3.12	16	14	2	0	92	100	55	32	29	44
*Tolar, Kevin	4	6	3.29	15	15	1	0	90	80	44	33	61	69

WATERTOWN

BATTING	AVG	G	AB	R	H	2B	3B	HR	RBI	BB	SO	SB
Canate, William, of	.261	57	199	28	52	5	2	2	15	10	43	9
*Charbonnet, Mark, of	.254	61	224	21	57	4	3	4	32	9	56	10
*Cotton, John, 2b	.210	73	286	53	60	9	4	2	27	40	71	24
*Davis, Mike, 1b-dh	.252	59	210	21	53	6	3	3	23	17	39	3
*Giles, Brian, of	.289	70	246	44	71	15	2	1	23	48	23	11
Hamm, Stacy, of	.260	21	54	16	14	1	0	0	6	10	20	2
Kluss, Dennis, of	.237	40	118	11	28	5	2	0	12	5	29	5
*Lorms, John, c	.178	32	73	10	13	2	1	0	4	29	21	3
*Morris, Aaron, 3b	.266	21	64	6	17	3	2	1	10	7	21	0
Perez, Joe, of-dh	.238	63	231	27	55	9	3	4	27	19	47	9
Pough, Clyde, 3b	.253	76	285	47	72	15	1	9	49	40	71	21
Shelton, Todd, c-dh	.083	4	12	2	1	0	0	0	1	2	3	2
Stinnett, Kelly, c	.240	60	192	29	46	10	2	2	21	40	43	3
Tena, Paulino, ss	.245	73	277	36	68	12	5	4	37	19	67	9
Welch, Ken, 1b-ss	.204	40	113	15	23	5	1	0	17	12	15	1

PITCHING	W	L	ERA	G	GS	CG	SV	IP	H	R	ER	BB	SO
Allen, Chad	7	6	3.48	15	15	1	0	93	90	49	36	30	62
*Bryant, Shawn	6	3	2.77	10	10	2	0	62	49	24	19	23	56
Cofer, Brian	0	1	9.82	8	0	0	0	15	15	16	16	21	12
*Ellis, Tim	0	1	10.38	2	1	0	0	4	8	5	5	6	3
Elston, Cary	0	0	40.50	1	0	0	0	1	3	3	3	1	1
Gonzales, Mike	0	0	0.00	7	0	0	2	15	8	2	0	6	17
Kallevig, Dane	2	4	3.06	15	5	1	3	62	65	30	21	16	46
*Langdon, Tim	1	4	2.92	9	9	0	0	49	49	24	16	19	46
Mlicki, Dave	3	0	3.38	7	4	0	0	32	33	15	12	11	28
Morgan, Scott	0	0	0.00	4	0	0	2	9	3	2	0	4	9
Munoz, Oscar	1	1	1.69	2	2	0	0	11	8	2	2	3	9
Person, Robert	1	0	1.10	5	2	0	0	16	8	2	2	7	19
*Rivera, Roberto	4	4	3.60	14	13	2	0	85	85	43	34	10	63
*Ryan, Bobby	5	3	0.73	27	0	0	9	62	47	11	5	20	69
Shepherd, Keith	3	3	2.48	24	0	0	3	54	41	22	15	29	55
Wertz, Bill	10	2	2.86	14	14	2	0	101	81	39	32	48	92
*Woodfin, Olonzo	0	2	5.14	5	3	0	0	14	14	14	8	20	5

WELLAND

BATTING	AVG	G	AB	R	H	2B	3B	HR	RBI	BB	SO	SB
Brown, Anthony, of	.247	59	182	26	45	6	3	0	20	27	40	6
*Brown, Mike, 1b	.295	65	193	23	57	7	0	2	32	22	35	5
*Bullett, Scott, of	.302	74	255	46	77	11	4	3	33	13	50	30
Campusano, Genaro, dh	.212	45	118	17	25	6	0	9	30	18	53	0
Curtis, John, of	.290	47	124	26	36	8	2	2	18	17	24	7
DelosSantos, Alberto, of	.375	5	8	1	3	0	1	0	1	0	0	0
Edge, Tim, c	.215	63	149	6	32	5	0	1	12	19	27	4
#Feliz, Janiero, 2b-ss	.165	48	85	13	14	2	2	0	4	7	33	6
Green, Tom, of	.278	16	36	3	10	2	0	0	4	3	7	3
Grisham, Wes, of	.265	46	147	16	39	7	0	1	20	8	24	3
Hanel, Marcus, c	.153	40	98	5	15	2	0	0	8	5	26	1
Johnson, Ben, ss-2b	.247	40	89	6	22	5	0	1	14	8	24	0
*Johnson, Mark, dh-1b	.375	5	8	2	3	1	0	0	2	2	0	0
Martin, Jon, 1b	.181	44	94	11	17	3	0	3	12	14	27	6
Martinez, Ramon, ss	.232	48	151	26	35	3	1	0	15	7	38	19
Osik, Keith, 3b-c	.278	29	97	13	27	4	0	1	20	11	12	2
Peterson, Rob, c-dh	.283	22	53	7	15	5	0	1	10	10	17	2
Polewski, Steve, 2b	.317	37	63	13	20	1	0	0	4	10	10	2
Ronca, Joe, of	.214	63	140	21	30	2	0	1	4	8	26	15
Schaefer, Cory, of	.279	23	61	15	17	2	0	0	7	11	12	7
*Schulte, John, 2b	.216	63	171	24	37	6	1	0	7	41	46	10
Young, Kevin, 3b	.244	72	238	46	58	16	5	0	31	36	10	10

PITCHING	W	L	ERA	G	GS	CG	SV	IP	H	R	ER	BB	SO
Carlson, Lynn	4	1	4.02	16	8	0	0	54	32	27	24	52	55
*Cooke, Stephen	2	3	2.35	11	11	0	0	46	36	21	12	17	43
Futrell, Mark	2	4	1.67	16	0	0	3	38	37	19	7	15	32
Lyle, Jeff	4	4	4.18	30	3	1	2	65	65	39	30	25	44
Miller, Kurt	3	2	3.29	14	12	0	0	66	59	39	24	37	62
Mooney, Troy	0	1	5.40	2	2	0	0	8	7	6	5	5	7
Pacheco, Alex	2	6	5.58	13	13	0	0	61	55	42	38	49	67
Redmond, Andre	1	1	5.00	15	8	0	0	45	37	32	25	60	46
*Robertson, Rich	3	4	3.08	16	13	0	0	64	51	34	22	55	80
Roeder, Steve	1	3	5.74	18	1	0	0	31	32	33	20	38	25
*Shouse, Brian	4	3	5.22	17	1	0	2	40	50	27	23	7	39
Simpson, Shelton	2	3	2.77	18	1	0	1	49	44	19	15	27	37
Tellers, Dave	4	2	1.36	20	0	0	5	40	23	9	6	7	53
*Way, Ron	1	1	3.38	9	0	0	2	13	12	5	5	8	15
White, Richard	1	4	3.26	9	5	1	0	39	39	19	14	14	43
Zimmerman, Mike	2	0	0.68	9	0	0	2	13	7	4	1	9	22

NORTHWEST LEAGUE

Nothing ever changes; Spokane wins again

By HOWIE STALWICK

The Northwest League remains a monument to stability. Franchises rarely move, attendance rarely drops, working agreements rarely change, and the Spokane Indians never lose.

The latter statement isn't entirely true, of course—it just seems that way. The Indians established a league record by winning their fourth straight championship in 1990, and Tom Romenesko thinks he's identified the formula for success.

"Environment," said Romenesko, director of minor league operations for the San Diego Padres, Spokane's parent club. "A great environment.

"Spokane is the best-kept secret in baseball. It starts with the ownership, the commitment from the community, the fans, how the players are treated, how the coaches are treated. People perform better in a good environment."

**Matt Mieske
...MVP**

Treated like grown-ups

As usual, the Padres did not stock Spokane with a flood of top draft picks or experienced pros. The Padres do load the Indians with college players in their 20s, and many of those players have lauded the instruction they receive in Spokane.

"We got great coaching," said relief pitcher Lance Painter. "Gino (Manager Gene Glynn) did a great job. He let us play the game. I know some situations where the managers force

LEAGUE CHAMPIONS

Playoff Champions, Where Applicable

1990—Spokane	1964—Yakima	1923-36—Did Not
1989—Spokane	1963—Yakima	Operate
1988—Spokane	1962—Wenatchee	1922—Calgary
1987—Spokane	1961—Lewiston	1921—Yakima
1986—Bellingham	1960—Yakima	1920—Victoria
1985—Everett	1959—Yakima	1919—Seattle
1984—Tri-Cities	1958—Yakima	1918—Seattle
1983—Medford	1957—Wenatchee	1917—Great Falls
1982—Salem	1956—Yakima	1916—Spokane
1981—Medford	1955—Eugene	1915—Seattle
1980—*Bellingham	1954—Vancouver	1914—Vancouver
—*Eugene	1953—Spokane	1913—Vancouver
1979—Central Ore.	1952—Victoria	1912—Seattle
1978—Grays Harbor	1951—Spokane	1911—Vancouver
1977—Bellingham	1950—Yakima	1910—Spokane
1976—Walla Walla	1949—Vancouver	1909—Seattle
1975—Eugene	1948—Spokane	1908—Vancouver
1974—Eugene	1947—Vancouver	1907—Aberdeen
1973—Walla Walla	1946—Wenatchee	1906—Tacoma
1972—Lewiston	1943-45—Did Not	1905—Everett
1971—Tri-City	Operate	1904—Boise
1970—Lewiston	1942—Vancouver	1903—Butte
1969—Rogue Valley	1941—Spokane	1902—Butte
1968—Tri-City	1940—Tacoma	1901—Portland
1967—Medford	1939—Tacoma	
1966—Tri-City	1938—Bellingham	*co-champions
1965—Tri-City	1937—Tacoma	

Todd Van Poppel, the $1.2 million draft pick, made a brief appearance in the NWL in 1990, going 1-1 in five games.

players to do things. He just let us play."

Glynn, who spent his previous 11 years in professional baseball as a minor league player, coach and manager with Montreal, was Spokane's fourth manager in as many years. He was impressed with the Padres' approach.

"The one thing this organization does is they're so personable with the players," Glynn said. "They give them confidence and let them play with what got them here the first year. I agree with that."

Spokane's Jay Gainer (.356-10-54) and Matt Mieske (.340-12-63) finished first or second in batting, homers and RBIs.

Gainer, a 24-year-old first baseman from South Alabama, became Spokane's third straight batting champion. Mieske, a right fielder from Western Michigan, gave Spokane its second straight MVP and fourth straight RBI champion.

Bellingham righthander Dave Adam led the league with a 1.43 ERA. He edged Boise southpaw Hilly Hathaway (1.46), who struck out a league-high 113, excluding 17 in one playoff game against Spokane.

Another attendance mark

The Indians weren't the only success story in the league, of course. The Boise Hawks, who never experienced a winning season in three years as an independent, posted a league-best 53-23 record (Spokane was 49-27) and won the Southern

Division in their first year as a California Angels farm club.

The eight teams drew 692,126 fans, setting a record for the fifth time in Jack Cain's six-year reign as president. Cain resigned after the season and was replaced by former league president Bob Richmond. Cain plans to devote more time to the Bend Bucks, the co-op team he operates with wife Mary.

Spokane, Eugene and Boise posted some of the highest attendance figures in league history. The Indians, who applied for a Triple-A expansion franchise after the season, led the league in attendance for the first time by drawing 129,999, an average of 3,714.

Eugene failed to lead in attendance for the first time since 1982, but drew 128,831 with a club that finished 30-46. Boise attracted 124,270 fans, down slightly from the year before, when the Hawks built their own stadium.

1990 *FINAL STANDINGS*

North	W	L	Pct.	GB
Spokane (Padres)	49	27	.645	—
Yakima (Dodgers)	36	40	.474	13
Everett (Giants)	35	41	.461	14
Bellingham (Mariners)	32	44	.421	17
South				
Boise (Angels)	53	23	.697	—
So. Oregon (Athletics)	40	36	.526	13
Eugene (Royals)	30	46	.395	23
Bend (Co-op)	29	47	.382	24

1990 *GENERAL INFORMATION*

Playoffs: Spokane defeated Boise 2-1 in best-of-3 final to win league championship.

Regular-Season Attendance: Spokane, 129,999; Eugene, 128,831; Boise, 124,270; Everett, 74,577; Yakima, 71,892; Southern Oregon, 69,247; Bellingham, 52,461; Bend, 40,849.

Managers: Bellingham—P.J. Carey; **Bend**—Mike Bubalo; **Boise**—Tom Kotchman; **Eugene**—Paul Kirsch; **Everett**—Deron McCue; **Southern Oregon**—Grady Fuson; **Spokane**—Gene Glynn; **Yakima**—Jerry Royster.

1990 Official All-Star Team: C—Eric Helfand, Southern Oregon. **1B**—Jay Gainer, Spokane. **2B**—Giovanni Miranda, Eugene. **3B**—Mike Galle, Yakima. **SS**—Kevin Farlow, Spokane. **OF**—Matt Mieske, Spokane; Eric Booker, Southern Oregon; Mark Dalesandro, Boise. **DH**—Brian Stephens, Bellingham. **RHP**—Randy Powers, Boise. **LHP**—Hilly Hathaway, Boise. **Most Valuable Player**—Matt Mieske, Spokane. **Manager of the Year**—Gene Glynn, Spokane.

Top 10 Major League Prospects (by Baseball America): 1. Todd Van Poppel, rhp, Southern Oregon; **2.** Kirk Dressendorfer, rhp, Southern Oregon; **3.** Derek Reid, of, Everett; **4.** Eric Helfand, c, Southern Oregon; **5.** Billy Lott, of, Yakima; **6.** Matt Mieske, of, Spokane; **7.** Hilly Hathaway, lhp, Boise; **8.** Joe Rosselli, lhp, Everett; **9.** Eric Christopherson, c, Everett; **10.** Jay Gainer, 1b, Spokane.

1990 *BATTING, PITCHING STATS*

CLUB BATTING

	AVG	G	AB	R	H	2B	3B	HR	SO	SB
Yakima	.263	76	2608	398	687	124	20	30	274	493	113
Southern Oregon	.259	76	2612	391	676	99	15	28	333	674	94
Spokane	.255	76	2627	394	669	107	17	40	338	694	106
Boise	.249	76	2543	425	634	86	17	49	404	646	70
Bend	.240	76	2545	348	610	84	11	29	305	649	183
Everett	.238	76	2563	349	611	121	9	35	326	597	105
Bellingham	.224	76	2562	273	574	100	11	44	236	675	76
Eugene	.224	76	2501	303	559	79	15	37	265	673	98

CLUB PITCHING

	ERA	G	CG	SHO	SV	IP	H	R	ER	BB	SO
Boise	2.43	76	4	10	21	679	570	250	183	225	664
Southern Oregon	3.32	76	1	8	15	684	588	325	252	293	677

	ERA	G	CG	SHO	SV	IP	H	R	ER	BB	SO
Eugene	3.62	76	2	2	15	674	636	372	271	306	595
Bellingham	3.67	76	6	4	9	680	577	342	277	353	624
Spokane	3.86	76	2	4	30	690	646	360	296	290	691
Yakima	3.91	76	2	2	17	678	642	403	295	335	638
Everett	4.13	76	4	3	13	669	662	369	307	305	664
Bend	4.60	76	1	2	18	667	701	460	341	375	549

INDIVIDUAL BATTING LEADERS

(Minimum 205 Plate Appearances)

	AVG	G	AB	R	H	2B	3B	HR	RBI	BB	SO	SB
*Gainer, Jay, Spokane	.356	74	281	41	100	21	0	10	54	31	49	4
Mieske, Matt, Spokane	.340	76	291	59	99	20	0	12	63	45	43	26
Dalesandro, Mark, Boise	.335	55	224	35	75	10	2	6	44	18	42	6
Galle, Mike, Yakima	.317	65	224	43	71	21	2	4	42	53	42	3
Booker, Eric, SO	.305	53	187	38	57	12	0	4	33	43	44	14
Hiatt, Phil, Eugene	.294	73	289	33	85	18	5	2	44	17	70	15
Reid, Derek, Everett	.288	62	215	35	62	15	1	5	40	20	49	21
*Helfand, Eric, SO	.285	57	207	29	59	12	0	2	39	20	49	4
Grebeck, Brian, Boise	.282	58	202	45	57	10	2	1	33	64	57	1
Lanfranco, Luis, SO	.278	69	259	37	68	10	2	2	28	25	74	6

INDIVIDUAL PITCHING LEADERS

(Minimum 61 Innings)

	W	L	ERA	G	GS	CG	SV	IP	H	R	ER	BB	SO
Adam, Dave, Bell	4	4	1.43	19	7	4	1	69	40	13	11	22	76
*Hathaway, Hilly, Boise	8	2	1.46	15	15	1	0	86	56	18	14	25	113
*Painter, Lance, Spokane	7	3	1.51	23	1	0	3	72	45	18	12	15	104
Peters, Doug, Eugene	7	2	1.73	15	14	1	0	83	76	23	16	20	74
Leftwich, Phil, Boise	8	2	1.86	15	15	0	0	92	88	36	19	22	81
Powers, Randy, Boise	7	3	2.56	15	15	4	0	102	87	40	29	19	76
Pakele, Louis, Boise	5	3	2.78	15	13	0	0	74	76	28	23	7	52
*Henrikson, Dan, Everett	10	3	3.08	15	15	1	0	102	103	43	35	39	77
Bradley, Mike, Spokane	7	2	3.34	15	15	2	0	89	68	37	34	43	91
Pollard, Damon, Eugene	3	3	3.34	14	14	1	0	70	46	35	26	42	77

BELLINGHAM

BATTING	AVG	G	AB	R	H	2B	3B	HR	RBI	BB	SO	SB
Hoffman, John, c	.250	4	12	1	3	0	0	0	0	1	4	0
*Hunter, Greg, 3b-ss	.213	56	183	21	39	5	2	1	13	22	36	2
Klavitter, Clay, dh-1b	.173	22	52	4	9	2	0	1	6	15	0	
Kluge, Matt, c	.242	34	99	9	24	7	0	0	7	3	34	2
Kounas, Tony, 1b	.231	19	65	9	15	4	0	1	11	8	13	1
Magallanes, Bobby, 3b-ss	.191	46	157	14	30	3	0	1	12	18	31	1
#McNair, Fred, dh	.205	50	176	16	36	8	0	3	17	15	55	7
Nava, Lipso, ss	.251	46	171	11	43	12	0	0	15	15	31	4
Nichols, Rob, 1b-3b	.225	57	209	22	47	13	0	3	23	12	59	0
Raasch, Glen, c	.190	47	163	16	31	4	0	6	13	5	56	0
Romay, Willie, of	.235	55	179	26	42	10	3	7	24	26	66	2
Santana, Ruben, 2b-3b	.252	47	155	22	39	3	2	4	13	18	39	10
*Stephens, Brian, of	.273	59	231	23	63	10	1	7	31	14	55	6
Terrell, Jim, of	.223	51	184	18	41	4	0	3	16	11	38	6
Twitty, Sean, of	.225	67	253	30	57	9	1	6	22	31	72	24
Wilder, Willie, of	.152	37	125	13	19	3	2	1	10	10	37	8
*Wilkerson, Willie, 2b	.243	47	148	18	36	3	0	0	10	21	34	5

PITCHING	W	L	ERA	G	GS	CG	SV	IP	H	R	ER	BB	SO
Adam, Dave	4	4	1.43	19	7	4	1	69	40	13	11	22	76
Callistro, Rob	2	2	5.55	22	0	0	2	36	35	28	22	34	35
Converse, Jim	2	4	3.92	12	12	0	0	67	50	31	29	32	75
*Cummings, John	1	1	2.12	6	6	0	0	34	25	11	8	9	39
*Duke, Kyle	4	5	3.71	12	11	0	0	61	57	30	25	46	40
*Fitzer, Doug	5	1	2.70	25	0	0	3	43	24	15	13	21	62
Green, Rick	1	3	2.17	7	7	0	0	37	24	19	9	19	34
*King, Kevin	3	2	4.78	6	6	0	0	32	37	18	17	10	27
Lodding, Rich	1	5	5.21	13	11	0	0	57	58	42	33	42	49
Magill, Jim	4	7	4.18	15	15	2	0	84	72	48	39	52	49
*McDonald, David	1	0	1.13	8	0	0	0	16	11	5	2	8	12
Rivera, Randy	0	0	0.00	3	0	0	1	6	2	0	0	1	6
Schanz, Scott	1	0	4.50	7	1	0	0	8	7	4	4	3	3
Tegtmeier, Doug	1	1	2.21	17	0	0	0	37	35	9	9	10	30
Williams, Tyler	0	1	4.55	17	0	0	2	32	29	18	16	9	23
*Yianacopolus, Kevin	2	5	4.46	23	0	0	0	36	37	22	18	18	42
Youngblood, Todd	0	3	7.71	17	0	0	0	26	34	29	22	17	24

BEND

BATTING	AVG	G	AB	R	H	2B	3B	HR	RBI	BB	SO	SB
Ahrens, Kelly, c	.231	43	121	16	28	7	0	6	13	17	55	4
Avent, Steve, c	.235	45	153	21	36	4	0	1	15	5	38	5
#Chevalier, Bonell, 2b-ss	.210	58	195	24	41	6	2	0	13	16	37	16
#Frias, Pedro, ss	.264	68	231	29	61	5	2	0	16	15	51	25
Grahovac, Mike, c	.423	7	26	5	11	3	0	0	1	3	2	0
Helms, Mike, 2b (9 Everett)	.159	32	82	6	13	1	0	0	7	12	31	1
Horan, Mike, of	.125	4	8	1	1	0	1	0	2	3	3	0
Hunt, Shannon, dh-1b	.141	38	92	9	13	2	0	2	7	15	46	2
Hyde, Mickey, of	.265	68	260	35	69	9	1	6	40	19	53	13
Krokroskia, Sean, of	.248	37	109	21	27	4	2	0	15	29	33	15
#Lyons, Mario, of	.179	46	123	19	22	5	1	1	10	19	45	14

Hilly Hathaway
...8-2, 1.46

Randy Powers
...7-3, 2.56

Mark Delesandro
... .335-8-44

	AVG	G	AB	R	H	2B	3B	HR	RBI	BB	SO	SB
McCormick, Glenn, 1b-3b	.239	72	251	37	60	6	1	3	24	39	67	2
Reyes, Amner, 3b	.236	57	199	28	47	3	0	2	27	22	24	11
Roa, Pedro, 2b	.156	11	32	4	5	0	0	0	2	3	13	2
Sammons, Lee, of	.261	69	253	49	66	5	1	1	20	46	50	45
Twitty, Doug, of	.240	57	192	17	46	8	0	2	22	24	38	14
*Varnell, Dan, of (4 Everett)	.298	39	104	10	31	11	0	2	15	16	34	2

PITCHING	W	L	ERA	G	GS	CG	SV	IP	H	R	ER	BB	SO
Blankenship, Bob	2	4	1.36	27	0	0	12	46	41	11	7	11	54
Boker, Mike (7 Everett)	1	2	5.50	19	0	0	0	34	35	25	21	27	33
Gibbs, Jim	0	0	0.00	4	0	0	2	11	1	0	0	3	18
Hill, Fred	0	0	2.38	6	0	0	0	11	12	3	3	5	12
*Klonoski, Jason	7	4	2.81	26	1	0	2	48	42	21	15	12	61
Miller, Russ	1	6	7.88	9	9	0	0	40	52	51	35	37	18
Minder, Troy	0	1	4.24	9	6	0	0	40	40	23	19	30	29
Nielson, Ken	1	1	4.70	2	0	0	0	8	8	4	4	5	7
Pena, Antonio	2	2	2.77	8	6	0	0	39	32	20	12	17	23
Potter, Lonnie	0	0	8.39	12	0	0	0	34	53	47	32	31	27
Reyes, Jose	3	7	3.67	21	5	1	0	76	80	41	31	23	64
Ross, Gary	5	7	5.61	16	16	0	0	85	93	62	53	44	42
Russell, Todd	1	4	6.02	15	13	0	0	64	78	57	43	45	34
Sims, Jon	0	0	2.70	3	0	0	1	3	2	2	1	1	2
*Wagner, Darrell	2	6	5.31	21	7	0	1	63	64	52	37	45	69
*Wanke, Chuck	0	3	4.88	6	6	0	0	28	27	22	15	26	25

BOISE

BATTING	AVG	G	AB	R	H	2B	3B	HR	RBI	BB	SO	SB
*Anderson, Garrett, of	.253	25	83	11	21	3	1	1	8	4	18	0
Dalesandro, Mark, of-3b	.335	55	224	35	75	10	2	6	44	18	42	6
Forbes, P.J., 2b	.249	43	169	29	42	9	1	0	20	23	22	11
*Garrett, Clifton, of	.203	53	148	28	30	1	1	0	7	42	27	15
Gil, Danny, c-dh	.309	51	152	27	47	12	0	5	34	25	43	0
Grebeck, Brian, ss-2b	.282	58	202	45	57	10	2	1	33	64	57	1
#Kotchman, Randy, 3b	.244	56	164	30	40	7	1	0	24	34	35	6
Lasher, Matt, 2b	.143	9	21	3	3	1	0	1	4	5	3	0
Ledinsky, Ray, of	.250	1	4	0	1	0	0	0	1	0	1	0
Markiewicz, Brandon, ph	.000	1	1	0	0	0	0	0	0	0	1	0
Partrick, Dave, of	.226	66	239	25	54	6	1	9	35	17	91	0
Percival, Troy, c	.203	29	79	12	16	0	0	0	5	19	25	0
*Phillips, J.R., 1b	.194	70	237	30	46	6	0	10	34	20	78	1
*Santana, Jose, dh-1b	.265	58	181	34	48	1	3	0	32	33	35	13
Shepperd, Rich, of	.300	16	40	9	12	2	0	0	2	7	8	1
Showalter, J.R., ss	.267	58	187	26	50	5	1	8	35	22	33	1
#Specyalski, Brian, of-2b	.250	25	68	18	17	2	1	1	8	17	10	8
Staydohar, David, of-dh	.284	53	169	31	48	7	2	6	18	13	51	4
Tejero, Fausto, c	.216	39	74	14	16	2	0	0	7	23	23	1
Williams, Joe, 3b	.123	40	81	14	10	2	1	1	5	15	36	0
#Williams, Kent, of	.056	5	18	4	1	0	0	0	2	4	7	2

PITCHING	W	L	ERA	G	GS	CG	SV	IP	H	R	ER	BB	SO
Ball, Jeff	2	0	5.02	13	0	0	0	14	17	11	8	6	12
Cobb, Marvin	0	0	0.00	2	0	0	0	4	3	0	0	1	6
Craven, Britt	1	0	3.77	6	0	0	0	14	14	6	6	6	9
Edenfield, Ken	8	4	1.65	31	0	0	9	55	38	15	10	17	57
*Gamez, Bob	3	0	2.91	14	7	0	0	46	42	19	15	15	38
*Hathaway, Hilly	8	2	1.46	15	15	0	0	86	56	18	14	25	113
Helm, Wayne	3	1	2.21	19	3	0	0	41	31	13	10	24	48
*James, Todd	0	1	13.50	1	1	0	0	3	8	5	5	3	3
Lachemann, Bret	0	1	1.50	2	0	0	0	6	4	1	1	3	3
*Leftwich, Phil	8	2	1.86	15	15	0	0	92	88	36	19	22	81
McCray, Todd	1	1	3.65	17	7	0	0	37	27	24	15	31	38
Mussett, Jose	0	0	0.00	1	0	0	0	1	0	0	0	1	0
Pakele, Louis	5	3	2.78	15	13	0	0	74	76	28	23	7	52
Powers, Randy	7	3	2.56	15	15	0	0	102	87	40	29	19	76
Scott, Darryl	2	1	1.34	27	0	0	6	54	41	11	9	19	57

	W	L	ERA	G	GS	CG	SV	IP	H	R	ER	BB	SO
*Search, Michael	4	2	2.04	16	0	0	0	18	14	6	4	8	21
*Stenz, Dan	1	1	7.50	18	0	0	0	18	19	16	15	13	25
Swingle, Paul	0	1	0.66	14	0	0	6	14	5	1	1	4	25

EUGENE

BATTING	AVG	G	AB	R	H	2B	3B	HR	RBI	BB	SO	SB
Alvarez, Javier, 2b-ss	.186	45	129	17	24	3	0	3	6	26	36	7
Brooks, Ray, c	.103	10	29	4	3	2	0	1	2	7	8	0
Carballo, Jay, ss	.216	53	148	18	32	3	1	2	11	24	25	4
Ebanks, Weddison, of	.188	8	16	2	3	0	0	0	2	1	5	0
Garcia, Francisco, of	.238	53	189	22	45	6	1	0	12	7	43	7
Guanchez, Harry, 1b	.263	66	194	13	51	6	0	6	35	14	51	0
Haber, Dave, of	.199	56	161	12	32	2	1	0	14	18	44	11
Harrel, Donny, c-dh	.223	55	184	17	41	8	2	4	25	12	57	2
Hiatt, Phil, 3b	.294	73	289	33	85	18	5	2	44	17	70	15
Jennings, Lance, c	.185	31	92	8	17	3	1	4	9	6	21	0
Johnson, Darron, 1b-dh ...	.171	42	117	9	20	6	0	2	14	8	40	0
Miranda, Giovanni, 2b	.338	42	145	30	49	3	0	0	15	15	30	16
Moser, Ricky, 3b-dh	.209	31	86	13	18	0	2	1	9	18	37	3
Rolls, David, c	.281	45	128	24	36	5	0	5	13	21	27	1
Sambel, Arnie, of	.143	8	28	1	4	0	0	0	1	4	7	0
Shields, Doug, of	.192	71	250	38	48	8	1	3	15	24	62	13
*Slater, Vernon, of	.190	53	137	15	26	1	1	4	9	19	62	9
Stewart, Brady, ss-2b	.165	34	85	15	14	2	0	0	2	10	16	6
*Strong, Shannon, of	.117	38	94	12	11	1	0	0	2	14	32	4

PITCHING	W	L	ERA	G	GS	CG	SV	IP	H	R	ER	BB	SO
*Baez, Francisco	0	3	3.40	11	8	0	0	40	38	22	15	25	32
Davis, Scott	3	2	7.07	17	0	0	0	28	34	24	22	16	22
*Franceschi, Sean	0	4	4.05	24	0	0	2	33	31	21	15	20	38
Frederick, Charles	1	6	3.67	22	0	0	0	34	33	26	14	19	26
Gill, Steve	0	1	4.39	13	0	0	3	27	28	13	13	6	27
Gutierrez, Rafael	2	2	3.71	22	1	0	0	44	39	24	18	20	44
Harris, Doug	4	5	4.41	15	15	0	0	69	74	46	34	28	46
Hierholzer, David	4	5	2.23	32	0	0	9	40	36	16	10	17	39
Holman, Brad	0	3	4.78	17	4	0	0	43	43	28	23	17	31
*Long, Tony	2	4	3.66	16	10	0	1	64	68	32	26	17	58
Myers, Rod	0	2	1.19	6	4	0	0	23	19	9	3	13	17
Peters, Doug	7	2	1.73	15	14	1	0	83	76	25	16	20	74
Pineda, Gabriel	2	0	3.57	20	0	0	0	45	39	29	18	24	43
Pollard, Damon	3	3	3.34	14	14	1	0	70	46	35	26	42	77
Rea, Shayne	2	4	5.28	9	6	0	0	31	32	24	18	22	21

EVERETT

BATTING	AVG	G	AB	R	H	2B	3B	HR	RBI	BB	SO	SB
*Alimena, Charles, 1b	.057	14	35	2	2	0	0	0	0	4	6	1
Borgogno, Mate, 2b-ss ...	.217	31	106	11	23	3	0	0	10	12	18	5
Christopherson, Eric, c ...	.265	48	162	20	43	8	1	1	22	31	29	7
#Dakin, Brian, 3b-2b	.243	35	107	14	26	4	0	2	15	16	23	1
Davis, Courtney, of	.091	4	11	4	1	0	0	0	1	3	7	0
#Davis, Matt, ss-2b	.270	39	141	23	38	9	0	4	18	14	21	8
Hart, Shelby, 1b-of	.203	54	182	12	37	5	0	0	17	18	35	3
Hyzdu, Adam, of	.245	69	253	31	62	16	1	6	34	28	78	2
*Jackson, John, of	.304	39	92	26	28	2	2	1	7	27	11	14
#Jensen, Marcus, dh-c ...	.170	51	171	21	29	3	0	2	12	24	60	0
Jones, Heath, 1b-dh	.000	6	18	1	0	0	0	0	0	2	8	0
Mesa, Audy, 2b (35 Bend) .	.251	67	239	27	60	8	0	4	35	13	55	9
*Miller, Barry, 1b	.265	38	136	19	36	12	0	2	15	13	25	1
Nes Smith, John, c-dh ...	.235	14	34	6	8	2	0	2	3	9	15	0
Reid, Derek, of	.288	62	215	35	62	15	1	5	40	20	49	21
Ringgold, Keith, of	.239	22	46	10	11	1	0	0	2	6	14	3
Sievers, Jason, c	.160	17	50	2	8	1	0	0	5	8	15	0
Spires, Tony, 3b-ss	.244	65	213	27	52	8	0	1	9	20	39	5
#Vega, Julio, of	.147	35	109	12	16	1	0	0	3	13	46	0
Ward, Ricky, ss	.262	39	149	25	39	11	1	1	22	17	28	7
Weber, Pete, of	.316	40	158	27	50	15	2	4	24	22	33	20
Young, Jason, 2b	.262	13	42	10	11	2	1	3	8	8	8	2

PITCHING	W	L	ERA	G	GS	CG	SV	IP	H	R	ER	BB	SO
Ayres, Lenny	3	3	1.73	22	0	0	4	36	25	10	7	24	42
Carlson, Dan	2	6	5.34	17	11	0	0	62	60	42	37	33	77
Ebert, Scott	1	1	5.68	5	5	1	0	25	25	19	16	23	21
Flanagan, Dan	0	0	0.00	4	0	0	2	3	2	1	0	0	2
*Gould, Frank	0	1	3.60	17	0	0	0	30	31	19	12	9	36
*Henrikson, Dan (7 Bend) ..	10	3	3.08	15	15	1	0	102	103	43	35	39	77
Huffman, Rod	1	0	3.66	21	0	0	2	39	41	20	16	12	30
Huisman, Rich	0	0	4.50	1	0	0	0	2	3	1	1	2	2
Huslig, Jim	0	1	4.50	2	1	0	0	8	9	4	4	9	4
McGehee, Kevin	4	8	4.76	15	14	0	0	74	74	47	39	38	86
McLeod, Brian	2	5	4.56	12	2	0	0	49	33	28	25	29	43
*Myers, Mike	4	5	3.90	15	14	1	0	85	91	43	37	30	73
*Peltzer, Kurt	3	1	4.31	18	5	0	0	48	58	30	23	23	39
*Rosselli, Joe	4	4	4.71	15	15	0	0	78	87	47	41	29	90
Whatley, Fred	0	1	4.11	8	0	0	0	15	16	8	7	8	15
*Yockey, Mark	5	2	3.86	23	1	0	3	47	45	22	20	15	53

BATTING

R	Matt Mieske, Spokane	59
H	Jay Gainer, Spokane	100
TB	Matt Mieske, Spokane	155
2B	Jay Gainer, Spokane	21
	Mike Galle, Yakima	21
3B	Darius Gash, Spokane	6
HR	Matt Mieske, Spokane	12
RBI	Matt Mieske, Spokane	63
SH	P.J. Forbes, Boise	7
SF	Garrett Beard, Yakima	10
BB	Brian Grebeck, Boise	64
IBB	Mike Galle, Yakima	5
HBP	Chris Hart, SO	11
SO	Dave Partrick, Boise	91
SB	Lee Sammons, Bend	45
CS	Pedro Frias, Bend	15
OB%	Brian Grebeck, Boise	.454

PITCHING

G	David Hierholzer, Eugene	32
	Bruce Bensching, Spokane	32
GS	Russ Garside, Spokane	17
CG	Dave Adam, Bellingham	4
	Randy Powers, Boise	4
ShO	Randy Powers, Boise	3
Sv	Bob Blankenship, Bend	12
W	Dan Henrikson, Everett	10
L	Kevin McGehee, Everett	8
IP	Dan Henrikson, Everett	102
	Randy Powers, Boise	102
H	Russ Garside, Spokane	111
R	Gary Ross, Bend	62
ER	Gary Ross, Bend	11
BB	Jim Magill, Bellingham	52
HB	Four tied at	7
SO	Hilly Hathaway, Boise	113
WP	Kevin McGehee, Everett	16
Bk	James Converse, Bell	9

SOUTHERN OREGON

BATTING	AVG	G	AB	R	H	2B	3B	HR	RBI	BB	SO	SB
Booker, Eric, of-dh	.305	53	187	38	57	12	0	4	33	43	44	14
Cabrera, Juan, ss-2b	.308	8	26	1	8	0	0	0	1	4	2	3
Campa, Eric, 2b-3b	.237	14	38	4	9	1	0	0	5	2	10	2
#Dattola, Kevin, of	.270	41	148	33	40	9	1	0	13	36	33	16
Hart, Chris, of	.264	67	239	50	63	14	2	6	32	37	86	15
*Helfand, Eric, c	.285	57	207	29	59	12	0	2	39	20	49	4
*Henry, Scott, c-1b	.294	6	17	4	5	1	0	0	2	3	4	1
#Hernandez, Carlos, ss-2b	.282	16	39	4	11	1	0	0	3	6	10	3
Lanfranco, Luis, 3b-2b	.278	69	245	37	68	10	2	2	28	25	74	6
Martinez, Manny, of	.246	66	244	36	60	5	0	2	17	16	59	6
Mercado, Rafael, 1b-of	.164	49	140	13	23	4	0	0	14	11	44	3
Muhlethaler, Mike, 1b-dh	.256	62	211	34	54	8	2	4	31	22	48	1
Osinski, Glenn, 2b-ss	.200	6	30	1	6	1	0	0	3	0	9	1
#Picketts, Bill, 2b-ss	.250	68	252	30	63	8	1	0	41	44	39	5
#Reid, Greg, ph	.333	3	3	0	1	0	0	0	0	0	1	0
Salazar, Carlos, 1b-c	.273	57	165	14	45	7	1	0	19	18	44	1
#Tamarez, Carlos, ss (2 Bend)	.220	60	200	23	44	0	4	0	17	15	54	7
Tredway, Ed, c	.250	22	60	7	15	0	0	1	7	1	15	4
Young, Ernie, of	.280	50	168	34	47	6	2	6	23	29	53	4

PITCHING	W	L	ERA	G	GS	CG	SV	IP	H	R	ER	BB	SO
Brimhall, Brad	2	6	5.10	16	16	0	0	67	74	49	38	44	64
Clifford, Jeff	2	1	3.93	20	0	0	0	50	42	30	22	26	52
Connolly, Craig	6	3	3.33	21	1	0	2	46	40	19	17	20	45
Craft, Mark	3	3	4.04	17	1	0	0	36	33	20	16	20	24
Dillon, Jim	4	1	1.54	9	7	1	0	35	25	9	6	5	31
Dressendorfer, Kirk	0	1	2.33	7	4	0	0	19	18	7	5	2	22
Garland, Chaon	4	3	3.08	11	9	0	0	50	40	21	17	15	42
*Johns, Doug	0	2	5.73	6	2	0	1	11	13	9	7	11	9
Myers, Eric	1	2	3.02	24	0	0	5	42	39	16	14	12	44
Peters, Don	1	1	0.76	11	7	0	0	36	20	7	3	17	34
Revenig, Todd	3	2	0.81	24	0	0	6	45	33	13	4	9	46
Scharff, Tony	0	0	12.54	4	2	0	0	9	13	16	13	14	12
*Shaw, Curtis	4	6	3.53	17	9	0	0	66	53	28	26	30	74
Sudbury, Craig	2	2	2.91	7	5	0	0	34	26	13	11	13	29
Tripp, Dave	3	2	4.28	16	0	0	0	40	39	26	19	15	34
Van Poppel, Todd	1	1	1.13	5	5	0	0	24	10	5	3	9	32
*Vizzini, Dan	1	0	2.20	16	0	0	1	29	19	10	7	16	41
*Zancanaro, David	3	0	3.86	10	8	0	0	44	44	22	19	13	42

SPOKANE

BATTING	AVG	G	AB	R	H	2B	3B	HR	RBI	BB	SO	SB
*Adams, Dave, of-1b	.218	46	156	23	34	5	1	1	20	31	38	3
Bish, Brent, 2b	.249	65	225	28	56	4	1	0	23	20	42	12
Bruno, Julio, 3b	.251	68	251	36	63	7	2	2	22	25	78	7
Elliott, Jim, c	.186	35	113	13	21	3	0	3	11	14	54	1
Farlow, Kevin, ss	.243	68	267	39	65	10	3	3	31	32	67	11
*Gainer, Jay, 1b	.356	74	281	41	100	21	0	10	54	31	49	4
#Gash, Darius, of	.236	64	254	47	60	7	6	2	27	37	71	20
*Gonzalez, Paul, 3b	.250	1	4	0	1	1	0	0	2	1	1	0
Hawks, Larry, c	.213	31	89	12	19	5	1	0	14	21	24	0
*McKoy, Keith, of	.242	64	236	39	57	8	2	1	24	16	59	18
Meury, Bill, ss	.111	5	18	1	2	0	0	0	2	0	5	0
Mieske, Matt, of	.340	76	291	59	99	20	6	12	63	45	43	26
Ordway, Jeff, inf-of	.218	39	101	19	22	3	1	0	4	11	35	2
Ostermann, Bill, dh-of	.221	46	145	16	32	6	0	6	18	19	52	0
*Pearce, Jeff, of-dh	.162	21	74	5	12	2	0	1	2	8	38	0
Siebert, Steve, 2b	.182	4	11	2	2	0	0	0	2	2	2	0
West, Jim, c	.216	42	111	14	24	5	0	0	6	25	36	2

PITCHING	W	L	ERA	G	GS	CG	SV	IP	H	R	ER	BB	SO
Bensching, Bruce	8	1	1.54	32	0	0	10	58	45	14	10	14	78
Bradley, Mike	7	2	3.34	15	15	2	0	89	68	37	34	43	91
Devore, Ted	1	3	3.07	10	5	0	1	44	33	16	15	20	34
Fredrickson, Scott	3	3	3.28	26	1	0	8	47	35	22	17	18	61
*Garside, Russ	8	3	5.66	17	17	0	0	83	111	60	52	22	57
Hays, Rob	2	0	4.15	10	2	0	0	30	26	18	14	14	30
*Mortensen, Tony	4	2	3.79	18	6	0	4	60	54	29	25	18	49
*Painter, Lance	7	3	1.51	23	1	0	3	72	45	18	12	15	104
Perez, Tirson	0	0	6.75	1	0	0	0	3	5	2	2	0	2
Sanders, Scott	2	1	0.95	3	3	0	0	19	12	3	2	5	21
Silcox, Rusty	3	1	6.43	16	16	0	0	71	79	58	51	43	61
*Thibault, Ryan	3	4	3.82	22	9	0	0	66	67	36	28	38	58
*Waldron, Joe	1	4	6.17	21	1	0	0	47	61	45	32	40	43

YAKIMA

BATTING	AVG	G	AB	R	H	2B	3B	HR	RBI	BB	SO	SB
Beard, Garrett, c-dh	.272	60	232	29	63	13	1	5	39	17	30	6
Bohringer, Helms, 3b	.327	21	49	9	16	2	2	0	10	6	6	1
*Brummer, Jeff, of	.270	70	274	46	74	10	4	3	32	36	61	33
Cardenas, Daniel, of-dh	.254	19	71	14	18	6	1	2	14	7	23	1
*Doffek, Scott, 2b	.257	61	202	23	52	7	4	4	30	11	14	1
Fowler, Yale, of-1b	.232	35	82	6	19	3	0	0	11	5	30	0
Galle, Mike, 3b	.317	65	224	43	71	21	2	4	42	53	42	3
Kliafas, Steve, ss	.186	39	118	8	22	2	0	1	12	8	19	4
Lott, Billy, of	.275	65	240	37	66	13	2	4	38	10	62	4
*Olson, Kurt, 1b-dh	.259	53	170	25	44	8	0	3	23	20	39	2
Ortiz, Hector, c	.272	52	173	16	47	3	1	0	12	5	15	1
#Perez, Jose, ss	.282	22	71	14	20	4	0	0	5	7	11	2
Rijo, Rafael, of	.260	51	200	30	52	9	1	1	13	12	32	23
Sena, Sean, 2b	.227	32	75	11	17	5	0	1	11	5	17	0
Troncoso, Nolberto, 1b-of	.250	66	228	51	57	9	2	1	32	40	40	22
#Vandebrake, Kevin, 2b	.167	5	12	1	2	0	0	0	2	1	4	0
*White, Craig, ss-3b	.241	52	133	23	32	5	0	0	7	24	32	6

PITCHING	W	L	ERA	G	GS	CG	SV	IP	H	R	ER	BB	SO
Astacio, Pedro	2	0	1.74	3	3	0	0	21	9	8	4	4	22
*Bishop, Craig	0	2	4.08	15	0	0	0	18	18	11	8	15	18
Branconier, Paul	1	4	5.28	18	6	0	1	61	85	44	36	16	35
Burroughs, Ken	0	1	9.64	12	0	0	0	14	10	18	15	25	17
Cantres, Jorge	3	2	3.89	24	0	0	3	42	29	20	18	19	34
Delahoya, Javier	3	5	4.46	14	14	0	0	71	65	52	35	39	71
Freeman, Scott	2	7	4.00	14	14	1	0	83	94	58	37	28	44
*Kelly, Joe	2	2	4.56	17	0	0	1	24	29	16	12	15	25
Madsen, Erik	1	0	3.38	13	1	0	1	24	17	15	9	22	23
*Mimbs, Mike	4	3	3.88	12	12	0	0	67	58	36	29	39	72
Mintz, Steve	2	3	2.42	20	0	0	3	26	21	9	7	16	38
*O'Connor, Ben	2	2	2.25	21	0	0	2	36	24	11	9	18	38
*Patrick, Tim	5	2	3.09	11	10	0	0	58	56	34	20	26	66
Perez, Pedro	6	3	2.34	24	0	0	8	42	24	14	11	18	47
Sampson, Mike	2	0	4.50	3	3	0	0	16	14	12	8	11	11
Tatis, Fausto	1	4	4.48	13	13	1	0	74	88	45	37	24	76

APPALACHIAN LEAGUE

20-game win streak propels Twins to title

By DEAN GYORGY

For the second straight year, Elizabethton emerged as the dominant team in the Appalachian League. The Twins became the first team to repeat as champions since 1981.

In 1989, there was a postseason playoff, so the Twins had to wait for a two-game sweep of Pulaski before they could celebrate. But in 1990, the Appalachian League did away with the playoffs, and went to a straight race for the top of the standings.

Paul Russo
. . . 22 homers

Elizabethton had it wrapped up early. The Twins won 20 straight games in one stretch, and were on pace to set the all-time mark for short-season winning percentage. They were chasing a ghost of their own league, as the 1979 Paintsville Yankees went 52-13 (.800). The Twins fell just short in the final week, going 51-16 (.761). But they won the title by 12 games over Huntington.

While there were some outstanding performances for the Twins, manager Ray Smith didn't see his team as simply overmatching the league.

"We just had the breaks during that streak," Smith said. "We're not the '27 Yankees, that's for sure."

League MVP Paul Russo, a 16th-round pick from the University of Tampa, slugged a franchise-record 22 home runs for the Twins. He also led the league in runs, total bases and RBIs.

Moving sale

Huntington, W.Va., welcomed professional baseball for the first time since 1942. The Cubs, located in Wytheville, Va. in 1989, moved west under a new ownership. The city's enthusiasm

LEAGUE CHAMPIONS

Playoff Champions, Where Applicable

1990—Elizabethton	1969—Pulaski	1949—Bluefield
1989—Elizabethton	1968—Marion	1948—Pulaski
1988—Kingsport	1967—Bluefield	1947—New River
1987—Burlington	1966—Marion	1946—New River
1986—Pulaski	1965—Salem	1945—Kingsport
1985—Bristol	1964—Johnson City	1944—Kingsport
1984—Elizabethton	1963—Bluefield	1943—Bristol
1983—Paintsville	1962—Bluefield	1942—Bristol
1982—Bluefield	1961—Middlesboro	1941—Elizabethton
1981—Paintsville	1960—Wytheville	1940—Johnson City
1980—Paintsville	1959—Morristown	1939—Elizabethton
1979—Paintsville	1958—Johnson City	1938—Greenville
1978—Elizabethton	1957—Bluefield	1937—Penning. Gap
1977—Kingsport	1956—Did Not	1926-36—Did Not
1976—Johnson City	Operate	Operate
1975—Johnson City	1955—Salem	1925—Greenville
1974—Bristol	1954—Bluefield	1924—Knoxville
1973—Kingsport	1953—Welch	1923—Knoxville
1972—Bristol	1952—Welch	1922—Bristol
1971—Bluefield	1951—Kingsport	1921—Johnson City
1970—Bluefield	1950—Bluefield	

Pulaski's Pat Dando hit .360 to win the Appalachian League batting crown.

was reflected in the attendance, as 66,042 fans jammed 80-year-old St. Cloud Commons. The Cubs drew only 16,839 in Wytheville in 1989.

The Philadelphia Phillies essentially had two teams in the league in 1990, as Princeton operated as a co-op with a distinctive Phillies flavor. The Pirates pulled out of Princeton after 1989, and farm directors wanted to keep a team there to maintain a balanced schedule. When no organization stepped forward with a full team, Philadelphia sent 18 players and manager Eli Grba.

Four first-round picks in the June draft began their professional careers in the Appalachian League. Elizabethton's Todd Ritchie (Twins) had the most success and was voted by managers as the league's second-best prospect. Catcher Mike Lieberthal (Phillies, Martinsville) got rave reviews for his defense. Shortstop Aaron Holbert (Cardinals, Johnson City) struggled, hitting .170 with one homer.

Tony Clark, picked second overall by Detroit, reported to Bristol after weeks of contract negotiations. Clark didn't do much on the field, but showed tremendous potential during batting practice.

1990 *FINAL STANDINGS*

	W	L	Pct.	GB
Elizabethton (Twins)	51	16	.761	—
Huntington (Cubs)	40	29	.580	12
Kingsport (Mets)	41	31	.569	12½
Bluefield (Orioles)	38	32	.543	14½
Pulaski (Braves)	37	35	.514	16½
Burlington (Indians)	35	37	.486	18½
Princeton (Co-op)	31	36	.463	20
Johnson City (Cards)	28	42	.400	24½
Martinsville (Phillies)	25	44	.362	27
Bristol (Tigers)	22	46	.324	29½

Playoffs: None

Regular-Season Attendance: Martinsville, 69,182; Burlington, 66,330; Huntington, 66,042; Kingsport, 37,363; Bluefield, 33,354; Princeton, 26,620; Bristol, 26,026; Johnson City, 24,153; Pulaski, 17,673; Elizabethton, 17,013.

Managers: Bluefield—Gus Gil; **Bristol**—Kenn Cunningham; **Burlington**—Dave Keller; **Elizabethton**—Ray Smith; **Huntington**—Steve Roadcap; **Johnson City**—Mark DeJohn; **Kingsport**—Jim Thrift; **Martinsville**—Rollie DeArmas; **Princeton**—Eli Grba; **Pulaski**—Randy Ingle.

1990 Official All-Star Team: C—Greg Zaun, Bluefield. **1B**—Pat Dando, Pulaski. **2B**—Jeff Borgese, Martinsville. **3B**—Jose Viera, Huntington. **SS**—Aaron Ledesma, Kingsport. **UTIL INF**—Jim Thome, Burlington. **OF**—Tracy Sanders, Burlington; Brian Kowitz, Pulaski; Rich Becker, Elizabethton. **UTIL OF**—Tim Sanders, Burlington. **DH**—Paul Russo, Elizabethton. **RHP**—Brad Hassinger, Princeton. **LHP**—Roger Dixon, Elizabethton. **RP**—Tom Benson, Elizabethton. **Player of the Year**—Paul Russo, Elizabethton. **Manager of the Year**—Ray Smith, Elizabethton.

Top 10 Major League Prospects (by Baseball America): 1. Jim Thome, 3b, Burlington; **2.** Todd Ritchie, rhp, Elizabethton; **3.** Jose Viera, 3b, Huntington; **4.** Tony Clark, of, Bristol; **5.** Butch Huskey, 3b, Kingsport; **6.** Aaron Ledesma, ss, Kingsport; **7.** Mike Lieberthal, c, Martinsville; **8.** Brian Kowitz, of, Pulaski; **9.** Sean Cheetham, rhp, Huntington; **10.** Denny Hocking, ss, Elizabethton.

1990 *BATTING, PITCHING STATS*

CLUB BATTING

	AVG	G	AB	R	H	2B	3B	HR	BB	SO	SB
Kingsport	.270	72	2429	370	655	114	12	53	206	520	132
Pulaski	.264	72	2458	361	649	112	23	41	273	457	88
Elizabethton	.262	67	2248	423	590	87	12	61	315	517	79
Bluefield	.259	70	2316	336	600	109	10	46	230	501	58
Huntington	.243	69	2217	308	540	103	6	42	263	465	58
Burlington	.234	72	2418	337	567	96	11	46	296	550	120
Martinsville	.230	69	2344	280	540	97	14	34	199	599	42
Princeton	.230	67	2238	299	515	88	19	35	240	530	82
Johnson City	.223	70	2287	301	505	78	12	33	301	564	98
Bristol	.211	68	2216	224	468	68	11	28	205	578	37

CLUB PITCHING

	ERA	G	CG	SHO	SV	IP	H	R	ER	BB	SO
Elizabethton	3.00	67	8	4	22	588	494	268	196	241	506
Huntington	3.32	69	6	6	18	586	517	288	215	246	577
Burlington	3.33	72	3	3	19	637	615	325	236	262	500
Kingsport	3.36	72	16	7	16	630	547	307	235	252	487
Pulaski	3.65	72	7	4	13	632	551	334	255	277	604
Princeton	3.67	67	12	4	13	586	562	321	239	253	411
Bluefield	3.81	70	13	6	11	603	592	344	255	222	549
Martinsville	4.00	69	11	3	10	601	584	341	267	264	583
Johnson City	4.19	70	2	2	14	599	588	371	276	249	484
Bristol	4.26	68	3	4	11	590	579	340	278	262	580

INDIVIDUAL BATTING LEADERS
(Minimum 194 Plate Appearances)

	AVG	G	AB	R	H	2B	3B	HR	RBI	BB	SO	SB
*Dando, Pat, Pulaski	.360	69	253	46	91	19	2	10	38	25	32	8
Russo, Paul, Eliz	.335	62	221	58	74	10	3	22	67	39	56	4
Garcia, Omar, Kingsport	.333	67	246	42	82	15	2	6	36	24	24	12
Ledesma, Aaron, Kingsport	.333	66	243	50	81	11	1	5	38	20	28	27
*Sandy, Tim, Kingsport	.331	49	163	31	54	6	3	3	14	32	16	9
Gavin, Tom, Eliz	.329	59	222	43	73	13	1	4	42	27	49	5
Viera, Jose, Hunt	.327	65	245	34	80	22	1	8	37	18	30	3
*Kowitz, Brian, Pulaski	.324	43	182	40	59	13	1	8	19	16	16	13
*Lockett, Ron, Prince	.310	63	229	32	71	12	5	6	34	15	51	11
#Zaun, Greg, Bluefield	.310	61	184	29	57	5	2	2	21	23	15	5

INDIVIDUAL PITCHING LEADERS
(Minimum 58 Innings)

	W	L	ERA	G	GS	CG	SV	IP	H	R	ER	BB	SO
Carpentier, Rob, Kings	6	1	1.87	22	8	2	1	82	53	24	16	30	56
Ritchie, Todd, Eliz	5	2	1.94	11	11	1	0	65	45	22	14	24	49
Hassinger, Brad, Prince	7	4	2.18	13	13	5	0	91	66	30	22	20	48
Cheetham, Sean, Hunt	4	2	2.38	12	12	0	0	68	55	27	18	27	76
Lira, Felipa, Bristol	5	5	2.41	13	10	2	1	78	70	26	21	16	71
Wegmann, Tom, Kingsport	5	4	2.45	14	12	4	0	84	53	34	23	30	103
*Snyder, Chris, Princeton	5	5	2.48	14	13	4	0	98	103	40	27	23	58
*Embree, Alan, Bristol	4	4	2.64	15	15	0	0	82	87	36	24	30	58

	W	L	ERA	G	GS	CG	SV	IP	H	R	ER	BB	SO
*Anderson, Matt, Bluefield	6	4	2.71	12	12	2	0	83	72	29	24	21	88
*Munoz, J.J., Martinsville	6	7	2.75	14	14	3	0	95	70	35	29	48	126

BLUEFIELD

BATTING	AVG	G	AB	R	H	2B	3B	HR	RBI	BB	SO	SB
*Alstead, Jason, of	.251	56	203	35	51	3	0	3	16	27	45	12
Asencio, Mattie, ss	.000	12	17	0	0	0	0	0	1	3	11	0
#Bell, Derek, c	.222	24	45	6	10	2	0	1	6	8	10	1
Burgillo, Robert, 1b	.150	18	20	1	3	0	0	0	0	1	2	0
Davis, Allen, of	.224	50	152	28	34	3	0	2	11	24	45	3
*DiMarco, Steve, dh	.273	43	150	18	41	13	1	0	18	15	23	1
Flowers, Doug, 1b	.269	39	104	13	28	5	0	2	12	8	25	1
Gordian, Carlos, c-3b	.125	8	8	2	1	0	0	0	1	0	2	0
*Graham, Gordon, 1b-dh	.281	24	64	10	18	2	1	2	8	3	26	2
Hodge, Roy, of	.229	26	48	4	11	0	0	0	3	3	8	0
McClain, Scott, 3b	.196	40	107	20	21	2	0	4	15	22	35	2
Millares, Jose, 2b	.273	48	176	25	48	12	0	3	25	10	28	6
*Miller, Brent, 1b	.325	32	117	21	38	10	1	10	28	7	22	0
Paredes, German, of	.266	60	218	24	58	11	0	6	30	6	42	2
Ramirez, Dan, ss-2b	.284	57	211	36	60	11	0	2	22	22	24	9
#Ruiz, Stewart, 2b	.206	22	34	4	7	1	0	0	5	14	1
*Schmidt, Keith, of	.278	55	169	24	47	12	2	5	24	17	62	5
*Sprick, Scott, ss-dh	.241	62	220	27	53	15	3	4	33	18	50	4
Thomas, Mike, of	.203	24	69	9	14	2	0	0	9	8	12	4
#Zaun, Greg, c	.310	61	184	29	57	5	2	2	21	23	15	5

PITCHING	W	L	ERA	G	GS	CG	SV	IP	H	R	ER	BB	SO
*Anderson, Matt	6	4	2.71	12	12	2	0	83	72	29	24	21	88
Benge, Brett	0	1	12.54	4	2	0	0	9	11	14	13	8	6
Chouinard, Bob	2	5	3.70	10	10	2	0	56	61	34	23	14	30
Egelston, Mike	1	0	4.03	11	0	0	1	22	26	12	11	3	15
Hays, Greg	2	1	3.42	14	0	0	3	24	20	11	9	6	21
Hebb, Mike	6	7	3.64	15	14	3	0	89	88	53	35	26	80
Heiden, Shawn	0	1	7.20	1	1	0	0	5	5	4	4	3	2
Marquez, Ihosvany	3	3	3.20	13	9	1	1	56	51	30	20	38	42
Medina, Victor	0	0	1.88	9	0	0	1	14	10	5	3	0	14
*Mercedes, Juan	3	2	5.35	15	5	0	0	37	42	40	25	38	27
O'Connell, Shawn	1	1	7.31	18	0	0	1	32	46	38	29	23	28
*O'Donoghue, John	4	2	2.01	10	6	2	0	49	49	13	11	10	67
Tippett, Brad	3	3	3.65	15	2	1	3	49	40	23	20	11	61
*Wiley, Mike	5	2	3.84	11	9	2	0	59	59	30	25	9	51
Williams, Jeff	2	0	1.59	9	0	0	0	11	7	3	2	5	14

BRISTOL

BATTING	AVG	G	AB	R	H	2B	3B	HR	RBI	BB	SO	SB
Alder, Jimmy, 3b-1b	.188	63	224	29	42	9	1	12	33	24	75	1
Bautista, Danny, of	.274	27	95	9	26	3	0	2	12	8	21	2
Bradford, Vince, of	.100	52	110	12	11	2	0	0	1	17	75	0
#Clark, Tony, of	.164	25	73	2	12	2	0	1	8	6	28	0
Cruz, Danny, of-p	.241	62	191	17	46	3	1	0	16	17	27	6
Debrand, Genaro, c	.230	32	113	11	26	3	2	1	10	4	14	1
*Dubose, Brian, 1b-of	.251	67	223	31	56	8	0	6	21	24	53	5
Fermin, Carlos, ss	.222	67	203	22	45	4	4	0	15	21	36	7
Hall, Chris, 3b-2b	.202	54	183	14	37	9	0	1	16	14	48	1
Hernandez, Luis, 2b	.203	54	182	21	37	5	1	0	11	13	46	7
*Jordan, Adrian, of	.102	16	49	7	5	1	0	0	1	8	9	1
Keating, Dave, of	.160	7	25	1	4	2	0	0	3	0	8	1
Mauro, Mike, 2b-ss	.157	18	51	6	8	1	0	0	3	5	14	1
Miller, Kevin, of-c	.269	61	212	21	57	6	0	5	22	20	45	1
#Roberts, Keith, of	.170	42	88	7	15	3	1	0	2	9	37	2
Ubina, Alex, c-1b	.256	39	78	9	20	3	1	0	8	6	10	0
*Wilson, Brad, c	.182	24	77	2	14	3	0	0	3	5	22	1

PITCHING	W	L	ERA	G	GS	CG	SV	IP	H	R	ER	BB	SO
Cruz, Danny	0	0	9.28	7	0	0	0	11	15	12	11	5	6
*Guilfoyle, Mike	4	6	3.06	16	7	0	1	65	54	35	22	25	80
*Haeger, Greg	0	2	5.15	24	2	0	3	37	37	25	21	24	51
*Henry, Jimmy	1	3	4.10	10	10	0	0	42	39	26	19	28	38
Lima, Jose	3	8	5.02	14	12	1	1	75	89	49	42	22	64
Lira, Felipa	5	5	2.41	13	10	2	0	78	70	26	21	16	71
Maietta, Ron	0	3	3.82	6	6	0	0	31	30	13	13	11	28
Nelson, Brian	0	1	13.06	5	1	0	0	10	7	16	15	25	8
Reinisch, Paul	2	1	1.52	15	0	0	1	24	24	6	4	5	26
Riker, Robert	2	5	6.12	19	5	0	0	60	68	46	41	21	60
*Rodriguez, Ed	0	3	4.60	13	1	0	0	31	32	22	16	10	45
Salazar, Luis	0	0	1.93	7	0	0	1	9	7	4	2	7	9
Stokes, Randy	1	0	2.13	21	0	0	3	38	25	10	9	18	43
Ubina, Alex	0	0	4.50	6	0	0	0	10	8	6	5	5	4
Warren, Brian	0	0	2.25	1	1	0	0	4	4	1	1	2	0
Withem, Shannon	3	9	5.23	14	13	0	0	62	70	43	36	35	48

BURLINGTON

BATTING	AVG	G	AB	R	H	2B	3B	HR	RBI	BB	SO	SB
Andujar, Hector, Inf	.200	10	30	1	6	0	0	0	0	2	4	1
Bell, David, 3b	.167	12	42	4	7	1	1	0	2	2	5	2
Brohm, Jeff, of-dh	.213	34	136	25	29	8	0	2	12	15	38	10
Bryant, Pat, of	.100	17	50	3	5	0	0	1	2	7	23	7

Burlington's Jim Thorne was hitting at a .373 clip when he was promoted out of the Appalachian League.

	AVG	G	AB	R	H	2B	3B	HR	RBI	BB	SO	SB
Flores, Miguel, 2b	.250	57	208	33	52	8	1	3	25	20	18	22
Gilmore, Matt, ss	.230	40	148	30	34	5	0	1	16	14	26	3
#Hardtke, Jason, ss	.268	39	142	18	38	7	0	4	16	23	19	11
Hence, Sam, of	.216	35	125	11	27	6	0	3	11	5	31	2
Henderson, Pedro, of	.221	43	140	22	31	7	1	3	18	18	46	5
Jimenez, Roberto, c	.241	40	137	12	33	7	1	0	10	10	29	2
#Martinez, John, c-3b	.263	41	156	14	41	5	0	1	18	9	24	0
*McCall, Rod, 1b	.163	31	92	8	15	5	0	1	11	10	43	0
Monastero, Frank, 2b	.151	21	53	6	8	1	0	0	6	4	6	1
Ortiz, Ramon, of	.200	9	20	0	4	0	0	0	2	2	3	1
Philyaw, Dino, of	.114	17	44	2	5	0	0	0	1	5	22	3
Pinckes, Mike, 1b-3b	.233	54	163	18	38	7	2	2	20	38	46	1
*Sanders, Tracy, of	.281	51	178	38	50	12	1	10	34	33	36	10
Shirley, Mike, of	.196	32	112	14	22	1	0	3	9	8	33	3
Smith, Rob, 2b-3b	.158	8	19	2	3	0	0	0	0	5	11	1
Thomas, Tim, 1b	.196	15	56	5	11	1	0	0	3	4	8	3
*Thome, Jim, 3b	.373	34	118	31	44	7	1	12	34	27	18	6
*Torres, Ramon, of-dh	.270	43	137	22	37	5	1	0	13	26	31	17
*Whitmore, Darrell, of	.241	30	112	18	27	3	2	0	13	9	30	9

PITCHING	W	L	ERA	G	GS	CG	SV	IP	H	R	ER	BB	SO
Baker, Sam	2	3	4.10	24	0	0	5	42	47	29	19	17	30
Brown, Dickie	3	4	5.75	13	12	0	0	67	76	45	43	30	53
*Bryant, Shawn	1	0	0.84	2	2	0	0	11	5	2	1	6	17
Elston, Cary	0	5	5.35	12	5	0	0	35	40	28	21	30	34
*Embree, Alan	4	4	2.64	15	15	0	0	82	87	36	24	30	58
Gajkowski, Steve	2	6	4.10	14	10	1	0	64	74	34	29	23	44
Johnson, Carl	2	1	1.08	27	0	0	14	50	35	8	6	28	46
*McElfish, Shawn	2	1	2.53	19	0	0	1	43	46	21	12	19	27
McLochlin, Mike	2	3	3.11	14	7	0	0	55	47	28	19	18	42
Mlicki, Dave	3	1	3.50	8	1	0	0	18	16	11	7	6	17
*Tillman, Tommy	7	2	2.89	30	0	0	0	53	51	24	17	12	47
Walden, Alan	5	6	2.80	15	15	1	0	93	67	45	30	33	72
Wechsberg, Von	2	1	2.92	5	5	1	0	25	24	14	8	10	13

ELIZABETHTON

BATTING	AVG	G	AB	R	H	2B	3B	HR	RBI	BB	SO	SB
#Becker, Richie, of	.289	56	194	54	56	5	1	6	24	53	54	18
*Blakeman, Todd, 1b	.233	49	180	27	42	11	0	5	34	13	39	0
*Brede, Brent, of	.245	46	143	39	35	5	0	0	14	30	30	14
Brown, Matt, c	.233	28	90	11	21	1	0	1	11	8	13	0
Bruno, Paul, dh-c	.184	28	103	15	19	3	0	4	22	14	32	0
Ewing, Brian, of	.148	8	27	2	4	0	0	0	0	4	8	2
Gavin, Tom, 3b	.329	59	222	43	73	13	1	4	42	27	49	5
Gumpf, John, of-1b	.236	51	191	31	45	9	1	7	28	12	71	4
#Hocking, Denny, ss-2b ...	.294	54	201	45	59	6	2	6	30	40	26	14

	AVG	G	AB	R	H	2B	3B	HR	RBI	BB	SO	SB
Miller, Damian, c	.222	14	45	7	10	1	0	1	6	9	3	1
#Morse, Matt, 2b	.251	63	235	34	59	9	3	3	29	26	31	8
Peppers, Devin, of	.143	17	42	5	6	0	0	0	2	7	28	0
Pfeffer, Kurt, of-dh	.281	29	96	16	27	5	1	2	21	13	30	0
Pichardo, Cisco, of	.229	33	105	16	24	3	0	0	15	9	18	6
Russo, Paul, 1b-dh	.335	62	221	58	74	10	3	22	67	39	56	4
Spaan, Tony, ss	.205	24	73	11	15	2	0	0	5	5	18	3
Wallgren, Chris, c	.263	23	80	9	21	4	0	0	7	6	11	0

PITCHING	W	L	ERA	G	GS	CG	SV	IP	H	R	ER	BB	SO
Benson, Tom	6	2	1.70	30	0	0	14	48	32	10	9	15	39
Bethancourt, Jose	4	2	3.65	13	4	1	2	49	34	27	20	19	40
*Bigham, Dave	6	2	4.15	29	0	0	5	56	50	35	26	35	66
Diaz, Sandy	4	2	3.07	13	12	1	0	70	67	40	24	32	61
*Dixon, Roger	7	2	2.79	13	13	1	0	84	66	34	26	48	57
Fritz, Scott	0	0	6.75	3	0	0	0	5	6	4	4	1	5
Henry, Jon	7	2	3.61	14	13	1	0	87	81	40	35	28	89
Persing, Tim	8	2	2.93	14	14	3	0	95	81	47	31	30	81
Ritchie, Todd	5	2	1.94	11	11	1	0	65	45	22	14	24	49
Taylor, Steve	4	0	2.30	10	0	0	1	27	32	9	7	5	22

HUNTINGTON

BATTING	AVG	G	AB	R	H	2B	3B	HR	RBI	BB	SO	SB
Biasucci, Joe, 2b	.188	6	16	2	3	1	0	0	1	2	3	0
*Craig, Morris, 1b	.310	48	155	22	48	11	0	1	14	16	26	0
Delgado, Pablo, of	.204	46	108	8	22	3	0	1	6	18	22	0
*Fernandez, Rolando, dh-of	.252	47	111	16	28	10	0	4	20	27	21	4
Ford, Calvin, of	.184	55	141	13	26	4	0	1	10	12	38	5
Gabbani, Michael, c	.275	50	178	25	49	7	1	5	18	17	36	2
Gardner, Willie, of	.298	52	168	18	50	7	1	3	27	8	50	2
Helms, Tommy, 2b	.211	27	71	9	15	3	0	0	3	6	15	0
Larregui, Edgardo, of	.186	34	102	13	19	3	0	2	16	7	12	3
Little, Mike, dh-of	.221	38	104	17	23	5	0	7	16	20	32	0
Montero, Cesar, 2b	.313	14	16	1	5	2	0	0	1	2	6	0
Moore, Tim, ss-2b	.281	54	178	28	50	10	1	2	17	27	22	5
*Murphy, Micah, 1b	.200	47	130	21	26	3	0	2	15	17	24	1
Postiff, J.P., 1b	.246	56	171	32	42	7	0	3	23	27	37	10
Saa, Humberto, ss-3b	.156	27	45	6	7	1	0	0	4	8	7	0
Sehorn, Jason, of	.184	49	125	21	23	3	1	1	10	8	52	9
Soto, Rafael, ss-3b	.085	42	59	10	5	1	0	0	3	11	15	4
Viera, Jose, 3b	.331	65	245	34	81	22	1	8	37	18	30	4
Wolff, James, c	.191	31	94	11	18	0	1	2	11	12	17	1

PITCHING	W	L	ERA	G	GS	CG	SV	IP	H	R	ER	BB	SO
Camarena, Miguel	0	0	3.18	13	0	0	2	28	27	16	10	14	21
Cheetham, Sean	4	2	2.38	12	12	0	0	68	55	27	18	27	76
Gardner, Scott	3	2	1.87	13	4	0	2	43	36	16	9	20	52
Godfrey, Tyson	9	2	3.29	13	13	2	0	82	76	34	30	31	57
Hawblitzel, Ryan	6	5	3.93	14	14	2	0	76	72	38	33	25	71
Kirk, Charles	2	1	2.84	10	0	0	1	13	10	5	4	1	9
Mann, Thomas	1	0	2.29	10	0	0	0	20	12	10	5	8	20
Perez, Leo (2 Prince)	5	1	1.90	22	1	0	3	52	36	12	11	11	72
*Ramirez, Nelson	0	0	9.53	3	0	0	0	6	7	6	6	4	7
Sanchez, Adrian	3	7	5.35	13	13	2	0	76	89	60	45	34	55
Stanley, Karl	1	1	2.19	9	1	0	0	25	17	7	6	14	35
Stevens, David	2	4	4.61	13	11	0	0	57	48	44	29	47	55
Taylor, Aaron	4	4	1.84	26	0	0	11	44	32	13	9	10	50

JOHNSON CITY

BATTING	AVG	G	AB	R	H	2B	3B	HR	RBI	BB	SO	SB
#Aversa, Joe, 3b-ss	.156	41	90	10	14	1	0	0	8	10	18	2
*Ball, Harry, 2b-3b	.200	66	225	43	45	7	2	5	26	37	54	8
Carpenter, Kevin, c-of	.135	23	52	2	7	1	0	0	1	9	20	1
Davis, Jerry, of	.112	39	116	9	13	6	0	0	6	6	39	0
*Dempsey, John, c	.249	52	173	16	43	4	1	0	15	24	30	1
*Donald, Tremayne, of-2b	.187	63	230	37	43	6	1	0	10	44	50	44
#Ealy, Tracey, dh-of	.276	57	214	33	59	8	0	2	18	27	58	17
#Ellsworth, Ben, 3b-ss	.183	41	115	10	21	2	1	0	10	8	22	0
French, Ron, of	.241	51	162	18	39	7	0	1	14	13	46	17
Hays, Kevin, c	.200	6	15	1	3	0	0	0	0	3	4	0
Holbert, Aaron, ss	.172	54	174	27	30	4	1	1	18	24	31	4
Jenkins, Anthony, of-dh	.167	16	48	5	8	2	0	2	4	6	21	0
*Jordan, Tim, of	.276	61	199	25	55	5	0	4	23	15	52	4
*Merrill, Larry, 3b	.083	5	12	0	1	0	0	0	0	2	5	0
Page, Sean, of	.244	49	160	26	39	8	1	6	18	29	47	0
*Rodriguez, Beto, 1b	.288	68	229	33	66	16	2	8	50	41	50	0
Spivey, Jim, c	.345	23	55	6	19	1	3	4	12	3	17	0

PITCHING	W	L	ERA	G	GS	CG	SV	IP	H	R	ER	BB	SO
Alberro, Hector	2	0	5.06	5	0	0	0	5	3	3	3	3	3
*Baker, Scott	4	2	2.28	32	0	0	0	51	44	21	13	29	62
Brumley, Duff	2	6	6.14	12	11	0	0	56	62	48	38	29	43
Gonzalez, Cecilio	2	7	4.18	13	13	0	0	71	74	41	33	20	52
Hays, Kevin	0	0	0.00	1	0	0	0	2	2	0	0	2	1
Hurst, Bill	0	0	1.69	2	2	0	0	11	5	2	2	6	12
Kelly, John	1	2	0.79	25	0	0	13	34	22	7	3	12	41
Lopez, Jose	5	5	2.76	14	14	1	0	82	86	40	25	24	43

BATTING

R	Paul Russo, Elizabethton	58
H	Pat Dando, Pulaski	91
TB	Paul Russo, Elizabethton	155
2B	Jose Viera, Huntington	22
3B	Jerome Edwards, Prin	6
HR	Paul Russo, Elizabethton	22
RBI	Paul Russo, Elizabethton	67
SH	Carlos Fermin, Bristol	9
SF	Rick Meyer, Martinsville	7
BB	Rich Becker, Elizabethton	53
IBB	Paul Russo, Elizabethton	5
	Pat Dando, Pulaski	5
HBP	J.P. Postiff, Huntington	13
SO	Jimmy Alder, Bristol	75
	Vince Bradford, Bristol	75
SB	Tremayne Donald, JC	43
CS	Tremayne Donald, JC	15
OB%	Rich Becker, Eliz	.448

PITCHING

G	Scott Baker, Johnson City	32
GS	Alan Embree, Bristol	15
	Alan Walden, Bristol	15
CG	Rob Rees, Kingsport	7
ShO	Four tied at	2
Sv	Tom Benson, Elizabethton	14
	Carl Johnson, Bristol	14
W	Tyson Godfrey, Huntington	9
L	Shannon Withem, Bristol	9
IP	Rob Rees, Kingsport	102
H	Chris Snyder, Princeton	103
R	Adrian Sanchez, Hunt	60
HR	J.J. Munoz, Martinsville	12
BB	Roger Dixon, Elizabethton	48
	J.J. Munoz, Martinsville	48
HB	Travis Dunlap, Pulaski	10
SO	J.J. Munoz, Martinsville	126
WP	Four tied at	12
Bk	Jimmy Henry, Bristol	9

	W	L	ERA	G	GS	CG	SV	IP	H	R	ER	BB	SO
McGarity, Jeremy	0	8	5.17	12	12	1	0	63	60	49	36	26	47
*Norris, David	2	2	4.50	24	5	0	0	52	49	28	26	29	48
Rodriguez, Manuel	2	1	7.83	19	3	0	0	46	64	44	40	17	27
Ruyak, Craig	1	4	5.49	24	1	0	0	41	47	37	25	21	30
Speek, Frank	3	2	1.78	27	0	0	1	35	23	9	7	12	33
*Urbani, Tom	4	3	3.35	9	0	0	0	48	43	35	18	15	40

KINGSPORT

BATTING

	AVG	G	AB	R	H	2B	3B	HR	RBI	BB	SO	SB
Davis, Darwin, dh	.000	1	4	0	0	0	0	0	0	0	3	0
*Davis, Gerrod, of	.230	68	261	39	60	7	0	5	28	8	37	20
#Franklin, Micah, 2b	.259	39	158	29	41	10	3	7	25	8	44	5
Fully, Ed, of	.278	66	237	29	66	18	1	0	35	16	57	16
Garcia, Omar, 1b	.333	67	246	42	82	15	2	6	36	24	24	12
Huskey, Butch, 3b	.269	72	279	39	75	13	0	14	53	24	74	1
Johnson, Marcel, dh-1b	.220	35	100	6	22	4	1	1	9	9	30	1
#Kinyoun, Travis, c	.000	5	17	0	0	0	0	0	0	1	6	1
Ledesma, Aaron, ss	.333	66	243	50	81	11	1	5	38	30	28	27
*Mathis, Wayne, of	.160	34	81	15	13	3	0	0	2	6	19	11
#Millan, Bernie, dh-ss	.311	57	183	14	57	5	1	0	20	12	17	2
Moore, Tony, of	.223	44	139	21	31	11	0	4	14	12	65	11
Rudolph, Mason, c	.175	48	154	26	27	5	0	7	21	8	65	0
*Sandy, Tim, of	.331	49	163	31	54	6	3	3	14	32	16	9
Steele, Steven, c	.500	2	4	0	2	0	0	0	1	0	1	0
#Veras, Quilvio, 2b	.383	24	94	21	36	5	0	1	14	13	14	9
Williams, Charles, c	.121	24	66	8	8	1	0	0	2	3	20	0

PITCHING

	W	L	ERA	G	GS	CG	SV	IP	H	R	ER	BB	SO
Anaya, Mike	0	0	0.00	3	1	0	0	7	3	1	0	3	11
Benson, Nate	6	4	3.38	13	10	1	1	61	56	42	23	37	33
Bristow, Rich	3	3	2.92	26	0	0	8	37	36	13	12	16	26
Carpentier, Rob	6	1	1.87	22	8	2	1	82	53	24	16	30	56
Carrasco, Hector	0	0	4.05	3	1	0	0	7	8	3	3	1	5
Engle, Tom	6	3	3.26	14	12	1	0	77	68	35	28	31	75
Lehnerz, Mike	0	2	32.40	3	2	0	0	3	4	12	12	16	2
*Lindsay, Darian	3	2	2.08	15	0	0	1	22	15	5	5	7	14
Martinez, Rey	0	3	7.41	20	1	0	4	34	43	33	28	22	26
Polanco, Nick	2	2	3.93	22	2	0	1	53	50	27	23	11	42
Rees, Rob	6	6	2.92	14	14	7	0	102	102	46	33	26	59
Van Rybach, Cap	4	1	4.01	12	9	1	0	61	56	32	27	22	35
Wegmann, Tom	5	4	2.67	14	12	0	0	84	53	34	25	30	103

MARTINSVILLE

BATTING

	AVG	G	AB	R	H	2B	3B	HR	RBI	BB	SO	SB
Bennett, Gary, c-dh	.269	16	52	3	14	2	1	0	10	4	15	0
Borgese, Jeff, 2b-3b	.300	61	223	36	67	13	2	2	28	37	25	2
Carmona, William, of	.225	43	151	15	34	8	0	3	17	4	52	1
Carson, Paul, of	.167	10	30	3	5	0	0	1	5	6	10	0
*Farmer, Mike, of	.268	55	194	33	52	11	5	10	34	13	56	11
*Foster, Lamar, 1b	.214	66	234	24	50	12	1	6	36	30	52	0
Grissom, Tony, of-dh	.176	5	17	1	3	1	0	0	0	2	3	0
Hedley, Darren, of	.200	41	125	14	25	7	0	0	8	30	48	1
*Hines, Maurice, dh-of	.191	15	47	3	9	2	0	0	0	2	10	0
*Larson, Dan, of-dh	.226	19	62	4	14	6	0	0	8	1	17	0
Lieberthal, Mike, c	.228	49	184	26	42	9	0	4	22	11	40	2
Medina, Facaner, of	.251	48	199	22	50	3	3	2	10	10	57	7
#Medina, Patricio, ss	.199	49	201	18	40	2	0	0	6	8	46	6
Meyer, Rick, 3b	.242	65	240	32	58	11	0	3	23	18	66	2
#Murphy, Mike, of	.097	9	31	4	3	0	0	0	1	7	17	1
Pascual, Jorge, 2b	.233	37	159	21	37	5	2	1	13	4	20	2
Pena, Porfirio, dh-c	.161	14	56	6	9	1	0	0	4	1	22	0

	AVG	G	AB	R	H	2B	3B	HR	RBI	BB	SO	SB
#Rosario, Francisco, ss	.184	21	76	11	14	2	0	1	2	8	27	6
Tewell, Terrance, dh-1b	.222	17	63	4	14	2	0	1	5	3	16	1

PITCHING	W	L	ERA	G	GS	CG	SV	IP	H	R	ER	BB	SO
Agado, David	2	5	3.98	14	14	1	0	81	80	43	36	46	64
Anderson, Chad	1	6	4.97	13	13	1	0	71	77	50	39	21	52
Badacour, Bob	3	6	3.53	12	12	2	0	74	65	37	29	20	53
Cooper, Darren	1	6	5.08	15	12	3	0	67	76	50	38	39	50
Croak, David	0	1	12.00	1	1	0	0	3	3	4	4	3	3
Domecq, Ray	5	2	2.18	26	0	0	8	33	21	9	8	17	40
Freeman, Pete	0	1	4.35	20	0	0	0	39	47	24	19	17	53
*Higgins, Bill	5	3	2.93	23	0	0	2	40	41	21	13	11	40
Kamerschen, Robbie	1	3	5.51	20	2	1	0	51	56	39	30	23	47
Lance, Garry	0	1	54.00	1	1	0	0	0	0	2	2	1	
*Munoz, J.J.	6	7	2.75	14	14	3	0	95	70	35	29	48	126
Wheeler, Winston	1	3	3.91	21	0	0	0	46	48	27	21	18	54

PRINCETON

BATTING	AVG	G	AB	R	H	2B	3B	HR	RBI	BB	SO	SB
#Brito, Luis, ss	.242	27	95	15	23	2	0	0	4	2	11	4
Cheek, Patrick, 3b-2b	.235	62	221	32	52	5	0	2	23	23	37	3
Edwards, Jerome, of	.192	64	229	39	44	4	6	1	20	30	66	27
Garces, Jesus, ss-2b	.149	49	161	18	24	1	1	0	10	12	34	7
Gunn, Jeffrey, of	.154	37	117	11	18	2	0	0	6	4	38	1
Hollins, James, 2b-ss	.265	54	204	27	54	17	2	2	28	24	24	3
Llanos, Aurelio, of	.221	47	154	18	34	8	0	4	17	9	51	12
*Lockett, Ron, 1b	.310	63	229	32	71	12	5	6	34	15	51	11
*Rusk, Troy, c-dh	.242	59	194	31	47	7	2	10	33	52	66	0
Silver, Chad, of	.234	47	167	18	39	6	1	0	8	7	26	4
#Smith, Terry, dh	.100	5	10	0	1	0	0	0	2	1	7	1
Sosa, Jose, of-dh	.156	14	32	0	5	1	0	0	3	2	18	0
*Steffens, Mark, of	.248	35	121	14	30	6	1	2	10	6	21	3
Tejada, Francisco, 3b-dh	.238	52	172	24	41	7	1	4	29	27	49	0
Vargas, Julio, c-dh	.244	43	131	20	32	10	0	4	17	26	30	1

PITCHING	W	L	ERA	G	GS	CG	SV	IP	H	R	ER	BB	SO
*Adamson, Joel	2	5	3.94	12	8	1	1	49	56	27	21	12	40
Blazier, Ron	3	5	4.46	14	13	1	0	79	79	46	39	29	45
Edwards, Samuel	0	2	9.75	9	0	0	0	12	17	13	13	11	8
Garcia, Mario	3	2	5.40	15	1	0	1	35	37	23	21	26	34
*Hammond, David	3	5	3.06	21	1	0	1	47	45	33	16	28	35
Hassinger, Brad	7	4	2.18	13	13	5	0	91	66	30	22	20	48
Manicchia, Bryan	2	1	2.16	22	0	0	8	50	33	22	12	21	47
Repoz, Jeff	2	0	3.54	4	4	0	0	20	23	9	8	10	7
*Snyder, Chris	5	5	2.48	14	13	4	0	98	103	40	27	23	48
*Stohr, Bill	4	7	4.30	16	12	1	1	75	77	45	36	42	59
Villareal, Juan	0	0	3.55	7	0	0	0	13	10	6	5	11	12
*Whisenant, Matt	0	0	11.40	9	2	0	0	15	16	27	19	20	25

PULASKI

BATTING	AVG	G	AB	R	H	2B	3B	HR	RBI	BB	SO	SB
Crump, Jamie, 3b-1b	.175	43	137	16	24	9	0	3	15	18	34	2
*Dando, Pat, 1b	.360	69	253	46	91	19	2	10	38	25	32	8
Fults, Nathan, of	.263	14	38	3	10	4	0	0	8	7	15	2
Gonzalez, Wallace, c-1b	.263	47	156	17	41	10	3	3	27	9	37	0
Graffagnino, Anthony, ss	.206	42	131	23	27	5	1	0	11	26	17	6
Hughes, Troy, of	.269	46	145	22	39	7	1	1	17	16	39	5
Jiminez, Vincent, c-dh	.245	29	98	11	24	4	2	1	5	15	22	1
Johnson, Anthony, of	.223	42	121	20	27	4	1	2	13	17	25	5
*Kowitz, Brian, of	.324	43	182	40	59	13	1	8	19	16	16	13
Mathis, Monte, 2b	.333	12	30	6	10	2	0	0	0	1	4	0
#Mongero, Trent, ss-3b	.222	44	144	17	32	2	2	1	9	14	35	4
Pullins, Jimmie, dh-of	.179	11	28	2	5	0	0	0	3	2	6	1
#Roa, Hector, ss	.348	21	92	23	32	3	2	3	14	5	17	7
*Rodriguez, Armando, dh-of	.277	46	137	21	38	8	2	2	19	21	29	5
Rudison, Karl, 3b	.218	47	133	20	29	4	3	0	12	24	25	6
Toth, Dave, c	.268	26	82	9	22	0	0	0	10	11	12	2
#Virgilio, George, 2b	.259	58	220	35	57	9	2	3	21	27	18	7
*Walker, Johnny, of	.212	39	132	12	28	6	0	4	11	8	28	5
*Williams, Juan, of	.273	58	198	18	54	6	1	0	22	11	45	9

PITCHING	W	L	ERA	G	GS	CG	SV	IP	H	R	ER	BB	SO
*Bark, Brian	2	2	2.66	5	5	0	0	24	17	19	7	13	33
*Bryan, Rusty	0	2	1.83	9	1	0	0	20	18	10	4	12	19
Chiles, Barry	4	2	3.99	17	6	1	3	56	46	36	25	26	44
Dunlap, Travis	1	3	3.83	17	4	0	2	52	34	26	22	30	60
*Ford, Stewart	0	1	6.20	15	0	0	0	20	18	17	14	16	11
Grebe, Brett	2	2	3.77	5	5	0	0	29	27	16	12	13	24
Mack, Ray	1	2	2.05	17	0	0	4	22	11	7	5	12	34
Morrison, Keith	6	6	4.10	13	13	2	0	79	77	46	36	37	79
*Owens, Larry	1	1	7.10	4	2	0	0	13	18	13	10	7	9
Place, Mike	4	3	2.61	22	1	0	3	48	41	20	14	17	38
Roa, Joe	4	2	2.97	14	11	3	0	76	55	29	25	26	49
Shepherd, Mike	2	5	4.02	18	1	0	1	40	42	20	18	19	35
*Werland, Henry	5	2	2.94	14	10	0	0	64	48	27	21	26	98
Williams, David	5	2	3.97	14	13	1	0	88	93	44	39	23	71

PIONEER LEAGUE

Dodgers fall short of own standard, but win

By ALLAN SIMPSON

At .704, the Great Falls Dodgers had the second-best winning percentage in professional baseball in 1990. They won their third straight Pioneer League title.

But by their own high standard, the Dodgers didn't stack up to some of the great Great Falls teams of the past, which have won at a combined .663 clip since the parent Los Angeles Dodgers began providing talent in 1984. The 1990 edition certainly fell short of the 1989 team, which went 53-14 (.791), and was hailed as one of the best short-season clubs ever fielded.

Raul Mondesi
. . . top prospect

"The talent was like night and day," said second-year Great Falls manager Joe Vavra, comparing the two clubs. "Last year, we had so much depth. We were much more experienced."

The rest of the Pioneer League managers, though, didn't see much drop in talent at Great Falls. In Baseball America's annual survey of the league's top major league prospects, Dodger players grabbed the top three spots and four of the first seven.

Great Falls also won the Northern Division race by a comfortable 9½ game margin over Helena, then swept Southern Division champ Salt Lake City, 3-0, in the league's best-of-5 championship series.

Dodger pitching proved too much for the Trappers, who were able to score only two runs in the three-game set. In the deciding game, won 4-1 by Great Falls, James Daspit and Gordie Tipton combined on a two-hitter.

Only two first-round draft picks appeared in the Pioneer League in 1990. Both were lefthanders whose stays were brief.

Ron Walden of Great Falls went 3-0 with a 0.42 ERA but lasted only four starts before he felt a twinge in his shoulder and was sent to the sidelines as a precautionary measure for the remainder of the season.

LEAGUE CHAMPIONS

Playoff Champions, Where Applicable

1990—Great Falls	1973—Billings	1956—Boise
1989—Great Falls	1972—Billings	1955—Magic Valley
1988—Great Falls	1971—Great Falls	1954—Great Falls
1987—Salt Lake City	1970—Idaho Falls	1953—Salt Lake City
1986—Salt Lake City	1969—Ogden	1952—Idaho Falls
1985—Salt Lake City	1968—Ogden	1951—Great Falls
1984—Helena	1967—Ogden	1950—Billings
1983—Billings	1966—Ogden	1949—Pocatello
1982—Medicine Hat	1965—Treasure Valley	1948—Twin Falls
1981—Butte	1964—Treasure Valley	1947—Twin Falls
1980—Lethbridge	1963—Magic Valley	1946—Salt Lake City
1979—Lethbridge	1962—Billings	1943-45—Did Not
1978—Billings	1961—Great Falls	Operate
1977—Lethbridge	1960—Boise	1942—Pocatello
1976—Great Falls	1959—Billings	1941—Ogden
1975—Great Falls	1958—Boise	1940—Ogden
1974—Idaho Falls	1957—Billings	1939—Twin Falls

Dan Smith (2-0, 3.65) made only five starts for Butte, before being promoted out of the league by the parent Texas Rangers.

Salt Lake City, operating again as an independent, enjoying another record-breaking season at the gate, drawing 192,366 fans. That broke their own short-season attendance record of 173,256, set in 1989.

Pocatello, which changed its name to the Gate City Pioneers when the San Francisco Giants dropping their affiliation following the 1989 season, also played without a full working agreement in 1990. The Montreal Expos provided manager Ed Creech and about half the team's players in a co-op arrangement, but it was a long season for the Pioneers, who won only 15 of 70 games.

That spared perennial doormat Medicine Hat the ignomy of finishing in last place again. The Blue Jays, who typically field the youngest team in the league, won 20 games.

1990 FINAL STANDINGS

North	W	L	Pct.	GB
Great Falls (Dodgers)	48	20	.706	—
Helena (Brewers)	37	28	.569	9½
Billings (Reds)	32	34	.485	15
Medicine Hat (Blue Jays) ...	20	46	.303	27
South				
Salt Lake (Independent)	42	26	.618	—
Idaho Falls (Braves)	39	31	.557	4
Butte (Rangers)	37	30	.552	4½
Gate City (Co-op)	15	55	.214	28

1990 GENERAL INFORMATION

Playoffs: Great Falls defeated Salt Lake City 3-0 in best-of-5 final to win league championship.

Regular-Season Attendance: Salt Lake City, 192,366; Billings, 94,245; Idaho Falls, 77,942; Great Falls, 72,609; Helena, 40,524; Butte, 30,116; Gate City, 20,926; Medicine Hat, 13,350.

Managers: Billings—Gerry Groninger; **Butte**—Bump Wills; **Gate City**—Ed Creech; **Great Falls**—Joe Vavra; **Helena**—Gary Calhoun; **Idaho Falls**—Steve Curry; **Medicine Hat**—Garth Iorg; **Salt Lake**—Nick Belmonte.

1990 Official All-Star Team: C—Todd Guggiana, Butte. **1B**—Mike Busch, Great Falls. **2B**—Vince Castaldo, Helena. **3B**—Tom Duffin, Salt Lake. **SS**—Grant Brittain, Idaho Falls. **OF**—David Hulse, Butte; K.C. Gillum, Billings; Raul Mondesi, Great Falls. **DH**—Kevin McMullan, Salt Lake. **P**—Pedro Martinez, Great Falls; Mike Ferry, Billings; Billy Ambos, Salt Lake. **Manager of the Year**—Steve Curry, Idaho Falls.

Top 10 Major League Prospects (by Baseball America): 1. Raul Mondesi, of, Great Falls; **2.** Ron Walden, lhp, Great Falls; **3.** Pedro Martinez, rhp, Great Falls; **4.** K.C. Gillum, of, Billings; **5.** Michael Carter, ss, Helena; **6.** Mike Ferry, rhp, Billings; **7.** Mike Busch, 1b, Great Falls; **8.** Howard Battle, 3b, Medicine Hat; **9.** Jon Shave, ss, Butte; **10.** Brent Bowers, of, Medicine Hat.

1990 BATTING PITCHING STATS

CLUB BATTING

	AVG	G	AB	R	H	2B	3B	HR	BB	SO	SB
Butte	.313	67	2355	437	738	112	27	37	286	361	95
Great Falls	.288	68	2402	435	692	111	36	45	276	451	107
Salt Lake City	.284	68	2357	447	671	105	29	31	328	429	79
Billings	.280	66	2290	391	642	96	16	44	280	491	81
Idaho Falls	.277	70	2439	395	665	115	21	38	316	527	105
Helena	.268	65	2210	365	593	108	17	41	279	446	100
Gate City	.251	70	2306	279	579	96	21	25	246	566	84
Medicine Hat	.239	66	2244	264	536	92	21	25	213	485	82

CLUB PITCHING

	ERA	G	CG	SHO	SV	IP	H	R	ER	BB	SO
Great Falls	3.07	68	0	4	20	609	554	257	208	261	559
Salt Lake City	4.04	68	9	2	20	606	689	354	272	208	417
Helena	4.27	65	4	2	13	575	622	325	273	251	477

Ron Walden
...3-0, 0.42

Jon Shave
... .352-2-42

Pedro Martinez
...8-3, 3.82

	ERA	G	CG	SHO	SV	IP	H	R	ER	BB	SO
Idaho Falls	4.50	70	4	5	18	608	653	376	304	301	477
Billings	4.55	66	2	2	16	580	589	380	293	294	450
Butte	4.78	67	8	1	15	576	614	384	306	282	461
Medicine Hat	5.12	66	1	2	9	573	623	427	326	348	465
Gate City	6.22	70	3	0	7	588	772	510	406	278	449

INDIVIDUAL BATTING LEADERS
(Minimum 189 Plate Appearances)

	AVG	G	AB	R	H	2B	3B	HR	RBI	BB	SO	SB
*Hulse, David, Butte	.358	64	257	54	92	12	2	2	36	25	31	24
*Gillum, K.C., Billings	.356	57	225	50	80	14	3	5	43	20	45	13
Shave, Jon, Butte	.352	64	250	41	88	9	3	2	42	25	27	21
*Guggiana, Todd, Butte	.351	66	248	50	87	23	5	4	52	26	22	6
#Bargas, Rob, SLC	.348	58	221	44	77	5	2	2	36	20	30	6
*Greer, Rusty, Butte	.345	62	226	48	78	12	6	10	50	41	23	9
Ingram, Garey, GF	.343	56	198	43	68	12	8	2	21	22	37	10
*Castaldo, Vince, Helena	.335	62	236	53	79	19	2	8	47	29	36	10
Moberg, Mike, SLC	.331	68	269	65	89	12	3	4	38	41	38	12
Quinones, Elliot, Bill	.330	54	215	38	71	8	1	6	46	17	27	10

INDIVIDUAL PITCHING LEADERS
(Minimum 56 Innings)

	W	L	ERA	G	GS	CG	SV	IP	H	R	ER	BB	SO
Ambos, Willie, SLC	7	3	2.57	14	12	3	0	88	89	33	25	21	47
Dease, Don'l, IF	4	2	2.91	13	13	0	0	59	58	25	19	29	55
Baumann, David, GF	7	3	3.03	13	11	0	0	68	66	25	23	26	48
*Nettnin, Rod, SLC	4	4	3.23	13	12	3	0	75	75	38	27	29	47
*Mimbs, Mark, GF	7	4	3.23	14	14	0	0	78	69	32	28	29	94
Whitworth, Ken, SLC	7	2	3.32	13	12	1	1	76	77	31	28	32	54
Whiteside, Matt, Butte	4	4	3.45	18	5	0	2	57	57	33	22	25	45
Martinez, Pedro, GF	8	3	3.62	14	14	0	0	77	74	39	31	40	82
Hamilton, Ken, GF	4	2	3.63	13	13	0	0	67	76	34	27	28	37
Zimbauer, Jason, Helena	3	6	3.67	12	12	0	0	74	70	38	30	27	64

BILLINGS

BATTING	AVG	G	AB	R	H	2B	3B	HR	RBI	BB	SO	SB
*Burroughs, Eric, of	.300	41	150	27	45	6	1	2	21	8	34	9
Filotei, Bobby, ss-2b	.197	57	183	33	36	3	2	1	18	35	36	5
*Gillum, K.C., of	.356	57	225	50	80	14	3	5	43	20	45	13
Gordon, Keith, ss	.234	49	154	21	36	5	1	1	14	24	51	6
Hammargren, Tucker, 1b-c	.296	57	189	36	56	12	0	9	45	36	68	1
#Jones, Kevin, 3b-1b	.278	46	162	24	45	8	0	5	22	9	36	2
Nichols, Brian, c-1b	.279	42	140	12	39	9	0	0	19	8	20	2
Perez, Victor, of-dh	.143	24	49	7	7	0	0	0	0	6	24	2
#Perna, Bobby, of-dh	.333	14	48	12	16	2	0	1	8	9	3	3
Quinones, Elliot, of	.330	54	215	38	71	8	1	6	46	17	27	10
*Riggs, Kevin, 2b	.318	57	192	49	61	9	2	1	21	47	27	16
*Vasquez, Chris, of	.286	54	182	25	52	9	2	5	34	14	29	4
Velez, Noel, 3b-of	.284	44	169	27	48	5	2	4	21	12	32	5
Wentz, Cuyler, 2b-ss	.500	6	12	3	6	1	0	0	4	5	4	1
Wheeler, Dave, c-1b	.137	38	117	10	16	2	0	2	15	15	32	1
*Wilson, Todd, 1b	.263	22	76	15	20	2	2	2	14	10	22	1

PITCHING	W	L	ERA	G	GS	CG	SV	IP	H	R	ER	BB	SO
Berry, Kevin	1	2	4.84	19	0	0	2	35	40	22	19	23	38
Doty, Sean	1	1	4.24	8	0	0	0	17	8	9	8	8	24
*Duff, Scott	2	2	3.58	13	0	0	1	28	23	12	11	13	32
Edwards, Ryan	0	1	5.55	20	0	0	0	36	50	33	22	21	21
Ferry, Mike	2	5	2.84	27	0	0	11	32	29	13	10	12	29
*Fry, Brian	3	2	6.00	22	0	0	1	21	23	16	14	22	19
*Keim, Chris	0	0	1.00	12	0	0	0	18	12	10	2	13	20
Luebbers, Larry	5	4	4.48	13	13	1	0	72	74	46	36	31	48
*Margheim, Greg	6	7	5.55	14	14	1	0	73	86	53	45	33	45
Nieves, Ernie	2	0	4.20	20	0	0	1	41	48	27	19	18	22
Robinson, Scott	4	3	5.37	12	12	0	0	59	63	53	35	35	38

	W	L	ERA	G	GS	CG	SV	IP	H	R	ER	BB	SO
Stewart, Carl	3	4	4.15	14	14	0	0	0	74	51	41	34	47	64
Tatar, Kevin	3	3	4.64	13	13	0	0	0	74	82	45	38	17	48
Wilburn, Trey (7 Gate City) .	0	1	3.52	8	0	0	0	1	15	12	6	6	7	15

BUTTE

BATTING	AVG	G	AB	R	H	2B	3B	HR	RBI	BB	SO	SB
Blevins, Greg, c	.237	41	118	17	28	7	0	3	20	10	28	0
Castellano, Miguel, of-1b ..	.273	60	216	33	59	4	1	4	32	20	29	4
*Greer, Rusty, of	.345	62	226	48	78	12	6	10	50	41	23	9
*Guggiana, Todd, c-3b	.351	66	248	50	87	23	5	4	52	26	22	6
*Hulse, David, of	.358	64	257	54	92	12	2	2	36	25	30	24
*Matachun, Paul, 3b-2b ...	.282	57	174	30	49	6	2	1	27	28	17	6
Matos, Malvin, of	.222	50	158	27	35	2	3	4	27	12	49	6
Mercado, Brian, dh	.324	52	148	29	48	9	2	3	26	35	32	0
Mouton, Brian, 1b	.294	55	194	34	57	10	1	2	33	28	34	5
Murray, Keith, of	.615	7	13	7	8	4	0	0	5	2	2	3
Penn, Shannon, 2b	.325	60	197	38	64	4	2	0	18	15	35	9
*Posey, Marty, dh-of	.321	46	109	21	35	8	0	2	18	18	23	0
Reyes, Victor, c	.217	23	46	7	10	1	0	0	5	1	10	2
Shave, Jon, ss	.352	64	250	41	88	9	3	2	42	25	27	21

PITCHING	W	L	ERA	G	GS	CG	SV	IP	H	R	ER	BB	SO
*Burrows, Terry	3	6	4.02	14	11	1	0	63	56	35	28	35	64
Busha, Rodney	2	1	5.44	15	5	1	0	41	44	35	25	30	32
Cardona, Jose	6	3	1.99	23	0	0	4	41	29	10	9	16	31
Dreyer, Steve	1	1	4.54	8	8	0	0	36	32	21	18	10	29
*Erickson, Scott	0	0	5.31	16	1	0	0	20	17	13	12	23	24
Gies, Chris	6	2	3.77	15	14	5	0	88	86	40	37	27	64
*Goetz, Barry	0	1	1.59	4	0	0	1	6	2	1	1	3	2
Patterson, Danny	0	3	6.35	13	3	0	1	28	36	23	20	14	18
*Ramharter, Steve	2	1	6.52	22	0	0	1	19	24	19	14	15	19
Scheetz, Brian	1	2	5.96	12	1	0	0	23	38	26	15	14	14
*Smith, Dan	2	0	3.65	5	5	0	0	25	23	10	10	6	27
St.Pe, Irving	3	0	11.30	15	1	0	0	29	57	48	36	15	24
*Surico, Steve	0	1	6.75	7	0	0	0	11	6	13	8	14	9
Washington, Tyrone ..	7	2	4.82	13	13	1	0	65	79	38	35	24	45
Watson, Andy	0	0	24.30	4	0	0	0	3	6	9	9	5	1
Wells, Tim	0	3	3.05	16	0	0	6	21	21	10	7	6	13
Whiteside, Matt	4	4	3.45	18	5	0	2	57	57	33	22	25	45

GATE CITY

BATTING	AVG	G	AB	R	H	2B	3B	HR	RBI	BB	SO	SB
*Adams, Gary, of	.263	65	217	26	57	7	3	9	31	16	58	5
*Asai, Itsuki, of	.253	58	162	26	41	7	4	2	21	26	32	10
*Atwater, Buck, 2b-dh	.245	59	192	28	47	7	1	1	16	25	52	7
Chiyomaru, Akihiko, 3b-2b .	.245	50	151	16	37	5	1	4	26	7	38	2
Heilgeist, Jim, of	.097	33	93	2	9	1	0	0	6	2	47	0
*Horne, Tyrone, of-dh	.282	56	202	26	57	11	2	1	13	24	62	23
*Marabella, Tony, 3b-2b ..	.252	59	206	18	52	9	0	0	32	25	23	2
Noce, Doug, c-of	.251	56	183	24	46	12	1	0	16	32	35	1
Ortega, Hector, of-3b	.283	65	244	34	69	6	5	1	17	22	60	20
#Phillips, Thomas, c	.311	25	74	7	23	5	1	0	6	5	20	1
Rivera, Hector, of	.095	10	21	1	2	1	0	0	0	1	13	0
*Sanchez, Perry, c-1b	.292	24	89	9	26	3	0	1	9	8	5	1
Santiago, Angelo, 1b	.241	60	191	35	46	7	1	5	26	37	76	3
Satoh, Hiroyuki, ss	.267	60	206	22	55	12	2	1	23	14	36	6
Simmerson, Pete, 2b-ss ..	.160	24	75	5	12	3	0	0	2	9	9	3

PITCHING	W	L	ERA	G	GS	CG	SV	IP	H	R	ER	BB	SO
Carter, David	2	2	6.15	26	0	0	0	45	65	45	31	23	27
Casey, Keith	0	0	15.68	7	0	0	0	10	26	23	18	9	4
Emerick, Chris	2	5	5.37	12	12	0	0	52	62	38	31	20	42
Espinoza, Carlos	1	2	6.70	24	3	0	1	50	70	41	37	17	40
*Fier, Mike	0	8	6.51	13	13	0	0	55	64	48	40	32	43
Foster, Kevin	1	7	4.58	10	10	0	0	55	43	42	28	34	52
Frederiksen, Kelly	1	7	5.43	20	5	0	3	56	78	48	34	30	37
Hutto, Paul	0	1	7.49	26	0	0	0	46	78	50	38	20	24
*Maema, Takashi	1	8	7.16	19	9	0	0	49	71	43	39	24	47
Martinez, William	2	7	7.90	24	3	0	2	49	70	47	43	21	37
Mizusawa, Hideki	2	3	7.44	17	5	1	0	42	68	42	35	15	10
Renko, Steve	3	4	3.92	11	10	2	0	60	56	32	26	23	68

GREAT FALLS

BATTING	AVG	G	AB	R	H	2B	3B	HR	RBI	BB	SO	SB
*Andrews, Dan, of	.276	41	98	12	27	1	0	0	9	8	12	1
*Blackwell, Eric, of	.313	60	163	33	51	7	5	4	31	36	40	12
Bohringer, Helmut, 2b-3b ..	.238	10	21	7	5	0	0	0	4	6	0	1
Busch, Mike, 1b	.327	61	220	48	72	18	2	13	47	38	49	3
Farrish, Keoki, of	.248	60	202	24	51	7	1	1	26	18	41	6
Frauenhoffer, Mike, 2b-ss ..	.231	41	108	16	25	2	1	0	12	12	23	4
Gray, Dan, c	.267	38	120	22	32	3	3	3	13	14	22	2
Griffin, Tim, 2b-3b	.329	40	143	26	46	11	0	3	25	10	33	2
Ingram, Garey, dh	.343	56	198	43	68	12	8	2	21	22	37	10
Lund, Ed, c	.162	31	68	11	11	3	1	1	8	4	8	1
Maurer, Ron, ss	.269	62	238	43	64	8	0	6	43	28	38	5
Meyers, Don, 3b-1b	.326	38	92	14	30	5	1	1	23	11	25	0
Mondesi, Raul, of	.303	44	175	35	53	10	4	8	31	11	30	30

PL DEPARTMENT LEADERS

BATTING

R	Mike Moberg, Salt Lake . .	65
H	David Hulse, Butte . .	92
TB	Mike Busch, Great Falls	133
2B	Todd Guggiana, Butte . .	23
3B	Garey Ingram, Great Falls .	8
HR	Mike Busch, Great Falls .	13
RBI	Tim Carter, Helena	58
SH	John Urcioli, Salt Lake . . .	9
SF	Rick Karcher, Idaho Falls .	8
BB	Grant Brittain, Idaho Falls	63
IBB	Kevin McMullen, Salt Lake	4
HBP	Several tied at	6
SO	Angelo Santiago, GC	76
SB	Chris Burton, Idaho Falls .	34
CS	Chris Burton, Idaho Falls .	10
OB%	Kevin Riggs, Billings	.463

PITCHING

G	Michael Hoog, Idaho Falls	29
GS	Several tied at	14
CG	Chris Gies, Butte	5
ShO	Three tied at	1
Sv	Mike Ferry, Billings	11
W	Scott Ryder, Idaho Falls .	9
L	Mike Fier, Gate City	8
	Takashi Maema, Gate City	8
IP	Gene Mirabella, Salt Lake	89
H	Don Pruitt, Helena	101
ER	Don Pruitt, Helena	54
HR	Don Pruitt, Helena	8
BB	Eric Patten, Helena	55
HB	Matt Whiteside, Butte	9
SO	Mark Mimbs, Great Falls .	94
WP	Carl Stewart, Billings	15
Bk	Kevin Tatar, Billings	7

	AVG	G	AB	R	H	2B	3B	HR	RBI	BB	SO	SB
Perez, Junior, c	.267	41	90	15	24	4	1	0	19	4	10	0
Smith, Ira, of	.261	54	142	31	37	7	3	1	28	25	33	8
Watts, Burgess, 3b	.267	51	176	26	47	9	1	2	22	14	24	3
Webb, Lonnie, 2b	.338	40	148	29	49	4	5	0	17	15	26	19

PITCHING	W	L	ERA	G	GS	CG	SV	IP	H	R	ER	BB	SO
Baumann, David	7	3	3.03	13	11	0	0	68	66	25	23	26	49
Daspitt, James	5	2	4.06	14	9	0	0	51	45	26	23	30	40
DeJarld, John	3	1	1.64	22	0	0	4	49	35	10	9	20	56
Hamilton, Ken	4	2	3.63	13	13	0	0	67	76	34	27	28	37
Jacinto, Larry	0	0	4.29	17	0	0	0	21	27	12	10	7	15
*Kerr, Jason	1	1	3.57	19	1	0	1	35	32	21	14	27	40
Martinez, Pedro	8	3	3.62	14	14	0	0	77	74	39	31	40	82
*Mimbs, Mark	7	4	3.23	14	14	0	0	78	69	32	28	29	94
*Mimbs, Mike	0	0	4.05	3	0	0	0	7	5	3	3	5	7
*O'Connor, Ben	0	1	8.10	1	1	0	0	3	7	4	3	0	4
Piotrowicz, Brian	2	1	1.74	22	0	0	7	41	29	15	8	8	41
Stryker, Ed	2	1	4.39	21	1	0	1	41	46	24	20	13	31
Tipton, Gordie	6	1	1.50	24	0	0	7	48	35	10	8	17	43
*Walden, Ron	3	0	0.42	4	4	0	0	22	9	4	1	11	20

HELENA

BATTING	AVG	G	AB	R	H	2B	3B	HR	RBI	BB	SO	SB
Baber, Larue, of	.150	23	80	7	12	1	0	1	3	7	28	2
Beck, Rob, c	.250	32	100	11	25	6	2	2	14	6	21	2
*Benjamin, Bobby, of	.311	20	61	14	19	4	1	2	10	20	20	6
Carter, Mike, ss	.307	61	241	45	74	11	3	0	30	16	20	22
Carter, Tim, 1b-dh	.279	63	233	40	65	15	0	12	58	32	56	3
*Castaldo, Vince, 2b-3b	.335	62	236	54	79	20	2	8	47	29	36	10
Coble, Tony, dh-of	.240	32	121	10	29	6	1	3	16	6	29	2
Couture, Mike, of	.217	42	120	27	26	4	1	3	17	25	39	7
#Diggs, Tony, of-2b	.256	42	129	18	33	5	0	0	13	11	19	10
*Edwards, Todd, of	.352	35	108	20	38	7	1	0	17	20	12	5
Flores, Juan, c	.287	33	108	15	31	5	0	0	11	10	14	3
*Glenn, Leon, 1b-dh	.235	42	153	19	36	6	2	4	26	29	41	12
Hood, Randy, of	.315	48	178	43	56	11	4	3	20	37	30	7
#Moseley, Scott, 2b	.143	3	7	2	1	0	0	0	1	1	1	0
*Norris, Mike, of	.179	32	67	8	12	1	0	0	1	6	17	3
Powell, Gordon, 3b	.217	45	152	17	33	4	0	3	18	8	41	5
Rambadt, Chuck, c	.107	15	28	4	3	1	0	0	1	10	7	0
Walker, Jimmy, inf	.143	3	7	0	1	0	0	0	0	0	3	0
Wheat, Chris, inf	.247	31	81	11	20	1	0	0	8	6	12	1

PITCHING	W	L	ERA	G	GS	CG	SV	IP	H	R	ER	BB	SO
Angelos, Phil	6	0	1.29	9	0	0	1	28	12	7	4	14	23
Archer, Kurt	0	2	3.66	10	0	0	3	20	19	9	8	3	23
*Brakeley, Bill	0	0	4.91	6	6	0	0	18	17	11	10	15	23
Hooper, Mike	0	1	4.22	5	5	0	0	21	29	12	10	8	15
Kellogg, Geoff	2	1	2.17	15	2	0	2	37	35	12	9	18	36
McDonald, Kevin	3	2	4.70	9	8	0	0	46	62	27	24	21	37
Miller, Pat	3	3	3.75	8	8	2	0	48	55	24	20	9	42
*Mobley, Jay	0	0	15.00	6	0	0	0	9	19	15	15	2	8
Patton, Eric	7	1	5.37	17	2	0	0	57	50	39	34	55	37
Pruitt, Don	5	4	5.60	13	13	1	0	72	102	54	45	16	52
Rupp, Mark	0	2	3.70	13	0	0	1	24	30	15	10	11	18
Souza, Brian	3	4	5.16	19	4	0	4	45	50	30	27	29	39
*Stephens, Mark	3	2	3.48	14	5	1	1	44	40	20	17	16	41
Wilson, Tim	2	0	2.93	13	0	0	1	31	32	12	10	7	19
Zimbauer, Jason	3	6	3.67	12	12	0	0	74	70	38	30	27	64

IDAHO FALLS

BATTING	AVG	G	AB	R	H	2B	3B	HR	RBI	BB	SO	SB
*Brittain, Grant, ss	.274	67	226	48	62	14	3	5	48	63	61	6
*Burton, Chris, of	.305	66	256	47	78	13	2	2	28	43	34	34

	AVG	G	AB	R	H	2B	3B	HR	RBI	BB	SO	SB
Chumbley, Steven, 2b-ss ..	.000	10	9	3	0	0	0	0	0	1	4	0
*Columbano, Jeff, c	.406	17	32	6	13	2	0	0	3	1	1	0
#Dipino, Paul, 3b	.222	4	9	0	2	0	0	0	0	1	2	0
Drabinski, Marek, c	.265	52	151	19	40	6	0	0	14	21	24	0
Fister, Corby, of	.208	38	106	19	22	6	0	1	13	19	17	2
Fults, Nathan, of	.065	13	31	2	2	0	0	0	1	2	12	0
*Giovanola, Ed, 2b	.388	25	98	25	38	6	0	0	13	17	9	6
*Gress, Loren, 1b	.330	53	197	26	65	10	2	4	33	13	53	1
*Karcher, Rick, 1b-dh	.304	68	247	34	75	15	4	6	45	26	43	8
Lucky, Keith, 3b-ss	.240	13	25	4	6	2	0	2	6	3	4	0
Markulike, Joe, 3b-1b	.132	23	38	6	5	0	0	0	7	5	2	0
McMillan, Stuart, of	.274	66	241	40	66	10	5	7	51	26	63	22
*O'Connor, Kevin, of	.234	12	47	6	11	2	0	1	4	0	5	4
Orr, Geoff, 3b	.289	67	242	44	70	13	1	7	39	33	54	10
Owen, Tommy, c	.091	6	11	1	1	0	0	0	2	2	7	0
Pullins, Jimmie, of	.304	37	92	12	28	3	2	1	13	13	20	2
Surane, John, 2b	.288	67	212	33	61	8	2	2	21	31	54	5
Sweeney, Michael, of	.147	26	68	9	10	2	0	0	2	3	34	1
Wood, John, c	.182	32	55	11	10	3	0	0	4	4	11	2
Zeller, William, c	.000	3	5	0	0	0	0	0	0	0	2	0

PITCHING	W	L	ERA	G	GS	CG	SV	IP	H	R	ER	BB	SO
Bates, Bill	2	4	5.44	21	7	0	1	50	52	36	30	20	62
Bourgeois, Jerry	0	0	9.39	4	0	0	0	8	10	9	8	10	7
Carter, Eric	2	1	7.94	18	0	0	0	23	27	22	20	21	14
*Creamer, Gerry	0	0	18.00	1	0	0	0	1	1	2	2	4	2
*Dare, Brian	3	6	4.05	15	13	1	0	80	85	49	36	24	36
Dease, Don'l	4	2	2.91	13	13	0	0	59	58	25	19	29	55
Gabriele, Mike	1	1	7.84	4	1	0	0	10	16	12	9	6	8
*Halliday, Allen	1	0	7.43	15	1	0	0	13	22	13	11	12	10
Hodges, Steven	4	3	3.56	25	0	0	2	43	35	20	17	23	45
*Hoog, Michael	4	1	3.86	29	0	0	5	42	47	19	18	21	38
Koolman, Bill	0	1	6.35	15	0	0	0	23	28	18	16	14	21
Langston, Keith	0	1	3.09	5	1	0	0	12	10	6	4	4	5
Lemon, Don	6	2	4.46	11	11	2	0	71	78	38	35	17	36
Mack, Ray	0	0	2.25	2	0	0	0	4	7	1	1	2	4
Newman, Tom	1	3	4.25	7	7	0	0	30	34	21	14	14	16
Rizzo, Thomas	1	1	6.49	14	2	0	0	26	36	23	19	18	16
Rohrwild, Shawn	1	0	2.65	24	0	0	10	37	26	12	11	23	43
*Ryder, Scott	9	5	4.29	14	14	0	0	78	81	50	37	39	59

MEDICINE HAT

BATTING	AVG	G	AB	R	H	2B	3B	HR	RBI	BB	SO	SB
Battle, Howard, 3b	.266	61	233	25	62	17	1	5	32	15	38	5
*Bowers, Brent, of	.274	60	212	30	58	7	3	3	27	30	35	19
Choate, Mark, 2b-ss	.234	62	214	30	50	7	1	2	22	33	51	11
Coolbaugh, Mike, ss-2b ..	.190	58	211	21	40	9	0	2	16	13	47	3
*Crump, Gerry, 1b	.000	1	5	0	0	0	0	0	0	0	2	0
Daniels, Lee, of	.168	31	95	3	16	3	0	0	9	7	39	4
Garcia, Anastacio, c	.188	18	48	3	9	3	0	0	3	5	12	0
*Harmes, Kris, c-1b	.261	50	165	18	43	8	1	1	18	24	21	2
Hines, Keith, of-dh	.262	38	126	15	33	2	4	3	14	14	41	4
*Hyers, Tim, 1b	.219	61	224	29	49	7	2	2	19	29	22	4
Loeb, Marc, c	.302	29	96	15	29	5	0	2	12	13	28	2
Reams, Ron, of-3b	.243	48	206	28	50	10	2	3	15	5	30	12
#Roberts, Lonell, of	.212	38	118	14	25	2	0	0	9	5	29	8
Septimo, Felix, of	.219	43	155	15	34	5	5	2	17	10	62	4
#Tavarez, Hector, ss	.279	39	136	18	38	7	2	0	12	9	28	4

PITCHING	W	L	ERA	G	GS	CG	SV	IP	H	R	ER	BB	SO
Adams, Morgan	0	1	8.49	13	2	0	0	23	37	26	22	21	17
Burley, Travis	3	4	6.69	12	7	0	0	36	34	32	27	37	23
Darley, Ned	0	4	4.71	9	8	0	0	29	29	24	15	26	13
Duey, Kyle	4	6	3.86	15	11	0	0	72	72	38	31	34	54
Fletcher, David	0	0	14.73	3	0	0	0	4	8	6	6	4	1
Garcia, Rafael	3	5	5.05	13	8	0	1	57	68	44	32	32	37
Gilligan, John	1	6	2.75	18	2	1	1	56	58	28	17	10	43
Hotchkiss, Tom	1	2	4.91	20	0	0	0	37	42	24	20	23	29
*Kistaitis, Dale	1	4	4.50	12	10	0	0	52	44	37	26	29	54
Miller, Scott	0	0	1.19	19	0	0	5	23	18	12	3	13	19
*Orman, Rick	1	2	8.42	19	0	0	1	26	39	28	24	16	24
Perez, Jose	0	3	10.74	11	4	0	0	31	47	44	37	15	21
Reese, Jason	1	0	6.48	17	0	0	0	25	31	19	18	26	19
*Spoljaric, Paul	3	7	4.34	15	13	0	1	66	57	43	32	35	62
Wilcox, Greg	2	2	4.21	13	1	0	0	36	39	22	17	27	49

SALT LAKE CITY

BATTING	AVG	G	AB	R	H	2B	3B	HR	RBI	BB	SO	SB
#Bargas, Rob, 1b	.348	58	221	44	77	5	2	2	36	20	30	6
*Beaulac, Joe, 1b-of	.080	13	25	2	2	0	0	0	1	3	10	0
Bielski, Rich, of-1b	.285	46	137	23	39	8	4	3	27	21	44	0
Biggers, Brian, 2b-ss	.296	38	98	19	29	2	1	0	11	9	18	1
#Briggs, Kenny, c	.227	35	88	15	20	6	1	3	17	14	22	2
Burnett, Joe, of	.200	27	45	9	9	0	0	0	5	15	16	7
Czarnetzki, Mike, of	.185	17	27	4	5	1	0	0	4	2	3	0
Doyle, Jim, 2b-of	.203	40	128	28	26	3	0	1	17	22	12	12
Duffin, Tom, 3b	.306	65	245	56	75	16	4	4	48	33	34	11

	AVG	G	AB	R	H	2B	3B	HR	RBI	BB	SO	SB
Garczyk, Ed, 2b	.214	12	28	6	6	1	0	0	3	6	1	4
Harris, Butch, 1b	.244	39	90	8	22	5	2	0	15	14	23	2
Keighley, Steve, c	.261	34	92	23	24	4	1	1	16	33	17	1
Kelly, Brian, of	.280	28	82	14	23	4	2	1	12	11	11	3
*Kidd, Dennis, of	.343	8	35	6	12	2	1	1	3	1	7	1
Martin, Jim, of	.286	19	84	13	24	5	1	0	13	9	16	2
McMullen, Kevin, dh-c	.299	60	234	44	71	14	4	10	56	30	56	2
Moberg, Mike, of	.331	68	269	64	89	12	3	4	38	41	38	12
#Montes, Dan, 2b	.235	31	81	10	19	4	0	0	12	7	12	5
*Reimsnyder, Brian, of	.200	10	20	1	4	1	0	0	1	4	8	0
Schifman, Jim, of	.464	8	28	8	13	0	1	0	6	3	3	2
Stofsky, Wayne, of	.310	21	87	19	27	5	0	0	8	4	13	1
Urcioli, John, ss	.258	63	213	30	55	7	2	1	35	25	35	5

PITCHING	W	L	ERA	G	GS	CG	SV	IP	H	R	ER	BB	SO
Alexander, Dave	3	0	4.67	15	0	0	1	35	48	30	18	7	13
Ambos, Willie	7	3	2.57	14	12	3	0	88	89	33	25	21	47
*Boone, Gary	2	3	5.40	20	0	0	4	28	34	22	17	13	26
*Gerstein, Ron	0	1	14.54	2	1	0	0	4	7	7	7	5	3
Hagy, Jeff	0	1	4.91	16	1	0	0	29	32	20	16	9	20
Jobes, Tracy	1	1	6.95	13	3	0	1	34	56	36	26	15	20
Jurado, Pat	3	1	0.83	13	0	0	7	33	24	7	3	7	28
Mirabella, Gene	7	5	3.93	14	14	2	0	89	98	47	39	34	90
*Nettnin, Rod	4	4	3.23	13	12	3	0	75	75	38	27	29	47
Sawaia, Joe	0	0	40.50	2	0	0	0	1	7	6	6	0	1
Steinkamp, Mike	6	4	4.54	13	12	0	0	69	89	46	35	19	29
*Sweet, Pat	1	0	3.38	4	0	0	0	8	6	3	3	5	4
White, Randy	1	1	5.45	18	1	0	6	36	47	28	22	13	35
Whitworth, Ken	7	2	3.32	13	12	1	1	76	77	31	28	32	54

GULF COAST LEAGUE

Dodgers sweep Expos; win titles at every level

By DEAN GYORGY

Putting on a Dodgers uniform seemed to go a long way toward winning a championship in 1990. Throughout the minor leagues, six of seven Los Angeles affiliates reached the postseason. Four won overall titles, including opposite ends of the spectrum, Triple-A Albuquerque and the Gulf Coast League entry.

The GCL team went 38-25, winning the Northern Division by two games, and then swept the Expos in a best-of-3 series.

Boosting the Dodgers' cause in a big way was Domingo Mota, a 31st-round draft pick in June and son of long-time Dodger Manny Mota. Domingo hit a league second-best .343, with 12 doubles and 34 RBIs.

The talent level was unusually strong in the GCL in 1990, as six No. 1 draft picks were sent to Florida for their professional debuts. The crop included the White Sox' Alex Fernandez, who didn't stay long. He was in the big leagues by August. The Braves' Chipper Jones, No. 1 overall, struggled a bit, hitting .229 with one homer and 18 errors in the field.

There were three no-hitters pitched in the GCL in 1990. The Mets' Ottis Smith beat the Twins 1-0 on July 24. The White Sox' Roosevelt Smith and Ted Marshall combined to shut down the Yankees for seven innings on Aug. 2. And Mariano Rivera of the Yankees, the league's ERA leader, had a seven-inning no-hitter against the Pirates on Aug. 31.

1990 *FINAL STANDINGS*

North	W	L	Pct.	GB
Dodgers	38	25	.603	—
Reds	36	27	.571	2
Red Sox	34	29	.540	4
Astros	33	30	.524	5
Royals	25	38	.397	13
Indians	23	40	.365	15
South				
Expos	40	23	.635	—
Rangers	36	27	.571	4
Braves	33	29	.532	6½
Yankees	32	30	.516	7½
Twins	32	30	.516	7½
Mets	29	30	.492	9
Pirates	25	37	.403	14½
White Sox	21	42	.333	19

1990 *GENERAL INFORMATION*

Playoffs: Dodgers defeated Expos 2-0 in best-of-3 final to win league championship.

Managers: Astros—Julio Linares; **Braves**—Jim Procopio; **Dodgers**—Ivan DeJesus; **Expos**—Lorenzo Bundy; **Indians**—Dean Treanor; **Mets**—John Tamargo; **Pirates**—Julio Garcia; **Rangers**—Chino Cadahia; **Reds**—Sammy Mejias; **Red Sox**—Felix Maldonado; **Royals**—Carlos Tosca; **Twins**—Joel Lepel; **White Sox**—Mike Gellinger; **Yankees**—Glenn Sherlock.

1990 Official All-Star Team: C—Jose Valdez, Dodgers. **1B**—Peter Laake, Rangers. **2B**—Claudio Ozario, Expos. **3B**—David Lowery, Rangers. **SS**—Tom Nevers, Astros. **OF**—Rondell White, Expos; Raul

Rondell White, left, and Domingo Mota were two of the GCL's top-rated outfielders.

Robinson, Braves; Domingo Mota, Dodgers. **SP**—John Roper, Reds. **RP**—Tony Bouton, Rangers. **Manager of the Year**—Sammy Mejias, Reds.

Top 10 Major League Prospects, combined Gulf Coast League and Arizona League (by Baseball America): 1. Rondell White, of, Expos; **2.** Marc Newfield, 1b, Mariners (Arizona); **3.** John Roper, rhp, Reds; **4.** Robbie Beckett, lhp, Padres (Arizona); **5.** Jamie Dismuke, 1b, Reds; **6.** Carl Everett, of, Yankees; **7.** Midre Cummings, of, Twins; **8.** Shane Andrews, 3b, Expos; **9.** Paul Brannon, c, Mariners (Arizona); **10.** Tom Nevers, ss, Astros.

1990 BATTING PITCHING STATS

CLUB BATTING

	AVG	G	AB	R	H	2B	3B	HR	BB	SO	SB
Astros	.273	64	2095	336	571	91	28	9	288	314	133
Dodgers	.265	64	2051	312	544	78	14	8	290	397	87
Expos	.250	63	2038	319	509	73	19	20	192	427	70
Red Sox	.248	63	2121	341	527	80	18	8	305	380	40
Braves	.246	62	2003	267	493	65	14	17	179	409	88
Rangers	.240	64	2053	263	492	69	18	6	201	358	118
Reds	.238	64	2110	293	503	83	14	26	237	382	121
Twins	.234	63	2108	295	493	63	33	16	190	570	116
Pirates	.233	63	2055	230	479	68	13	9	141	425	58
Royals	.232	64	2003	241	465	78	17	9	249	430	104
Yankees	.223	62	1980	251	442	60	19	11	229	468	79
Indians	.219	63	1933	242	423	56	9	9	336	390	96
Mets	.219	60	1881	225	411	54	25	17	201	475	90
White Sox	.203	63	1942	216	394	64	14	9	217	500	122

CLUB PITCHING

	ERA	G	CG	SHO	SV	IP	H	R	ER	BB	SO
Yankees	2.44	62	4	8	13	528	388	221	143	193	505
Mets	2.64	60	8	6	14	509	427	226	146	156	432
Expos	2.89	63	1	6	14	533	457	218	171	185	421
Rangers	2.92	64	2	8	26	543	491	229	176	153	484
White Sox	3.04	63	1	4	14	541	471	285	183	189	514
Braves	3.15	62	7	2	14	534	470	287	187	231	415
Dodgers	3.36	64	3	5	17	551	501	257	206	247	413
Pirates	3.43	63	3	5	11	531	491	280	202	209	425
Reds	3.54	64	1	5	23	564	503	278	222	284	402
Astros	3.61	64	2	5	6	551	445	275	221	300	413
Twins	3.66	63	5	3	19	550	518	320	224	232	436
Royals	3.67	64	0	3	13	545	496	291	222	320	360
Red Sox	3.98	63	8	5	11	564	562	311	249	258	315
Indians	4.21	63	6	0	10	539	526	353	252	296	390

INDIVIDUAL BATTING LEADERS
(Minimum 170 Plate Appearances)

	AVG	G	AB	R	H	2B	3B	HR	RBI	BB	SO	SB
Houk, Tom, Twins	.344	46	157	25	54	10	5	3	37	22	18	3
Mota, Domingo, Dodgers	.343	61	213	46	73	12	2	1	34	36	19	23
*Laake, Peter, Rangers	.322	64	214	36	69	15	2	1	37	39	38	2
#Schmidt, David, Red Sox	.322	50	180	44	58	8	8	0	28	37	36	3
#Cummings, Midre, Twins	.316	47	177	28	56	3	4	5	28	13	32	13
Valdez, Jose, Dodgers	.320	59	206	31	66	15	1	1	43	22	29	1
Williams, Leroy, Dodgers	.313	58	198	25	62	8	0	0	25	26	26	5
Hennessey, Scott, Royals	.313	48	160	21	50	7	1	0	14	21	18	6
#Lowery, David, Rangers	.300	62	240	41	72	8	0	0	18	27	14	40
White, Rondell, Expos	.299	57	221	33	66	7	4	5	34	17	33	10

INDIVIDUAL PITCHING LEADERS
(Minimum 50 Innings)

	W	L	ERA	G	GS	CG	SV	IP	H	R	ER	BB	SO
Rivera, Mariano, Yankees	5	1	0.17	22	1	1	1	52	17	3	1	7	58
Roper, John, Reds	7	2	0.97	13	13	0	0	74	41	10	8	31	76
*Smith, Ottis, Mets	6	5	1.47	13	13	3	0	79	53	21	13	28	89
Martinez, Jose, Mets	8	3	1.57	13	13	4	0	92	68	27	16	9	90
*Rumer, Tim, Yankees	6	3	1.70	12	12	2	0	74	34	23	14	6	86
Griffen, Leonard, Reds	4	2	1.71	11	8	1	1	58	44	15	11	9	38
*Vanryn, Ben, Expos	5	3	1.74	10	9	0	0	52	44	13	10	15	56
Garcia, Fermin, Reds	4	0	1.76	21	0	0	2	51	44	12	10	18	25
*Hines, Richard, Yankees	5	2	1.77	11	9	0	0	61	44	18	12	19	73
Perez, Dario, Royals	2	4	1.95	10	10	0	0	51	43	20	11	11	37

ASTROS

BATTING	AVG	G	AB	R	H	2B	3B	HR	RBI	BB	SO	SB
Basey, Marsallis, 2b	.000	1	5	0	0	0	0	0	0	0	0	0
Bennington, Jeff, c	.296	31	71	13	21	8	1	0	12	4	10	1
Cabrera, Ruben, of	.246	20	57	8	14	2	0	0	7	4	15	3
Chavez, Raul, ss-2b	.323	48	155	23	50	8	1	0	23	7	12	5
Christopherson, Gary, 3b-dh	.273	53	187	24	51	12	0	2	31	24	12	4
*Cruz, Ruben, of	.255	39	141	12	36	5	3	0	13	11	2	3
Diggs, Corey, 2b	.275	29	80	16	22	3	2	0	10	14	10	5
#Harley, Al, of	.321	35	109	19	35	6	1	0	12	23	11	17
Jarad, Samir, dh	.000	1	3	0	0	0	0	0	0	0	1	0
Lanfranco, Raphael, c	.217	26	69	6	15	2	0	0	7	10	16	3
#Montero, Alberto, 3b	.262	36	126	21	33	6	0	1	16	13	20	1
Nevers, Tom, ss	.238	50	185	23	44	10	5	2	32	27	38	13
*Petagine, Roberto, 1b	.289	55	187	35	54	5	4	2	24	26	23	9
Pickering, Norbert, dh-1b	.383	16	47	9	18	4	1	0	9	3	8	2
#Reyes, Glen, 2b	.313	20	48	6	15	0	1	0	7	5	7	5
Richison, David, inf	.186	25	43	10	8	0	0	0	8	6	7	7
*Sabino, Guillermo, 2b	.179	10	28	3	5	0	1	0	2	6	7	4
Smith, Lance, c	.271	23	70	12	19	2	0	1	9	13	6	1
Swinton, Jermaine, of	.320	39	122	29	39	8	0	1	12	27	34	15
*Vandemark, John, dh-1b	.217	9	23	2	5	1	0	0	4	8	4	1
Wallace, David, of	.270	50	159	33	43	3	4	0	24	28	21	23
*White, Jimmy, of	.244	52	180	32	44	6	4	0	18	29	50	11

PITCHING	W	L	ERA	G	GS	CG	SV	IP	H	R	ER	BB	SO
August, Sam	4	2	1.53	7	7	0	0	29	25	10	5	2	22
Bennett, Brian	2	1	4.58	22	0	0	0	37	39	23	19	26	22
Black, Scott	0	0	1.50	9	0	0	0	12	11	3	2	4	8
Boatman, Steve	3	4	3.12	13	10	1	0	58	36	23	20	39	50
Brown, Duane	1	2	6.43	4	3	0	0	14	18	10	10	6	12
Bullard, Scott	2	1	1.64	4	0	0	0	11	5	3	2	7	6
Correa, Jorge	1	3	6.12	9	8	0	0	32	25	26	22	23	26
DelaCruz, Juan	4	1	2.15	18	0	0	0	29	21	8	7	5	14
Farmer, Gordon	1	0	0.00	3	3	0	0	12	5	0	0	1	19
Hampton, Mark	0	0	0.00	1	1	0	0	6	4	0	0	2	2
Hernandez, Javier	0	3	3.49	15	0	0	2	28	27	13	11	10	21
Kemp, Doug	0	0	2.45	3	0	0	0	4	1	2	1	3	3
Locke, Joe	0	0	11.57	3	0	0	0	2	4	3	3	3	1
*Mallicoat, Rob	0	1	4.96	7	4	0	0	16	15	15	9	15	21
*Navarro, Luis	3	6	4.72	13	11	1	0	55	49	34	29	42	31
Nieves, Fionel	2	3	5.52	10	7	0	1	31	26	23	19	23	18
*Nix, David	2	1	2.90	13	4	0	1	40	31	18	13	27	30
*Prats, Mario	2	0	3.16	20	1	0	2	43	32	17	15	19	48
*Quaid, John	3	1	2.28	12	1	0	0	28	17	8	7	17	17
*Rinaldi, Kevin	3	0	2.38	13	1	0	0	42	29	17	11	15	29
Vejar, Max	0	1	6.86	13	0	0	0	21	25	19	16	11	13

BRAVES

BATTING	AVG	G	AB	R	H	2B	3B	HR	RBI	BB	SO	SB
Anderson, Tony, c-1b	.273	24	77	7	21	1	0	2	13	2	12	1
Anthony, Alexander, of	.065	17	31	3	2	0	0	1	3	5	15	1
Archer, Carl, p-dh	.222	27	45	3	10	3	0	0	4	5	6	1
Arendt, James, of	.000	3	4	0	0	0	0	0	0	0	2	0
Ayrault, Joe, c	.276	30	87	8	24	2	2	0	12	9	15	1
Chambers, Mark, of	.258	30	66	15	17	0	0	0	2	4	13	12
Correa, Miguel, of	.229	33	109	19	25	6	0	0	10	6	20	10
Ellis, Jason, c	.286	4	7	0	2	0	0	0	1	1	1	0
Garcia, Adrian, c	.234	17	47	2	11	3	0	0	5	2	9	3
*Garr, Ralph Jr., of	.265	21	34	7	9	0	0	0	1	5	8	1
Hurford, Jeff, of	.179	21	56	6	10	0	0	0	3	3	11	3
Jester, Brian, 1b	.277	43	119	23	33	8	1	2	16	23	25	2
#Jones, Chipper, ss	.229	44	140	20	32	1	1	1	18	14	25	5
#Lemke, Mark, 2b-3b	.364	4	11	2	4	0	0	1	5	1	3	0
Marks, Lance, 3b-dh	.230	42	152	19	35	6	0	1	19	8	22	3
Mathis, Cory, of	.212	19	33	5	7	2	0	0	1	2	10	1
Mendez, Miguel, 3b	.180	15	50	6	9	1	0	0	8	8	14	1
Moore, Doyle, of	.182	7	11	0	2	0	0	0	1	0	0	0
Owen, Tommy, c	.217	10	23	1	5	1	0	0	2	3	11	0
Paulino, David, 2b-ss	.216	31	97	13	21	3	1	1	11	2	18	4
Rivera, Melvin, of-3b	.220	24	50	8	11	1	0	0	7	9	21	3
Roa, Hector, 2b-ss	.209	13	43	7	9	1	0	1	2	5	5	4
*Robinson, Don, of	.195	41	118	13	23	3	2	0	15	13	36	5

	AVG	G	AB	R	H	2B	3B	HR	RBI	BB	SO	SB
Robinson, Raul, of	.385	42	135	24	52	6	1	4	22	11	19	11
*Ross, Sean, dh-of	.385	6	26	6	10	1	3	1	3	0	3	0
Santoya, Cristobal, 2b-ss	.410	31	122	21	50	7	1	0	12	5	8	10
*Sly, Kian, of	.185	17	27	3	5	2	0	0	3	2	7	0
*Trevino, Gerald, 2b	.180	23	61	7	11	2	0	0	5	12	15	1
#Waldenberger, David, 3b	.188	35	112	10	21	4	1	0	8	8	22	5
*Walling, Kevin, 1b	.196	38	107	9	21	1	1	2	13	11	27	1

PITCHING	W	L	ERA	G	GS	CG	SV	IP	H	R	ER	BB	SO
Archer, Carl	2	2	2.51	14	3	0	1	28	24	13	8	15	32
Bridges, Brad	1	1	4.08	11	0	0	0	18	23	16	8	11	12
*Bryan, Rusty	0	0	3.60	6	3	0	0	20	17	12	8	10	14
*Creamer, Gerald	1	1	3.86	6	1	0	0	14	14	11	6	6	12
Cronin, Jeff	4	0	2.13	7	5	1	0	38	25	14	9	6	28
Garcia, Franklin	0	2	4.24	7	2	0	0	17	17	8	8	4	6
*Honeycutt, Ron	3	4	2.25	13	10	0	0	52	32	23	13	43	42
Kempfer, Jason	4	0	3.27	16	3	0	0	41	34	19	15	18	28
Koller, Jerry	4	3	2.12	13	8	1	0	51	45	24	12	13	45
Ledwik, Shannon	1	1	1.72	22	0	0	8	31	26	14	6	4	19
Lemon, Don	1	0	2.25	2	2	1	0	12	14	5	3	1	13
Petit, Ricardo	0	0	6.48	6	0	0	0	8	6	9	6	12	6
Potts, Michael	5	2	3.46	23	1	0	4	39	30	23	15	25	39
Rutter, Samuel	3	4	3.59	16	6	1	0	58	54	29	23	17	49
*Smith, Mike	0	0	3.38	7	0	0	0	13	8	5	5	6	12
Spires, Stuart	1	4	3.76	8	5	0	1	26	36	26	11	9	11
Vasquez, Julio	3	5	4.19	13	13	3	0	67	65	36	31	31	47

DODGERS

BATTING	AVG	G	AB	R	H	2B	3B	HR	RBI	BB	SO	SB
Blanco, Henry, 3b	.219	60	178	23	39	8	0	1	19	26	41	7
#Brown, Jimmy, 2b	.204	28	49	9	10	0	0	0	8	13	12	3
*Carroll, Donnie, p-of	.333	21	3	0	1	0	0	0	0	0	0	1
Diaz, Andres, 1b-of	.267	60	191	27	51	6	4	1	30	28	23	12
*Gorman, Dirk, of	.212	27	52	8	11	0	1	1	2	6	12	3
Graves, Randall, ss-2b	.284	57	190	38	54	10	4	0	28	40	42	5
Hoffman, Robert, c	.208	13	24	3	5	0	0	0	2	4	7	1
Kliafas, Steve, ss	.342	20	79	9	27	7	0	0	17	3	5	2
*Macu, Andres, of	.274	38	117	20	32	1	1	2	16	11	37	4
Mota, Domingo, of-2b	.343	61	213	46	73	12	2	1	34	36	19	23
Nurre, Peter, c	.238	29	63	11	15	0	0	0	8	8	12	3
*Perez, Francisco, of	.067	7	15	0	1	0	0	0	0	0	6	0
#Perez, Jose, ss	.217	26	60	12	13	1	0	0	5	15	7	3
*Pinkney, Alton, of	.167	35	90	7	15	2	1	0	7	10	22	4
*Puchales, Javier, of	.200	29	55	7	11	0	0	0	4	7	20	4
Smith, Frank, of	.222	50	162	18	36	3	0	1	17	24	47	6
Sweeney, Robert, c	.125	21	32	1	4	0	0	0	2	4	16	0
Valdez, Jose, c-dh	.320	59	206	31	66	15	1	1	43	22	29	1
#Vandebrake, Kevin, 2b	.247	24	73	17	18	5	0	0	6	7	14	2
Williams, Leroy, of-1b	.313	58	198	25	62	8	0	0	25	26	26	5

PITCHING	W	L	ERA	G	GS	CG	SV	IP	H	R	ER	BB	SO
Botts, Jake	5	5	4.60	15	7	0	1	43	35	26	22	33	50
Broyles, Jason	4	2	2.58	11	11	0	0	59	50	29	17	40	38
*Carroll, Donnie	2	1	4.11	18	4	0	1	46	43	26	21	19	23
Castro, Nelson	3	1	4.25	10	10	0	0	55	65	30	26	7	35
Cruz, Jose	0	4	4.79	17	1	0	0	41	45	24	22	33	35
*Daniel, Keith	2	1	2.86	17	2	0	6	28	16	11	9	18	21
Davis, Greg	2	2	2.88	17	1	0	3	41	29	16	13	23	28
Farnsworth, Ross	3	2	2.60	12	7	1	1	52	33	18	15	22	49
*Maldonado, Albert	6	1	3.71	17	0	0	3	34	43	17	14	6	31
*Matthews, Thomas	5	3	3.69	11	11	1	0	63	69	31	26	20	35
Parra, Jose	5	3	2.67	10	10	1	0	57	50	22	17	18	50
Racobaldo, Mike	1	0	1.26	16	0	0	2	29	22	7	4	8	18

EXPOS

BATTING	AVG	G	AB	R	H	2B	3B	HR	RBI	BB	SO	SB
Andrews, Shane, 3b	.242	56	190	31	46	7	1	3	24	29	46	11
Benitez, Yamil, of	.229	22	83	6	19	1	0	1	5	8	18	0
Callari, Ray, ss-2b	.257	35	113	28	29	4	0	1	11	16	10	6
*Clow, Craig, 1b	.281	46	153	14	43	6	2	1	22	12	35	3

	AVG	G	AB	R	H	2B	3B	HR	RBI	BB	SO	SB
Hardge, Michael, ss-2b ...	.222	53	176	33	39	5	0	1	13	15	43	6
#Jones, Brian, of	.127	36	102	16	13	0	0	0	5	9	36	3
Malinowski, Chris, dh-3b ..	.295	26	78	16	23	3	1	0	14	8	12	2
Murphy, Sean, dh-of	.353	22	68	9	24	4	2	0	9	14	19	1
Ozario, Claudio, 2b	.294	54	204	43	60	9	4	5	30	17	51	9
Pacheco, Gaspar, 1b-c ..	.190	27	79	2	15	3	1	0	9	4	9	2
Pages, Javier, c	.221	34	104	14	23	8	0	2	17	11	27	0
Phillips, Tom, c-1b	.176	15	51	7	9	3	0	0	7	6	16	1
Powell, Corey, dh-p	.181	33	83	6	15	3	0	1	10	3	21	0
Robertson, Stan, of	.224	48	161	25	36	5	3	0	18	5	32	10
*Sanchez, Perry, c	.255	15	51	11	13	1	0	0	7	8	5	1
Santana, Raul, c	.200	5	20	3	4	1	0	0	1	2	4	0
Weimerskirch, Mike, of ...	.317	30	101	22	32	3	1	0	10	8	10	5
White, Rondell, of	.299	57	221	33	66	7	4	5	34	17	33	10

PITCHING	W	L	ERA	G	GS	CG	SV	IP	H	R	ER	BB	SO
Alvarez, Cesar	5	2	2.60	11	10	0	0	52	42	17	15	16	47
Ashley, Duane	2	1	1.17	10	0	0	0	23	13	4	3	9	28
Batista, Miguel	4	3	2.06	9	6	0	0	39	33	16	9	17	21
Clelland, Ricky	2	6	4.50	12	12	0	0	58	51	39	29	36	45
Conley, Matt	1	2	4.15	10	3	0	0	17	18	12	8	12	13
Foster, Kevin	2	0	5.06	4	0	0	0	11	9	6	6	6	11
*Ortega, Oscar	3	1	2.63	20	0	0	3	38	34	12	11	10	21
Pacheco, Alex	1	0	5.19	6	0	0	0	9	11	7	5	4	5
*Perez, Carlos	3	1	2.52	13	2	0	2	36	24	14	10	15	38
Powell, Corey	3	1	4.30	10	9	0	0	52	49	30	25	14	28
Renko, Steve	1	0	1.80	2	0	0	0	5	6	1	1	1	5
*Shehan, Brian	1	1	1.52	16	1	0	3	30	27	9	5	12	25
*Vanryn, Ben	5	3	1.74	10	9	0	0	52	44	13	10	15	56
*White, Gabe	4	2	3.14	11	11	1	0	57	50	21	20	12	41
Whitman, Ryan	1	0	1.17	14	0	0	3	23	14	3	3	0	23
Wicks, Raymond	2	0	3.16	18	0	0	3	31	32	14	11	2	14

INDIANS

BATTING	AVG	G	AB	R	H	2B	3B	HR	RBI	BB	SO	SB
Andujar, Hector, ss	.252	38	119	13	30	4	0	0	12	23	14	6
Ashford, Bubba, c-3b ...	.163	16	43	2	7	0	0	0	5	5	5	0
Bell, David, 3b	.261	30	111	18	29	5	1	0	13	10	8	1
Bryant, Pat, of	.196	17	51	3	10	2	0	0	3	8	18	2
#Carrera, Mahaly, 2b-3b ..	.147	26	75	3	11	2	0	0	9	11	14	1
Cofer, Brian, p-2b	.750	8	4	1	3	1	0	0	0	1	0	0
#Couvertier, Ed, of	.169	31	89	8	15	1	0	1	12	16	8	1
Guerra, Pete, c	.262	38	107	8	28	6	0	0	10	13	15	1
Hamm, Stacy, of	.357	5	14	6	5	0	0	0	1	5	5	4
*Hernandez, Keith, dh-1b ..	.455	5	11	3	5	1	0	1	2	1	2	0
Lachmann, Brian, dh-c ..	.333	5	18	1	6	2	0	0	4	1	1	0
*McCall, Rod, 1b	.278	10	36	5	10	2	0	0	6	5	10	0
*Minter, Larry, of-dh	.203	26	69	6	14	3	0	0	5	4	19	1
Monastero, Frank, 3b-2b ..	.300	22	70	9	21	2	0	0	13	16	11	2
Morgan, James, of	.180	41	133	20	24	4	0	0	10	22	38	13
*Morris, Aaron, 1b	.354	27	96	14	34	5	1	4	17	10	22	2
O'Neil, Barry, of	.200	6	15	1	3	1	0	0	3	2	0	0
Person, Robert, of-dh	.087	24	46	6	4	0	0	0	3	10	12	1
Philyaw, Dino, of	.259	25	81	15	21	3	1	0	3	14	17	15
*Powell, Rick, of	.214	31	70	19	15	3	0	0	8	42	16	14
Ramirez, Omar, of	.172	18	58	6	10	0	0	0	2	11	10	2
Romero, Richard, ss-2b ...	.111	40	126	12	14	1	1	0	3	17	26	9
*Schultz, Bobby, of	.264	31	87	9	23	3	0	0	8	14	18	5
Schwartz, Brian, c	.140	24	57	5	8	0	0	0	4	14	13	0
Shirley, Mike, of	.080	7	25	1	2	0	1	0	4	3	10	2
Smith, Rob, 2b	.333	20	57	11	19	2	0	0	7	20	11	2
Sued, Nick, c	.229	11	35	0	8	1	0	0	2	2	8	0
Thomas, Tim, 1b	.239	19	71	10	17	2	0	2	9	2	23	6
Whitehurst, Todd, dh-ss ..	.273	7	11	1	3	0	1	0	2	7	4	0
*Wilson, Dwayne, 3b-1b ...	.164	43	140	25	23	0	3	1	10	25	28	5

PITCHING	W	L	ERA	G	GS	CG	SV	IP	H	R	ER	BB	SO
Cofer, Brian	1	1	0.96	7	2	1	0	28	10	6	3	13	21
Crawford, Carlos	2	3	4.36	10	9	0	0	54	68	43	26	25	39
Day, Kenny	1	3	3.55	19	1	0	1	51	56	31	20	17	32
*Ferran, Alex	0	4	11.22	12	5	0	0	22	25	34	27	27	22
Fleet, Joseph	1	6	6.65	12	7	1	0	45	46	38	33	44	31
*Hasenzahl, Kirk	2	3	5.23	20	3	0	0	53	63	40	31	34	38
Hernandez, Fernando	4	4	4.00	11	11	2	0	70	61	36	31	30	43
*Langdon, Tim	3	2	0.61	6	4	0	0	29	21	10	2	12	20
Morgan, Scott	2	0	0.69	6	0	0	1	13	5	1	1	7	10
Person, Robert	0	2	7.36	8	0	0	2	7	10	7	6	4	8
Rosado, Jose	0	1	6.48	3	2	0	0	8	15	11	6	5	2
Sawyer, Rick	3	1	2.87	22	0	0	5	38	32	16	12	10	30
Sides, Craig	0	1	9.45	3	3	0	0	7	7	7	7	11	3
Sweeney, Mark	2	6	3.15	10	10	1	0	60	45	34	21	36	50
Winiarski, Chip	2	3	4.62	13	6	1	1	51	59	39	26	19	35

METS

BATTING	AVG	G	AB	R	H	2B	3B	HR	RBI	BB	SO	SB
#Allison, Tom, 2b	.000	1	4	0	0	0	0	0	0	0	1	0
Casanova, Raul, c	.077	23	65	4	5	0	0	1	4	16	0

BATTING

R	Amadoz Arias, Reds	46
	Domingo Mota, Dodgers	46
H	Domingo Mota, Dodgers	73
TB	Rondell White, Expos	97
2B	Jose Valdez, Dodgers	15
	Peter Laake, Rangers	15
3B	David Schmidt, Red Sox	8
HR	James Dismuke, Reds	7
RBI	Jose Valdez, Dodgers	43
SH	Three tied at	7
SF	Steven Thomas, Reds	5
	Tom Houk, Twins	5
BB	Rick Powell, Indians	42
IBB	James Dismuke, Reds	5
HBP	Three tied at	8
SO	Paul Meyer, Mets	62
SB	David Lowery, Rangers	37
CS	Domingo Mota, Dodgers	15
OB%	Domingo Mota, Dodgers	.453

PITCHING

G	Danny Miceli, Royals	27
GS	Several tied at	13
CG	Melvin Gonzales, Red Sox	4
	Jose Martinez, Mets	4
ShO	Jose Martinez, Mets	2
Sv	Tony Bouton, Rangers	16
W	Melvin Gonzales, Red Sox	9
L	Glenn Coombs, Pirates	8
	Joe Borowski, White Sox	8
IP	Jose Martinez, Mets	92
	Melvin Gonzales, RS	92
H	Melvin Gonzales, RS	88
R	Joe Borowski, White Sox	47
HR	Chip Winiarski, Indians	5
	Dave Giberti, Rangers	5
BB	Jackie Abel, Twins	62
HB	Three tied at	8
SO	Jose Martinez, Mets	90
WP	Samuel Rutter, Braves	12
	Daniel Tobin, Reds	12
Bk	Troy Hooper, Pirates	11

	AVG	G	AB	R	H	2B	3B	HR	RBI	BB	SO	SB
*Daubach, Bryan, 1b-dh	.270	45	152	26	41	8	4	1	19	22	41	2
Davis, Darwin, 3b	.309	30	94	10	29	5	2	2	13	10	16	4
Garcia, Guillermo, 2b-3b	.184	42	136	9	25	1	2	0	6	7	34	1
Hernandez, Rafael, 3b-ss	.198	28	86	6	17	1	0	0	5	7	21	4
Luciano, Sullivan, of	.181	46	160	19	29	2	0	4	13	11	35	3
Meyer, Paul, 1b-dh	.215	46	177	18	38	7	4	1	20	12	62	4
Mompres, Danilo, ss	.193	50	187	26	36	4	2	2	19	13	47	9
Moreno, Juan, of	.208	32	77	7	16	3	1	0	5	15	31	4
Patrizi, Mike, c	.178	29	90	7	16	3	0	0	7	7	34	6
*Quillin, Ty, c	.134	34	119	10	16	2	0	0	5	12	23	1
#Smith, Demond, of	.261	46	153	19	40	9	2	1	7	20	34	17
Steele, Steve, c	.311	15	45	6	14	0	0	0	3	5	8	1
Tolliver, Jerome, of	.272	55	184	26	50	5	4	5	37	30	36	16
#Veras, Quilvio, 2b	.296	30	98	26	29	3	3	1	5	19	16	16
Williams, Charles, c	.182	5	11	0	2	1	0	0	1	0	4	1
#Williams, Terrell, ss	.186	18	43	6	8	0	1	0	1	4	16	1

PITCHING	W	L	ERA	G	GS	CG	SV	IP	H	R	ER	BB	SO
Belmonte, Pedro	3	2	2.62	18	3	0	1	45	36	23	13	17	28
Corbell, Eric	1	3	2.02	17	3	0	4	36	35	15	8	10	19
Hernandez, Hermes	0	0	7.45	7	1	0	0	10	18	12	8	7	5
Langan, Richard	2	2	4.44	12	1	0	0	26	24	17	13	12	26
Lehnerz, Mike	0	0	0.00	3	0	0	0	0	0	0	0	2	0
*Lindsay, Darian	0	1	2.89	6	0	0	2	9	7	4	3	2	11
Manfred, Jim	1	3	3.18	14	3	0	3	40	31	16	14	17	28
Martinez, Jose	8	3	1.57	13	13	4	0	92	68	27	16	9	90
Ramirez, Hector	3	5	4.09	11	8	1	0	51	54	34	24	21	43
Schorr, Brad	2	3	2.97	12	8	0	3	58	44	23	19	7	47
Seymour, Steve	3	1	1.91	9	6	0	0	33	34	19	7	13	27
*Smith, Ottis	6	5	1.36	13	13	3	0	79	53	21	12	28	89
Wegmann, Tom	0	0	0.00	1	0	0	0	1	0	0	0	0	3
Williams, Scotty	0	2	2.73	15	1	0	1	30	23	15	9	11	16

PIRATES

BATTING	AVG	G	AB	R	H	2B	3B	HR	RBI	BB	SO	SB
*Arace, Pascual, of	.212	36	99	10	21	3	0	0	10	4	15	7
Calder, Joseph, 1b	.237	57	211	17	50	9	2	4	34	12	50	6
*Capriotti, Joe, of	.234	33	77	6	18	1	0	0	7	9	8	2
#Cintron, Miguel, 3b	.133	34	113	10	15	1	1	0	6	7	20	3
Colon, Angel, ss-2b	.228	39	101	6	23	3	0	0	10	2	13	2
*Conger, Jeffrey, of	.183	46	120	19	22	3	1	0	6	17	52	4
*Davis, Brad, c	.212	35	66	4	14	2	0	0	5	8	12	2
Gallego, Chris, 2b	.238	38	105	11	25	6	0	0	9	7	7	2
Hinson, Dean, c	.177	36	79	7	14	2	0	0	9	4	15	0
House, Jeffrey, dh-3b	.284	55	201	25	57	13	2	2	20	16	39	4
Leavell, Barry, of	.245	39	106	15	26	4	1	0	7	3	25	1
#Martinez, Javier, 2b	.150	18	20	2	3	0	0	0	1	0	4	1
Martinez, Ramon, ss	.362	15	58	8	21	2	1	0	5	2	6	2
McLin, Joseph, 1b-dh	.189	31	95	17	18	3	1	1	8	13	26	1
#Mitchell, Antonio, of	.294	44	102	18	30	4	2	3	13	8	21	3
Nixon, Jason, c	.222	32	63	6	14	1	1	0	5	4	11	3
*Peppers, Cedrick, of	.194	48	139	7	27	1	0	0	6	8	27	5
Perez, William, of	.250	5	12	4	3	1	0	0	1	0	2	0
Rodriguez, Hector, 3b-ss	.241	17	58	9	14	1	1	1	6	3	10	0
Schaefer, Cory, of	.273	26	55	6	15	0	0	0	4	4	19	2
Sondrini, Joseph, 2b	.358	24	53	9	19	2	0	0	10	4	12	4
Tooch, Charles, ss-2b	.246	43	122	14	30	6	0	0	7	6	31	3

PITCHING	W	L	ERA	G	GS	CG	SV	IP	H	R	ER	BB	SO
*Arias, Alexander	3	1	2.30	17	0	0	0	27	21	9	7	12	26

	W	L	ERA	G	GS	CG	SV	IP	H	R	ER	BB	SO
Bradley, Dave	3	5	3.73	10	9	0	0	51	56	30	21	12	29
Coombs, Glenn	1	8	5.02	12	11	1	0	52	66	39	29	20	47
Fajardo, Hector	1	1	3.86	5	4	0	0	21	23	10	9	8	17
French, Tim	1	6	4.40	14	8	0	0	47	40	29	23	26	42
*Gobel, Donnie	1	2	4.05	18	1	0	3	33	29	21	15	16	43
Goytia, Victor	1	1	4.76	11	0	0	0	17	23	12	9	12	5
Hooper, Troy	3	5	2.71	13	13	2	0	66	56	29	20	22	67
Hunter, Bobby	0	2	2.06	9	5	0	2	35	17	13	8	14	30
Mejia, Juan	0	0	67.50	1	0	0	0	1	1	5	5	4	0
Pike, David	0	1	6.17	8	0	0	1	12	12	10	8	7	12
*Ramirez, Roberto	2	1	0.53	11	3	0	0	34	20	4	2	18	27
Shade, Derek	0	0	7.50	4	0	0	0	6	7	7	5	6	4
Sosa, Jose	2	2	4.82	16	1	0	0	37	42	27	20	13	15
Sparks, Shane	3	1	3.51	16	2	0	1	41	39	18	16	14	19
*Way, Ron	1	0	1.80	12	0	0	4	15	13	6	3	1	15
White, Rick	3	1	0.50	7	6	0	0	36	26	11	2	4	27

RANGERS

BATTING	AVG	G	AB	R	H	2B	3B	HR	RBI	BB	SO	SB
#Antoine, Junior, of	.212	17	52	3	11	1	0	0	4	1	16	1
#Crespo, Michael, c	.429	5	14	3	6	1	2	0	5	2	2	0
Douglas, Arthur, of	.500	2	4	0	2	0	0	0	0	0	2	0
Evangelista, George, 2b-3b	.219	32	105	13	23	3	1	0	9	7	21	1
*Flinn, Geoff, dh	.207	20	58	5	12	1	1	1	7	9	13	0
Gonzalez, Efrain, of	.135	33	89	9	12	1	0	0	11	4	17	2
*Haughney, Trevor, of	.214	48	140	18	30	5	0	0	12	19	37	14
Hodge, Lee, 2b	.264	54	193	27	51	11	2	1	25	6	19	14
Holland, Sidney, dh-of	.213	53	174	20	37	3	4	2	24	22	35	14
*Jones, Lance, of-dh	.247	29	97	14	24	3	0	0	6	8	20	11
*Laake, Peter, 1b	.322	64	214	36	69	15	2	1	37	39	38	2
*Lindsay, Jon, c	.134	21	67	2	9	1	0	0	2	1	12	0
#Lowery, David, 3b	.300	62	240	41	72	8	0	0	18	27	14	40
McMullan, Chris, c	.246	24	57	6	14	0	0	0	2	11	8	0
#Parra, Franklin, ss	.259	37	116	11	30	2	1	0	9	4	28	9
Texidor, Jose, of	.232	50	168	29	39	5	3	1	19	20	23	3
Turco, Frank, ss	.300	5	10	1	3	1	0	0	1	1	2	0
Williams, Cliff, c	.219	28	64	8	14	2	0	0	7	8	15	2
*Wiseman, Greg, of	.212	34	99	8	21	5	2	0	10	8	24	2
Woodall, Kevin, ss	.141	30	92	9	13	1	0	0	3	3	12	3

PITCHING	W	L	ERA	G	GS	CG	SV	IP	H	R	ER	BB	SO
Ayala, Jason	2	5	6.82	18	0	0	2	32	34	27	24	21	31
Berthau, Terrell	4	1	2.33	12	4	0	0	39	38	12	10	7	24
Bouton, Tony	4	1	0.94	26	0	0	17	29	19	6	3	9	45
Cain, Tim	0	3	3.75	16	1	0	1	36	27	22	15	5	37
Devaughan, Jeff	2	1	1.27	15	1	0	3	28	23	7	4	14	26
*Devereaux, Brandon	0	0	16.20	1	0	0	0	2	5	3	3	0	1
Duval, Avery	1	0	5.65	6	2	0	0	14	24	12	9	1	13
*Giberti, Dave	4	5	2.66	13	12	0	0	64	59	29	19	16	60
Henson, Micky	0	1	3.86	4	4	0	0	12	9	6	5	7	8
*Holcomb, Lou	1	0	5.40	2	0	0	0	3	4	2	2	1	3
Johnson, Johnny	1	1	2.82	15	0	0	0	22	25	8	7	10	27
*Kunz, Richard	2	2	2.86	9	2	0	0	22	17	10	7	9	20
Madrigal, Victor	3	1	2.11	12	9	0	0	47	40	13	11	10	43
McGough, Keith	4	2	2.73	13	11	1	0	59	44	20	18	17	48
*Oliver, Darren	0	0	0.00	3	3	0	0	6	1	1	0	1	7
Phillips, Brad	0	0	0.00	3	0	0	1	6	6	0	0	1	6
*Quero, Juan	5	1	2.12	13	11	1	0	64	59	18	15	8	54
Rhoades, Troy	1	0	4.30	8	1	0	0	15	18	12	7	4	4
Stafford, Tim	2	1	2.25	8	3	0	1	28	20	8	7	6	16
Watson, Andy	0	2	5.74	10	0	0	0	16	19	13	10	7	11

REDS

BATTING	AVG	G	AB	R	H	2B	3B	HR	RBI	BB	SO	SB
#Arias, Amadoz, 2b	.254	61	248	46	63	8	3	1	27	21	37	25
Aubin, Kevin, c-dh	.154	5	13	1	2	0	0	0	1	0	4	0
Burris, Pierre, of	.242	52	194	27	47	5	0	0	10	20	30	21
*Cabral, Irene, of	.230	48	126	21	29	1	0	0	9	21	34	5
Cartagena, Ivan, 1b	.152	32	99	11	15	3	0	1	5	3	18	2
*Dismuke, James, 1b	.355	39	124	22	44	8	4	7	28	28	8	3
Duncan, Enrique, of-2b ..	.217	15	46	6	10	2	0	0	5	2	13	5
Gianni, Guy, c	.250	2	4	1	1	0	0	0	0	0	0	0
Gibralter, Steve, of	.259	52	174	26	45	11	3	4	27	23	30	9
*Giegling, Matt, c-1b	.286	53	189	21	54	11	1	3	37	14	20	1
Graham, Derrick, of-ss ...	.168	44	125	20	21	2	0	0	7	20	28	10
Hammond, Greg, of	.200	42	130	12	26	6	0	0	6	20	20	6
Hernandez, Ramon, ss ...	.222	60	221	22	49	10	1	4	29	12	47	4
Loyola, Juan, of	.086	29	70	3	6	1	0	1	5	10	24	0
Munoz, Jesus, c	.333	2	3	0	1	0	0	0	1	0	0	0
#Perna, Bobby, 3b-of	.290	46	169	29	49	6	1	2	31	25	22	5
Thomas, Steven, 3b	.236	49	174	25	41	9	1	3	18	18	47	12

PITCHING	W	L	ERA	G	GS	CG	SV	IP	H	R	ER	BB	SO
Balentine, Brian	2	3	5.03	12	10	0	0	48	48	33	27	33	44
Brothers, John	1	3	5.55	17	1	0	3	36	40	28	22	16	37
*Diaz, Rafael	4	1	5.95	13	4	0	1	39	44	29	26	23	32
Fenton, Todd	1	2	12.86	10	1	0	1	14	24	20	20	9	4

	W	L	ERA	G	GS	CG	SV	IP	H	R	ER	BB	SO
Garcia, Fermin	4	0	1.76	21	0	0	2	51	44	12	10	18	25
Griffen, Leonard	4	2	1.71	11	8	1	1	58	44	15	11	9	38
Langford, Rich	3	3	2.35	15	0	0	2	31	27	10	8	17	27
McClain, Charles	4	2	2.76	12	12	0	0	65	44	27	20	38	57
Roper, John	7	2	0.97	13	13	0	0	74	41	10	8	31	76
Tobin, Daniel	3	3	4.11	13	13	0	0	57	54	38	26	36	26
Vivas, Domingo	0	5	3.29	23	0	0	12	38	41	17	14	8	18
Wiggins, James	2	0	2.56	14	0	0	1	32	26	13	9	21	8
Wyatt, Charles	1	1	9.30	11	2	0	0	20	26	26	21	25	10

RED SOX

BATTING	AVG	G	AB	R	H	2B	3B	HR	RBI	BB	SO	SB
Awkard, Herman, of	.263	8	19	4	5	2	0	0	1	1	5	1
#Berni, Denny, 1b-dh	.258	24	93	11	24	5	0	0	11	12	11	0
#Bethea, Scott, ss-3b	.236	43	161	24	38	4	0	0	8	31	21	6
Borrero, Rikchy, c	.211	34	109	13	23	6	0	1	10	16	28	0
Chick, Bruce, of	.323	24	93	12	30	5	2	1	23	12	11	4
Colon, Felix, 1b	.278	29	108	22	30	11	0	1	22	16	21	0
Crimmins, John, c-dh	.258	31	97	16	25	1	3	2	13	13	18	0
Dekneef, Mike, ss-2b	.249	47	189	25	47	7	1	0	17	20	25	8
Dorante, Lou, dh	.333	5	9	2	3	0	0	0	2	2	1	0
Feno, Quinn, of	.169	26	71	10	12	0	0	0	8	9	16	0
Fowler, Jake, 1b	.178	41	146	20	26	5	0	1	10	11	24	0
#Graham, Greg, 3b-ss	.226	26	93	16	21	2	0	0	11	21	13	1
Guzman, Eddie, dh-3b	.195	13	41	5	8	1	0	0	4	0	6	1
Marin, Jose, ss	.226	15	31	3	7	1	0	0	4	1	8	0
McKeel, Walt, c-dh	.250	13	44	2	11	3	0	0	6	3	8	0
*Mitchell, Tim, 1b	.000	3	7	0	0	0	0	0	0	0	3	0
*Norris, Bill, 3b	.309	28	97	20	30	7	0	0	13	20	13	2
*Rappoli, Paul, of	.284	53	162	31	46	4	0	1	22	34	16	4
#Schmidt, David, 2b	.322	50	180	44	58	8	8	0	28	37	36	3
Soto, Emirson, of-c	.254	39	126	19	32	2	1	0	16	13	17	3
Tackett, Tim, c	.056	6	18	3	1	1	0	0	3	2	5	0
Vann, Troy, of	.192	8	26	7	5	1	0	0	2	3	8	0
Witherspoon, Richard, of ...	.200	11	40	5	8	0	0	0	2	3	11	1
Younker, Jason, of	.231	47	156	27	36	4	3	1	27	25	53	6

PITCHING	W	L	ERA	G	GS	CG	SV	IP	H	R	ER	BB	SO
Allen, Tracy	0	3	8.47	7	2	0	2	17	23	17	16	11	14
Anacki, Paul	0	1	6.46	12	4	0	0	23	32	20	17	13	20
Brown, Ernie	0	1	8.05	10	1	0	0	19	21	20	17	23	18
Burgo, Dale	2	1	1.55	5	5	1	0	29	22	7	5	9	18
Centeno, Luis	2	2	6.25	16	1	0	1	41	52	35	28	23	21
Curry, Steve	1	2	2.57	3	3	0	0	14	11	5	4	2	12
Delgado, Richard	4	5	3.59	25	0	0	6	53	54	25	21	14	30
Gonzales, Melvin	9	1	3.04	14	12	4	0	92	88	45	31	22	42
Kite, Dan	0	1	12.27	4	0	0	0	4	3	5	5	13	3
Konopki, Mark	0	0	9.00	1	0	0	0	1	2	1	1	1	1
Lemaster, Matt	0	2	11.05	9	1	0	0	15	19	20	18	10	7
*Maloney, Ryan	7	0	2.26	17	8	0	2	64	52	20	16	35	28
Miller, Todd	2	0	0.64	3	2	0	0	14	6	1	1	5	10
*Mitchelson, Mark	2	2	3.92	5	1	0	0	21	19	10	9	6	15
*Mosley, Tony	0	0	0.00	2	0	0	0	4	1	0	0	1	4
Niemeyer, Bryan	3	3	3.56	14	7	2	0	66	64	32	26	31	20
Painter, Gary	2	0	1.38	5	5	1	0	33	23	8	5	9	27
Powers, Terry	0	1	2.77	3	3	0	0	13	10	5	4	3	10
Sosa, Juan	0	4	5.19	12	8	0	0	43	60	35	25	27	15

ROYALS

BATTING	AVG	G	AB	R	H	2B	3B	HR	RBI	BB	SO	SB
#Andrews, Jay, of-dh	.277	33	112	15	31	4	3	4	21	15	24	6
Burton, Darren, of	.207	15	58	10	12	0	1	0	2	4	17	6
Cerda, Jose, 3b	.118	16	34	3	4	1	0	0	2	2	7	1
Day, George, 2b-3b	.291	57	196	27	57	5	1	0	19	23	24	12
Ebanks, Weddison, of	.207	11	29	4	6	0	0	0	5	3	9	3
Garcia, Francisco, of	.481	7	27	5	13	2	0	0	7	4	1	0
Gerald, Ed, of	.216	15	51	8	11	1	2	1	5	6	15	5
Hennessey, Scott, of	.313	48	160	21	50	7	1	0	14	21	18	6
#Indriago, Juan, 3b-2b	.161	41	124	16	20	2	0	0	9	24	19	11
#Isava, Jesus, c-dh	.202	31	84	4	17	4	2	0	11	6	21	2
Jabalera, Miguel, ss-3b	.123	25	57	4	7	2	0	0	5	5	10	0
Jennings, Lance, c	.292	15	48	4	14	4	0	0	5	4	12	0
Mays, Terrance, of	.125	45	104	20	13	2	0	0	7	20	33	11
Melendez, Luis, of	.252	37	111	9	28	3	0	0	9	5	23	3
#Morillo, Cesar, ss	.270	55	185	21	50	6	2	1	17	22	45	7
Newhouse, Andre, of	.200	20	40	7	8	3	0	0	2	12	15	0
*Perez, Pablo, 1b	.192	53	151	22	29	7	3	0	9	32	35	6
Schreiner, John, 1b-3b	.361	24	83	11	30	10	1	3	20	10	16	9
#Smith, Thomas, of-3b	.142	39	134	11	19	4	1	0	4	11	49	7
Stewart, Andy, dh-3b	.192	21	52	5	10	4	0	0	1	9	13	3
Strickland, Chad, c	.221	50	163	14	36	7	0	0	12	11	24	6

PITCHING	W	L	ERA	G	GS	CG	SV	IP	H	R	ER	BB	SO
Baaske, Keith	1	2	4.63	15	0	0	5	23	22	12	12	16	13
Berumen, Andres	0	2	2.38	5	4	0	1	23	24	9	6	8	18
*Brea, Julio	0	1	1.32	6	0	0	0	14	9	5	2	1	9
Budnick, Alan	1	5	5.59	18	5	0	1	37	50	34	23	23	12

	W	L	ERA	G	GS	CG	SV	IP	H	R	ER	BB	SO
Chrisman, Jim	2	0	3.86	8	0	0	1	16	14	8	7	8	10
Foster, Clint	0	1	8.35	9	3	0	0	18	18	18	17	20	11
Fyock, Wade	1	2	2.45	11	10	0	0	55	49	24	15	30	27
Henn, Jonathan	2	1	4.91	13	0	0	0	18	18	12	10	17	13
Jacobs, John	1	1	1.77	11	0	0	0	20	20	11	4	16	19
Lee, Anthony	4	3	4.47	12	12	0	0	54	57	29	27	36	36
Lee, Thomas	3	3	2.90	14	6	0	1	50	43	25	16	34	37
Miceli, Danny	3	4	3.91	27	0	0	4	53	45	27	23	29	48
Perez, Dario	2	4	1.95	10	10	0	0	51	43	20	11	11	37
Stewart, Reggie	1	3	6.98	13	0	0	0	19	13	18	15	21	14
Toth, Robert	2	2	1.66	7	7	0	0	38	34	8	7	4	22
West, Eric	2	4	4.42	16	7	0	0	55	37	31	27	46	34

TWINS

BATTING	AVG	G	AB	R	H	2B	3B	HR	RBI	BB	SO	SB
#Blanco, Pedro, ss	.202	34	104	11	21	0	1	0	5	8	27	10
Brown, Alvin, c-of	.286	36	112	18	32	2	3	0	15	12	45	6
Caridad, Ron, p-dh	.167	10	18	2	3	1	0	0	0	2	3	0
#Cummings, Midre, of	.316	47	177	28	56	3	4	5	28	13	32	13
#Evans, Glenn, 3b-of	.175	41	126	13	22	2	1	0	7	12	35	2
Fernandez, Manuel, 2b	.000	2	1	0	0	0	0	0	0	0	1	0
Fimbres, Javier, 1b-c	.246	48	142	20	35	10	0	1	11	24	18	1
#Hawkins, Craig, 2b	.217	37	129	16	28	3	2	0	8	4	35	9
Hayes, Allen, of-dh	.145	27	76	8	11	3	2	0	9	6	47	1
Hoerner, Troy, dh-of	.278	40	126	22	35	4	4	3	21	11	44	2
Houk, Tom, 3b-1b	.344	46	157	25	54	10	5	3	37	22	18	3
King, Karl, c	.120	33	75	7	9	3	0	0	5	6	16	0
#Moore, Tim, of	.260	27	77	19	20	2	3	3	15	13	24	6
#Norman, Ken, of	.252	44	131	22	33	6	2	1	9	9	47	24
*Ogden, Jamie, 1b	.198	28	101	11	20	1	2	0	5	7	41	2
Portu, Richard, of	.168	37	101	10	17	3	2	0	8	10	37	0
Prater, Steve, c	.000	1	1	0	0	0	0	0	0	0	0	0
Ramirez, Francisco, c	.160	27	81	7	13	1	0	0	8	4	19	1
Rivera, David, 2b-3b	.252	40	127	29	32	5	1	0	8	13	35	25
Rumsey, Derrell, of	.176	39	136	15	24	2	1	0	8	11	25	8
Valette, Ramon, ss	.257	34	109	12	28	2	0	0	10	2	21	3

PITCHING	W	L	ERA	G	GS	CG	SV	IP	H	R	ER	BB	SO
Abel, Jackie	3	2	2.74	23	9	0	1	69	49	35	21	63	61
Asp, Bryan	4	3	4.62	13	8	1	2	51	57	32	26	21	41
*Berson, Candido	0	0	8.53	5	0	0	0	6	9	8	6	3	5
Caridad, Ron	0	0	7.71	5	1	0	0	7	5	6	6	8	2
Correa, Jose	4	5	4.55	14	8	1	0	59	55	37	30	13	47
Fritz, Scott	2	2	3.44	8	6	1	0	37	26	18	14	17	31
Hayes, Allen	0	0	6.00	3	0	0	0	6	9	7	4	9	5
Hoppe, Denny	4	1	2.76	9	7	1	0	49	51	23	15	9	28
Juarbe, Javier	2	4	4.50	23	0	0	4	48	51	31	24	13	52
Landis, Kipp	4	3	3.17	18	1	0	0	48	47	22	17	8	23
Lindaman, Chad	2	1	4.50	10	1	0	1	18	18	10	9	8	8
Mieses, Melanio	0	5	3.58	25	3	0	11	38	38	28	15	13	24
Roskom, Bryan	4	2	1.39	10	6	0	0	45	33	19	7	14	46
Taylor, Kerry	3	1	3.57	14	13	1	0	63	57	37	25	33	59

WHITE SOX

BATTING	AVG	G	AB	R	H	2B	3B	HR	RBI	BB	SO	SB
Andujar, Robert, of-2b	.214	36	117	15	25	4	1	1	9	10	38	11
Coachman, James, 3b	.218	57	193	20	42	9	0	1	12	21	43	10
#Durham, Ray, 2b	.276	35	116	18	32	3	3	0	13	15	36	23
Garcia, Manuel, of-dh	.240	7	25	2	6	1	1	1	5	3	2	0
Gilligan, Lawrence, ss-2b	.158	19	57	3	9	3	0	0	7	6	10	0
*Green-Shornock, Tim, 1b	.225	44	138	10	31	2	4	0	17	14	21	10
Guzman, Ramon, of	.119	36	101	8	12	3	0	0	6	9	33	4
*Jackson, Muzzy, 1b	.227	33	88	11	20	2	0	0	5	15	24	1
#James, Nathaniel, of-2b	.146	41	103	15	15	2	0	0	4	9	33	7
*McGough, Greg, c-1b	.181	28	72	13	13	2	0	1	6	8	24	3
*Moye, Wayne, of	.218	27	78	11	17	5	0	0	3	2	16	5
Poe, Charles, of-dh	.177	46	147	13	26	3	2	0	15	16	38	11
Robledo, Nilson, c	.190	35	105	10	20	3	0	4	11	5	34	4
Sheppard, Don, of	.179	46	151	15	27	6	1	0	6	12	40	12
Story, Jonathan, ss-3b	.282	44	149	25	42	7	1	1	22	15	40	6
Taylor, Jonathan, c	.143	18	35	2	5	0	0	0	0	4	10	1
#Vogel, Michael, c-dh	.175	43	103	13	18	5	0	0	7	31	26	5
Wilson, Brandon, ss-2b	.268	11	41	4	11	1	0	0	5	4	5	3
Zarate, Vince, of-ss	.187	42	123	12	23	3	1	0	10	18	27	6

PITCHING	W	L	ERA	G	GS	CG	SV	IP	H	R	ER	BB	SO
*Altaffer, Todd	1	0	3.09	6	0	0	2	12	10	7	4	3	14
Baldwin, James	1	6	4.10	9	7	0	0	37	32	29	17	18	32
Bere, Jason	0	4	2.37	16	2	0	1	38	26	19	10	19	41
Borowski, Joe	2	8	5.58	12	11	0	0	61	74	47	38	25	67
Cortes, Conde	0	0	0.64	6	1	0	1	14	12	2	1	3	17
Culberson, Donald	0	1	1.59	3	0	0	0	6	6	1	0	1	9
DelaCruz, Carlos	0	0	0.00	3	2	0	0	8	7	0	0	1	9
Dinuzzo, Jeff	0	0	0.00	3	0	0	1	5	0	0	0	1	9
Dorsey, Carl	0	0	0.00	1	0	0	0	1	1	1	0	0	0
Fernandez, Alex	1	0	3.60	2	2	0	0	10	11	4	4	1	16
*Fritz, Greg	0	1	3.80	12	0	0	1	24	32	14	10	4	17

	W	L	ERA	G	GS	CG	SV	IP	H	R	ER	BB	SO
Hoey, Andrew	2	1	0.45	9	0	0	1	20	7	5		1	17
Hulme, Pat	1	1	2.18	10	0	0	1	20	17	8	5	8	18
Jean, Domingo	2	5	2.29	13	13	1	0	79	55	32	20	16	65
*Locklear, Dean	0	2	4.07	14	0	0	1	24	25	17	11	7	29
*Marshall, Ted	2	1	3.56	14	5	0	1	44	36	20	17	13	33
McGraw, Walter	4	6	3.44	10	10	0	0	50	49	32	19	21	33
Micucci, Ron	0	1	5.14	4	0	0	0	7	5	4	4	10	4
Middaugh, Scott	0	0	2.25	2	0	0	0	4	3	1	1	1	5
Perigny, Donald	1	1	0.54	7	1	0	3	17	9	1	1	6	19
Ruiz, Jorge	1	0	1.42	7	0	0	1	13	19	7	2	5	10
Smith, Roosevelt	1	3	3.50	7	7	0	0	36	26	23	14	20	35
Vanderwel, Bill	0	1	0.00	2	0	0	0	2	2	2	0	1	2
Wickman, Bob	2	0	2.45	2	2	0	0	11	7	4	3	1	15

YANKEES

BATTING	AVG	G	AB	R	H	2B	3B	HR	RBI	BB	SO	SB
Cerone, Rick, c	.143	3	7	0	1	0	0	0	0	0	1	0
Cooper, Tim, 3b-ss	.268	53	179	27	48	9	3	2	22	27	39	7
#Cumberbatch, Abdiel, of	.197	45	122	13	24	1	0	1	4	21	39	11
Demerson, Tim, of	.223	42	139	15	31	8	1	1	14	12	19	9
#Eberly, Ryan, 2b	.179	17	39	2	7	1	0	0	3	10	1	1
#Everett, Carl, of	.259	48	185	28	48	8	5	1	14	15	38	15
Felix, Nathanael, 2b	.226	42	133	19	30	0	1	0	11	21	22	7
Figga, Michael, c	.285	40	123	19	35	1	1	2	18	17	33	4
Harris, Adolfo, of-dh	.236	39	127	11	30	3	2	1	22	7	35	0
*Ledee, Ricardo, of	.108	19	37	5	4	2	0	0	1	6	18	2
Leon, Johnny, dh-3b	.294	54	204	40	60	10	1	1	25	22	20	4
Matouzas, Jeff, c	.146	29	82	9	12	0	0	1	9	15	34	1
Salcedo, Edwin, c-dh	.152	16	33	0	5	2	1	0	2	1	16	1
Sanchez, Daniel, ss-2b	.186	14	43	5	8	2	0	0	2	1	12	0
*Seefried, Tate, 1b	.157	52	178	15	28	3	0	0	20	22	53	2
*Smith, Tom, 2b	.258	9	31	5	8	2	1	0	4	2	8	0
Spencer, Shane, of	.184	42	147	20	27	4	0	0	7	20	23	11
Turrentine, Rich, ss-2b	.211	50	171	18	36	4	3	1	15	17	48	4

PITCHING	W	L	ERA	G	GS	CG	SV	IP	H	R	ER	BB	SO
*Dunbar, Matt	0	0	3.00	3	0	0	1	6	4	2	2	3	7
Faw, Brian	7	5	2.13	12	12	1	0	80	56	27	19	16	66
Gilbert, Brent	0	2	3.50	10	1	0	2	18	15	9	7	5	16
Hayes, Jim	1	0	4.15	11	0	0	1	13	3	9	6	19	24
*Hines, Richard	5	2	1.77	11	9	0	0	61	44	18	12	19	73
*Kindall, Scott	0	1	5.68	4	0	0	0	6	8	4	4	1	6
Laviano, Frank	1	3	4.61	17	1	0	0	27	36	21	14	17	14
Rivera, Mariano	5	1	0.17	22	1	1	1	52	17	3	1	7	58
*Rumer, Tim	6	3	1.70	12	12	2	0	74	34	23	14	21	88
Santaella, Alexis	3	2	3.35	14	5	0	0	38	30	19	14	23	39
Santiago, Sandi	1	1	1.82	23	0	0	4	40	38	13	8	7	27
*Seiler, Stuart	2	1	2.18	16	0	0	4	21	18	5	5	3	23
Smith, Mike S.	0	2	5.09	6	6	0	0	23	22	21	13	18	12
Springer, Russell	0	2	1.20	4	4	0	0	15	10	6	2	4	17
Thibert, John	1	5	4.67	13	11	0	0	54	53	41	28	30	35

ARIZONA LEAGUE

Mariners outfield prospect Tommy Boudreau led the Rookie Arizona League with a .378 average.

Ho hum . . . Brewers win another league title

By DEAN GYORGY

The Milwaukee Brewers were instrumental in turning a dream into reality with the creation of the Arizona League in 1988. Fittingly, the Brewers are the only champions the league has ever known.

Six teams battled each other and the Arizona heat during the 1990 season, and Milwaukee turned in the best record for the third straight year, besting the rest of the six-team field by 3½ games.

Marc Newfield . . . MVP

Leading the club to its 36-17 record were outfielder Orlando Barrios, who hit .321, and righthanders Phil Angelos, who went 7-1 with a 2.48 ERA, and Don Blair, who went 4-1, 0.91.

The Arizona League had two first-round picks make their debuts: Mariners' first baseman Marc Newfield (.318-6-38) and Padres' lefthander Robbie Beckett (2-5, 4.38). Newfield was named league MVP and the No. 2 prospect in a combined poll of Arizona and Gulf Coast League managers. Beckett was named the No. 4 prospect.

1990 FINAL STANDINGS

	W	L	Pct.	GB
Brewers	36	17	.679	—
Mariners	32	20	.615	3½
Cardinals	28	24	.538	7½
Athletics	25	27	.481	10½
Angels	19	35	.352	17½
Padres	18	35	.340	18

1990 GENERAL INFORMATION

Playoffs: None

Managers: Angels—Bill Lachemann; **Athletics**—Gary Jones; **Brewers**—Alex Taveris; **Cardinals**—Larry Milbourne; **Mariners**—Dave Myers; **Padres**—Jaime Moreno.

1990 Official All-Star Team: C—Don Pryblinski, Cardinals; Jose Stella, Angels. **1B**—Marc Newfield, Mariners. **2B**—Julian Salazar, Brewers; Carlos Polanco, Angels. **3B**—John Halland, Mariners. **SS**—Israel Seda, Mariners. **OF**—Orlando Barrios, Brewers; Jose Velez, Cardinals; Tony Pritchett, Athletics. **DH**—Paul Brannon, Mariners. **RHP**—Phil Angelos, Brewers. **LHP**—Derron Spiller, Cardinals. **RHRP**—Jonas Hamlin, Cardinals. **LHRP**—Bill Kostich, Mariners; Victor Rojas, Angels. **Most Valuable Player**—Marc Newfield, Mariners. **Manager of the Year**—Jaime Moreno, Padres; Bill Lachemann, Angels.

Top 10 Major League Prospects (by Baseball America): See Gulf Coast League. page 227.

1990 BATTING PITCHING STATS

CLUB BATTING

	AVG	G	AB	R	H	2B	3B	HR	BB	SO	SB
Mariners	.277	54	1955	354	542	85	33	21	246	370	43
Brewers	.267	53	1844	334	492	60	36	13	220	329	64
Angels	.262	55	1876	281	491	52	26	6	248	399	52
Cardinals	.259	53	1862	312	483	60	25	17	220	301	46
Athletics	.256	53	1855	292	474	74	21	17	213	477	77
Padres	.214	54	1773	261	379	66	12	10	250	463	117

CLUB PITCHING

	ERA	G	CG	SHO	SV	IP	H	R	ER	BB	SO
Brewers	3.42	53	7	3	14	471	434	238	179	184	369
Mariners	3.54	54	0	2	10	490	442	280	193	261	459
Athletics	3.93	53	1	3	6	474	472	309	207	232	415
Cardinals	4.17	53	3	3	8	468	501	277	217	200	371
Angels	4.61	55	1	1	6	476	472	351	244	281	382
Padres	5.29	54	0	1	5	466	540	379	274	239	343

INDIVIDUAL BATTING LEADERS
(Minimum 151 Plate Appearances)

	AVG	G	AB	R	H	2B	3B	HR	RBI	BB	SO	SB
Boudreau, Tommy, Mariners	.378	36	135	27	51	8	2	4	29	19	34	1
Johnson, Wayne, Angels	.366	39	131	33	48	3	1	1	13	32	23	19
Hamlin, Jonas, Cardinals	.344	53	221	45	76	11	4	9	39	13	30	0
Stela, Jose, Angels	.331	48	169	25	56	9	4	0	23	16	17	2
Prybylinski, Don, Cards	.325	46	154	32	50	13	1	1	28	26	16	2
Barrios, Orlando, Brewers	.313	42	166	34	52	5	4	2	22	14	14	10
Newfield, Marc, Mariners	.313	51	192	34	60	13	2	6	38	25	20	4
*Velez, Jose, Cardinals	.317	46	183	26	58	7	6	0	29	8	12	5
Spears, Brian, Brewers	.300	52	210	33	63	9	2	5	45	11	21	2
Bobo, Elgin, Angels	.297	42	145	20	43	6	5	0	19	18	30	2

INDIVIDUAL PITCHING LEADERS
(Minimum 45 Innings)

	W	L	ERA	G	GS	CG	SV	IP	H	R	ER	BB	SO
*Kostich, Bill, Mariners	3	1	0.40	23	0	0	6	45	28	7	2	6	39
*Montoya, Norm, Angels	3	3	2.11	10	6	1	1	47	49	20	11	7	28
*Spiller, Derron, Cards	4	2	2.18	9	9	1	0	58	46	18	15	15	46
*Urso, Sal, Mariners	3	2	2.31	20	0	0	1	51	36	25	17	23	63
Angelos, Phil, Brewers	7	1	2.48	9	7	4	0	65	51	26	18	9	45
*Hampton, Mike, Mariners	7	2	2.66	14	13	0	0	64	52	32	19	40	59
Gamez, Francisco, Brewers	2	3	2.66	11	7	1	0	51	42	21	15	20	31
Lynch, Mike, Brewers	4	2	2.74	13	13	1	0	76	66	31	24	31	69
Russell, Lee, Mariners	5	1	3.11	19	5	0	0	55	51	33	19	26	51
Jolley, Mike, Cards	1	0	3.33	28	0	0	0	49	55	24	20	22	37

ANGELS

BATTING	AVG	G	AB	R	H	2B	3B	HR	RBI	BB	SO	SB
Alcaraz, Vladimiro, dh-1b	.228	17	57	10	13	2	0	0	10	10	14	0

	AVG	G	AB	R	H	2B	3B	HR	RBI	BB	SO	SB
*Anderson, Garrett, of	.213	32	127	5	27	2	0	0	14	2	24	3
Baez, Hector, of	.167	2	6	2	1	0	0	0	0	1	0	0
Bertucci, Joe, 3b-of	.180	31	100	12	18	0	1	0	6	17	32	1
Bobo, Elgin, of-c	.297	42	145	20	43	6	5	0	19	18	30	2
Brito, Frank, 2b	.300	4	20	2	6	1	0	0	1	0	2	0
Buldier, Nelson, c	.333	1	3	0	1	0	0	0	0	0	2	0
Guzik, Brian, ss	.242	18	62	11	15	2	1	1	9	8	18	2
House, Ken, of-1b	.246	42	130	17	32	5	5	0	20	28	31	4
Johnson, Wayne, ss-of	.366	39	131	33	48	3	1	1	13	32	23	19
*Jorge, Genaro, of	.200	18	50	5	10	1	0	0	6	12	12	0
Markiewicz, Brandon, ss	.162	31	99	14	16	2	0	0	4	10	22	1
Minnis, Billy, 2b	.269	24	78	16	21	4	1	1	8	7	18	2
Oliver, Felix, of	.300	3	10	1	3	0	0	0	0	0	4	0
*Osuna, Julio, c	.370	16	46	9	17	1	2	0	8	5	6	0
Peterson, Drew, 3b	.276	7	29	4	8	1	0	0	3	1	6	1
Pineiro, Mike, c-of	.333	28	69	11	23	2	1	0	9	3	10	0
Polanco, Carlos, 2b-of	.301	42	136	28	41	2	0	2	21	26	18	8
Rios, Chris, of	.400	14	45	9	18	1	3	0	11	8	2	1
Rodriguez, Pascual, of-3b	.250	4	4	1	1	0	0	0	0	0	2	0
Sierra, Domingo, 2b-of	.268	23	71	8	19	1	1	0	7	4	15	2
Simmons, Mark, 3b-of	.194	29	103	14	20	1	0	0	11	15	27	3
Stela, Jose, c-of	.331	48	169	25	56	9	4	0	23	16	17	2
Stowell, Jim, of	.225	19	71	11	16	3	1	1	12	12	17	1
Tallent, Ron, 1b	.161	33	112	12	18	3	0	0	7	10	47	0

PITCHING	W	L	ERA	G	GS	CG	SV	IP	H	R	ER	BB	SO
Heredia, Julian	2	2	3.81	5	5	0	0	26	25	14	11	10	18
Heusman, Theron	1	2	1.06	10	1	0	0	17	8	6	2	16	18
Kelso, Jeff	2	4	8.93	16	8	0	0	41	51	54	41	42	32
Lachemann, Bret	2	1	4.40	14	2	0	0	29	32	22	14	13	36
*Lyke, Jim	0	1	7.33	13	0	0	0	23	38	32	19	16	9
Martinez, Eric	0	3	4.56	14	1	0	0	24	29	19	12	10	22
Martinez, Francisco	3	2	6.55	17	3	0	0	33	31	40	23	32	29
Montoya, Norm	3	3	2.11	10	6	1	1	47	49	20	11	7	28
Musset, Jose	2	7	8.89	13	13	0	0	63	63	54	42	41	49
Refnes, Todd	0	1	4.20	3	3	0	0	15	19	7	7	3	15
Rice, David	0	1	3.00	12	1	0	0	24	26	12	8	14	14
Rojas, Victor	0	0	2.81	23	0	0	5	26	12	14	9	20	30
Severino, Blas	0	2	2.30	7	5	0	0	31	24	13	8	14	32
Silverio, Victor	2	4	5.08	13	7	0	0	44	39	30	25	29	29
Watson, Ron	2	3	3.27	20	0	0	0	33	26	14	12	14	21

ATHLETICS

BATTING	AVG	G	AB	R	H	2B	3B	HR	RBI	BB	SO	SB
Aracena, Luinis, of	.293	49	164	27	48	9	1	0	21	29	45	11
Bailey, Reggie, 1b-of	.146	43	137	11	20	2	0	2	17	4	30	0
#Cabrera, Juan, ss-2b	.254	18	67	9	17	1	1	0	8	4	14	3
Carlsen, Bobby, 2b-3b	.367	36	120	34	44	9	0	1	20	23	14	9
Dionicio, Eurben, of-3b	.167	37	108	16	18	2	0	2	11	13	41	2
*Duncan, Jeff, 3b	.250	42	152	30	38	12	4	2	27	25	45	5
#Francisco, Vicente, ss	.246	43	175	23	43	3	2	0	14	6	42	5
Fuentes, Nelson, c	.205	16	44	5	9	1	0	1	6	2	11	0
Hust, Gary, of	.200	44	150	13	30	1	2	1	9	11	60	3
Keathley, Don, 1b-c	.254	45	130	17	33	2	0	2	10	19	36	0
Kennedy, Mike, c-dh	.227	13	44	1	10	1	0	1	7	2	5	0
Lydy, Scott, dh-1b	.340	18	50	8	17	6	0	2	11	10	14	0
Mercado, Rafael, 1b	.286	5	21	4	6	0	0	0	6	2	6	1
Molina, Islay, c	.339	39	127	20	43	12	2	0	18	9	22	5
Moriso, Pablo, 1b	.000	1	1	0	0	0	0	0	0	0	1	0
Olofson, Chris, of	.231	24	52	10	12	0	0	2	4	17	5	5
#Pritchett, Tony, of-2b	.274	51	197	44	54	6	9	3	35	32	42	20
#Reid, Greg, dh-of	.257	34	105	19	27	6	0	0	8	18	29	8

PITCHING	W	L	ERA	G	GS	CG	SV	IP	H	R	ER	BB	SO
Acosta, Jose	5	5	3.92	12	12	0	0	62	71	45	27	20	27
Floyd, Tony	2	0	2.25	13	0	0	0	32	28	10	8	8	35
*Fults, Tony	1	1	6.35	4	1	0	0	6	5	5	4	10	6
Gechter, Tony	0	0	1.42	10	0	0	0	19	13	8	3	9	14
Hill, Fred	1	1	2.70	9	0	0	2	13	15	7	4	7	14
Hokuf, Ken	3	4	5.40	20	0	0	0	37	43	33	22	26	36
Johns, Doug	3	1	1.84	8	7	1	0	44	36	17	9	9	38
*Lara, Nelson	0	1	5.09	15	0	0	0	18	24	17	10	10	12
Lynch, Jeff	0	1	11.05	5	2	0	0	7	5	10	9	15	6
McCarty, Scott	0	5	4.24	10	9	0	0	51	52	35	24	32	59
*Miller, Rick	4	0	3.38	7	2	0	0	29	22	11	11	12	28
Morillo, Santiago	1	1	4.30	13	3	0	0	29	37	20	14	15	27
Newson, Mike	0	0	5.40	3	0	0	0	3	2	2	2	3	1
Orr, Dan	0	0	38.57	2	0	0	0	2	1	10	10	9	3
Phoenix, Steve	3	1	1.45	6	6	0	0	31	25	14	5	4	31
Rose, Scott	0	0	1.47	9	1	0	0	18	12	5	3	3	21
Scharff, Tony	1	1	5.01	14	0	0	2	23	26	19	13	13	27
Sturtze, Tanyon	2	5	5.44	12	10	0	0	48	55	41	29	27	30

BREWERS

BATTING	AVG	G	AB	R	H	2B	3B	HR	RBI	BB	SO	SB
Baber, Larue, of	.180	31	128	23	23	4	1	0	7	11	27	8
Barrios, Orlando, of-dh	.313	42	166	34	52	5	4	2	22	14	14	10

AZL DEPARTMENT LEADERS

BATTING

R	Jonas Hamlin, Cardinals .	45
H	Jonas Hamlin, Cardinals .	76
TB	Jonas Hamlin, Cardinals	119
2B	Marc Newfield, Mariners .	13
3B	Tony Pritchett, Athletics . . .	9
HR	Jonas Hamlin, Cardinals . .	8
RBI	Brian Spears, Brewers . .	45
SH	Pedro Vasquez, Padres . . .	4
	Julian Salazar, Brewers . . .	4
SF	Juan Cabrera, Brewers . . .	6
	Brian Spears, Brewers . . .	6
BB	Duane Singleton, Brewers	41
IBB	David Howry, Padres	4
HBP	Elgin Bobo, Angels	9
SO	Gary Hust, Athletics	60
SB	Tony Pritchett, Athletics . .	20
CS	Sam Shannon, Padres . .	14
OB%	Wayne Johnson, Angels .497	

PITCHING

G	Matt Tomso, Cardinals . . .	29
GS	Four tied at	13
CG	Phil Angelos, Brewers	4
ShO	Three tied at	1
Sv	Tom Kinney, Cardinals . . .	7
W	Mike Hampton, Mariners . .	7
	Phil Angelos, Brewers . . .	7
L	Jose Musset, Angels	7
	Jeffrey Brown, Padres . . .	7
IP	Mike Lynch, Brewers	76
H	Andy Peterson, Cardinals .	83
R	Three tied at	54
HR	Three tied at	5
BB	Robbie Beckett, Padres . . .	45
HB	Mike Lynch, Brewers	7
	Jose Davila, Padres	7
SO	Mike Lynch, Brewers	69
WP	Mike Hampton, Mariners . .	10
Bk	Jose Davila, Padres	9

	AVG	G	AB	R	H	2B	3B	HR	RBI	BB	SO	SB
*Benjamin, Bobby, of	.296	26	81	19	24	3	6	0	14	19	19	3
Cabrera, Juan, 3b	.255	44	165	27	42	6	3	1	26	10	27	7
Diaz, Steve, c	.148	25	81	8	12	2	0	1	11	7	18	0
#Enriquez, Graciano, of	.231	43	169	30	39	10	4	1	19	19	37	5
Flores, Carlos, ss	.257	23	70	9	18	0	1	0	12	9	9	1
Hood, Randy, ss-3b	.231	4	13	2	3	0	0	0	1	2	4	0
*Irwin, Ryan, c	.271	23	70	13	19	1	0	0	8	8	12	1
Rodriguez, Frank, dh-c	.276	31	98	16	27	1	5	0	14	11	28	2
Salazar, Julian, 2b	.288	47	156	29	45	6	1	1	18	23	30	7
Siglock, Steven, of-2b	.239	27	67	16	16	2	3	1	12	11	12	3
*Singleton, Duane, of	.238	45	126	30	30	6	1	1	12	43	37	7
Spears, Brian, 1b	.300	52	210	33	63	9	2	5	45	11	21	2
Tatum, John, 3b-dh	.280	21	75	10	21	0	1	0	10	7	16	0
Vargas, Trinidad, ss	.336	36	128	30	43	0	3	0	20	15	13	5
Walker, Jimmy, of	.375	9	40	5	15	1	1	0	3	0	5	3

PITCHING	W	L	ERA	G	GS	CG	SV	IP	H	R	ER	BB	SO
Angelos, Phil	7	1	2.48	9	7	4	0	65	51	26	18	9	45
Blair, Don	4	1	0.91	6	6	1	0	40	24	5	4	6	46
Boze, Marshall	1	0	7.40	15	0	0	3	21	27	22	18	13	17
Bumgarner, Wes	6	3	5.05	11	11	0	0	57	54	38	31	24	27
Coffey, Mike	0	1	4.71	13	0	0	1	21	25	16	11	13	17
Gamez, Francisco	2	3	2.66	11	7	1	0	51	42	21	15	20	31
Griego, Orlando	2	2	3.33	20	0	0	3	27	30	13	8	8	14
Kiefer, Mark	0	0	3.86	1	1	0	0	3	3	1	1	1	2
Lynch, Mike	4	2	2.74	13	13	1	0	76	66	31	24	31	69
McCreadie, Brant	0	0	6.55	7	0	0	1	11	11	10	8	11	17
McCutchen, Jim	4	3	3.06	13	3	0	2	35	29	13	12	19	28
Nichols, Doug	3	0	3.70	7	3	0	1	24	25	17	10	12	29
*Rolfes, Mike	1	1	4.42	16	0	0	2	18	20	13	11	12	17
Stone, Brad	2	0	3.50	8	0	0	1	18	25	10	7	1	8
White, Dave	0	0	2.08	2	2	0	0	4	2	2	1	4	2

CARDINALS

BATTING	AVG	G	AB	R	H	2B	3B	HR	RBI	BB	SO	SB
#Aversa, Joe, ss-3b	.235	9	34	5	8	1	0	0	4	8	8	2
Carpenter, Kevin, of-c	.182	10	33	4	6	0	0	0	4	2	5	0
#Colon, Hector, 2b	.174	23	46	6	8	0	0	0	6	19	8	3
Davenport, Jim, of-dh	.183	40	115	16	21	3	3	1	14	15	39	5
*Dudek, Steve, of-dh	.304	31	125	19	38	4	1	0	11	4	19	3
Gale, Bill, of	.239	40	155	29	37	8	2	1	21	22	21	3
Gonzalez, Rich, of	.226	8	31	3	7	0	0	0	0	3	0	1
Hamlin, Jonas, 1b	.344	53	221	45	76	11	4	9	39	13	30	0
Keating, Mike, ss-3b	.180	29	89	16	16	1	0	1	8	12	16	1
Landinez, Carlos, 2b	.260	28	104	30	27	5	2	2	14	29	12	16
*Lowman, Sydney, c-dh	.301	20	73	9	22	1	0	0	6	4	16	0
*Meek, Darryl, of	.186	43	113	20	21	3	1	1	18	26	37	1
Meza, Lorenzo, 3b	.245	50	204	29	50	1	1	1	22	5	19	0
Prybylinski, Don, c	.325	46	154	32	50	13	1	1	28	26	16	2
Ugueto, Jesus, ss	.179	34	112	13	20	1	0	0	14	11	31	2
Vargas, Victor, 2b	.269	18	67	10	18	1	2	0	5	13	10	2
*Velez, Jose, of	.317	46	183	26	58	7	4	1	0	29	8	5

PITCHING	W	L	ERA	G	GS	CG	SV	IP	H	R	ER	BB	SO
Anderson, Paul	0	0	1.29	5	1	0	0	14	10	2	2	3	15
Avram, Brian	2	0	4.68	19	3	0	0	42	57	34	24	26	24
*Davis, Jeff	1	0	10.97	6	1	0	0	11	11	14	13	15	4
Eaton, Dann	5	2	5.94	8	7	0	0	36	39	24	22	15	42
Glover, Greg	3	2	5.67	7	7	0	0	27	27	24	17	17	31
Jolley, Mike	1	0	3.33	28	0	0	0	49	55	24	20	22	37
*Kinney, Tom	4	1	3.26	25	1	0	7	39	42	14	14	10	19
Marchesi, Jim	3	5	4.64	17	6	0	0	46	50	33	25	16	23

	W	L	ERA	G	GS	CG	SV	IP	H	R	ER	BB	SO
*Nielsen, Kevin	2	3	1.91	7	7	2	0	42	43	20	9	17	41
Peterson, Andy	3	5	4.83	15	11	0	0	69	83	49	37	26	45
*Spiller, Derron	4	2	2.18	9	9	1	0	58	46	18	15	15	46
Tomso, Matt	0	4	4.89	29	0	0	1	35	38	21	19	18	44

MARINERS

BATTING	AVG	G	AB	R	H	2B	3B	HR	RBI	BB	SO	SB
Barlow, Clemmon, of	.245	37	102	23	25	8	4	1	16	13	37	2
Boudreau, Tommy, of-dh	.378	36	135	27	51	8	2	4	29	19	34	1
Brannon, Paul, c-dh	.278	25	97	11	27	5	3	1	15	4	16	3
Candelario, Frank, c	.212	24	66	4	14	2	0	0	5	2	26	0
Fermaint, Mike, 2b	.299	33	117	26	35	4	1	0	8	28	18	3
*Fernandez, Julio, of	.303	38	109	24	33	3	5	0	12	20	23	4
Halland, Jon, 3b	.296	38	159	28	47	6	6	4	33	12	35	3
Johnson, John, 3b	.277	13	47	9	13	2	0	0	5	4	7	0
Klavitter, Clay, c-2b	.289	11	45	4	13	4	0	1	7	2	7	0
*Lawson, David, of	.170	34	112	22	19	2	1	0	15	23	24	5
List, Paul, of	.292	15	48	7	14	3	3	1	9	12	6	1
#Lozano, Jose, c-1b	.255	22	51	6	13	1	0	0	6	7	11	0
Moncion, Pedro, ss	.253	31	99	23	25	2	1	0	9	19	15	0
Newfield, Marc, 1b-of	.313	51	192	34	60	13	2	6	38	25	20	4
Powell, L.V., dh	.214	18	42	10	9	1	0	0	5	2	10	2
Ramos, Martin, of	.261	22	69	13	18	3	1	2	14	9	21	2
*Robertson, Tom, of	.254	38	130	25	33	4	2	0	16	8	19	1
Seda, Israel, ss	.266	31	124	21	33	5	1	1	19	13	13	7
Valentin, Jose, 2b	.289	27	97	24	28	4	0	0	8	11	11	4
Valverde, Osvaldo, 3b-1b	.262	21	65	6	17	4	0	0	6	2	10	1
Walles, Todd, 1b-dh	.306	19	49	7	15	1	1	0	1	11	7	0

PITCHING	W	L	ERA	G	GS	CG	SV	IP	H	R	ER	BB	SO
*Gargagliano, Dion	0	0	0.00	1	0	0	0	1	0	1	0	2	1
*Hampton, Mike	7	2	2.66	14	13	0	0	64	52	32	19	40	59
*Hartman, Kelly	0	2	6.59	7	2	0	0	14	22	14	12	12	15
*Kostich, Bill	3	1	0.40	23	0	0	6	45	28	7	2	6	39
*Neugent, Jim	1	0	1.53	14	0	0	1	18	14	8	4	13	23
Pena, Antonio	2	1	2.88	5	5	0	0	25	17	9	8	13	24
Perkins, Paul	5	4	4.18	13	13	0	0	71	74	54	39	31	62
Polanco, Giovanni	0	3	6.75	8	4	0	0	19	38	25	18	16	17
*Roberts, Tim	1	1	7.77	13	1	0	0	22	25	21	19	18	8
Russell, Lee	5	1	3.11	19	5	0	0	55	51	33	19	26	51
*Urso, Sal	3	2	2.31	20	0	0	1	51	36	25	17	23	63
Wallace, Stafford	0	1	0.86	12	0	0	1	21	9	2	2	14	11
Whitney, Mike	0	1	3.05	16	0	0	1	21	18	12	7	13	18
Wiley, Chuck	5	2	3.64	15	11	0	0	64	58	37	27	34	68

PADRES

BATTING	AVG	G	AB	R	H	2B	3B	HR	RBI	BB	SO	SB
Abercrombie, John, of	.288	43	156	35	45	10	1	7	23	20	23	10
*Anthony, Mark, of-dh	.161	27	87	14	14	0	0	0	5	11	31	10
Bullock, Craig, 3b	.169	48	148	19	25	7	0	0	9	27	44	6
#Carion, German, 2b	.179	13	39	2	7	0	0	0	2	4	8	0
Cruz, Juan, of	.214	46	159	18	34	8	1	0	16	9	53	15
Decareau, Thomas, of	.262	29	103	16	27	8	0	0	13	17	31	5
Joyce, James, c	.161	30	93	4	15	2	0	0	6	9	17	1
#Mateo, Jose, ss-of	.000	5	1	0	0	0	0	0	0	0	0	0
Matos, Alberto, of	.135	32	104	14	14	2	2	0	8	11	48	8
*McDavid, Ray, of	.146	13	41	4	6	0	2	0	1	6	5	3
Mowry, David, 1b	.239	50	180	25	43	6	0	1	28	38	34	9
Shannon, Sam, 2b-3b	.244	39	127	23	31	2	2	0	9	26	30	19
Siebert, Steve, 2b-ss	.154	28	91	15	14	1	0	1	8	14	28	6
#Stephens, Reggie, dh-2b	.231	35	117	20	27	1	0	0	12	23	26	10
Thurston, Jerrey, c	.228	43	149	23	34	6	1	0	16	16	38	6
Vasquez, Pedro, ss	.242	49	178	28	43	13	1	1	27	18	47	16

PITCHING	W	L	ERA	G	GS	CG	SV	IP	H	R	ER	BB	SO
*Beckett, Robbie	2	5	4.38	10	10	0	0	49	40	28	24	45	54
*Brown, Jeffrey	1	7	5.40	17	7	0	1	65	76	53	39	15	66
Davila, Jose	2	3	6.09	16	5	0	0	44	55	46	30	21	24
Devore, Ted	3	2	6.84	7	2	0	1	25	37	24	19	10	22
*Ellis, Tim	0	0	6.43	8	0	0	1	14	18	14	10	8	7
Eubanks, Craig	5	4	4.13	19	9	0	1	52	49	34	24	32	37
*Huber, Jeff	1	4	3.03	9	7	0	1	36	32	19	14	15	21
*Ivie, Ryan	3	0	3.38	13	4	0	0	35	39	17	13	11	24
Martin, Paul	1	1	9.10	19	0	0	0	30	41	36	31	21	23
Narcisse, Tyrone	0	0	5.06	7	1	0	0	11	13	11	6	6	6
*O'Neill, Kevin	1	3	4.82	15	4	0	0	37	37	23	20	14	16
Perez, Tirson	0	3	5.81	16	1	0	0	31	44	29	20	16	18
Ploeger, Tim	0	3	6.49	16	4	0	0	35	56	45	25	25	24

DOMINICAN SUMMER LEAGUE

Pirates capture top prize in rookie league

By ALLAN SIMPSON

Pittsburgh's entry in the Dominican Summer League walked away with the league title in 1990, beating teams fielded by San Francisco and Cleveland in a three-team double-elimination final. The Pirates, champions of the league's Santo Domingo Division, won three of four games, edging the Indians (1-2) and Giants (1-2).

All but four major league teams—the Cubs, Cincinnati, Philadelphia and Minnesota—participated in the three-division alignment. Several teams fielded joint entries. Both Los Angeles and Toronto, traditionally the most active teams in signing Dominican talent, fielded two teams.

San Francisco posted the league's best overall record (56-13), winning the San Pedro de Macoris Division by 14 games. Cleveland qualified for post-season play by taking the Cibao Division.

The Giants had the league's top pitcher, Salomon Torres, who led the league in wins (11-1), ERA (0.50) and strikeouts (101, in 90 innings).

Cleveland had the league's top hitter, Gonzalo Vargas (.378), while Jose Diaz of the White Sox led with 13 homers and Roberto Mejia of the Dodgers' Cibao Division entry had a league-best 74 RBIs.

The Dominican Summer League, a feeder program used largely for Hispanic players who are not ready to participate in American professional leagues, was in its sixth year of sponsorship by major league clubs.

1990 *FINAL STANDINGS*

San Pedro de Macoris Division	W	L	Pct.	GB
Giants	56	13	.812	—
Braves	42	27	.609	14
Dodgers	36	31	.537	19
Orioles/White Sox	31	39	.443	25½
Astros/Cardinals	23	47	.329	33½
Rangers	19	50	.275	37

Santo Domingo Division	W	L	Pct.	GB
Pirates	48	22	.686	—
Mariners	40	28	.588	7
Angels	38	30	.559	9
Blue Jays	37	31	.544	10
Athletics	36	32	.529	11
Expos	35	35	.500	13
Yankees	34	36	.486	14
Tigers/Padres/Red Sox	8	62	.114	40

Cibao Division	W	L	Pct.	GB
Indians	44	28	.611	—
Dodgers	43	29	.597	1
Royals/Mets	30	42	.417	14
Blue Jays/Brewers	27	45	.375	17

AND THERE'S MORE

Other Pro Baseball

College Baseball

Amateur Baseball

The 1990 Draft

MEXICAN LEAGUE

Third-place Leon wins first Mexican title

By ALLAN SIMPSON

The upstart Leon Braves overcame a third-place finish in the Southern Zone to capture their first-ever Mexican League title in 1990. The Braves, in their eighth year in the league, defeated Union Laguna, 4-1, in the best-of-7 final.

Leon got two wins and a save in the championship series from workhorse Jaime Orozco, who thereupon left to join the Baltimore Orioles organization. The veteran righthander, who led the league in starts and innings pitched, went the distance in the deciding game, beating the Cottongrowers 5-3.

Jaime Orozco
. . . wins final

To reach the championship series, Leon defeated the Mexico City Reds, 4-1, in the Southern Zone semi-finals, then edged Campeche, 4-2, in the zone finals.

Julio Purata won five straight games in post-season play for Leon, including a 7-0, three-hit shutout over Union Laguna in Game Two of the finals.

Union Laguna, third-place finishers in the North, stopped defending champion Los Dos Laredos, 4-2, in the other semi-final. Laredos, bidding to become the first team since the 1960 Mexico City Tigers to win a championship with all native players, had finished with the league's best record (81-50) in regular-season play.

The Owls began the season with three players on loan from the Cincinnati Reds, but abruptly severed their working agreement during the season.

Americans shine

Yucatan DH Nick Castaneda won the batting title with a .388 average. It was the second title for the 27-year-old native of San Pedro, Calif., who originally signed with the Pittsburgh Pirates in 1980 and was in his fifth year in the Mexican League.

Castaneda also won the 1988 title, at .374, then took a year out to play in the Kansas City Royals organization in 1989, but missed most of the season when he was hurt in a brawl. He rejoined the Royals organization in 1990, once the Mexican League season was over.

LEAGUE CHAMPIONS

Playoff Champions, Where Applicable

1990—Leon	1978—Aguascalientes	1965—M.C. Tigers
1989—Dos Laredos	1977—Nuevo Laredo	1964—M.C. Reds
1988—M.C. Reds	1976—M.C. Reds	1963—Puebla
1987—M.C. Reds	1975—Tampico	1962—Monterey
1986—Puebla	1974—M.C. Reds	1961—Veracruz
1985—M.C. Reds	1973—M.C. Reds	1960—M.C. Tigers
1984—Yucatan	1972—Cordoba	1959—M.C. Reds
1983—Campeche	1971—Jalisco	1958—Nuevo Laredo
1982—Ciudad Juarez	1970—Aguila	1957—M.C. Reds
1981—*M.C. Reds	1969—Reynosa	1956—M.C. Reds
—*Reynosa	1968—M.C. Reds	1955—M.C. Tigers
1980—No champion	1967—Jalisco	
1979—Puebla	1966—M.C. Tigers	*co-champions

Castaneda, whose best season in Mexico came for San Luis Potosi in 1986 when a livelier ball was used and he hit .412 with 53 homers and 147 RBIs, finished three points ahead of Mexico City Tigers outfielder Eric Mangham, 24, in the batting race.

Mangham, property of the Los Angeles Dodgers, missed a month of the season with a broken finger suffered during the league's all-star game, won by the South Zone, 9-8.

American-developed players led the league in most other categories.

San Luis Potosi had the worst overall record in the league but outfielder Alex Sanchez led with 28 homers. Union Laguna's David Stockstill was tops with 109 RBIs, while Saltillo's Trench Davis led with 189 hits. Campeche outfielder Roy Johnson had the most doubles (35) and total bases (257), and also slugged a league-high six homers in post-season play.

Monterrey's Mike Cole led in stolen bases for the fourth year in a row, but his 56 thefts were far off his league record of 100 set a year earlier.

Aikens productive again

Leon DH Willie Aikens, who missed winning a triple crown in 1989 by two RBIs, led the champion Braves with a .358 average. The two-time batting champ, whose .454 mark in 1986 remains a league record, had 21 homers and 106 RBIs.

Meanwhile, Braves manager Francisco Estrada, who once caught for the New York Mets, played in 23 games in 1990, hitting .193. It was Estrada's 22nd active season, tying him with legendary Hector Espino, the league's all-time home run leader.

Saltillo righthander Armando Reynoso pitched one of three no-hitters during the Mexican League season, a 1-0 perfecto over the Monterrey Industrials. Ten days later, he became the league's only 20-game winner. Reynoso finished with a 20-3 record, 2.60 ERA and a league-leading 170 strikeouts.

Controversy broke out on the final day of the regular season when Yucatan pulled its team off the field to protest a reversal of an umpire's home run call, and forfeited the second game of a doubleheader to the Mexico City Tigers.

The fracas started when Castaneda, the league's top hitter, hit a drive over the fence near the foul pole. At first, umpires ruled a home run, but later changed the call. The Lions cried foul, a heated argument ensued and the team refused to return to the field.

Yucatan, which led the league in attendance for the fourth year in a row, was fined 10 million pesos (about $3,300) and was threatened with a one-year expulsion from the league for a repeat incident.

1990 *FINAL STANDINGS*

North	W	L	Pct.	GB
Los Dos Laredos	81	50	.618	—
Union Laguna	71	54	.568	7
Monterrey Sultans	70	62	.560	11½
Monclova	63	66	.488	17
Saltillo	64	68	.485	17½
Monterrey Industrials	49	82	.374	32
San Luis Potosi	42	87	.326	38
South				
Mexico City Tigers	73	50	.593	—
Mexico City Reds	72	54	.571	2½
Leon	74	57	.565	3
Campeche	66	57	.537	7
Yucatan	65	64	.504	11
Aguascalientes	54	69	.439	19
Tabasco	52	76	.406	23½

MEXICAN LEADERS

Alex Sanchez
...28 homers

Dave Stockstill
...RBI leader

Roy Johnson
...346-28-95

1990 GENERAL INFORMATION

Playoffs: Laredo defeated Monclova 4-3 in best-of-7 quarterfinal; Union Laguna defeated Monterrey Sultans 4-2 in best-of-7 quarterfinal; Campeche defeated Mexico City Tigers 4-2 in best-of-7 quarterfinal; Leon defeated Mexico City Reds 4-1 in best-of-7 quarterfinal; Leon defeated Campeche 4-2 in best-of-7 semifinal; Union Laguna defeated Laredo 4-2 in best-of-7 semifinal; Leon defeated Union Laguna 4-1 in best-of-7 final for league championship.

Regular-Season Attendance: Yucatan, 250,358; Monclova, 230,554; Union Laguna, 210,147; Campeche, 198,885; Saltillo, 197,528; Leon, 195,938; San Luis Potosi, 195,502; Tabasco, 194,972; Mexico City Reds, 190,733; Laredo, 183,500; Aguascalientes, 182,750; Mexico City Tigers, 181,758; Monterrey Industrials, 171,264; Monterrey Sultans, 160,066.

Managers: Aguascalientes—Carlos Paz; **Campeche**—Roberto Mendez, Sergio Robles; **Laredo**—Jose "Zacatillo" Guerrero; **Leon**—Francisco Estrada; **Mexico City Reds**—Benjamin "Cananea" Reyes; **Mexico City Tigers**—Ossie Alvarez; **Monclova**—Gregorio Luque; **Monterrey Industrials**—Hector Espino; **Monterrey Sultans**—Leobardo Figueroa Rodriguez; **Saltillo**—Aurelio Monteagudo, Mercelo Juarez; **San Luis Potosi**—Rodolfo Sandoval; **Tabasco**—Miguel Sotelo, Joel Serna; **Union Laguna**—Marco Antonio Vazquez; **Yucatan**—Roberto Castellon Yuen.

1990 BATTING PITCHING STATS

INDIVIDUAL BATTING LEADERS
(U.S. Players and Players with 300 At-Bats)

	AVG	G	AB	R	H	2B	3B	HR	RBI	BB	SO	SB
Gainey, Ty, MC Reds	.400	36	235	22	54	14	2	9	53	14	33	3
Castaneda, Nick, Yucatan . .	.388	104	330	67	128	24	3	22	80	90	59	0
Mangham, Eric, MC Tigers . .	.385	97	361	83	139	17	4	6	48	41	36	50
Davis, Trench, Saltillo	.380	127	498	84	189	33	4	5	50	56	32	20
Reid, Jessie, MC Reds	.379	27	95	22	36	5	1	7	28	22	18	1
Brown, Todd, Monclova	.374	101	348	78	130	24	4	19	76	52	55	19
Smith, Greg, Saltillo	.372	121	452	73	168	15	0	6	49	46	38	32
Steels, James, MC Reds . . .	.372	23	86	22	32	5	1	0	14	13	6	3
Alyea, Brant, Tabasco	.364	11	44	6	16	2	1	1	7	4	8	0
Garbey, Barbaro, MC Tigers .	.362	120	423	63	153	23	1	12	90	46	48	1
Aikens, Willie, Leon	.358	130	419	83	150	32	1	21	106	101	61	0
Johnson, Roy, Campeche . . .	.346	118	416	81	144	35	0	26	95	63	59	2
Tillman, Rusty, Sultans	.344	74	244	48	84	9	5	11	40	45	46	19
Stockstill, Dave, Laguna	.341	127	451	76	154	30	2	17	109	72	42	2
Threadgill, George, Monclova	.339	30	109	23	37	3	3	0	18	18	27	0
Sanchez, Alex, San Luis . . .	.337	108	392	80	132	24	5	28	79	41	95	15
Cole, Mike, Campeche	.336	123	452	91	152	15	2	0	34	64	34	56
Vargas, Hedi, Aguas	.332	105	370	81	123	19	1	25	92	65	76	1
Cazarin, Manuel, Leon	.329	117	423	51	139	25	0	9	73	23	46	7
Fernandez, Daniel, MC Reds .	.328	123	445	113	146	24	11	3	61	87	56	43
Paris, Kelly, MC Reds	.326	27	95	17	31	10	0	4	20	16	21	0
Villaescusa, Fernando, Aguas	.325	92	366	46	119	17	4	2	43	22	16	9
Navarrete, Juan, Indus	.325	132	504	71	164	24	4	3	55	38	15	9
Elizondo, Fernando, Aguas . .	.323	110	415	63	124	18	1	10	54	30	38	4
Green, David, Tabasco	.322	110	385	59	124	20	1	17	67	51	54	6
Brown, Darrell, Industrials . .	.322	45	180	30	58	8	0	1	12	13	12	9
Wright, George, Yucatan . . .	.322	127	459	96	148	31	4	15	73	68	83	4
Valencia, Carlos, Aguas	.320	101	344	69	110	18	6	3	48	44	35	3
Shepherd, Ron, Leon	.318	108	400	75	127	22	4	17	72	32	72	5

	AVG	G	AB	R	H	2B	3B	HR	RBI	BB	SO	SB
Griffin, Dave, Monclova	.316	17	57	9	18	2	0	1	9	9	9	1
Aguilar, Enrique, Sultans	.316	127	462	72	146	24	3	9	59	55	31	6
Tubbs, Greg, MC Reds	.315	57	213	37	67	5	9	4	33	36	45	11
Valenzuela, Leo, Monclova ..	.315	117	419	55	132	18	6	6	54	50	67	8
Tellez, Alonso, Industrials ...	.312	128	475	75	148	29	10	14	78	41	66	5
Monell, John, San Luis	.311	49	183	27	57	10	0	6	17	14	18	15
Diaz, Luis, Laredo	.311	104	367	67	114	13	6	6	46	46	70	9
Blocker, Terry, Leon	.310	121	451	77	140	21	11	5	74	34	48	21
Reyes, Juan, Sultans	.309	115	408	59	126	27	1	18	86	28	108	5
Castro, Eddie, Saltillo	.308	124	399	93	123	24	1	25	91	112	91	5
Ortiz, Alejandro, Laredo	.307	129	423	87	130	20	0	27	104	102	61	9
Morones, Martin, MC Reds ..	.307	118	368	78	113	14	7	7	39	45	51	13
Mora, Andres, Laredo	.306	121	422	54	129	19	1	16	68	53	57	2
Wong, Julian, Saltillo	.306	125	470	78	144	17	6	0	47	39	29	7
Vizcarra, Roberto, Leon	.305	131	525	89	160	28	4	12	64	37	23	16
Aguilera, Antonio, Sultans ..	.305	132	465	93	142	30	8	7	40	67	61	48
Miller, Eddie, Aguas	.304	39	148	28	45	4	4	6	23	8	30	9
Guzman, Marco, Campeche .	.304	117	404	52	123	16	5	7	54	39	34	1
Reyna, Luis, Saltillo	.303	80	300	46	91	17	5	10	41	25	49	13
Walker, Bernie, Laredo	.301	69	246	49	74	12	5	4	18	49	62	33
Tiquet, Lazaro, Tabasco	.301	127	462	43	139	18	2	2	41	28	74	5
Valdez, Baltazar, Yucatan ...	.300	127	453	60	136	20	0	22	87	47	52	1
See, Larry, Sultans	.297	86	300	40	89	17	2	10	49	36	35	7
Villela, Carlos, Industrials ...	.296	125	466	54	138	21	10	1	30	32	54	5
Estrada, Hector, MC Reds ..	.296	110	409	47	121	18	2	10	69	8	64	4
Alvarez, Heriberto, Yucatan .	.295	111	349	49	103	12	7	7	43	22	52	3
Guerrero, Francisco, Laguna	.293	119	443	95	130	21	6	3	39	73	59	11
Machiria, Pablo, MC Tigers .	.293	114	423	68	124	17	5	11	83	28	44	1
Cruz, Luis, Laguna	.293	127	475	62	139	29	3	15	76	25	61	3
Romero, Marco, Laredo	.293	125	434	82	127	11	5	10	57	55	56	16
Valverde, Raul, Laguna	.293	114	482	64	112	15	8	4	39	22	41	3
Esquer, Ramon, Leon	.292	127	438	86	128	12	10	2	36	51	58	23
Abril, Ramon, Laguna	.292	119	411	65	120	13	1	0	28	27	19	10
Rodriguez, Juan, Sultans ...	.292	124	424	73	124	22	4	4	55	69	21	12
Hernandez, Leo, Campeche .	.291	124	437	66	127	17	2	24	88	57	40	4
Camacho, Adulfo, MC Tigers	.291	103	313	65	91	16	3	3	53	65	57	7
Saiz, Heminio, Laguna	.289	123	356	61	103	18	2	5	46	31	51	3
Rodriguez, Guillermo, MC Tigers	.289	117	433	75	125	21	2	15	65	25	67	5
Serratos, Miguel, Aguas	.287	98	317	35	91	16	3	5	43	19	47	1
Estrada, Roberto, Tabasco ..	.287	116	422	58	121	15	3	2	37	29	51	10
Valencia, Armando, Saltillo ..	.284	122	423	47	120	14	4	0	51	25	46	4
Pacho, Juan, Yucatan	.284	126	450	58	128	16	3	0	29	25	46	9
Verdugo, Vicente, MC Reds .	.283	121	452	58	128	13	2	3	37	25	24	2
Hernandez, Rodolfo, Sultans	.282	115	383	41	108	21	2	7	62	51	45	1
Soto, Carlos, San Luis	.282	92	308	32	87	10	0	14	62	33	44	2
Arce, Francisco, Saltillo	.279	109	348	40	97	19	3	6	51	52	51	2
Leyva, German, Monvlova ...	.279	124	448	74	125	11	7	0	47	60	38	11
Alvarez, Hector, MC Tigers .	.279	123	441	57	123	20	2	1	52	30	46	10
Barrera, Nelson, MC Reds ..	.278	124	464	61	129	26	2	20	82	35	64	5
Ramirez, Gustavo, Monclova	.277	111	364	34	101	19	3	2	53	26	31	1
Mere, Pedro, Laredo	.277	106	375	58	104	9	0	15	64	48	65	4
Shines, Razor, MC Reds ...	.276	78	268	51	74	15	0	6	49	55	28	6
Ramirez, Enrique, Laredo ...	.272	129	449	61	122	8	7	1	37	39	31	13
Dominguez, David, San Luis	.272	126	445	60	121	21	2	8	63	46	75	2
Saenz, Ricardo, Saltillo	.272	110	356	47	97	16	5	9	54	40	61	7
Valenzuela, Horacio, Leon ..	.271	123	447	52	121	23	2	16	83	32	78	4
Leal, Jose, Sultans	.271	111	332	25	90	14	4	4	51	25	48	3
Baca, Manuel, Aguas	.270	108	378	51	102	12	1	12	61	29	58	2
Castelan, Miguel, Indus	.269	116	391	35	105	12	3	1	32	22	56	17
Felice, Jason, Laguna	.268	40	123	15	33	7	0	5	18	24	27	1
Martinez, Grimaldo, Monclova	.268	117	351	57	94	18	1	1	33	43	46	13
Gutierrez, Felipe, Campeche	.266	116	399	42	106	18	1	9	50	17	44	1
Uzcanga, Ali, Industrials	.265	105	339	32	90	13	1	0	20	28	48	1
Garcia, Martin, San Luis	.264	107	314	28	83	12	5	1	32	39	48	3
Rivera, Eleazar, San Luis ...	.263	102	316	30	83	7	2	4	37	24	69	2
Moreno, Roberto, Monclova .	.262	126	413	51	108	16	3	0	33	25	109	3
Kinnard, Ken, San Luis	.262	12	42	7	11	1	0	1	6	3	11	4
Pena, Luis, Campeche	.262	123	412	60	108	17	0	17	61	48	56	1
Sanchez, Gerardo, Laredo ..	.261	132	464	69	121	15	4	11	58	51	54	7
Almodobar, Ricardo, MC Tigers	.258	116	314	42	81	12	2	0	36	26	35	8
Rabb, John, Laguna	.257	56	187	32	48	11	0	9	36	31	47	11
Washington, Randy, Monclova	.256	38	125	25	32	6	0	4	25	23	30	2
Payton, Eric, Tabasco	.254	51	181	20	46	7	1	3	23	18	31	2
Sandoval, Jose, MC Reds ...	.252	122	408	55	103	19	5	5	36	37	80	9
Luna, Jose, Saltillo	.249	122	333	31	83	9	3	0	34	27	21	4
Gonzalez, Jesus, Tabasco ...	.247	122	465	38	115	16	0	2	31	26	28	1
Sanchez, Andres, Tabasco ..	.246	122	378	32	93	9	6	1	27	37	70	3
Jarrell, Joe, Sultans	.242	18	66	12	16	3	0	2	4	7	14	2
Herrera, Ricardo, Campeche	.238	100	349	62	83	15	2	0	23	47	41	21
Samaniego, Manuel, Indus ..	.235	96	310	25	73	7	2	2	39	13	34	2
Garza, Gerardo, Laredo	.234	113	376	26	88	10	1	1	34	19	32	5
Torres, Eduardo, Saltillo	.232	113	353	59	82	16	4	6	43	64	73	8
Gonzalez, Noe, Leon	.229	101	340	27	78	9	0	4	31	27	56	3
Clayton, Leonardo, Monclova	.224	124	361	48	81	14	2	7	41	66	70	4
Torres, Ray, Yucatan	.222	103	334	52	74	22	0	20	63	59	83	1
Douglas, Arthur, Tabasco ...	.220	30	109	10	24	3	0	3	7	10	28	6

	AVG	G	AB	R	H	2B	3B	HR	RBI	BB	SO	SB
Peralta, Amado, San Luis . . .	.218	121	349	53	76	13	2	10	48	84	83	1
Sconiers, Daryl, Indus . . .	.218	41	133	14	29	5	1	2	16	22	27	0
Cosey, Don, Tabasco	.190	30	100	4	19	4	0	0	12	5	14	2
St.Laurent, Jim, Tabasco . . .	.186	13	43	3	8	2	0	0	4	4	11	0

INDIVIDUAL PITCHING LEADERS

(U.S. Players and Players with 100 Innings)

	W	L	ERA	G	GS	CG	SV	IP	H	R	ER	BB	SO
Normand, Guy, Monclova . . .	14	4	2.08	21	21	7	0	143	114	42	33	64	107
Browning, Mike, Monclova . .	7	4	2.10	25	0	0	10	56	50	17	13	17	37
Barraza, Ernesto, Laredo . .	6	6	2.46	27	15	4	2	117	102	44	32	83	63
Navarro, Adolfo, Sultans . . .	9	5	2.57	23	23	3	0	133	137	53	38	41	98
Reynoso, Armando, Saltillo .	20	3	2.60	27	27	12	0	201	174	61	58	73	170
Gonzalez, Arturo, Sultans . .	14	5	2.61	22	21	9	0	166	156	58	48	30	114
Dozier, Tom, Yucatan	15	7	2.66	25	25	12	0	189	165	62	56	60	120
Cervantes, Lauro, Laguna . .	17	6	2.71	26	26	9	0	170	180	72	51	58	86
Alvarez, Juan, Laredo	9	7	2.76	24	22	2	0	134	122	60	41	81	70
Moreno, Angel, MC Tigers . .	10	5	2.81	23	23	7	0	151	160	61	47	49	107
Retes, Lorenzo, Laredo	6	5	2.82	24	11	9	1	108	95	41	34	48	40
Raygoza, Martin, Campeche	13	8	2.90	27	24	11	1	189	180	76	61	59	109
Osuna, Roberto, Sultans . . .	11	6	2.92	22	21	4	0	139	109	54	45	31	107
Orozco, Jaime, Leon	17	8	2.98	27	27	21	0	214	224	78	71	29	93
Perry, Jeff, Laguna	6	6	2.99	46	5	1	27	99	85	39	33	42	117
Huerta, Luis, Campeche. . . .	10	9	3.01	27	24	7	1	146	154	70	49	54	82
Mendez, Luis, MC Reds	16	5	3.04	25	25	6	0	166	172	67	56	42	63
Valdez, Armando, Industrials	11	12	3.04	37	19	5	4	172	164	70	58	65	120
Lazorko, Jack, San Luis	0	0	3.14	5	1	0	3	14	15	7	5	4	11
Esquer, Mercedes, Yucatan .	8	4	3.18	20	19	5	0	141	126	56	50	36	114
Cook, Glen, Monclova	0	2	3.25	4	4	0	0	28	27	13	10	11	19
Garza, Alejandro, Sultans . . .	9	8	3.27	19	15	1	0	107	99	48	39	40	76
Moreno, Jesus, Laredo	16	7	3.29	26	26	15	0	192	155	72	70	43	132
Camerena, Martin, Tabasco .	7	9	3.32	25	24	8	0	154	157	66	57	42	62
Purata, Julio, Leon	11	9	3.47	28	27	7	0	174	182	90	67	76	131
Colorado, Salvador, Yucatan	14	10	3.49	31	23	10	2	173	205	79	67	23	66
Renteria, Hilario, Laguna . . .	11	8	3.60	25	24	9	0	170	183	74	68	42	90
Castellanos, Humberto, Sal .	6	7	3.64	34	10	3	1	116	126	56	47	53	72
Dominquez, Herminio, Campeche	12	5	3.66	22	22	4	0	135	124	58	55	52	95
Sosa, Mario, Tabasco	6	13	3.68	23	22	7	1	142	157	74	58	63	68
Rodriguez, Raul, MC Tigers .	10	2	3.71	24	21	5	0	133	136	66	55	54	71
Morrow, Ben, Industrials	8	9	3.79	32	18	4	6	145	137	76	61	45	136
Solis, Ricardo, Saltillo	9	7	3.82	22	19	4	1	127	141	62	54	31	62
Couoh, Enrique, Laredo	14	8	3.83	25	25	11	0	167	143	78	71	74	121
Williams, Roger, MC Reds . .	9	6	3.89	18	18	6	0	123	124	60	53	47	58
Hernandez, Encarnacion, Lag	11	8	3.97	30	26	3	1	152	176	84	67	65	62
Grovom, Carl, Laredo	2	0	4.01	14	4	1	1	34	28	15	15	17	38
Osuna, Ricardo, MC Reds . .	7	6	4.03	18	17	5	0	114	118	60	51	43	61
Cosio, Mario, Monclova	8	9	4.10	27	25	6	0	145	157	79	66	79	66
Munoz, Miguel, Saltillo	9	15	4.14	26	26	6	0	165	214	107	67	33	54
Carranza, Javier, Aguas	8	11	4.19	26	26	7	0	150	158	85	70	92	100
Zamudio, Aurelio, Tabasco . .	8	10	4.20	24	24	2	0	150	148	80	70	68	69
Chavez, Guadalupe, Leon . .	5	5	4.25	20	20	2	0	102	121	63	48	37	47
Soto, Fernando, Leon	11	8	4.31	27	27	9	0	173	210	87	83	48	95
Lizarraga, Hugo, San Luis . .	6	11	4.35	27	18	1	0	120	148	69	58	51	46
Saldana, Edgardo, Tabasco .	10	12	4.36	25	24	4	0	138	161	74	67	82	67
Velazquez, Ildefonso, Cam . .	11	10	4.38	27	26	7	0	148	171	86	72	45	73
Garcia, Rene, Campeche . . .	6	8	4.40	24	15	1	0	102	123	62	50	55	56
Rios, Jesus, MC Tigers	9	10	4.42	24	24	2	0	149	157	83	73	54	89
Lopez, Emigdio, MC Tigers .	7	6	4.43	26	14	4	1	102	118	59	50	30	58
Aguilar, Miguel, Saltillo	5	8	4.47	25	22	2	0	109	122	66	54	45	66
Montano, Francisco, Aguas .	4	14	4.48	21	21	6	0	127	143	78	63	50	58
Palafox, Juan, Laguna	7	11	4.52	25	23	6	1	125	128	69	63	47	48
Straker, Les, Sultans	6	6	4.52	15	15	3	0	98	118	60	49	40	52
Garcia, Jorge, Indus	12	15	4.53	27	26	9	0	163	205	91	82	49	71
Veliz, Francisco, San Luis . .	6	9	4.55	22	20	1	1	115	149	75	58	56	58
Kinnunen, Mike, San Luis . .	2	7	4.66	13	11	3	1	77	77	45	40	36	53
Sinohui, David, Leon	10	9	4.88	32	13	6	5	135	151	76	73	56	71
Martinez, Ramon, MC Reds .	11	10	5.08	28	24	6	0	142	153	86	80	63	71
Pulido, Alfonso, MC Reds . .	6	4	5.18	19	19	2	0	106	132	66	61	30	24
Rodriguez, Ignacio, Mon . . .	7	12	5.32	27	26	3	0	115	125	78	68	82	95
Castaneda, Aurelio, San Luis	2	3	5.36	48	2	0	2	101	128	77	60	57	48
Quinones, Enrique, Aguas . .	11	8	5.36	30	20	5	0	128	156	90	82	71	81
Lopez, Raul, Monclova.	3	9	5.38	22	22	2	0	110	138	86	66	41	80
Acosta, Martin, Aguas	7	7	5.46	31	17	2	1	119	130	83	72	66	63
Serafin, Hector, Indus	7	12	5.55	28	26	1	0	136	190	104	84	53	69
Chambers, Travis, Aguas . . .	1	2	5.79	9	0	0	4	14	19	9	9	5	11
Lara, Eddie, Aguas	4	9	6.13	22	18	2	1	101	137	77	69	58	53
Meagher, Tom, San Luis . . .	1	2	6.30	5	5	0	0	20	22	20	14	17	16
Rodriguez, Mario, Saltillo . . .	3	7	6.34	31	12	1	2	104	149	88	73	48	61
Mack, Tony, Industrials	0	2	6.86	4	4	1	0	20	29	19	15	6	15
Moore, Robert, Laredo	0	2	9.45	4	0	0	1	7	10	7	7	3	6

JAPANESE LEAGUES

Seibu smashes Giants for sixth win in 9 years

By WAYNE GRACZYK

Perhaps inspired by the Cincinnati Reds sweep of the Oakland Athletics in the 1990 World Series, the underdog Seibu Lions dominated the Yomiuri Giants in the Japan Series. The Pacific League Lions knocked off the defending Central League and Japan champion Giants in four straight games to win the Far East version of the Fall Classic.

Jim Paciorek
...CL bat king

Led by former New York Yankees and Pittsburgh Pirates player Orestes Destrade, the Lions made quick work of defeating the Giants by scores of 5-0, 9-5, 7-0 and 7-3 to win their sixth Japan Series title in the last nine years and continue their dominance of Japan pro baseball.

Destrade, the Pacific League regular season home run champ with 42 and the co-RBI leader (tied with Orix Braves slugger Kazuhiko Ishimine with 106), was named the MVP in the Japan Series and walked away with a new automobile, cash and other prizes worth 9.25 million yen (about $74,000).

Paciorek wins batting crown

The Lions and Giants ho-hummed their way to clinching their respective league pennants with Yomiuri securing the C.L. flag on Sept. 8 and Seibu wrapping up the P.L. banner on Sept. 23. The Giants won by 22 games over the Hiroshima Carp and the Lions spaced 12 games between themselves and the second place Orix Braves.

In addition to the titles won by Destrade, the Central League batting crown went to another U.S. player, former Milwaukee Brewers outfielder Jim Paciorek of the Taiyo Whales. The brother of Chicago White Sox broadcaster Tom Paciorek was the runner-up in 1989 but won the title this time with a .326 average.

1990 FINAL STANDINGS

Central League	W	L	T	Pct.	GB
Yomiuri Giants	88	42	0	.677	—
Hiroshima Carp	66	64	2	.508	22
Taiyo Whales	64	66	3	.492	24
Chunichi Dragons	62	68	1	.477	26
Yakult Swallows	58	72	0	.446	30
Hanshin Tigers	52	78	0	.400	36
Pacific League					
Seibu Lions	81	45	4	.643	—
Orix Braves	69	57	4	.548	12
Kintetsu Buffaloes	67	60	3	.532	14½
Nippon Ham Fighters	66	63	1	.512	16½
Lotte Orions	57	71	2	.445	25
Fukuoka Daiei Hawks	41	85	4	.325	40

Playoffs: Seibu Lions defeated Yomiuri Giants 4-0 in best in best-of-7 final for league championship.

CENTRAL LEAGUE

INDIVIDUAL BATTING LEADERS
(Minimum 403 Plate Appearances)

	AVG	AB	R	H	HR	RBI
Paciorek, Jim, Whales	.326	527	78	172	17	94
Takagi, Yutaka, Whales	.323	406	61	131	10	55
Hirosawa, Katsumi, Swallows	.317	496	81	157	25	72
Law, Vance, Dragons	.313	457	69	143	29	78
Wada, Yutaka, Tigers	.304	496	72	151	8	36
Tatsunami, Kazuyoshi, Dragons	.303	511	73	155	11	45
Hara, Tatsunori, Giants	.303	366	58	111	20	68
Ikeyama, Takahiro, Swallows	.303	502	83	152	31	97
Shoda, Kozo, Carp	.301	462	48	139	3	39
Sumi, Fujio, Swallows	.301	366	26	110	6	51

(Remaining U.S. Players)

	AVG	AB	R	H	HR	RBI
Allen, Rod, Carp	.313	326	56	102	25	68
Cromartie, Warren, Giants	.293	450	68	132	14	55
Brown, Mike, Giants	.282	227	24	63	7	29
Meyer, Joey, Whales	.275	378	59	104	26	77
Parrish, Larry, Tigers	.249	381	56	95	28	80
Young, Mike, Carp	.234	222	27	52	11	35
Rowdon, Wade, Carp	.230	87	7	20	2	15
Murphy, Dwayne, Swallows	.229	109	19	25	5	22
Distefano, Benny, Dragons	.215	181	18	39	5	14
Wieligman, Rich, Tigers	.196	46	2	9	1	4
Ponce, Carlos, Whales	.193	57	3	11	0	3

INDIVIDUAL PITCHING LEADERS
(Minimum 130 Innings)

	W	L	ERA	G	SV	IP	SO
Saito, Masaki, Giants	20	5	2.17	27	0	224	146
Kuwata, Masumi, Giants	14	7	2.51	23	0	186	115
Kida, Masao, Giants	12	8	2.71	32	7	183	182
Koda, Isao, Giants	11	5	2.90	23	0	130	106
Sasaoka, Shinji, Carp	13	11	3.15	44	17	151	129
Miyamoto, Kenji, Swallows	11	7	3.16	22	0	159	76

(Remaining U.S. Players)

	W	L	ERA	G	SV	IP	SO
Bannister, Floyd, Swallows	3	2	4.04	9	0	49	31
Keough, Matt, Tigers	7	9	5.00	24	0	130	72
Rochford, Mike, Swallows	0	3	8.61	9	0	23	17

PACIFIC LEAGUE

INDIVIDUAL BATTING LEADERS
(Minimum 403 Plate Appearances)

	AVG	AB	R	H	HR	RBI
Nishimura, Norifumi, Orions	.338	438	78	148	3	38
Oishi, Daijiro, Buffaloes	.314	471	93	148	20	69
Diaz, Mike, Orions	.311	454	74	141	33	101
Kiyohara, Kazuhiro, Lions	.307	436	99	134	37	94
Traber, Jim, Buffaloes	.303	495	64	150	24	92
Ishige, Hiromichi, Lions	.298	359	48	107	8	47
Brewer, Tony, Fighters	.295	407	65	120	17	63
Arai, Hiromasa, Buffaloes	.292	363	58	106	6	34
Tanaka, Yukio, Fighters	.287	450	63	129	18	52
Fujii, Yasuo, Braves	.285	463	81	132	37	96

(Remaining U.S. Players)

	AVG	AB	R	H	HR	RBI
Wells, Boomer, Braves	.307	163	25	50	7	31
Winters, Matt, Fighters	.278	468	73	130	35	97
Bernatard, Tony, Hawks	.275	276	36	76	13	40
Destrade, Orestes, Lions	.263	476	81	125	42	106
Bryant, Ralph, Buffaloes	.245	412	67	101	29	73
Upshaw, Willie, Hawks	.220	191	22	42	6	17
Dayett, Brian, Fighters	.208	53	5	11	3	11
Van Burkleo, Ty, Lions	.196	112	20	22	9	22
Hengel, Dave, Orions	.179	67	6	12	4	12
Wilson, Jim, Hawks	.059	17	1	1	1	2

INDIVIDUAL PITCHING LEADERS
(Minimum 130 Innings)

	W	L	ERA	G	SV	IP	SO
Nomo, Hideo, Buffaloes	18	8	2.91	29	0	235	287
Watanabe, Hisanobu, Lions	18	10	2.97	30	0	224	172
Shibata, Yasumitsu, Fighters	12	10	3.11	27	0	202	150
Komiyama, Satoru, Orions	6	10	3.27	30	2	171	126
Watanabe, Tomio, Lions	13	7	3.38	24	1	176	130
Ishii, Takehiro, Lions	8	6	3.38	23	0	133	99

(Remaining U.S. Players)

	W	L	ERA	G	SV	IP	SO
Schulze, Don, Braves	6	4	2.58	20	3	70	32
Hoffman, Guy, Braves	8	9	4.13	24	0	153	111
Gossage, Rich, Hawks	2	3	4.40	28	8	47	40

WINTER BASEBALL

Miami's Orange Bowl, with its 250-foot left field line, proved inadequate as a CWS site.

New U.S. site hardly suited for baseball

By ALLAN SIMPSON

The Caribbean World Series took on a decidedly new look in 1990. For the first time in its 42-year history, the CWS was played in a location foreign to the competing teams—that's foreign, as in the United States.

Miami's Orange Bowl was selected as the site of the four-nation series, which matches champions from baseball's recognized winter leagues and previously had been hosted on a rotating basis by the participating countries.

Escogido, the Dominican League representative, won the double-elimination competition, finishing with a 5-1 record. It was the Lions second series triumph in three years. Puerto Rico and defending champion Venezuela finished in a two-way tie for second, at 3-3, while Mexico brought up the rear, winning only one of six games.

Ongoing financial problems in the competing Caribbean countries, aggravated by a devalued currency against the American dollar, sent CWS organizers searching for a new home in 1990. Officials were faced with a real threat that no country might have resources sufficient to host the series, so Miami, with its heavy Hispanic population, was selected as a compromise site.

The series was a fiasco from the start. The Orange Bowl, a football facility which last was used for a baseball exhibition featuring ageless Satchel Paige in 1956, was hastily converted into a makeshift baseball stadium. But a 250-foot left field foul line, all-grass infield and nuances foreign to a major international competition made it hopelessly inadequate.

Crowds in the 75,000-seat facility totalled little more than 50,000 for the seven-day event, far short of expectations.

"The people involved in this project have a long-term commitment (a three year-deal) that's grounded in modest expectations in the first year," said Rick Horrow, head of the

Miami organizing group. "All of us are entering it with that attitude. My thought is to survive and establish credibility the first year. But I think in the long run, the series will turn out to be a great success."

Home run haven

Escogido, making its third straight appearance at the CWS, won the tournament with relative ease. It went into the final night of the competition needing only to defeat San Juan, the Puerto Rican League champion, to win the title. Earlier, the Lions had defeated Caracas, the Venezuelan League champion, and Hermosillo, the Mexican Pacific League entry, twice each.

Escogido unleashed a blistering 18-hit attack in the deciding game against Puerto Rico, and won handily, 16-5. The barrage included two home runs and five RBIs by Geronimo Berroa (Braves), who was named the tournament's most valuable player. In all, Berroa hit four home runs in the series, batted .300 and drove in eight runs.

Nelson Liriano (Blue Jays) also homered for the Dominican champions. All five Puerto Rican runs came on solo home runs, including two by second baseman Carlos Baerga (Indians). Outfielder Barry Jones (Braves) belted his fifth of the tournament.

The eight homers in the championship game was a single-game record, and raised the total for the series to 48 in 12 games, shattering the old mark of 30 in 1987.

Playing conditions at the Orange Bowl were widely criticized. With the short porch in left field only 250 feet away, teams regularly disdained the bunt and a running game for the long ball.

"(The short fence) takes away from a lot of things that you normally would do," said Hermosillo manager Tim Johnson. "You're not going to bunt when you need to."

The 1991 series, scheduled Feb. 2-10, is to undergo another facelift, though it will remain in Miami for a second year. It will be known as Winterball I and be played at 10,000-seat Robert Maduro Miami Stadium.

DOMINICAN REPUBLIC

The Escogido Lions became champions of the 1990 Caribbean Series, but never found the going as easy during the Dominican League season.

Dave Hansen
... MVP

The Lions finished second during the regular season. In the league's 18-game playoffs which determined two finalists for the league's championship series, they went 9-9, winning a spot opposite Aguilas with a 10-8 victory on the final night as outfielder Geronimo Berroa had an RBI single and his fifth home run of the round-robin.

From there, the Lions swept aside Aguilas, 4-2, in the best-of-7 championship series to earn their third straight trip to the Caribbean Series. They followed by winning five of six games to capture their second CWS championship in three years.

Aguilas second baseman Angel Gonzalez (Red Sox) won the league's regular season batting title with a .434 mark, a whopping 101 points ahead of Estrellas' Daved Segui (Orioles). Gonzalez hit only .204 during the 1988-89 season. He became only the third player in league history to bat over .400, following Ralph Garr's .457 in 1970-71 and Pedro Hernandez' .408 mark in 1982-83.

Licey's Dave Hansen (Dodgers), who hit .326, was named the league's MVP. Licey won the regular season title, but quickly bowed out in the playoffs.

1990 *FINAL STANDINGS*

Regular Season	W	L	Pct.	GB
Licey	28	19	.596	—
Escogido	27	21	.563	1½
Aguilas	25	23	.521	3½
Estrellas	24	24	.500	4½
Azucareros	15	32	.319	13
Playoffs	**W**	**L**	**Pct.**	**GB**
Aguilas	11	6	.647	—
Escogido	9	9	.500	2½
Estrellas	8	10	.444	3½
Licey	7	10	.412	4

LEAGUE CHAMPIONSHIP SERIES: Escogido defeated Aguilas 4-2 in best-of-7 final.

INDIVIDUAL BATTING LEADERS
(Minimum 100 At-Bats)

	AVG	G	AB	R	H	2B	3B	HR	RBI	BB	SO	SB
Gonzalez, Angel, Agu	.434	33	122	14	53	7	1	1	15	7	12	3
#Segui, David, Est	.333	42	147	21	49	10	2	2	22	28	12	0
*Hansen, Dave, Licey	.326	46	184	31	60	9	0	3	21	21	22	5
Jose, Felix, Licey	.324	41	148	22	48	8	3	1	20	25	23	7
Michel, Domingo, Licey	.318	45	151	28	48	5	1	2	23	31	16	6
Mercedes, Luis, Est	.302	42	162	27	49	2	2	0	8	13	22	8
Delacruz, Hector, Esc	.300	42	110	18	33	6	2	3	16	10	24	3
#Sambo, Ramon, Azu	.298	35	131	17	39	1	0	0	8	20	23	17
Noboa, Junior, Esc	.295	40	156	21	46	6	1	0	18	11	12	5
Nunez, Mauricio, Est	.292	40	130	15	38	8	0	2	21	13	10	4
Sosa, Sammy, Esc	.285	37	151	14	43	4	2	2	19	5	29	13
Bournigal, Rafael, Est	.281	38	114	12	32	4	0	0	13	6	11	2
Gonzalez, Denny, Agu	.280	41	143	12	40	4	2	5	25	25	27	3
Delossantos, Luis, Esc	.276	43	163	26	45	4	4	2	30	18	18	3
Rosario, Victor, Azu	.275	30	102	15	28	6	2	0	6	4	21	3
Chance, Tony, Est	.269	47	160	18	43	9	1	4	17	16	46	4
Eusebio, Raul, Azu	.263	36	118	8	31	1	2	0	15	6	19	0
*Fletcher, Darrin, Licey	.260	32	104	9	27	4	0	0	12	12	15	0
Grissom, Marquis, Esc	.258	47	178	33	46	6	1	2	11	24	29	16
#Vizcaino, Jose, Esc	.257	41	140	21	36	2	0	0	14	18	21	3
#Offerman, Jose, Azu	.250	43	152	22	38	10	1	0	8	21	34	23
*Neel, Troy, Agu	.248	44	149	18	37	6	0	3	17	20	40	2
*Tatis, Bernie, Esc	.246	47	167	31	41	8	2	3	16	30	31	11
Meulens, Hensley, Azu	.237	33	118	10	28	7	0	0	14	15	31	1
Brito, Bernardo, Licey	.236	39	157	17	37	12	0	1	38	6	42	1
Berroa, Geronimo, Esc	.233	41	146	20	34	7	1	2	16	22	31	1
Alexander, Manny, Est	.230	42	135	18	31	3	2	0	9	6	31	6
#Pena, Geronimo, Licey	.226	40	137	31	31	2	1	3	12	21	26	5
Alou, Moises, Agu	.226	43	168	21	38	5	2	2	17	12	29	3
Bernhardt, Cesar, Est	.226	33	124	16	28	5	1	1	16	7	16	3
*Sabino, Miguel, Est	.224	40	125	12	28	5	3	0	9	9	22	2
Tejada, Wil, Esc	.214	39	103	10	22	2	0	0	11	9	12	1
Cabrera, Francisco, Azu	.212	31	113	8	24	2	0	4	12	7	25	1
Fermin, Felix, Agu	.204	27	103	10	21	2	0	0	1	9	1	1

INDIVIDUAL PITCHING LEADERS
(Minimum 35 Innings)

	W	L	ERA	G	GS	CG	SV	IP	H	R	ER	BB	SO
*Edwards, Jeff, Agu	4	3	2.17	14	10	1	0	66	57	20	16	20	76
Acosta, Jose, Azu	3	2	2.25	16	3	1	0	44	35	14	11	11	22
Smith, Mike, Est	4	2	2.26	10	10	0	0	60	46	21	15	29	40
Shaw, Jeff, Agu	6	2	2.28	13	11	1	0	71	64	34	18	24	44
Araujo, Andy, Licey	2	2	2.31	13	4	0	1	47	46	17	12	5	18
Delacruz, Carlos, Est	3	2	2.38	10	9	0	0	45	44	17	12	15	22
Rojas, Mel, Esc	6	1	2.57	12	12	0	0	63	55	26	18	29	36
Del, Rosario, Maximo, Est	0	1	2.60	30	0	0	9	35	33	13	10	9	19
Skalski, Joe, Agu	2	5	2.82	13	11	0	0	54	47	26	17	17	38
*Frey, Steve, Esc	5	3	2.82	11	11	1	0	54	47	22	17	25	42
Rivera, Ben, Est	2	5	2.93	16	3	0	1	40	37	20	13	15	18
Valdez, Efrain, Licey	2	1	2.95	14	5	0	1	37	39	15	12	15	18
Pena, Ramon, Agu	2	2	2.95	30	0	0	10	40	36	14	13	7	28
*Cavers, Mike, Est	5	2	3.17	11	11	0	0	60	55	21	21	19	30
*Alba, Gibson, Esc	2	1	3.38	16	5	0	2	48	36	19	18	31	40
Nunez, Jose, Esc	4	3	3.42	11	10	0	0	53	47	25	20	27	38
Galvez, Balvino, Licey	2	1	3.58	8	6	0	0	38	38	19	15	18	25
Holmes, Darren, Licey	6	4	3.82	12	12	1	0	64	56	28	27	34	63
Wetteland, John, Licey	2	0	3.86	11	8	0	0	42	41	21	18	18	43
Hernandez, Manny, Azu	0	5	3.96	8	8	0	0	39	50	29	17	16	13
Cano, Jose, Azu	2	5	4.18	10	9	0	0	47	52	30	22	23	33
Beasley, Chris, Azu	4	5	4.42	11	9	2	0	55	65	34	27	17	34
Wagner, Hector, Agu	1	4	5.59	14	7	0	0	39	56	32	24	13	12

PUERTO RICO

San Juan's Edgar Martinez became the first Puerto Rican League player in more than 40 years to hit over .400. The Seattle Mariners third base prospect finished the 1989-90 season with a .424 average, far ahead of Santurce outfielder Mark Ryal's .342 mark.

Edgar Martinez
. . . .424 hitter

Martinez was named the league's co-MVP with teammate Carlos Baerga (Indians), who hit .343 with four homers. Baerga and Ponce's Luis Aguayo tied for the league lead with 35 RBIs.

Ponce, managed by Sandy Alomar Sr. and featuring sons Roberto (Padres) and Sandy Jr. (Indians) finished in first place in the league's regular season, but player defections and a porous infield defense caused a collapse in the first round of the playoffs. The Lions lost 16 of 18 games.

That opened the door for San Juan, which won the league's 18-game round robin playoff with a 13-4 record, then defeated Caguas, 5-3, in the best-of-9 championship series.

1990 *FINAL STANDINGS*

Regular Season	W	L	Pct.	GB
Ponce	31	19	.620	—
Caguas	28	22	.560	3
San Juan	27	23	.540	4
Mayaguez	23	27	.460	8
Santurce	22	28	.440	9
Arecibo	19	31	.380	12
Playoffs				
San Juan	13	4	.765	—
Caguas	12	6	.667	1½
Mayaguez	8	9	.471	5
Ponce	2	16	.111	11½

LEAGUE CHAMPIONSHIP SERIES: San Juan defeated Caguas 5-3 in best-of-9 final.

INDIVIDUAL BATTING LEADERS
(Minimum 100 At-Bats)

	AVG	G	AB	R	H	2B	3B	HR	RBI	BB	SO	SB
Martinez, Edgar, SJ	.424	43	132	28	56	8	1	3	25	37	15	4
*Ryal, Mark, Snt	.342	40	149	20	51	13	0	3	26	10	20	3
#Baerga, Carlos, SJ	.341	50	179	28	61	13	1	4	35	24	24	8
#Hall, Albert, Snt	.326	49	187	34	61	9	2	1	16	30	24	22
Alomar, Sandy, Ponce	.321	42	156	33	50	7	0	3	21	13	15	3
Morris, Angel, Snt	.320	39	122	17	39	6	0	4	22	8	23	1
#Silver, Roy, May	.317	45	145	21	46	8	3	2	26	15	9	0
Aguayo, Luis, Ponce	.316	48	171	15	54	7	1	3	35	17	23	1
Ortiz, Junior, SJ	.316	41	133	18	42	6	0	4	21	15	12	1
*Francona, Terry, Ponce	.310	49	187	26	58	10	1	1	30	19	16	1
#Diaz, Alex, May	.309	45	175	21	54	4	0	1	16	10	24	5
#Howard, Tom, Ponce	.308	48	156	35	48	9	2	5	27	32	24	15
#Barrett, Tom, Cag	.306	33	111	16	34	9	3	1	12	10	8	7
Vargas, Hector, Are	.301	40	153	24	46	8	1	1	16	21	21	12
Cotto, Henry, Cag	.301	46	173	43	52	7	1	7	18	27	29	13
#Burgos, Paco, Ponce	.300	40	140	24	42	10	1	0	6	3	9	6
#Cora, Joey, Ponce	.293	49	198	42	58	6	1	1	19	26	11	15
McGriff, Terry, Snt	.292	48	161	27	47	15	0	1	13	26	30	1
Lindeman, Jim, May	.287	49	178	17	51	14	1	4	29	12	25	4
Lopez, Luis, Snt	.286	49	182	24	52	12	0	3	26	20	24	3
*Jones, Barry, SJ	.285	50	207	28	59	10	3	4	32	6	26	6
Cuevas, Angelo, Cag	.282	41	124	21	35	11	0	1	18	12	17	2
Vaughn, Greg, Ponce	.274	46	164	31	45	6	1	10	30	36	31	7
*Cortes, Hernan, Are	.270	41	115	16	31	8	1	1	16	27	14	3
Gonzalez, Juan, Cag	.269	44	156	36	42	7	1	9	34	18	31	9
Tubbs, Greg, SJ	.266	47	177	34	47	8	2	0	9	24	29	3
*Sanchez, Osvaldo, Snt	.262	46	130	18	34	4	0	2	18	20	18	1

	AVG	G	AB	R	H	2B	3B	HR	RBI	BB	SO	SB
Calderon, Ivan, Ponce	.261	33	134	15	35	10	1	3	26	6	17	4
*Lankford, Ray, May	.261	48	184	30	48	6	8	3	15	15	29	7
Wilson, Jim, Are	.259	50	185	17	48	10	0	4	27	11	38	3
*Canale, George, Cag	.250	45	152	23	38	9	0	5	21	33	31	2
*Escalera, Ruben, SJ	.250	45	140	19	35	4	1	1	12	8	22	2
Lind, Jose, Snt	.250	37	128	16	32	6	1	0	14	13	5	8
Rivera, Luis, May	.244	33	119	13	29	6	2	1	16	13	19	2
*Thornton, Lou, May	.242	37	132	20	32	8	1	3	15	5	22	6
#Valentin, Jose, Snt	.239	38	117	17	28	6	0	1	10	16	25	5
Virgil, Ozzie, Snt	.238	38	101	13	24	4	0	2	15	20	8	0
#Williams, Bernie, Are	.235	45	153	29	36	4	2	5	14	31	33	13
#Alicea, Edwin, Are	.234	47	175	33	41	12	2	5	23	29	30	2
Pagnozzi, Tom, May	.231	42	143	8	33	9	0	0	20	6	28	2

INDIVIDUAL PITCHING LEADERS
(Minimum 35 Innings)

	W	L	ERA	G	GS	CG	SV	IP	H	R	ER	BB	SO
Gray, Jeff, May	1	1	1.24	26	0	0	10	36	26	6	5	9	28
Murphy, Dan, Ponce	1	3	2.08	21	1	0	11	39	30	13	9	24	33
Bockus, Randy, Cag	2	1	2.25	25	2	0	10	40	33	15	10	17	32
Calderon, Jose, Snt	1	0	2.61	20	1	0	1	38	37	12	11	20	14
Lind, Orlando, SJ	4	3	2.72	10	8	1	0	53	39	17	16	23	31
*Figueroa, Fernando, Are ...	3	5	2.75	12	8	1	0	59	46	31	18	31	45
Hanson, Erik, Are	3	2	2.83	8	7	0	0	48	45	19	15	12	38
*Rosario, David, SJ	2	2	3.06	17	5	0	4	50	46	24	17	16	41
Reed, Rick, Snt	6	4	3.12	14	12	3	0	84	82	33	29	20	53
Nunez, Edwin, Ponce	5	2	3.15	11	11	2	0	60	64	23	21	10	41
Bones, Ricky, Ponce	8	2	3.19	12	12	2	0	79	74	34	28	25	42
Sebra, Bob, Snt	2	5	3.30	20	6	0	6	57	45	32	21	26	43
Oliveras, Francisco, Cag ...	3	4	3.34	9	9	2	0	57	55	30	21	12	31
Rivera, Lino, May	3	2	3.35	18	5	0	0	51	54	26	19	29	33
*Miranda, Angel, Are	1	2	3.44	18	4	0	1	37	27	14	14	30	33
Burtt, Dennis, May	5	3	3.48	12	10	1	1	62	69	32	24	15	22
*Stewart, Hector, Cag	3	1	3.50	21	2	0	0	44	46	20	17	16	23
Nezelek, Andy, Cag	3	3	3.51	24	1	0	2	41	36	20	16	18	16
Melendez, Jose, Cag	5	2	3.57	14	11	1	0	71	57	30	28	15	42
Olivares, Omar, Cag	3	5	3.71	13	11	0	0	70	65	33	29	32	35
Sanchez, Geraldo, Cag	2	0	3.82	13	3	0	0	35	35	21	15	16	10
Harris, Gene, Are	1	3	3.86	17	4	0	2	40	34	20	17	18	24
Chavez, Rafael, Ponce	5	2	4.04	26	0	0	3	56	62	25	25	13	29
*Vesling, Don, SJ	4	2	4.35	11	11	0	0	60	56	30	29	24	26
Rodriguez, Gabriel, Ponce ..	3	3	4.42	18	3	0	2	39	38	24	19	25	24
Sierra, Candy, Snt	4	4	4.43	12	11	0	0	61	71	36	30	24	38
Tirado, Aris, Are	2	9	4.55	12	9	1	1	55	62	32	28	28	37
Deleon, Luis, May	2	4	4.64	8	7	0	0	43	46	25	22	7	30
Moore, Brad, Cag	5	4	4.82	14	9	1	0	47	55	30	25	28	22
Taylor, Terry, Are	1	3	4.91	12	8	0	1	48	40	31	26	30	32
Montalvo, Rafael, SJ	3	3	4.91	22	1	0	0	37	40	21	20	12	18
Valera, Julio, May	5	4	4.96	12	12	0	0	69	71	45	38	25	44
Krawczyk, Ray, Ponce	3	0	5.45	7	7	0	0	36	51	24	22	8	27
Schwabe, Mike, SJ	3	4	5.50	9	8	0	0	36	47	24	22	6	25

VENEZUELA

Caracas won its third Venezuelan League title in four years, edging Lara 4-3 in the league's best-of-7 championship series. Jim Neidlinger (Dodgers), working on two day's rest, came out of the bullpen to pitch the final 4⅔ innings as Caracas hung on to win the deciding game, 5-3.

Luis Sojo
....351 hitter

Neidlinger, the Venezuelan League pitcher of the year, had pitched a complete-game victory over Lara in Game Five of the series, and asked manager Phil Regan if he could return to the U.S. to be with his pregnant wife. Regan encouraged Neidlinger to stick around, and he went to his ace in the deciding game with one out in the fourth and Caracas down 2-1. Neidlinger allowed only one hit over the last three innings.

Veteran outfielder Tony Armas hit four homers for Caracas in the seven-game series, including an insurance blast in the deciding game.

Lara infielder Luis Sojo (Blue Jays) was named the league's MVP. He led the league in batting, runs scored and hits.

The Zulia Eagles, winners of the 1989 Caribbean World Series, finished a disappointing fifth. They lost a one-game playoff with LaGuaira for the league's fourth and final playoff berth.

1990 FINAL STANDINGS

Regular Season	W	L	Pct.	GB
*Magallanes	33	27	.550	—
*Lara	33	27	.550	—
Caracas	32	28	.533	1
LaGuaira	32	29	.525	1½
Zulia	31	30	.508	2½
Aragua	20	40	.333	13
Playoffs	**W**	**L**	**Pct.**	**GB**
Caracas	8	4	.667	—
Lara	8	4	.667	—
LaGuaira	7	5	.583	1
Magallanes	1	11	.083	7
*co-champions				

LEAGUE CHAMPIONSHIP SERIES: Caracas defeated Lara, 4-3, in best-of-7 series for league championship.

INDIVIDUAL BATTING LEADERS
(Minimum 100 At-Bats)

	AVG	G	AB	R	H	2B	3B	HR	RBI	BB	SO	SB
Sojo, Luis, Lara	.351	57	231	45	81	8	7	4	20	20	19	18
Estarda, Asdrubal, Lara	.328	55	204	31	67	9	3	2	40	16	32	4
Naveda, Edgar, Mag	.327	46	171	28	56	7	1	1	29	12	21	1
Rohde, Dave, Mag.	.327	48	165	28	54	4	2	0	21	35	15	3
Cacares, Edgar, Car.	.324	48	185	26	60	9	0	0	15	18	17	13
Sharperson, Mike, Car.	.321	32	112	28	36	8	2	0	15	23	20	2
Olivares, Ossie, Mag.	.319	57	182	35	58	8	4	0	22	31	13	4
Arndt, Larry, Mag.	.310	30	113	21	35	7	2	3	14	13	28	1
Quintana, Carlos, Zulia	.308	33	117	21	36	6	2	3	25	25	10	2
Uribe, Jorge, Caracas	.305	53	174	24	53	7	4	2	27	12	44	4
Mendez, Jesus, Aragua	.304	59	217	27	66	12	3	0	27	19	10	3
Carrasco, Norm, LaG.	.303	54	221	23	67	12	1	0	28	6	16	4
Traxler, Brian, Car.	.300	57	203	25	61	16	2	4	39	38	23	2
Manrique, Fred, Aragua	.297	45	165	20	49	14	1	3	30	19	19	0
Barnes, Skeeter, Mag.	.296	34	135	23	40	7	1	4	26	7	13	5
Infante, Alex, Mag.	.296	45	159	30	47	7	1	0	10	18	11	15
Soto, Fernando, Zulia	.290	40	131	19	38	3	2	0	8	21	24	3
Rincones, Hector, Aragua	.289	48	152	13	44	7	1	0	13	17	8	2
Tovar, Raul, LaGuaira	.289	58	232	41	67	12	5	6	32	22	27	2
Willard, Jerry, Mag.	.289	46	135	27	39	7	2	4	24	54	24	3
Amaro, Ruben, Zulia	.288	25	104	17	30	5	2	3	12	16	10	6
Hernandez, Carlos, Car.	.287	53	178	20	51	7	2	1	22	9	27	3
Vizquel, Omar, Caracas	.286	45	175	29	50	11	4	0	16	15	13	8
Espinoza, Andres, Lara	.282	55	163	13	46	10	0	3	23	14	23	0
Martinez, Carlos, LaG.	.281	60	221	29	62	18	3	3	34	29	30	4
Chavez, Pedro, Mag.	.279	36	104	15	29	6	0	0	14	10	9	0
Whiten, Mark, Lara	.272	55	206	37	56	6	3	4	25	19	49	10
Galindo, Luis, LaG.	.272	57	202	29	55	3	2	0	13	22	22	1
Salazar, Luis, LaG.	.268	36	138	14	37	5	2	5	18	13	16	2
Magallanes, Willie, Mag.	.267	58	232	31	62	12	1	8	41	24	64	2
Cole, Alex, Aragua	.267	49	180	36	48	3	4	0	3	42	19	26
Espinoza, Alvaro, Aragua	.265	46	170	15	45	8	0	1	15	3	18	2
Sprague, Ed, Lara	.265	55	215	22	57	9	3	5	31	10	29	2
Labastidas, Mario, Zulia	.263	49	137	15	36	1	1	0	11	8	13	4
Hill, Glenallen, Lara	.257	42	152	25	39	6	1	5	23	27	36	5
Alfaro, Jesus, Caracas	.256	60	207	20	53	12	2	3	28	36	33	1
Zambrano, Eduardo, Zulia	.255	55	188	22	48	12	0	2	26	23	34	1
Delima, Rafael, Aragua	.253	54	190	22	48	4	4	1	11	36	27	2
Garcia, Carlos, Mag.	.250	51	168	18	42	7	2	1	25	17	21	1
Castellano, Pedro, Zulia	.249	60	217	33	54	16	3	2	37	25	53	2
Perez, Robert, Lara	.247	58	170	17	42	4	2	1	13	8	29	0
Azocar, Oscar, Caracas	.245	57	220	34	54	14	3	6	30	17	16	2
Hamelin, Bob, LaGuaira	.241	37	108	23	26	8	1	6	22	38	32	0
Little, Scott, LaG.	.239	59	213	28	51	6	1	3	22	33	36	5
Salazar, Luis E., LaG.	.238	44	147	12	35	10	1	0	16	5	21	0
Torres, Al, Aragua	.235	38	136	13	32	7	0	6	16	18	33	3

INDIVIDUAL PITCHING LEADERS
(Minimum 40 Innings)

	W	L	ERA	G	GS	CG	SV	IP	H	R	ER	BB	SO
Aponte, Luis, Lara	6	1	1.99	29	0	0	9	50	39	15	11	19	29
Upshaw, Lee, Aragua	2	3	2.08	8	7	0	0	48	43	15	11	15	20
Blankenship, Kevin, Zulia	6	1	2.13	14	12	1	1	84	67	29	20	37	41
Medvin, Scott, Caracas	4	2	2.20	25	0	0	7	41	31	14	10	19	34
Baller, Jay, LaGuaira	1	3	2.23	25	0	0	10	40	38	13	10	17	33

	W	L	ERA	G	GS	CG	SV	IP	H	R	ER	BB	SO
Tapia, Jose, Caracas	2	0	2.25	21	0	0	1	48	34	13	12	17	15
Straker, Les, Mag.	6	3	2.29	13	13	1	0	71	59	23	18	27	33
Conde, Argenis, Mag.	6	4	2.68	13	12	2	0	77	69	30	23	31	37
Machado, Julio, Zulia	3	1	2.84	29	0	0	12	44	32	15	14	28	36
Harkey, Mike, Zulia	2	3	2.84	9	7	1	0	51	48	17	16	15	43
Lugo, Urbano, Car.	3	4	2.87	14	14	0	0	78	61	32	25	32	45
Lynch, Dave, LaGuaira	6	2	2.91	13	10	0	1	53	50	20	17	33	33
Neidlinger, Jim, Car.	8	2	2.99	15	12	4	1	84	78	36	28	19	65
Blair, Willie, Lara	3	3	3.00	15	10	1	0	69	67	30	23	28	36
Leal, Luis, Lara	4	3	3.04	15	13	0	1	77	87	30	26	17	33
Hernandez, Xavier, Lara	2	6	3.06	21	8	0	3	68	75	40	23	22	38
Bohanon, Brian, Mag.	2	7	3.10	11	11	1	0	67	60	31	23	30	42
Cardona, Jose, LaG.	1	2	3.21	23	0	0	2	48	50	23	17	15	27
Carreno, Amalio, Car.	3	3	3.30	14	13	0	1	71	57	31	26	30	40
Heredia, Ubaldo, Car.	4	4	3.48	11	9	0	0	52	58	30	20	15	32
Vasquez, Luis, Mag.	6	3	3.49	11	11	0	0	59	63	26	23	17	16
Espinoza, Roberto, Aragua ..	3	6	3.61	13	10	1	0	67	77	36	27	17	37
McGrath, Chuck, Aragua	5	7	3.68	15	12	3	0	73	87	42	30	19	36
Cook, Mike, Caracas	5	5	3.70	29	0	0	5	41	36	18	17	23	26
Garcia, Ramon, Mag.	5	3	3.70	19	7	0	0	58	54	30	24	28	24
Castillo, Tony, Lara	7	3	3.88	18	12	0	0	72	71	34	31	34	81
Bencomo, Omar, Lara	8	5	3.94	20	6	0	0	59	70	33	28	21	25
Strauss, Julio, Car.	3	4	4.33	18	8	0	1	52	57	28	25	27	23
Castillo, Frank, Zulla	3	5	4.38	14	10	0	0	82	82	39	30	29	42

MEXICAN PACIFIC LEAGUE

Hermosillo survived an opening-round scare in the Mexican Pacific League playoffs and went on to land its first berth in the Caribbean World Series in seven years. It was the ninth league title overall for Hermosillo.

The Orange Growers won both halves of the Northern Division race, and finished with a 46-23 record in the regular season. But they immediately found themselves in trouble in the first round of the league's eight-team playoff. They lost the first two games of their best-of-9 series to Obregon, but rallied to win five of the next six.

Narciso Elvira
... top pitcher

From there, they swept aside Guaymas 5-0 in the semi-finals and whipped Navojoa, 4-1, in the league's best-of-7 championship series.

Hermosillo lefthander Narciso Elvira (Brewers) was the league's top pitcher. He fashioned a 9-2 record and 1.41 ERA, and had a streak of 39 consecutive scoreless innings in one stretch. He also led the league in strikeouts, with 94 in 89 innings.

Mexicali's Dave Hollins, drafted by Philadelphia at the 1989 Winter Meetings, won the batting title with a .327 average.

1990 *FINAL STANDINGS*

Overall	W	L	Pct.	GB
Hermosillo	46	23	.667	—
Mexicali	40	30	.571	6½
Mazatlan	37	31	.544	8½
Navojoa	36	31	.537	9
Guasave	36	32	.529	9½
Los Mochis	36	33	.522	10
Culiacan	35	34	.507	11
Obregon	31	36	.463	14
Guaymas	28	40	.412	17½
Tijuana	17	52	.246	29

PLAYOFFS: Quarter-finals (best-of-9)—Guaymas defeated Mexicali, 5-4; Navojoa defeated Guasave, 5-3; Hermosillo defeated Obregon, 5-3; Mazatlan defeated Los Mochis, 5-2. **Semi-finals (best-of-9)**—Hermosillo defeated Guaymas, 5-0; Navojoa defeated Mazatlan, 5-4. **Championship Series (best-of-7)**—Hermosillo defeated Navojoa, 4-1.

INDIVIDUAL BATTING LEADERS
(Minimum 125 At-Bats)

	AVG	G	AB	R	H	2B	3B	HR	RBI	BB	SO	SB
#Hollins, Dave, Mex	.327	52	162	44	53	14	2	9	40	52	22	0
*Carter, Jeff, Nav	.324	67	241	54	78	3	5	2	16	51	37	33
Rojas, Homar, Herm	.317	65	249	34	79	10	1	10	54	17	33	0
Smith, Greg, LM	.300	68	270	39	81	16	2	8	48	24	27	5
*Newson, Warren, Mex	.299	70	231	59	69	11	0	12	37	63	49	19
*Grunhard, Dan, Obr	.298	36	131	24	39	5	0	8	24	11	24	0
Tellez, Alonso, Guay	.297	68	269	33	80	13	1	5	36	19	26	2
*DeShields, Delino, Herm . . .	.297	67	246	38	73	18	2	9	48	42	51	18
*Sanchez, Armando, Maz . . .	.296	68	257	45	76	6	1	1	19	40	25	1
See, Larry, Maz	.295	35	149	27	44	10	1	4	23	7	23	1
Jimenez, Houston, Mex	.292	68	260	48	76	12	2	6	20	41	29	9
Renteria, Rick, Nav	.290	52	193	27	56	8	2	1	28	21	13	8
#Walker, Chico, Herm	.289	49	166	41	48	9	0	11	26	46	33	10
Garcia, Cornelio, Herm	.289	49	180	29	52	11	0	3	26	29	37	11
*Navarrete, Juan, Guay	.288	68	267	35	77	8	1	1	33	24	8	4
*Tolentino, Jose, Guay	.285	65	221	38	63	13	0	5	27	48	27	4
Garbey, Barbaro, Gsv	.285	60	200	30	57	9	0	12	28	21	18	1
#Smith, Greg, Herm	.285	62	267	34	76	10	2	0	37	15	35	12
Pacho, Juan, Maz	.283	68	237	21	67	11	0	0	21	17	17	1
Clark, Phil, LM	.281	66	242	31	68	7	1	4	36	17	33	2
Ortiz, Alejandro, Obr	.279	66	219	41	61	8	0	16	43	40	29	3
Cazarin, Manuel, Maz	.278	58	205	16	57	9	0	3	28	15	34	1
*Velazquez, Guillermo, Mex . .	.277	69	260	34	72	17	0	13	74	25	37	1
#Cuyler, Milt, LM	.277	64	260	51	72	13	3	2	31	50	35	35
*Cole, Michael, Gsv	.275	51	182	32	50	2	1	1	16	44	15	13
Ramirez, Enrique, Guay	.274	59	186	26	51	5	5	0	17	10	9	3
#Frazier, Lou, Cul-Nav	.272	63	217	44	59	9	4	2	15	59	36	47
Walters, Dan, Mex	.272	60	195	21	53	6	0	9	25	18	29	2
Guzman, Marco, Herm	.272	67	243	31	66	15	0	4	30	33	24	0
*Farmer, Reggie, Mex-Tij . . .	.271	52	177	35	48	11	2	3	23	26	55	7
Hansen, Terrel, Nav	.270	65	233	27	63	14	0	7	33	30	69	4
*Carter, Steve, Maz	.268	61	243	35	66	10	3	5	42	16	30	9
Machiria, Pablo, Mex	.267	67	247	29	66	10	0	4	28	14	34	2
Aldrich, Tom, LM	.265	55	211	32	56	16	1	9	37	23	43	3
Romero, Marco, Guay	.264	55	174	21	46	5	1	0	16	26	29	5
*Longmire, Tony, Maz	.264	61	212	28	56	12	1	3	24	36	21	10
Mendoza, Mario, Nav	.263	61	209	19	55	5	1	0	20	17	34	1
Rodriguez, Juan, LM	.263	66	236	32	62	5	0	1	21	35	07	3
Dominguez, David, LM	.262	56	183	24	48	7	0	6	25	36	41	0
Martinez, Grimaldo, Maz-Gsv .	.262	51	141	17	37	6	1	0	8	15	16	0
*Kirby, Wayne, LM	.261	68	283	41	74	10	1	2	31	19	25	17
Verdugo, Vicente, Obr	.261	67	241	33	63	11	0	1	26	24	21	2
*May, Derrick, Gsv	.261	59	222	34	58	6	0	13	43	18	29	1
Torres, Ray, Cul	.261	67	238	23	62	11	0	9	34	37	57	2
Gonzalez, Jesus, Cul	.259	68	263	27	68	5	0	2	26	24	19	2
Mora, Andres, LM	.258	62	229	21	59	11	0	9	31	30	32	0

INDIVIDUAL PITCHING LEADERS
(Minimum 50 Innings)

	W	L	ERA	G	GS	CG	SV	IP	H	R	ER	BB	SO
*Elvira, Narciso, Herm	9	2	1.41	14	14	3	0	89	51	14	14	30	94
Barojas, Salome, Maz	4	2	1.54	34	0	0	17	58	33	12	10	25	44
*Rodriguez, Rosario, Mex . . .	4	2	1.56	10	7	4	2	52	29	15	9	29	30
*Solis, Ricardo, Herm	9	2	1.79	15	15	5	0	106	94	31	21	25	55
Gonzalez, Arturo, Nav	10	1	1.89	12	12	4	0	91	63	22	19	31	65
Castillo, Luis, Cul	8	5	2.23	15	15	5	2	105	103	32	26	24	58
*Ilsley, Blaise, Cul	9	2	2.29	17	16	6	0	114	83	31	29	38	58
Ochoa, Porfirio, Cul	3	0	2.59	22	0	0	2	59	60	21	17	16	21
Ohnoutka, Brian, Mex	7	3	2.70	15	13	2	1	93	76	29	28	26	67
*Jimenez, Isaac, Maz	4	2	2.77	12	10	1	0	62	57	23	19	30	27
*Dominguez, Herminio, Nav . .	5	6	2.79	14	14	2	0	84	73	35	26	31	43
Ibarra, Carlos, Gsv	7	7	2.83	18	15	3	0	115	100	40	36	52	52
Munoz, Miguel, LM	7	2	2.83	14	14	2	0	99	88	36	31	15	33
LeMasters, Jim, Obr	5	4	2.83	15	11	2	0	70	57	30	22	38	35
Sandoval, Guillermo, Gsv . . .	7	2	2.84	12	10	1	0	70	45	23	22	44	42
Orozco, Jaime, Obr	7	7	3.03	14	14	7	0	104	103	41	35	24	54
Cruz, Andres, Maz	6	5	3.08	16	15	2	0	102	92	36	35	33	66
*Esquer, Mercedes, Mex	8	4	3.12	14	14	1	0	95	85	36	33	30	75
Enriquez, Martin, Nav	6	5	3.13	14	11	3	0	83	62	36	29	33	46
Palacios, Vicente, Mex	3	7	3.15	16	10	1	0	66	54	26	23	28	38
Reynoso, Armando, Obr	4	5	3.16	14	14	4	0	94	76	40	33	29	72
*Ruiz, Cecilio, Obr	5	4	3.17	15	15	3	0	102	93	41	36	41	50
Loubier, Steve, Mex	6	3	3.19	12	12	0	0	73	63	33	26	35	57
*Walsh, Dave, Guay-Tij	5	4	3.30	15	14	4	0	85	74	43	31	57	54
Mendez, Luis, Herm	5	4	3.30	15	14	1	0	79	72	37	29	29	57
Raygoza, Martin, LM	7	6	3.33	15	15	4	0	103	98	41	38	31	48
Velazquez, Ildefonso, Guay . .	6	5	3.39	17	15	4	0	98	89	50	37	22	38
Springer, Dennis, Herm	5	4	3.39	13	13	2	0	80	83	39	30	28	41
Osuno, Roberto, LM	2	1	3.44	18	4	1	0	55	62	21	21	28	39
Pacholec, Joe, Maz	5	2	3.55	8	8	2	0	51	42	22	20	28	41
Barron, Avelino, Tij	1	6	3.58	17	5	1	0	60	53	35	24	24	25
Renteria, Hilario, Nav	6	3	3.60	15	15	1	0	95	88	43	38	30	43
Chadwick, Ray, Guay-Cul . . .	5	7	3.67	18	17	1	0	103	96	56	42	62	90
*Pulido, Alfonso, Tij	2	9	3.74	13	13	4	0	87	96	38	36	12	61

COLLEGE BASEBALL

Georgia scores big upset; wins first CWS crown

By JIM CALLIS

In the best College World Series tradition, Mike Rebhan stepped to the fore in 1990.

The CWS spotlight always seems to find the underdog. Names like Eddie Delzer and Greg Ellena and Dave Shermet don't ring a bell anymore. But for a brief time in Omaha, Neb., they meant championships.

So did Rebhan. Georgia's senior righthander never will pitch in the major leagues, or even the minors for that matter. He wasn't drafted, and because he already has a wife and two children, decided to complete his degree in computer science rather than pursue any free-agent opportunities.

But he closed his baseball career in style. Rebhan won two games

**Mike Rebhan
... Series MVP**

against Stanford superprospect Mike Mussina and was named MVP after the Bulldogs captured an improbable championship.

Peaked at the right time

Georgia had been ranked as high as No. 5 by Baseball America, but then lost three games at Louisiana State to blow the Southeastern Conference title and dropped two straight in the SEC tournament. Going into the Northeast Regional in Waterbury, Conn. with seven losses in its last eight games, the Bulldogs appeared in no position to win its first championship.

Georgia righted itself in time, surviving a scare from Rutgers to clinch their second CWS berth. The Bulldogs advanced to Omaha in 1987, the only other year they've made the regionals. They lost two quick CWS games that year, despite the presence of future major leaguers Cris Carpenter, Steve Carter and Derek Lilliquist.

COLLEGE WORLD SERIES

(All Time Champions)

Year — Champion	Record	Year — Champion	Record
1990—Georgia	52-19	1968—USC	39-12
1989—Wichita State	68-16	1967—Arizona State	53-12
1988—Stanford	46-23	1966—Ohio State	27- 6
1987—Stanford	53-17	1965—Arizona State	54- 8
1986—Arizona	49-19	1964—Minnesota	31-12
1985—Miami, Fla.	64-16	1963—USC	35-10
1984—Cal St. Fullerton	66-20	1962—Michigan	34-15
1983—Texas	66-14	1961—USC	36- 7
1982—Miami, Fla.	54-18	1960—Minnesota	34- 7
1981—Arizona State	55-13	1959—Oklahoma State	27- 5
1980—Arizona	43-25	1958—USC	29- 3
1979—Cal St. Fullerton	60-14	1957—California	35-10
1978—USC	54- 9	1956—Minnesota	33- 9
1977—Arizona State	57-12	1955—Wake Forest	29- 7
1976—Arizona	56-17	1954—Missouri	22- 4
1975—Texas	59- 6	1953—Michigan	21- 9
1974—USC	50-20	1952—Holy Cross	23- 6
1973—USC	51-11	1951—Oklahoma	19- 9
1972—USC	47-13	1950—Texas	27- 6
1971—USC	46-11	1949—Texas	23- 7
1970—USC	45-13	1948—USC	26- 4
1969—Arizona State	56-11	1947—California	31-10

Georgia coach Steve Webber, named Baseball America's 1990 college coach of the year, clutches CWS trophy.

"This team is probably not as good," said Georgia's Steve Webber, Baseball America's College Coach of the Year. "But there's a difference between talent and baseball players. And we have a lot of baseball players who perform and give it all they got."

Five Bulldogs seniors had been to the 1987 CWS, and though none had played, they knew what to expect.

"I think in 1987 we came in really just happy to be here," third baseman Jeff Cooper said. "This year, coach Webber talked to the team and we had the attitude that these teams here are just like us. We talked to the guys several times, telling them not to get caught up in the stuff going on, and just focus on playing the games."

That philosophy, along with excellent pitching (1.40 ERA) and defense (six double plays vs. five errors) and just enough offense (.261), worked in Omaha.

Third-team All-American Dave Fleming, who had ended Mississippi State's 177-game scoring streak earlier in the year, shut out the fellow SEC Bulldogs again in the opener, 3-0. That set up a meeting with No. 1-ranked and top-seeded Stanford.

The Cardinal seemed poised for its third championship in four seasons after it held a 2-0 lead through five innings behind the pitching of soon-to-be Baltimore Orioles first-round pick Mussina. Then Georgia exploded for a Series record-tying 11 runs and Rebhan cruised to a 16-2 win.

Rebhan said the win was especially meaningful because it meant his wife Patricia could see him pitch. She couldn't get off work and had to care for their two children up to that point, but would fly to Omaha for the rest of the CWS.

Stanford rallied in the seventh inning against Fleming for a 4-2 win in the next game, creating a rubber match for the right to advance to the championship game. The Cardinal had won 13 consecutive elimination games since 1987, Stanford coach Mark Marquess called this team his most consistent ever and Mussina hadn't lost to the same opponent twice all year.

Rebhan came to Georgia's rescue again, outpitching Mussina for a 5-1 victory. He finished the CWS with two wins, two complete games and a 1.00 ERA.

"I was sorry my wife wasn't here for the first game," Rebhan said. "You always want to share special moments. I was just glad she was here to see me pitch my last collegiate ballgame."

Gunning down the Cowboys

In the other bracket, Oklahoma State batted .390 and won three straight games by a combined score of 35-8. No team ever had stormed into the final game so dominant.

LSU coach Skip Bertman compared the Cowboys to the great Southern California and Arizona State teams of the 1970s. Oklahoma State's only close call came in their second game against LSU, when a Strategic Air Command looking-glass jet buzzed Rosenblatt Stadium.

Few expected Georgia to beat the Cowboys, especially with freshman Stan Payne getting the start because Fleming and Rebhan didn't have enough rest. The Omaha World-Herald picked the Bulldogs to lose for the fifth time in five games.

Webber said he didn't think Payne would be nervous. Payne's roommate, first baseman Doug Radziewicz, said the lefthander got little sleep the night before the game.

Georgia players celebrate the school's first victory in CWS.

Arizona State outfielder Mike Kelly hit .376 with 21 homers and was named Baseball America's 1990 player of the year.

"He kept me up," Radziewicz said. "He was rolling, tossing and turning until 3 a.m., and that's when I fell asleep. But then we got up in the morning and watched the Smurfs, and everything was OK."

Payne allowed only one run in six innings, and Cooper scored the first run and drove in the second for a 2-1 lead. Fleming entered after a leadoff double by DH Brian Kelly in the seventh, and catcher Terry Childers withstood a violent home-plate collision one out later to keep the tying run from scoring.

Fleming got a double play in the eighth and struck out the side in the ninth to close out the win. The loss was the record fifth for Oklahoma State in the championship game, its third under Gary Ward.

"How can you compare knife wounds?" said Ward when asked how much the loss hurt. "By how deep it goes? Three inches? Four inches? Five inches?"

Changing of the guard

For the first time since the CWS adopted its eight-team format in 1948, no representative from the states of Arizona, Florida and Texas was present. Georgia's win further pointed out the parity that now exists in college baseball.

The Bulldogs became the second straight team from outside the Sun Belt to win college baseball's biggest prize. Before Wichita State did so in 1989, it had been 23 years since Ohio State accomplished the feat in 1966.

And more teams than ever appear capable of making it to Omaha. Just check 1990 contestants The Citadel, Georgia Southern and Cal State Fullerton. Only Fullerton at No. 21 was ranked before the regionals, yet the teams pulled off upsets at Miami, Wichita State and Texas (respectively), three of the toughest places to play in the nation.

Clemson's Bill Wilhelm (left) and Washington State's Chuck 'Bobo' Brayton each won their 1000th game in 1990.

The SEC mounted a challenge to the Pacific-10 Southern Division's standing as the pre-eminent baseball conference. Georgia won the conference's first title, and league rivals LSU and Mississippi State also were on hand at the CWS. Only the Six-Pac in 1988 had sent three teams to Omaha.

Heavenly Sun Devil

Center fielder Mike Kelly became the third Arizona State star to be named Baseball America's College Player of the Year. He hit .376 with 21 home runs, 82 RBIs and 20 stolen bases. "He's the best I've had," Sun Devils coach Jim Brock said. "And he's the best I ever hope to have." ... Stanford center fielder Jeff Hammonds was named Baseball America's Freshman of the Year. He hit .355 with a Cardinal-record 48 stolen bases, and had a 37-game hitting streak that tied Clemson's Brian Kowitz for the longest of the season ... Wichita State won the inaugural Hall of Fame Tournament, created by the American Baseball Coaches Association to give baseball a season-opening event. The tournament didn't draw well in Baseball City, Fla., and will be held in 1991 at LSU's Alex Box Stadium ... The Big Ten Conference placed the Michigan baseball program on two years probation after uncovering more than 40 violations of conference and NCAA rules from 1983-88 under former coach Bud Middaugh. The Wolverines were banned from postseason play and television appearances for two years, and voluntarily reduced scholarships and restricted recruiting activities to avoid a third year of probation ... Several coaches notched the 1,000th win of their careers. Miami-Dade CC North's Demie Mainieri (March 12) became the first junior college coach to do so, and was followed by Seminole (Okla.) JC coach Lloyd Simmons (March 19). Washington State's Bobo Brayton (April 11) and Clemson's Bill Wilhelm (April 29) pulled off the trick at the Division I level ... Florida sophomore righthander Steve Georgiadis died March 17 from heart

THE TOP 25

(Final 1990 Ranking, by Baseball America)

1. Georgia	52-19	14. Southern Illinois	49-14
2. Oklahoma State	56-17	15. North Carolina	51-14
3. Stanford	59-12	16. Illinois	43-21
4. Louisiana State	54-19	17. San Diego State	49-22
5. Arizona State	52-16	18. Washington State	48-19
6. Southern California	40-22	19. Wichita State	45-19
7. Mississippi State	50-21	20. The Citadel	46-14
8. Florida State	57-15	21. Houston	44-23
9. Cal State Fullerton	36-23	22. Loyola Marymount	45-17
10. Texas	51-17	23. South Alabama	44-19
11. Georgia Southern	50-19	24. UCLA	41-26
12. Arkansas	47-15	25. Creighton	48-22
13. Miami, Fla.	52-13		

UCLA catcher Paul Ellis emerged as the top slugger in the college ranks, hitting 29 homers.

complications arising from rotator-cuff surgery. He was 19 . . . Some big coaching names switched jobs after the season. Cal State Fullerton's Larry Cochell went to Oklahoma, with Illinois' Augie Garrido returning to the scene of his two CWS championships to replace Cochell. Longtime Southern Illinois coach Itchy Jones replaced Garrido.

Warriors win again

As usual, Lewis-Clark State made the most of its automatic entry into the NAIA World Series held annually at its Harris Field in Lewiston, Idaho. The Warriors beat Auburn-Montgomery 9-4 for its fourth straight championship and sixth in seven years.

Senior right fielder Mark Rasmussen hit .542 (13-for-24) with five RBIs in six games to win MVP honors. Freshman Kevin Logsdon allowed one unearned run in 5⅔ innings of relief to pick up the final win.

After the World Series, the NAIA announced the event would move to Canton, Ohio as part of a spring sports festival in 1992. Lewis-Clark State had put up unprecedented attendance numbers since landing the tournament in 1984, but teams had complained about the Warriors' automatic bid and home-field advantage.

1990 ALL-AMERICA TEAM

Dan Wilson
... .370-8-49

Jeff Hammonds
... .355, 48 SB

Sean Rees
... 13-3, 2.67

Kirk Dressendorfer
... 12-4, 3.16

Dan Smith
... 14-3, 1.96

Oscar Munoz
... 15-2, 2.39

FIRST TEAM

1990 Statistics

Pos.	Player, School	Yr.	Avg	AB	R	H	2B	3B	HR	RBI	SB
C	Dan Wilson, Minnesota	Jr.	.370	181	43	67	15	2	8	49	10
1B	Don Barbara, Long Beach State	Sr.	.474	215	69	102	27	1	7	61	9
2B	Anthony Manahan, Arizona St.	Jr.	.366	284	66	104	22	5	10	81	9
3B	Greg D'Alexander, Arkansas	Sr.	.387	212	51	82	18	2	14	65	10
SS	Tim Costo, Iowa	Jr.	.372	196	59	73	15	1	16	64	5
OF	Mike Kelly, Arizona State	So.	.376	258	83	97	17	6	21	82	20
	Jeff Hammonds, Stanford	Fr.	.355	301	83	107	15	7	7	44	48
	Wes Grisham, Louisiana State	Sr.	.360	278	65	100	18	4	11	72	5
DH	Paul Ellis, UCLA	Jr.	.360	247	61	89	8	1	29	83	3

Pos.	Player, School	Yr.	W	L	ERA	G	Sv	IP	H	BB	SO
P	Sean Rees, Arizona State	So.	13	3	2.67	22	0	138	98	54	162
	Stan Spencer, Stanford	Jr.	14	1	2.73	20	0	142	126	28	145
	Dan Smith, Creighton	Jr.	14	3	1.96	17	0	120	84	48	134
	Oscar Munoz, Miami	Jr.	15	2	2.39	20	1	128	98	57	115
	Kirk Dressendorfer, Texas	Jr.	12	4	3.16	22	2	125	98	33	152

SECOND TEAM

1990 Statistics

Pos.	Player, School	Yr.	Avg	AB	R	H	2B	3B	HR	RBI	SB
C	Mike Harrison, California	So.	.341	232	53	79	10	1	21	63	4
1B	Steve Estroff, North Carolina	Jr.	.389	229	51	89	20	3	15	73	0
2B	David Tollison, Texas	Jr.	.350	263	60	92	21	3	12	69	17
3B	Tim Griffin, Stanford	Jr.	.306	268	63	82	20	0	21	75	9
SS	Chris Martin, Pepperdine	Sr.	.358	218	65	78	17	2	14	65	31
OF	Paul Carey, Stanford	Sr.	.335	260	71	87	21	1	16	51	8
	Marc Ronan, Florida State	Jr.	.356	250	75	89	25	1	6	60	34
	Brian Kowitz, Clemson	Jr.	.403	253	87	102	22	6	3	60	34
DH	Mark Dalesandro, Illinois	Sr.	.395	223	61	88	14	1	16	73	4

Pos.	Player, School	Yr.	W	L	ERA	G	Sv	IP	H	BB	SO
P	Joey Hamilton, Ga. Southern	So.	18	4	3.07	25	1	161	160	36	138
	Randy Powers, Southern Cal	Sr.	11	3	2.20	23	2	138	120	15	90
	Mike Zimmerman, So. Alabama	Jr.	12	7	1.59	27	5	158	102	50	170
	Gar Finnvold, Florida State	Sr.	15	3	2.77	19	1	136	120	41	136
	Paul Byrd, Louisiana State	So.	17	6	3.84	29	1	141	147	52	130

THIRD TEAM

C—Eric Christopherson, San Diego State. **1B**—Chris Pritchett, UCLA. **2B**—Kevin Jordan, Nebraska. **3B**—Jeff Ball, San Jose State. **SS**—Robert Eenhoorn, Davidson. **OF**—Todd Greene, Georgia Southern; Doug Shields, Southern Illinois; Darren Bragg, Georgia Tech. **DH**—Gary Daniels, Brigham Young. **P**—Mike Hostetler, Georgia Tech; Phil Stidham, Arkansas; Aaron Sele, Washington State; Rich Robertson, Texas A&M; Dave Fleming, Georgia.

Sam Militello
... small college ace

Kelly Stinnett
... juco RBI king

Gamecocks step forward

Junior Tim VanEgmond emerged at the right time for Jacksonville State (Ala.). VanEgmond entered the postseason as the Gamecocks' No. 4 pitcher, but collected two saves and a shutout, winning MVP honors as Jacksonville State won the Division II World Series in Montgomery, Ala.

The Gamecocks outlasted Cal State Northridge, which moves up to Division I in 1991, 12-8 in the finale for their first title ever. Reliever Craig Holman pitched 6⅓ innings for the win to improve his record to 8-0.

Tampa finished third at the World Series and featured Baseball America's Small College Player of the Year. Righthander Sam Militello went 15-2 with a 1.75 ERA and broke Spartans season records for wins, complete games (eight), innings (144) and strikeouts (182). He set career records in each category as well, and signed with the New York Yankees as a sixth-round draft pick.

More Warriors

Eastern Connecticut State received a victory from each of its four senior starting pitchers to win the Division III World Series in Battle Creek, Mich. Chris Kebalka pitched his first complete game of the year in the finale, an 8-1 win over Aurora (Ill.) that gave the Warriors their first title since 1982.

Steve Boskus tied a school record with his ninth win in the opener; Norm Worthington, who missed all of 1989 recovering from Hodgkin's Disease, won the next game; and Rusty Greer pitched a shutout in the semifinal. Shortstop Brian Mercado was named MVP after hitting three home runs in the opener and another in the final game.

Gators, Seahawks win JUCO titles

San Jacinto (Texas) North won its second straight Junior College World Series, coming out of the losers brackets to beat Middle Georgia twice in Grand Junction, Colo. The Gators, who have won five of the last six titles, were led by shortstop Randy Brown, the Series MVP after batting .455 with three home runs and 15 runs scored.

Seminole (Okla.) JC finished third, powered by Baseball America's Junior College Player of the Year, catcher Kelly Stinnett. Stinnett hit .399 with 22 home runs and a national-best 97 RBIs. As a freshman, he hit .418, led the nation with 30 home runs and 124 RBIs and was an 11th-round pick of the Cleveland Indians, with whom he signed in 1990.

In California, Los Angeles Harbor JC won its first state championship since 1984. The Seahawks cracked the 50-win barrier at 51-5, and beat Chabot JC 5-2 in the final game at Irvine. Harbor coach Jim O'Brien retired after the win, deciding to concentrate on his duties as athletic director.

DIVISION I LEADERS

TEAM BATTING
BATTING AVERAGE

	G	AVG
Long Island	40	.354
New Mexico State	59	.343
Loyola Marymount	62	.341
Long Beach State	59	.335
Central Michigan	57	.335
Maine	62	.333
Bucknell	33	.329
Fordham	50	.328
Southern Illinois	63	.328
St. Mary's	58	.328

RUNS SCORED

	G	R
Oklahoma State	73	631
Louisiana State	73	587
Washington State	67	560
Mississippi State	71	560
Florida State	72	555
Brigham Young	69	553
Arizona State	68	552
Georgia	71	552
Stanford	71	551
Georgia Tech	71	547

HOME RUNS

	G	HR
Arizona State	68	101
Brigham Young	69	96
Georgia Tech	71	95
Stanford	71	93
Oklahoma State	73	90
New Mexico State	59	89
UCLA	67	88
Georgia Southern	69	88
Wake Forest............	61	86
Georgia	71	86

STOLEN BASES

	G	SB	ATT
Jackson State	50	241	287
Nicholls State	54	231	300
Fla. International ...	60	227	280
Illinois-Chicago	57	173	231
Texas	68	166	224
Florida State	72	165	246
San Diego State	71	160	230
Tennessee	59	159	226
Coastal Carolina ...	59	158	189

TEAM PITCHING
EARNED RUN AVERAGE

	G	ERA
Miami (Fla.)................	65	2.57
Jackson State	50	2.69
Texas A&M	60	2.80
South Alabama	64	2.80
Central Florida	60	2.80
SW Missouri State	57	2.91
McNeese State	55	2.92
Nicholls State	54	2.93
Texas	68	2.99
Notre Dame	58	3.00

TEAM FIELDING
FIELDING AVERAGE

	G	PCT
Northwestern State	51	.981
Stanford	71	.972
Loyola Marymount	62	.972
Southern Illinois	63	.971
Miami (Fla.)............	65	.971
Michigan	57	.970
Cal State Fullerton	59	.970
Long Beach State	59	.969
New Hampshire	37	.969
Davidson	51	.969

INDIVIDUAL BATTING LEADERS
(Minimum 120 At-Bats)

	AVG	G	AB	R	H	2B	3B	HR	RBI	BB	SO	SB
Don Barbara, Long Beach St.	.474	59	215	69	102	27	1	7	61	52	17	9
Tom Nuneviller, West Chester	.470	43	151	51	71	17	2	11	50	25	7	10
Mike Sciortino, C. Conn. ...	.457	38	138	31	63	11	2	4	34	16	6	3
Joe Markulike, Bucknell ...	.454	33	130	38	59	8	8	3	28	7	10	20
Mike Migliarese, St. Joseph's	.453	42	148	28	67	15	3	8	49	14	11	6
Marc Marini, Jacksonville ..	.439	54	171	55	75	15	3	0	31	44	20	20
Sal Conti, Long Island	.438	40	146	42	64	14	3	13	55	10	32	7
John Belicka, Georgetown .	.438	46	176	46	77	13	6	10	51	25	18	18
Gary Daniels, BYU	.437	69	270	84	118	27	10	24	91	28	29	14
Ray Montgomery, Fordham .	.429	48	175	46	75	15	0	4	48	35	12	42
Eric Danapilis, Notre Dame .	.429	40	140	39	60	14	1	6	31	22	22	12
Brad Owens, W. Ill.	.429	39	133	37	57	9	5	10	33	23	17	8
Grant Brittain, W. Car.	.428	58	180	67	77	14	2	20	68	49	44	15
Scott Waugh, Appy St.	.426	41	141	30	60	9	2	1	27	22	14	13
James Ruocchio, Long Island	.424	40	170	45	72	21	3	7	44	11	10	3
Mike Clarke, Chicago State .	.422	43	161	40	68	14	3	13	56	12	21	11
Jason Giambi, Long Beach St.	.422	46	154	31	65	10	1	0	29	25	23	5
Frankie Watts, Southern ...	.421	43	133	49	56	9	4	3	13	37	11	20
Russ Mushinsky, Penn St. .	.417	43	139	46	58	16	5	3	41	20	13	6
Vinnie Hughes, N.C. State .	.417	54	156	30	65	6	0	6	35	11	15	4
Scott Stahoviak, Creighton .	.417	67	228	63	95	25	2	6	51	41	31	10
Rick Mediavilla, Loyola Mary	.416	61	269	72	112	11	1	1	25	18	17	18
Mark Robert, Wyoming ...	.415	54	195	56	81	10	1	16	67	24	20	13
Scott Campbell, Oklahoma .	.415	57	205	57	85	15	4	6	59	42	20	21
Ciro Ambrosio, Long Island .	.415	40	159	52	66	10	4	13	35	24	16	8
Carlton Hardy, Grambling ..	.415	45	135	27	56	16	4	4	33	21	16	5
Andy Hartung, Maine	.414	61	210	59	87	12	3	15	76	38	32	9
John Adams, E. Car.	.413	55	208	61	86	15	3	5	46	27	16	3
Denny McNamara, C. Mich.	.412	55	199	62	82	17	1	16	60	19	15	29
Randy Wilstead, BYU	.411	68	241	78	99	20	4	22	64	53	38	7
Paul Prosser, W. Va.	.409	52	171	46	70	13	2	6	46	17	30	10
Jason Geis, Portland	.407	50	177	39	72	14	2	9	48	20	22	8
Glenn Donelin, Army	.406	41	155	39	63	14	3	0	27	12	18	12
Todd Schroeder, Ill. St. ...	.405	56	200	42	81	20	10	4	32	32	31	4
Rich Juday, Mich. State ...	.405	50	173	40	70	10	4	12	49	21	21	1
Paul Bruno, NY Tech	.405	53	190	42	77	10	0	20	68	27	29	0
Jim Whitman, NY Tech	.404	49	193	53	78	15	0	10	30	23	22	7
Brian Kowitz, Clemson ...	.403	66	253	87	102	22	6	3	60	44	20	34
Tim Flannelly, Michigan ...	.402	56	194	38	78	9	3	5	40	24	13	3
Carlton Thompson, Georgetown	.402	44	179	48	72	6	4	0	14	21	11	23
Bill Ostermeyer, Centenary .	.401	58	187	51	75	19	2	11	41	29	27	12

	AVG	G	AB	R	H	2B	3B	HR	RBI	BB	SO	SB
Jason Martinez, Georgetown	.401	44	147	13	59	4	0	0	12	8	29	1
Joe Williams, New Mex. St. .	.401	59	192	77	77	10	2	25	78	53	37	12
Rob Leary, Long Island	.400	39	150	43	60	13	7	6	41	18	15	6
Dan Ferrira, Sac. State	.400	40	140	34	56	12	0	6	33	19	17	16
Brian Kelley, Bos.Coll.....	.399	43	168	32	67	7	0	0	23	18	21	9
Scott Thomson, ODU	.399	58	203	48	81	17	8	7	40	11	19	7
Dave Preikszas, Miami (O.) .	.398	52	161	48	64	12	4	4	31	23	29	15
Mike Neill, Villanova	.398	46	171	43	68	11	1	5	30	26	25	3
Anthony Jenkins, Citadel ...	.397	60	224	70	89	16	4	16	68	44	30	12
Darren Bragg, Georgia Tech	.397	71	239	61	95	17	2	10	73	62	42	14
Efrain Lara, New Mex. St. ..	.397	51	141	44	55	13	3	9	48	21	22	8
Bill Mueller, SW Mo. St.....	.397	47	126	41	50	5	0	0	20	27	15	11

RUNS SCORED

	G	R
Mitch Simons, Okla. State ..	73	89
Brian Kowitz, Clemson	66	87
Joe Burnett, SW La.	63	84
Gary Daniels, BYU	69	84
Mike Kelly, Arizona State ..	68	83
Jeff Hammonds, Stanford ..	69	83
Randy Wilstead, BYU	68	78
Joe Williams, New Mex. St.	59	77
Mark Sweeney, Maine	61	76
Marc Ronan, Fla. State ...	70	75
J.R. Showalter, Georgia ...	71	75
David McCarty, Stanford ...	71	74

HITS

	G	H
Gary Daniels, BYU	69	118
Rick Mediavilla, Loy. Mary. .	61	112
Fernando Vina, Arizona St. .	63	108
Troy Paulsen, Stanford	71	108
Jeff Hammonds, Stanford ..	69	107
Anthony Manahan, Arizona St.	68	104
Don Barbara, Long Beach St.	59	102
Brian Kowitz, Clemson	66	102
Chris Pritchett, UCLA	67	102
Chris Gomez, Loy. Mary....	60	100
Todd Greene, Ga. So.......	69	100
Wes Grisham, LSU	73	100

TOTAL BASES

	G	TB
Gary Daniels, BYU	69	237
Todd Greene, Ga. So.	69	203
Randy Wilstead, BYU	68	193
Mike Kelly, Arizona St.	68	189
Paul Ellis, UCLA..........	66	186
Jim Austin, Arizona St.	66	179
Andy Bruce, Georgia Tech .	71	178
Rob Fitzpatrick, Ga. So. ...	68	172
Kevin Young, S. Miss.	67	168
Joe Williams, New Mex. St. .	59	166
Anthony Manahan, Arizona St.	68	166
Tim Griffin, Stanford	70	165
J.R. Showalter, Georgia ...	71	163
Tommy Raffo, Miss. State ..	70	161
Steve Estroff, North Carolina	63	160

DOUBLES

	G	2B
Scott Hatteberg, Wash. St. .	66	29
Troy Paulsen, Stanford	71	29
Geoff Martinez, USIU	60	28
Don Barbara, Long Beach St.	59	27
Kevin Young, S. Miss.	67	27
Gary Daniels, BYU	69	27
Glenn Osinski, New Orleans	63	26
Scott Stahoviak, Creighton .	67	25
Pete Grifol, Fla. State	68	25
Marc Ronan, Fla. State	70	25
Chris Gomez, Loy. Mary....	60	24
Jeff Antoon, UCSB	61	24
Bruce Chick, Georgia	70	24

TRIPLES

	G	3B
Roger Ahrens, Bucknell ...	33	10
Rob Newman, Louisville ...	43	10
Todd Schroeder, Ill. St.	56	10
Steve Gill, Arizona	59	10
Gary Daniels, BYU	69	10
Charles Johnson, Miami (Fla.)	64	9
Shawn Buchanan, Nebraska	68	9

HOME RUNS

	G	HR
Paul Ellis, UCLA..........	66	29

Don Barbara
...nation's top hitter

	G	HR
Todd Greene, Ga. So.......	69	26
Joe Williams, New Mex. St. .	59	25
Anthony Maisano, Ga. Tech .	64	25
Gary Daniels, BYU	69	24
Mike Daniel, Okla. State ...	61	23
Randy Wilstead, BYU	68	22
Mike Harrison, Cal	59	21
Mike Kelly, Arizona St.	68	21
Rob Fitzpatrick, Ga. So. ...	68	21
Tim Griffin, Stanford	70	21
Paul Bruno, NY Tech	53	20
Grant Brittain, W. Car.	58	20
Eric Macrina, Clemson	53	18
Mike Seda, New Mex. St. ..	56	18
Bobby Benjamin, Nebraska .	68	18

RUNS BATTED IN

	G	RBI
Mike Daniel, Okla. State ...	61	92
Gary Daniels, BYU	69	91
Jeff Ball, San Jose St.	60	83
Paul Ellis, UCLA..........	66	83
Mike Kelly, Arizona St.	68	82
Anthony Manahan, Arizona St.	68	81
Joe Williams, New Mex. St. .	59	78
Andy Bruce, Georgia Tech .	71	78
Andy Hartung, Maine	61	76
Greg Blevins, SW Louisiana	64	75
Kevin Young, S. Miss.	67	75
Todd Greene, Ga. So.	69	75
Tim Griffin, Stanford	70	75
J.R. Showalter, Georgia ...	71	74
Mark Dalesandro, Illinois...	59	73
Jake Austin, Wake Forest ..	61	73
Steve Estroff, North Carolina	63	73
Bobby Benjamin, Nebraska .	68	73
Darren Bragg, Georgia Tech	71	73
Wes Grisham, LSU	73	72
John Cohen, Miss. State ...	71	71

BASES ON BALLS

	G	BB
Eric Cruz, Fla. Int.	58	87
Paul Carey, Stanford	71	67
Bobby Benjamin, Nebraska .	68	66
Marc Ronan, Fla. State	70	66
Mitch Simons, Okla. State ..	73	64

STRIKEOUTS

	G	SO
Shaun Thomas, Va. Tech . .	57	80
Todd Steverson, Arizona St.	63	80
Mike Skaggs, Vanderbilt . . .	58	66
Shaun Murphy, UNLV	51	64
Bo Loftin, New Orleans	56	61

TOUGHEST TO STRIKE OUT
(Minimum 125 At-Bats)

	AB	SO	Ratio
Dave Stewart, New Hamp.	139	1	139.0
Eric Macrina, Clemson. . .	189	4	47.3
Fernando Vina, Arizona St.	279	7	39.9
Dave Scheitlen, Purdue . .	197	5	39.4
Phil Aiello, Seton Hall	157	4	39.3
David Gogal, Portland St. .	216	6	36.0
Frank Tremmel, Ala.-Birm.	196	6	32.7

STOLEN BASES

	G	SB	ATT
Roger Bowman, Fla. Int . .	58	58	64
Jerrold Rountree, UCSB .	62	57	78
Allen Battle, So. Ala. . . .	64	54	63
Joe Burnett, SW Louisiana	63	52	61
Eric Cruz, Fla. Int	58	51	65
Calvin Murray, Texas . . .	67	49	58
Kevin Dattola, So. Fla. . . .	65	49	62
Jeff Hammonds, Stanford	69	48	59
Mark Romer, Coas. Carolina	59	45	51
Ray Montgomery, Fordham	48	45	52
John Boccieri, St. Bona . .	43	43	47
Jimmy Davenport, Jackson St.	49	43	48
Mike Lemitola, Seton Hall	52	43	49
Darren Thorpe, TCU	55	43	53
Mike Basse, Tennessee . .	45	43	55
Pat Karlin, Kansas	56	42	53
Eddie Anderson, Nebraska	62	41	47
Fletcher Thompson, Nich. St.	50	40	49

**Mike Daniel
...top RBI man**

	G	SB	ATT
Thomas Coates, Austin Peay	56	40	50
Jeff Barry, San Diego St. .	66	40	53
James Mouton, St. Mary's	58	39	49
Bob Braddy, Jackson St. .	50	39	50

HIT BY PITCH

	G	HBP
Andy Small, Illinois	37	19
Allen Battle, So. Ala.	64	18
Greg McGough, NE La.	42	16
Jim Bell, Florida	47	16
Jim Alexander, San Diego . .	53	16
Brian Roberts, Illinois	59	16

INDIVIDUAL PITCHING LEADERS
(Minimum 60 Innings)

	W	L	ERA	G	GS	CG	SV	IP	H	R	ER	BB	SO
David Sinnes, Notre Dame . .	9	2	1.05	18	8	3	1	69	39	18	8	35	77
Brian Kenny, Villanova	10	1	1.54	14	12	10	0	93	80	24	16	20	88
Terry Burrows, McNeese St. .	10	3	1.59	20	14	5	1	96	60	29	17	46	116
Mike Zimmerman, So. Ala. .	12	7	1.59	26	16	13	5	158	102	43	28	50	170
Craig Sands, SW Mo. St. . .	8	2	1.60	17	6	4	2	68	49	24	12	30	41
Todd Pick, New Orleans . . .	8	5	1.63	27	1	1	3	83	58	19	15	31	93
Jim Dougherty, North Carolina	12	2	1.71	17	15	6	0	116	88	30	22	32	87
Tom Migliozzi, St. John's . .	6	3	1.76	9	9	6	0	61	57	17	12	14	49
Rich Robertson, Texas A&M .	10	1	1.77	15	13	7	1	91	53	24	18	45	106
Jon Henry, C. Fla.	5	3	1.81	15	8	0	0	65	52	21	13	27	54
Dave Leonard, Holy Cross .	4	3	1.85	9	7	6	1	63	57	26	13	8	34
Brian Piotrowicz, Notre Dame .	7	3	1.90	16	11	1	1	80	77	31	17	18	53
Jeff Alkire, Miami (Fla.)	7	1	1.92	24	5	1	0	70	39	16	15	29	61
Dan Smith, Creighton	14	3	1.96	17	16	12	0	120	84	33	26	48	134
Jeff Post, Oregon St.	10	4	1.96	26	7	4	4	83	76	23	18	17	45
Jim O'Connor, NY Tech	7	3	2.04	14	12	6	0	97	84	33	22	17	48
Kevin Legault, Seton Hall . .	6	3	2.09	17	6	1	3	60	46	19	14	20	41
Mike Maxey, Xavier	3	6	2.10	13	11	2	0	73	68	45	17	44	40
Dave Hutcheson, So. Fla. . .	3	3	2.11	29	8	0	1	81	62	22	19	20	55
Craig Connolly, Penn	7	1	2.13	12	12	5	0	72	54	26	17	23	80
Greg Wilcox, Davidson	12	2	2.14	17	16	7	0	118	82	32	28	46	125
Tim Langdon, E. Car.	11	2	2.16	17	16	4	0	104	72	43	25	37	86
Dave Matranga, Nebraska .	10	3	2.16	34	2	0	4	87	81	30	21	36	75
Ben O'Connor, Md.-Balt. Co. .	5	6	2.19	13	10	4	0	78	61	26	19	43	65
Doug Harris, Jas. Madison .	7	4	2.21	15	12	3	0	90	69	36	22	41	70
Jim Harden, Miss. St.	5	0	2.21	30	0	0	3	73	60	22	18	12	58
Anthony Laszaic, C. Fla.	8	1	2.22	14	12	5	0	81	77	38	20	23	61
Shawn Purdy, Miami (Fla.) . .	11	3	2.22	21	17	4	0	126	116	38	31	43	81
Aaron Sele, Wash. State . .	12	2	2.22	17	16	9	0	122	102	45	30	41	121
Mark Mimbs, Mercer	8	7	2.26	19	18	8	1	111	97	46	28	47	102
Randy Powers, USC	11	3	2.29	23	18	8	2	138	120	47	35	15	90
Karl Dunson, Jackson St. . .	6	6	2.29	14	11	4	0	75	63	33	19	34	69
Todd Pittman, Wright St. . . .	3	2	2.30	10	8	3	0	63	47	25	16	37	34
John Lewis, Winthrop	5	5	2.30	15	11	4	0	82	78	34	21	20	57
Al Benavides, Houston	8	1	2.34	30	1	0	2	81	81	27	21	22	73
Brian Lucas, NWestern St. . .	9	4	2.34	16	13	4	1	77	61	23	20	26	51
Ronnie Allen, Texas A&M . .	6	4	2.35	13	13	8	0	100	78	36	26	28	70
Frank Speek, Liberty	9	4	2.36	17	17	10	0	126	100	45	33	29	93
Scott Sanders, Nich. St.	11	6	2.37	24	14	10	4	122	80	44	32	58	133
Oscar Munoz, Miami (Fla.) . .	15	2	2.39	20	19	4	1	128	98	42	34	57	115
Craig Saccavino, Richmond .	4	2	2.40	11	9	3	1	64	62	30	17	20	33
Chad Elder, Jacksonville . . .	7	1	2.41	19	11	3	2	82	73	31	22	35	63
Scott Brow, Washington . . .	9	5	2.42	14	13	4	0	104	96	43	28	31	75
Kurt Archer, San Diego St. .	9	2	2.42	25	11	5	2	104	97	37	28	38	64
Tom McGraw, Wash. State . .	10	5	2.43	20	17	4	0	111	102	39	30	41	121

WINS

	W	L
Joey Hamilton, Ga. So.	18	4
Paul Byrd, LSU	17	6
Todd Douma, Arizona St.	16	3
Oscar Munoz, Miami (Fla.)	15	2
Gar Finnvold, Fla. State	15	3
Bobby Reed, Miss. State	15	4
Stan Spencer, Stanford	14	1
Chad Ogea, LSU	14	2
Dan Smith, Creighton	14	3
Mike Mussina, Stanford	14	3
Sean Rees, Arizona St.	13	3
Ken Whitworth, UC Irvine	13	4
Jon Willard, Loy. Mary.	13	4
Paul Anderson, Fla. Int.	13	5
Damon Pollard, S. Miss.	13	5
Mike Rebhan, Georgia	13	5
Jim Dougherty, North Carolina	12	2
Greg Wilcox, Davidson	12	2
Britt Craven, Pepperdine	12	2
Steve Duda, Pepperdine	12	3
Aaron Sele, Wash. State	12	3
Billy Walker, Gonzaga	12	3
John O'Donoghue, LSU	12	3
Darryl Scott, Loy. Mary.	12	4
Mike Hostetler, Georgia Tech	12	4
Darrin Paxton, Wichita St.	12	4
Jason Schira, East. Ky.	12	4
Kirk Dressendorfer, Texas	12	4
Andy Croghan, Long Beach St.	12	4
James Popoff, CS Fullerton	12	5
Dave Fleming, Georgia	12	6
Mike Zimmerman, So. Ala.	12	7

LOSSES

	W	L
Michael Mimbs, Mercer	4	13
Bill O'Neill, LaSalle	0	11
Danny Clark, ETSU	2	11
Henri Saunders, Tulane	4	11
Mike Whisonant, USIU	5	11

APPEARANCES

	G
Tom Hickox, Stetson	39
Winston Wheeler, So. Fla.	38
Rusty Filter, San Diego St.	37
Tom Cheek, San Diego	37
Jeff Richards, Illinois	36

COMPLETE GAMES

	GS	CG
Mike Zimmerman, So. Ala.	16	13
Dave Fleming, Georgia	19	13
Dan Smith, Creighton	16	12
Matt Whiteside, Ark. St.	14	11
Darren Dreger, SW Texas	15	11
Donovan Osborne, UNLV	16	11
Damon Pollard, S. Miss.	21	11

SAVES

	G	SV
Ted Ward, Miami (O.)	27	15
Bob Undorf, So. Fla.	32	15
Mike Call, Washington	23	13
Darek Braunecker, UALR	25	13
Al Levine, So. Ill.	29	13
Mike Grohs, ODU	30	13
Brian Beatson, S. Car.	26	12
Tom Hickox, Stetson	39	12
Mike Ericson, Mich. State	19	11
Robert Teague, East. Ky.	30	11
Brad Gregory, Fla. State	31	11
Phil Stidham, Ark.	33	11

INNINGS PITCHED

	G	IP
Joey Hamilton, Ga. So.	25	161
Dave Fleming, Georgia	21	160
Mike Zimmerman, So. Ala.	27	158
Steve Wolf, Fresno State	23	154
Tim Lindsay, UCLA	28	149
Mike Mussina, Stanford	20	149
Damon Pollard, S. Miss.	21	148
Stan Spencer, Stanford	20	142
Ken Whitworth, UC Irvine	22	141
Paul Byrd, LSU	29	141

BASES ON BALLS

	IP	BB
Damon Pollard, S. Miss.	148	90
Shane Hale, So. Ala.	105	82
Mike Whisonant, USIU	106	79
Dave Zancanaro, UCLA	121	78
Rob DeMayo, Boston	58	77
Steve Surico, Loy. Mary.	70	77
Lance Price, Liberty	80	77
Troy Chacon, USIU	85	77
Shawn Loucks, UCSB	93	76

STRIKEOUTS

	IP	SO
Steve Wolf, Fresno State	154	171
Mike Zimmerman, So. Ala.	158	170
Dave Fleming, Georgia	160	163
Sean Rees, Arizona St.	138	162
Kirk Dressendorfer, Texas	125	152
Damon Pollard, S. Miss.	148	152
Erik Schullstrom, Fresno State	122	148
Stan Spencer, Stanford	142	145
Lance Dickson, Arizona	120	141
Joey Hamilton, Ga. So.	161	138
Gar Finnvold, Fla. State	136	136
Donovan Osborne, UNLV	139	135
Dan Smith, Creighton	120	134
Scott Sanders, Nich. St.	122	133
Paul Byrd, LSU	141	130
Scott Ryder, Ga. So.	140	128
Billy Walker, Gonzaga	107	127

Steve Wolf
... 171 strikeouts

	IP	SO
Michael Mimbs, Mercer	104	126
Doug Creek, Georgia Tech	126	126
Greg Wilcox, Davidson	118	125
Brian Williams, S. Car.	107	125
Todd Douma, Arizona St.	137	124
Chad Ogea, LSU	132	123
Rod Bolton, Kentucky	112	121
Aaron Sele, Wash. State	122	121
Terry Burrows, McNeese St.	96	116
Darrin Paxton, Wichita St.	121	116
Levon Largusa, Hawaii	102	115
Bobby Jones, Fresno State	122	115
Oscar Munoz, Miami (Fla.)	128	115

STRIKEOUTS/9 INNINGS
(Minimum 50 Innings)

	IP	SO	AVG
John Burke, Florida	50	73	13.1
Bryant Ballentine, UNC-W	67	85	11.4
Dave Norwood, Lehigh	50	62	11.2
Matt Ruebel, Oklahoma	85	104	11.0
Terry Burrows, McNeese St.	96	116	10.9
Kirk Dressendorfer, Texas	125	152	10.9
Mike Mimbs, Mercer	104	126	10.9
Brett Roberts, Morehead St.	56	68	10.9
Erik Schullstrom, Fresno St.	122	148	10.9
Billy Walker, Gonzaga	107	127	10.7
Paul Shuey, North Carolina	66	78	10.7
Sean Rees, Arizona St.	138	162	10.6
Mark Kubicki, S. Miss.	72	85	10.6
Lance Dickson, Arizona	120	141	10.6

CONFERENCE STANDINGS, LEADERS

(Select NCAA Division I conferences only)

ATLANTIC COAST CONFERENCE

	Conference		Overall	
	W	L	W	L
*North Carolina	17	4	51	14
Clemson	14	6	43	23
North Carolina State..........	14	7	48	20
Wake Forest	10	10	35	24
Georgia Tech....................	9	9	46	25
Virginia..........................	7	11	21	32
Duke	4	15	28	25
Maryland.........................	2	15	22	26

*Won conference tournament

ALL-CONFERENCE TEAM: C—Kevin O'Sullivan, Virginia. **1B**—Steve Estroff, UNC. **2B**—Bobby Rivell, Virginia. **3B**—Andy Bruce, Georgia Tech. **SS**—Ron Maurer, UNC. **OF**—Warren Sawkiw, Wake Forest; Brian Kowitz, Clemson; Darren Bragg, Georgia Tech. **DH**—Anthony Maisano, Georgia Tech. **Util**—Brian Bark, N.C. State. **SP**—Mike Hostetler, Georgia Tech. **RP**—Paul Shuey, UNC.

INDIVIDUAL BATTING LEADERS
(Minimum 125 At-Bats)

	AVG	G	AB	R	H	2B	3B	HR	RBI	BB	SO	SB
Hughes, Vinnie, NC St.	.417	54	156	30	65	6	0	6	35	11	15	4
Kowitz, Brian, Clemson ...	.403	66	253	87	102	22	6	3	60	44	20	34
Bragg, Darren, Ga. Tech ...	.397	71	239	61	95	17	2	10	73	62	42	14
Estroff, Steve, UNC	.389	63	229	51	89	20	3	15	73	33	25	0
Martz, Danny, Wake Forest .	.367	48	158	45	58	11	1	8	37	21	20	4
Rivell, Bobby, Virginia	.365	50	200	58	73	8	3	11	43	28	22	20
Bruce, Andy, Ga. Tech.....	.363	71	267	58	97	20	5	17	78	24	35	3
McCracken, Quinton, Duke ..	.363	48	204	46	74	7	5	2	32	22	12	26
Pierce, Jeff, NC St.	.359	68	262	70	94	19	2	13	64	34	37	5
Sawkiw, Warren, Wake Forest	.359	61	237	66	85	12	3	16	69	46	24	11
DeBerry, Joe, Clemson	.359	60	237	52	85	8	2	15	70	28	43	4
Norman, David, Duke	.359	51	184	41	66	14	1	11	41	12	17	2
Scharff, Richie, Virginia	.352	49	165	36	58	8	0	1	20	25	16	9
Kenney, Doug, Ga. Tech ...	.352	62	193	40	68	10	1	8	34	29	31	3

INDIVIDUAL PITCHING LEADERS
(Minimum 60 Innings)

	W	L	ERA	G	GS	CG	SV	IP	H	R	ER	BB	SO
Dougherty, Jim, UNC	12	2	1.71	17	15	6	0	116	88	30	22	32	87
Woodall, Brad, UNC	7	2	2.54	26	0	0	5	60	53	19	17	22	69
Shuey, Paul, UNC	8	1	2.73	31	1	0	8	66	50	29	20	45	78
Hostetler, Mike, Ga. Tech ...	12	4	2.76	18	18	6	0	130	111	61	40	37	97
Rumer, Tim, Duke	6	1	2.83	17	8	0	0	60	53	24	19	37	49
Colson, Brent, Ga. Tech	3	2	2.93	20	7	0	1	61	41	26	20	33	57
Parker, Tim, Clemson	7	5	2.97	17	17	5	0	97	70	44	32	53	90
Frazier, Ron, Clemson	6	3	3.40	24	9	1	4	77	77	41	29	32	60
Fernandez, Rich, UNC	8	2	3.42	29	3	1	5	79	75	44	30	43	68

BIG EIGHT CONFERENCE

	Conference		Overall	
	W	L	W	L
*Oklahoma State	18	6	56	17
Kansas State	13	11	30	27
Nebraska......................	12	12	42	26
Iowa State....................	11	13	33	27
Missouri	11	13	28	27
Kansas........................	10	14	27	31
Oklahoma	9	15	31	26

*Won conference tournament

ALL-CONFERENCE TEAM: C—Mike Daniel, Oklahoma State. **1B**—Bobby Benjamin, Nebraska. **2B**—Mitch Simons, Oklahoma State. **3B**—Bobby Carlsen, Oklahoma State. **SS**—Brad Beanblossom, Oklahoma State. **OF**—Mike Weimerskirch, Iowa State; Pat Karlin, Kansas; Scott Campbell, Oklahoma. **Util**—Kevin Jordan, Nebraska. **DH**—Darnel Hawkins, Missouri. **SP**—Steve Renko, Kansas; John Dettmer, Missouri; Gordie Tipton, Oklahoma State; Dave Hierholzer, Kansas State. **RP**—Curtis Shaw, Kansas; Dave Matranga, Nebraska.

INDIVIDUAL BATTING LEADERS
(Minimum 125 At-Bats)

	AVG	G	AB	R	H	2B	3B	HR	RBI	BB	SO	SB
Campbell, Scott, Oklahoma	.415	57	205	57	85	15	4	6	59	42	20	21
Hawkins, Darnel, Missouri	.368	55	190	50	70	9	6	11	54	32	33	7
Carlsen, Bobby, Okla. State	.363	71	234	68	85	17	1	6	62	62	27	9
Daniel, Mike, Okla. State	.362	61	196	60	71	13	1	23	92	46	34	3
Vantiger, Tom, Iowa State	.356	57	216	57	77	18	2	1	39	26	24	27
Stewart, Denard, Kansas	.356	56	180	35	64	19	0	9	37	14	33	8
McArn, Brian, Nebraska	.354	62	212	60	75	10		5	41	31	28	34
Simons, Mitch, Okla. State	.353	73	272	89	96	22	1	11	58	64	30	29
Jordan, Kevin, Nebraska	.348	68	250	51	87	19	3	14	70	31	30	8
Beanblossom, Brad, Okla. State	.343	72	265	62	91	19	0	4	50	47	24	14
Champagne, Andre, Oklahoma	.339	57	186	52	63	23	3	6	30	29	25	6
Karlin, Pat, Kansas	.339	56	192	42	65	8	2	0	24	33	19	42
Vosik, Bill, Nebraska	.339	67	224	42	76	18	2	3	52	31	25	5
Bohrofen, Brent, Oklahoma	.338	43	145	33	49	5	2	5	36	17	27	12
Benjamin, Bobby, Nebraska	.335	68	221	61	74	14	1	18	73	66	47	0

INDIVIDUAL PITCHING LEADERS
(Minimum 60 Innings)

	W	L	ERA	G	GS	CG	SV	IP	H	R	ER	BB	SO
Matranga, Dave, Nebraska	10	3	2.26	34	2	0	4	87	81	30	21	36	75
Tipton, Gordie, Okla. State	10	1	2.53	20	7	2	2	92	69	30	26	30	71
Hierholzer, David, Kansas St.	7	5	3.13	15	14	8	1	98	86	40	34	46	90
Burbank, Dennis, Okla. State	10	2	3.19	18	17	4	0	99	86	45	35	46	41
Schreckengast, Denny, Iowa St.	7	2	3.50	14	11	2	1	77	65	33	30	28	59
Bullock, Josh, Nebraska	5	4	3.68	17	13	3	1	86	79	44	35	48	66
Renko, Steve, Kansas	6	7	3.77	17	14	2	0	93	79	54	39	59	89
Powers, Steve, Missouri	6	2	3.77	11	11	1	0	62	72	33	26	27	45
Ruebel, Matt, Oklahoma	6	4	4.01	20	9	4	1	85	79	51	38	55	104
Shaw, Curtis, Kansas	10	4	4.03	29	1	0	3	60	56	54	39	59	89

BIG TEN CONFERENCE

	Conference		Overall	
	W	L	W	L
Iowa	22	6	38	19
*Illinois	19	9	43	21
Minnesota	19	9	36	24
Ohio State	16	12	32	29
Michigan	14	14	33	24
Indiana	14	14	30	27
Michigan State	13	15	28	24
Purdue	8	19	27	31
Wisconsin	8	20	16	41
Northwestern	6	21	24	32

*Won conference tournament

ALL-CONFERENCE TEAM: C—Dan Wilson, Minnesota. **1B**—Brian Roberts, Illinois. **2B**—Brian Raabe, Minnesota. **3B**—Keith Noreen, Iowa. **SS**—Tim Costo, Iowa. **OF**—Brian Wujcik, Iowa; Phil Dauphin, Indiana; Chris Hatcher, Iowa. **DH**—Mark Dalesandro, Illinois. **P**—Kirt Ojala, Michigan; John DeJarld, Iowa.

INDIVIDUAL BATTING LEADERS
(Minimum 125 At-Bats)

	AVG	G	AB	R	H	2B	3B	HR	RBI	BB	SO	SB
Juday, Rich, Mich. State	.405	50	173	40	70	10	4	12	49	21	21	1
Flannelly, Tim, Michigan	.402	56	194	38	78	9	3	5	40	24	13	3
Dalesandro, Mark, Illinois	.395	59	223	61	88	14	1	16	73	23	24	4
Hatcher, Chris, Iowa	.393	57	206	54	81	11	3	11	50	14	37	18
Wujcik, Brian, Iowa	.391	57	179	34	70	8	2	7	48	31	26	13
Noreen, Keith, Iowa	.373	50	166	52	62	11	1	12	45	27	11	4
Costo, Tim, Iowa	.372	57	196	59	73	15	1	16	64	26	24	5
Mulligan, Sean, Illinois	.371	57	143	37	53	10	1	15	42	14	31	3
Wilson, Dan, Minnesota	.370	57	181	43	67	15	2	8	49	42	18	10
Gates, Brent, Minnesota	.368	61	223	46	82	17	1	7	63	30	20	10
Dauphin, Phil, Indiana	.368	57	190	56	70	12	5	13	52	39	30	23
Perona, Joe, N'western	.368	56	182	36	67	20	6	5	37	17	23	8
Pfaff, Mark, Ohio State	.363	56	160	39	58	9	5	6	44	28	27	3
Mayes, Craig, Mich. State	.351	47	154	35	54	10	2	3	27	11	16	1

INDIVIDUAL PITCHING LEADERS
(Minimum 60 Innings)

	W	L	ERA	G	GS	CG	SV	IP	H	R	ER	BB	SO
DeJarld, John, Iowa	11	3	2.56	18	14	10	3	105	92	44	30	40	78
Pfaff, Jason, Michigan	6	2	2.71	13	10	3	0	70	70	26	21	14	46
Williams, Craig, Indiana	7	3	3.15	12	11	6	0	69	79	35	24	18	40
Ojala, Kirt, Michigan	6	4	3.20	15	12	6	0	70	76	29	25	22	52
Hyde, Rich, Illinois	9	2	3.56	19	13	5	0	104	113	53	41	36	41
Lowery, John, Minnesota	4	4	4.14	19	13	4	1	83	90	45	38	44	62
Kennedy, Brian, Iowa	7	3	4.19	14	12	4	1	73	75	40	34	25	50
Klingenbeck, Scott, Ohio St.	10	4	4.28	16	14	8	1	88	71	54	42	56	76
Brock, Russell, Michigan	6	4	4.37	16	13	6	0	82	97	47	40	27	56

BIG WEST CONFERENCE

	Conference		Overall	
	W	L	W	L
Cal State Fullerton	13	5	36	23
UC Santa Barbara	13	8	40	22
Fresno State	13	8	38	24
Long Beach State	12	9	36	22
UC Irvine	10	11	34	25
Nevada-Las Vegas	10	11	29	24
San Jose State	9	12	43	17
Pacific	1	17	14	40

ALL-CONFERENCE TEAM: C—Todd Johnson, Fresno State. **1B**—Don Barbara, Long Beach State. **2B**—Mate Borgogno, Cal State Fullerton. **3B**—Jeff Antoon, UC Santa Barbara. **SS**—Al Rodriguez, UC Irvine. **OF**—Rich Gonzales, Cal State Fullerton; Eric Booker, San Jose State; Mike Czarnetski, UC Santa Barbara. **Util**—Todd Guggiana, Long Beach State. **DH**—Jason Giambi, Long Beach State. **SP**—Huck Flener, Cal State Fullerton; James Popoff, Cal State Fullerton; Steve Wolf, Fresno State; Andy Croghan, Long Beach State; Ken Whitworth, UC Irvine. **RP**—Bobby Jones, Fresno State.

INDIVIDUAL BATTING LEADERS
(Minimum 125 At-Bats)

	AVG	G	AB	R	H	2B	3B	HR	RBI	BB	SO	SB
Barbara, Don, Long Beach St.	.474	59	215	69	102	27	1	7	61	52	17	9
Giambi, Jason, Long Beach St.	.422	46	154	31	65	10	1	0	29	25	23	5
Gonzales, Rich, CS Fullerton	.386	58	223	46	86	12	0	5	42	21	18	5
Booker, Eric, San Jose State	.383	58	201	69	77	17	3	5	39	63	23	22
Borgogno, Mate, CS Fullerton	.374	58	235	45	88	16	1	3	56	27	23	8
Gallego, Chris, UC Irvine ...	.370	59	238	58	88	11	4	2	39	30	12	3
Johnson, Todd, Fresno State	.367	62	251	51	92	15	6	7	56	16	28	0
Czarnetski, Mike, UCSB	.366	62	235	48	86	12	1	4	45	56	24	37
Combs, Fred, UC Irvine	.366	53	175	55	64	14	4	4	34	50	34	10
DeChavez, Osmar, UC Irvine	.365	58	197	52	72	17	2	3	44	49	22	4
Johnson, Tim, UNLV	.362	53	213	47	77	20	1	7	32	17	19	6
Nevin, Phil, CS Fullerton ...	.358	59	240	59	86	12	5	14	52	44	29	14
Guggiana, Todd, Long Beach St.	.354	59	243	64	86	17	5	9	54	31	31	11

INDIVIDUAL PITCHING LEADERS
(Minimum 60 Innings)

	W	L	ERA	G	GS	CG	SV	IP	H	R	ER	BB	SO
Andrakin, Rob, San Jose State	7	4	2.55	21	9	2	2	92	71	34	26	31	76
Hays, Greg, Long Beach State	5	2	2.71	28	1	0	4	70	63	23	21	14	63
Ringkamp, Mark, San Jose St.	10	3	2.87	17	14	4	2	100	78	35	32	15	68
Whitworth, Ken, UC Irvine	13	4	3.00	22	18	9	1	141	151	60	47	39	96
Grewal, Ranbir, Fresno State	10	6	3.08	23	12	4	0	105	96	51	36	51	96
Colarusso, Sam, CS Fullerton	7	3	3.24	15	14	2	0	86	89	37	31	38	57
Brownholtz, Joe, Pacific	3	5	3.30	19	11	3	1	101	94	55	37	41	71
Jones, Bobby, Fresno State .	9	3	3.38	30	13	5	5	122	126	76	46	36	115
Wolf, Steve, Fresno State ...	9	6	3.74	23	19	8	0	154	156	79	64	53	171

METRO CONFERENCE

	Conference		Overall	
	W	L	W	L
*Florida State.................	17	4	57	15
Southern Mississippi	16	5	42	25
South Carolina	10	6	33	25
Virginia Tech	9	9	36	22
Memphis State	7	12	31	25
Cincinnati	5	10	23	29
Louisville	4	10	15	29
Tulane......................	4	16	19	35

*Won conference tournament

ALL-CONFERENCE TEAM: C—Pete Grifol, Florida State. **1B**—Tony Elsbrock, Cincinnati. **2B**—Allen Bevis, Florida State. **3B**—Len Wentz, Virginia Tech. **SS**—Jamie Baker, Cincinnati. **OF**—Skeets Thomas, South Carolina; Marc Ronan, Florida State; Rod Emmons, Virginia Tech. **Util**—Brian Williams, South Carolina. **DH**—Buddy Cribb, Florida State. **P**—Gar Finnvold, Florida State; Damon Pollard, Southern Mississippi.

INDIVIDUAL BATTING LEADERS
(Minimum 125 At-Bats)

	AVG	G	AB	R	H	2B	3B	HR	RBI	BB	SO	SB
Thomas, Skeets, So. Carolina	.383	58	214	43	82	14	2	11	59	32	32	7
Young, Kevin, So. Mississippi	.379	67	253	58	96	27	3	13	75	28	30	17
Nace, Todd, So. Mississippi .	.376	61	234	48	88	14	2	2	20	35	43	4
Bargas, Rob, Florida State ..	.376	57	210	40	79	22	1	5	58	27	19	1

	AVG	G	AB	R	H	2B	3B	HR	RBI	BB	SO	SB
Wentz, Len, Virginia Tech . .	.365	58	211	53	77	20	1	8	53	41	23	10
Ronan, Marc, Florida State . .	.356	70	250	75	89	25	1	6	60	66	25	34
Elsbrock, Tony, Cincinnati . .	.353	51	170	35	60	10	0	9	28	22	32	2
Moss, Steve, Memphis State	.351	55	202	37	71	21	1	7	46	25	30	1
Bevis, Allen, Florida State . .	.350	67	226	68	79	20	5	2	39	50	40	33
Schneider, Ken, Cincinnati . .	.349	47	146	32	51	16	0	3	27	12	10	10
Kross, Chris, Memphis State	.341	56	211	39	72	17	1	0	24	19	16	11

INDIVIDUAL PITCHING LEADERS
(Minimum 60 Innings)

	W	L	ERA	G	GS	CG	SV	IP	H	R	ER	BB	SO
Gregory, Brad, Florida State	5	2	2.43	31	6	2	11	93	94	32	25	20	85
Bailey, Roger, Florida State . .	9	1	2.65	15	13	0	0	75	73	33	22	30	54
Finnvold, Gar, Florida State .	15	3	2.77	19	18	9	1	136	120	53	42	41	136
Williams, Brian, So. Carolina .	8	4	3.03	15	15	4	0	107	75	40	36	55	125
Pollard, Damon, So. Miss.	13	5	3.34	21	21	11	0	148	115	68	55	90	152
Carson, Mark, So. Miss.	7	3	3.41	22	7	2	4	74	66	33	28	38	43
Gilligan, John, So. Miss.	11	3	3.50	19	18	8	0	134	139	72	52	36	111
Goodson, Kirk, Va. Tech	6	5	3.59	13	12	3	0	73	66	40	29	33	47
Kimball, Ricky, Florida State .	7	4	3.75	25	11	2	9	96	102	52	40	34	90

MISSOURI VALLEY CONFERENCE

	Conference		Overall	
	W	L	W	L
Wichita State	14	6	45	19
*Southern Illinois	14	6	49	14
Creighton	13	7	48	22
Indiana State	8	12	43	21
Bradley	6	13	31	32
Illinois State	4	15	26	31

*Won conference tournament

ALL-CONFERENCE TEAM: C—Doug Mirabelli, Wichita State. **1B**—Scott Stahoviak, Creighton. **2B**—Tim Davis, Southern Illinois. **3B**—Pat Meares, Wichita State. **SS**—Dave Wrona, Southern Illinois. **OF**—Doug Shields, Southern Illinois; John Pivovar, Creighton; Chris Wimmer, Wichita State. **Util**—Todd Schroeder, Illinois State. **DH**—Mike Farrell, Indiana State. **P**—Sean Bergman, Southern Illinois; Dan Smith, Creighton; Kennie Steenstra, Wichita State.

INDIVIDUAL BATTING LEADERS
(Minimum 125 At-Bats)

	AVG	G	AB	R	H	2B	3B	HR	RBI	BB	SO	SB
Stahoviak, Scott, Creighton .	.417	67	228	63	95	25	2	6	51	41	31	10
Schroeder, Todd, Illinois St. .	.405	56	200	42	81	20	10	4	32	32	31	7
Wrona, Dave, So. Illinois . . .	.395	62	228	43	90	17	0	9	56	16	18	4
Ruckman, Steve, Indiana St. .	.391	50	128	29	50	5	3	3	28	14	15	2
Farrell, Mike, Indiana St.	.377	68	191	63	72	7	5	0	27	53	25	0
Endebrock, Kurt, So. Illinois .	.357	62	241	71	86	13	3	2	33	31	32	24
Shields, Doug, So. Illinois . . .	.351	61	225	64	79	14	7	9	64	27	34	12
McDonald, Chad, Indiana St. .	.349	62	215	50	75	14	1	4	53	28	19	5
Davis, Tim, So. Illinois	.346	63	231	64	80	20	4	5	64	24	18	6
Hollenkamp, Brad, So. Illinois	.345	60	198	41	68	12	1	7	44	28	40	1
McCafferty, Mike, Creighton .	.343	58	175	38	60	20	5	7	49	20	40	4
McCloughan, Scot, Wichita St.	.340	62	209	43	71	9	3	2	34	40	29	11

INDIVIDUAL PITCHING LEADERS
(Minimum 60 Innings)

	W	L	ERA	G	GS	CG	SV	IP	H	R	ER	BB	SO
Smith, Dan, Creighton	14	3	1.96	17	16	12	0	120	84	33	26	48	134
Steenstra, Kennie, Wichita St.	9	2	2.47	17	11	2	0	84	76	32	23	23	56
Bergman, Sean, So. Illinois .	9	3	2.76	15	14	6	0	98	86	36	30	40	62
Giaudrone, Charlie, Wich. St.	8	3	2.92	14	13	0	0	62	64	21	20	42	47
Stryker, Ed, Illinois St.	8	6	3.36	17	14	7	0	104	99	46	39	17	65
Heathcott, Mike, Creighton . .	7	3	3.46	16	16	2	0	94	102	48	36	51	61
Paxton, Darrin, Wichita St. . .	12	4	3.49	19	19	4	0	121	98	56	47	57	116
Green, Tyler, Wichita State . .	6	5	3.55	15	15	4	0	91	63	46	36	48	104

PACIFIC-10 CONFERENCE

	Conference		Overall	
North	W	L	W	L
*Washington State	19	5	47	19
Oregon State	15	9	30	22
Washington	14	10	30	19
Gonzaga	13	11	37	21
Portland	10	14	26	25
Portland State	9	15	30	24
Eastern Washington.	4	20	14	36

*Won conference tournament

ALL-CONFERENCE TEAM: C—Scott Hatteberg, Washington State. **1B**—Rob Nichols, Washington State. **2B**—Greg Hunter, Washington State. **3B**—John Tsoukalas, Gonzaga. **SS**—Kevin Stocker, Washington. **OF**—Dane Walker, Portland State; Jim Connor, Washington State; Gary Van Tol, Gonzaga; Brad Clem, Portland. **Util**—Jim Straw, Eastern Washington. **DH**—Jason Geis, Portland. **SP**—Billy Walker, Gonzaga; Jeff Post, Oregon State; Aaron Sele, Washington State; Scott Brow, Washington.

INDIVIDUAL BATTING LEADERS
(Minimum 125 At-Bats)

	AVG	G	AB	R	H	2B	3B	HR	RBI	BB	SO	SB
Geis, Jason, Portland	.407	50	177	39	72	14	2	9	48	20	22	8
Walker, Dane, Port. St.	.393	53	196	45	77	13	6	4	46	33	20	13
Van Tol, Gary, Gonzaga	.382	56	191	33	73	13	0	2	36	25	12	12
Hatteberg, Scott, Wash. St.	.381	66	231	59	88	29	2	8	51	43	18	4
Tsoukalas, John, Gonzaga	.378	56	180	51	68	8	0	8	45	33	17	10
Connor, Jim, Wash. St.	.369	67	236	70	87	23	3	8	58	55	40	6
Clem, Brad, Portland	.360	51	197	54	71	17	3	8	49	24	23	18
Neitzel, R.A., Oregon St.	.355	52	211	49	75	14	2	3	20	27	26	20
Ahart, Corey, Gonzaga	.337	58	199	44	67	12	4	1	30	39	19	23
Lutz, Brent, Washington	.335	49	170	41	57	13	3	2	38	27	25	16
Anderson, Aaron, Oregon St.	.333	48	192	37	64	7	1	1	23	13	19	11
Loomis, Geoff, Portland	.333	47	156	32	52	11	1	1	28	21	12	3
Fromdahl, Aric, Portland	.332	50	193	37	64	15	0	0	24	18	28	2
Nichols, Rob, Wash. State	.330	63	224	63	74	17	1	14	60	23	39	1
Thompson, Tad, Wash. State	.330	62	182	38	60	12	2	7	42	34	29	3

INDIVIDUAL PITCHING LEADERS
(Minimum 60 Innings)

	W	L	ERA	G	GS	CG	SV	IP	H	R	ER	BB	SO
Post, Jeff, Oregon St.	10	4	1.96	26	7	4	4	83	76	23	18	17	45
Sele, Aaron, Wash. St.	12	3	2.22	17	16	9	0	122	102	45	30	41	121
Brow, Scott, Washington	9	5	2.42	14	13	4	0	104	96	43	28	31	76
McGraw, Tom, Wash. St.	10	5	2.43	20	17	4	0	110	102	39	30	46	91
Walker, Billy, Gonzaga	12	3	2.52	18	16	9	1	107	81	38	30	54	127
McCarthy, Craig, Oregon St.	4	1	2.96	22	7	1	3	70	64	29	23	9	52
Johnson, Tod, Washington	6	3	3.10	13	13	4	0	87	86	44	30	26	40
Gower, Tim, Gonzaga	10	4	3.57	24	13	2	6	111	114	50	44	18	78
Peterson, Mark, Port. St.	10	3	3.64	17	13	7	0	96	85	48	39	20	73
Fredrickson, Aaron, Port.	4	3	3.75	14	13	0	0	60	52	33	25	26	64

PACIFIC-10 CONFERENCE

	Conference		Overall	
South	**W**	**L**	**W**	**L**
Stanford	20	7	59	12
Arizona State	20	10	52	16
Southern California	18	12	40	22
UCLA	14	16	41	26
Arizona	11	19	26	34
California	3	27	18	43

ALL-CONFERENCE TEAM: C—Paul Ellis, UCLA; Mike Harrison, Cal. **1B**—Chris Pritchett, UCLA. **INF**—Tim Griffin, Stanford; Anthony Manahan, Arizona State; Troy Paulsen, Stanford; Fernando Vina, Arizona State. **OF**—Mike Kelly, Arizona State; Jim Austin, Arizona State; Jeff Hammonds, Stanford; Paul Carey, Stanford; Joel Wolfe, UCLA. **Util**—Troy Bradford, Arizona; Jeff Cirillo, USC; Jon Zuber, Cal. **SP**—Randy Powers, USC; Sean Rees, Arizona State; Stan Spencer, Stanford.

INDIVIDUAL BATTING LEADERS
(Minimum 125 At-Bats)

	AVG	G	AB	R	H	2B	3B	HR	RBI	BB	SO	SB
Vina, Fernando, ASU	.387	63	279	69	108	17	7	2	34	18	7	20
Zuber, Jon, Cal	.386	58	228	53	88	21	2	4	40	31	30	10
Kelly, Mike, ASU	.376	68	258	83	97	17	6	21	82	54	61	20
Wolfe, Joel, UCLA	.376	60	197	51	74	14	6	10	44	32	43	30
Pritchett, Chris, UCLA	.368	67	277	73	102	14	1	13	67	28	36	3
Manahan, Anthony, ASU	.366	68	284	66	104	22	5	10	81	37	24	9
Ellis, Paul, UCLA	.360	66	247	61	89	8	1	29	83	38	22	3
Austin, Jim, ASU	.358	66	271	71	97	17	7	17	57	36	40	19
Hammonds, Jeff, Stanford	.355	69	301	83	107	15	7	7	44	35	32	48
Neumann, Reid, Cal	.352	59	227	44	80	10	2	3	37	28	20	13
Mashore, Damon, Arizona	.352	58	233	59	82	13	2	4	31	30	49	17
Harrison, Mike, Cal	.341	59	232	53	79	10	1	21	63	31	57	4
Paulsen, Troy, Stanford	.340	71	318	53	108	29	3	5	58	21	36	7
Owens, Billy, Arizona	.339	53	186	26	63	10	2	2	31	15	32	1
McCarty, David, Stanford	.336	71	268	74	90	21	4	12	69	54	48	3

INDIVIDUAL PITCHING LEADERS
(Minimum 60 Innings)

	W	L	ERA	G	GS	CG	SV	IP	H	R	ER	BB	SO
Powers, Randy, USC	11	3	2.29	23	18	8	2	138	120	47	35	15	90
Rees, Sean, Arizona St.	13	3	2.67	22	20	8	0	138	98	58	41	54	162
Spencer, Stan, Stanford	14	1	2.73	20	19	9	0	142	126	52	43	28	145
Yaughn, Kip, ASU	11	5	2.98	28	15	3	4	115	96	58	38	51	88
Reid, John, Stanford	7	1	3.03	19	13	1	0	86	90	36	29	41	54

	W	L	ERA	G	GS	CG	SV	IP	H	R	ER	BB	SO
Zancanaro, Dave, UCLA	11	6	3.19	30	13	4	5	121	111	72	43	78	100
Dickson, Lance, Arizona	7	8	3.46	16	16	7	0	120	101	66	46	55	141
Nickell, Jackie, USC	7	4	3.49	29	3	0	2	70	71	33	27	20	45
Mussina, Mike, Stanford ...	14	5	3.50	20	20	9	0	149	158	70	58	35	111
Cirillo, Jeff, USC	6	2	3.50	23	9	0	3	71	73	36	28	31	42

SOUTHEASTERN CONFERENCE

	Conference		Overall	
	W	L	W	L
*Louisiana State	20	7	54	19
Georgia	18	9	52	19
*Mississippi State	17	9	50	21
Auburn	13	13	34	24
Vanderbilt	12	13	28	30
Florida	11	12	29	30
Alabama	10	13	34	21
Mississippi	10	16	23	29
Tennessee	9	18	28	31
Kentucky	8	18	27	29

*Co-champions, conference tournament

ALL-CONFERENCE TEAM: C—Tim Edge, Auburn. **1B**—Tommy Raffo, Mississippi State. **2B**—Tookie Johnson, LSU. **3B**—Keith Osik, LSU. **SS**—J.R. Showalter, Georgia. **OF**—John Cohen, Mississippi State; Jim Schifman, Vanderbilt; Wes Grisham, LSU. **DH**—Brian Jester, Georgia. **P**—Dave Fleming, Georgia; Chad Ogea, LSU; JoJo Smith, Vanderbilt.

INDIVIDUAL BATTING LEADERS
(Minimum 125 At-Bats)

	AVG	G	AB	R	H	2B	3B	HR	RBI	BB	SO	SB
Edge, Tim, Auburn	.387	57	191	43	74	15	2	9	48	40	21	0
Harris, Mike, Kentucky	.371	51	175	54	65	11	4	5	36	32	18	16
Vitiello, Joe, Alabama	.364	54	184	52	67	14	2	11	53	46	35	3
Jester, Brian, Georgia	.364	54	198	50	72	11	0	17	64	35	38	3
Schifman, Jim, Vanderbilt ..	.362	57	229	61	83	12	5	9	38	28	22	18
Grisham, Wes, LSU	.360	73	278	65	100	18	4	11	72	34	41	5
Raffo, Tommy, Miss. State .	.358	70	271	58	97	19	3	13	69	37	51	7
Farrell, John, Alabama	.354	52	209	49	74	11	5	8	36	22	19	17
DeFelice, Mike, Tennessee .	.353	51	173	36	61	15	1	10	45	15	34	2
Mouton, Lyle, LSU	.351	57	174	44	61	18	1	10	41	33	39	5
Cordani, Rich, LSU	.348	71	273	69	95	23	6	9	59	36	38	6
Doyle, Phil, Alabama	.346	49	191	35	56	8	0	10	33	14	29	4
Powell, Jeff, Auburn	.345	39	142	33	49	6	1	4	33	19	12	5
Johnson, Tookie, LSU	.344	69	270	59	93	13	2	2	59	26	18	8
Ramirez, Danny, Tennessee	.343	58	210	52	72	6	0	2	29	36	20	38

INDIVIDUAL PITCHING LEADERS
(Minimum 60 Innings)

	W	L	ERA	G	GS	CG	SV	IP	H	R	ER	BB	SO
Harden, Jon, Miss. State	5	0	2.21	30	0	0	3	73	60	22	18	12	58
Smith, JoJo, Vanderbilt	9	3	2.67	22	13	6	6	98	79	44	29	49	75
Pricher, John, Florida	6	3	2.71	23	7	1	2	83	79	32	25	29	67
Fleming, Dave, Georgia	12	6	2.86	21	19	13	2	160	134	63	51	55	163
O'Donoghue, John, LSU	12	3	2.88	20	18	2	0	109	118	46	35	27	85
Bolton, Rod, Kentucky	8	7	2.90	20	14	8	2	112	101	51	36	36	121
Rebhan, Mike, Georgia	13	5	3.01	22	18	9	1	138	131	61	46	47	92
Sullivan, Grant, Mississippi .	6	6	3.01	18	16	5	0	105	99	45	35	26	62
Reed, Bobby, Miss. State ...	15	4	3.01	25	22	7	3	140	122	58	47	39	98
Roberts, Mark, Alabama	7	4	3.15	18	15	3	1	91	82	42	32	51	90

SOUTHWEST CONFERENCE

	Conference		Overall	
	W	L	W	L
Arkansas	16	5	47	15
*Texas	15	5	51	17
Houston	12	9	44	23
Rice	11	9	33	29
Texas A&M	11	10	43	17
Baylor	9	12	33	19
Texas Tech	5	16	31	29
Texas Christian	4	17	27	32

*Won conference tournament

ALL-CONFERENCE TEAM: C—Tony Gilmore, Arkansas. **1B**—James Wambach, Houston. **2B**—David Tollison, Texas. **3B**—Greg D'Alexander, Arkansas. **SS**—Steve Kliafas, Baylor. **OF**—Bubba Carpenter, Arkansas; Paul Gonzalez, Texas

Christian; Mike Robison, Baylor. **Util**—Scott Pugh, Texas. **DH**—Keith Darter, Houston. **P**—Kirk Dressendorfer, Texas; Rich Robertson, Texas A&M; Mark Swope, Arkansas; Phil Stidham, Arkansas; Al Benavides, Houston.

INDIVIDUAL BATTING LEADERS
(Minimum 125 At-Bats)

	AVG	G	AB	R	H	2B	3B	HR	RBI	BB	SO	SB
Darter, Keith, Houston	.396	67	235	57	93	14	3	2	44	24	19	10
D'Alexander, Greg, Arkansas	.387	60	212	51	82	18	2	14	65	37	31	10
Jones, Lance, Texas	.380	68	250	71	95	17	7	3	54	56	40	34
Piskor, Kirk, Arkansas	.360	62	247	56	89	13	3	13	63	25	38	12
Carpenter, Bubba, Arkansas	.360	56	161	44	58	15	2	2	34	43	31	13
Malone, Scott, TCU	.358	59	215	41	77	10	3	6	42	18	21	9
Losa, Mike, TCU	.355	59	220	45	78	10	6	13	49	20	16	9
Pugh, Scott, Texas	.351	51	171	42	60	17	1	6	32	21	24	2
King, Clay, Texas	.351	61	231	49	81	18	1	2	45	20	23	6
Tollison, Dave, Texas	.350	68	263	60	92	21	3	12	69	30	30	17
Wambach, James, Houston .	.349	64	212	35	74	18	1	4	52	23	15	0
Johnson, Mark, Arkansas . . .	.343	57	178	44	61	7	4	1	36	26	17	26
Dietrich, Derrick, Houston . .	.340	61	141	37	48	3	4	2	21	27	18	11
Morland, Mike, Texas	.340	43	141	23	48	11	1	1	33	13	29	1
Ellis, Kevin, Baylor	.338	46	145	37	49	4	2	10	41	10	24	4

INDIVIDUAL PITCHING LEADERS
(Minimum 60 Innings)

	W	L	ERA	G	GS	CG	SV	IP	H	R	ER	BB	SO
Robertson, Rich, Texas A&M	10	1	1.77	15	13	7	1	91	53	24	18	45	106
Benavides, Al, Houston	8	1	2.34	30	1	0	2	81	81	27	21	22	73
Allen, Ronnie, Texas A&M . .	6	4	2.35	13	13	8	0	100	78	36	26	28	70
Ruffcorn, Scott, Baylor	9	3	2.60	16	14	7	0	93	73	29	27	52	78
Gaskill, Chris, Texas	7	4	2.86	24	6	1	7	66	71	24	21	21	55
Darter, Keith, Houston	8	6	2.78	27	12	2	4	81	66	29	25	35	56
Bradley, Mike, Texas	7	2	2.87	21	13	1	1	78	80	38	25	47	60
Weber, Ben, Houston	8	5	2.89	22	14	4	0	97	90	44	31	33	66
Dare, Brian, Texas	8	2	3.00	23	12	2	2	87	90	42	29	30	80
Dressendorfer, Kirk, Texas . .	12	4	3.16	22	18	6	2	125	98	55	44	33	152

SUN BELT CONFERENCE

	Conference		Overall	
East	**W**	**L**	**W**	**L**
Jacksonville	13	5	42	20
Old Dominion	11	6	40	19
UNC Charlotte	8	9	33	29
Virginia Commonwealth	2	14	18	29
West	**W**	**L**	**W**	**L**
South Alabama	12	6	44	20
*South Florida	8	10	41	24
Western Kentucky	8	10	32	28
Alabama-Birmingham	8	10	27	26

*Won conference tournament

ALL-CONFERENCE TEAM: C—Kris Gresham, UNC Charlotte. **1B**—Jonathan Camilo, Western Kentucky. **2B**—Joe Lis, South Florida. **3B**—Chris Vlasis, Virginia Commonwealth. **SS**—Brad Worley, Western Kentucky. **OF**—Marc Marini, Jacksonville; Scott Thomson, Old Dominion; Kristin Metheny, Alabama-Birmingham. **DH**—Alex Moreno, South Florida. **P**—Mike Zimmerman, South Alabama; Jeff Ware, Old Dominion; Chris Haney, UNC Charlotte.

INDIVIDUAL BATTING LEADERS
(Minimum 125 At-Bats)

	AVG	G	AB	R	H	2B	3B	HR	RBI	BB	SO	SB
Marini, Marc, Jacksonville . .	.439	54	171	55	75	15	3	0	31	44	20	20
Thomson, Scott, ODU	.399	58	203	48	81	17	8	7	40	11	19	7
Camilo, Jonathan, W. Ky. . . .	.366	60	227	32	83	23	1	5	37	18	28	1
Metheny, Kristin, UAB	.360	52	203	42	73	6	3	0	15	19	18	13
Lis, Joe, South Florida	.357	65	221	47	79	11	4	1	36	49	28	10
Vlasis, Chris, VCU	.356	47	160	42	57	9	3	2	26	34	20	11
Sells, George, ODU	.347	59	193	44	67	11	1	9	35	36	50	3
Haney, Chris, UNC Charlotte	.340	55	200	38	68	11	0	2	35	26	21	8
Moreno, Alex, South Florida .	.338	58	195	28	66	14	1	7	38	33	34	9
Worley, Brad, W. Ky.	.335	60	239	37	80	13	4	3	36	12	26	10

INDIVIDUAL PITCHING LEADERS
(Minimum 60 Innings)

	W	L	ERA	G	GS	CG	SV	IP	H	R	ER	BB	SO
Zimmerman, Mike, USA . . .	12	7	1.59	27	16	13	5	158	102	43	28	50	170
Hutcheson, David, So. Florida	3	3	2.11	29	8	0	1	81	62	22	19	20	55
Elder, Chad, Jacksonville . . .	7	1	2.41	19	11	3	2	82	73	31	22	35	63
Flanagan, Danny, VCU	4	2	2.49	31	0	0	1	65	44	23	18	24	44
Edenfield, Ken, W. Kentucky .	8	8	2.59	25	14	5	4	118	113	47	34	34	94
Haney, Chris, UNC Charlotte .	6	7	2.62	17	13	9	0	96	94	35	28	18	82
Treadwell, Jody, Jacks.	11	3	2.65	18	13	4	0	99	86	43	29	38	78
Reed, Mark, South Florida . .	5	3	2.79	16	12	3	0	74	74	33	23	23	39

WESTERN ATHLETIC CONFERENCE

	Conference		Overall	
	W	L	W	L
*San Diego State..............	21	7	49	22
Brigham Young	20	7	43	25
Wyoming	20	8	37	18
Hawaii......................	17	10	37	24
New Mexico	10	16	25	31
Utah	10	16	19	33
Air Force	7	21	26	34
Colorado State	4	24	9	42

*Won conference tournament

ALL-CONFERENCE TEAM: C—Mark Robert, Wyoming. **1B**—Randy Wilstead, BYU. **2B**—Victor Vargas, Wyoming. **3B**—Mike Edwards, Utah. **SS**—Brian Grebeck, San Diego State. **OF**—Gary Daniels, BYU; Jeff Barry, San Diego State; Terance Frazier, New Mexico. **DH**—Eric Christopherson, San Diego State. **P**—Kurt Archer, San Diego State; Scott Freeman, Wyoming; Craig Sudbury, Utah.

INDIVIDUAL BATTING LEADERS
(Minimum 125 At-Bats)

	AVG	G	AB	R	H	2B	3B	HR	RBI	BB	SO	SB
Daniels, Gary, BYU	.437	69	270	84	118	27	10	24	91	28	29	14
Robert, Mark, Wyoming	.415	54	195	56	81	10	1	16	67	24	20	13
Wilstead, Randy, BYU	.411	68	241	78	99	20	4	22	64	53	38	7
Beck, Rob, Utah	.372	51	183	43	68	12	2	13	45	16	19	5
Schwankl, Darren, Air Force .	.370	58	189	35	70	21	3	1	42	26	21	8
Call, Burt, BYU	.367	67	215	61	79	14	6	11	55	45	42	12
Vargas, Victor, Wyoming ...	.364	55	184	55	67	17	1	7	41	41	28	7
Simpson, Brian, BYU	.363	58	182	47	66	10	2	9	56	29	21	2
Dennison, Brian, San Diego St.	.362	68	232	70	84	15	3	4	34	38	29	34
DeGrange, Mark, Air Force	.360	60	175	38	63	11	1	3	44	29	26	5
Milne, Blaine, BYU	.358	52	162	35	58	11	1	5	36	21	24	2
Boucher, Steve, San Diego St.	.351	64	191	40	67	10	0	1	30	27	17	8
Beltran, Rigo, Wyoming ...	.351	47	154	35	54	13	2	5	42	20	8	4
Christopherson, Eric, SD St.	.348	69	230	50	80	18	5	7	51	58	38	6

INDIVIDUAL PITCHING LEADERS
(Minimum 60 Innings)

	W	L	ERA	G	GS	CG	SV	IP	H	R	ER	BB	SO
Archer, Kurt, San Diego St. ..	9	2	2.42	25	11	5	2	104	97	37	28	38	64
Navarro, Rick, San Diego St. .	3	3	2.59	20	13	2	1	83	74	32	24	19	43
Petersen, Andy, San Diego St.	10	2	2.80	23	8	5	1	90	88	31	28	26	61
Clark, Lance, BYU	8	6	2.84	24	9	4	1	92	101	46	29	40	60
Plantenberg, Erik, SD St. ..	10	5	3.06	21	19	3	0	115	96	46	39	54	101
Largusa, Levon, Hawaii	10	4	3.28	17	16	1	0	102	67	40	37	68	115
Nealon, Greg, Hawaii	5	2	3.39	15	11	0	0	72	78	38	27	30	39
Alexanderson, Russ, UNM ..	5	7	3.41	13	13	10	0	92	97	51	35	27	41

CONFERENCE STANDINGS

Remaining Division I Conferences

American South

	Conf.		Overall	
	W	L	W	L
*SW Louisiana	11	4	47	18
New Orleans	11	4	37	27
Louisiana Tech	8	7	29	31
Arkansas State.....	7	8	11	38
Texas-Pan Am.	5	10	30	24
Lamar	3	12	16	37

Atlantic Ten

	Conf.		Overall	
East	W	L	W	L
*Rutgers	14	2	37	19
Massachusetts	12	4	26	20
Rhode Island.......	6	10	11	23
Temple	5	11	17	31
St. Joseph	3	13	19	26
West				
George Washington	13	3	23	31
West Virginia.......	12	4	33	20
St. Bonaventure	7	9	22	19
Penn State	6	10	22	23
Duquesne..........	2	14	5	22

Big East

	Conf.		Overall	
	W	L	W	L
Seton Hall	16	4	35	18
St. John's	15	6	29	18
Villanova..........	13	8	33	16
*Connecticut	12	9	27	19
Providence.........	11	10	27	21
Boston College.....	8	13	21	22
Georgetown........	4	16	17	30
Pittsburgh.........	4	17	8	23

Big South

	Conf.		Overall	
	W	L	W	L
Coastal Carolina ...	14	2	40	19
Radford	8	7	24	27
UNC Asheville	8	9	25	25
Baptist	6	7	12	36
*Campbell	6	8	15	33
Augusta............	5	8	22	30
Winthrop...........	5	11	22	28

Colonial Athletic Association

	Conf.		Overall	
	W	L	W	L
*East Carolina	11	2	47	9
Richmond..........	9	4	27	19
UNC Wilmington ...	5	6	23	25
George Mason	6	8	28	30
James Madison	3	5	27	19
William & Mary	1	10	9	31

East Coast

	Conf.		Overall	
	W	L	W	L
Delaware	12	2	26	18
*Lafayette...........	12	2	26	17

	Conf.		Overall	
	W	L	W	L
Rider	9	5	22	22
Towson State	7	7	18	29
Bucknell	6	8	13	20
Lehigh	4	10	10	14
Hofstra	3	11	6	25
Drexel	3	11	6	26

ECAC

North Atlantic

	Conf.		Overall	
	W	L	W	L
Maine	12	3	42	20
Central Connecticut	9	5	25	14
Northeastern	9	6	26	20
Vermont	5	9	18	13
New Hampshire	4	10	18	19
Hartford	4	10	15	20

Northeast

	Conf.		Overall	
Long Island	12	3	27	13
St. Francis	9	6	17	18
Wagner	6	6	17	15
Monmouth	7	8	16	19
Mount St. Mary's	4	7	12	19
Fairleigh Dickinson	3	11	15	23

Diamond

	Conf.		Overall	
New York Tech	11	0	32	20
C.W. Post	7	5	20	23
Pace	4	7	15	25
Brooklyn	3	8	9	24
West Chester	3	8	24	17

MAAC North

	Conf.		Overall	
LeMoyne	10	1	18	12
Canisius	6	6	11	20
Siena	5	6	6	24
Colgate	4	8	15	19
Niagara	4	8	11	22

MAAC South

	Conf.		Overall	
*Fordham	16	2	36	14
Holy Cross	10	7	17	13
Fairfield	9	9	13	22
Iona	9	9	22	21
Manhattan	7	11	11	21
St. Peter's	6	12	19	18
LaSalle	5	12	11	36

EIBL

	Conf.		Overall	
	W	L	W	L
Pennsylvania	13	5	23	17
Army	11	7	23	17
Brown	11	7	19	21
Princeton	11	7	23	18
Dartmouth	10	8	21	17
Harvard	9	9	15	20
Yale	8	10	21	24
Cornell	7	11	21	23
Navy	6	12	16	20
Columbia	4	14	12	24

Mid-American

	Conf.		Overall	
	W	L	W	L
Central Michigan	19	9	38	19
Western Michigan	16	9	30	20
Kent	17	10	35	18
Eastern Michigan	20	12	32	25
Miami (Ohio)	14	14	34	22
Ohio	12	16	29	27
Bowling Green St.	10	17	29	25
Ball State	8	19	21	33
Toledo	7	17	21	27

Mid-Continent Universities

	Conf.		Overall	
	W	L	W	L
Blue				
*Illinois-Chicago	8	3	33	24
Akron	7	5	25	29
Cleveland State	3	6	13	27
Valparaiso	3	7	20	35
Gray				
SW Missouri State	11	0	42	15
Eastern Illinois	4	7	24	30
Western Illinois	4	8	19	20
Northern Iowa	4	8	20	39

Midwestern Collegiate

	Conf.		Overall	
	W	L	W	L
East				
Notre Dame	20	2	46	12
Detroit	11	11	24	25
Xavier	7	13	18	36
Dayton	4	16	15	46

West

	Conf.		Overall	
*Evansville	10	2	27	25
Butler	5	7	18	30
Saint Louis	1	7	18	38

Ohio Valley

	Conf.		Overall	
	W	L	W	L
*Middle Tenn. State	14	0	42	15
Eastern Kentucky	15	3	42	15
Tennessee Tech	7	9	26	25
Austin Peay	6	8	31	25
Morehead State	6	9	23	24
Murray State	2	11	16	25
Tennessee State	2	12	12	29

Southern

	Conf.		Overall	
	W	L	W	L
*The Citadel	13	1	46	14
Western Carolina	10	7	37	25
Marshall	10	7	20	19
Virginia Military	6	8	12	26
Appalachian State	6	9	19	22
Furman	6	11	20	24
East Tennessee	4	12	10	31

Southland

	Conf.		Overall	
	W	L	W	L
Texas-Arlington	11	5	31	30
Sam Houston	11	6	34	22
McNeese State	10	7	35	20
NE Louisiana	10	8	28	17
Northwestern St.	9	9	38	13
SW Texas State	7	11	31	22
Stephen F. Austin	3	15	11	46

Southwest Athletic

	Conf.		Overall	
	W	L	W	L
East				
*Jackson State	17	1	33	16
Alcorn State	12	10	13	25
Miss. Valley State	8	11	11	29
Alabama State	4	17	16	26
West				
Southern	17	5	26	17
Grambling State	13	9	20	25
Texas Southern	10	14	15	33
Prairie View	6	18	12	45

Trans America

	Conf.		Overall	
	W	L	W	L
East				
Georgia Southern	17	1	50	19
*Stetson	10	8	33	31
Samford	5	11	25	28
Mercer	2	14	15	34
West				
Centenary	12	3	40	18
Ark.-Little Rock	8	7	33	20
Hardin-Simmons	3	9	16	41

West Coast

	Conf.		Overall	
	W	L	W	L
Loyola Marymount	25	9	45	17
Pepperdine	24	12	37	23
Nevada-Reno	15	14	33	22
Santa Clara	17	19	26	30
San Diego	16	19	24	32
St. Mary's	15	19	30	28
San Francisco	7	27	14	39

INDEPENDENTS

	Overall	
	W	L
Miami	52	13
Nicholls State	36	17
New Mexico State	40	19
Central Florida	40	20
Florida International	40	20
Wright State	35	20
Sacramento State	34	25
Davidson	27	23
Florida A&M	18	17
Liberty	23	24
SE Louisiana	22	25
Maryland-Balt. Co.	16	20
Delaware State	14	18
Northern Colorado	18	28
U.S. International	15	44
Boston	9	35

*—Won conference tournament

Team USA's reputation takes one on the chin

By JIM CALLIS

Team USA's 1988 Olympic gold medal seemed much further than two years away in 1990. At the two major international events on the calendar, the U.S. finished third at the Goodwill Games and seventh at the World Championships.

U.S. coach Jim Morris (Georgia Tech) wanted to avoid the problems Charlie Greene (Miami-Dade CC South) ran into in 1989, when several players left his roster late in the summer. So Morris decided to avoid juniors and seniors selected in the June draft and cast his lot with college freshmen and sophomores.

Much to his chagrin, he found that he couldn't even get the best underclassmen. Take outfielders Mike Kelly (Arizona State), Jeff Hammonds (Stanford) and Calvin Murray (Texas), for example.

Kelly, Baseball America's College Player of the Year, didn't want to travel and wanted to use wood bats in the Cape Cod League. Hammonds, BA's Freshman of the Year, just took the summer off.

Jim Morris
... limited recources

Murray, who went on to become BA's Summer Player of the Year, opted for summer school and then the Alaska League.

"It shouldn't be like that," Morris said. "In my opinion, when an athlete gets the opportunity to play for his country, it should be the biggest honor that can be bestowed upon him. That's the way it is in Japan and Cuba. We have to do something to promote it in our country."

"We won't force the issue with a player," United States Baseball Federation executive director Dick Case said. "He's going to have to decide. We're not going to beg him to be a part of it."

First baseman David McCarty (Stanford) didn't have to be begged, and led the U.S. with a .445 average. He said he not only became a better player, but also learned to deal with the stress of international competition and grueling travel. But he also could see why elite players with definite futures as professionals would pass up Team USA.

"The only time when U.S. national players become household names is during the Olympics," McCarty said. "Teams from the Pan Am Games and the World Championships don't get the media coverage. Everyone grows up with their priorities as the Olympics and then pro ball.

"Most of us plan on getting drafted and signing rather than come back next year, just because it's not in a high-profile position that being in the Olympics is."

Some positives

Team USA, the youngest team in international competition, went 25-13 overall in 1990.

On the plus side, they beat Cuba in a three-game series for the first time since the sides initiated the rivalry five years ago. U.S. ace Aaron Sele (Washington State) pitched a 1-0 three-hitter in the finale. And Morris said he never has had a team

SUMMER BASEBALL

INTERNATIONAL CHAMPIONS

1990 Goodwill Games at Tacoma, Wash. **Champion:** Cuba. **Runner-up:** Japan.

1990 World Championship at Edmonton, Alberta. **Champion:** Cuba. **Runner-up:** Nicaragua.

1990 World Junior Championship (18 and under) at Havana, Cuba. **Champion:** Cuba. **Runner-up:** Taiwan.

NATIONAL CHAMPIONS

National Baseball Congress World Series (unlimited) at Wichita, Kan. **Champion:** Wichita, Kan. **Runner-up:** Midlothian, Ill.

U.S. Olympic Festival IX (18 and under) at Minneapolis. **Champion:** USA North. **Runner-up:** USA West.

American Legion World Series (19 and under) at Corvallis, Ore. **Champion:** Mayo, Md. **Runner-up:** Bayamon, P.R.

All-American Amateur Baseball Association (21 and under) at Johnstown, Pa. **Champion:** Baltimore, Md. **Runner-up:** Youngstown, Ohio.

Junior Olympic Super Series (16 and under) at Coral Springs, Fla. **Champion:** Norwalk, Calif. (Mickey Mantle League World Series champions). **Runner-up:** Akron, Ohio (NABF Junior World Series champions).

LITTLE LEAGUE

Big League World Series (16-18) at Ft. Lauderdale, Fla. **Champion:** Taiwan. **Runner-up:** Maracaibo, Venezuela.

Senior League World Series (13-15) at Kissimmee, Fla. **Champion:** Taiwan. **Runner-up:** Danville, Calif.

Little League World Series (13) at Taylor, Mich. **Champion:** Yabucoa, P.R. **Runner-up:** San Antonio, Texas.

Little League World Series (11-12) at Williamsport, Pa. **Champion:** Taiwan. **Runner-up:** Shippensburg, Pa.

AMERICAN AMATEUR BASEBALL CONGRESS

Stan Musial World Series (unlimited) at Battle Creek, Mich. **Champion:** Dallas. **Runner-up:** Auburn, Calif.

Connie Mack World Series (17-18) at Farmington, N.M. **Champion:** Dallas. **Runner-up:** Carolina, P.R.

Mickey Mantle World Series (15-16) at Waterbury, Conn. **Champion:** Norwalk, Calif. **Runner-up:** Cincinnati.

Sandy Koufax World Series (13-14) at Spring, Texas. **Champion:** Fayetteville, Ga. **Runner-up:** Duncanville, Texas.

Pee Wee Reese World Series (11-12) at Jonesboro, Ga. **Champion:** Arrevica, P.R.. **Runner-up:** Lakewood, Calif.

Willie Mays World Series (9-10) at Hapeville, Ga. **Champion:** Dallas. **Runner-up:** California.

NATIONAL AMATEUR BASEBALL FEDERATION

Major World Series (unlimited) at Louisville, Ky. **Champion:** Cincinnati. **Runner-up:** Dayton, Ohio.

College World Series (21 and under) at Sterling Springs, Mich. **Champion:** Ann Arbor, Mich. **Runner-up:** New York City.

Senior World Series (17-18) at Youngstown, Ohio. **Champion:** Baltimore, Md. **Runner-up:** Chicago.

Junior World Series (15-16) at Northville, Mich. **Champion:** Akron, Ohio. **Runner-up:** Lexington, Ky.

Sophomore World Series (13-14) at Northville, Mich. **Champion:** Beaver Creek, Ohio. **Runner-up:** Birmingham, Mich.

BABE RUTH LEAGUE

Babe Ruth World Series (16-18) at Niles, Mich. **Champion:** Staten Island, N.Y. **Runner-up:** San Antonio, Texas.

Babe Ruth World Series (13-15) at Houma, La. **Champion:** Youngstown, Ohio. **Runner-up:** Manchester, N.H.

Babe Ruth World Series (13 Prep) at Jamestown, N.Y. **Champion:** Oakland, Calif. **Runner-up:** Pine Bluff, Ark.

Bambino World Series (12 and under) at Longview, Wash. **Champion:** Oakland, Calif. **Runner-up:** Pueblo, Colo.

PONY LEAGUE

Palomino World Series (17-18) at Greensboro, N.C. **Champion:** Houston. **Runner-up:** Weirton, W.Va.

Colt League World Series (15-16) at Lafayette, Ind. **Champion:** Tampa, Fla. **Runner-up:** Caguas, P.R.

Pony League World Series (13-14) at Washington, Pa. **Champion:** Seoul, South Korea. **Runner-up:** Lakewood, Calif.

Bronco League World Series (11-12) at Sacramento, Calif. **Champion:** Manila, Philipines. **Runner-up:** Shorewood, Ill.

DIXIE BASEBALL ASSOCIATION

Majors World Series (17-18) at Avon Park, Fla. **Champion:** Montgomery, Ala. **Runner-up:** Una, Tenn.

Pre-Major World Series (15-16) at Shreveport, La. **Champion:** Angelina County, Texas. **Runner-up:** Hattiesburg, Miss.

Boys World Series (13-14) at Eufala, Ala. **Champion:** South Gwinnett County, Ga. **Runner-up:** Lancaster, S.C.

Youth World Series (11-12) at Lakeland, Fla. **Champion:** Albany, Ga. **Runner-up:** Bossier City, La.

Led by star third baseman Omar Linares, Cuba again dominated the international baseball scene in 1990.

play harder for him.

Intensity wasn't enough when it counted, however. At the Goodwill Games, held July 26-31 in Tacoma, Wash., the U.S. could do no better than a third-place finish. After trouncing the sad-sack Soviet national team 17-0 in the first meeting between the two teams, Team USA lost to Japan in extra innings. That forced a semifinal game with the powerful Cubans.

Cuba, which went undefeated, pounded Team USA 16-2, with center fielder Victor Mesa sacrificing with a 10-0 lead. Reliever Darrin Paxton (Wichita State) drilled Mesa his next time up. Cuba coach Servio Borges said his team bunted because of the international 10-run rule which can shorten games by two innings, an explanation that didn't placate Morris.

"I wasn't too excited about that," Morris said. "I guess we'll consider doing the same thing at a later time."

The U.S. didn't get the chance at the World Championships held Aug. 4-19 in Edmonton, Alberta. Cuba crushed Team USA 23-1 and won 10 straight games. In 15 games at the two big summer events, the Cubans outscored their opponents 192-32.

A quirky format that featured two pairs of round-robins before medal competition contributed to a U.S. downfall, but a 5-4 record didn't help matters. Puerto Rico was truly a victim of injustice, going 7-1 before the medal games but playing for (and losing) only a bronze medal due to a bizarre tie-breaker.

A hot finish brought utilityman Jorge Fabregas (Miami), who made Team USA as a walk-on, within one point of McCarty in the team batting race. Infielder Brent Gates (Minnesota) turned in another strong summer by batting .373, while Sele and closer

Golden Spikes Award goes to Juco star, Alex Fernandez

Alex Fernandez, who enjoyed a brilliant freshman season in 1989 at the University of Miami then transferred to Miami-Dade Community College South to be eligible for the draft, was named winner of the 1990 Golden Spikes Award.

Alex Fernandez
. . . Golden spikes

The award is the highest honor bestowed an amateur player in the United States, and past winners have included such major leaguers as Will Clark, Ben McDonald, Tim Wallach, Robin Ventura and Jim Abbott.

Fernandez went 15-2 with a 2.01 ERA in his only season at Miami, then was 12-2 with a 1.19 ERA at nearby Miami-Dade and led the nation's junior college pitchers with 154 strikeouts in 121 innings. He was the first college player selected in the 1990 draft, going fourth overall to the Chicago White Sox. The 20-year-old righthander reached the big leagues after eight minor league appearances.

Other finalists included Iowa shortstop Tim Costo, UCLA catcher Paul Ellis, Georgia pitcher Dave Fleming, Arizona State outfielder Mike Kelly, Tampa pitcher Sam Militello, Miami pitcher Oscar Munoz, Minnesota catcher Dan Wilson and Georgia Southern pitcher Joey Hamilton.

Murray wins top summer award

Texas center fielder Calvin Murray's electrifying performance as an Anchorage Buc earned him Baseball America's 1990 Summer Player of the Year Award.

Calvin Murray
. . . great summer

Murray sparked Anchorage to an easy Alaska League championship by hitting .370 with eight home runs and a team-best 49 RBIs from the leadoff spot. He also stole 49 bases.

Of the 10 previous winners, nine became first-round draft picks. John Olerud, who went in the third round before winning the award last year, would have been the tenth if he hadn't been considered unsignable.

Murray already has been a first-round pick. The Cleveland Indians ignored his stated desire to attend Texas and wasted the 11th pick in the 1989 draft on him. He hit .298 with three homers as a Longhorns freshman, and stole a Southwest Conference-record 49 bases.

Baseball America's Summer All-America first team:

C—Tommy Eason (East Carolina/Staunton, Shenandoah Valley), .367-17-49.

1B—David McCarty (Stanford/Team USA), .445-3-31. **2B**—Brent Gates (Minnesota/Team USA), .373-4-28. **3B**—Jorge Fabregas (Miami/Team USA), .444-5-30. **SS**—Brian Eldridge (Arizona/Anchorage Bucs, Alaska), .406-10-52.

OF—Calvin Murray (Texas/Anchorage Bucs, Alaska), .370-8-52, 49 SB; Mark Smith (Southern California/Wareham, Cape Cod), .408-6-33; Jim Austin (Arizona State/Team USA), .369-6-27.

DH—Scott Stahoviak (Creighton/Wichita, Jayhawk), .386-12-69.

P—Aaron Sele (Washington State/Team USA), 5-2, 2.60; Bobby Jones (Anchorage Bucs, Alaska), 10-2, 3.28; Bill Wissler (Penn/Bourne, Cape Cod), 8-2, 1.56; Phil Stidham (Arkansas/Team USA), 5-3, 2.39; Brad Woodall (North Carolina/Wareham, Cape Cod), 2-1, 1.03.

First baseman David McCarty, who hit a team high .445, was one of the few bright spots for Team USA in 1990.

Philip Stidham (Arkansas) tied for the lead with five victories apiece.

Juniors settle for bronze

The U.S. junior team, which won the last two titles, finished third at the World Junior Championships held Aug. 25-Sept. 5 in Havana, Cuba. The Cubans won the tournament for players 18 and younger, employing mind games to their advantage.

"A lot of gamesmanship went on," Team USA coach Bernie Walter (Arundel, Md., High) said. "It was a masterpiece. It was a work of art."

Cuba played all of its games in the evening while the U.S. played all of its games except the final in the hotter morning and afternoon. Five of those games started at 9:30 a.m., meaning the team had to get up at 6 a.m. And for all of those games, Team USA's dugout faced the sun while its opponents rested in the shade.

Walter was also displeased with the living conditions: one 15-foot-by-30-foot room for 18 players. The coup de grace came in the last game, which the U.S. had to win against Cuba to force another game for the championship.

"The Cuba national TV man called the pitches for the hitters," said Walter, the first man chosen to coach the junior team. He led Team USA to its first championship in December 1988 in Australia.

Aided by the cameraman, Cuba broke open a close game with six runs in two innings against Jose Prado (Miami) and Mike Schiefelbein (Arizona), and won 7-1. Prado and Schiefelbein were both second-round picks in the June draft.

Prado led all pitchers at the tournament with 29 strikeouts in 22 innings. Right fielder Shawn Green (rising senior at Tustin, Calif., High) hit .486 and had a tournament-high 17 hits, and first baseman Jay Powell (Mississippi State) led all players with four home runs and 19 RBIs. Green, Powell, catcher Willie Morales (Arizona) and second baseman Paul Petrulis (Mississippi State) earned all-tournament honors for the U.S.

North defends Festival title

The junior Team USA was formed by players from the U.S. Olympic Festival held July 6-15 in Minneapolis. For the second straight year, the North team emerged victorious.

Aaron Knieper (Saginaw, Mich./Central Michigan) and Casey Whitten (Haubstadt, Ind./Indiana State), who went on to pitch for the junior team, pitched the North to victory. Knieper picked up two of the North's three wins, while Whitten contributed the other. Knieper beat the West 7-4 in the final, with Whitten picking up a save.

East first baseman Scott Bartucca (Phelps, N.Y./Onondaga, N.Y., CC) was the offensive star of the tournament. He hit .600 (9-for-15) with 10 RBIs in four games.

Another repeat

The North wasn't the only amateur team to defend a prestigious title in 1990. The Wichita Broncos of the Jayhawk League became the first team since the Grand Rapids (Mich.) Sullivans in 1983-84 to win consecutive National Baseball Congress World Series.

Wichita beat the Midlothian (Ill.) White Sox 11-4 in the final game, derailing an offensive juggernaut that hit .350 with a record 28 home runs and averaged nearly 10 runs a game. The Broncos used a Series-best 3.17 ERA to win eight of nine games in the 35-team, double-elimination tournament held Aug. 3-19 in Wichita, Kan.

Wichita used only college players to win the top prize of $12,500. Three Creighton players—first baseman Scott Stahoviak and outfielders Chad McConnell and John Pivovar—combined to hit .418 with five home runs and 39 RBIs.

Midlothian DH Kirk Vucsko, who played two years in the Los Angeles Dodgers organization, broke Series records for home runs (9) and RBIs (25). He hit three home runs, tying a record most recently set by John Olerud in 1988, in a 15-5 semifinal win over the top-seeded Mat-Su Miners of the Alaska Central League.

And another repeat

The Yarmouth-Dennis Red Sox, who went 29 years between Cape Cod League titles, won their second straight by beating the Wareham Gatemen two games to one.

Playoff MVP Kirk Piskor (Arkansas) hit three home runs in the opening game of the final round to lead the Red Sox to a 14-8 victory. Wareham's Tommy Carter (Auburn) then pitched a 6-0 six-hitter to set the stage for a dramatic third game.

One strike away from defeat, Wareham tied the finale 7-7 on a two-run home run by outfielder Doug Glanville (Penn). In the bottom of the ninth, Red Sox outfielder Mark Sweeney (Maine), the 1989 playoff MVP, homered off the league's top reliever, Brad Woodall (North Carolina), for the victory.

Mark Smith
. . . .400 hitter

Wareham outfielder Mark Smith (Southern Cal) was named league MVP after hitting .408 with six home runs and 33 RBIs. No player had hit .400 since the Cape switched to wood bats in 1985.

In Alaska, the Anchorage Bucs won the Alaska League in a walk and capped a 49-13 season by winning the six-team Hawaiian International Tournament in Honolulu. Anchorage won the final game 10-1 against a team from Tokyo as Bobby Jones (Fresno State) pitched a five-hitter.

In the wacky two-league set-up in The Land of the Midnight Sun, the Mat-Su Miners won the Alaska Central League by one game over the Anchorage Glacier Pilots. Mat-Su finished third at the NBC World Series.

Jorge Fabregas
... .444 hitter

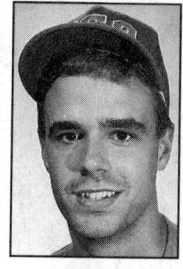
Brent Gates
... .373-4-28

Jim Austin
... .369-6-27

TEAM USA
(Cumulative summer statistics)

BATTING	AVG	G	AB	R	H	2B	3B	HR	RBI	BB	SO	SB
McCarty, David, 1b	.445	32	110	26	49	13	6	3	31	20	19	1
Fabregas, Jorge, 3b-c	.444	35	126	30	56	10	4	5	30	9	24	2
Gates, Brent, ss-2b	.373	31	118	24	44	10	3	4	28	12	7	1
Austin, Jim, of	.369	32	122	43	45	6	3	6	27	23	30	7
Bragg, Darren, of	.367	33	109	30	40	8	1	7	25	14	33	6
Hatteberg, Scott, c	.353	10	34	9	12	4	0	1	8	3	7	1
Gomez, Chris, 2b-ss	.336	36	119	29	40	6	0	6	34	15	10	7
Mashore, Damon, of	.311	35	106	24	33	8	2	1	8	21	31	12
Ciccarella, Joe, of-1b	.298	34	114	26	34	10	2	5	34	7	31	1
Wilson, Pookie, of	.262	27	61	12	16	3	0	0	7	7	9	7
Flannelly, Tim, 3b	.259	18	54	9	14	2	1	4	15	4	7	0
Melendez, Dan, 1b	.239	17	46	8	11	3	0	1	7	6	11	2
Nevin, Phil, 3b	.237	14	38	3	9	3	0	0	10	2	7	0
Burnett, Roger, ss	.217	26	60	11	13	1	1	2	10	8	12	4
Harrison, Mike, c	.125	11	24	1	3	1	0	0	2	5	9	0
Tallman, Troy, c	.123	26	57	9	7	1	0	0	4	14	24	2
Totals	**.328**	**38**	**1302**	**305**	**427**	**89**	**23**	**45**	**281**	**171**	**272**	**53**

PITCHING	W	L	ERA	G	GS	CG	SV	IP	H	R	ER	BB	SO
Rees, Sean	1	0	0.00	1	1	0	0	2	1	0	0	0	1
Stidham, Phil	5	3	2.39	30	0	0	2	49	46	17	13	6	38
Allen, Ronnie	0	1	2.46	4	1	0	0	7	5	2	2	2	3
Sele, Aaron	5	2	2.60	13	10	1	0	52	38	20	15	23	53
Bennett, Doug	3	0	2.72	10	4	0	0	30	23	13	9	11	30
Smith, JoJo	4	1	4.54	16	1	0	0	34	31	19	17	14	31
Hostetler, Mike	4	2	4.71	14	9	1	0	42	47	27	22	12	23
Klingenbeck, Scott	0	0	4.91	4	1	0	0	9	7	4	2	2	6
Paxton, Darrin	0	0	4.96	21	1	0	0	33	28	24	18	18	38
Hamilton, Joey	2	3	5.15	14	9	0	0	37	37	29	21	16	24
Gavaghan, Sean	0	0	8.10	8	0	0	0	10	11	10	9	10	8
Byrd, Paul	1	1	10.24	7	1	0	0	19	32	22	22	10	13
Totals	**25**	**13**	**4.24**	**38**	**38**	**2**	**2**	**322**	**310**	**191**	**152**	**138**	**268**

1990 WORLD CHAMPIONSHIPS

Edmonton, Alberta
August 4-19, 1990

POOL A	W	L	POOL B	W	L
Cuba	5	0	Puerto Rico	5	0
Nicaragua	3	2	United States	4	1
Japan	3	2	Taiwan	3	2
South Korea	2	3	Canada	2	3
Mexico	1	4	Netherlands	1	4
Italy	1	4	Venezuela	0	5

POOL C	W	L	POOL D	W	L
Cuba	3	0	Nicaragua	2	1
South Korea	2	1	Puerto Rico	2	1
Taiwan	1	2	Japan	2	1
United States	0	3	Canada	0	3

PLAYOFFS: Seventh Place—United States 9, Canada 4. **Fifth Place**—Japan 14, Taiwan 3. **Bronze Medal**—South Korea 7, Puerto Rico 4. **Gold Medal**—Cuba 14, Nicaragua 0; Cuba 11, Nicaragua 5 (Cuba wins best-of-3 series, 2-0).

ALL-STAR TEAM: C—Pedro Rodriguez, Cuba. **1B**—Lourdes Gourriel, Cuba. **2B**—Julio Medina, Nicaragua. **3B**—Omar Linares, Cuba. **SS**—German Mesa, Cuba. **OF**—Shinniti Sato, Japan; Angel Morales, Purto Rico; Rikkert Faneyte, The Netherlands. **DH**—Orestes Kindelan, Cuba. **RHP**—Kuo Lee Chien-Fu, Taiwan. **LHP**—Omar Ajete, Cuba.

INDIVIDUAL BATTING LEADERS
(Minimum 25 At-Bats)

	AVG	G	AB	R	H	2B	3B	HR	RBI	BB	SO	SB
Kindelan, Orestes, Cuba ...	.581	10	43	23	25	7	0	9	25	3	6	0
Sato, Shinniti, Japan	.556	9	36	7	20	3	3	1	14	3	1	0
Linares, Omar, Cuba	.512	10	41	20	21	4	1	6	18	5	7	0
Gates, Brent, USA	.500	9	38	10	19	4	2	3	11	5	1	0
Gomez, Chris, USA	.500	9	36	11	18	2	0	3	11	2	4	2
Fabregas, Jorge, USA	.500	9	36	7	18	1	1	0	8	1	6	0
Mesa, German, Cuba	.475	9	40	17	19	5	3	2	7	1	6	4
Curran, Randy, Canada	.471	9	34	7	16	4	1	2	10	4	3	1
Gourriel, Lourdes, Cuba	.463	10	41	12	19	6	0	4	19	3	1	0
Bragg, Darren, USA	.448	7	29	9	13	1	0	1	6	3	7	2
McCarty, David, USA	.448	8	29	6	13	3	1	0	9	3	5	0
Lo Kuo-Chong, Taiwan	.441	9	34	8	15	3	0	2	5	3	2	1
Rodriguez, Pedro, Cuba	.429	10	35	11	15	5	0	2	9	1	4	0
Villegas, Richart, Venezuela	.429	8	28	5	12	2	1	1	4	2	2	0
Urrutia, Ermidelio, Cuba	.419	8	31	10	13	2	1	3	9	2	2	1
Faneyte, Rikkert, Netherlands	.419	8	31	9	13	5	0	3	9	5	5	4
Nakamoto, Hiroshi, Japan ..	.417	9	36	10	15	4	0	0	6	4	4	1
Morales, Angel, PRico	.417	9	36	8	15	3	1	0	10	4	0	0
Bianchi, Roberto, Italy	.417	7	24	6	10	0	0	2	7	6	4	0
Huan Chung-Yi, Taiwan	.400	9	35	7	14	1	0	1	8	4	1	0
Medina, Julio, Nicaragua	.395	10	43	8	17	4	2	1	8	2	2	2
Ku Kuo-Chian, Taiwan	.393	9	28	8	11	0	0	1	7	2	4	0
Mesa, Victor, Cuba	.390	10	41	10	16	2	3	3	15	2	4	0
Gambuti, Elio, Italy	.385	8	26	5	10	2	0	2	8	4	4	0

INDIVIDUAL PITCHING LEADERS
(Minimum 15 Innings)

	W	L	ERA	G	GS	CG	SV	IP	H	R	ER	BB	SO
Valle, Lazaro, Cuba	3	0	0.00	4	3	1	0	21	11	3	0	5	19
Feliciano, Jesus, PRico	1	0	0.56	2	2	1	0	16	11	1	1	6	5
Valle, Fulvio, Italy	1	0	1.31	3	1	1	0	21	17	3	3	0	7
Ajete, Omar, Cuba	2	0	1.53	3	3	1	0	18	13	5	3	3	22
Sanchez, Rasbony, Nicaragua	1	1	1.56	4	2	1	1	17	13	3	3	5	7
Chung Min-Tae, So. Korea	3	1	2.02	5	3	3	1	36	27	10	8	11	29
Hebert, Carlos, Nicaragua	2	0	2.25	2	2	1	0	16	16	4	4	3	8
Ishidaira, Eiichi, Japan	2	0	2.55	5	2	0	0	18	16	5	5	1	15
Kuo Lee Chien-Fu, Taiwan	4	0	3.24	5	4	3	0	33	31	13	12	9	24
Kim Do-Wan, So. Korea	2	0	3.26	4	3	0	0	19	18	7	7	7	23

1990 WORLD JUNIOR CHAMPIONSHIPS

Havana, Cuba
Aug. 25-Sept. 5, 1990

GROUP A	W	L		GROUP B	W	L
United States	4	0		Cuba	5	0
Canada	3	1		Mexico	4	1
Taiwan	2	2		Venezuela	3	2
Italy	1	3		Australia	2	3
France	0	4		Brazil	1	4
				Holland	0	5

MEDAL GROUP	W	L
Cuba	5	0
Taiwan	3	2
United States	3	2
Venezuela	2	3
Canada	1	4
Mexico	1	4

TEAM USA

BATTING	AVG	G	AB	R	H	2B	3B	HR	RBI	BB	SO	SB
Green, Shawn, of	.486	9	35	14	17	4	0	0	11	2	2	8
Marrillia, Tony, of	.476	8	21	5	10	3	1	0	3	4	3	2
Powell, Jay, 1b-3b	.444	9	36	11	16	2	1	4	19	1	7	1
Petrulis, Paul, 2b	.432	9	37	11	16	2	0	2	10	7	2	4
Ortega, Randy, c	.417	6	12	5	5	3	0	0	4	3	0	0
Kieschnick, Brooks, 1b-of	.414	8	29	8	12	2	0	2	10	4	4	0
Morales, Willie, c-of	.316	7	19	5	6	2	0	1	2	3	1	1
Fernandez, Tony, ss	.292	9	24	9	7	1	1	0	3	10	0	2
Spiezio, Scott, 3b	.320	8	25	5	8	3	0	1	7	1	2	0
Thompson, Bruce, of	.267	7	15	8	4	1	0	1	3	6	2	1
Brohawn, Troy, of	.214	6	14	6	3	0	0	0	1	3	0	0
Wyngarden, Bubba, c	.211	6	18	2	3	0	0	0	0	1	3	1
Totals	.361	9	310	97	112	22	3	11	81	52	36	20

PITCHING	W	L	ERA	G	GS	CG	SV	IP	H	R	ER	BB	SO
Kieschnock, Brooks	0	0	0.00	2	0	0	0	2	1	0	0	1	0
Whitten, Casey	2	0	0.68	3	1	1	0	13	6	1	1	5	14
Kneiper, Aaron	2	1	1.56	4	2	1	0	17	16	3	3	4	13
Schiefelbein, Mike	1	0	2.08	3	2	0	0	9	6	4	2	3	15
Prado, Jose	1	0	2.45	4	3	1	0	22	17	8	6	6	29
Lorraine, Andrew	0	1	6.00	4	0	0	0	3	1	2	2	3	3
Adams, Willie	1	0	9.45	2	1	0	0	7	12	7	7	2	9
Totals	7	2	2.71	9	9	3	0	73	59	25	22	24	83

CAPE COD LEAGUE

East	W	L	T	Pts.	West	W	L	T	Pts.
Yarmouth-Dennis	24	16	3	51	Wareham	24	19	1	49
Orleans	24	20	0	48	Cotuit	22	19	3	47
Brewster	23	20	1	47	Hyannis	20	13	1	41
Harwich	22	21	1	45	Bourne	19	24	1	39
Chatham	17	24	2	36	Falmouth	17	26	1	35

PLAYOFFS: Wareham defeated Cotuit, 2-0, in best-of-3 semi-final; Yarmouth-Dennis defeated Orleans, 2-0, in best-of-3 semi-final. Yarmouth-Dennis defeated Wareham, 2-1, in best-of-3 final for league championship.

ALL-STAR TEAM: C—Pete Grifol (Florida State), Brewster. **1B**—Billy Owens (Arizona), Brewster. **2B**—Mike Losa (Texas Christian), Yarmouth-Dennis. **3B**—Mike Groppuso (Seton Hall), Orleans. **SS**—Ted Corbin (Auburn), Orleans. **OF**—Mark Smith (Southern California), Wareham; Mark Sweeney (Maine), Yarmouth-Dennis; Doug Glanville (Penn), Wareham; Mike Kelly (Arizona State), Orleans. **Util**—Brett Jenkins (Southern California), Wareham. **DH**—Lyle Mouton (Louisiana State), Brewster. **P**—Bill Wissler (Penn), Bourne; Mike Juhl (Florida), Hyannis; Tim Smith (Ohio State), Yarmouth-Dennis; Marc Pisciotta (Georgia Tech), Yarmouth-Dennis; Brad Woodall (North Carolina), Wareham.

INDIVIDUAL BATTING LEADERS
(Minimum 125 At-Bats)

	AVG	G	AB	R	H	2B	3B	HR	RBI	BB	SO	SB
Smith, Mark, Wareham	.408	44	169	32	69	14	3	6	33	16	25	6
Jenkins, Brett, Wareham	.344	40	157	24	54	11	1	4	29	7	16	1
Solomon, Steve, Hyannis	.341	33	129	16	44	11	1	0	9	14	27	5
Mouton, Lyle, Brewster	.340	43	162	36	55	12	1	8	26	17	31	6
Glanville, Doug, Wareham	.331	44	178	29	59	7	2	1	20	19	25	13
Piskor, Kirk, Y-D	.329	43	155	24	51	11	1	3	31	6	33	8
Rogers, Lamarr, Chatham	.313	39	128	40	46	2	2	0	4	27	23	15
Sweeney, Mark, Y-D	.310	43	155	25	48	10	1	4	24	28	21	2
Suplee, Ray, Cotuit	.307	39	150	16	46	10	0	1	22	12	31	3
Groppuso, Mike, Orleans	.305	43	151	29	46	6	1	6	26	21	38	13
Basse, Mike, Bourne	.293	41	150	30	44	6	4	0	20	18	32	28
Lis, Joe, Bourne	.292	41	137	20	40	8	0	0	15	18	26	7
Vitiello, Joe, Hyannis	.292	44	161	31	47	5	0	10	35	31	38	2
Burke, Matt, Orleans	.291	42	141	19	41	6	1	3	19	23	28	2
Simpson, Casey, Bourne	.289	41	149	17	43	9	2	2	19	8	34	2
Cunha, Steve, Wareham	.281	40	146	19	41	9	4	1	19	12	26	8
Sheff, Chris, Cotuit	.273	44	154	21	42	7	4	5	27	17	28	8
Seitzer, Brad, Y-D	.272	41	136	17	37	7	0	2	17	16	27	3
Clapinski, Chris, Wareham	.271	40	133	20	36	4	1	0	9	22	24	5
Hartmann, Brian, Harwich	.270	44	148	19	40	8	0	4	23	18	46	4
Owens, Billy, Brewster	.268	42	153	27	41	7	0	7	26	17	35	1
Mayes, Craig, Falmouth	.266	42	139	18	37	6	0	3	12	13	29	3
Hickey, Mike, Wareham	.266	41	139	11	37	8	2	1	21	10	38	2
Austin, Jake, Y-D	.266	41	128	21	34	9	1	5	23	11	32	2
Kelly, Mike, Orleans	.264	39	144	22	38	5	1	6	14	15	35	16
Brown, Ronnie, Brewster	.262	36	122	17	32	9	0	3	14	25	37	1
Losa, Mike, Y-D	.261	42	153	17	40	4	0	0	15	16	29	11
Langer, Bob, Falmouth	.261	39	138	18	36	6	3	0	14	18	28	5
Seguin, Brian, Cotuit	.255	42	153	20	39	7	3	0	17	11	16	1
Fleming, Carlton, Cotuit	.252	36	127	15	32	6	1	0	13	10	7	4

INDIVIDUAL PITCHING LEADERS
(Minimum 35 Innings)

	W	L	ERA	G	GS	CG	SV	IP	H	R	ER	BB	SO
Woodall, Brad, Wareham	2	1	1.03	19	0	0	8	35	24	8	4	18	47
Hutchins, Jason, Wareham	3	1	1.37	13	4	0	0	46	19	11	7	34	45
Wissler, Bill, Bourne	8	2	1.56	11	11	5	0	86	66	23	15	19	77
Hubbard, Mark, Orl.	2	1	1.66	8	5	1	2	38	24	9	7	22	36
Nickell, Jack, Chat.	5	2	1.74	9	8	3	0	62	47	16	12	10	47
Carter, Tommy, Wareham	5	3	1.74	10	9	0	0	52	45	20	10	28	39
Maguire, Mike, Brew-Orl.	1	2	1.78	12	2	1	0	35	24	10	7	13	43
Pfaff, Jason, Cotuit	4	1	1.81	9	8	2	0	65	54	18	13	12	40
George, Chris, Hyan.	4	2	1.85	9	6	2	0	49	37	13	10	26	48
Juhl, Mike, Hyannis	7	2	1.85	12	10	6	0	83	51	22	17	21	65
MacNeil, Doug, Cotuit	2	3	2.47	9	9	1	0	55	34	17	15	17	59
Smith, Tim, Y-D	7	5	2.47	12	11	6	0	91	70	35	25	23	92
Stuart, Brad, Y-D	4	2	2.58	9	8	0	1	59	48	26	17	25	50
Kenny, Brian, Harwich	6	5	2.62	11	11	7	0	82	67	32	24	14	49
Sproviero, Nick, Harwich	7	2	2.65	12	10	4	0	75	62	23	22	35	44
Greene, Rich, Brew.	8	2	2.66	14	7	3	0	74	63	27	22	19	49
Shoppe, David, Orl.	3	2	2.68	13	3	1	2	40	29	16	12	10	28
Alston, Garvin, Brew.	3	1	2.72	9	7	0	0	50	30	18	15	29	34
Moody, Richie, Chatham	2	2	2.72	8	7	0	0	43	32	18	13	21	48
Walania, Alan, Harwich	2	1	2.74	17	2	1	5	43	48	17	13	6	15

AMATEUR DRAFT 1990

Van Poppel signing highlights expensive year

By ALLAN SIMPSON

Triggered by a lucrative new television deal, major league clubs went on a lavish spending spree in 1990.

They spent freely at the major league level, signing Jose Canseco and numerous other players to multi-year contracts yielding in excess of $3 million a year. They spent freely in acquiring amateur talent, paying out some of the largest bonuses in draft history.

Todd Van Poppel
... $1.2 million

The biggest bonus recipient of 1990 was schoolboy pitching sensation Todd Van Poppel, who signed a rich three-year guaranteed deal with the defending World Series champion Oakland Athletics that provided a $500,000 bonus and $1.2 million overall. It was the first multi-year contract ever signed by a high school player and only the fourth in draft history. The $1.2 million package was the largest ever.

Van Poppel's bonus jumped the average bonus for first-round picks to more than $250,000—up 37 percent from 1989, when bonuses took a sharp upward spiral. Every first-round pick in 1990 was given a bonus of at least $175,000. Not coincidentally, for the first time since 1985, every first-round pick was signed.

Van Poppel in demand

Competition for players was intense, none more so than for Van Poppel, a 6-5 righthander from Martin High School in Arlington, Texas. He was singled out as the top prospect prior to the draft, but complicated the picture by stating his desire to forego the draft and attend the University of Texas.

Atlanta had the No. 1 overall pick and met frequently with Van Poppel and his family prior to the draft to establish his signability. The last meeting took place a day before the draft.

Convinced that Van Poppel wouldn't budge in his desire to go to college, the Braves compromised by taking Larry (Chipper) Jones, a high school shortstop from Pierson, Fla., with the first pick.

The next 12 clubs also passed on Van Poppel, but Oakland, drafting 14th overall, decided it was worth the gamble, particularly since it had stockpiled seven draft picks in the first two rounds.

Van Poppel initially expressed displeasure at being drafted by Oakland.

"If they think they can buy me, they're wrong," Van Poppel said. "Money's not everything. The things I want to do, money can't buy. I've got to mature as a person and as a ballplayer. I think I can do that in college."

Smooth move by A's

Oakland officials took a calculated, low-pressure approach in negotiations with Van Poppel.

A's general manager Sandy Alderson, player development director Karl Kuehl and instructor-counselor Harvey Dorfman first met with Van Poppel and his family for three hours in

Atlanta bypassed Todd Van Poppel with the No. 1 pick and went for shortstop Chipper Jones, above.

their Arlington home on June 18—two weeks after he was selected.

"It was a very positive discussion," Alderson said. "We talked about the virtues of the Oakland A's, not other factors. The focus of our discussion was that Todd was in a very enviable position, that he could choose among dreams: pitching for the A's in the World Series, or pitching at the University of Texas and in the Olympics. We stressed that he had a choice among positives."

With input from his father Hank and advisor Scott Boras, Van Poppel began to reconsider his options over the next several weeks. Finally, on July 16, he signed a contract with Oakland that included a $500,000 cash signing bonus, plus $100,000 in salary for the rest of the 1990 season. He will be paid $200,000 in 1991 and $400,000 in 1992.

A's, Expos get multiple picks

By getting Van Poppel and six other picks in the first two rounds, it was a case of the rich getting richer. Never before had a defending World Series champion profited so handsomely in the draft as the Athletics.

Because of their failure to resign free agents Dave Parker, Storm Davis and Tony Phillips the previous winter, the A's were compensated with five draft picks. They used the first of their two picks for Parker to draft Van Poppel.

No team, however, had a windfall draft of the order of the Montreal Expos, who had 10 selections in the first two rounds. The Expos gained two picks each for the loss of Type A free agents Hubie Brooks, Pascual Perez and Mark Langston, one for Type B free agent Bryn Smith, and an additional pick for the club's failure to sign Charles Johnson, their No. 1 pick in the 1989 draft.

The Expos spent in excess of $1.2 million to sign all 10 picks. They also went on to sign every pick through the first 14 rounds, 22 in all.

Expensive draft

Van Poppel's rich signing bonus highlighted a spending spree in which the 10 largest bonuses of the draft era were paid out in a 12-month period, ending July, 1990.

Beginning with '89 draftees Ben McDonald and John Olerud, who signed multi-year deals in excess of $800,000 late in August, 1989, the wave of large bonus payments continued when Atlanta signed Jones moments after it drafted him to a $275,000 bonus. Throw in $60,000 for the college scholarship plan, a life insurance annuity and Jones' total package amounted to more than $400,000.

From there bonus payments continued to escalate.

Alex Fernandez, who two years earlier turned down $150,000 as Milwaukee's No. 1 pick, signed with the Chicago White Sox for a pre-arranged figure of $350,000. He was the fourth overall selection. Cleveland, drafting eighth, spent $300,000 for University of Iowa shortstop Tim Costo, regarded as the top power hitter in the college ranks.

Detroit, with the second pick, had to go as high as $500,000 to sign 6-foot-8 outfielder Tony Clark. At that, the Tigers had to make key concessions.

The Tigers got Clark to agree to a contract five days before Van Poppel signed with Oakland, but had to agree to let him play basketball at the University of Arizona. That meant he would be available to the Tigers from mid-May to mid-August only over the next several years.

Toronto also gambled its first two picks on pitcher Steve Karsay and third baseman Chris Weinke.

Karsay had written to the commissioner's office prior to the draft requesting that his name be withdrawn from consideration because he wanted to attend college at Louisiana State. The Blue Jays selected the Queen's, N.Y., righthander anyway and eventually signed him for $325,000. Late in August, the Jays also corraled Weinke, one of the nation's top prep quarterbacks who had already begun fall football practice at Florida State. He signed for $375,000.

Boston slowed in early rounds

The highest unsigned pick was pitcher-shortstop Frankie Rodriguez, selected by Boston with the very first pick in the second round. Rodriguez elected to attend Howard (Texas) Junior College, but remains under control to the Red Sox because of baseball's junior college rule. He will be eligible to sign with the Red Sox following completion of his team's season in the spring of 1991.

Boston, which forfeited its first-round pick to St. Louis for signing catcher Tony Pena as a free agent, also failed to sign three other picks in the first 10 rounds. Overall, only 30 picks in the first 10 rounds did not sign.

Milwaukee had the greatest success in signing its draft picks. Though the Brewers spent nowhere near the bonus money Oakland or Montreal did and lost their first-round pick to the A's for signing Parker, they managed to sign their first 25 selections. Montreal, which made 10 selections before the Brewers made their first, signed its first 22.

Overall, 1,487 players were drafted, three fewer than the record 1,490 selected in 1989. 823 had signed professional contracts by Oct. 1. It is projected that another 30-50 players attending junior college programs will sign in the spring.

Houston, which drafted 87 players in 1989, topped that figure by selecting a record 100 players in 1990. The Astros signed only 29 of the 100, but 52 enrolled in junior colleges making them eligible to sign in the spring.

Big leaguers in '90

Two players selected in the 1990 draft made their mark in the big leagues by the conclusion of the season.

Fernandez, 20, drafted as a sophomore out of Miami-Dade

Tony Clark
... No. 2 pick overall

Tim Costo
... selected eighth

South Community College, and Arizona lefty Lance Dickson, 21, each made stops with three minor league clubs on a whirlwind trip to Chicago. Fernandez was drafted by the White Sox, Dickson by the Cubs.

Jones, the No. 1 overall pick, shared little of the first-year success Fernandez and Dickson enjoyed. He was assigned to the Braves' entry in the Gulf Coast League and batted only .229.

His adjustment to pro ball was compounded by a broken hand he received in a scuffle with a teammate the day before his high school team played in the Florida state 2-A state championship. His hand was wrapped in a cast the day the Braves drafted him.

Jones gained notoriety as an all-state football and baseball player at The Bolles School, an elite private school in Jacksonville. He became the first Florida player ever to be drafted No. 1, after batting .488 with five homers and 25 RBIs. As a pitcher, he was 7-3 with a 1.00 ERA.

"Good middle infielders are hard to find," Braves general manager Bobby Cox said, justifying his club's selection of Jones. "I think we have found a good one. About eight people in our organization have seen him, and they all came to the same conclusion. He's pretty much a polished ballplayer at this time."

Prior to the draft, the Braves made little secret of their preference for Van Poppel, but when Van Poppel repeatedly told the Braves that he was committed to attending Texas, the Braves thought it better to take the sure sign rather than risk an embarasing impasse. Reportedly, their offers to Van Poppel reached as high as $900,000.

"I know there are some people who will say I was the Braves second choice," Jones said, "but that's better than being the ninth or 10th. If Todd Van Poppel doesn't want to play for the Atlanta Braves, I'm more than happy to take his place."

Detroit takes Peete, McMurtry

As always, there was an assortment of athletes who have made a name for themselves in other sports who were selected in the '90 draft.

Besides taking Clark, who averaged more than 43 points per game on the basketball court his senior year, Detroit went for former Michigan All-American wide receiver Greg McMurtry in the 27th round and Detroit Lions quarterback Rodney Peete in the 28th. Neither player signed.

The California Angels took a flyer on two players who played no baseball in college: Notre Dame quarterback Tony Rice and Virginia Tech basketball star Bimbo Coles, an ex-Olympian.

Houston had to cough up $250,000 to sign its first draft pick, Tom Nevers, who was a fifth-round pick of the National Hockey League's Pittsburgh Penguins in 1989.

Among sons of ex-major leaguers who were drafted: Gary (Astros) and Domingo Mota (Dodgers), the third and fourth sons of Manny Mota to join the pro ranks; Bret Boone (Mariners), son of Bob and grandson of Ray; Chris Haney (Expos), son of Brewers' pitching coach Larry.

It's a miracle

An interesting development in the 1990 draft was the inclusion of two independently-operated Class A clubs in the selection process. Rule IV draft regulations permit minor league clubs to participate and both the Florida State League's Miami Miracle and the New York-Penn League's Erie Sailors took part in the proceedings, beginning with the fourth round.

Erie selected only one player, 24-year-old Brigham Young outfielder Gary Daniels. Miami, to the dismay of several major league clubs, chose 16 players, many of whom were bonafide top prospects. Miracle owner Marvin Goldklang said his club decided to participate in the draft when he was unable to secure adequate talent from major league clubs for his struggling Florida State League franchise.

"It was absolutely a last resort," Goldklang said. "In life, you do what you have to do. If the help was forthcoming, there's a good chance we would not have participated in the draft."

The Miracle began by selecting Stanford All-American outfielder Paul Carey in the fourth round and continued raking in some of the top undrafted college talent. They paid out bonuses totalling about $250,000 and signed 15 of their 16 picks.

Since drafted players are prohibited from being traded for a period of one year, all players signed by Miami will remain its property until Draft Day, 1991. It is anticipated that several players will be sold to major league organizations after that date.

TEAM-BY-TEAM SELECTIONS

(Boldface type indicates player signed with selecting club; order of selection in parenthesis after team name.)

ATLANTA BRAVES (1)

1. **Chipper Jones, ss, The Bolles School, Jacksonville, Fla.**
2. (Choice to Red Sox as compensation for Type 'B' free agent Nick Esasky).
3. **Lance Marks, of, Dana Hills HS, Dana Point, Calif.**
4. **Johnny Walker, of, University of Texas.**
5. **Joe Ayrault, c, Sarasota (Fla.) HS.**
6. Ken Reed, 3b-1b, Hamilton (Ohio) HS.
7. **Ed Giovanola, ss, Santa Clara University.**
8. **Armando Rodriguez, of, San Mateo (Calif.) JC.**
9. **Brian Kowitz, of, Clemson University.**
10. **Anthony Graffagnino, ss, East Islip (N.Y.) HS.**
11. Phil Stidham, rhp, University of Arkansas.
12. **Brian Bark, lhp-of, North Carolina State University.**
13. Damon Lembi, 3b-1b, Burlingame (Calif.) HS.
14. **Kian Sly, of-1b, San Diego (Calif.) HS.**
15. **Adrian Garcia, c, Elizabeth (N.J.) HS.**
16. Michael Tarter, c, Walton HS, Marietta, Ga.
17. **Jerome Koller, rhp, Martinsville (Ind.) HS.**
18. **Michael Potts, lhp, Gordon (Ga.) JC.**
19. **Juan Williams, of, Ramona HS, Riverside, Calif.**
20. **Ralph Garr, of, Bellaire HS, Missouri City, Texas.**
21. James King, rhp, Gordon (Ga.) JC.
22. **Stewart Ford, lhp, Ranger (Texas) JC.**
23. Matthew Wagner, rhp, Cedar Falls (Iowa) HS.
24. **Jason Kempfer, rhp, Sparta HS, Baldwin, Ill.**
25. **Cory Mathis, of, Gonzales (Texas) HS.**
26. **Michael Place, rhp, St. Petersburg (Fla.) JC.**
27. **Larry Owens, lhp, Armstrong State University.**
28. **Loren Gress, 1b, Hutchinson (Kan.) JC.**
29. **Scott Ryder, rhp, Georgia Southern College.**
30. David Hollingsworth, rhp, Middle Georgia JC.
31. **Gerald Trevino, ss, Pleasanton (Texas) HS.**
32. **Kevin O'Connor, of, University of Illinois.**
33. **Doyle Moore, rhp, Madison Heights HS, Anderson, Ind.**
34. Dustin Longenecker, of, Parkview HS, Stone Mountain, Ga.
35. Scott Watkins, lhp, Seminole (Okla.) JC.
36. **Brian Dare, lhp, University of Texas.**
37. Adrian Jones, of-rhp, Universtiy of Missouri-St. Louis.

38. **Don Robinson, of, Haynesville (La.) HS.**
39. Jason Wood, ss, Fresno (Calif.) CC.
40. Chris Chandler, ss, Beverly Hills (Calif.) HS.
41. Amauri Rodriguez, 2b, Caguas, P.R.
42. John Wilder, rhp-ss, South Florence HS, Florence, S.C.
43. William Maitland, rhp, Dinwiddie County HS, Sutherland, Va.
44. Christopher Robbins, rhp, Union County HS, Blairsville, Ga.
45. Ja'Rad Hunt, 2b-3b, McNair HS, Atlanta Ga.
46. **Samuel Rutter, rhp, Abingdon (Va.) HS.**
47. **Shannon Ledwick, rhp, Ranger (Texas) JC.**
48. Jake Green, ss-rhp, Suwannee HS, Live Oak, Fla.
49. Adan Garcia, rhp, Gadsden HS, Anthony, N.M.
50. Joseph Hiller, rhp, Strafford Academy HS, Macon, Ga.
51. Reed Garwood, 1b, Deerfield Winds HS, Albany, Ga.
52. Mark Beeman, 3b, Carlsbad (N.M.) HS.
53. Richard Freeman, 3b, Bellaire HS, Houston, Texas.
54. Kelly Wunsch, lhp, Bellaire HS, Houston, Texas.
55. **Tommy Owen, c, University of Georgia.**
56. Jason Gonzales, ss, Blinn (Texas) JC.
57. Gary Herrmann, lhp, Blinn (Texas) JC.
58. Brad Riddle, of, Morton (Ill.) JC.
59. Darrett Robinson, of, Bellaire HS, Houston, Texas.
60. **James Arendt, of, Montezuma (Iowa) HS.**
61. Jamine Adams, of, Canyon Springs HS, Moreno Valley, Calif.
62. **Mark Chambers, of, University of Northern Iowa.**
63. **Anthony Johnson, of, Huston Tillotson College.**
64. Robert Valdez, lhp, El Dorado HS, Albuquerque, N.M.
65. Greg Quinn, of, Shadow Mountain HS, Phoenix.
66. Victor McCraney, of, Taft (Calif.) JC.
67. James Richardson, of, Westark (Ark.) JC.
68. Robert Hooker, ss, Norland HS, Miami.

BALTIMORE ORIOLES (20)

1. **Mike Mussina, rhp, Stanford University.**
2. **Erik Schullstrom, rhp, Fresno State University.**
2. **Jeff Williams, rhp, Wichita State University** (Supplemental choice—69th— for loss of Type 'C' free agent Dave Schmidt).
3. **Mike Thomas, of, Richmond County HS, Rockingham, N.C.**
4. Chris West, 1b-3b, Eastern Wayne HS, Goldsboro, N.C.
5. **Bob Chouinard, rhp, Forest Grove (Ore.) HS.**
6. **Brad Tyler, ss, University of Evansville.**
7. **John Hale, lhp, University of South Alabama.**
8. Michael Daniel, c, Oklahoma State University.
9. **Roy Hodge, of, St. Thomas, V.I.**
10. **Damon Buford, 2b-of, University of Southern California.**
11. **Gordon Graham, 1b, Hershey (Pa.) HS.**
12. **Jason Alstead, of, St. Cloud State University.**
13. **Kip Yaughn, rhp, Arizona State University.**
14. **Scott Miley, of, Mission HS, San Jose, Calif.**
15. Duane Page, rhp, Ocean View HS, Westminster, Calif.
16. Willie Speakman, c, Fullerton (Calif.) JC.
17. **Steve Godin, of, East Carolina University.**
18. **Brett Benge, rhp, Rend Lake (Ill.) JC.**
19. **Brent Miller, 1b, Middle Georgia JC.**
20. **Steve DiMarco, 3b, C.W. Post.**
21. **Daniel Ramirez, ss, University of Tennessee.**
22. **Scott McClain, rhp, Atascadero (Calif.) HS.**
23. **Justin Evans, of, Betheny (Okla.) HS.**
24. **Scott Sprick, ss, Jacksonville State University.**
25. **Michael Hebb, rhp, Anne Arundel (Md.) CC.**
26. **David Paveloff, rhp, Chapman College.**
27. **Michael Lamitola, 2b, Seton Hall University.**
28. Dom DeSantis, rhp, University of New Orleans.
29. Jason Hutchins, of, Golden West (Calif.) JC.
30. Robin Jennings, of, Annandale HS, Alexandria, Va.
31. **Todd Unrein, lhp, University of Southwestern Louisiana.**
32. **Greg Hays, rhp, Long Beach State University.**
33. **James Dedrick, rhp, University of Southern California.**
34. Matt Jarvis, lhp, La Cueva HS, Albuquerque, N.M.
35. Anthony Simas, of, St. Joseph HS, Santa Maria, Calif.
36. Kyle Allred, ss, Murray State (Okla.) JC.
37. **Ihosvany Marquez, rhp, Miami Springs HS, Hialeah, Fla.**
38. **Jose Millares, 3b, Azusa Pacific University.**
39. Jonathan Nunnally, c, Hargrave Military Academy, Pelham, N.C.
40. Kevin Ryan, rhp, Seminole (Okla.) JC.
41. David McLaughlin, ss, Milwaukie (Ore.) HS.
42. Dennis Van Pelt, of-1b, Long Branch (N.J.) HS.
43. Doug McConathy, 1b-3b, Cypress (Calif.) JC.
44. **Doug Flowers, c, North Carolina Wesleyan.**

BOSTON RED SOX (18)

1. (Choice to Cardinals as compensation for Type 'A' free agent Tony Pena)
2. Frankie Rodriguez, rhp-ss, Eastern District HS, Brooklyn, N.Y. (Choice from Braves as compensation for Type 'B' free agent Nick Esasky).
2. (Choice to Twins as compensation for Type 'A' free agent Jeff Reardon).
3. **Walt McKeel, c, Greene Central HS, Snow Hill, N.C.**

4. Greg Thomas, of, Lake Brantley HS, Altamonte Springs, Fla.
5. **Tim Tackett, c, Waverly (Ohio) HS.**
6. **Gar Finnvold, rhp, Florida State University.**
7. **Todd Miller, rhp, Temple University.**
8. Aaron Knieper, rhp, Nouvel Catholic HS, Saginaw, Mich.
9. John Collett, rhp, Citrus (Calif.) JC.
10. **Rikchy Borrero, c, Hormigueros, P.R.**
11. **Terry Powers, rhp, Volunteer State (Tenn.) CC.**
12. **David Schmidt, 2b, Southwestern (Calif.) CC.**
13. **Greg Graham, ss, University of Louisville.**
14. **Quinn Feno, 1b-of, New Bedford (Mass.) HS.**
15. **Bruce Chick, of, University of Georgia.**
16. **Erik Plantenberg, lhp, San Diego State University.**
17. Evan Pratte, 2b-ss, Southwest Missouri State University.
18. Robert Henkel, lhp, San Jacinto (Texas) JC.
19. **Brian Young, rhp, Ohio University.**
20. **Mike DeKneef, ss, Lewis Clark State College.**
21. Chad Trahan, rhp, Seminole (Okla.) JC.
22. **David Kivac, lhp, San Jacinto (Texas) JC.**
23. **Ryan Maloney, lhp, Lancaster (Ohio) HS.**
24. **Timothy Smith, rhp, Boston College.**
25. **William Norris, 3b, Eckerd College.**
26. Les Norman, of, College of St. Francis (Ill.)
27. **Chris Davis, rhp, JC of the Sequoias.**
28. **John Crimmins, c, Norwood (Mass.) HS.**
29. **Scott Bethea, ss, Louisiana State University.**
30. Jerry Burns, rhp, Napa Valley (Calif.) JC.
31. Jeffrey Johnson, rhp, Fresno (Calif.) CC.
32. Joseph Mondello, c, San Jacinto (Texas) JC.
33. James Young, rhp, Weaver (Ala.) HS.
34. Nicolas Ortiz, 3b-ss, Cidra, P.R.
35. (selection voided)
36. **Tim Davis, 2b, Southern Illinois University.**
37. Greg Sorrell, 1b-of, Poway HS, San Diego.

CALIFORNIA ANGELS (24)

1. (Choice to Expos as compensation for Type 'A' free agent Mark Langston).
2. **Phil Leftwich, rhp, Radford University.**
3. **Brandon Markewicz, ss, Dixie Hollins HS, St. Petersburg, Fla.**
4. **Garrett Anderson, of, Kennedy HS, Granada Hills, Calif.**
5. Doug Creek, lhp, Georgia Tech.
6. **Troy Percival, c, UC Riverside.**
7. **Randy Powers, rhp, University of Southern California.**
8. **Dan Gil, c, University of Southern California.**
9. **Mark Simmons, 3b, Morgan Park HS, Chicago.**
10. **J.R. Showalter, ss, University of Georgia.**
11. **Mike Pineiro, 3b, West Covina (Calif.) HS.**
12. **Joe Bertucci, 3b, Ridgewood HS, Port Richey, Fla.**
13. Ryan Hancock, rhp, Monta Vista HS, Cupertino, Calif.
14. **Fausto Tejero, c, Florida International University.**
15. Jermaine Allensworth, ss, Madison Heights HS, Anderson, Ind.
16. **Wayne Johnson, ss, Oklahoma Christian College.**
17. **Todd McCray, rhp, University of Florida.**
18. **Mark Dalesandro, c, University of Illinois.**
19. **Brian Grebeck, ss, San Diego State University.**
20. **P.J. Forbes, 2b, Wichita State University.**
21. **Ken Edenfield, rhp, Western Kentucky University.**
22. **Brian Guzik, ss, Greater Latrobe (Pa.) HS.**
23. **Joe Williams, 3b, New Mexico State University.**
24. **Don Barbara, 1b, Long Beach State University.**
25. Drew Christman, of, Midwest City (Okla.) HS.
26. **Britt Craven, rhp, Pepperdine University.**
27. **Vladimiro Alcaraz, 1b, West Valley HS, Spokane, Wash.**
28. Brian Toney-Gay, of, Morrilton (Ark.) HS.
29. Mark Ledinsky, lhp-of, Lake County (Ill.) JC.
30. Kevin Lewis, c, Indian River (Fla.) CC.
31. **Louis Pakele, rhp, University of Hawaii-Hilo.**
32. David Berg, 2b, Sacramento (Calif.) CC.
33. **Jeff Ball, rhp, University of Hawaii.**
34. Todd Hall, ss, Sacramento (Calif.) CC.
35. **Theron Heusman, lhp, El Reno (Okla.) JC.**
36. **Joseph Hardwick, of, Nahsua (N.H.) HS.**
37. **Ronald Watson, rhp, Eckerd College.**
38. **Elgin Bobo, 1b-c, Sonoma State University.**
39. Todd Blyleven, rhp, Villa Park (Calif.) HS.
40. John Deremer, rhp, San Jose (Calif.) CC.
41. Joshua Hurst, lhp, Glendale (Ariz.) CC.
42. Jay Hassel, rhp, Rancho Santiago (Calif.) JC.
43. Tony Gonzales, ss, Rubidoux HS, Mira Loma, Calif.
44. **Todd Refnes, rhp, Cal Poly San Luis Obispo.**
45. Alfredo Diaz, ss, El Monte (Calif.) HS.
46. Steven Morgan, of, Tate HS, Gonzales, Fla.
47. Earl Partrick, c, Tate HS, Gonzales, Fla.
48. Martin Malloy, ss-2b, Trenton (Fla.) HS.
49. **Eric Buechele, c, Fresno State University.**
50. Tony Rice, c, Notre Dame University.

The Chicago teams drafted Lance Dickson, left, and Alex Fernandez, and promoted them to the big leagues in 1990.

51. Jerry McLemore, of, Waxahachie (Texas) HS.
52. Brian Duva, 2b-of, Oak Hall HS, Gainesville, Fla.
53. Joe Davis, ss, Central Arizona JC.
54. Bimbo Coles, ss, Virginia Tech University.

CHICAGO CUBS (23)

1. **Lance Dickson, lhp, University of Arizona.**
2. **Ryan Hawblitzel, rhp, Leonard HS, West Palm Beach, Fla.**
2. **Troy Bradford, rhp, University of Arizona** (Supplemental choice—72nd— for loss of Type 'C' free agent Scott Sanderson).
3. **Tim Parker, rhp, Clemson University.**
4. **Sean Cheetham, rhp, Woodbridge (Va.) HS.**
5. **Tyson Godfrey, rhp, Aberdeen (Wash.) HS.**
6. Ronnie Brown, of, Manatee (Fla.) JC.
7. **Adrian Sanchez, rhp, Rio Grande HS, Albuquerque, N.M.**
8. **Phil Dauphin, of, Indiana University.**
9. **Jim Wolff, c, Palm Beach (Fla.) JC.**
10. Randy Ortega, c, Lincoln HS, Stockton, Calif.
11. **Michael Young, rhp, Anderson University.**
12. Pedro Valdes, lhp, Loiza, P.R.
13. Steve Gurtner, rhp, Holy Cross HS, Chalmette, La.
14. **Scott Gardner, rhp, Imperial Valley (Calif.) JC.**
15. **Joe Porcelli, lhp, Iona College.**
16. Travis Woods, of, Santa Monica (Calif.) CC.
17. **Willie Gardner, of, Tupelo (Miss.) HS.**
18. **Mike Gabbani, c, Cal State Dominguez Hills.**
19. **Ken Krahenbuhl, rhp, San Bernardino (Calif.) HS.**
20. **Steve Coffey, ss, University of Massachusetts.**
21. **Jim Robinson, c, Mississippi State University.**
22. **Joe Biasucci, 2b, Palm Beach (Fla.) JC.**
23. **Brian Wilson, ss, Modesto (Calif.) JC.**
24. Glenn Delafield, of, Denham Springs (La.) HS.
25. **John DeRicco, 1b, University of Nevada-Reno.**
26. Kurt Bierek, 3b, Glencoe HS, Hillsboro, Ore.
27. Patrick Huston, 3b, Los Angeles Pierce JC.
28. Angel Abreu, rhp, Guaynabo, P.R.
29. Jay Meyer, lhp, Johnson County (Kan.) CC.
30. **Andy Hartung, 3b, University of Maine.**
31. **Charles Kirk, rhp, Jacksonville University.**
32. Benjamin Bryant, rhp, San Jacinto (Texas) JC.
33. **J.P. Postiff, 3b, Fresno State University.**
34. Steven Walker, of, Lee County HS, Leesburg, Ga.
35. Jorge Santiago, 3b, Bayamon, P.R.
36. Ramon Martinez, ss, Toa Alta, P.R.
37. Edwin Zayas, rhp, Luquillo, P.R.
38. Darren Stumberger, 3b-1b, Spanish River HS, Boca Raton, Fla.
39. Mike Schmitz, 1b, Coconut Creek (Fla.) HS.
40. James Riggio, rhp, Chamberlain HS, Tampa, Fla.
41. Ricardo Serpa, of-lhp, Bayamon, P.R.
42. **Tommy Helms, 2b, Western Hills HS, Cincinnati.**
43. Travis Champion, of, Hibriten HS, Lenoir, N.C.
44. Jeff Mapson, c, Palmdale (Calif.) HS.
45. **Rolando Fernandez, of, Northwestern State University.**

CHICAGO WHITE SOX (4)

1. **Alex Fernandez, rhp, Miami-Dade South CC.**
2. **Bob Wickman, rhp, University of Wisconsin-Whitewater.**
2. Eric Maloney, rhp, Carmel HS, Mundelein, Ill. (Supplemental choice—67th— for loss of Type 'C' free agent Richard Dotson).
3. **Robert Ellis, rhp, Panola (Texas) JC.**
4. **James Baldwin, rhp, Pinecrest HS, Southern Pines, N.C.**

5. Ray Durham, 2b, Harding HS, Charlotte, N.C.
6. Charles Poe, of, West Covina (Calif.) HS.
7. Mike Vogel, c-of, Cretin HS, Brooklyn Park, Minn.
8. Nathaniel James, of, Lake Mary HS, Altamonte Springs, Fla.
9. Doug McGraw, rhp, Duncanville (Texas) HS.
10. Jonathon Taylor, c, Alcorn Central HS, Corinth, Miss.
11. Keith Strange, c, Oregon Tech.
12. Jimmy Hurst, of, Central HS, Tuscaloosa, Ala.
13. Rod Bolton, rhp, University of Kentucky.
14. Fred Starks, rhp, Brevard (Fla.) CC.
15. Mike Bradish, 1b, Christ College-Irvine (Calif.).
16. Jeff DiNuzzo, rhp, Seton Hall University.
17. Larry Gilligan, 2b, Brookdale (N.J.) CC.
18. Brandon Wilson, ss, University of Kentucky.
19. Kerry Valrie, of, University of Southern Mississippi.
20. Jonathan Jenkins, rhp, East Carolina University.
21. Muzzy Jackson, 1b, Mercer University.
22. Terry Marshall, lhp, Sweet Water HS, Nanafalia, Ala.
23. Todd Altaffer, lhp, Jacksonville State University.
24. Mark Gilreath, rhp, Brevard (Fla.) JC.
25. Jonathan Story, ss-2b, Southern University.
26. Vince Zarate, of, Kennedy HS, New York, N.Y.
27. James Coachman, 1b, Troy State University.
28. Dennis McCaffery, of, Villanova University.
29. Dan Magee, lhp, Jackson State University.
30. Roosevelt Smith, rhp, Southern University.
31. Todd Hotz, lhp, University of Texas.
32. Corey Austin, 1b-of, Faulkner State (Ala.) JC.
33. Jason Hisey, rhp, University of Arizona.
34. Billy Warner, rhp, Central Private HS, Greenell Springs, La.
35. Cedrick Thomas, lhp, Gulf Coast (Fla.) CC.
36. Jason Bere, rhp, Middlesex (Mass.) CC.
37. Ron Scott, lhp, Sarasota (Fla.) HS.
38. Tim Green-Shornock, 1b, Marlboro HS, Morganville, N.J.
39. Mike Potter, rhp, Central Arizona JC.
40. Greg McGough, c, Northeast Louisiana University.
41. Matt Skrometta, rhp, Satellite Beach (Fla.) HS.
42. Mike Hancock, lhp, Volunteer State (Tenn.) CC.
43. Donald Culberson, rhp, East Central University.
44. Karun Jackson, ss, Bishop State (Ala.) JC.
45. Allen Battle, of, University of South Alabama.
46. Eric Chapman, of, Garrett (Md.) CC.
47. William Zerbe, lhp, Gaither HS, Tampa, Fla.
48. Emanuel Hayes, ss, Forest Brook HS, Houston.
49. Andrew Hoey, rhp, Central Washington University.
50. John Timko, c, Clearwater (Fla.) HS.
51. Clemente Gordan, c, Grambling State University.
52. Steve Davis, rhp, Angelina (Texas) JC.
53. Chris Hitt, lhp, Jersey Village HS, Houston.
54. Brad Kantor, 3b-c, Manatee (Fla.) JC.
55. Mike Badorek, rhp, Olivet Nazarene College.
56. Greg Elliott, ss, Pearl River (Miss.) JC.
57. Anthony Box, ss-of, Brookwood (Ala.) HS.

CINCINNATI REDS (7)

1. Dan Wilson, c, University of Minnesota.
2. Keith Gordon, ss, Wright State University.
3. Dan Tobin, rhp, Dowagiac Union HS, Dowagiac, Mich.
4. Mike Ferry, rhp, Auburn University.
5. Kevin Aubin, c, Drury HS, Stamford, Vt.
6. Steve Gibralter, of, Duncanville (Texas) HS.
7. Juan Loyola, of, Canuy, P.R.
8. Larry Luebbers, rhp, University of Kentucky.
9. Ken Carlyle, rhp, University of Mississippi.
10. Clifton Foster, rhp, Angelina (Texas) JC.
11. Shannon Jones, ss, Aurora (Colo.) Central HS.
12. John Roper, rhp, Hoke County HS, Raeford, N.C.
13. Derick Graham, rhp, Hoke County HS, Raeford, N.C.
14. Bobby Perna, 3b, Cumberland (Tenn.) University.
15. Randy Albaladejo, c, Vega Alta, P.R.
16. Shane Halter, ss, Seminole (Okla.) HS.
17. Tucker Hammargren, 1b-c, Arizona State University.
18. Brian Carlin, of, Angelina (Texas) JC.
19. Kevin Berry, rhp, Northwestern State University.
20. Marc Valdes, rhp, Jesuit HS, Tampa, Fla.
21. Mark Fields, of, Washington HS, Los Angeles.
22. Martis Aviles, lhp, Levittown, P.R.
23. Joseph Wallace, c, Granite City (Ill.) HS.
24. Ryan Towns, rhp, Gonzales (Texas) HS.
25. Greg Margheim, lhp, Virginia Tech.
26. Brian Hierholzer, c, Blue Valley North HS, Overland Park, Kan.
27. Scott Connor, rhp, Gateway HS, Aurora, Colo.
28. Kevin Riggs, 2b, East Carolina University.
29. Mark Mann, rhp, McNicholas HS, Cincinnati.
30. Craig Bolcerek, c, Brenham (Texas) HS.
31. Jorge Ortiz, rhp, Carolina, P.R.

32. Edwin Corps, rhp, San Juan, P.R.
33. Charles McClain, rhp, University of Tennessee.
34. John Gast, 3b, East Carolina University.
35. Bo Loftin, c, University of New Orleans.
36. Chad Hodge, of, Marcus HS, Flower Mound, Texas.
37. Michael Carlton, c, Texas City (Texas) HS.
38. James Rushworth, rhp, Panola (Texas) JC.
39. Pierre Burris, of-3b, Kansas City (Kan.) CC.

CLEVELAND INDIANS (8)

1. Tim Costo, ss, University of Iowa.
1. Sam Hence, of, Stone County HS, Wiggins, Miss. (Supplemental choice—39th—for failure to sign 1989 No. 1 pick Calvin Murray).
2. Darrell Whitmore, of, West Virginia University (Choice from Mariners as compensation for Type 'B' free agent Pete O'Brien).
2. Pat Bryant, of, Cleveland HS, Reseda, Calif.
3. Jason Hardtke, ss, Leland HS, San Jose, Calif.
4. Jeff Brohm, ss, University of Louisville.
5. Oscar Munoz, rhp, University of Miami.
6. Paul Bako, c, Lafayette (La.) HS.
7. David Bell, 3b, Moeller HS, Cincinnati.
8. Shawn Bryant, lhp, Oklahoma City University.
9. Rodrick McCall, 1b, Orange Coast (Calif.) JC.
10. Robert Smith, 2b, Allen County (Kan.) CC.
11. Carl Johnson, rhp, Lassen (Calif.) JC.
12. Craig Sides, rhp, Jefferson Davis (Ala.) JC.
13. Todd Whitehurst, rhp, North Monterey HS, Salinas, Calif.
14. Dino Philyaw, of, Southern Wayne HS, Dudley, N.C.
15. Samuel Baker, rhp, Hill (Texas) JC.
16. James Morgan, of, North Marion HS, Sparr, Fla.
17. Dave Milcki, rhp, Oklahoma State University.
18. Stephen Gajkowski, rhp, Bellevue (Wash.) CC.
19. Ricky Powell, of, Tioga HS, Alexandria, La.
20. Robert Schultz, of, Walton HS, Marietta, Ga.
21. Matt Carpenter, c, Euclid (Ohio) Senior HS.
22. Jerry Ashford, 3b-c, Everman (Texas) HS.
23. Baylor Alexander, c, Florida JC.
24. Roynal Coleman, of, Kishwaukee (Ill.) JC.
25. Timothy Thomas, 1b-of, Ohio University.
26. Scott Morgan, rhp, Middle Tennessee State University.
27. Oscar Resendez, rhp, Texas Southmost JC.
28. Bart Peterson, rhp, Brigham Young University.
29. David Vindivich, of, Mount Tahoma HS, Tacoma, Wash.
30. Eric Trice, of, LaGrande (Ore.) HS.
31. Victor Ramirez, of, Hill (Texas) JC.
32. Pete Guerra, c, Laredo (Texas) JC.
33. Kenneth Day, rhp, Washington State University.
34. Larry Minter, of, Harlan HS, Chicago.
35. Jose Sued, c, Hill (Texas) JC.
36. Edwin Couvertier, of, Urb Las Virtude, P.R.
37. Cesar Ramirez, of, Phoenixville (Pa.) Area HS.
38. Joseph Fleet, rhp, Southeastern Louisiana University.
39. Tim Langdon, lhp, East Carolina University.
40. Michael Zollars, ss, Western Oklahoma State JC.
41. Joseph Frias, 2b, Oklahoma City University.
42. Mark Martin, of, Connors State (Okla.) JC.
43. David Chisum, of, Laredo (Texas) JC.
44. John Rodgers, c, Panola (Texas) JC.
45. Efrain Montero, lhp, Ponce, P.R.
46. Charles Hickman, 1b, San Jacinto (Texas) JC.
47. (selection voided)
48. Ron Vaught, rhp, Deer Park (Texas) HS.
49. Joseph Chastain, lhp, Florida JC.
50. DeWayne Wilson, 2b, Lockhart HS, Sharon, S.C.
51. Carlos Crawford, rhp, Montreat-Anderson (N.C.) JC.
52. Chad Brown, lhp, North Gaston HS, Gastonia, N.C.
53. James Warwick, ss, Colfax (Wash.) HS.
54. Lance Martin, of, Tumwater (Wash.) HS.
55. Brian Coleman, rhp, Bainbridge Island (Wash.) HS.
56. Aaron Morris, of-1b, Lakeland (Ohio) CC.
57. John Lorms, c, Eastern Kentucky University.
58. Tracy Sanders, of, Limestone College.
59. Frank Monastero, 2b, West Chester University.

DETROIT TIGERS (2)

1. Tony Clark, of, Christian HS, El Cajon, Calif.
2. (Choice to Athletics as compensation for Type 'B' free agent Tony Phillips).
2. Keith Grunewald, ss, Walton HS, Marietta, Ga. (Choice from Padres as compensation for Type 'B' free agent Fred Lynn).
3. Vince Bradford, of, Malvern (Ark.) HS
4. Jimmy Alder, 3b, Dobyns-Bennett HS, Kingsport, Tenn.
5. Shannon Withem, rhp, Willow Run HS, Ypsilanti, Mich.
6. Steve Wolf, rhp, Fresno State University.
7. Randy Curtis, of, Riverside (Calif.) CC.
8. Dan Rogers, 1b, Missouri Southern University.
9. Greg Coppeta, lhp, University of Southern Maine.

10. Roger Luce, c, University of Texas.
11. **Sean Sadler, 3b, Missouri Baptist College.**
12. Aaron Seja, of, Millikan HS, Long Beach, Calif.
13. Charlie Greene Jr., c, Miami-Dade South CC.
14. Benjamin Blomdahl, rhp, Riverside (Calif.) CC.
15. Toby McFarland, lhp, Petoskey (Mich.) HS.
16. **Brian Nelson, rhp, George Mason University.**
17. **Tom Drell, rhp, Florida Southern College.**
18. Keith Kinsey, of, Santa Fe HS, Lakeland, Fla.
19. **Michael Guilfoyle, lhp, St. Peter's College.**
20. **Warren Sawkiw, 2b, Wake Forest University.**
21. **Greg Haeger, 1b-lhp, University of Michigan.**
22. **David Mastropietro, of, LaSalle University.**
23. **Douglas Kimbler, ss, College of St. Rose (N.Y.).**
24. **Brian Saltzgaber, of-2b, Western Michigan University.**
25. **Gregg Radachowsky, c, Boston College.**
26. Kerry Collins, ss-3b, Wilson HS, West Lawn, Pa.
27. Greg McMurtry, of, University of Michigan.
28. Rodney Peete, 3b, Marina Del Ray, Calif.
29. Darwin Traylor, of, Poly HS, Riverside, Calif.
30. John Rosengren, lhp, Rye (N.Y.) HS.
31. **Paul Reinisch, 1b, Wake Forest University.**
32. **Brian Schubert, rhp, Kent State University.**
33. **Bob Undorf, rhp, University of South Florida.**
34. Thomas Paskievitch, rhp, Central Michigan University.
35. **Dennis McNamara, of, Central Michigan University.**
36. **Kirk Mendenhall, ss, Westminster (Mo.) College.**
37. **Kevin Miller, c, Chico State University.**
38. **Rob Fazekas, rhp, Rutgers University.**
39. **Robert Riker, rhp, Central Michigan University.**
40. **Eric Leimeister, rhp, St. John's University.**
41. **Tim Kirt, of, Missouri Baptist College.**
42. **Keith Roberts, of, West Nassau HS, Callahan, Fla.**
43. **Brian Warren, rhp, New Mexico State University.**
44. Matthew Hammett, lhp, Macomb (Mich.) JC.
45. David Bowden, c, Martin Luther King HS, Detroit.
46. Rodney Tisdale, of, University Christian HS, Jacksonville, Fla.
47. Steven Hughart, lhp, Brevard (Fla.) JC.
48. Arthur Johnson, ss, Texarkana (Texas) CC.
49. Gregory Steele, rhp, Homer (Mich.) HS.
50. Karry Riley, rhp, Suwannee HS, Live Oak, Fla.
51. Dan Ruff, of, University of Michigan.
52. Willie Adams, rhp, La Serna HS, La Mirada, Calif.
53. Tim Goodwin, of, Burlington (Iowa) HS.
54. Doug Newstrom, rhp, Woodson HS, Fairfax, Va.
55. **John Sutey, rhp, Kentwood HS, Kent, Wash.**
56. Willie Morales, c, Tucson (Ariz.) HS.

HOUSTON ASTROS (15)

1. (Choice to Giants as compensation for Type 'B' free agent Ken Oberkfell).
1. **Tom Nevers, ss, Edina (Minn.) HS** (Choice from Giants as compensation for Type 'A' free agent Kevin Bass).
1. **Brian Williams, rhp, University of South Carolina** (Supplemental choice—31st—for loss of Type 'A' free agent Kevin Bass).
2. **Gary Mota, of, Fullerton (Calif.) JC.**
3. **Chris Hatcher, of, University of Iowa.**
4. **Perry Berry, 2b, University of Southwestern Louisiana.**
5. **Al Harley, of, Sheldon HS, Eugene, Ore.**
6. **Jimmy White, of, Brandon HS, Tampa, Fla.**
7. **David Nix, lhp, Harrison HS, Evansville, Ind.**
8. **Tony Gilmore, c, University of Arkansas.**
9. **Jorge Correa, rhp, Miami (Fla.) Senior HS.**
10. Brian Boehringer, rhp, University of Nevada-Las Vegas.
11. **Fletcher Thompson, 2b, Nicholls State University.**
12. **Jeff Ball, 3b, San Jose State University.**
13. **Ray Montgomery, of, Fordham University.**
14. James Evans, rhp, Hancock (Calif.) JC.
15. **Layne Lambert, 3b, University of Nevada-Las Vegas.**
16. **Marsalis Basey, ss, Martinsburg (W.Va.) HS.**
17. **Jon Quaid, lhp, Chabot (Calif.) JC.**
18. Frank Jacobs, 1b, Notre Dame University.
19. **Steven Bottoms, lhp, Overton HS, Nashville, Tenn.**
20. **Juan Martinez, rhp, Huston Tillotson College.**
21. Anthony Griffin, 1b, Washington HS, Hawthorne, Calif.
22. **Dennis Reed, rhp, Cal Poly San Luis Obispo.**
23. Jason Varitek, c, Lake Brantley HS, Longwood, Fla.
24. Johnny Mitchell, of, Sprayberry HS, Marietta, Ga.
25. James Martin, of, Seminole (Okla.) JC.
26. Jim Dougherty, rhp, University of North Carolina.
27. **Lincoln Gumbs, ss, Clarke (Miss.) JC.**
28. **Douglas Ketchen, rhp, Cal State Fullerton.**
29. Bret Hemphill, c, Cupertino HS, Santa Clara, Calif.
30. Chris Singleton, of, Pinole Valley HS, Hercules, Calif.
31. **Michael Irwin, rhp, University of Portland.**
32. **Lance Smith, c, McNeese State University.**
33. Robert Baldwin, of, DeLand HS, Lake Helen, Fla.

34. Joe Gonzalez, rhp, Miami (Fla.) Senior HS.
35. Dax Winslett, rhp, Plano (Texas) Senior HS.
36. **Scott Black, rhp, University of Missouri.**
37. Rodney Foster, of-2b, Midwest City (Okla.) HS.
38. **Jose Flores, ss, Cidra, P.R.**
39. **Jason Wall, lhp, Louisiana State University.**
40. **Vincent Roman, of, Ithaca College.**
41. **Scott Bullard, rhp, Florida JC.**
42. **Stephen McCumiskey, c, University of Rhode Island.**
43. Raymond Dault, rhp, Austin (Texas) HS.
44. Robert McCloud, rhp, Palomar (Calif.) JC.
45. Steve Williams, of, Santa Cruz HS, Arizona City, Ariz.
46. Christopher Milton, ss, Wilson HS, Hacienda Heights, Calif.
47. Derek Davis, of, Ellison HS, Fort Hood, Texas.
48. Greg Almond, c, Middle Georgia JC.
49. Cleveland Ladell, 2b-of, Texarkana (Texas) HS.
50. Mark Prather, of, McLennan (Texas) CC.
51. Malcolm Huckaby, 3b, Bristol (Conn.) Central HS.
52. James Davis, 3b, Lincoln HS, San Diego.
53. Brian McGlone, ss, Hillsborough (Fla.) CC.
54. Todd Coburn, c, Wooster HS, Carson City, Nev.
55. Scott Smith, of, Coppell (Texas) HS.
56. Michael Belcher, c, Broad Run HS, Sterling, Va.
57. Carey Lundstrom, rhp, Los Angeles Harbor JC.
58. David Maize, c, Triton (Ill.) JC.
59. William Paragin, c, Hamilton (Ohio) HS.
60. Bernard Bellard, rhp, Acadiana HS, Lafayette, La.
61. Johnny Booker, of, Tucson (Ariz.) HS.
62. David Angotti, c, Grossmont (Calif.) JC.
63. Kevin Ehl, rhp, Cypress (Calif.) JC.
64. Kevin Cook, of, Cypress (Calif.) JC.
65. Steven Hernandez, ss, Orange Coast (Calif.) JC.
66. Brian Thompson, of, Chabot (Calif.) JC.
67. Jason Rathburn, rhp, Westlake HS, Austin, Texas.
68. Ron Cacini, ss, Triton (Ill.) JC.
69. Donald Miller, rhp, Sprayberry HS, Marietta, Ga.
70. Michael Lustyk, rhp-3b, Interlake HS, Bellevue, Wash.
71. Joseph Miller, of, Los Angeles Harbor JC.
72. Todd Mancini, of, LaSalle Academy, Cranston, R.I.
73. Mike Condon, c, Southern Union State (Ala.) JC.
74. William Adams, of, John Jay HS, San Antonio, Texas.
75. Jeffrey Brown, rhp, Schenectady (N.Y.) CC.
76. Travis Driskill, rhp, Anderson HS, Austin, Texas.
77. Anastoshio Navarro, 3b, El Rancho HS, Pico Rivera, Calif.
78. Darious Carter, ss, Glenn Oaks HS, Baton Rouge, La.
79. Dennis Colon, ss, Manati, P.R.
80. Kenneth Jackson, 1b, Polk (Fla.) CC.
81. Eric Mooney, lhp, St. Anthony HS, Long Beach, Calif.
82. Jose Matos, rhp, Rio Piedras, P.R.
83. Daniel Young, lhp, Cannon County HS, Woodbury, Tenn.
84. Patrick Bettancourt, 3b, Mission Bay HS, San Diego.
85. Marc Claus, ss, Broward (Fla.) CC.
86. George Wyles, c, Permian HS, Odessa, Texas.
87. Daniel Pagan, 3b-1b, Rio Piedras, P.R.
88. Greg Guell, lhp, Miami-Dade CC South.
89. Adam West, of, Hudson Valley (N.Y.) CC.
90. Sean Garrison, lhp, Berlin HS, Kensington, Conn.
91. Geoff Grenert, rhp, Mesa (Ariz.) CC.
92. Brian Whyburn, rhp, Ukiah (Calif.) HS.
93. Scott Mowl, rhp, Cerritos (Calif.) JC.
94. Matthew Martinez, 2b, Sacramento (Calif.) CC.
95. Chad Phillips, rhp, Orange Coast (Calif.) JC.
96. Michael Houck, rhp, El Camino (Calif.) JC.
97. Floyd White, 1b-of, Middle Georgia JC.
98. Cedric Moore, of, Westwood HS, Fort Pierce, Fla.
99. Jeff Caldwell, of, Bogalusa (La.) HS.

KANSAS CITY ROYALS (25)

1. (Choice to Padres as compensation for Type 'A' free agent Mark Davis).
2. (Choice to Athletics as compensation for Type 'A' free agent Storm Davis).
3. **Shayne Rea, rhp, Henry Ford (Mich.) CC.**
4. **Doug Harris, rhp, James Madison University.**
5. **Darren Burton, of, Pulaski County HS, Somerset, Ky.**
6. **Wade Fyock, rhp, Somerset (Pa.) HS.**
7. **Tom Smith, inf, Avon Park (Fla.) HS.**
8. **Philip Hiatt, 3b, Louisiana Tech.**
9. **Anthony Lee, rhp, El Dorado HS, Las Vegas, Nev.**
10. **Robert Toth, rhp, Pacifica HS, Cypress, Calif.**
11. Chad Drown, ss, La Mirada HS, Placentia, Calif.
12. **Rod Myers, rhp, University of Wisconsin.**
13. **Chad Strickland, c, Carl Albert HS, Oklahoma City.**
14. **Damon Pollard, rhp, University of Southern Mississippi.**
15. **Thomas Lee, rhp, Los Angeles CC.**
16. **David Haber, of, Catonsville (Md.) CC.**
17. **Victor Gonzalez, 3b-of, Carolina, P.R.**
18. **Donald Harrel, c, Taft (Calif.) JC.**

19. Doug Shields, of, Southern Illinois University.
20. Doug Peters, rhp, Indiana University.
21. Brady Stewart, ss, Ohio State University.
22. William Long, lhp, Montgomery (Md.) JC.
23. Vernon Slater, of, Polk (Fla.) CC.
24. Andre Newhouse, ss, Sterling HS, Houston.
25. Raymie Brooks, c, El Reno (Okla.) JC.
26. Alan Budnick, rhp, University of Detroit.
27. Rafael Gutierrez, rhp, East Los Angeles JC.
28. Arnie Sambel, of, University of San Francisco.
29. Charles Frederick, rhp, Parkland (Ill.) JC.
30. Brian Bevil, rhp, Angelina (Texas) JC.
31. Weddison Ebanks, of, Utah Valley CC.
32. Marcelio Hansen, lhp, Olympic (Wash.) JC.
33. Scott Davis, rhp, Adelphi University.
34. Sean Franceschi, lhp, Univeristy of New Orleans.
35. Brad Holman, rhp, Auburn University.
36. Damon Daniels, of, Texarkana (Texas) CC.
37. John Schreiner, 1b, Penn State University.
38. David Hierholzer, rhp, Kansas State University.
39. Kevin Sisk, 3b, James Madison University.
40. Mitch Simons, 2b, Oklahoma State University.
41. Shannon Strong, of, Treasure Valley (Ore.) CC.
42. Terrance Mays, of, Kaskaskia (Ill.) CC.
43. Scott Hennessey, of, Johnson County (Kan.) CC.
44. Tyres Blackburn, c-of, Bryan Adams HS, Dallas.
45. Chris Moten, rhp, Bellflower (Calif.) HS.
46. Brian Gelzheiser, rhp, Baldwin HS, Pittsburgh.
47. Sean Strade, rhp, Grant HS, Portland, Ore.
48. Reggie Ingram, of, Coffee HS, Douglas, Ga.
49. Craig Tucker, rhp, Klamath HS, Klamath Falls, Ore.
50. Richard Parker, rhp, Los Angeles JC.
51. Gerald Sharko, 1b, Phoenix (Ariz.) JC.
52. Brian Parks, rhp, Skagit Valley (Wash.) CC.
53. Shane Gilder, 2b, San Jacinto (Texas) JC.
54. Lyle Mouton, of, Louisiana State University.
55. John Jacobs, rhp, Chino (Calif.) HS.
56. Nick Kaiser, 2b-ss, Cuesta (Calif.) JC.
57. Jonathan Mathews, 1b-of, Centerville (Iowa) HS.

LOS ANGELES DODGERS (9)

1. Ron Walden, lhp, Blanchard (Okla.) HS.
2. (Choice to Expos as compensation for Type 'A' free agent Hubie Brooks).
2. Leroy Williams, ss, East St. John HS, Reserve, La. (Supplemental choice—68th—for loss of Type 'C' free agent Dave Anderson).
2. Scott Freeman, rhp, University of Wyoming (Supplemental choice—73rd—for loss of Type 'C' free agent John Tudor).
3. (Choice to Pirates as compensation for Type 'A' free agent Jim Gott).
4. Mike Busch, 1b, Iowa State University.
5. Frank Smith, of, Poly HS, Riverside, Calif.
6. Alton Pinkney, of, Glynn Academy, Brunswick, Ga.
7. Daniel Gray, c, State University of New York-Binghamton.
8. C.J. Kerr, lhp, Cerritos (Calif.) JC.
9. Jake Botts, rhp, North Monterey HS, Salinas, Calif.
10. Kenneth Hamilton, rhp, Patrick Henry (Ala.) JC.
11. William Mapp, of, Natrona County HS, Casper, Wyo.
12. Keoki Farrish, of, Ohlone (Calif.) JC.
13. Greg Davis, rhp, El Camino (Calif.) CC.
14. Warren Daspit, rhp, Cal State Sacramento.
15. Tim Griffin, 3b, Stanford University.
16. Donn Cunnigan, of, Gahr HS, Los Angeles.
17. Stephen Mintz, c, Mt. Olive (N.C.) JC.
18. Lonnie Webb, ss, South Georgia JC.
19. Burgess Watts, 3b-rhp, JC of Du Page (Ill.).
20. Peter Nurre, c, Cabrillo (Calif.) JC.
21. Wayne Lindemann, lhp, Lower Columbia (Wash.) JC.
22. Michael Racobaldo, rhp, Pennsauken (N.J.) HS.
23. Ron Maurer, ss, University of North Carolina.
24. Michael Mimbs, lhp, Mercer University.
25. Mark Mimbs, lhp, Mercer University.
26. Gordie Tipton, rhp, Oklahoma State University.
27. Jody Treadwell, rhp, Jacksonville University.
28. Randall Graves, ss, Riverside (Calif.) CC.
29. David Baumann, rhp, Western New England College.
30. Benjamin O'Connor, lhp, University of Maryland.
31. Domingo Mota, of, Cal State Fullerton.
32. Anthony Rodriguez, c, Aguadilla, P.R.
33. Albert Maldonado, lhp, Yauco, P.R.
34. Kurt Ehmann, ss, Mendocino (Calif.) Calif.
35. Steve Matos, c, Chaminade HS, Hollywood, Fla.
36. Mike Brady, lhp, Florida State University.
37. Ira Smith, of-2b, University of Maryland-Eastern Shore.
38. Brady Raggio, rhp, San Ramon HS, Danville, Calif.
39. Mark Sweeney, of, University of Maine.
40. Larry Jacinto, rhp, Southern California College.
41. John Cranford, 2b, Middle Georgia JC.

FIRST-ROUND PICKS

| Mike Mussina | Ron Walden | Shane Andrews |
| ... Orioles pick | ... Dodgers draft | ... Expos choice |

42. Clint Minear, lhp, East Mississippi JC.
43. Charles Williams, of, Meridian (Miss.) JC.
44. **Ed Lund, c, Notre Dame University.**
45. Jason Sengbusch, rhp, Westfield HS, Oxford, Wis.
46. **Thomas Matthews, lhp, University of Edinboro.**
47. Joseph Jacobsen, rhp, Clovis (Calif.) West HS.
48. **Robert Sweeney, 3b, Waukesha (Wis.) County Technical JC.**
49. **Dirk Gorman, of, State University of New York-Binghamton.**
50. Ismael Castaneda, lhp, Hanford (Calif.) HS.
51. Mario Johnson, ss, Simmons HS, Hollandale, Miss.
52. Gordon Hockett, 1b, Union HS, Tulsa Okla.
53. Robert Calton, lhp, Lehi (Utah) HS.
54. Todd Williams, rhp, Onondaga (N.Y.) CC.
55. Brett Kim, 3b, Marin (Calif.) CC.
56. Joseph Wagner, rhp, Adams Friendship (Wis.) HS.
57. Patrick Reed, ss, Mt. Hood (Ore.) CC.
58. Melvin Warren, of, Solano (Calif.) CC.
59. **Daniel Andrews, of, Cal Poly Pomona.**
60. David Madsen, 3b, Murray (Utah) HS.
61. Greg Raisola, c, Nogales HS, Walnut, Calif.
62. Roger Sweeney, of, Marin (Calif.) JC.
63. Fausto Abad, of, Jupiter (Fla.) HS.

MILWAUKEE BREWERS (14)

1. (Choice to Athletics as compensation for Type 'A' free agent Dave Parker).
2. **LaRue Baber, of, Grant HS, Sacramento, Calif.**
3. **Michael Carter, ss, Livingston (Ala.) University.**
4. **Don Blair, rhp, Wabash (Ind.) HS.**
5. **Duane Singleton, of, McKee Vocational Tech, Staten Island, N.Y.**
6. **Tom McGraw, lhp, Washington State University.**
7. **Bobby Benjamin, 1b-of, University of Nebraska.**
8. **Tim Clark, of, Louisiana State University.**
9. **Kevin McDonald, rhp, University of Southwestern Louisiana.**
10. **Kurt Archer, rhp, San Diego State University.**
11. **Brian Souza, rhp, University of Hawaii.**
12. **Marshall Boze, rhp, Southwestern (Calif.) CC.**
13. **Dave Wrona, ss, Southern Illinois University.**
14. **Tim Carter, 1b, Miami (Ohio) University.**
15. **John Tatum, 3b, Grossmont HS, Santee, Calif.**
16. **Mike Couture, c, Clemson University.**
17. **Mark Stephens, lhp, Central Arizona JC.**
18. **Orlando Barrios, of, High Point College.**
19. **Patrick Miller, rhp, University of Detroit.**
20. **David White, rhp, University of South Florida.**
21. **Michael Norris, of, Richland (Texas) CC.**
22. **Charles Rambadt, c, Dominican College.**
23. **Don Pruitt, rhp, University of Arizona.**
24. **Orlando Griego, rhp, New Mexico State University.**
25. **Christopher Wheat, ss, Monmouth College.**
26. Brendt Newbill, lhp, McNary HS, Salem, Ore.
27. Michael Killimet, of, Fort Walton Beach (Fla.) HS.
28. **Anthony Coble, of, Wingate College.**
29. **Todd Edwards, of, University of Arizona.**
30. Sam Taylor, of, El Cerrito HS, Richmond, Calif.
31. **Mike Lynch, rhp, Rollins College.**
32. **Julian Salazar, ss, Pasadena (Calif.) CC.**
33. **Vince Castaldo, 3b, Universtiy of Kentucky.**
34. Alonso Beltran, rhp, Socorro HS, El Paso, Texas.
35. Robert Dickerson, of, Harrison Central HS, Gulfport, Miss.
36. **Carlos Flores, ss, Sierra Vista HS, Baldwin Park, Calif.**
37. Luis Melendez, 3b, Ponce, P.R.
38. Steve Boyd, rhp, Central Arizona JC.
39. David Repass, 1b-lhp, Forest HS, Ocala, Fla.
40. Ernie Nietzke, of, Saddleback (Calif.) JC.
41. **David Acevedo, rhp, San Sebastian, P.R.**

42. Reid Mizuguchi, rhp, Univeristy of Southern Claifornia.
43. Steven Sigloch, 2b, University of Utah.
44. Clinton Brown, rhp, Taft (Calif.) CC.

MINNESOTA TWINS (12)

1. Todd Ritchie, rhp, Duncanville (Texas) HS.
1. Midre Cummings, of, Edison HS, Miami (Supplemental choice—29th—for loss of Type 'A' free agent Jeff Reardon to Red Sox).
2. Jay Owens, c, Middle Tennessee State University.
2. Ron Caridad, rhp, Westminster HS, Miami (Choice from Red Sox as compensation for Type 'A' free agent Jeff Reardon).
3. Jamie Ogden, 1b, White Bear Lake (Minn.) HS (Choice from Pirates as compensation for Type 'C' free agent Wally Backman).
3. Richie Becker, of, Aurora West HS, Aurora, Ill.
4. Silvio Censale, lhp, Catholic HS, Paramus, N.J.
5. Brent Brede, of, Wesclin HS, Trenton, Ill.
6. Craig Hawkins, 2b, Simeon HS, Chicago.
7. Tim Persing, rhp, Mansfield University.
8. James Mouton, of, St. Mary's (Calif.) College.
9. Trevor Humphry, rhp, Delight (Ark.) HS.
10. Andrew Prater, c, Travis HS, Austin, Texas.
11. Mark Swope, rhp, University of Arkansas.
12. Pat Meares, 3b, Wichita State University.
13. Steve Whitaker, lhp, Merced (Calif.) JC.
14. Jeff Granger, lhp, Orangefield (Texas) HS.
15. Jon Henry, rhp, University of Central Florida.
16. Paul Russo, c-1b, University of Tampa.
17. Fred Smith, rhp, Roosevelt HS, Brooklyn, N.Y.
18. Scott Weiss, rhp, Stanford University.
19. Matt Morse, 2b, University of Michigan.
20. Damian Miller, c, Viterbo (Wis.) College.
21. Ed Guardado, lhp, San Joaquin Delta (Calif.) CC.
22. John Cohen, of, Mississippi State University.
23. David Schwartz, rhp, University of California.
24. Tom Gavin, 3b, Rider College.
25. Clint Jensen, of, Naperville (Ill.) Central HS.
26. Robert Welles, rhp, Beverly Hills (Calif.) HS.
27. Dicky Dixon, lhp, University of Mississippi.
28. Devin Peppers, of, College of the Desert (Calif.).
29. Steve Kimble, of, Mount Zion HS, Decatur, Ill.
30. Charles MacKendrick, rhp, Grand Junction (Colo.) HS
31. Glenn Evans, ss, Harlan HS, Chicago.
32. Brian Ewing, of, College of Idaho.
33. Geoff Edsell, rhp, Montoursville (Pa.) HS.
34. Kurt Pfeffer, rhp, Marin (Calif.) CC.
35. James Belcher, rhp, Spring Hill HS, Olathe, Kan.
36. Alex Pereira, lhp, Southwest HS, Miami.
37. Brian Klepper, lhp, Iola (Kan.) HS.
38. Richard Portu, of, Westminster HS, Miami.
39. Paul Bruno, c, New York Tech.
40. Matt Brown, c, San Jose State University.
41. Brian Raabe, 2b, University of Minnesota.
42. Derrell Rumsey, of, Sonoma State University.
43. Mike Neal, ss, Hammond (La.) HS.
44. Greg Stephens, rhp, South HS, Fargo, Mo.
45. Hiram Ramirez, c, Ensenada, P.R.
46. Jason Luttges, of, DeAnza (Calif.) CC.
47. Chris Gump, 2b, Mesa (Ariz.) CC.
48. David Garrow, ss, South Mountain (Ariz.) CC.
49. Clarke Rea, c, Scottsdale (Ariz.) CC.
50. Anthony Lacy, of-ss, Foothill HS, Sacramento, Calif.
51. Larry Lucchetti, rhp, San Joaquin Delta (Calif.) CC.
52. Kevin Rawitzer, lhp, Diablo Valley (Calif.) CC.
53. Brian Henderson, of, Boone HS, Orlando, Fla.
54. Blake Byers, c, Seabreeze HS, Daytona Beach, Fla.

MONTREAL EXPOS (11)

1. Shane Andrews, 3b, Carlsbad (N.M.) HS.
1. Rondell White, of, Jones County HS, Gray, Ga. (Choice from Angels as compensation for Type 'A' free agent Mark Langston).
1. Gabe White, lhp, Sebring (Fla.) HS (Supplemental choice—28th—for loss of Type 'A' free agent Mark Langston).
1. Stan Spencer, rhp, Stanford University (Supplemental choice—35th—for loss of Type 'A' free agent Hubie Brooks).
1. Ben Vanryn, lhp, East Noble HS, Kendallville, Ind. (Supplemental choice—37th—for loss of Type 'A' free agent Pascual Perez).
1. Stan Robertson, of, Plainview (Texas) HS (Supplemental choice—40th—for failure to sign 1989 No. 1 pick Charles Johnson).
2. Michael Hardge, ss, Ellison HS, Killeen, Texas (Choice from Dodgers as compensation for Type 'A' free agent Hubie Brooks).
2. Tavo Alvarez, rhp, Tucson (Ariz.) HS (Choice from Yankees as compensation for Type 'A' free agent Pascual Perez).
2. Chris Haney, lhp, University of North Carolina-Charlotte.
Chris Martin, ss, Pepperdine University (Choice from Cardinals as ...tion for Type 'B' free agent Bryn Smith).
Mathile, rhp, Wright State University.

4. Jeff Barry, of, San Diego State University.
5. Ricky Clelland, rhp, Buckeye North HS, Brilliant, Ohio.
6. Steve Long, rhp, St. Xavier College.
7. Rob Fitzpatrick, c, Georgia Southern College.
8. Javier Pages, c, Stranahan HS, Fort Lauderdale, Fla.
9. Craig Clow, 1b, Western Oregon University.
10. William Samples, of, Liberty University.
11. Brian Jones, of, Barstow (Calif.) HS.
12. Bob Baxter, lhp, Harvard University.
13. Ted Ciesla, ss, Rutgers University.
14. Robbie Katzaroff, of, UCLA.
15. Troy Kopp, c, University of the Pacific.
16. Randy Wilstead, 1b, Brigham Young University.
17. Jackie Ross, of, Edison HS, Miami.
18. Frederick Collier, 1b, Abbeville (S.C.) HS.
19. Thomas Philips, c, Fresno State University.
20. Perry Sanchez, c, Long Beach State University.
21. Scott Brocail, rhp, Lamar (Colo.) HS.
22. David Bingham, ss-of, Walla Walla (Wash.) CC.
23. Steve Renko, rhp, University of Kansas.
24. Marc Tsitouris, 1b-c, Wingate College.
25. Mathew Haas, c, St. Mary's HS, Paducah, Ky.
26. Ranbir Grewal, rhp, Fresno State University.
27. Darrin Kotch, lhp, Rutgers University.
28. Billy Brewer, lhp, Dallas Baptist University.
29. Kenya Hunt, 1b, Oceanside (Calif.) HS.
30. Brian Shehan, lhp, UNC Asheville.
31. Dean Madsen, of, Yuba (Calif.) JC.
32. Kelton Jacobson, rhp, Bellevue (Wash.) CC.
33. Robert Navarro, rhp, Pomona (Calif.) HS.
34. Trenton Hauswirth, c, Palm Desert (Calif.) HS.
35. Ryan Whitman, rhp, Jupiter HS, Lake Park, Fla.
36. Mike Morland, c, University of Texas.
37. Benjamin Boulware, of, Los Gatos (Calif.) HS.
38. John Polasek, lhp, Rice University.
39. Jose Diaz, Jose, Guayama, P.R.
40. David Schultz, of, Marina HS, Huntington Beach, Calif.
41. Doug Noce, c, Cal Poly San Luis Obispo.
42. Jacob Benz, lhp, College Park HS, Pleasant Hill, Calif.
43. John Rogers, lhp, East Los Angeles HS.
44. Todd Anderson, of, Lewis-Clark State College.
45. Alex Miranda, 1b, Columbus HS, Miami.
46. Victor Llanos, 3b, Carolina, P.R.
47. Jason Jensen, of, McLane HS, Fresno, Calif.
48. Mark Palfalvi, 1b, Chabot (Calif.) JC.
49. Ronald Jones, of, Mesa (Ariz.) CC.
50. Jorge Adame, c, Bell HS, Maywood, Calif.
51. Archie Jean, of, Mendocino (Calif.) CC.
52. Allen Gallagher, ss, Centennial HS, Gresham, Ore.
53. Charles Lee, of, Currituck HS, Poplar Branch, N.C.
54. Clinton Oltjenbruns, 1b, Willits (Calif.) HS.
55. Gregg Press, rhp, Cabrillo (Calif.) JC.
56. Stephen Mitchell, rhp, Saratoga HS, Los Gatos, Calif.
57. Brett Brown, c, Mesa (Ariz.) CC.
58. Randy Collins, c, Mt. San Jacinto (Calif.) JC.
59. Christopher Lowen, rhp, Moreno Valley (Calif.) HS.
60. Paul Carpentier, rhp, Chaffey (Calif.) JC.
61. Martin Colunga, c, Colton (Calif.) HS.
62. Matthew Jones, 1b, Red Land HS, Lewisberry, Pa.
63. Michael Grigsby, rhp, Lassen (Calif.) JC.

NEW YORK METS (17)

1. Jeromy Burnitz, of, Oklahoma State University.
2. Aaron Ledesma, ss, Chabot (Calif.) JC.
3. Micah Franklin, ss, Lincoln HS, San Francisco.
4. Mike Petrizi, c, Pennsauken (N.J.) HS.
5. Darwin Davis, 3b, Simeon HS, Chicago.
*6. Demond Smith, of, Eisenhower HS, Rialto, Calif.
7. Pete Walker, rhp, University of Connecticut.
8. Raul Casanova, c, Ponce, P.R.
9. Fernando Vina, 2b, Arizona State University.
10. Michael Quillin, of, Nickerson HS, Buhler, Kan.
11. Darren Dreifort, of, Wichita (Kan.) Heights HS.
12. Caspar Van Rynbach, rhp, Iowa Western CC.
13. Tom Hamilton, of, South Fork HS, Indiantown, Fla.
14. Todd Douma, lhp, Arizona State University.
15. Steve Soderstrom, rhp, Turlock (Calif.) HS.
16. Eric Corbell, rhp, Incarnate Word (Texas) College.
17. Brian Daubach, 1b, Belleville (Ill.) Township HS.
18. Trey Cheek, rhp, Broughton HS, Raleigh, N.C.
19. Anthony Phillips, rhp, University of Southern Mississippi.
20. Steven Steele, c, Millikan HS, Long Beach, Calif.
21. Jason King, ss, Washington State University.
22. Brad Schorr, rhp, Columbus (Ga.) HS.
23. Mike Sciortino, lhp, Central Connecticut State University.
24. Steven Seymour, rhp, Ocean County (N.J.) CC.

25. Steve Thomas, rhp, **University of Alabama.**
26. Robert Carpenter, rhp, **University of New Hampshire.**
27. Englebert Bull, of, Fairfax HS, Los Angeles.
28. **Terrell Williams, 3b, Harlan HS, Chicago.**
29. William Brunson, lhp, Eastfield (Texas) JC.
30. **Philip Scott, ss, Wittenberg University.**
31. Joseph Sewell, rhp, UC Irvine.
32. Michael Holtz, lhp, Central Cambria HS, Ebensburg, Pa.
33. James Northeimer, c, Sacramento (Calif.) HS.
34. Aaron Richards, rhp-ss, Westlake HS, Austin, Texas.
35. **James Manfred, rhp, Indian Hills (Iowa) CC.**
36. Maceo Mitchell, of, Fresno (Calif.) CC.
37. Anthony Richardson, 1b, Simeon HS, Chicago.
38. Andrew Lorraine, lhp, Hart HS, Valencia, Calif.
39. Thomas King, of, Albany (Ga.) HS.
40. Todd Pridy, 1b, Napa Valley (Calif.) JC.
41. Shaun Watson, rhp, Southwestern HS, Brighton, Ill.
42. Shane Bushard, 3b, North Idaho JC.
43. Karl Carswell, 2b, Shawnee Mission HS, Overland Park, Kan.
44. Douglas Yartz, lhp, Yuba (Calif.) CC.
45. **Ricardo Otero, of, Vega Baja, P.R.**
46. **Scotty Williams, rhp, Morristown (Tenn.) HS.**
47. Thomas Daniel, of, Prairie HS, Vancouver, Wash.
48. **Tom Allison, 2b, Chapman (Calif.) JC.**
49. Claude Allen, rhp, Hogan HS, Vallejo, Calif.
50. Rick Helling, rhp, Kishwaukee (Ill.) JC.
51. Christopher Eckley, of-1b, Burke HS, Omaha, Neb.
52. Randy Farmer, 2b-ss, Meridian (Miss.) JC.

NEW YORK YANKEES (10)

1. **Carl Everett, of, Hillsborough HS, Tampa, Fla.**
2. **Robert Eenhoorn, ss, Davidson University** (Choice from Pirates as compensation for Type 'B' free agent Walt Terrell).
2. (Choice to Expos as compensation for Type 'A' free agent Pascual Perez).
3. **Tate Seefried, 1b, El Segundo (Calif.) HS.**
4. **Kirt Ojala, lhp, University of Michigan.**
5. **Rick Lantrip, inf, Fresno State University.**
6. **Sam Militello, rhp, University of Tampa.**
7. **Jalal Leach, of, Pepperdine University.**
8. **Tim Rumer, lhp, Duke University.**
9. Matthew Terrell, of, Sturgis (Mich.) HS.
10. **Darren Hodges, rhp, Ferrum College.**
11. **Richard Hines, lhp, University of Mississippi.**
12. **Ron Frazier, rhp, Clemson University.**
13. **Jeff Motuzas, c, Nashua (N.H.) HS.**
14. **Bo Siberz, rhp, Texas A&M University.**
15. **Michael Smith, rhp, Seekonk HS, Pawtucket, R.I.**
16. **Ricardo Ledee, of, Salinas, P.R.**
17. **Bryan Faw, rhp, Clemson University.**
18. **Bob Deller, of, Texas Wesleyan University.**
19. **Brent Gilbert, rhp, Texas A&M University.**
20. **Kevin Jordan, 2b, University of Nebraska.**
21. **Stuart Seiler, lhp, University of Virginia.**
22. Andrew Pettitte, lhp, Deer Park (Texas) HS.
23. Thomas Wilson, of, Fullerton (Calif.) JC.
24. Jorge Posada, ss, Rio Piedras, P.R.
25. **Matt Dunbar, lhp, Florida State University.**
26. Shannon Knighton, 1b, Bleckley County HS, Cochran, Ga.
27. James Musselwhite, rhp-1b, Apopka (Fla.) HS.
28. **Shane Spencer, of, Granite Hills HS, El Cajon, Calif.**
29. Corey Hayes, of, Pattonville HS, Florissant, Mo.
30. Brad Stuart, rhp, University of New Orleans.
31. Kent Donnelly, rhp, Foothill HS, Santa Ana, Calif.
32. **Mike Hankins, ss, UCLA.**
33. John Sutherland, rhp, UCLA.
34. **Pat Morphy, rhp, Northeastern Louisiana University.**
35. Kevin Ohme, lhp, Indian River (Fla.) CC.
36. Brett King, ss, Apopka (Fla.) HS.
37. Ernie Yaroshuk, of-1b, Miami-Dade CC South.
38. **John Thibert, rhp, Mesa (Ariz.) JC.**
39. Mike Heathcott, rhp, Creighton University.
40. Wesley Hawkins, of, Mansfield (La.) HS.
41. John Wasdin, rhp, Godby HS, Tallahassee, Fla.
42. **Barry Smith, 2b, Cumberland (Ky.) University.**
43. Daniel Redovian, rhp, Brevard (Fla.) JC.
44. William Lawrence, lhp, Gulf Breeze (Fla.) HS.
45. Albert Perez, rhp, Ohlone (Calif.) JC.
46. Matthew Ruoff, 3b, Santa Rosa (Calif.) JC.
47. James Ramminger, 1b, Goodrich HS, Fond Du Lac, Wis.
48. James Spero, of, Santa Rosa (Calif.) JC.
49. Tim Kester, rhp, Coral Springs (Fla.) HS.
50. Alex McCoy, of, Culver Military HS, Wilmington, N.C.
    Rich Haley, of, Rancho Cordova (Calif.) HS.
    ...rt Alderman, c, Sacramento (Calif.) CC.
    ...Patrick, rhp, Indian River (Fla.) CC.
    ...ndrich, rhp, Edison (Fla.) CC.

55. Franklyn Johnson, 1b, Howard (Texas) JC.
56. Mark Saugstad, ss-3b, University of California.
57. Sean Palmer, of, Ganesha HS, Diamond Bar, Calif.
58. Andres Texidor, c, Canovanas, P.R.
59. Tracy Latimer, rhp, Westwood HS, Fort Pierce, Fla.
60. **Scott Kendall, lhp, Central HS, Fort Pierce, Fla.**
61. Joe Smith, rhp, Cardinal Newman HS, West Palm Beach, Fla.
62. Anthony Crueger, lhp, Texarkana (Texas) CC.
63. Kortney Paul, c, Southwest HS, Fort Worth, Texas.
64. Derek January, lhp, Miami-Dade CC South.
65. Joseph Long, rhp, Citrus (Calif.) JC.
66. Joel Grimes, 1b, Barbers Hill HS, Mount Bellviue, Texas.
67. Kevin Bosse, 3b-1b, Navasota (Texas) HS.
68. Eric Methner, rhp, Michigan State University.
69. Rodd Kelley, ss, Brandon (Fla.) HS.
70. Pedro Lewis, 3b, McClatchy HS, Sacramento, Calif.
71. Terry Vaughn, of, Oceanside (Calif.) HS.
72. Danny Rios, rhp, Pace HS, Hialeah, Fla.
73. Ray Gossett, lhp, Glendora HS, San Dimas, Calif.
74. Eric Taylor, lhp, Mingo HS, Mingo Junction, Ohio.

OAKLAND ATHLETICS (26)

1. **Todd Van Poppel, rhp, Martin HS, Arlington, Texas** (Choice from Brewers as compensation for Type 'A' free agent Dave Parker).
1. **Don Peters, rhp, College of St. Francis (Ill.)**
1. **David Zancanaro, lhp, UCLA** (Supplemental choice—34th—for loss of Type 'A' free agent Storm Davis).
1. **Kirk Dressendorfer, rhp, University of Texas** (Supplemental choice—36th—for loss of Type 'A' free agent Dave Parker).
2. **Curtis Shaw, lhp, University of Kansas** (Choice from Tigers as compensation for Type 'B' free agent Tony Phillips).
2. **Eric Helfand, c, Arizona State University** (Choice from Royals as compensation for Type 'A' free agent Storm Davis).
2. **Gary Hust, of, Petal (Miss.) HS.**
3. **Chaon Garland, rhp, Haverford (Pa.) College.**
4. **Jeff Duncan, 3b, Jackson State (Tenn.) CC.**
5. **Chris Hart, of, Auburn University.**
6. **Creighton Gubanich, c, Phoenixville (Pa.) Area HS.**
7. **Dan Vizzini, lhp, Francis Marion College.**
8. Andy Bruce, 3b, Georgia Tech.
9. **Mike Kennedy, c, Elon College.**
10. **Ernie Young, of, Lewis University.**
11. **Mark Craft, rhp, Virginia Military Institute.**
12. **Bill Picketts, 2b, Cal State Los Angeles.**
13. **Eric Myers, rhp, Seminole (Okla.) JC.**
14. **Jim Dillon, rhp, University of Maine.**
15. **Kevin Dattola, of, University of South Florida.**
16. **Doug Johns, lhp, University of Virginia.**
17. Scott Dodd, lhp, Glendale (Ariz.) CC.
18. **Greg Reid, of, Cal State Los Angeles.**
19. **Carlos Salazar, 1b-c, Azusa Pacific University.**
20. **Chris Olofson, of, Bakersfield (Calif.) JC.**
21. **Rick Miller, lhp, Grand Canyon College.**
22. **Islay Molina, c, Columbus HS, Miami.**
23. **Tanyon Sturtze, rhp, Quinsigamond (Mass.) CC.**
24. Dwayne Fowler, rhp, Long Beach State University.
25. **David Tripp, rhp-of, Clemson University.**
26. Shawn Purdy, rhp, University of Miami.
27. **Eric Booker, of, San Jose State University.**
28. **Glenn Osinski, ss, University of New Orleans.**
29. **Craig Connolly, rhp, University of Pennsylvania.**
30. **Mike Newson, rhp, Crenshaw HS, Los Angeles.**
31. **Scott Rose, rhp, Hillsborough (Fla.) CC.**
32. **Craig Sudbury, rhp, University of Utah.**
33. **Jeff Clifford, rhp, Assumption College.**
34. **Tony Gechter, rhp, Trinidad (Colo.) JC.**
35. Tim Mathews, rhp, St. Louis CC-Meramec.
36. **Tony Scharff, rhp, Oklahoma City University.**
37. **Todd Revenig, rhp, Mankato State University.**
38. **Reggie Bailey, 1b, Coffee HS, Douglas, Ga.**
39. **Mike Muhlethaler, 3b, University of California.**
40. Chris Oscar, lhp, Valley HS, Las Vegas.
41. **Tony Fults, lhp, Franklin County HS, Decherd, Tenn.**
42. Carlos James, of, Pine Bluff (Ark.) HS.
43. Jonathan Lowe, rhp, McLennan (Texas) CC.
44. Marcus Maple, of, Central HS, Beaumont, Texas.
45. Michael Bumpers, of, McCrory (Ark.) HS.
46. Marcus Miller, rhp, Bay HS, Panama City, Fla.
47. Oscar Draper, rhp, Johnson HS, Huntsville, Ala.
48. Robert Pierce, rhp, Dixie (Utah) JC.
49. John White, 3b, Long Beach (Calif.) CC.

PHILADELPHIA PHILLIES (3)

1. **Mike Lieberthal, c, Westlake HS, Westlake Village, Calif.**
2. Tim Schweitzer, lhp, Reedsport (Ore.) HS.
3. **Dan Larson, of, Birmingham (Calif.) HS.**

4. John Ingram, lhp, Los Angeles Harbor JC.
5. Tom Nuneviller, of, West Chester University.
6. Mike Murphy, of, St. Pius X HS, Albuquerque, N.M.
7. Joel Adamson, lhp, Cerritos (Calif.) JC.
8. Ron Lockett, 1b, Jackson State University.
9. Derrick White, 3b, Santa Rosa (Calif.) JC.
10. Jorge Pascual, 2b-3b, Aquinas (Tenn.) JC.
11. Gary Bennett, c, Waukegan (Ill.) East HS.
12. Chad Anderson, rhp, Roseburg (Ore.) HS.
13. Jerome Edwards, of, Jackson State University.
14. Mike Williams, rhp, Virginia Tech.
15. Scott Coleman, lhp, Orange Glen HS, Valley Center, Calif.
16. Eric Spann, of, Stamford (Conn.) HS.
17. Maurice Hines, 1b, Rose HS, Greenville, N.C.
18. Darren Hedley, of, American River (Calif.) CC.
19. Antonio Grissom, of, South Georgia JC.
20. Marvin Benard, of, Los Angeles Harbor JC.
21. Robert Waszgis, c, Fort Scott (Kan.) CC.
22. Robert Lamb, rhp, Central HS, Tuscaloosa, Ala.
23. James Koehler, 1b, De Anza (Calif.) JC.
24. R.A. Neitzel, 2b, Oregon State University.
25. Steve McGovern, rhp, Cal State Los Angeles.
26. Omar Washington, rhp, Samuell HS, Dallas, Tex.
27. Terrell Smith, ss, Stanhope Elmore HS, Millbrook, Ala.
28. Mark Graham, lhp, Santa Monica (Calif.) CC.
29. Gary Lance, rhp, American River (Calif.) CC.
30. Ryan Ridenour, c, Oregon Tech.
31. Erik Judson, ss-2b, UC San Diego.
32. Samuel Edwards, rhp, Gateway HS, Kissimmee, Fla.
33. Thomas Jones, rhp-of, Sam Houston State University.
34. Danny Miller, rhp, Poway (Calif.) HS.
35. John Salamon, rhp, Sto-Rox HS, McKees Rocks, Pa.
36. Bill Higgins, lhp, Clinch Valley County HS, Castlewood, Va.
37. Mike Montgomery, rhp, East Tennesee State University.
38. Sean Ryan, 1b, Rutgers University.
39. Troy Paulsen, ss, Stanford University.
40. Jeff Borgese, of, Fresno State University.
41. Steven Hollins, ss, Appalachian State University.
42. Chadwick Silvers, of, Carson Newman College.
43. Eric Hill, rhp, Walters State (Tenn.) CC.
44. Troy Rusk, c-1b, University of South Florida.
45. Jeffery Gunn, of, Grambling State University.
46. Pat Cheek, 3b, U.S. International University.
47. Patrick Garrigan, ss, Miami (Ohio) University.
48. Eric Maudlin, of, American River (Calif.) CC.
49. Julio Cruz, c, American River (Calif.) JC.
50. Lawrence Novey, c, Grant HS, Sacramento, Calif.
51. Jeff Richardson, 3b, St. Bernards HS, Culver City, Calif.
52. Jeffrey Wagner, 3b, Federal Way (Wash.) HS.
53. Scott Eggleston, rhp, Maple Woods (Mo.) CC.
54. Demetrius Comeaux, of, Gahr HS, Cerritos, Calif.
55. Manuel Evans, of, Pasadena (Calif.) HS.
56. Ron Ollison, 2b, Angelina (Texas) JC.
57. Michael Myers, of, Donegal HS, Mt. Joy, Pa.

PITTSBURGH PIRATES (5)

1. Kurt Miller, rhp, West HS, Bakersfield, Calif.
1. Mike Zimmerman, rhp, University of South Alabama (Supplemental choice—27th—for loss of Type 'A' free agent Jim Gott).
2. (Choice to Yankees as compensation for Type 'B' free agent Walt Terrell).
3. (Choice to Twins as compensation for Type 'B' free agent Wally Backman).
3. John Schulte, of, Brenham (Texas) HS (Choice from Dodgers as compensation for Type 'A' free agent Jim Gott).
4. Norm House, c, Castlewood (Va.) HS.
5. Glenn Coombs, rhp, Cypress Creek HS, Houston.
6. Tim Edge, c, Auburn University.
7. Kevin Young, 3b, University of Southern Mississippi.
8. Jeff Conger, lhp-of, Charlotte (N.C.) Latin HS.
9. Rich Robertson, lhp, Texas A&M University.
10. Cedrick Peppers, of, Hughes Springs HS, Avinger, Texas.
11. Artis Johnson, of, Delray Beach (Fla.) HS.
12. Wes Grisham, of, Louisiana State University.
13. Brian Shouse, lhp, Bradley University.
14. Jeff McCurry, rhp, San Jacinto (Texas) CC.
15. Richard White, rhp, Paducah (Ky.) JC.
16. Lynn Carlson, rhp, Greenville (Ill.) College.
17. John Douris, rhp, Orange Coast (Calif.) CC.
18. Charles Tooch, ss, Forest Hill HS, West Palm Beach, Fla.
19. Jason Leto, of-2b, St. Petersburg (Fla.) JC.
20. Mark Johnson, 1b, Dartmouth College.
    Shelton Simpson, rhp, Eastern Kentucky University.
    ___ Murray, of, Beaver Dam (Wis.) HS.
    ___ Trimble, of-rhp, Carthage (Texas) HS.
    ___lk, c-3b, Louisiana State University.
    ___r, rhp, Shorter (Ariz.) CC.
    ___fer, of, University of Wisconsin-Oshkosh.

FIRST-ROUND PICKS

Kurt Miller
...Pirates pick

Eric Christopherson and Adam Hyzdu
...Giants first two selections

27. **Brad Davis, c, Columbus College.**
28. **Dave Tellers, rhp, San Jose State University.**
29. **Ben Johnson, 3b, Oregon State University.**
30. **Tom Green, of, Georgia Tech.**
31. Mark LaRosa, lhp, Louisiana State University.
32. Aaron Wofford, ss, Lindhurst HS, Olivehurst, Calif.
33. **David Pike, rhp, Riverview HS, Sarasota, Fla.**
34. Shawn Buchanan, of, University of Nebraska.
35. Angel Delgado, ss-3b, East Chicago (Ind.) Central HS.
36. Mike Russell, rhp, Fort Vancouver HS, Vancouver, Wash.
37. John Carter, rhp, Simeon HS, Chicago, Ill.
38. **Tim French, rhp, Northern Kentucky University.**
39. **Joe Sondrini, 2b, North Adams State College.**
40. **Steven Polewski, ss-2b, Chicago State University.**
41. **Javier Martinez, ss, Levittown, P.R.**

ST. LOUIS CARDINALS (13)

1. **Donovan Osborne, lhp, University of Nevada-Las Vegas.**
1. **Aaron Holbert, ss, Jordan HS, Long Beach, Calif.** (Choice from Red Sox as compensation for Type 'A' free agent Tony Pena.)
1. **Paul Ellis, c, UCLA** (Supplemental choice—30th—for loss of Type 'A' free agent Tony Pena).
2. (Choice to Expos as compensation for Type 'B' free agent Bryn Smith).
3. **Marc Ronan, c-of, Florida State University.**
4. **Andrew Beasley, c, Virginia Military Institute.**
5. Jimmy Lewis, rhp, Florida JC.
6. **George Sells, lhp, Old Dominion University.**
7. **Scott Baker, lhp, Taft (Calif.) JC.**
8. **Mark MacArthur, ss, The Master's College.**
9. **Terry Bradshaw, of, Norfolk State University.**
10. **Mark Smith, of-rhp, University of Texas.**
11. **Jose Velez, of, Mayaguez, P.R.**
12. **Jimmy Davenport, of, Jackson State University.**
13. **Tom Urbani, lhp, Long Beach State University.**
14. Keith Adaway, 2b-of, St. Louis CC-Meramec.
15. **Brad Beanblossom, ss, Oklahoma State University.**
16. Pat Treend, rhp, El Camino Real, West Hills, Calif.
17. Ricky Kimball, rhp, Florida State University.
18. **David Norris, lhp, St. Mary's (Calif.) College.**
19. **Jimmy Marchesi, rhp, El Capitan HS, Lakeside, Calif.**
20. **Don Prybylinski, c, Illinois State University.**
21. **Troy Salvior, rhp, Hillsdale College.**
22. **Steve Dudek, of, Rancho HS, Las Vegas, Nev.**
23. **Kevin Carpenter, c, West Virginia University.**
24. **Duff Brumley, rhp, Cleveland (Tenn.) State CC.**
25. **Skeets Thomas, of, University of South Carolina.**
26. Joe Wise, rhp, Georgia Tech.
27. **Bill Gale, of, Central Connecticut State University.**
28. **Lorenzo Meza, ss, Sweetwater HS, National City, Calif.**
29. **Anthony Jenkins, of, The Citadel.**
30. **Harry Ball, 2b, Rollins College.**
31. **Brian Sullivan, lhp, Cumberland Univeristy.**
32. **Rich Gonzalez, of, Cal State Fullerton.**
33. **Brian Avram, rhp, JC of Southern Idaho.**
34. **John Kelly, rhp, Kennesaw College.**
35. **Frank Speek, rhp, Liberty University.**
36. Kevin Morgan, 2b, Southeastern Louisiana University.
37. **Tom Fusco, lhp, Long Island University.**
38. **Darryl Meek, rhp, Parkway South HS, St. Louis.**
39. **Michael Jolley, rhp, Dixie (Utah) JC.**
40. **Beto Rodriguez, 1b, U.S. International University.**
41. **Andy Petersen, rhp, San Diego State University.**
42. **Kevin Nielsen, lhp, San Diego State University.**
43. Chris Turner, 3b-of, Western Kentucky University.
44. **Craig Ruyak, rhp, College of William & Mary.**

45. **Joe Aversa, ss, Southern California College.**
46. Ryan Martindale, c, Creighton University.
47. Doak Wishon, of, Seminole (Okla.) JC.
48. John Coletti, lhp, Seminole (Okla.) JC.
49. **Sydney Lowman, c, Draughon's (Tenn.) JC.**
50. Gilberto Torres, of, Florida International University.
51. **Matthew Tomso, rhp, Mount Olive (Ill.) HS.**
52. **Jonas Hamlin, 1b, JC of Southern Idaho.**
53. Bart Evans, rhp, Three Rivers (Mo.) CC.
54. **Victor Vargas, 2b, University of Wyoming.**
55. Steven Afenir, c, Escondido HS, San Marcos, Calif.
56. Joseph Merritt, c, Volunteer State (Tenn.) CC.
57. Travis Hunter, rhp, JC of Southern Idaho.
58. Greg Jones, of, Southeastern Illinois JC.
59. Jackie Sosa, 1b-of, Castle Park Heights HS, Chula Vista, Calif.
60. Nicholas DeLuca, ss, Taylorsville HS, Salt Lake City, Utah.

SAN DIEGO PADRES (19)

1. (Choice to Giants as compensation for Type 'A' free agent Craig Lefferts).
1. **Robbie Beckett, lhp, McCallum HS, Austin, Texas** (Choice from Royals as compensation for Type 'A' free agent Mark Davis).
1. **Scott Sanders, rhp, Nicholls State University** (Supplemental choice—32nd—for loss of Type 'A' free agent Mark Davis).
2. (Choice to Tigers as compensation for Type 'B' free agent Fred Lynn).
3. **Jerrey Thurston, c, Lake Brantley HS, Altamonte Springs, Calif.**
4. **Rusty Silcox, rhp, Arizona State University.**
5. **Mark Anthony, 3b, Lancaster (S.C.) HS.**
6. **Jeff Pearce, of, Pepperdine University.**
7. **Craig Bullock, 3b, Aldine HS, Houston.**
8. **Keith McKoy, 2b, Southeastern (N.C.) CC.**
9. **Tyrone Narcisse, rhp, Lincoln HS, Port Arthur, Texas.**
10. **Paul Gonzalez, 3b, Texas Christian University.**
11. Jay Powell, rhp-3b, West Lauderdale HS, Collinsville, Miss.
12. **David Mowry, 1b, Glendora (Calif.) HS.**
13. **Steve Gill, of, University of Arizona.**
14. **Scott Frederickson, rhp, University of Texas.**
15. **Kevin Farlow, ss, Cal State Fullerton.**
16. **Brent Bish, ss, Cal State Los Angeles.**
17. **Matt Mieske, of, Western Michigan University.**
18. Todd Evers, rhp, University of Wisconsin.
19. Keith Stafford, ss-2b, Swainsboro (Ga.) HS.
20. **Billy Meury, ss, University of Maryland.**
21. Scott Emerson, lhp, Shadow Mountain HS, Phoenix, Ariz.
22. Jon Ratliff, rhp, Liverpool Central HS, Clay, N.Y.
23. **James Elliott, c, University of Denver.**
24. **Jay Gainer, 1b, University of South Alabama.**
25. **Lance Painter, lhp, University of Wisconsin.**
26. **Bruce Bensching, rhp, Lewis-Clark State College.**
27. **Jon Bellamy, 3b, Lassen (Calif.) JC.**
28. **Reginald Stephens, 2b, Forest Park CC.**
29. Greg Cushman, 3b, Monterey HS, Lubbock, Texas.
30. **Ryan Ivie, lhp, Tumwater HS, Olympia, Wash.**
31. **Mike Bradley, rhp, University of Texas.**
32. **Darius Gash, of, Middle Tennessee State University.**
33. **Lawrence Hawks, 1b-c, Central Missouri State University.**
34. **Paul Martin, rhp, Florida CC.**
35. Thomas Quinn, rhp, Mississippi State University.
36. **Joseph Waldron, lhp, Southwestern Oklahoma State University.**
37. Shawn Pagee, c, JC of San Mateo (Calif.).
38. **James West, c, University of San Francisco.**
39. **Aaron Frederickson, lhp, University of Portland.**
40. Aldren Sadler, rhp, Rockdale County HS, Conyers, Ga.
41. **David Adams, of, Cal State Los Angeles.**
42. Stephen Grack, of, Rancho Santiago (Calif.) JC.
43. **Thomas DeCareau, of, Harvard University.**
44. **German Carion Vega, 2b, Gurabo, P.R.**
45. **Steve Siebert, 2b-of, Georgia Southern College.**
46. **Jeffrey Brown, lhp, Navarro (Texas) JC.**
47. Phillip Haney, c, Radford University.
48. **Tim Ploeger, c, Western HS, Las Vegas, Nev.**
49. Alan Benes, rhp, Lake Forest (Ill.) HS.
50. Gary Frank, 2b, La Jolla (Calif.) HS.
51. **Robert Hays, rhp, Chico State University.**
52. **Jeffrey Ordway, ss-2b, Oregon Tech.**
53. Alan Levine, rhp, Southern Illinois University.

SAN FRANCISCO GIANTS (21)

1. **Adam Hyzdu, of, Moeller HS, Cincinnati** (Choice from Astros as compensation for Type 'B' free agent Ken Oberkfell).
1. **Eric Christopherson, c, San Diego State University** (Choice from Padres ... compensation for Type 'A' free agent Craig Lefferts).
...hoice to Astros as compensation for Type 'A' free agent Kevin Bass).
...cus Jensen, c-rhp, Skyline HS, Oakland, Calif. (Supplemental ...—for loss of Type 'A' free agent Craig Lefferts).
... rhp, Coral Gables (Fla.) HS.
...elli, lhp, Alemany HS, Mission Hills, Calif. (Supplemental

choice—70th—for loss of Type 'C' free agent Candy Maldonado).

3. **Rich Huisman, rhp, Lewis University.**
4. **Mike Myers, lhp, Iowa State University.**
5. **Julio Vega, of, Shoreham-Wading River HS, Shoreham, N.Y.**
6. **John Jackson, of, University of Southern California.**
7. Gregory Norton, ss, Bishop O'Dowd HS, Orinda, Calif.
8. **Kevin McGehee, rhp, Louisiana Tech.**
9. Nate Holdren, of, Richland (Wash.) HS.
10. **Derek Reid, of, Triton (Ill.) JC.**
11. **Kurt Peltzer, lhp, University of Wisconsin.**
12. **Shelby Hart, of, Golden West (Calif.) JC.**
13. Shawn Henrichs, rhp, Linn-Benton (Ore.) JC.
14. Stacy Hollins, rhp, Willis (Texas) HS.
15. **Mark Yockey, lhp, Lewis-Clark State College.**
16. Rikkert Faneyte, of, Miami-Dade South CC.
17. **Jason Sievers, c, Lees Summit (Mo.) HS.**
18. **Mate Borgogno, 2b, Cal State Fullerton.**
19. John Davis, rhp, Georgia Tech.
20. **Tony Spires, ss, Coastal Carolina College.**
21. **Daniel Flanagan, rhp, Virginia Commonwealth University.**
22. Craig Bauer, rhp, Grand Canyon College.
23. **Jim Huslig, rhp, Universtly of Oklahoma.**
24. Jarrod Smith, 3b-of, Winter Haven (Fla.) HS.
25. Alan Dosty, c, Grant HS, Sacramento, Calif.
26. Lance Chambers, ss-3b, St. Petersburg (Fla.) JC.
27. **Michael Helms, ss-of, University of Oregon.**
28. **Rodney Huffman, rhp, McLennan (Texas) CC.**
29. Luis Pote, lhp, Kishwaukee (Ill.) JC.
30. Shawn Ramion, c, Lakeland (Ohio) CC.
31. Vince Beall, of, Sacramento (Calif.) HS.
32. Andre Keene, 1b, Lanham, Md.
33. Marcus Lee, of, U.S. Naval Academy Prep School, San Diego.
34. **Daniel Varnell, of, Foothill (Calif.) JC.**
35. Matt Castles, lhp, Davis (Calif.) HS.
36. **Brian Dakin, c-inf, University of San Francisco.**

SEATTLE MARINERS (6)

1. **Marc Newfield, 1b, Marina HS, Huntington Beach, Calif.**
1. **Anthony Manahan, ss, Arizona State University** (Supplemental choice—38th—for failure to sign 1989 No. 1 draft pick Scott Burrell).
2. (Choice to Indians as compensation for Type 'B' free agent Pete O'Brien).
3. **Dave Fleming, lhp, University of Georgia.**
4. **Paul Brannon, of, Kings Mountain (N.C.) HS.**
5. **Bret Boone, 2b, University of Southern California.**
6. **Michael Hampton, lhp, Crystal River (Fla.) HS.**
7. **Kevin King, lhp, University of Oklahoma.**
8. **John Cummings, lhp, University of Southern California.**
9. **David Lawson, 1b-of, West Covina (Calif.) HS.**
10. **Stafford Wallace, rhp, Lufkin (Texas) HS.**
11. **Tommy Robertson, of, Fairfield Central HS, Ridgeway, S.C.**
12. Luis Victoria, rhp, Isla Verde, Puerto Rico.
13. Kekoa Kaluhiokalani, rhp, Waianae (Hawaii) HS.
14. **Lipso Nava, ss, Miami-Dade New World Center CC.**
15. **Scott Schanz, rhp, UCLA.**
16. **Jim Converse, rhp, Casa Roble HS, Orangevale, Calif.**
17. **Richard Russell, rhp, Campbell University.**
18. **David Adam, rhp, Central Connecticut State University.**
19. Albert Lopez, rhp, Mesa (Ariz.) CC.
20. **Jim Neugent, lhp, Mustang HS, Yukon, Okla.**
21. **Tony Kounas, of, Loyola Marymount University.**
22. Pat Bojcun, rhp, Central Michigan University.
23. **Greg Hunter, 2b, Washington State University.**
24. **Willie Wilder, of, Murray State University.**
25. **Douglas Fitzer, lhp, University of Detroit.**
26. Jeff Tucker, rhp, Allen County (Kan.) CC.
27. Christopher Terry, ss, Tokay HS, Stockton, Calif.
28. Brad Gay, c, Dixie Hollins HS, St. Petersburg, Fla.
29. **David McDonald, lhp, Brandeis University.**
30. Renaldo Bullock, of, Triton (Ill.) JC.
31. Damon Bihm, of, University HS, Los Angeles.
32. Ron Rico, 1b, Cerritos (Calif.) JC.
33. **Dion Gargagliano, lhp, CC of Morris (N.J.).**
34. Michael Bond, ss, Allegany (Md.) CC.
35. **Clay Klavitter, 3b, Glendale (Ariz.) CC.**
36. **Salvy Urbo, lhp, Plant HS, Tampa.**
37. Alfred Rivers, of, Tallassee (Ala.) HS.
38. Miguel Nolasco, ss, Lely HS, Naples, Fla.
39. Kenny Williams, rhp, Elk Grove (Calif.) HS.
40. Bernard Erhard, ss-2b, Spartanburg Methodist (S.C.) JC.
41. Gary Miller, rhp, Penn State University.
42. Armando Morales, rhp, Indian Hills (Iowa) CC.
43. Anthony Maisano, 1b, Georgia Tech University.
44. Michael Gilmore, of-1b, Broomfield (Colo.) HS.
45. Brian Fontes, rhp, Fresno (Calif.) CC.
46. **Charles Wiley, rhp, Johnson County (Kan.) CC.**
47. Scott Bedford, c, Edmonds (Wash.) CC.

48. Rodney Mazion, ss, Hillsborough HS, Tampa.
49. George Glinatsis, rhp, University of Cincinnati.
50. Richard Wrobel, of, Upland (Calif.) HS.
51. Daniel Stanley, ss, Yakima Valley (Wash.) CC.
52. **Jon Halland, 2b, Arizona State University.**
53. Brian Klomp, rhp, McLane HS, Fresno, Calif.
54. **Rob Nichols, 1b, Washington State University.**
55. Roger Johnson, c, San Pedro (Calif.) HS.
56. Eddie Miller, rhp, Compton (Calif.) CC.
57. Dennis Shrum, 3b, Bullard HS, Fresno, Calif.
58. **James Bonnici, ss, Adams HS, Rochester, Mich.**
59. Robert Lewis, c, Los Angeles Harbor JC.
60. Marcus Drake, of, Arroyo Grande HS, Oceano, Calif.
61. Ron Stanford, rhp, Crisp County HS, Cordele, Ga.
62. Hector Hernandez, rhp, Carolina, P.R.
63. Thomas Borio, rhp, Plainville (Conn.) HS.
64. Brandon Newell, 3b, Nooksack Valley HS, Everson, Wash.
65. Matthew Pontbriant, lhp, St. Bernard's HS, Norwich, Conn.
66. Bryan Lundberg, rhp, Glendale (Ariz.) CC.
67. Silas Grinstead, c, Cardinal Neumann HS, Lake Worth, Fla.
68. Tim Cornish, of-ss, Camarillo (Calif.) HS.
69. Keith Tippett, ss, Indian River (Fla.) CC.
70. Daniel Ricabal, rhp, San Gabriel HS, Rosemead, Calif.
71. Shawn Sanderfer, 3b, Upland (Calif.) HS.
72. Toraino Golston, of, Gateway HS, Aurora, Colo.
73. Craig Gienger, 1b, Otero (Colo.) JC.
74. Michael Bruce, c, Canoga Park (Calif.) HS.
75. **Tim Roberts, lhp, Duke University.**

TEXAS RANGERS (16)

1. **Dan Smith, lhp, Creighton University.**
2. Mike Schiefelbein, rhp, Chatfield HS, Littleton, Colo.
3. **Bobby Reed, rhp, Mississippi State University.**
4. **Mickey Henson, rhp, South Point HS, Belmont, N.C.**
5. **Jon Shave, ss, Mississippi State University.**
6. Kevin Woodall, ss, Georgetown (S.C.) HS.
7. **Terry Burrows, lhp, McNeese State University.**
8. Steve Dreyer, rhp, University of Northern Iowa.
9. Tim Wells, rhp, Southwest Missouri State University.
10. **Rusty Greer, of, University of Montevallo (Ala.).**
11. Efrain Gonzalez, of, Margarita River HS, Gurabo, P.R.
12. **Andy Watson, rhp, Crowder (Mo.) CC.**
13. **David Hulse, of, Schreiner (Texas) College.**
14. **Brian Mercado, rhp-3b, Eastern Connecticut State University.**
15. **Greg Blevins, c, University of Southwestern Louisiana.**
16. Harold Berrios, of, Ottawa Hills HS, Grand Rapids, Mich.
17. **Frank Turco, ss, Barry University.**
18. **Rodney Busha, rhp, University of North Alabama.**
19. **Todd Guggiana, 3b, Long Beach State University.**
20. Tim Kubinski, lhp, San Luis Obispo (Calif.) HS.
21. Jarod Juelsgaard, rhp, Waldorf (Iowa) CC.
22. **Marty Posey, c-of, Tulane University.**
23. **Keith Murray, of, University of South Alabama.**
24. Shawn Kennedy, rhp, El Monte (Calif.) HS.
25. **Matt Whiteside, rhp, Arkansas State University.**
26. **Johnny Johnson, rhp, Birmingham-Southern University.**
27. **Troy Rhoades, rhp, Greenwood (Ark.) HS.**
28. **Chris McMullan, c, University of Richmond.**
29. **Steve Ramharter, lhp, Rice University.**
30. Noe Najera, lhp, Cypress (Calif.) CC.
31. **Scott Erickson, lhp, Kearney State (Neb.) College.**
32. Bryan Judice, of, Poly HS, Riverside, Calif.
33. **Mark Finney, rhp, Glendale (Ariz.) CC.**
34. **Greg Wiseman, of, Crowder (Mo.) CC.**
35. **Junior Antoine, of, St. Croix, V.I.**
36. **Lee Hodge, 2b, University of Mississippi.**
37. Chris Alexander, c, Southside HS, Memphis, Tenn.
38. **Chris Gies, rhp, Seminole (Okla.) JC.**
39. **Tim Cain, rhp, University of Connecticut.**
40. Damian Grossie, 3b, University of Southwestern Louisiana.
41. **Tim Stafford, rhp, McNeese State University.**
42. Brad Haley, 3b-of, El Toro (Calif.) HS.
43. Donavon Hopper, rhp, Goldendale (Wash.) HS.
44. Reggie Moore, ss, UCLA.
45. **Sidney Holland, of, University of Texas-Pan American.**
46. **Lance Jones, of, University of Texas.**
47. **George Evangelista, ss, Merrimack (Mass.) College.**
48. **Peter Laake, 1b-of, University of Maryland.**
49. **Richard Kunz, lhp, Brigham Young University.**
50. **Steve Surico, lhp, Loyola Marymount University.**
51. **Anthony Bouton, rhp, University of South Carolina.**
Paul Matachun, 3b-2b, Eastern Connecticut State University.
Dawley, rhp, Canyon Springs HS, Moreno Valley, Calif.
Hepworth, of, North Florida CC.
uarez, lhp, Fresno (Calif.) CC.
slasken, of, Clear Creek HS, League City, Texas.

57. Gary Beashore, 3b-rhp, Kansas City (Mo.) CC.
58. Mark Lummus, lhp, Cleburne (Texas) HS.
59. Quran Strane, of, Westmoore HS, Oklahoma City, Okla.
60. Jerry Garrett, Oceanside (Calif.) HS.

TORONTO BLUE JAYS (22)

1. **Steve Karsay, rhp, Christ The King HS, Queens, N.Y.**
2. **Chris Weinke, 3b, Cretin HS, St. Paul, Minn.**
2. **Tim Hyers, 1b-of, Newton County HS, Covington, Ga.** (Supplemental choice—71st—for loss of Type 'C' free agent Lloyd Moseby).
3. **Felipe Crespo, of, Notre Dame HS, Caguas, P.R.**
4. **Howard Battle, of, Mercy Cross HS, Ocean Springs, Miss.**
5. **Scott Burrell, University of Connecticut.**
6. **David Tollison, 2b, University of Texas.**
7. **Scott Brow, rhp, University of Washington.**
8. **Paul Menhart, rhp, Western Carolina University.**
9. **Huck Flener, lhp, Cal State Fullerton.**
10. **Tom Singer, lhp, St. John's University.**
11. **Daniel Viitala, of, Northern Michigan University.**
12. **Mark Choate, ss, North HS, Bakersfield, Calif.**
13. Craig Holman, rhp, Jacksonville State University.
14. **Matt Watson, rhp, Cal State Fullerton.**
15. **Travis Burley, rhp, Miramar HS, Hollywood, Fla.**
16. **Mike Coolbaugh, ss, Roosevelt HS, San Antonio, Texas.**
17. **Allen Rhea, lhp, Milligan College.**
18. **Ron Reams, of, Laney (Calif.) JC.**
19. **Carlos Santiago, of, Comerio, P.R.**
20. Matthew Wilke, ss, University of North Dakota.
21. **Rafael Garcia, rhp, Southern California College.**
22. **Sam Mandia, rhp, Seton Hall University.**
23. **Jason Reese, rhp, UC Riverside.**
24. Deron Pointer, of, Curtis HS, Tacoma, Wash.
25. **Matthew Hudik, 2b, Ohio University.**
26. **David Marcon, lhp, Oral Roberts University.**
27. **Tom Hotchkiss, rhp, Santa Clara University.**
28. **Robert Adkins, rhp, Manatee HS, Bradenton, Fla.**
29. **Dale Kistaitis, lhp, University of Nebraska.**
30. **Ciro Ambrosio, ss, Long Island University.**
31. **Greg Wilcox, rhp, Davidson College.**
32. **Kyle Duey, rhp, University of Portland.**
33. **Bob Aylmer, lhp, Fordham University.**
34. **Scott Miller, ss-rhp, Elon College.**
35. **Rusty Filter, rhp, San Diego State University.**
36. **John Gilligan, rhp, University of Southern Mississippi.**
37. Ricardo Jordan, lhp, Miami-Dade CC South.
38. **Frank Kower, rhp, UNC Charlotte.**
39. **D.J. Boston, 1b, San Jacinto (Texas) JC.**
40. Darian Hagan, ss, University of Colorado.
41. **Joe Ganote, rhp, UNC Charlotte.**
42. **Roberto Duran, of, Seward Park HS, New York.**
43. Patrick Valero, lhp, Kent State University.
44. Todd Weinberg, lhp, Somerset (Mass.) HS.
45. **Travis Baptist, lhp, Hillsboro HS, Aloha, Ore.**
46. Robert Barber, c, American River (Calif.) JC.
47. John Allan, lhp, Yakima Valley (Wash.) CC.
48. Chris Laiche, lhp, St. Martin's Episcopal HS, Metairie, La.
49. Ryan Henderson, rhp, Citrus (Calif.) JC.
50. David Pearlman, rhp, Fullerton (Calif.) HS.
51. Jonathan Holsgrove, ss, Mineola HS, Williston Park, N.Y.
52. Martin Thomas, 1b, Kendrick HS, Columbus, Ga.
53. David Burke, rhp, Clay HS, Green Cove Springs, Fla.
54. Jeffery Gatland, rhp, Northport HS, East Northport, N.Y.
55. Bob Ippolito, rhp, Helix HS, La Mesa, Calif.

ERIE SAILORS

Class A
4. **Gary Daniels, of, Brigham Young University.**

MIAMI MIRACLE

Class A
4. **Paul Carey, of, Stanford University.**
5. **Miah Bradbury, c, Loyola Marymount University.**
6. **Mike Lansing, ss, Wichita State University.**
7. **Greg D'Alexander, 3b, University of Arkansas.**
8. **Tommy Raffo, 1b, Mississippi State University.**
9. **Brad Gregory, rhp, Florida State University.**
10. **Ken Whitworth, rhp, UC Irvine.**
11. **Mike Czarnetski, of, UC Santa Barbara.**
12. **Rod Nettnin, lhp, University of Nevada-Reno.**
13. **Tim Rigsby, ss, Clemson University.**
14. Todd Pick, rhp, University of New Orleans.
15. **John Urcioli, ss, New York Tech.**
16. **Mike Ericson, rhp, Michigan State University.**
17. **Joe Burnett, of, University of Southwestern Louisiana.**
18. **Charlie Rogers, lhp, University of North Alabama.**
19. **Billy Walker, rhp, Gonzaga University.**

INDEX

AMERICAN LEAGUE CLUBS

NATIONAL LEAGUE CLUBS

INDEPENDENT CLUBS

NOTES

_____
_____
_____
_____
_____
_____
_____
_____
_____
_____
_____
_____
_____
_____
_____
_____
_____
_____
_____
_____
_____
_____
_____
_____
_____
_____
_____
_____
_____
_____
_____
_____
_____
_____
_____
_____
_____
_____
_____
_____

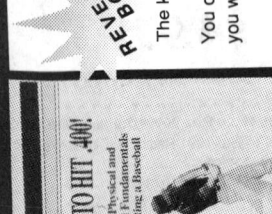

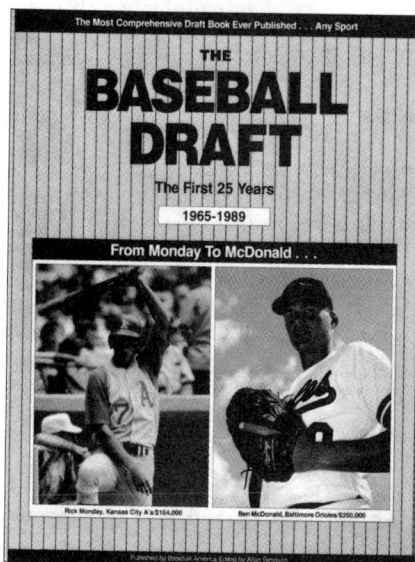